What Is a Thesaurus?

"A *Thesaurus* is the opposite of a dictionary. You turn to it when you have the meaning already but don't yet have the word. It may be on the tip of your tongue, but what it is you don't yet know. It is like the missing piece of a puzzle. You know well enough that the other words you try out won't do. They say too much or too little. They haven't the punch or have too much. They are too flat or too showy, too kind or too cruel. But the word which just fills the bill won't come, so you reach for the *Thesaurus*."

—*From the Introduction by* I. A. RICHARDS

ROGET'S

Pocket Thesaurus

BASED ON
ROGET'S International Thesaurus
of English Words and Phrases

Edited by
C. O. SYLVESTER MAWSON

Assisted by
KATHARINE ALDRICH WHITING

PUBLISHED BY POCKET BOOKS NEW YORK

ROGET'S POCKET THESAURUS

Based on *Roget's International
Thesaurus of English Words and Phrases*

Crowell edition published December, 1923
POCKET BOOK edition published September, 1946
96th printing..........July, 1971

This POCKET BOOK edition includes every word
contained in the original, higher-priced edition. It is printed
from brand-new plates made from completely reset, clear, easy-to-read
type. POCKET BOOK editions are published by POCKET BOOKS, a division
of Simon & Schuster, Inc., 630 Fifth Avenue, New York, N.Y. 10020.
Trademarks registered in the United States and other countries.

L

INTRODUCTION

A *Thesaurus*, says the dictionary, is "a treasury or storehouse; hence a repository, especially of words, as a dictionary." But, in a sense, this book is the opposite of a dictionary. You turn to a dictionary when you have a word but are not sure enough what it means—how it has been used and what it may be expected to do. You turn to the *Thesaurus* when you have your meaning already but don't yet have the word. It may be on the tip of your tongue, or in the back of your mind or the hollow of your thought, but what it is you don't yet know. It is like the missing piece of a puzzle. You know well enough that the other words you try out won't do. They are not the right shape. They say too much or too little. They haven't the punch or have too much. They are too flat or too showy, too kind or too cruel. But the word which just fills the bill won't come, so you reach for the *Thesaurus*.

Like the dictionary, it is a dangerous book in all sorts of ways. Sometimes you wake up—after half an hour— and realize that the problem of the missing word is still where it was. You have just been wandering happily about in the treasure house looking its riches over, forgetting what you came in for. It has worse dangers. Sometimes the words you find start new streams of thought which wash everything out.

Then not the word only but the idea too will be missing. In this "Lost Chord" situation, the best thing to conclude is that so evanescent an idea was hardly worth keeping. Sometimes, worse still, Temptation assails you. Instead of the right word—the word your thought was yearning for as its mysterious predestined mate—some

v

brazen hussy or wastrel of a vocable, never met and never thought of before, seizes your regard.

> *O these encounterers*
> *That give a coasting welcome ere it comes*

Beware! As Confucius' pupil said, "For one word a man is often deemed to be wise and for one word he is often deemed to be foolish. We ought to be careful indeed what we say."

A big vocabulary is a grand thing when well understood and resourcefully used. But all grandeurs have their penalties. It is the business of a *Thesaurus* to take us into all verbal company—to introduce us to every sort and condition of word, with no guarantee, expressed or implied, as to what they may not do to us if we trust them without proper inquiry.

> *Who hath given man speech*
> *Or who hath set therein*
> *A thorn for peril and a snare for sin*

cries the Chorus in *Atalanta in Calydon*.

The great Railway strike in England turned upon the phrase "definitive terms." One side took it to mean "unchangeable"; the other explained too late that they only meant "full and detailed." Well does Peter Mark Roget observe, "A misapplied or misapprehended term is sufficient to give rise to fierce and interminable disputes; a misnomer has turned the tide of popular opinion; a verbal sophism has decided a party question; an artful watchword, thrown among combustible materials has kindled the flame of deadly warfare and changed the destiny of an empire."

That is the tragic side. The comic possibilities more concern us here. People who swagger about in borrowed words may, like Porthos in *The Three Musketeers*, impress the inexperienced. They bring the wrong sorts of smiles to the lips of the discerning.

To know the words without the things is perilous indeed. "How often," said the lecturer, "have I dallied by the shores of Lac Leman or strolled on the delightful slopes overlooking Lake Geneva." "Pardon me," said a member of the audience, "but are they not synonymous?" "You may think so, Sir," replied the speaker, "but for my part I consider Lac Leman by far the more synonymous of the two." Awful warnings of this sort abound. "I always tell my children to look it up in the dictionary or the encyclopedia," said the Sea Captain. "That is what they are there for. Always be exact . . . No, I don't wear my ribbons in public places. Seems to me they are a bit promiscuous."

But when is a word our own? What is a mastery of language? How in fact do we acquire a vocabulary worthy of the name?

The answer of course is: By experience with words, by living with great books and good talkers, by watching their words at work and at play—in brief, by becoming *familiar* with words. Mere acquaintanceship with them is not profitable here. An acquaintance is one whose name and face you know, without more than a rough idea of his being and business. A familiar is one about whom you know as much as possible. Words are astonishingly like people. They have characters, they almost have personalities—are honest, useful, obliging . . . or treacherous, vain, stubborn . . . They shift, as people do, their conduct with their company. They are an endless study in which we are studying nature and ourselves at that meeting point where our minds are trying to give form to or take it from the world.

Peter Mark Roget a century ago had high hopes of the help his arrangement of words might be to thought and to the construction of a common second language such as Basic English may become. There is nothing fantastic about such hopes. In drawing up his scheme of divisions his model was biological classification. He was a physician and Secretary of the Royal Society. But we need not take Roget's actual categories too seriously. To criticize them would be to bring up all the hardest problems there are. They serve their purpose—which is to remind us systematically of all that we know about words. "It is not sufficiently considered," said Dr. Johnson, "that men require more often to be reminded than to be informed." For information about words we go to the dictionary— the bigger it is the better. We go to the *Thesaurus* in the hope that something we really know already will come back to us in our need. How vast is the realm of our current oblivion. "I know," said Benjamin Paul Blood, "as having known, the secret of existence." Nothing will better make us realize how nearly true this is than an hour spent in the treasury. How incredibly much we understand if only we can mobilize our understanding. Roget's *Thesaurus* is one of the greatest of all *memoria technica*. It is an astonishing thought that we can carry it in the pocket.

I. A. RICHARDS

CONTENTS

POCKET THESAURUS AND WORD FINDER

CLASS I
WORDS EXPRESSING ABSTRACT RELATIONS

CLASS II
WORDS RELATING TO SPACE

CLASS III
WORDS RELATING TO MATTER

CLASS IV
WORDS RELATING TO THE INTELLECTUAL FACULTIES

CLASS V
WORDS RELATING TO THE VOLUNTARY POWERS

CLASS VI
WORDS RELATING TO THE SENTIENT & MORAL POWERS

ABBREVIATIONS USED IN THIS BOOK

abbr. abbreviated, abbreviation
adj. adjective, adjectival expression
adv. adverb, adverbial expression
Am. *or* **Amer.** America, American
Am. hist. American history
Am. Ind. American Indian
anat. anatomy
anon. anonymous
Ar. Arabic
arch. architecture
archæol. archæology
arith. arithmetic
astrol. astrology
astron. astronomy
Bib. Biblical
biol. biology
bot. botany
Brit. British
Can. Canada, Canadian
chem. chemistry
Chin. Chinese
class. classical
colloq. colloquial
com. commerce, commercial
conj. conjunction
Du. Dutch
Dan. Danish
dial. dialect, dialectal
dim. diminutive
E. East
eccl. ecclesiastical
Eng. English, England
erron. erroneous, -ly
esp. especially
exc. except
F. French
fem. feminine
fig. figurative, -ly
G. *or* **Ger.** German
Gr. Greek
Gr. Brit. Great Britain
her. heraldry
Hind. Hindustani
hist. history, historical
Icel. Icelandic
Ind. Indian
Ir. Irish, Ireland
int. interjection
It. Italian

Jap. Japanese
joc. jocular
L. Latin
l.c. lower case
masc. masculine
math. mathematics
mil. military
Moham. Mohammedan
myth. mythology
n. noun
naut. nautical
neut. neuter
Norw. Norwegian
obs. obsolete
opp. opposed
orig. original, -ly
parl. parliamentary
path. pathology
Pg. Portuguese
pharm. pharmacy
philos. philosophy
physiol. physiology
pl. plural
pol. *or* **polit.** political
pop. popular, -ly
prep. preposition
prov. proverb, provincial
psychol. psychology
R. C. Ch. Roman Catholic Church
relig. religion
rhet. rhetoric, rhetorical
Russ. Russian
S. Am. South American
Scand. Scandinavian
Scot. Scottish, Scotland
sing. singular
Skr. Sanskrit
Sp. Spanish
surg. surgery
Sw. Swedish
tech. technical
theat. theatrical
theol. theology
typog. typography
Univ. University
U. S. United States
v. verb
zool. zoology

HOW TO USE THE BOOK

I. To find a synonym or antonym for any given WORD:

Turn to the Index* and find the particular word or any term of
kindred meaning; then refer to the category indicated (the numbers printed in bold face at the top corner of each page).
There in its proper grouping, the indexed word will be found, together with a wide selection of related terms. Synonyms and
antonyms are placed in adjoining positions. For example, suppose a
synonym is wanted for the word "cold" in the sense of "indifferent."
Turn to the Index, where the following references will be found:

> cold, *adj.*
> *frigid* **383**
> *insensible* 823
> *indifferent* 866

The italicized words give the general sense of the synonyms in the
respective categories. The bold-faced figures denote that the indexed word is itself the heading or keyword of a distinct group.
Thus, in this example, under **383** we find a list of adjectives
grouped under the word "cold" in the literal sense of the term.

Turning to No. **866** (the sense required), we read through the varied list of
synonyms ("indifferent, frigid, lukewarm," etc.) and select the most appropriate
expression. To widen the selection, suggested references are given to allied lists;
while in the adjoining category (No. **865**) are grouped the corresponding antonyms
("eager, keen, burning, ardent," etc.). The groups are arranged, not merely to
supply synonyms for some special word, but also to suggest new lines of thought
and to stimulate the imagination.

II. To find suitable words to express a given IDEA:

Find in the Index some word relating to the idea, and the categories referred to will supply the need.

For example, suppose a writer wishes to convey the idea of "rest." Turning to
No. **265**, he will find *nouns* giving such associated senses as "quiet," "pause,"
"resting place," or *verbs* with the sense of "be still," "remain," "quell," or *adjectives* such as "quiescent," "still," "silent," and the like. The mere reading of the
entire list will help to crystallize the idea and give it utterance.

**III. To find appropriate words or new ideas on any given SUB-
JECT:**

Turn up the subject or any branch of it. The Index itself will
frequently suggest various lines of thought, while reference to the
indicated groups will provide many words and phrases that
should prove helpful.

Thus, suppose "poetry" is the theme, No. **597** will be found most suggestive.
Or again, the subject may be "the drama" (**599**), "music" (**415**), "the vegetable
kingdom" (**367**), "national legislatures" (**696**), "psychical research" (**992a**), or

*(page 311)

"mythology" **(979)**. The writer may perhaps be hazy about the titles of the ruling chiefs of India. Reference to **875** will prevent his applying a Hindu title to a Mohammedan prince. He may wish to know the term for a "plain" in different parts of the world; No. **344** will tell him exactly. The subject may be such an everyday one as "food" **(298)**, "automobiles" **(272)**, "aviation" **(267** and **269a)**, or various kinds of "amusements" **(840)**; whatever it is, the search will not prove altogether unprofitable.

N.B.—To grasp the underlying principle of the classification, study the *Tabular Synopsis of Categories* (pp. xiv-xxviii).

The guide numbers always refer to the *section* numbers in the text, and *not* to pages.

PLAN OF CLASSIFICATION

TABULAR SYNOPSIS OF CATEGORIES

Class I. ABSTRACT RELATIONS

I. EXISTENCE

1. Existence	2. Nonexistence
3. Substantiality	4. Unsubstantiality
5. Subjectiveness	6. Objectiveness
7. State	8. Circumstance

II. RELATION

9. Relation	10. Irrelation
11. Consanguinity	
12. Correlation	
13. Identity	14. Contrariety
15. Difference	
16. Uniformity	16a. Want of Uniformity
17. Similarity	18. Dissimilarity
19. Imitation	20. Nonimitation
20a. Variation	
21. Copy	22. Prototype
23. Agreement	24. Disagreement

III. QUANTITY

25. Quantity	26. Degree
27. Equality	28. Inequality
29. Mean	
30. Compensation	
31. Greatness	32. Smallness
33. Superiority	34. Inferiority
35. Increase	36. Decrease
37. Addition	38. Deduction
39. Adjunct	40. Remainder
	40a. Decrement
41. Mixture	42. Simpleness
43. Junction	44. Disjunction
45. Vinculum	
46. Coherence	47. Incoherence
48. Combination	49. Decomposition
50. Whole	51. Part
52. Completeness	53. Incompleteness
54. Composition	55. Exclusion (from a compound)
56. Component	57. Extraneousness

IV. ORDER

58. Order	59. Disorder
60. Arrangement	61. Derangement
62. Precedence	63. Sequence
64. Precursor	65. Sequel

Class III. MATTER

I. MATTER IN GENERAL

II. INORGANIC MATTER

(1) Solids

(2) Fluids

CLASS IV. **INTELLECT**

I. FORMATION OF IDEAS

Class V. VOLITION

I. INDIVIDUAL VOLITION

600. Will
602. Willingness
604. Resolution
604a. Perseverance
606. Obstinacy

601. Necessity
603. Unwillingness
605. Irresolution

607. Apostasy
608. Caprice

609. Choice

609a. Absence of Choice
610. Rejection

611. Predetermination
613. Habit
615. Motive
617. Plea
618. Good
620. Intention
622. Pursuit

612. Impulse
614. Desuetude
615a. Absence of Motive
616. Dissuasion
619. Evil
621. Chance
623. Avoidance
624. Relinquishment

625. Business
626. Plan
627. Method
628. Mid-course
630. Requirement
631. Instrumentality
632. Means
633. Instrument
634. Substitute
635. Materials
636. Store
637. Provision
639. Sufficiency
641. Redundance
642. Importance
644. Utility
646. Expedience
648. Goodness
650. Perfection
652. Cleanness
654. Health
656. Healthiness
658. Improvement
660. Restoration
662. Remedy
664. Safety
666. Refuge
668. Warning
669. Alarm
670. Preservation

629. Circuit

638. Waste
640. Insufficiency

643. Unimportance
645. Inutility
647. Inexpedience
649. Badness
651. Imperfection
653. Uncleanness
655. Disease
657. Unhealthiness
659. Deterioration
661. Relapse
663. Bane
665. Danger
667. Pitfall

II. INTERSOCIAL VOLITION

CLASS VI. **AFFECTIONS**

I. AFFECTIONS IN GENERAL

II. PERSONAL AFFECTIONS

V. RELIGIOUS AFFECTIONS

ROGET'S POCKET THESAURUS AND WORD FINDER

CLASS I

WORDS EXPRESSING ABSTRACT RELATIONS

I. EXISTENCE

1. EXISTENCE. — *N.* **existence**, being, entity, subsistence, presence, omnipresence, ubiquity.

reality, actuality, fact, matter of fact, truth, verity.

essence, inner reality, vital principle.

Science of existence: ontology.

V. **exist**, be, subsist, live, breathe; vegetate; happen, take place; occur, prevail.

consist in, lie in; be comprised in.

abide, continue, endure, last, remain.

Adj. **existent**, subsistent, extant; afloat, on foot, current, prevalent.

real, actual, positive, absolute; veritable, true; substantial, essential.

well founded, well grounded, authentic.

Adv. **actually**, in fact, in reality; indeed.

2. NONEXISTENCE. — *N.* **nonexistence**, inexistence; nonentity; nullity; nihilism; blank; absence, emptiness, void, vacuum; nothingness.

annihilation, extinction, destruction, abolition, extirpation, nirvana, obliteration.

V. **not exist**, be null and void; cease to exist; pass away, perish, be *or* become extinct; die out; disappear, vanish, fade, melt away, dissolve, be no more; die, etc., 360.

annihilate, nullify; abrogate, etc., 756; destroy, etc., 162; remove, displace, vacate; obliterate, extirpate.

Adj. **inexistent**, nonexistent; negative, blank; null, missing, absent, etc., 187.

unreal, baseless, unsubstantial, shadowy, spectral, visionary.

unborn, uncreated, unbegotten.

extinct, gone, lost, departed; defunct, etc. (*dead*), 360.

fabulous, ideal, etc. (*imaginary*), 515.

3. SUBSTANTIALITY.—*N.* substantiality; person, thing, object, article; something, a being, creature, body, substance, matter, etc., 316; groundwork, materiality.

Adj. substantial, essential; personal, bodily, corporeal, tangible, etc. (*material*), 316.

4. UNSUBSTANTIALITY.—*N.* unsubstantiality, nothingness, nihility; bubble, etc., 353.

nothing, naught, *nil* [L.], nullity, zero, cipher; blank, void, hollowness.

thing of naught, man of straw, lay figure; nonentity.

phantom, apparition, specter, shadow, dream, vision, will-o'-the-wisp, *ignis fatuus* [L.].

V. vanish, evaporate, fade, sink, fly, dissolve, melt away; die away; die out; disappear, etc., 449.

Adj. unsubstantial; baseless, groundless; ungrounded; without foundation.

visionary, imaginary, immaterial, spectral, etc., 980*a*; dreamy; shadowy; ethereal, airy, gaseous, imponderable, tenuous, vague, vaporous, dreamlike, illusory, unreal.

vacant, vacuous; empty, void, blank, hollow.

5. SUBJECTIVENESS.—*N.* subjectiveness, intrinsicality, inherence, immanence, indwelling; ego; essence, quintessence, elixir; gist, pith, core, kernel, marrow, backbone, heart, soul, life, substance.

principle, nature, constitution.

temper, temperament; spirit, humor, quality, disposition.

aspect, mood, feature, peculiarity, idiosyncrasy.

Adj. intrinsic, subjective; fundamental, implanted, inherent, essential, natural; innate, inborn, inbred, ingrained, indwelling, immanent, inwrought; radical, incarnate, hereditary, inherited, congenital, indigenous, native; in the grain, bred in the bone, instinctive; characteristic, ineradicable, fixed.

Adv. practically, virtually, substantially, in effect.

6. OBJECTIVENESS.—*N.* objectiveness, extraneousness, extrinsicality.

Adj. extrinsic, objective; extraneous, external, incidental, accidental, nonessential, unessential, accessory; contingent, fortuitous, casual.

implanted, ingrafted; inculcated, infused.

7. STATE.—*N.* state, condition, category; estate, lot, mood, temper.

dilemma, pass, predicament, quandary, corner, fix [*colloq.*], plight.

frame, fabric, stamp, mold; constitution.

form, shape; tone, tenor, trim, guise, fashion, mode, style, character.

8. CIRCUMSTANCE.—*N.* **circumstance,** situation, phase, position; footing, standing, status.

occasion, juncture, contingency.

predicament, emergency; exigency, crisis, pinch, pass, plight.

Adj. **circumstantial,** conditional, provisional; contingent, incidental; adventitious.

Adv. **thus,** in such wise; in *or* under the circumstances (*or* conditions).

accordingly, that being the case; since, seeing that.

conditionally, provided, if, in case; if so, unless, in the event of; provisionally.

II. RELATION

9. RELATION.—*N.* **relation,** bearing, relativity, reference, connection, concern; analogy; similarity; homogeneity, affinity, alliance, nearness, association; consanguinity, etc., 11; relationship, relevancy.

ratio, proportion; comparison.

link, tie, bond.

V. **relate to,** refer to; bear upon, regard, concern, touch, affect, pertain to, belong to; correlate.

associate, connect; link, bind.

Adj. **relative,** relating to, referable to; belonging to.

related, connected, associated, affiliated; allied, collateral, cognate, affinitive.

relevant, applicable, in the same category.

Adv. **as regards,** concerning, with relation to, with regard to; by the way, in the matter of.

10. [Want or absence of relation] IRRELATION.—*N.* **irrelation,** dissociation; inapplicability; disconnection, disjunction; inconsequence, disagreement, heterogeneity; irrelevancy.

V. **have no relation to,** have no bearing upon, have nothing to do with.

Adj. **unrelated,** irrespective, unallied, disconnected, unconnected, heterogeneous; isolated.

extraneous, strange, alien, foreign, outlandish, exotic.

irrelevant, inapplicable, not pertinent, unessential, inapposite, beside the mark.

remote, farfetched, out-of-the-way, forced, detached, apart.
incidental, parenthetical, episodic.

Adv. parenthetically, by the way, by the by; incidentally, without regard to.

11. [Relations of kindred] CONSANGUINITY.—*N.* **consanguinity,** relationship, kindred, blood; parentage, paternity; lineage, connection, alliance; people [as, *my people*], family, ties of blood, blood relation.

kinsman, kinsfolk; kith and kin; relative, relation; connection; next of kin; near relation, distant relation.

family, fraternity; brotherhood, sisterhood.

race, stock, generation; clan, tribe; strain, breed.

V. be related to, claim kinship with.

Adj. related, akin, consanguineous, allied, affiliated; kindred.

12. [Double or reciprocal relation] CORRELATION.—*N.* **correlation,** interdependence, reciprocity, mutuality, correspondence, interchange, exchange, barter.

alternation, seesaw, to-and-fro.

V. reciprocate, alternate, interact; interchange, exchange; correlate.

Adj. **reciprocal,** mutual, correlative; correspondent, corresponding; alternate; interchangeable; equivalent, complementary.

13. IDENTITY.—*N.* **identity,** sameness, unity, convertibility; equality, etc., 27; homogeneity; self, oneself.

monotony, repetition, etc., 104.

facsimile, etc. *(copy)*, 21; similarity, etc., 17; exactness, fidelity; same, selfsame, counterpart.

V. coincide, coalesce.

treat as identical (*or* the same), render identical; identify.

Adj. **identical,** self, selfsame, ditto.

coincident, coinciding, coalescent, indistinguishable; one; equivalent, convertible, equal.

14. CONTRARIETY.—*N.* **contrariety,** contrast, foil, antithesis, counterpart, complement; oppositeness; antagonism, opposition, clashing, repugnance, antipathy.

inversion, subversion, reversal, the opposite, the reverse, the inverse, the converse, antipodes.

V. be contrary, contrast with, oppose, differ from.

invert, reverse, turn topsy-turvy, turn upside down, transpose.
contradict, contravene; antagonize, etc., 708.

Adj. **contrary,** opposite, counter, adverse, averse, converse, reverse; opposed, antithetical, contrasted, antipodean, diametrically opposite; antagonistic, conflicting, inconsistent, contradictory; hostile, inimical.

15. DIFFERENCE.—*N.* **difference,** dissimilarity, variance, variation, variety; diversity, divergence, heterogeneity, contrast, antithesis; disagreement, disparity, inequality, distinction, contradiction, contrariety.

nice (*or* fine, subtle) distinction, discrimination; modification.

V. **differ,** vary; mismatch, contrast; diverge from, depart from, deviate from; modify, change, alter.

discriminate, distinguish, etc., 465.

Adj. **different,** diverse, heterogeneous; varied, variant, divergent, incongruous, modified; diversified, various.

other, another, not the same; unequal, etc., 28; unmatched, widely apart.

distinctive, characteristic, discriminative, distinguishing; diagnostic.

16. UNIFORMITY.—*N.* **uniformity;** homogeneity, stability, continuity, permanence, consistency, accordance, conformity; agreement, etc., 23; consonance.

regularity, constancy, evenness, sameness, unity, even tenor, routine.

V. **accord with,** etc., 23; conform to; assimilate; level, smooth.

Adj. **uniform,** homogeneous, of a piece, consistent; even, equable, constant, level; invariable, regular, unvaried, undiversified, unvarying, singsong, dreary, monotonous.

Adv. **always,** ever, evermore, perpetually, forever, everlastingly, invariably.

16a. WANT OF UNIFORMITY.—*N.* diversity, irregularity, unevenness; uncomformity, dissimilarity, dissimilitude, divergence, heterogeneity.

Adj. **diversified,** varied, irregular, checkered, uneven; multifarious, of various kinds.

17. SIMILARITY.—*N.* **similarity,** resemblance, likeness, semblance, affinity, approximation, parallelism; agreement, etc., 23; analogy, correspondence; brotherhood, family likeness.

repetition, etc., 104; sameness, etc. (*identity*), 13; uniformity, etc., 16.

the like; match, fellow, companion, pair, mate, twin, double, counterpart, brother, sister; one's second self, *alter ego* [L.]; chip of the old block, birds of a feather.

simile, parallel, type, image, etc. (*representation*), 554.

V. **resemble,** look like, favor [*colloq.*], follow, echo, reproduce, bear resemblance; savor of, smack of; approximate; parallel, match, rhyme with; take after; imitate, etc., 19.

Adj. **similar,** resembling, like, alike; twin.

analogous, parallel, of a piece; such as.

akin to, etc. (*consanguineous*), 11; correlative, corresponding, cognate, allied to.

approximate, near, close, something like, near [as, *near* silk, *colloq.*], mock, pseudo, simulating, representing.

exact, etc. (*true*), 494; lifelike, faithful, true to life; the very image of, cast in the same mold.

Adv. as if, so to speak; as it were, as if it were; *quasi* [L.], just as.

18. DISSIMILARITY.—*N.* dissimilarity, dissimilitude; unlikeness, diversity, disparity, divergence, variation; difference, etc., 15; novelty, originality.

V. vary, etc. (*differ*), 15; differ from; diversify.

Adj. dissimilar, unlike, disparate; divergent, nonidentical, unique, new, novel, unprecedented, original; diversified, etc., 16a.

Adv. otherwise, alias.

19. IMITATION.—*N.* imitation, copying; repetition, duplication; quotation; reproduction.

mockery, aping, mimicry.

simulation, impersonation; parrotism, parrotry; representation, etc., 554; semblance, pretense; copy, etc., 21.

paraphrase; parody, etc., 21.

plagiarism; forgery, etc., 544.

imitator, echo, cuckoo, parrot, ape, monkey, mimic; copyist.

V. imitate, copy, mirror, reflect, reproduce, repeat; do like, echo, re-echo, catch; match, parallel; forge, counterfeit.

mimic, ape, simulate, impersonate, act, etc. (*drama*), 599; represent, etc., 554; parody, travesty, caricature, burlesque, take off, mock; borrow.

follow in the steps (*or* wake) of, take pattern by, follow suit [*colloq.*], follow the example of, walk in the shoes of, take after, model after; emulate.

Adj. imitative, modeled after; molded on, borrowed, counterfeit, imitation, false, pseudo, near [as, *near* silk, *colloq.*]; mock, mimic.

Adv. literally, verbatim, word for word, exactly, precisely.

20. NONIMITATION.—*N.* nonimitation, originality, creativeness.

Adj. unimitated, uncopied; unmatched, unparalleled; inimitable, etc., 33; unique, original, primordial, creative; exceptional, rare, uncommon, unexampled, out-of-the-way, unwonted.

20a. VARIATION.—*N.* variation, alteration, change, imitation; modification; discrepancy.

divergency, deviation, deflection; aberration; innovation.

V. vary, etc. (*change*), 140; deviate, etc., 279; diverge; alternate.

Adj. **varied,** modified; diversified, etc., 16*a*; dissimilar, etc., 18.

21. [Result of imitation] COPY.—*N.* **copy,** facsimile, counterpart, effigy, form, likeness, similitude, semblance, cast, tracing; imitation, etc., 19; model, representation, study; portrait, etc., 554; duplicate, transcript, transcription; reflection, shadow, echo; reprint, replica, transfer, reproduction, repetition.

servile copy, counterfeit, forgery.

parody, caricature, burlesque, travesty, paraphrase; cartoon.
Adj. **faithful,** lifelike, similar, close, exact.

22. [Thing copied] PROTOTYPE.—*N.* **prototype,** original, model, pattern, precedent, standard; type; archetype, exemplar, example.

copy, text, design; keynote.

die, mold; matrix, last, mint, seal, punch, stamp, intaglio, negative.

V. be an example, set an example.

23. AGREEMENT.—*N.* **agreement,** accord, accordance, unison, harmony, concord, union, unity, unanimity; understanding, *entente cordiale* [F.], concert [as, the *concert* of Europe].

conformity, uniformity, consistency; correspondence, parallelism, apposition.

fitness, aptness, relevancy; pertinence, aptitude, propriety, applicability, admissibility, compatibility.

adaptation, adjustment, accommodation; assimilation.

consent, etc. (*assent*), 488; concurrence, consensus; co-operation.

V. **agree,** accord, harmonize; correspond, tally, consent, etc. (*assent*), 488; suit, fit, befit; square with, dovetail, match, resemble, parallel.

adapt, accommodate, graduate; adjust, etc. (*render equal*), 27; regulate, reconcile.

Adj. **agreeing,** accordant, correspondent, congenial; coherent; harmonious, reconcilable, conformable; consistent, compatible; in accordance with, in harmony with, in keeping with.

apt, apposite, pertinent, pat; to the point; happy, felicitous, germane, applicable, relevant, admissible.

fit, adapted, appropriate, suitable; meet, etc. (*expedient*), 646.

24. DISAGREEMENT.—*N.* **disagreement,** discord, dissonance, disunion, discrepancy, unconformity, incongruity, dissension, conflict, opposition, antagonism, difference, misunderstanding.

disparity, disproportion; inequality, variance, divergence.

unfitness, inaptitude, impropriety, inapplicability, irrelevancy.

V. **disagree,** clash, conflict, dispute, quarrel, jar, interfere.

Adj. **disagreeing,** discordant, inharmonious; hostile, antagonistic, repugnant, clashing, jarring, factious, dissentient, incompatible, irreconcilable, inconsistent with; incongruous; repugnant to.

inapt, inept, inappropriate, improper, unsuited, unsuitable, inapplicable; unfit, unbefitting, unbecoming; ill-timed, unseasonable, ill-adapted, infelicitous, irrelevant.

uncongenial, unsympathetic, ill-assorted, mismatched.

Adv. in defiance of, in contempt of, in spite of.

III. QUANTITY

25. [Absolute quantity] **QUANTITY.—***N.* quantity, magnitude; size, bulk, volume, mass, amount, measure, measurement, substance, strength.

[Science of quantity] mathematics.

[Definite quantity] armful, handful, mouthful, spoonful, stock, batch, lot, dose; quota, pittance, driblet.

Adj. quantitative, some, any, more or less.

26. [Relative quantity] **DEGREE.—***N.* degree, grade, step, extent, measure, amount, ratio, standard, height, pitch; reach, mark, stage, rate, range, scope, caliber; gradation, shade; tenor, compass; sphere, station, rank, standing; interval, space [*music*]; intensity, strength.

V. graduate, calibrate, measure.

Adj. comparative, gradual, shading off.

Adv. by degrees, gradually, step by step, little by little, inch by inch, drop by drop; to some extent.

27. [Sameness of quantity or degree] **EQUALITY.—***N.* equality, parity, symmetry, balance, poise; evenness, monotony, level; equivalence, equipoise, equilibrium; par, quits; distinction without a difference, identity, similarity.

tie, dead heat; drawn game, drawn battle; neck-and-neck race.

match, peer, compeer, equal, mate, fellow, brother; equivalent.

V. equal, match, keep pace with, run abreast; come up to; balance.

equalize, level, dress [*mil.*], balance, handicap, trim, adjust, poise; strike a balance; restore equilibrium.

Adj. equal, even, level, monotonous, symmetrical, co-ordinate; on a par with, on a level with, up to the mark.

equivalent, tantamount; quits; synonymous; convertible; all one, all the same; drawn [as, *a game*].

Adv. equally, to all intents and purposes.

28. [Difference of quantity or degree] **INEQUALITY.—***N.* inequality, disparity, odds; difference, etc., 15; unevenness, shortcoming; superiority, etc., 33; inferiority, deficiency, inadequacy.

V. **be unequal,** have the advantage, turn the scale; overmatch, etc., 33; fall short of.

Adj. **unequal,** uneven, partial, inadequate, deficient; overbalanced, unbalanced, top-heavy, lopsided.

unequaled, unparalleled, unrivaled, unique, matchless, inimitable, peerless.

29. MEAN.—*N.* mean, medium, average, balance, rule, run, golden mean, middle; compromise, neutrality.

V. **average,** split the difference, strike a balance, pair off.

Adj. **mean,** intermediate; middle, etc., 68; average, normal, standard; neutral.

mediocre, middle class, bourgeois, commonplace.

Adv. **on an average,** in the long run; in round numbers.

30. COMPENSATION.—*N.* compensation, equation; indemnification; compromise, measure for measure, retaliation, equalization.

setoff, offset; makeweight, counterpoise, ballast; indemnity, equivalent, *quid pro quo* [L.]; amends, counterbalance, counterclaim.

pay, payment, reward, etc., 973.

V. **compensate,** indemnify; counterpoise, balance, counterbalance, offset, set off; square, make up for, equalize, etc., 27; recoup, redeem; pay, reward, etc., 973.

Adj. **compensating,** compensatory, equivalent, equal.

Adv. **notwithstanding,** but, however, yet, still, nevertheless, although, though; howbeit, albeit; at all events, in spite of, despite, on the other hand, at the same time.

31. GREATNESS.—*N.* greatness, vastness, magnitude; size, etc., 192; multitude; immensity, enormity, might, strength, intensity, fullness.

great quantity, quantity, deal [*colloq.*], volume, bulk, mass, heap; stock, store, load, shipload; abundance, sufficiency.

fame, distinction, grandeur, dignity; importance, etc., 642.

V. **be great,** soar, tower, loom, rise above, transcend; bulk, bulk large.

enlarge, etc. (*increase*), 35; wax, magnify, grow, expand, swell, dilate.

Adj. **great,** large, considerable, big, bulky, huge, etc., 192; titanic; voluminous, ample, abundant; many, etc., 102; full, intense; signal.

goodly, noble, precious, mighty; extraordinary; important, etc., 642; supreme, etc., 33; complete, etc., 52; arrant, downright; uttermost; profound, intense, consummate; rank, unmitigated, glaring, flagrant.

world-wide, widespread, far-famed, extensive.

august, grand, dignified, sublime, majestic.

vast, immense, enormous, extreme; inordinate, excessive, extravagant, monstrous, crass, gross; towering, stupendous, prodigious.

unlimited, etc. (*infinite*), 105; unutterable, indescribable, ineffable, unspeakable, inexpressible, fabulous.

absolute, positive, stark, decided, unequivocal, essential, perfect.

remarkable, notable, noticeable, noteworthy, renowned.

Adv. **in a great or high degree:** greatly, much, indeed, very, very much, most; pretty, enough, in a great measure, passing, richly; on a large scale; by wholesale; mightily, powerfully; extremely, exceedingly, intensely, indefinitely, immeasurably, incalculably, infinitely.

in a positive degree: truly, etc. (*truth*), 494; decidedly, unequivocally, absolutely, essentially, fundamentally, radically, downright, in all conscience.

in a complete degree: entirely, completely, wholly; abundantly, amply, fully, widely.

in a supreme degree: pre-eminently, superlatively, supremely, incomparably.

in a too great degree: immoderately, monstrously, preposterously, exorbitantly, excessively, enormously, out of all proportion.

in a marked degree: particularly, remarkably, singularly, curiously, uncommonly, unusually, peculiarly, notably, signally, strikingly, pointedly, chiefly; famously, egregiously, prominently, glaringly, emphatically, incredibly.

in a violent degree: furiously, violently, severely, desperately, tremendously, extravagantly.

in a painful degree: painfully, sadly, sorely, bitterly, piteously, grievously, miserably, cruelly, woefully, lamentably, shockingly, frightfully, dreadfully, fearfully, terribly, horribly, distressingly, balefully.

32. SMALLNESS.—*N.* **smallness**, littleness, paucity; fewness, sparseness, scarcity, insignificance, unimportance.

small quantity, modicum, minimum; atom, particle, trifle, electron, molecule, corpuscle, point, speck, dot, mote, jot, iota; minutiæ, details; tittle, spark; grain, scruple, minim; drop, sprinkling, dab, dash, tinge, dole, mite, bit, morsel, crumb, scrap, shred, tag, splinter, rag; snip, sliver, paring, shaving, hair; thimbleful, handful, capful, mouthful; fragment, fraction.

V. **be small**, lie in a nutshell.

diminish, etc. (*decrease*), 36; contract, shrink, dwindle, wane.

Adj. **small**, little, stunted; diminutive, etc. (*small in size*), 193; minute, miniature, inconsiderable, paltry, etc. (*unimportant*), 643; scanty, scant, limited, meager, sparing; few, etc., 103; moderate, modest.

inappreciable, infinitesimal, atomic, microscopic, molecular.

mere, simple, sheer, stark, bare.

Adv. **in a small degree:** to a small extent, on a small scale; a little, slightly, imperceptibly; miserably, wretchedly; insufficiently, imperfectly, faintly, feebly, passably.

in a certain or limited degree: partially, in part, in a certain degree, to a certain degree *or* extent; comparatively, rather, in some degree *or* measure; somewhat; simply, only, purely, merely; at least, at most, ever so little, thus far, after a fashion.

almost, nearly, well-nigh, not quite, all but, near upon, close upon, near the mark; within an ace (*or* inch) of, on the brink of; scarcely, hardly, barely, only just, no more than.

in an uncertain degree: about, thereabouts, somewhere about, nearly.

in no degree: noway, nowise, not at all, not in the least, not a bit, not a jot, in no wise, in no respect, by no means, on no account.

33. SUPERIORITY.—*N.* superiority, majority, plurality; advantage; preponderance, prevalence.

nobility, etc. (*rank*), 875; superman, overman.

supremacy, supremeness, primacy, pre-eminence, lead; maximum, record; crest, climax, culmination, summit, peak, transcendence; lion's share, excess, surplus, overweight, redundance.

V. **exceed,** excel, transcend, outdo, outbalance, overbalance, outweigh, outrank, outrival, out-Herod Herod; pass, surpass, overtop, overmatch; cap, culminate, beat, cut out [*colloq.*]; beat hollow [*colloq.*], outstrip, eclipse, throw into the shade; predominate, prevail; precede, take precedence, come first, bear the palm, break the record.

Adj. **superior,** greater, major, higher, exceeding; distinguished, ultra.

supreme, greatest, maximum, utmost, paramount, pre-eminent, foremost, crowning, excellent, peerless, matchless; unrivaled, unparalleled, unequaled, unapproached, unsurpassed; superlative, incomparable, transcendent.

Adv. **beyond,** more, over; over and above; at its height.

in a superior or supreme degree: eminently, pre-eminently, surpassing, superlatively, supremely, principally, especially, particularly, peculiarly.

34. INFERIORITY.—*N.* inferiority, shortcoming, deficiency; minimum; imperfection; meanness, poorness, baseness, shabbiness.

Personal inferiority: the people, etc., 876; subordination.

V. **be inferior,** fall short of, come short of, not come up to; become smaller, decrease, yield the palm, play second fiddle.

Adj. **inferior,** smaller; less, lesser, deficient, reduced, lower, subordinate, secondary, junior, minor, humble; second rate; unimportant, etc., 643.

Adv. **less,** short of, under.

35. INCREASE.—*N.* **increase,** augmentation, addition, enlargement, extension, expansion, growth, increment, accretion, development, accumulation, inflation, enhancement, aggravation, exaggeration.

gain, produce, product, profit, advantage, booty, plunder.

V. **increase,** augment, add to, enlarge, etc., 31; advance, rise, mount, ascend.

aggrandize, raise, exalt; deepen, heighten, lengthen, thicken; inflate, intensify, enhance, magnify, redouble, double; aggravate, exaggerate.

Adj. **increasing,** growing, crescent, multiplying, intensifying, intensive.

Adv. **crescendo,** increasingly.

36. DECREASE.—*N.* **decrease,** diminution, lessening, subtraction, reduction, abatement, declension; shrinkage, contraction, curtailment, abridgment.

subsidence, wane, ebb, decline; ebb tide, neap tide, ebbing.

V. **decrease,** diminish, lessen; abridge, shorten, shrink, contract; dwindle, fall away, waste, wear; wane, ebb, decline, subside, languish, decay, crumble.

discount, belittle, minimize, depreciate, extenuate, lower, weaken, attenuate; dwarf, reduce, shorten, subtract; mitigate, ease, moderate.

Adv. **decrescendo,** decreasingly.

37. ADDITION.—*N.* **addition,** annexation, accession, re-enforcement; increase, etc., 35; increment.

affix, codicil, tag, appendage, postscript, adjunct, supplement; accompaniment, insertion.

V. **add,** annex, affix, subjoin, tack to, append, tag, attach; interpose, introduce, insert.

compute, total, cast (*or* sum, count) up.

re-enforce, strengthen, augment.

Adj. **additional,** supplemental, supplementary; extra, spare, further, fresh, more, other, auxiliary, contributory, accessory.

Adv. **in addition,** more; and, also, likewise, too, furthermore, further; besides, to boot; over and above, moreover; as well as, together with, along with, in conjunction with.

38. DEDUCTION.—*N.* **deduction,** subtraction, retrenchment; abstraction, mutilation, amputation, curtailment, abbreviation.

rebate, etc. (*decrement*), 40*a*; minuend, subtrahend; decrease, etc., 36.

V. **deduct,** subtract, retrench; withdraw; take from, take away; detract, reduce, eliminate, diminish, curtail, shorten; deprive of, etc. (*take*), 789; weaken.

mutilate, amputate, cut off, cut away, excise.

pare, thin, prune, scrape, file.

Adv. **less;** short of; minus, without, except, excepting, with the exception of, save, exclusive of.

39. [Thing added] ADJUNCT.—*N.* adjunct, addition, affix, suffix, appendage, annex, augmentation, increment, re-enforcement, accessory, accompaniment, etc., 88; addendum (*pl.* addenda); complement, supplement, sequel.

rider, offshoot, episode, side issue, corollary, codicil, etc. (*addition*), 37.

V. **add,** annex, etc., 37.

Adj. **additional,** etc., 37.

40. [Thing remaining] REMAINDER.—*N.* remainder, residue, remains, remnant, rest, relic; leavings, odds and ends, residuum, dregs, refuse, stubble, ruins, wreck, skeleton, fossil, stump, rump.

surplus, excess; balance [*commercial slang*], result; superfluity, redundance; survival.

V. **remain,** survive, be left; exceed.

Adj. **remaining,** left, residual, residuary; over, odd; surviving; net; superfluous, etc. (*redundant*), 641.

40a. [Thing deducted] DECREMENT.—*N.* decrement, discount, rebate, defect, loss, deduction; waste.

41. MIXTURE.—*N.* mixture, admixture, junction, etc., 43; amalgamation, combination, etc., 48; infusion, transfusion; infiltration; interlarding, interpolation, etc., 228; adulteration.

Thing mixed: tinge, tincture, touch, dash, smack, spice, seasoning, infusion.

Compounds: alloy, amalgam; brass, pewter; miscellany, medley, mess, hash, hodgepodge, patchwork, jumble; potpourri, mosaic.

half-blood, half-breed, half-caste, crossbreed; mulatto, quadroon, octoroon, Eurasian; mule, cross, hybrid, mongrel.

V. **mix,** join, etc., 43; combine, etc., 48; mingle, commingle, intermingle, interlard, interpolate, intertwine, interweave; associate with.

imbue, infuse, diffuse, suffuse, transfuse, instill, infiltrate, dash, tinge, tincture, season, blend, cross; alloy, amalgamate, compound, adulterate.

Adj. **mixed,** composite, half-and-half, hybrid, mongrel, heterogeneous; motley, variegated, miscellaneous, promiscuous, indiscriminate.

Adv. **among,** amid, with; in the midst of.

42. [Freedom from mixture] SIMPLENESS.—*N.* **simpleness,** purity, homogeneity.

elimination, sifting, purification, etc. (*cleanness*), 652.

V. **render simple,** simplify.

sift, winnow, bolt, eliminate; exclude, get rid of; clear, purify, etc. (*clean*), 652.

Adj. **simple,** uniform, homogeneous, single, pure, clear; elemental, elementary.

43. JUNCTION.—*N.* **junction,** joining, union; connection, conjunction, annexation, attachment; marriage, wedlock; confluence, communication, meeting, reunion; assemblage, etc., 72; coherence, etc., 46; combination, etc., 48.

joint, joining, juncture, pivot, hinge, articulation; seam, gore, gusset, link, bond.

contingency, emergency, predicament, crisis, concurrence.

V. **join,** unite, connect; associate; put together, piece together, embody.

attach, fix, fasten, bind, secure, tighten, clinch, tie, strap, sew, lace, stitch, knit, button, buckle, hitch, lash, splice, gird, tether, moor, picket, chain; fetter, hook, link, yoke, bracket; marry; bridge over, span.

pin, nail, screw, bolt, hasp, clasp, clamp, rivet; solder, cement, etc., 46.

entwine, interlace, intertwine, interweave; entangle.

Adj. **joined,** joint; corporate, compact.

firm, fast, close, tight, taut, secure, inseparable, indissoluble.

Adv. **jointly,** in conjunction with, etc. (*in addition to*), 37; fast, firmly.

44. DISJUNCTION.—*N.* **disjunction,** disconnection, disunion, disengagement, dissociation, discontinuity, etc., 70; isolation, insularity, insulation, separateness; dispersion.

separation, parting; detachment, segregation; divorce; cæsura, division, subdivision, break, fracture, rupture; dismemberment, dissection, disintegration, severance, disruption, cleavage.

fissure, breach, rent, rift, crack, slit, cut, incision.

V. **disjoin,** disconnect, disengage, disunite, dissociate, divorce, part, detach, unfasten, separate, disentangle, cut off, segregate; set apart, keep apart; insulate, isolate; cut adrift, loose, set free. liberate.

divide, sunder, subdivide, sever, dissever, cut, chop, saw, snip, nip, cleave, rive, rend, slit, rip, split, splinter, chip, crack, snap, break, tear, burst; wrench, rupture, hack, hew, slash, slice, carve, quarter, dissect, anatomize; partition, parcel.

disintegrate, dismember, disband; disperse, etc., 73; dislocate, break up.

part, part company; separate, leave; alienate, estrange.

Adj. disjoined, discontinuous, disjunctive; isolated, insular; separate, apart, asunder, loose, free, adrift.

Adv. separately, one by one, severally, apart, asunder.

45. [Connecting medium] VINCULUM.—*N.* vinculum, link; connective, connection; junction, etc., 43; hyphen; bracket; bridge, steppingstone; bond, cord; rope, line, cable, hawser, painter; chain; string, etc. (*filament*), 205.

fastening, tie; ligament, ligature; strap; tackle, rigging; yoke, band, headband, fillet, snood, brace, thong, girdle, noose, lariat, lasso, knot, girth, cinch.

cement, glue, gum, paste, size, solder, mortar, plaster, putty.

shackle, rein, etc. (*means of restraint*), 752.

V. bridge over, span; connect, etc., 43.

46. COHERENCE.—*N.* coherence, cohesion, cohesiveness, adherence, adhesion, adhesiveness; conglomeration, aggregation, consolidation, soldering, connection; relativity.

tenacity, toughness; stickiness; inseparability.

conglomerate, concrete, etc., 321.

V. cohere, adhere, coagulate, stick, cling, cleave, hold, close with, clasp, hug.

glue, agglutinate, cement, paste, gum; solder, weld; cake, consolidate, solidify, agglomerate.

Adj. adhesive, cohesive, adhering, tenacious, tough; sticky, etc., 352.

47. INCOHERENCE.—*N.* incoherence, nonadhesion; looseness, laxity, relaxation; loosening, disjunction, etc., 44.

V. loosen, make loose, slacken, relax; unglue, etc., 46; detach, etc., 44.

Adj. nonadhesive, noncohesive, incoherent, detached, loose, baggy, slack, lax, relaxed, segregated, unconsolidated; uncombined, etc., 48.

48. COMBINATION.—*N.* combination, mixture, etc., 41; junction, etc., 43; union, unification, synthesis, incorporation, amalgamation, coalescence, fusion, brew, blend, blending; centralization.

alloy, compound, amalgam, composition, resultant.

V. **combine,** unite, incorporate, alloy, intermix, interfuse, interlard, amalgamate, embody, absorb, blend, merge, fuse, consolidate, coalesce, solidify, impregnate, centralize.

league, federate, confederate, fraternize, club, associate, amalgamate, couple, pair, ally.

Adj. **combined,** conjoint; ingrained, imbued.

allied, amalgamated, federate, confederate, corporate, leagued.

49. DECOMPOSITION.—*N.* **decomposition,** analysis, dissection, dissolution, breakup; disjunction, etc., 44; disintegration.

decay, rot, putrefaction, putrescence, putridity, caries, corruption.

V. **decompose,** analyze, dissolve; resolve into its elements, dissect, disintegrate, disperse; crumble into dust.

rot, decay, consume, putrefy.

50. [Principal part] WHOLE.—*N.* **whole,** totality, integrity, entirety, completeness; integer, integral.

all, the whole, total, aggregate, sum, sum total.

bulk, mass, lump, tissue, staple, body, greater part, main part; lion's share.

V. **form a whole,** embody, amass; aggregate, assemble; amount to.

Adj. **whole,** total, gross, entire; complete, etc., 52; wholesale, sweeping; comprehensive.

indivisible, indissoluble, indissolvable.

Adv. **wholly,** altogether; as a whole, totally, completely, entirely, all, all in all, wholesale, in a body, collectively, in the aggregate, in the main, on the whole, bodily, substantially.

51. PART.—*N.* **part,** portion; item, particular; aught, any; division; sector, segment; fraction, fragment; detachment, subdivision.

section, chapter, verse; article, clause.

piece, lump, bit, cut, cutting; chip, chunk, slice, scrap, crumb, morsel, moiety, particle; installment, dividend; share.

member, limb, arm, wing, scion, branch, bough, joint, link, offshoot, ramification, twig, spray, spring; runner, tendril; leaf, leaflet; stump.

V. **part,** divide, disjoin, etc., 44; partition, etc. (*apportion*), 786.

Adj. **fractional,** fragmentary, sectional; incomplete, partial.

divided, broken, cut, cropped, shorn.

divisible, dissoluble, dissolvable.

Adv. **partly,** in part, partially; piecemeal, by installments, in detail.

52. COMPLETENESS.—*N.* **completeness,** intactness, completion, etc., 729; fill, saturation, entirety; totality, integrity; perfection, etc., 650; solidarity, unity, all, high tide, flood tide, spring tide.

V. **complete,** etc. (*accomplish*), 729; fill, charge, load, replenish; make up, eke out, supply deficiencies; fill up, fill in, satiate; saturate.

Adj. **complete,** entire, whole, intact, perfect, full, absolute, thorough; solid, undivided.

brimful, brimming, chock-full; saturated, crammed; replete, etc. (*redundant*), 641; fraught, laden.

exhaustive, radical, sweeping, thoroughgoing.

regular, unmitigated, sheer, unqualified, unconditional, free, abundant, etc. (*sufficient*), 639.

completing, supplemental, supplementary.

Adv. **completely,** altogether, outright, wholly, totally, utterly, quite; effectually, fully, in all respects, in every respect; out and out; throughout, from first to last, from head to foot, from top to toe, every whit, every inch.

53. INCOMPLETENESS.—*N.* **incompleteness,** deficiency, shortcoming, want, lack, insufficiency, imperfection, etc., 651; immaturity.

Part wanting: defect, deficit, omission; shortage; break, etc. (*discontinuity*), 70; missing link.

V. **be incomplete,** fall short of, lack, etc. (*be insufficient*), 640.

Adj. **incomplete,** uncompleted, imperfect, unfinished; defective, deficient, wanting, failing, in arrear, short, short of; perfunctory, sketchy, crude, immature.

mutilated, garbled, hashed, mangled, butchered, docked, truncated.

in progress, in hand; going on, proceeding.

54. COMPOSITION.—*N.* **composition,** constitution; make-up; combination, etc., 48; embodiment; formation.

authorship, compilation, composition, production, invention; writing.

painting, etching, design, etc. (*painting*), 556; relief, etc. (*sculpture*), 557.

typesetting, typography, etc., 591.

V. **be composed of,** consist of.

include, etc., 76; contain, hold, comprehend, admit, embrace, embody.

compose, constitute, form, make; fabricate, weave, construct; compile, scribble, draw, write.

55. EXCLUSION.—*N.* **exclusion,** omission, exception, rejection, repudiation; exile, seclusion, lockout, ostracism, prohibition.

separation, segregation, elimination, expulsion.

V. **exclude,** bar; leave out, shut out; reject, repudiate, black-ball, ostracize; lay aside, put aside, set apart; relegate, segregate; strike off, strike out; neglect, banish, etc. (*seclude*), 893; separate, etc. (*disjoin*), 44.

pass over, omit; eliminate, weed out.

Adj. **exclusive,** inadmissible, preclusive, preventive, prohibitive.

Adv. **except,** exclusive of, save.

56. COMPONENT.—*N.* **component,** integral part, element, constituent, ingredient, contents; feature; member, etc. (*part*), 51; personnel.

V. **enter into,** be *or* form part of, etc., 51; merge in, share in, participate; belong to, appertain to; combine, unite.

form, make, constitute, compose, fabricate, etc., 54.

Adj. **inherent,** intrinsic, essential.

inclusive, all-embracing, comprehensive.

57. EXTRANEOUSNESS.—*N.* **extraneousness,** extrinsicality; exclusion; alienism.

foreign body (substance *or* element).

alien, stranger, intruder, interloper, foreigner, newcomer; immigrant, emigrant; outsider, barbarian, tenderfoot [*slang*].

Adj. **extraneous,** foreign, alien, exterior, external; outlandish, barbaric, barbarian.

excluded, inadmissible; exceptional.

Adv. **abroad,** in foreign parts, in foreign lands; oversea, overseas.

IV. ORDER

58. ORDER.—*N.* **order,** regularity, uniformity, symmetry, harmony; course, routine; method, disposition, arrangement, array, system, economy, discipline, orderliness, subordination.

gradation, progression; series, etc. (*continuity*), 69.

rank, place, etc. (*term*), 71.

V. **adjust,** regulate, systematize, standardize; time.

Adj. **orderly,** regular; in order, in trim, neat, tidy, methodical, uniform, symmetrical, shipshape, businesslike, systematic, normal, habitual.

Adv. **in order,** methodically, in turn, in its turn; step by step; systematically, by clockwork.

59. DISORDER.—*N.* **disorder,** derangement; irregularity; untidiness; anomaly, etc. (*unconformity*), 83; anarchy, anarchism; disunion; discord.

confusion, disarray, jumble, botch, litter, farrago, mess, muddle, hodgepodge, imbroglio, chaos, clutter, medley.

complexity, complication, entanglement, intricacy; perplexity; network, maze, labyrinth; wilderness, jungle; tangled skein.

turmoil, ferment, etc. (*agitation*), 315; trouble, disturbance, convulsion, tumult, uproar, riot, rumpus [*colloq.*], fracas, pandemonium, Babel, saturnalia.

V. **disorder,** botch, disturb, derange, etc., 61; entangle, ravel, ruffle, rumple.

Adj. **disorderly,** out of order, out of place, irregular, desultory; anomalous, etc. (*unconformable*), 83; disorganized; straggling; unmethodical, unsystematic; untidy, slovenly, messy [*colloq.*], indiscriminate, chaotic, confused; deranged, etc., 61; topsy-turvy, disjointed, out of joint.

complex, intricate, complicated, perplexed, involved, entangled, knotted, tangled, inextricable.

troublous, tumultuous, turbulent; riotous, etc. (*violent*), 173.

60. [Reduction to Order] ARRANGEMENT.—*N.* arrangement, plan, etc., 626; preparation, provision; disposal, disposition; distribution, sorting, assortment, allotment, apportionment, graduation, organization, groupings; analysis, classification, division, systematization, codification.

Result of arrangement: orderliness, form, array, digest; synopsis, etc. (*compendium*), 596; table; register, etc. (*record*), 551; organism; stipulation, settlement.

V. **arrange,** dispose, fix, place; form; set in order, set out; compose, space, range, graduate, marshal, array, rank, group, parcel out, allot, apportion, distribute, assign the parts; dispose of, assort, sort; tidy [*colloq.*].

classify, class, file, list; register, etc. (*record*), 551; catalogue, tabulate, index, alphabetize, grade, codify.

methodize, regulate, systematize, co-ordinate, organize; unravel, disentangle.

Adj. **arranged,** embattled, in battle array; cut and dried; methodical, orderly, regular, systematic, on file; tabular.

61. [Bringing into disorder] DERANGEMENT.—*N.* derangement, muss [*colloq.* U. S.], mess; disorder, etc., 59; discomposure, disturbance; disorganization, dislocation; inversion, etc., 218; insanity, etc., 503.

V. **derange,** disarrange, discompose, displace, misplace; mislay, disorder; disorganize; embroil, convulse, unsettle, disturb, confuse, trouble, perturb, disconcert, jumble; muddle; unhinge, dislocate, put out of joint, throw out of gear.

turn topsy-turvy, etc. (*invert*), 218; bedevil; complicate, involve, perplex, confound; tangle, entangle; tousle [*colloq.*], dishevel, ruffle; rumple, etc. (*fold*), 258; become insane, etc., 503.

litter, scatter; mix, etc., 41.

62. [Consecutive Order] **PRECEDENCE.**—*N.* precedence, the lead, superiority, etc., 33; importance, consequence; premise; antecedence, precursor, etc., 64; priority, preference.

prefix, affix; preamble; prelude, overture, voluntary.

V. **precede,** forerun, come before, come first; head, lead, lead the way; introduce, usher in; rank, outrank; take precedence.

prefix; premise, prelude, preface; affix.

Adj. **preceding,** precedent, antecedent; anterior; prior, etc., 116; before; former, foregoing, aforesaid, said; introductory, etc., 64.

Adv. **before;** in advance, etc. (*precession*), 280.

63. SEQUENCE.—*N.* sequence, train; following, succession; afterclap, afterglow, aftermath, afterpiece, aftertaste.

continuation, prolongation; order of succession.

V. **succeed,** come after, ensue, come next.

follow, tag [*colloq.*], heel, dog, shadow, hound, hunt; trace, retrace.

append, place after, subjoin.

Adj. **succeeding,** sequent; subsequent; proximate, next; consecutive, etc. (*continuity*), 69.

latter, posterior, etc., 117.

Adv. **after,** subsequently; behind, etc. (*rear*), 235.

64. PRECURSOR.—*N.* precursor, antecedent, precedent, predecessor; forerunner, pioneer; outrider; leader, bellwether; herald, harbinger.

prelude, preamble, preface, prologue, foreword, proem, exordium, introduction; heading, frontispiece, groundwork; preparation, etc., 673; overture, voluntary; premises.

prefigurement, etc., 511; omen, etc., 512.

Adj. **introductory,** preludial, prefatory, precursory, inaugural, preliminary.

65. SEQUEL.—*N.* sequel, suffix, tail, queue, train, wake, trail, rear; retinue, suite; appendix, postscript, postlude, conclusion, epilogue; peroration; codicil; continuation; appendage, tag, aftergrowth, afterpiece, afterthought, second thoughts; outgrowth.

follower, successor, pursuer, adherent, partisan, disciple, client; sycophant, parasite.

66. BEGINNING.—*N.* beginning, commencement, opening, outset, incipience, inception; introduction, etc. (*prelude*), 64; initial; inauguration, embarkation, rising of the curtain; curtain raiser, maiden speech; exordium; outbreak, onset, brunt; initiative, first move; start, starting point; dawn, etc. (*morning*), 125.

origin, etc. (*cause*), 153; source, rise; bud, germ, egg, embryo, rudiment; genesis, birth, nativity, cradle, infancy.

head, heading; title page; van, etc. (*front*), 234.

entrance, entry; inlet, orifice, mouth, porch, portal, portico, door; gate, gateway; postern, wicket, threshold, vestibule; border, frontier.

rudiments, elements, outlines, grammar, alphabet, ABC.

V. **begin,** commence; rise, arise; originate, initiate, open, start; dawn, set in, take its rise, enter upon; set out, etc. (*depart*), 293; embark in; make one's debut; institute; set about, set to work; make a start; break ground, cross the Rubicon; undertake, etc., 676.

usher in, lead the way, take the lead *or* initiative; inaugurate, head; lay the foundations, etc. (*prepare*), 673; found, etc. (*cause*), 153; set up, set on foot, launch, broach; open up, open the door to.

come into existence, take birth; burst forth, break out; spring up, crop up.

recommence; begin at the beginning, begin again, start afresh.

Adj. **initial,** prime, introductory, incipient; inaugural; embryonic, rudimentary; primal, primary, primeval, etc. (*old*), 124; aboriginal; natal.

first, maiden, foremost, front, head, leading.

Adv. **first,** in the first place, in the bud, in embryo, from the beginning, formerly.

67. END.—*N.* **end,** close, termination, conclusion, finish, completion, finis, finale, period, term, terminus, last, extreme, extremity; fag end, tip, nib, point, tail, tag, peroration, appendix, epilogue; consummation, denouement, fall of the curtain; goal, destination, terminal, limit, stoppage; expiration; dissolution, death, etc., 360; doomsday.

last stage, evening (*of life*); *coup de grâce* [F.], deathblow; knockout.

V. **end,** close, finish, terminate, conclude; expire, die, etc., 360; come to a close, perorate; run out, pass away.

bring to an end, put an end to, make an end of; achieve, etc. (*complete*), 729; stop, etc., 142.

Adj. **final,** terminal; conclusive; crowning, etc. (*completing*), 729; last, ultimate; hindermost; rear, etc., 235.

ended, settled, decided, over.

Adv. **finally,** in fine; at the last; once for all.

68. MIDDLE.—*N.* **middle,** midst, thick, midmost; mean, etc., 29; medium, middle term; center, core, kernel, nucleus, hub, heart, bull's-eye; mid-course, neutrality, compromise.

equidistance, bisection; equator, diaphragm, midriff.

Adj. **middle,** medial, mid, midmost; intermediate, equidistant, central, pivotal, mediterranean, equatorial.

Adv. **midway,** halfway, in the middle; amidships.

69. [Uninterrupted sequence] CONTINUITY.—**continuity,** continuousness, succession, round, suite, progression, series, train, chain; scale; gradation, course; perpetuity.

procession, cavalcade, parade; column; retinue, cortege, funeral, ovation.

pedigree, genealogy, lineage, history, family tree, race; ancestry, descent, family, house; line, line of ancestors; strain.

rank, file, line, row, range, tier.

V. **arrange in a series,** string together, file, list, thread, tabulate.

Adj. **continuous,** continued; consecutive, progressive, gradual, serial, successive; uninterrupted, unbroken, entire; linear; perennial. constant.

Adv. **continuously,** in a line, in succession, in turn; running, gradually, in file, in single file, in Indian file.

70. [Interrupted sequence] DISCONTINUITY.—*N.* **discontinuity,** disconnectedness; disconnection, etc., 44; interruption, break, fracture, flaw, fault, crack, cut; gap, etc. (*interval*), 198; intermission, alternation.

V. **alternate,** interchange, intermit.

discontinue, pause, interrupt, intervene; break, break off; interpose, etc., 228; disconnect, etc. (*disjoin*), 44; dissever.

Adj. **discontinuous,** disconnected, broken, interrupted, fitful, irregular, spasmodic, desultory; intermittent, alternate, recurrent, periodic.

Adv. **at intervals,** by snatches, by jerks, by fits and starts.

71. TERM.—*N.* **term,** rank, station, stage, step; degree, etc., 26; scale, grade, status, state, position, standing, footing, place, mark, period, range.

72. [Collective Order] ASSEMBLAGE.—*N.* **assemblage,** collection, levy, gathering, ingathering, mobilization, meet, forgathering, muster, team; concourse, conflux, congregation.

meeting, levee, reunion, drawing room, at home; social gathering, 892; assembly, congress, house, senate, legislature, etc., 696; convocation, caucus, convention.

company, platoon, faction, caravan, posse, watch, squad, corps, troop, troupe; army, regiment.

miscellany, miscellanea, compilation; symposium; library, etc. (*store*), 636.

crowd, throng; flood, rush, deluge; rabble, mob, host, etc. (*multitude*), 102; rout, press, crush, horde, body, tribe; crew, gang, knot, squad, force, band, party; bunch, drive, roundup.

clan, brotherhood, association, etc. (*party*), 712.

group, cluster, clump, set, batch, lot, pack; budget, assortment, bunch; parcel, packet, bundle, package, bale, fagot, wisp, truss, tuft, shock, clump; grove, thicket; rick, stack, sheaf, swath; volley, shower, storm, cloud.

accumulation, etc. (*store*), 636; heap, lump, pile, mass, pyramid; drift, snowball, snowdrift; amassment; conglomeration, aggregation, concentration, convergence, congestion, quantity, etc. (*greatness*), 31.

V. **be** *or* **come together,** assemble, collect, muster; meet, unite, join, rejoin; cluster, flock, swarm, surge, stream, herd, crowd, huddle, throng, associate; congregate, concentrate, resort, forgather.

bring together, assemble, muster, collect, gather; hold a meeting, convene, convoke; rake up, dredge, heap, mass, pile; pack, cram, lump together; compile, group, concentrate, unite, amass, accumulate, hoard, store.

Adj. **dense,** serried, teeming, swarming, populous.

73. DISPERSION.—*N.* **dispersion,** disjunct on, etc., 44; divergence, radiation, broadcast, spread, dissemination, diffusion, dissipation, distribution; apportionment, allotment.

V. **disperse,** scatter, sow, disseminate, sow broadcast, diffuse, radiate, broadcast, shed, spread, bestrew, dispense, disband, dismember, distribute; apportion, etc., 786; dispel, cast forth, draft off; strew, cast, sprinkle; issue, deal out, retail, utter.

Adj. **scattered,** disseminated, strown, strewn, dispersed, diffuse, diffusive, sparse, broadcast, sporadic, widespread; epidemic, etc. (*general*), 78; adrift, stray; disheveled.

74. [Place of meeting] FOCUS.—*N.* **focus,** center, gathering place, rendezvous, rallying point, headquarters, resort, haunt, retreat, club; tryst, trysting place, place of meeting.

V. **focus,** bring to a point, bring to a focus; rally, meet.

75. [Distributive Order] CLASS.—*N.* **class,** division, subdivision, category, head, order, section; department, province, domain, sphere.

kind, sort, type, estate, genus, species, variety, family, race, tribe, caste, clan, breed, kin; clique, coterie, set; sect, gender, sex.

description, denomination, persuasion, connection, designation, character, stamp; selection, specification.

76. INCLUSION.—*N.* **inclusion,** admission, incorporation, comprisal, reception.

composition, embodiment, formation.

V. **include,** comprise, comprehend, contain, admit, embrace, receive, inclose, etc. (*circumscribe*), 229; incorporate, cover, embody, encircle; reckon among, number among; refer to; place under, arrange under, take into account.

Adj. **inclusive,** included, including; comprehensive, sweeping, all-embracing.

77. EXCLUSION [from a class].—*N.* **exclusion,** rejection, *see* exclusion (*from a compound*), 55.

78. GENERALITY.—*N.* **generality,** universality, catholicity, miscellany, miscellaneousness; common run, prevalence. rifeness.

everyone, everybody, all hands [*colloq.*], all the world and his wife [*humorous*], anybody.

V. **be general,** prevail.

render general, spread, broaden, universalize, generalize.

Adj. **general,** generic, collective; current, wide, broad, comprehensive, sweeping; encyclopedic, panoramic; widespread, etc. (*dispersed*), 73; common, prevalent, prevailing, rife, epidemic.

universal, catholic, world-wide.

every, all, unspecified, miscellaneous, indefinite.

Adv. **generally,** always, in general, generally speaking; for the most part.

79. SPECIALTY.—*N.* **specialty,** speciality, individuality. peculiarity; personality, characteristic, mannerism, idiosyncrasy, singularity, originality; trait, distinctive feature.

particulars, details, items, counts; minutiæ.

V. **specify,** particularize; individualize, specialize; designate, determine; denote, indicate, point out, select, differentiate; itemize, enter into detail.

Adj. **special,** especial, particular, individual, specific, proper, personal, original, private, respective, definite, minute, certain, peculiar, marked, appropriate, characteristic, exclusive, restricted; singular, exceptional; typical, representative.

Adv. **each,** apiece, one by one, severally, respectively, in detail.

namely, that is to say, viz.; to wit.

80. RULE.—*N.* **regularity,** uniformity, constancy, clockwork precision; punctuality, etc. (*exactness*), 494; even tenor, rut; system; routine, custom; formula; canon, convention, maxim, rule, regulation; standard, model, precedent; conformity, etc., 82.

law, order of things; normality, normalcy, normal state, ordinary condition, standing order; hard and fast rule.

Adj. **regular,** uniform, symmetrical, constant, steady; according to rule, etc., 82; normal, habitual, customary, etc., 613; methodical, orderly, systematic.

81. MULTIFORMITY.—*N.* **multiformity,** variety, diversity.

Adj. **multiform,** multifold, multifarious, multiplex; manifold, many-sided; protean, heterogeneous, motley, mosaic.

indiscriminate, irregular, diversified, diverse; of every description.

82. CONFORMITY.—*N.* **conformity,** observance; conventionality, etc. (*custom*), 613; agreement, accord.

example, instance, exemplification, illustration, specimen, sample.

conventionalist, formalist, bromide [*slang*], Philistine.

V. **conform to,** adapt oneself to.

be regular, travel in a rut; obey rules; agree with, comply with, fall in with; be guided by, harmonize, conventionalize, follow the fashion; do at Rome as the Romans do; swim with the stream.

exemplify, illustrate, cite, quote.

Adj. **conformable to rule,** adaptable, consistent, agreeable, compliant; regular, etc., 80; according to rule, well regulated, orderly, uniform, symmetric.

conventional, etc. (*customary*), 613; ordinary, common, habitual, usual; strict, rigid, uncompromising.

typical, normal, formal; canonical, orthodox, exemplary, illustrative, in point.

Adv. **conformably,** by rule; in accordance with, in keeping with; according to; as usual, as a matter of course.

invariably, etc. (*uniformly*), 16.

83. UNCONFORMITY.—*N.* **nonconformity,** unconformity, nonobservance, unconventionality, informality; anomaly, anomalousness, exception, peculiarity; breach *or* violation of custom; eccentricity, oddity, rarity.

individuality, singularity, originality, idiosyncrasy, mannerism.

aberration, irregularity; singularity; exemption; qualification, proviso.

nonconformist, Bohemian, nondescript character, original, freak, prodigy, wonder, miracle, curiosity.

mongrel, half-caste, etc., 41.

outcast, outlaw, Ishmael, pariah.

V. **be uncomfortable,** leave the beaten path; break (*or* violate). a law *or* custom; stretch a point.

Adj. **uncomfortable,** exceptional, eccentric; abnormal, unnatural, anomalous, misplaced, out of order, irregular, arbitrary, lawless; informal, stray, eccentric, peculiar, exclusive, egregious.

unusual, unaccustomed, unwonted, uncommon; rare, singular, unique, curious, odd, extraordinary, strange, monstrous; wonderful, etc., 870; remarkable, noteworthy, queer, quaint, nondescript, original, unorthodox, unconventional, Bohemian, unprecedented, unparalleled, unexampled, unheard of; fantastic, newfangled, eccentric, grotesque, bizarre; unfamiliar, outlandish.

heterogeneous, amorphous, mongrel, hybrid; unsymmetric, etc., 243.

Adv. unconformably; except, unless, save.

V. NUMBER

84. NUMBER.—*N.* **number,** symbol, numeral, figure, cipher, digit, integer, round number; series.

sum, product, total, aggregate, difference.

ratio, proportion, percentage; progression; arithmetical progression.

power, root, exponent, index, logarithm.

85. NUMERATION.—*N.* **numeration,** numbering; tale, tally, enumeration, reckoning, computation, calculation, calculus; measurement, etc., 466; statistics.

arithmetic, algebra, differential calculus, calculus of differences.

muster, poll, census, roll call; account, etc. (*list*), 86.

Instruments: abacus, calculating machine, adding machine, cash register.

arithmetician, calculator, algebraist, geometrician, trigonometrician, mathematician, actuary, statistician.

V. **number,** count, enumerate; call over, run over; take an account of, call the roll, muster, poll; sum up, cast up; tell off, cipher, reckon, reckon up, estimate, compute, calculate.

check, prove, demonstrate, balance, audit, overhaul, take stock.

total, amount to, come to.

Adj. **numeral,** numerical; arithmetical, analytic, algebraic, statistical, computable, calculable, commensurable, commensurate.

86. LIST.—*N.* **list,** catalogue, card index; inventory, schedule; register, etc. (*record*), 551; account; bill, bill of costs; tally, file, index, table, contents; book, ledger; synopsis, syllabus; scroll, screed, invoice, manifest, bill of lading; prospectus, program; bill of fare, menu; score, bulletin, census, statistics, returns; directory, atlas, gazetteer; calendar, almanac.

dictionary, lexicon, glossary, vocabulary, wordbook, thesaurus.

roll; muster roll; roll of honor; roster, slate, poll, panel.

V. **list,** enroll, schedule, inventory, register, catalogue, invoice, bill, book, slate, post, docket; empanel, tally, file, index, tabulate, enter, census.

87. UNITY.—*N.* **unity,** oneness; individuality; unification, etc., 48; completeness, completion.

one, unit; individual.

V. isolate, insulate.

render one; unite, etc. (*join*), 43, (*combine*), 48.

Adj. **one,** sole, lone, single, solitary; individual, apart, alone; unaccompanied, unattended, singlehanded; singular, odd, unique, isolated; insular.

88. ACCOMPANIMENT.—*N.* **accompaniment,** adjunct, accessory; context; appendage, appurtenance; attribute.

company, association, partnership; companionship.

attendant, companion, associate, colleague, partner; consort, spouse; satellite, hanger-on, shadow; escort, suite, train, retinue, convoy, follower, etc., 65.

V. **accompany,** attend, convoy, chaperon; associate with, couple with.

Adj. **accompanying,** fellow, twin, joint; associated with, coupled with; accessory, attendant.

Adv. **with,** withal; together with, along with, in company with; therewith, herewith; and, etc. (*addition*), 37.

together, in a body, collectively, in conjunction.

89. DUALITY.—*N.* **duality,** dualism; duplicity; polarity.

two, deuce, couple, couplet, both, twain, brace, pair, twins, Castor and Pollux, gemini, fellows; yoke, span; distich.

V. **pair,** mate, couple, bracket, yoke.

Adj. **two,** twain, both; dual, twin; duplex, etc., 90; tête-à-tête.

90. DUPLICATION.—*N.* **duplication,** doubling, reduplication; iteration, etc. (*repetition*), 104; renewal.

duplicate, facsimile, copy, replica, counterpart, etc. (*copy*), 21.

V. **double;** redouble, reduplicate; repeat, etc., 104; renew, renovate.

Adj. **double;** doubled; twofold, two-sided, duplex; double-faced, double-headed; twin, duplicate, second; dual.

Adv. **twice,** once more; over again, etc. (*repeatedly*), 104.

91. [Division into two parts] BISECTION.—*N.* **bisection,** halving, bifurcation, forking, branching, ramification, dichotomy.

half, moiety.

V. **bisect,** halve, divide, separate, split, cut in two, cleave.

fork, bifurcate, branch off *or* out, ramify.

Adj. **bisected,** cloven, cleft; bifurcated; semi-, demi-, hemi-.

92. TRIALITY.—*N.* **triality** [*rare*], trinity,[1] triunity.

three, triad, triplet, trio; triangle, trident, tripod, trireme, triumvirate.

third power, cube.

Adj. **three;** triform, tertiary.

93. TRIPLICATION.—*N.* **triplication,** triplicity; trilogy.

V. **treble,** triple; cube.

Adj. **treble,** triple; threefold; third.

[1]*Trinity* is hardly ever used except in a theological sense; *see* Deity, 976.

Adv. **three times,** thrice; in the third place, thirdly; threefold, triply, trebly.

94. [Division into three parts] **TRISECTION.**—*N.* trisection, tripartition, third, third part.

V. **trisect,** divide into three parts, third.

95. QUATERNITY.—*N.* quaternity [*rare*], four, quartet, quadruplet; square, quadrilateral; quadrangle.

V. **square,** biquadrate, reduce to a square.

Adj. **four;** quadratic; quadrangular, quadrilateral.

96. QUADRUPLICATION.—*N.* quadruplication.

V. **quadruplicate,** multiply by four.

Adj. **fourfold,** quadruple; fourth.

Adv. **four times,** in the fourth place, fourthly.

97. [Division into four parts] **QUADRISECTION.**—*N.* quadrisection, quadripartition; quartering; fourth; quart, quarter; farthing; quarto.

V. **quarter,** divide into four parts, quadrisect.

98. FIVE, ETC.—*N.* **five,** quintet, pentagon, pentameter.

six, half a dozen; hexagon, hexameter, sextet.

seven, heptagon, heptameter, heptarchy.

eight, octave, octagon, octameter, octavo, octet.

nine, nonagon.

ten, decade, decagon, decasyllable, decemvir, decemvirate, decennium.

twelve, dozen; **thirteen,** long dozen, baker's dozen; **twenty,** score; **fifty,** half a hundred; **sixty,** threescore; **seventy,** threescore and ten; **eighty,** fourscore; **ninety,** fourscore and ten.

hundred, centenary, century; bicentenary, tercentenary.

thousand, millennium; myriad.

V. **quintuplicate,** sextuple; centuplicate.

Adj. **five,** fifth, quintuple; pentangular, pentagonal. **sixth,** sextuple, hexagonal, hexangular. **seventh,** septuple, heptagonal, heptangular. **eight,** octuple, octagonal, octangular. **tenth,** tenfold, decimal, decagonal, decasyllabic. **eleventh,** undecennial, undecennary. **twelfth,** duodenary, duodenal. **sixtieth,** sexagesimal. **seventieth,** septuagesimal.

centuple, centuplicate, centennial, centenary; hundredth; thousandth, millenary, millennial, etc.

99. QUINQUESECTION, ETC.—*N.* **quinquesection,** division by five, etc., 98; decimation; tithe; fifth, etc.

Adj. **decimal,** tenth; duodecimal, twelfth; sexagesimal, sexagenary; hundredth, centesimal; millesimal, etc.

100. [More than one] **PLURALITY.**—*N.* **plurality,** one or two, two or three, etc.; a few, several; multitude, etc., 102; majority.

Adj. **plural,** more than one, upwards of, some, certain.

100a. [Less than one] FRACTION.—*N.* **fraction,** fractional part; part, portion, fragment, etc., 51.

Adj. **fractional,** fragmentary, inconsiderable, partial.

101. ZERO.—*N.* **zero,** nothing; naught, nought; cipher; none, nobody.

102. MULTITUDE.—*N.* **multitude,** multitudinousness, multiplicity; profusion, etc. (*plenty*), 639; legion, host, array, army, galaxy; numbers, scores; heap, power, sight, lot, lots [*all five colloq.*], swarm, bevy, cloud, flock, herd, drove, shoal, school, flight, covey, hive, brood, litter, farrow, fry, nest; mob, crowd, etc. (*assemblage*), 72.

V. **be numerous,** swarm with, teem with, be alive with, crowd, swarm, outnumber, multiply; people.

Adj. **many,** several, sundry, various, alive with; numerous; profuse, manifold, multitudinous, teeming, populous, outnumbering, crowded, thick, galore [*colloq.*]; thick-coming, endless, etc. (*infinite*), 105.

103. FEWNESS.—*N.* **fewness,** paucity, scarcity, sparseness, sparsity; handful; small quantity, etc., 32; rarity, infrequency; minority.

Diminution of number: reduction, weeding, elimination; decimation; eradication.

V. **render few,** reduce, diminish, weed out, eliminate, thin, decimate.

Adj. **few,** scant, scanty; thin, rare, scarce, sparse, few and far between; exiguous; infrequent.

104. REPETITION.—*N.* **repetition,** iteration, recapitulation, reiteration; monotone; duplication, reduplication, monotony, harping, recurrence; reappearance, reproduction; periodicity, etc., 138; succession, run; alliteration; rhythm, tautology; diffuseness, redundancy.

echo, encore, burden of a song, refrain, undersong.

cuckoo, etc. (*imitation*), 19; reverberation, vibration, resonance; drumming, etc. (*roll*), 407; renewal, etc. (*restoration*), 660.

V. **repeat,** iterate, reiterate, redouble, reproduce, echo, re-echo, drum, harp upon, hammer; rehearse; resume, return to, recapitulate.

recur, revert, return, reappear; renew, etc. (*restore*), 660.

duplicate, reduplicate.

Adj. **repeated,** repetitious, recurrent, recurring; frequent, incessant; redundant, tautological; another.

monotonous, harping, iterative, unvaried; habitual, etc., 613.

aforesaid, aforenamed; said.

Adv. **repeatedly,** often, again, anew, afresh, once more; ditto, encore, again and again; over and over, frequently, etc., 136.

105. INFINITY.—*N.* **infinity,** infinitude, infiniteness; perpetuity, immortality; inexhaustibility, immensity, boundlessness.

V. **be infinite,** have no limits (*or* bounds), go on forever.

Adj. **infinite,** immense; numberless, countless, measureless, innumerable, immeasurable, incalculable, illimitable, interminable, unfathomable; without limit, without end, limitless, endless, boundless; untold, unnumbered, unmeasured, unbounded, unlimited; perpetual, etc., 112.

VI. TIME

106. TIME.—*N.* **time,** duration; period, term, stage, space, span, spell, snap, season; course.

intermediate time, while, interim, interval; intermission, interregnum, interlude; respite.

era, epoch, eon, cycle, age, reign, dynasty, administration.

V. **continue,** last, endure, stay, go on, remain, persist, abide, stand, stick [*colloq.*], hold out; intervene; elapse, etc., 109.

pass time, spend *or* while away time, tide over; employ time; seize an opportunity; linger on, drag on; tarry, etc., 110; waste time, etc. (*be inactive*), 683; procrastinate, etc., 133.

Adj. **permanent,** etc. (*durable*), 110; timely, opportune, seasonable.

Adv. **while,** whilst, during; in the course of; in the time of, when; meantime, meanwhile, in the meantime, in the interim; from day to day; for a time, for a season; till, until, up to, yet; the whole time, all the time; throughout; for good, permanently, always.

then, hereupon, thereupon, whereupon.

107. Absence of time.—*N.* no time.

Adv. **never,** ne'er; at no time, at no period; on no occasion, nevermore.

108. [Definite duration or portion of time] PERIOD.—*N.* **period;** octave, semester, quarter, moon, year, decennial, decennium; decade, lifetime, generation; epoch, era, century, age, millennium.

109. [Indefinite duration] COURSE.—*N.* **corridors** (*or* sweep, vista, halls, progress, process, lapse, flow, tide, march, flight) of time; duration, etc., 106.

Indefinite time: eon, age.

V. **elapse,** lapse, flow, run, proceed, advance, pass; fly, slip, slide, glide; crawl, drag; expire, go by, pass by, be past.

Adv. **in time,** in due time (*or* season, course); in course of time, in the fullness of time.

110. [Long duration] **DURABILITY.**—*N.* durability, durableness, permanence, continuance, persistence, lastingness, standing; immutability, stability; survival; longevity, etc. (*age*), 128; delay, etc. (*lateness*), 133; slowness.

an age, a long time, eon, century, an eternity; perpetuity, etc., 112.

V. **last,** endure, stand, remain, abide, continue, etc., 106.

tarry, etc., 133; drag on, protract, prolong; spin out, eke out, draw out; temporize, gain time.

outlast, outlive, survive.

Adj. **permanent,** durable, lasting; chronic, long-standing; persistent; lifelong, livelong; endless, fixed, long-lived, perennial; perpetual, etc., 112.

prolonged, protracted, spun out; lingering, long-winded; slow, etc., 275.

Adv. **long,** for a long time; long ago, etc. (*in a past time*), 122; all the day long, the livelong day; all the year round; permanently.

111. [Short duration] **TRANSIENCE.**—*N.* transience, transiency, evanescence, impermanence; changeableness, etc., 149; mortality; span; nine days' wonder, bubble; interregnum, interim.

velocity, etc., 274; suddenness, abruptness.

V. **be transient,** flit, pass away, fly, gallop, vanish, sink, melt, fade, evaporate.

Adj. **transient,** transitory, passing, evanescent, fleeting, fugitive; temporal, temporary, provisional, provisory; cursory; short-lived, ephemeral; deciduous; perishable, mortal; precarious; impermanent.

brief, quick, brisk, fleet; meteoric, volatile, summary; pressed for time, etc. (*haste*), 684; sudden, momentary, spasmodic, instantaneous.

Adv. **temporarily,** for the moment, for a time; awhile, soon, etc. (*early*), 132; briefly.

112. [Endless duration] **PERPETUITY.**—*N.* perpetuity, eternity, aye; immortality, perpetuation.

V. **eternalize,** immortalize, eternize, perpetuate.

Adj. **perpetual,** eternal, everlasting, continual, endless, unending; ceaseless, incessant, uninterrupted, unceasing; interminable; unfading, never-ending, deathless, immortal, undying, imperishable.

Adv. **perpetually,** always, ever, evermore, aye; forever, in all ages, without end, to the end of time; till doomsday; constantly, etc. (*very frequently*), 136.

113. [Point of time] INSTANTANEITY.—*N.* instantaneity, instantaneousness; suddenness, abruptness.

moment, instant, second, twinkling, flash, breath.

V. be instantaneous; flash.

Adj. instantaneous, momentary, extempore, sudden, abrupt.

Adv. instantaneously, in no time; presto, instanter, in a trice, in a jiffy [*colloq.*], suddenly, in the same breath; at once, plump; immediately, etc. (*early*), 132; extempore, on the spur of the moment; slapdash, etc. (*haste*), 684.

114. [Estimation, measurement, and record of time] CHRONOMETRY.—*N.* chronometry, chronology, horology.

almanac, calendar; register, registry; chronicle, annals, journal, diary.

timekeeper, clock, watch, repeater; chronometer, timepiece; dial, sundial, hourglass.

V. **register,** date, chronicle; measure time, beat time, mark time.

Adj. chronologic *or* chronological, temporal.

115. [False estimate of time] ANACHRONISM.—*N.* anachronism, error in time, error in chronology, misdate; anticipation; disregard (*or* neglect, oblivion) of time.

V. **misdate;** antedate, postdate, anticipate; take no note of time.

Adj. **misdated;** undated; overdue; out of date, anachronistic, behind time, ahead of time.

116. PRIORITY.—*N.* priority, predecessor, precedence, pre-existence; precursor, antecedent, forerunner; the past, etc., 122.

V. **precede,** come before; pre-exist, forerun; go before, lead, head; presage, herald, usher in, introduce, announce.

be beforehand, etc. (*be early*), 132; anticipate, forestall.

Adj. **prior,** previous, preceding, anterior, antecedent; pre-existent; former, aforementioned, foregoing, before-mentioned, aforesaid, said; introductory, etc. (*precursory*), 64.

Adv. **before,** prior to; earlier; previously, ere, already, yet, beforehand; on the eve of.

117. POSTERIORITY.—*N.* posteriority; succession, sequence; following, continuance, prolongation; futurity, future; successor; sequel, etc., 65; remainder.

V. **follow after,** pursue, come after, go after; succeed, supervene; ensue, result.

Adj. **subsequent,** posterior, following, after, later, succeeding, successive, ensuing, posthumous; future, etc., 121; after-dinner.

Adv. **subsequently,** after, afterward, since, later; next, close upon, thereafter, thereupon.

118. PRESENT TIME.—*N*. the present time, the present juncture *or* occasion; the times, time being; twentieth century.

Adj. present, actual, instant, current, latest, existing.

Adv. at this time, at this moment, etc., 113; now, at present; today, nowadays; already; even now, but now, just now; for the time being.

119. DIFFERENT TIME.—*N*. different time, other time.

Adv. then, at that time (*or* moment, instant); on that occasion.

when; whenever, whensoever; whereupon, upon which; at various times.

once, formerly, once upon a time.

120. SIMULTANEOUSNESS.—*N*. simultaneousness, synchronism, coexistence, coincidence, concurrence.

contemporary, coeval.

V. coexist, concur, accompany, keep pace with; synchronize.

Adj. simultaneous, coexisting, coincident, synchronous, concomitant, concurrent; coeval; contemporary, contemporaneous.

Adv. simultaneously, together, in concert; in the same breath.

121. THE FUTURE.—*N*. future, futurity, hereafter, time to come; morrow, tomorrow, by and by, doomsday, day of judgment, crack of doom.

approach of time, advent; destiny, etc., 152.

heritage, heirs, posterity, descendants.

prospect, anticipation, expectation; foresight, etc., 510.

V. anticipate, expect, await, foresee; forestall, etc. (*be early*), 132.

approach, await, threaten; impend, etc. (*be destined*), 152; come on, draw near.

Adj. future, to come; coming, impending, overhanging, imminent; next, near, close at hand; eventual, ulterior; prospective, in prospect.

Adv. prospectively, hereafter, in future; in course of time, eventually, ultimately, sooner or later.

soon, early; on the eve of, on the point of, about to.

122. THE PAST.—*N*. the past, past time, days of yore, days of old, times past, former times, yesterday, the olden time; retrospection, memory, priority.

antiquity, antiqueness, time immemorial, history, remote time; remote past; paleontology, archeology, antiquarianism.

antiquary, antiquarian, archeologist.

ancestry, lineage, forefathers.

V. pass, lapse, blow over.

Adj. past, gone, gone by, over, passed away, bygone, elapsed,

lapsed, expired, extinct, exploded, forgotten, irrecoverable; obsolete, antiquated, outworn.

former, pristine, quondam, late; ancestral.

foregoing, last, latter; recent.

looking back, retrospective, retroactive; archeological.

Adv. **formerly,** of old, of yore, time was, ago; anciently, long ago; lately, latterly, of late; ere now, before now, hitherto, heretofore; already, yet, up to this time.

123. NEWNESS.—*N.* **newness,** novelty; youth, juvenility, immaturity.

innovation; renovation, restoration.

upstart, *nouveau riche* [F.], parvenu.

modernism, modernness, modernity; modernization; latest fashion.

V. **renew,** renovate; rejuvenate; modernize.

Adj. **new,** novel, recent, fresh, green; young, etc., 127; raw, immature; virgin, untried; **modern,** late; newborn, new-fashioned, newfangled, newfledged; just out [*colloq.*], unhandled; brand-new, up-to-date [*colloq.*], renovated, spick-and-span.

Adv. **newly,** afresh, anew, lately, just now, latterly, of late.

124. OLDNESS.—*N.* **oldness,** age, antiquity.

maturity, matureness, ripeness.

decline, decay; senility, superannuation, dotage.

archaism, antiquarianism; thing of the past, relic of the past.

tradition, custom, immemorial usage, common law; folklore.

V. **be old,** have had its day, have seen its day.

become old, age, fade.

Adj. **old,** ancient, antique; time-honored, venerable, hoary; elder, eldest; firstborn; senile, etc., 128.

primitive, prime, primeval, aboriginal; antediluvian, prehistoric, dateless, patriarchal, archaic, classic, medieval; ancestral.

immemorial, traditional, unwritten, inveterate, rooted.

antiquated, of other times, of the old school, old world; obsolete, out-of-date, out-of-fashion, gone by, stale, old-fashioned, exploded, extinct, timeworn, crumbling, secondhand.

125. MORNING. [Noon]—*N.* **morning,** morn, forenoon, ante-meridian, A.M., prime, dawn, daybreak; dayspring, peep of day, break of day, aurora, sunrise, daylight, cockcrow.

noon, midday, noonday, noontide, meridian, prime; nooning, noontime.

spring, springtide, springtime, seedtime; vernal equinox.

summer, summertide, summertime, midsummer.

Adj. **matin,** matutinal.

noon, noonday, midday.

spring, vernal.

summer, estival.

126. EVENING. [Midnight]—*N.* evening, eve, decline of day, close of day, eventide, vespers, nightfall, curfew, dusk, gloaming, twilight, sunset, sundown, bedtime.

afternoon, post meridiem [L.], P.M.

midnight; dead of night, witching time.

autumn, fall; harvesttime; autumnal equinox; Indian summer. winter.

Adj. vesper, nightly, nocturnal; autumnal.

wintry, winterly.

127. YOUTH.—*N.* youth; juvenility; infancy, babyhood; child-hood; boyhood, girlhood; rising generation; minority, imma-turity, teens, tender age, bloom.

cradle, nursery.

flower of life, springtide of life, seedtime of life, golden season of life; heyday of youth, school days.

Adj. young, youthful, juvenile, green, callow, sappy, beardless, underage, in one's teens; younger, junior; newfledged, unfledged, unripe.

128. AGE.—*N.* age; oldness, old age, advanced age, senility, years, gray hairs, declining years, decrepitude, superannuation, second childhood, dotage; vale of years, decline of life; green old age, ripe age; longevity.

seniority, eldership, primogeniture; elders, etc. (*veteran*), 130; dean, father.

V. age, grow old, decline, wane.

Adj. aged; old, etc., 124; elderly, senile; ripe, mellow, declining, waning, past one's prime; gray, gray-headed, hoar, hoary, vener-able, patriarchal, timeworn, antiquated, effete, decrepit, super-annuated; advanced in life (*or* years); stricken in years; doting, etc. (*imbecile*), 499.

older, elder, oldest, eldest; senior; firstborn.

129. INFANT.—*N.* infant, babe, baby; nursling, suckling.

child, tot, mite, chick, kid [*slang*], little one, brat, pickaninny [*colored child*], urchin, elf.

youth, boy, lad, laddie, slip, sprig, stripling, youngster, cub, whippersnapper [*colloq.*], schoolboy, hobbledehoy, young hopeful, cadet, minor.

girl, lass, lassie, wench, damsel; maid, maiden, virgin; nymph, colleen, flapper, minx, schoolgirl; hoyden, tomboy, romp.

Adj. infantile, infantine, puerile, boyish, girlish, childish, babyish, kittenish; boylike, girllike, newborn; young, etc., 127.

130. VETERAN.—*N.* veteran, old man, patriarch, graybeard;

grandfather, sexagenarian, octogenarian, nonagenarian, centenarian; Methuselah; elders, forefathers; dotard, etc., 501.

granny, crone, hag, beldam.

Adj. veteran; aged, etc., 128.

131. ADOLESCENCE.—*N.* adolescence, majority, adulthood, womanhood, manhood, virility; flower of age; full bloom; spring of life.

man, etc., 373; woman, etc., 374; adult.

middle age, maturity, full age, prime of life, meridian of life.

V. come of age, come to man's estate, come to years of discretion; attain majority; come out [*colloq.*].

Adj. adolescent, pubescent, of age, of full age, of ripe age; out of one's teens, grown up, full-grown, manly, manlike, virile, adult; womanly; marriageable.

middle-aged, mature, in one's prime; matronly.

132. EARLINESS.—*N.* earliness, punctuality, promptitude, readiness, expedition, quickness, haste, etc. (*velocity*), 274; suddenness.

prematurity, precocity, precipitation, anticipation.

V. be early, be beforehand.

anticipate, forestall, take time by the forelock, steal a march upon; bespeak, secure, engage, pre-engage.

accelerate, expedite, etc. (*quicken*), 274; make haste, etc. (*hurry*), 684.

Adj. early, timely, seasonable, punctual, forward; prompt, etc. (*active*), 682.

premature, precipitate, precocious, anticipatory.

sudden, instantaneous, immediate; unexpected, etc., 508.

imminent, impending, near.

Adv. early, soon, anon, betimes, ere long, before long; punctually, in time; on time, on the dot [*slang*].

beforehand; prematurely, too soon; precipitately, hastily; in anticipation; unexpectedly, unawares.

suddenly, etc. (*instantaneously*), 113; at short notice, extempore; on the spur of the moment, at once; on the spot, on the instant, at sight, offhand, straight, straightway; forthwith, immediately, quickly, speedily, apace; presently, by and by, directly.

133. LATENESS.—*N.* lateness; tardiness, etc. (*slowness*), 275.

delay, procrastination, postponement, adjournment, prorogation, retardation; protraction, prolongation; moratorium; aftertime; respite, truce, reprieve, stop, stay, suspension, remand.

V. be late, tarry, wait, stay, bide, take time; dawdle, etc. (*be inactive*), 683; linger, loiter, gain time; hang fire; stand over, lie over; hang.

put off, defer, delay, lay over, suspend; stave off; retard, postpone, adjourn, prorogue, procrastinate; dally, prolong, protract, spin out, draw out, table, lay on the table, shelve; reserve, temporize, filibuster, stall [*slang*].

be kept waiting, dance attendance; cool one's heels [*colloq.*]; await, expect, wait for.

Adj. **late,** tardy, dilatory; slow, leisurely, behindhand, backward, unpunctual; overdue, belated, delayed; posthumous.

Adv. **late;** backward, at the eleventh hour, at length, at last; ultimately; behind time; too late.

slowly, deliberately, at one's leisure.

134. TIMELINESS.—*N.* **timeliness,** opportunity, opening, occasion, show [*colloq.*]; suitable time *or* season, high time; nick of time; golden opportunity, clear stage, fair field; spare time, leisure.

crisis, turn, emergency, juncture, conjuncture; turning point.

V. **improve the occasion;** seize an opportunity; use (*or* profit by) an opportunity; give (*or* grant) an opportunity; suit the occasion, etc. (*be expedient*), 646; strike the iron while it is hot, make hay while the sun shines.

Adj. **timely,** well timed, opportune, seasonable; appropriate, suitable.

lucky, providential, fortunate, happy, favorable, propitious, auspicious.

occasional, accidental, extemporaneous, extemporary; contingent, provisional.

Adv. **opportunity,** in due time; for the nonce; in the nick of time, just in time; at the eleventh hour, now or never.

by the way, by the by; while on this subject, speaking of; extempore; on the spur of the moment.

135. UNTIMELINESS.—*N.* **untimeliness,** unseasonableness, unsuitable time, improper time; evil hour; intrusion; anachronism.

V. **be ill-timed,** mistime, intrude, come amiss, break in upon; be busy, be occupied, be engaged.

lose an opportunity; neglect an opportunity; allow *or* suffer the opportunity to pass (*or* slip, go by, escape); waste time; let slip through the fingers.

Adj. **ill-timed,** mistimed, ill-fated, ill-omened, ill-starred; untimely, unseasonable, out of season; inopportune, inconvenient, untoward, unlucky, inauspicious, unpropitious, unfortunate, unfavorable, unsuited; inexpedient.

unpunctual, etc. (*late*), 133; premature, etc. (*early*), 132.

136. FREQUENCY.—*N.* **frequency,** repetition, iteration, reiteration.

V. keep on; reiterate, repeat, recur, etc., 104; do nothing but.

Adj. frequent, not rare, thick-coming, incessant, perpetual, continual, constant, habitual, etc., 613.

Adv. often, oft, ofttimes, frequently; repeatedly, in quick succession; daily, every day; habitually, commonly.

perpetually, continually, constantly, incessantly, at all times.

sometimes, occasionally, at times, now and then, again and again.

137. INFREQUENCY.—*N.* infrequency, infrequence, rarity; uncommonness.

Adj. infrequent, uncommon, sporadic; rare, few, scant, scarce; unprecedented.

Adv. seldom, rarely, scarcely, hardly; not often, infrequently, uncommonly, sparsely, scarcely ever, hardly ever.

138. REGULARITY [of recurrence].—*N.* periodicity, intermittence; oscillation, vibration; beat, pulse, pulsation; rhythm, alternation; round, revolution, rotation, regularity, bout, turn; routine; cycle.

anniversary, biennial, triennial, quadrennial, quinquennial, sextennial, septennial, octennial, decennial; tricennial, jubilee, centennial, centenary, bicentennial, bicentenary, tercentenary; birthday, natal day, fete day, saint's day, feast, festival, fast, holiday.

Christmas, Yuletide, New Year's Day, Ash Wednesday, Maundy Thursday, Good Friday, Easter; Halloween, All Saints' Day; All Souls' Day; Candlemas; Memorial *or* Decoration Day, Independence Day, Labor Day, Thanksgiving, ground-hog day, woodchuck day, leap year, St. Swithin's Day, Midsummer Day; May Day.

V. return, revolve, recur, come round again; beat, pulsate; alternate; intermit.

Adj. periodic, periodical; serial, recurrent, cyclic, cyclical, rhythmic, recurring, intermittent; alternate, every other; every.

regular, steady, constant, methodical, punctual.

Adv. by turns, in turn, in rotation, alternately, off and on, round and round.

139. IRREGULARITY [of recurrence].—*N.* irregularity, uncertainty, unpunctuality; fitfulness, capriciousness.

Adj. irregular, uncertain, unpunctual, capricious, erratic, desultory, fitful, flickering; rambling, spasmodic; unmethodical, unsystematic, unequal, uneven, variable.

Adv. by fits and starts.

VII. CHANGE

140. CHANGE.—*N.* change, alteration, mutation, permutation, variation, modification, modulation, inflection, mood, qualification, innovation, deviation, shift, turn; diversion, variety, break.

conversion, etc. (*gradual change*), 144; revolution, etc., 146; inversion, reversal; displacement, transposition, removal, transference.

transformation, metamorphosis, transfiguration, transmutation; transubstantiation; transmigration, metempsychosis; avatar.

changeableness, etc., 149.

V. **change,** alter, vary, modulate, diversify, qualify, tamper with; turn, shift, veer, jibe, jib, tack, chop, warp, swerve, deviate, dodge; turn aside; take a turn, turn the corner.

modify, work a change, patch, piece, transform, transfigure, transmute, convert, revolutionize; metamorphose, ring the changes; innovate, introduce new blood, shuffle the cards; shift the scene, turn over a new leaf.

recast, remodel; reverse, etc., 218; convert into, etc., 144.

Adj. **changed,** newfangled; changeable, changeful, variable, devious, transitional.

141. PERMANENCE.—*N.* **permanence,** fixity, persistence, endurance; durability; standing, *status quo* [L.]; maintenance, preservation, conservation; conservatism; stability, constancy; quiescence, etc., 265; obstinacy, inflexibility.

V. **endure,** persist, remain, stay, tarry, rest, hold, last, bide, abide, dwell, maintain, keep; stand fast, subsist, live, outlive, survive; hold one's ground (*or* footing).

Adj. **permanent,** stable, fixed, settled, established, irremovable, durable; unchanged, intact, inviolate; persistent; conservative; unfailing, unfading.

Adv. for good, at a stand, at a standstill, as you were!

142. CESSATION.—*N.* **cessation,** discontinuance; intermission, remission; suspense, suspension; interruption; stop; hitch [*colloq.*]; stoppage, halt.

pause, rest, lull, respite, truce, armistice, stay; interregnum. **In debate:** closure, cloture.

deadlock, checkmate, dead center, dead stand, dead stop; end. **punctuation:** comma, semicolon, colon, period, full stop; cæsura.

V. **cease,** discontinue, desist, stay; break off, leave off; hold, stop, pull up, stop short; check, stick, hang fire; halt, pause, rest; come to a stand; arrive, etc., 292; go out, die away, wear away, pass away, lapse; be at an end.

have done with, give over; give up, etc. (*relinquish*), 624.

interrupt, suspend, intermit, remit; put an end to, bring to a stand (*or* standstill), stop, cut short, arrest.

143. CONTINUANCE [in action].—*N.* **continuance,** continuation; pursuance, maintenance, extension, perpetuation, prolongation; persistence, perseverance; repetition.

V. **continue,** persist, go on, keep on, hold on; abide, pursue; stick to; maintain its course; keep up, drag on, stick [*colloq.*], persevere, endure, carry on; keep the field, keep the ball rolling.

sustain, uphold, hold up, follow up, perpetuate, prolong, maintain; preserve.

Adj. **continuing,** uninterrupted, unvarying, persistent, unceasing, unvaried, sustained, chronic; undying, immortal, perpetual.

144. [Gradual change to something different] **CONVERSION.** —*N.* conversion, reduction, transmutation, assimilation; chemistry, alchemy; growth, progress; naturalization; transportation.

passage, transit, transition, transmigration; shifting, flux; phase.

convert, neophyte, proselyte; pervert, renegade, apostate, turncoat.

V. **be converted into;** become, turn to *or* into; turn out, lapse, shift; pass into, grow into, merge into; melt, grow, wax, mature, mellow.

convert into, resolve into; make, render; mold, form, remodel, reform, reorganize; bring to, reduce to.

145. REVERSION.—*N.* reversion, return; revulsion; turning point, turn of the tide; alternation, rotation; inversion, etc., 218; recoil, reaction; retrospection, retrogression; restoration, relapse, atavism, throwback.

V. **revert,** reverse, return, turn back; relapse; invert; recoil; retreat; restore; undo, unmake; turn the scale.

146. [Sudden or violent change] **REVOLUTION.**—*N.* revolution, revolt; breakup; destruction, etc., 162; clean sweep, debacle, overturn, overthrow, rebellion, rising, uprising, mutiny, counter-revolution, bolshevism.

spasm, convulsion, throe, revulsion; earthquake, eruption, upheaval, cataclysm, explosion.

V. **revolutionize,** revolt, rebel, rise; remodel, recast.

Adj. **revolutionary,** catastrophic, cataclysmic, cataclysmal, insurgent, Red, insurrectionary, mutinous, rebellious; bolshevistic *or* bolshevik.

147. [Change of one thing for another] **SUBSTITUTION.**—*N.* substitution, commutation, supplanting.

substitute, scapegoat; alternative; makeshift, temporary expedient, shift, apology, stopgap; alternate; dummy, double; changeling; representative, deputy.

price, purchase money, consideration, equivalent.

V. **substitute,** put in the place of, change for, give place to; take the place of, supplant, supersede, replace, cut out [*colloq.*]; commute, redeem, compound for.

Adj. substituted, vicarious.

Adv. instead; by proxy; in place of, in lieu of.

148. [Double or mutual change] INTERCHANGE.—*N.* **interchange,** exchange; commutation, permutation; transposition, shuffle; alternation, reciprocity; swap [*colloq.*], barter, exchange; retaliation, reprisal; retort, requital, cross fire.

V. **interchange,** exchange, bandy, barter, transpose, swap [*colloq.*], reciprocate, commute; give and take, retaliate; retort; requite.

Adj. **reciprocal,** mutual; interchangeable.

international, interstate, interurban, interdenominational; interscholastic, intercollegiate.

Adv. in exchange, vice versa, conversely, by turns, turn about.

149. CHANGEABLENESS.—*N.* **changeableness,** mutability, inconstancy; versatility, mobility; instability, vacillation, irresolution, indecision; fluctuation, vicissitude; alternation, oscillation.

Comparisons: moon, kaleidoscope, chameleon, quicksilver, shifting sands, weathercock, vane, weathervane, harlequin, turncoat; wheel of fortune.

restlessness, fidgets, disquiet; disquietude, unrest; agitation, etc., 315.

V. **fluctuate,** vary, waver, flicker, flutter, shift, shuffle, shake, totter, tremble, vacillate, shift to and fro; oscillate, pulsate, vibrate; alternate.

Adj. **changeable,** changeful; changing, mutable, variable, kaleidoscopic; protean, versatile, mobile.

inconstant, unsteady, unstable, unfixed, unsettled; fluctuating, wavering, vibratory, restless, tremulous; erratic, fickle; mercurial, irresolute, indecisive; capricious, fitful, spasmodic; vagrant, wayward; desultory, transient, etc., 111.

150. STABILITY.—*N.* **stability,** immutability, unchangeableness, constancy; immobility; soundness, vitality, stabilization; stiffness, solidity; permanence, etc., 141; obstinacy, obduracy.

fixture, establishment; leopard's spots.

standpatter [*politics*].

V. **be firm,** stick fast; stand firm, remain firm; stand pat [*colloq.*].

establish, settle, fix, set, stabilize; retain, keep hold; make good, make sure; fasten, etc. (*join*), 43; perpetuate.

settle down; strike root, take root.

Adj. **unchangeable,** immutable; unaltered, unalterable, constant; permanent, persistent, invariable, undeviating; stable, durable, perennial; irretrievable, irrevocable, indissoluble, indestructible, imperishable, indelible.

fixed, steadfast, firm, solid; deep-rooted, ineradicable; fast, steady, confirmed, inveterate; immovable, rooted; settled, stereo-typed, established, vested; obstinate, etc., 606; incontrovertible, valid.

stuck fast, transfixed, aground, stranded.

151. PRESENT EVENTS.—*N.* **eventuality,** event, occurrence, incident, affair, transaction, proceeding, fact; phenomenon.

circumstance, particular; happening, adventure; crisis, pass, emergency, contingency; concern, business.

consequence, issue, result, termination, conclusion.

affairs, matters; the world, life, things, doings; the times.

V. **happen,** occur; take place, come to pass, take effect; present itself; fall out, turn out, befall, betide; turn up, crop up, arrive; ensue, result; arise, start; take its course, pass off.

experience; meet with; fall to the lot of; be one's lot; find, en-counter; undergo, pass through, go through, endure, bear, suffer, abide, stand, brook.

Adj. **eventful,** stirring, full of incident; memorable, momen-tous, signal; current, on foot, at issue, in question; incidental.

Adv. **eventually,** ultimately, finally; in the event of, in case.

152. FUTURE EVENTS.—*N.* **destiny,** fatality, fate, lot, doom, fortune; future, future state; future existence, hereafter· next world, world to come; life to come; prospect.

V. **impend,** hang over, threaten, loom, await, approach; fore-ordain, preordain; destine, predestine, doom.

Adj. **impending,** destined; coming, in store, to come, instant, at hand, near, imminent; in the wind, in prospect.

Adv. **in time,** in the long run; all in good time; eventually.

VIII. CAUSATION

153. CAUSE.—*N.* **cause,** origin, source, principle, element; prime mover, ultimate cause; author, producer, creator, determi-nant; mainspring, agent; leaven; groundwork, foundation, support.

causality, causation; origination; production, etc., 161.

spring, fountain, well; fountainhead, reservoir, wellspring; genesis; derivation; remote cause; influence.

pivot, hinge, turning point; heart, hub, focus.

reason, reason why; ground, occasion; final cause; under-currents.

rudiment, egg, germ, nucleus, seed.

nest, cradle, nursery, birthplace, hotbed.

V. **cause,** originate, give rise to, occasion, sow the seeds of; bring to pass, bring about; produce; create, develop; set on foot, entail; found, institute.

procure, induce. draw down, superinduce. evoke, elicit, provoke.

contribute, conduce to, have a hand in, influence; determine, decide, turn the scale.

Adj. causal, original; primary, originative, generative, productive, creative; formative; radical; in embryo, embryonic.

Adv. from the beginning, in the first place; because, etc., 155.

154. EFFECT.—*N.* effect, consequence; aftergrowth, afterclap, aftermath; derivative; derivation; result; resultant; upshot, issue, outcome, conclusion; catastrophe, end; development, outgrowth; fruit, crop, harvest, product.

production, work, handiwork, fabric, performance; creature, creation; offspring, offshoot; first fruits.

V. be the effect of, be due to, be owing to; originate in *or* from; rise from, spring from, emanate from, come from, issue from, flow from, result from; depend upon, hang upon, hinge upon, turn upon.

Adj. owing to; resulting from; due to; caused by; derived from, evolved from; derivative; hereditary.

Adv. consequently, it follows that, as a consequence, in consequence; necessarily, eventually.

155. [Assignment of cause] ATTRIBUTION —*N.* attribution, theory, assignment, reference to, accounting for; imputation; derivation.

explanation, interpretation, reason why.

V. attribute to, ascribe to, impute to, refer to, lay to, trace to; blame; saddle; account for, derive from; theorize.

Adj. attributed; attributable, referable; due to; owing to.

Adv. hence, thence, therefore, for, since, on account of, because, owing to; forasmuch as; whence.

why? wherefore? whence? how comes it? how is it? how so?

156. [Absence of assignable cause] CHANCE[1].—*N.* chance, accident, fortune, hazard, luck, fluke [*cant*], casualty, hit; fate, lottery, tossup [*colloq.*]; throw of the dice; heads or tails, wheel of fortune.

probability, possibility, contingency, odds, run of luck; main chance.

gamble, speculation, gaming, game of chance.

V. chance, turn up; fall to one's lot; be one's fate; stumble on, light upon; blunder upon, hit, hit upon.

Adj. casual, fortuitous, accidental, chance, haphazard, random, incidental, unintentional, unpremeditated.

[1]The word *chance* has two distinct meanings: the first, the absence of assignable *cause*, as above; and the second, the absence of *design*—for the latter see 621.

Adv. **by chance,** by accident; at random, casually; perchance, etc. (*possibly*), 470.

157. POWER.—*N.* **power;** potency, efficacy, puissance, might, energy, vigor, force; ascendancy, sway, almightiness, omnipotence; authority, weight, control; influence, predominance.

ability, competence, efficiency, efficacy; validity, cogency; vantage ground.

capability, capacity: faculty, quality, attribute, endowment, virtue, gift, property, qualification.

V. **empower;** give *or* confer power; invest, endue; endow, arm; strengthen, etc., 159.

electrify, magnetize, energize, galvanize.

Adj. **powerful,** puissant, potent, capable, able; cogent, valid, effective, effectual, efficient, efficacious, adequate, competent; predominant; mighty, omnipotent, almighty.

forcible, energetic; influential; productive.

electric, magnetic, galvanic, dynamic, potential.

Adv. **by virtue of,** by dint of.

158. IMPOTENCE.—*N.* **impotence;** inability, disability. incapacity, incapability; ineptitude; inefficiency, incompetence, disqualification; inefficacy, etc. (*inutility*), 645; failure, etc., 732.

helplessness, prostration, paralysis, collapse, exhaustion, senility, superannuation, decrepitude, imbecility, inanition.

mollycoddle, old woman, milksop, sissy [*colloq.*], mother's darling.

collapse, faint, swoon, drop; go by the board; end in smoke, etc. (*fail*), 732.

render powerless, disable, disarm, incapacitate, disqualify, unfit, invalidate, undermine, deaden, cramp, tie the hands; prostrate, paralyze, muzzle, cripple, maim, lame, throttle, strangle, silence, spike the guns; unhinge, unfit; put out of gear.

unman, unnerve, devitalize, attenuate, enervate.

shatter, exhaust; weaken, enfeeble.

Adj. **powerless,** impotent, helpless; incapable, incompetent, inefficient, ineffective, unfit, unfitted, unqualified, disqualified; crippled, disabled; senile, decrepit, superannuated; paralytic, paralyzed, nerveless, out of joint, out of gear; unnerved, unhinged; done up [*colloq.*], done for [*colloq.*], dead-beat [*colloq.*], exhausted, shattered, prostrate, demoralized, harmless; unarmed, weaponless, defenseless.

nugatory, null and void, inoperative, good for nothing, ineffectual, inadequate, inefficacious, etc. (*useless*), 645.

159. STRENGTH.—*N.* **strength;** power, etc., 157; energy, vigor, force; main (*or* physical, brute) force; spring, elasticity.

vitality, virility, lustihood, stamina, nerve, muscle, sinews, physique; grit.

athletics, athleticism; gymnastics, calisthenics.

athlete, gymnast, acrobat; Atlas, Hercules.

strengthening, invigoration, refreshment.

Science of forces: dynamics, statics.

V. **strengthen,** invigorate, brace, nerve, fortify, buttress, sustain, harden, steel; gird, set up, gird up one's loins; recruit, set on one's legs [*colloq.*]; vivify; refresh, reinforce, restore.

Adj. **strong,** mighty, vigorous, forcible; hard, stout, robust, sound, sturdy, husky [*colloq.*], hardy, powerful, potent, puissant.

resistless, irresistible, invincible, impregnable, unconquerable, indomitable, incontestable, valid; overpowering, overwhelming, all-powerful.

able-bodied; athletic, Herculean, muscular, brawny, wiry, well knit, sinewy, strapping, stalwart, lusty.

manly, manful; masculine, male, virile, in the prime of manhood.

Adv. **strongly,** by force, by main force.

160. WEAKNESS.—*N.* **weakness,** debility, relaxation, languor, enervation; impotence, etc., 158; infirmity, effeminacy; fragility; inactivity, etc., 683.

anemia, bloodlessness, deficiency of blood, poverty of blood.

loss of strength, delicacy; decrepitude; invalidism.

V. **be weak;** drop, crumble, give way; totter, dodder; tremble, shake; halt, limp; fade, languish, decline, flag, fail.

weaken, enfeeble, debilitate, shake, relax, sap, enervate, unnerve; cripple, unman; cramp, reduce, sprain, strain, dilute, impoverish.

Adj. **weak,** faint, feeble, infirm; impotent; relaxed, unnerved, unstrung, limp, strengthless, powerless; weakly, sickly, flaccid.

soft, effeminate, womanish.

frail, fragile; flimsy, sleazy, papery, unsubstantial, gimcrack, rickety, jerry-built; broken, decrepit, lame, shattered, shaken, crazy, shaky, tumbledown.

unsound, spent, effete; decayed, rotten, worn, seedy, languishing, wasted, laid low, the worse for wear; on its last legs.

161. [Power in operation] PRODUCTION.—*N.* **production,** creation, construction, formation, fabrication, manufacture; building, architecture, erection; organization; establishment; workmanship, performance; achievement; flowering, efflorescence, fruition; genesis, birth; evolution, development, growth; breeding; propagation.

publication; works, opus (*pl.* opera) [L.]; authorship.

structure, building, edifice, fabric, erection, pile.

V. **produce,** perform, operate, do, make, form, construct, fabricate, frame, contrive, manufacture; build, raise, rear, erect; establish, constitute, compose, evolve, coin, organize, institute; achieve, accomplish.

flower, blossom, bear fruit, bear, bring forth, give birth to, usher into the world; generate, propagate, engender, create; breed, develop, bring up.

induce, superinduce; cause, etc., 153.

Adj. **productive;** prolific, etc., 168; creative, formative, constructive; generative; teeming.

162. [Nonproduction] DESTRUCTION.—*N.* destruction; waste, dissolution, breaking up, disruption; disorganization; demolition, overthrow, subversion, suppression; abolition, etc., 756; sacrifice; ravage, devastation, incendiarism; revolution, etc., 146; road to ruin; sabotage.

fall, downfall, ruin, perdition; breakdown, breakup; cave-in [*colloq.*]; wreck, shipwreck, cataclysm.

extinction, extermination, annihilation; doom, crack of doom.

V. **perish,** fall, fall to the ground, tumble, topple; fall to pieces, break up, crumble, go to wrack and ruin; go by the board, be all over with, go to pieces, totter to its fall.

destroy, do (*or* make) away with, waste; nullify, annul, sacrifice, demolish, overturn, overthrow, overwhelm; upset, subvert, put an end to; do for [*colloq.*], undo, break down, cut down, pull down, dismantle, mow down, blow down; suppress, quash, put down, crush, blot out, efface, obliterate, cancel, erase, strike out, expunge, delete; dispel, dissipate, dissolve; consume.

smash, crash, quell, squash [*colloq.*], shatter, shiver, batter; tear (*or* pull, crush) to pieces; ruin, fell; sink, swamp, scuttle, wreck, shipwreck, engulf, submerged; lay in ruins, raze, level; deal destruction, lay waste, ravage, gut; devour, desolate, devastate, blast, exterminate, eradicate, annihilate.

Adj. **destructive,** subversive, cataclysmic, ruinous, incendiary, suicidal, deadly, all-destroying, all-devouring.

163. REPRODUCTION.—*N.* reproduction, renovation; restoration, etc., 660; renewal, revival, regeneration, revivification; apotheosis; resuscitation, reanimation, resurrection, reappearance.

V. **reproduce,** restore, etc., 660; revive, renovate, renew, repeat, regenerate, revivify, resuscitate, reanimate, refashion, multiply.

Adj. **reproductive,** resurgent, reappearing; renascent; Hydra-headed.

164. PRODUCER.—*N.* producer, originator, inventor, author, founder, generator, mover, architect, grower, raiser, introducer, creator; maker, etc. (*agent*), 690; prime mover.

165. DESTROYER.—*N.* **destroyer,** wrecker, annihilator; cankerworm, etc. (*bane*), 663; assassin, etc. (*killer*), 361; executioner, etc. (*punish*), 975; iconoclast, vandal, nihilist.

166. PATERNITY.—*N.* **paternity,** fathership, fatherhood; parentage.

parent, father, sire, dad [*colloq.*], papa, pater [*colloq.*], daddy [*colloq.*], paterfamilias; ancestor.

motherhood, maternity, mother, dam, mamma, mammy, mam [*colloq.*], matriarch, materfamilias.

stem, trunk, tree, stock, pedigree, house, lineage, line, family, race, tribe, clan; genealogy, family tree, descent, extraction, birth, ancestry; forefathers, forebears.

Adj. **parental;** paternal; maternal; ancestral, linear, patriarchal; racial.

167. POSTERITY.—*N.* **posterity,** progeny, breed, issue, offspring, brood, family, children, heirs; rising generation.

descendant, scion, offshoot, chip of the old block, heir, heiress, heir apparent, heir presumptive.

child, son, daughter, baby, kid [*colloq.*], imp, brat, cherub, tot, innocent, urchin, chit [*colloq.*]; infant, etc., 129.

lineage, line, straight descent, heredity, sonship, primogeniture.
Adj. **hereditary,** lineal.
filial, sonlike, daughterly, dutiful.

168. PRODUCTIVENESS.—*N.* **productiveness,** fecundity, fertility, luxuriance; multiplication, propagation, fructification.

V. **fructify;** generate, impregnate; teem, spawn, multiply; produce, etc., 161; conceive.

Adj. **productive,** prolific, copious; teeming, fertile, fruitful, plenteous, luxuriant; generative, life-giving; originative.

169. UNPRODUCTIVENESS.—*N.* **unproductiveness,** infertility, sterility, barrenness, unfruitfulness; unprofitableness, etc. (*inutility*), 645.

waste, desert, Sahara, wild, wilderness.

V. **be unproductive;** hang fire, flash in the pan, come to nothing.

Adj. **unproductive,** barren, unfertile, arid, sterile, unfruitful, fruitless, useless, fallow; unprofitable, etc. (*useless*), 645.

170. AGENCY.—*N.* **agency,** operation, force, function, office, maintenance, exercise, work, swing, play.

causation, impelling force; mediation, intervention, instrumentality; influence, etc., 175; action, etc. (*voluntary*), 680; method, procedure.

V. **operate,** work; act, perform, play, support, sustain, maintain, take effect, quicken, strike; have play, have free play; bring to bear upon.

Adj. **operative,** efficient, efficacious, practical, effectual; at work, on foot; acting, in operation, in force, in action.

171. ENERGY.—*N.* **energy,** force; intensity, vigor, strength, backbone [*colloq.*], vim [*colloq.*], mettle, pep [*slang*], fire, go [*colloq.*], high pressure; human dynamo.

activity, agitation, effervescence, ferment, fermentation, ebullition, stir, bustle; voluntary, energy, etc., 682; mental energy, etc., 604; resolution, stimulation; exertion, etc. (*effort*), 686.

V. **give energy,** energize, stimulate, strengthen, invigorate, kindle, excite, inflame, exert; sharpen, intensify.

Adj. **energetic,** strong, forcible, active, strenuous, brisk, forceful, mettlesome, enterprising, go-ahead [*colloq.*]; potent, etc. (*powerful*), 157; intense, keen, sharp, acute, incisive, trenchant.

poignant, virulent, caustic, corrosive, mordant; harsh, stringent, drastic.

172. INERTNESS.—*N.* **inertness,** inertia, inactivity, torpor, languor, quiescence, inaction, passivity, stagnation.

mental inertness; sloth; inexcitability, etc., 826; irresolution, indecision, vacillation; obstinacy, etc., 606.

V. **be inert,** hang fire, be inactive; smolder.

Adj. **inert,** inactive, passive; torpid, etc., 683; sluggish, logy, stagnant, dull, heavy, slack, tame, slow, lifeless, dead.

latent, dormant, smoldering, unexerted.

Adv. in suspense, in abeyance.

173. VIOLENCE.—*N.* **violence,** vehemence, might, impetuosity, boisterousness, disorder, effervescence, ebullition; turbulence, bluster; uproar, riot, row [*colloq.*], rumpus [*colloq.*].

ferocity, rage, fury, exasperation; malignity; severity, etc., 739; force, brute force; outrage.

fit, paroxysm, spasm, convulsion, throe; hysterics, passion, etc., 825.

outbreak, outburst, discharge, volley, explosion, blast, detonation, eruption, volcano, earthquake, thunderstorm.

fury, berserk, dragon, demon, tiger, wild beast; fire-eater [*colloq.*], etc. (*blusterer*), 887.

V **be violent;** ferment, effervesce; rampage; run wild, run amuck, rage, roar, riot, storm; boil, boil over; fume, foam, ride roughshod, out-Herod Herod.

explode, go off, detonate, fulminate, let off, let fly, discharge, thunder, blow up, flash, flare, burst.

render violent; stir up, quicken, excite, incite, urge, lash, stimulate; irritate, inflame, kindle, foment, exasperate, convulse, infuriate, madden, lash into fury.

Adj. violent, vehement, acute, sharp; rough, tough [*colloq.*], rude, bluff, brusque, abrupt, boisterous, wild, impetuous, rampant; savage, fierce, ferocious.

turbulent, tumultuous; disorderly, raging, troublous, riotous, obstreperous, uproarious; frenzied, mad, insane; desperate, rash; infuriate, furious, frantic, outrageous; stormy, etc. (*wind*), 349.

fiery, flaming, scorching, hot, red-hot.

unbridled, unruly; headstrong, ungovernable, uncontrollable, irrepressible.

spasmodic, convulsive, explosive; detonating; volcanic, meteoric.

Adv. violently, amain; by storm, by force, by main force, with might and main, at one fell swoop; in desperation, with a vengeance.

174. MODERATION.—*N.* moderation; lenity, etc., 740; temperateness, temperance, gentleness, mildness, quiet, sobriety; mental calmness, composure, etc. (*inexcitability*), 826.

alleviation, assuagement, mitigation, relaxation, tranquilization, pacification.

moderator; sedative, lenitive, palliative; opiate, balm.

V. moderate, slacken, soften, mitigate, palliate, alleviate, allay, assuage, appease, temper, mollify, lull, soothe, compose, still, calm, cool, quiet, tranquilize, hush, quell, sober, pacify, smooth, deaden, smother; blunt, subdue, chasten; weaken, etc., 160; lessen, decrease; check, tame, curb, restrain.

Adj. moderate, gentle, mild; cool, sober, temperate, reasonable, lenient, measured; calm, unruffled, quiet, tranquil, still, halcyon; peaceful, peaceable, pacific.

Adv. in moderation, within bounds.

175. [Indirect Power] INFLUENCE.—*N.* influence; importance, etc., 642; weight, pressure, pull [*colloq. or slang*]; interest; preponderance, prevalence, sway; predominance, upper hand, ascendancy; dominance, reign; control, domination, hold; authority, power, potency, capability, spell, magic, magnetism.

footing; purchase, support; play, leverage, vantage ground, advantage.

patronage, protection, auspices; patron, etc. (*auxiliary*), 711; tower of strength.

V. be influential, carry weight, sway, bias, actuate, weight, tell; magnetize, work upon; take root, take hold; pervade, run through; be rife.

dominate, subject; predominate, outweigh; override, overbear; have *or* gain the upper hand, prevail.

lead, control, rule, manage, master, get control of, make one's influence felt; take the lead, pull the strings; turn the scale; set the fashion.

Adj. **influential,** effective, potent; important, etc., 642; weighty; prevalent, rife, rampant; dominant, predominant, authoritative, recognized.

Adv. with telling effect, with authority.

176. TENDENCY.—*N.* **tendency,** aptness, aptitude, proneness, proclivity, bent, turn, tone, bias, set, warp, leaning (*with* to *or* toward), predisposition, inclination, liability, propensity, susceptibility; quality, nature, temperament; idiosyncrasy; cast, vein, grain, humor, mood, trend, drift.

V. **tend,** contribute, conduce, lead, influence, dispose, incline, verge, bend to, warp, turn, work toward, gravitate toward, trend; affect; carry, redound to, bid fair to; promote, etc. (*aid*), 707.

Adj. **tending;** conducive, working toward, in a fair way to, likely to, calculated to; liable, etc., 177; subservient, instrumental, useful; subsidiary, accessory.

177. LIABILITY.—*N.* **liability,** susceptibility; possibility, contingency.

V. **be liable,** incur, lay oneself open to, be subjected to, run the chance, stand a chance; lie under, expose oneself to, open a door to.

Adj. **liable,** subject, in danger, open to, exposed to; answerable, responsible, accountable, amenable; apt to; dependent on.

contingent, incidental, possible, on the cards, within range of, at the mercy of.

178. CONCURRENCE.—*N.* **concurrence,** co-operation, collaboration; conformity, agreement, accord; alliance; complicity, collusion, partnership, union.

V. **concur,** conduce, conspire, contribute; agree, unite, harmonize, combine; hang *or* pull together, co-operate; keep pace with, run parallel.

Adj. **concurrent,** conformable, joint, co-operative, concordant, harmonious, in alliance with, of one mind, at one with.

179. COUNTERACTION.—*N.* **counteraction,** opposition; contrariety, contradiction; antagonism, polarity; clashing, collision, interference, resistance, friction; reaction, recoil; counterblast, neutralization, check, hindrance; repression, restraint.

V. **counteract,** clash, cross, interfere with, conflict with; contravene; jostle; militate against, stultify, antagonize, frustrate, oppose, overcome, overpower, withstand, resist, impede, hinder, repress, restrain; recoil, react.

neutralize, offset, undo, cancel; counterpoise, counterbalance.
Adj. **antagonistic,** conflicting, reactionary; contrary, etc., 14.
Adv. **although,** notwithstanding; in spite of; against.

CLASS II

Words Relating To SPACE

I. SPACE IN GENERAL

180. [Indefinite space] SPACE.—*N.* **space,** extension, extent,
proportions, expanse, stretch; room, accommodation, capacity;
scope, compass, range, latitude, field; sweep, play, swing; spread,
expansion.

elbowroom, leeway, seaway, headway; margin; sphere, arena.

open space, free space, void, waste, desert, wild, wilderness;
moor, down, downs, upland, moorland; prairie, steppe, llano,
campagna.

unlimited space; heavens, ether, infinity; world, wide world.

Adj. **spacious,** roomy, extensive, extended, expansive, capacious, ample; widespread, vast, world-wide, wide, far-flung,
boundless, limitless, endless, infinite; shoreless, trackless, pathless.

Adv. **extensively;** by and large; everywhere, far and near (*or* wide), here, there,
and everywhere; from pole to pole, from the four corners of the earth, from all
points of the compass; to the four winds, to the uttermost parts of the earth.

181. [Definite space] REGION.—*N.* **region,** sphere, ground,
soil, area, realm, hemisphere, quarter, orb, circuit, circle; pale,
etc. (*limit*), 233; tract, clearing; domain.

county, shire, canton, province, department, parish, diocese, township, commune,
ward, bailiwick; principality, duchy, palatinate, archduchy, dukedom, dominion,
colony, commonwealth, territory, country; fatherland, motherland; kingdom,
empire.

precinct, arena, district, beat; patch, plot, inclosure, close, enclave, field, paddock, etc. (*inclosure*), 232; street.

clime, climate, zone, meridian, latitude.

Adj. **territorial,** provincial, regional, insular; local, parochial.

182. [Limited space] PLACE.—*N.* **place,** spot, whereabouts,
point; niche, nook, corner, hole, pigeonhole, etc. (*receptacle*), 191;
compartment; premises, courtyard, square, place, piazza, plaza,
forum; hamlet, village, etc. (*abode*), 189; pen, etc. (*inclosure*),
232; location, site, locality, situation.

Adv. **somewhere,** in some place, here and there, in various places.

183. SITUATION.—*N.* **situation,** position, locality, latitude
and longitude; footing, status, standing; standpoint; stage;
aspect, attitude, posture, pose.

place, site; station, post, seat, whereabouts; environment, ground; bearings, direction, spot, etc. (*limited space*), 182.

topography, geography; map, plan, chart.

V. **be situated**, be situate, be located; lie; have its seat in.

Adj. **situate**, situated; local, topical, topographical.

Adv. hereabouts, thereabouts, whereabouts; in place, here, there.

184. LOCATION.—*N.* **location**, situation, lodgment; stowage; packing, lading; establishment, settlement, installation; insertion, etc., 300.

anchorage, roadstead, mooring.

settlement, plantation, colony; habitation, etc. (*abode*), 189.

domestication; colonization; naturalization.

V. **place**, situate, locate, localize, put, lay, set, seat; station, park (as, *an automobile*), lodge, quarter, post, install; house, stow, pack; load, lade; establish, fix, root; graft; plant, etc. (*insert*), 300; deposit, store, store away.

billet on, quarter upon, saddle with.

settle, domesticate, colonize, found, people; take root, strike root, anchor, cast anchor, moor, tether, picket; settle down; take up one's abode, establish *or* locate oneself; keep house; squat, burrow, get a footing; bivouac, encamp, pitch one's tent; inhabit, etc., 186.

Adj. **placed**; situate, ensconced, imbedded, rooted; moored, at anchor.

185. DISPLACEMENT.—*N.* **displacement**, misplacement, dislocation, derangement, transposition.

ejection, expulsion, eviction; exile, banishment, ostracism.

removal, etc. (*transference*), 270; transshipment, moving, shift.

V. **displace**, dislodge, disestablish; misplace, unseat, disturb; set aside, remove, take away, cart away, draft off; exile, etc. (*seclude*), 893.

unload, empty, etc. (*eject*), 297; transfer, etc., 270; dispel.

vacate, depart, evacuate.

Adj. **displaced**; unplaced, unhoused, unsettled; houseless, homeless, out of place; out of a situation.

186. PRESENCE.—*N.* **presence**, attendance; occupancy, occupation; ubiquity, omnipresence.

permeation, pervasion; diffusion.

bystander, etc. (*spectator*), 444.

V. **be present**, make one of; look on, attend, remain find *or* present oneself; lie, stand.

inhabit, occupy, dwell, reside; stay, sojourn; live, abide; lodge, tenant; people.

frequent, resort to, haunt; revisit.

pervade, permeate; overspread; fill, run through.

Adj. **present;** situate; moored, at anchor; resident, domiciled; ubiquitous, omnipresent.

peopled, inhabited, populous.

Adv. here, there, everywhere; aboard, on board, at home, afield; on the spot; in presence of, before.

187. ABSENCE.—*N.* **absence,** nonresidence, absenteeism; nonattendance, cut [*colloq.*]; alibi.

emptiness; void, vacuum. vacancy.

interval, hiatus, interruption; interregnum.

truant, absentee.

V. **be absent;** keep away, play truant, absent oneself, stay away, hold aloof.

withdraw, retreat, retire; go away.

Adj. **absent,** not present, away, nonresident, gone, from home; missing; lost; wanting; omitted.

empty, void; vacant, vacuous, blank; untenanted, unoccupied, uninhabited, tenantless; desert, deserted, uninhabitable.

Adv. without, minus, nowhere; elsewhere; in default of; sans.

188. INHABITANT.—*N.* **inhabitant;** resident, dweller, indweller, addressee, occupier, occupant, householder; inmate; tenant, incumbent; settler, squatter, backwoodsman, planter, habitant, colonist; islander; denizen, citizen; burgher, townsman, burgess; villager; cottager, cotter; boarder, lodger.

native, aborigine, aboriginal.

people, etc. (*mankind*), 372; population; colony, settlement; household.

V. **inhabit,** dwell, etc., 186.

Adj. **indigenous,** native, domestic; domiciled; naturalized; vernacular.

189. HABITATION.—*N.* **habitation,** abode, dwelling, lodging, domicile, residence, address, berth, housing, quarters, headquarters.

home, fatherland, motherland, country; homestead, hearth, chimney corner; roof, household, housing, native soil, native land.

county, parish, etc. (*region*), 181.

retreat, haunt, habitat, resort; nest, arbor, bower, grotto; lair, den, cave, hole, hiding place, cell, sanctum sanctorum, eyrie, rookery, hive; covert, perch, roost.

anchorage, roadstead, roads; dock, basin, wharf, quay, port, harbor.

camp, bivouac, encampment, cantonment, barracks, quarters; tent, wigwam, tepee; igloo.

farm, farmhouse, grange.

cot, cabin, hut, hovel; shanty, dugout, chalet, log cabin, log house; shack [colloq], shed, booth, stall, pen, fold; stable, barn; kennel, sty, cote, dovecote, coop, hutch; cowhouse, cowshed.

house, mansion, place, villa, cottage, lodge, hermitage, rotunda, tower, château, castle, pavilion, hotel, court, manor house, hall, palace; kiosk, bungalow, country seat; apartment (or brownstone, duplex, frame, shingle, flat, tenement) house; three-decker; building, buildings.

hamlet, village, dorp [Dutch], rancho [Sp. Amer.].

town, borough, city, capital, metropolis; suburb; province, country; county town, county seat.

street, place, terrace, parade, esplanade, boardwalk, embankment, road, row, lane, alley, court, quadrangle, close, yard, passage.

square, polygon, circus, crescent, block, arcade, colonnade, cloister; market place.

assembly room, auditorium, concert hall, armory, gymnasium; cathedral, church, chapel, meetinghouse, etc. (temple), 1000; parliament, etc. (council), 696.

inn, hotel, tavern, caravansary, alehouse, saloon, club, clubhouse; grill room, chophouse, coffeehouse, eating house; canteen, restaurant, buffet, café, cabaret.

sanatorium, health resort, sanitarium; spa, watering place.

V. inhabit, etc., 186; take up one's abode, etc. (locate oneself), 184.

Adj. urban, metropolitan; cosmopolitan; suburban.

provincial, rural, rustic, country, countrified.

190. [Things contained] CONTENTS.—*N.* contents; cargo, lading, freight, shipment, load, bale, burden; cartload, shipload; stuffing.

V. load, lade, ship, pile, fill, stuff.

191. RECEPTACLE.—*N.* receptacle, container; inclosure, etc., 232; recipient, receiver; compartment, cell; hole, corner, niche, recess, nook, crypt; stall; pigeonhole; mouth.

stomach, paunch, belly, crop, craw, maw.

bag, sack, wallet, pocket, pouch; purse; knapsack, haversack, satchel, reticule; saddlebags; portfolio; valise, grip [colloq.], suitcase, handbag, schoolbag, brief case, traveling bag, Gladstone bag.

case, chest, box, coffer, caddy, casket; reliquary, shrine; caisson; desk, bureau; trunk, portmanteau, bandbox.

vessel, utensil; vase, canister, jar; basket, pannier, hamper; crate; creel; cradle, bassinet.

For liquids: cistern, reservoir; vat, caldron, barrel, cask, keg, tun, butt, firkin, tub; bottle, jar, decanter, ewer, carafe, canteen, flagon; demijohn; flask, vial, phial; cruet, caster; urn, percolator, coffeepot, teapot, samovar; bucket, pail; pot, tankard, jug, pitcher, mug, porringer; receiver, retort, alembic, crucible; can, kettle; bowl, basin; punch bowl, cup, goblet, beaker, chalice, tumbler, glass.

plate, platter, dish, tray, waiter, salver.

ladle, dipper; shovel, trowel, spatula.

cupboard, closet; locker, bin, buffet, sideboard; drawer, chest of drawers, chiffonier; till, safe; bookcase, cabinet.

chamber, apartment, room, cabin; office, court, hall, suite of rooms, apartment, flat, tenement; parlor, living (or sitting, drawing, reception) room; best room [colloq]; boudoir; sanctum; bedroom, dormitory; refectory, dining room; nursery, schoolroom; library, study, studio; smoking room, den.

attic, loft, garret, cellar, vault, hold, cockpit; cubbyhole; basement, kitchen, pantry, scullery, storeroom, lumber room; dairy, laundry; garage; hangar; outhouse, penthouse; lean-to, shed.

portico, porch, stoop, veranda, piazza.

bower, arbor, summerhouse; grotto; conservatory, greenhouse.

II. DIMENSIONS

192. SIZE.—*N.* **size,** dimensions, proportions; magnitude, bulk, volume; largeness, greatness; expanse, amplitude, mass; capacity; tonnage; cordage; caliber.

lump, block, mass; clod, mountain, mound; heap, etc. (*assemblage*), 72.

corpulence, obesity, plumpness.

immensity, hugeness, monstrosity, enormity.

giant, Titan, Hercules, Gargantua; monster, mammoth, whale, behemoth, leviathan, elephant, jumbo [*colloq.*]; colossus.

V. **be large,** become large, etc. (*expand*), 194.

Adj. **large,** big, great, considerable, bulky, voluminous, ample, massive; capacious, comprehensive, spacious; mighty, towering.

stout, corpulent, fat, plump, chubby; portly, burly, brawny, fleshy.

unwieldy, hulky, hulking, lumpish, overgrown; puffy, swollen, bloated.

huge, immense, enormous, titanic, mighty; vast; stupendous; monster, monstrous; gigantic; elephantine, mammoth; giant, colossal, cyclopean, Gargantuan.

193. LITTLENESS.—*N.* **littleness,** smallness; epitome; microcosm; vanishing point.

dwarf, pygmy, midget; Lilliputian, elf; doll, puppet, manikin; Tom Thumb.

mite, insect, arthropod, ephemerid, ephemera, bug [*pop.*], larva.
atom, monad, animalcule, animalculum (*pl.* animalcula), molecule, microbe, germ, micro-organism, bacterium (*pl.* bacteria), amoeba.

particle, speck, dot, mote; scrap; spark; scintilla; fragment, fraction; grain, powder, dust; minutiæ, etc. (*unimportance*), 643.

V. **belittle,** lie in a nutshell; become small, decrease; contract, etc., 195.

Adj. **little,** small, minute, diminutive, microscopic; inconsiderable, petty; limited, cramped; puny, runty, tiny, wee [*colloq.*], elfin, miniature, pocket; undersized, stunted, dwarf, dwarfed, dwarfish, pygmy; Lilliputian; invisible, infinitesimal, homeopathic.

Adv. in a small compass, in a nutshell; on a small scale.

194. EXPANSION.—*N.* **expansion,** dilation; growth, increase, enlargement, amplification; extension, augmentation, aggrandizement; spread, increment, development, swell, dilatation; obesity, corpulence; dropsy, swelling, distension, puffiness, inflation.

V. **enlarge,** expand, widen, extend, grow, increase, swell, fill out; dilate, stretch, spread; wax; bud, shoot, sprout, germinate, put forth, open, burst forth; outgrow; overrun.

spread, augment, aggrandize; distend, develop, amplify, spread out, widen, magnify; inflate, blow up; stuff, fatten, pad, cram, bloat; exaggerate.

Adj. **expanded,** larger; swollen, expansive, widespread, overgrown, exaggerated, bloated, fat, tumid, dropsical; corpulent, obese; puffy, distend, bulbous; full-blown, full-grown; big, etc., 192.

195. CONTRACTION.—*N.* **contraction,** reduction, diminution; decrease, etc., 36; lessening, shrinking; atrophy; emaciation, attenuation.

compression, condensation, constraint, compactness; compendium, abstract, epitome; strangulation; astringency.

V. **decrease,** lessen, grow less, dwindle, shrink, contract, narrow, shrivel, collapse, wither, fall away, waste, wane, ebb.

diminish, boil down; deflate, exhaust, empty; constrict, condense, compress, squeeze, crush; pinch, tighten, strangle; cramp; dwarf; shorten, etc., 201; circumscribe, limit, bound, confine.

pare, reduce; attenuate; rub down, scrape, file, grind, chip, shave, shear.

Adj. **contracting,** astringent; shrunk, shrunken, contracted; strangulated; wizened; stunted; waning; compact.

196. DISTANCE.—*N.* **distance,** remoteness; space, etc., 180; far cry to; elongation; drift, offing, background; remote region; reach, span.

outpost, outskirt; horizon, skyline; foreign parts, antipodes.

V. **be distant;** extend to, stretch to, reach to, spread to, stretch away to; range, outreach.

Adj. **distant,** far, far off, far away, remote; telescopic; yon, yonder; ulterior; transatlantic, transalpine; ultramundane, antipodean; inaccessible, out-of-the-way; unapproachable.

Adv. **far off,** far away, afar, afar off; away; beyond range, aloof; wide of, clear of; abroad, yonder, farther, further, beyond; far and wide, from pole to pole; out of range, out of hearing.

apart, asunder; at arm's length.

197. NEARNESS.—*N.* **nearness,** proximity, propinquity; vicinity, vicinage, neighborhood, contiguity, etc., 199.

short distance, short cut; earshot, close quarters, range, stone's throw; gunshot, hair's breadth, span.

purlieus, neighborhood, vicinage, environs, suburbs, confines.

bystander, spectator; neighbor.

approach, approximation, access; convergence, meeting.

V. **be near,** adjoin, abut, neighbor, trench on; border upon, verge upon; approximate; stand by, hang about; cling to, clasp, hug; huddle; hover over.

bring *or* draw near; converge, etc., 290; crowd, pack, huddle.

Adj. **near,** nigh, close (*or* near) at hand, close, neighboring, bordering upon, contiguous, adjacent, adjoining; proximate, approximate; at hand, handy; intimate.

Adv. **near,** nigh, hard by, close to, close upon; hard upon; at the point of; next door to; within reach (*or* call, hearing, earshot, range); on the verge of; in sight of; at close quarters; beside, alongside, side by side; in juxtaposition; at the heels of.

about; thereabouts; roughly, in round numbers; approximately, as good as, well-nigh.

198. INTERVAL.—*N.* **interval,** space; separation, division; hiatus, cæsura; interruption; interregnum; interstice.

parenthesis; void, vacuum; incompleteness, deficiency.

cleft, break, gap, opening; hole, puncture; chasm, mesh, crevice, chink, cranny, crack, slit, fissure, rift, fault, flaw, breach, fracture, rent, gash, cut.

gorge, defile, pass, ravine, canyon, crevasse; abyss, abysm; gulf; inlet, strait; furrow, etc., 259; gully, gulch, notch.

V. **gape,** yawn; separate, etc., 44.

199. CONTACT.—*N.* **contact,** contiguity, contiguousness, proximity, apposition, abuttal, abutment, juxtaposition, touching, meeting; conjunction, adhesion, etc., 46.

borderland; frontier, etc. (*limit*), 233.

V. **adjoin,** join, abut on, neighbor, border, march with; graze, touch, meet; coincide; coexist; adhere, etc., 46.

Adj. **contiguous,** touching, in contact, conterminous, end to end; close, etc. (*near*), 197.

200. [Linear Dimensions] LENGTH.—*N.* **length,** longitude, extent, span; mileage.

line, bar, rule, stripe, streak.

lengthening, prolongation, production, protraction; tension, extension.

Measures of length: line, nail, inch, hand, palm, foot, cubit, yard, ell, fathom, rood, pole, furlong, mile, knot, league; chain; meter, kilometer, centimeter, etc. pedometer, odometer, odograph, viameter, log [*naut.*], speedometer, telemeter, scale.

V. **be long,** stretch out, sprawl; extend to, reach to, stretch to.

lengthen, let out, extend, elongate; stretch; prolong, protract; draw out, spin out.

Adj. **long,** elongate, lengthy, outstretched, extended; lengthened, interminable.

linear, lineal; longitudinal.

lanky, lank, slab-sided [*slang*], rangy; tall; long-limbed.

Adv. **lengthwise,** at length, longitudinally, along, tandem; in a line; from end to end, from stem to stern, from head to foot, from top to toe; fore and aft; over all.

201. SHORTNESS.—*N.* **shortness,** brevity, littleness, etc., 193; a span.

abridgment, shortening, abbreviation, retrenchment, curtailment, epitomization, condensation; reduction, etc. (*contraction*), 195; epitome, etc. (*compendium*), 596.

elision, ellipsis; conciseness, brevity.

V. **shorten,** curtail, retrench, abridge, abbreviate; take in, reduce; compress, contract; epitomize, abstract, summarize, condense; cut, pare down, clip, dock, lop, prune, shear, shave, mow, crop, stunt; nip, check the growth of, foreshorten [*drawing*].

Adj. **short,** brief, curt; compendious, compact; stubby, pudgy, squatty; stumpy [*colloq.*], thickset, chunky, scrub, stocky, squat, dumpy; pug, turned up; little, etc., 193; concise, etc., 572; summary.

202. BREADTH, THICKNESS.—*N.* **breadth,** width, latitude, amplitude.

diameter, bore, caliber; radius.

thickness; corpulence, etc. (*size*), 192; expansion, dilatation.

V. expand, etc., 194; thicken, widen.

Adj. **broad,** wide, ample, extended, outspread, outstretched.

thick, dumpy, squat, thickset, stubby, etc., 201.

203. NARROWNESS, THINNESS.—*N.* **narrowness,** slenderness; closeness.

line; hair's breadth.

thinness, tenuity; leanness, lankiness, emaciation.

shaving; strip, etc. (*filament*), 205; thread, skeleton, shadow, scrag, mere skin and bone.

narrowing, tapering; contraction, etc., 195.

V. **narrow,** taper; contract, etc., 195.

Adj. **narrow,** close; slender, thin, fine, delicate, threadlike, finespun, taper, slim; scant, scanty, spare; contracted.

lean, emaciated, skinny, scrawny, meager, gaunt, rawboned, lank, lanky, weedy [*colloq.*]; starved, starveling; attenuated, shriveled, pinched, spindle-legged, spindle-shanked, spindling; worn to a shadow; hatchet-faced; lantern-jawed.

204. LAYER.—*N.* **layer,** stratum, course, bed, coping, substratum, floor, stage, story, tier.

leaf, sheet, flake, scale, coat, peel, membrane, film, slice, shaving, wafer.

stratification, lamination, foliation; scaliness.

V. **slice,** shave, pare, peel.

plate, coat, veneer; cover, etc., 223.

Adj. **scaly,** filmy, membranous, flaky, foliated, stratified.

205. FILAMENT.—*N.* **filament,** line; fiber, vein, hair, cobweb, capillary, strand, tendril, gossamer.

thread, yarn, packthread, cotton.

string, twine, twist, cord, rope, tape, ribbon, wire.

strip, shred, slip, band, fillet, lath, splinter.

Adj. **fibrous,** threadlike, wiry, stringy, ropy; capillary, wire-drawn; hairy, etc. (*rough*), 256.

206. HEIGHT.—*N.* **height,** altitude, elevation, eminence, pitch; loftiness, sublimity.

tallness, stature; prominence, etc., 250; apex, zenith, culmination.

colossus, etc. (*size*), 192; giant.

height, mount, mountain, hill; headland, foreland, promontory; ridge, dune, rising ground, down, uplands, highlands; knoll, hummock, hillock, mound; bluff, cliff, peak.

tower, pillar, column, obelisk, monument, belfry, steeple, spire, minaret, campanile, turret, dome, cupola; pyramid, pagoda.

pole, pikestaff, Maypole, flagstaff; mast, mainmast, topmast.

high water; high (*or* flood, spring) tide.

V. **tower,** soar, hover; cap, culminate; overhang, surmount, rise above, command, overtop, rise, ascend.

heighten, uprear, uplift, upraise, elevate.

Adj. **high,** elevated, eminent, exalted, lofty, sublime; tall, gigantic, big, colossal; towering, beetling, soaring, elevated; higher, superior, upper, supernal; highest, etc. (*topmost*), 210.

lanky, etc. (*thin*), 203.

upland, hilly, mountainous, alpine, heaven-kissing, cloud-capped.

overhanging, impending, incumbent, overlying; superimposed.

Adv. **on high,** high up, aloft, up, above, overhead; in the clouds.

207. LOWNESS.—*N.* **lowness,** levelness, flatness; debasement, prostration; depression, hollow; lowlands.

basement, cellar, vault, crypt, cavern; hold; base, etc., 211.

low water, low (*or* ebb, neap) tide.

V. **be low,** lie low, underlie; crouch, wallow, grovel; lower, etc. (*depress*), 308.

Adj. **low,** low-lying, level; flat; crouched, squat, prostrate, depressed, debased.

lower, inferior, under, nether.

lowest, nethermost, lowermost.

Adv. **under,** beneath, underneath, below, down, downward; underfoot, underground; downstairs, belowstairs; at a low ebb; below par.

208. DEPTH.—*N.* **depth,** profundity, depression, hollow.

pit, shaft, well, crater, chasm, crevasse, deep, abyss, bowels of the earth, bottomless pit.

soundings, draft, submersion, plunge, dive; plummet, lead.

V. deepen, sink, excavate, mine, sap, dig, burrow.

sound, heave the lead, take soundings.

Adj. deep, deep-seated, profound, buried; sunk, submerged, subaqueous, submarine, subterranean, underground.

bottomless, fathomless, unfathomed, unfathomable, abysmal, down-reaching, yawning.

Adv. out of one's depth, beyond one's depth; over head and ears.

209. SHALLOWNESS.—*N.* shallowness, superficiality; shoals.

Adj. shallow, slight, superficial; skin-deep, ankle-deep, knee-deep, shoal.

210. SUMMIT.—*N.* summit, top, vertex, apex, zenith, pinnacle, acme, crown; height, pitch, maximum; goal, consummation; climax, turning point; culmination; turn of the tide, fountainhead.

tip, tiptop; crest, crow's-nest, cap, peak; brow, head.

architrave, frieze, cornice, coping, coping stone, capital, headpiece, capstone, pediment, entablature; attic, loft, garret, housetop, upper story, roof (*covering*), 223.

V. crown, top, cap, crest, surmount, overtop; culminate.

Adj. highest (high, etc., 206), top, topmost, overmost, uppermost, tiptop; capital, head, polar; supreme, supernal.

211. Base.—*N.* base, basement; plinth, dado, wainscot; baseboard, mopboard; bedrock, hardpan; foundation, substructure, substratum, ground, earth, pavement, floor, paving; footing, groundwork, basis.

bottom, nadir, foot, sole, toe, hoof, root; keel.

Adj. bottom, undermost, nethermost; fundamental; founded on, based on.

212. VERTICALITY.—*N.* verticality, perpendicularity, erectness.

cliff, steep, crag, bluff, palisades; wall, precipice.

V. be vertical, stand erect *or* upright, stick up, cock up.

render vertical, set up, raise up, erect, rear, raise, pitch.

Adj. vertical; upright, erect, perpendicular, plumb, bolt upright.

Adv. on end; endwise; at right angles.

213. HORIZONTALITY.—*N.* horizontality; flatness; level, plane, stratum.

recumbency; lying down, reclination, proneness, supination, prostration.

V. be horizontal, lie, recline, lie flat; sprawl, loll.

render horizontal, lay, level, flatten, even, raze, smooth, align.

prostrate, knock down, floor, fell, ground, cut (*or* hew) down, mow down.

Adj. **horizontal,** level, even, plane, flush; flat, smooth.

recumbent, prone, supine, prostrate.

Adv. on one's back; on all fours; on its beam ends.

214. PENDENCY.—*N.* **pendency,** dependency; suspension, hanging.

pendant, drop, eardrop, tassel, lobe; tail, train, queue, pigtail; pendulum.

chandelier, gaselier.

V. **be pendent;** hang, depend, swing, dangle, lower, droop; flap, trail, beetle, jut, overhang.

suspend, hang, sling, hook up, hitch, fasten to, append.

Adj. **pendent,** pendulous, hanging; dependent; beetling, jutting over, overhanging; lowering; suspended.

215. SUPPORT.—*N.* **support,** ground, foundation, base, basis, fulcrum, purchase, footing, hold; stage, platform; rest, resting place; groundwork, substratum; floor.

supporter; aid, etc., 707; prop, truss, stand, stalk; bracket; ledge, shelf, table, trestle; rung, round; staff, stick, crook, crutch.

post, pillar, column, pediment, pedestal; caryatid; buttress, jamb, mullion, stile, abutment.

frame, framework; scaffold, skeleton, beam, rafter, girder, lintel, joist; keystone; arch; mainstay.

seat, throne, dais; divan, ottoman, sofa, davenport, couch, daybed; stall; chair, wing chair, armchair, easy chair, elbowchair, rocking chair, Morris chair; settee, form, bench; saddle, sidesaddle, pillion; packsaddle; pommel, horn.

stool, hassock, footstool.

bed, bedstead, four-poster; pallet; cot; hammock, shakedown; crib, trundle bed, cradle; litter, stretcher; bunk, berth; mat, rug, cushion; lap.

V. **support,** bear, carry, hold, sustain, shoulder; hold up, back up, bolster up, shore up, uphold, brace, truss, stay, prop; maintain; aid, etc., 707.

Adj. **supporting,** supported; fundamental.

216. PARALLELISM.—*N.* **parallelism,** equidistance, concentricity.

V. **be parallel,** parallel, equal.

Adj. **parallel,** coextensive, equidistant; collateral, concentric, concurrent; abreast, equal, even, alongside.

Adv. alongside, abreast, broadside on.

217. OBLIQUITY.—*N.* **obliquity,** inclination, incline, slope, slant; leaning, tilt; bias, diagonal, zigzag, list, twist, sag, cant, lurch; distortion, etc., 243; bend, curve.

acclivity, steepness; rise, ascent, pitch, grade, rising ground, hill, bank; cliff, precipice, etc. (*vertical*), 212; shelving beach; declivity, dip, fall.

V. **be oblique;** slope, slant, lean, cant, incline, shelve, decline, descend, bend; heel over, careen; sag, slouch, sidle, skid.

render oblique; sway, bias; slope, slant, tilt; incline, bend, crook; distort, etc., 243; zigzag, stagger [*mech.*].

Adj. oblique, inclined; sloping, tilted; askew, asquint, bias, aslant, diagonal, transverse, athwart; indirect, wry, awry, crooked; sinuous, zigzag; knock-kneed, etc. (*distorted*), 243.

uphill, rising, ascending; steep, abrupt, precipitous.

downhill, falling, descending; declining, shelving, declivitous.

Adv. obliquely; on one side, askew, askance, awry, edgewise, at an angle; sidelong, sidewise, slantwise.

218. INVERSION.—*N.* inversion, subversion, reversion; opposition, polarity; contrariety, contradiction, reversal, transposition, transposal; turn of the tide; overturn, revolution; somersault; revulsion.

V. be inverted, turn (*or* go, wheel) about, turn (*or* tilt, topple) over; capsize, turn turtle.

invert, subvert; reverse; upturn, overturn, upset, overset, turn topsy-turvy; transpose.

Adj. inverted, wrong side out (*or* up); inside out, upside down; on one's head, topsy-turvy.

inverse; reverse, etc. (*contrary*), 14; opposite.

Adv. inversely, conversely; heels over head, head over heels.

219. CROSSING.—*N.* crossing; intersection, grade crossing.

network, reticulation; net, web, mesh, netting, lace, plait; sieve, screen; wicker; mat, matting; trellis, lattice, grating, grille, gridiron, tracery, fretwork, filigree; entanglement.

crucifix, cross, rood, crisscross.

V. cross, intersect, interlace, intertwine, intertwist, interweave, interlink, crisscross; twine, entwine, weave, twist, wreathe; dovetail, mortise, splice, link.

plait, pleat, plat, braid; entangle, ravel; net, knot.

Adj. crossed, matted, transverse, intersected, cross; cross-shaped, cruciform; netlike, retiform, latticed, grated, barred, streaked.

Adv. cross, athwart, thwart, transversely; at grade; crosswise, across.

220. EXTERIORITY.—*N.* exteriority; outside, exterior; surface superficies; skin, covering; face, facet.

V. be exterior, lie around, environ, encircle.

externalize, objectify, visualize, envisage, actualize.

Adj. exterior, external, extraneous; outer, outermost; outward, outlying, outside, outdoor.

outstanding: extrinsic, incidental: superficial, skin-deep.

Adv. externally, out, without, over, outwards, out of doors, in the open air.

221. INTERIORITY.—*N.* **interiority**; inside, interior; interspace, subsoil.

contents, etc., 190; substance, pith, marrow; heart, bosom, breast; recesses, innermost recesses; cave, etc. (*concavity*), 252.

inmate, intern, inhabitant, etc., 188.

V. **inclose**, etc. (*circumscribe*), 229; intern; embed, etc. (*insert*), 300; place within, keep within.

Adj. **interior**, internal; inner, intimate, inside, inward, inmost, innermost; deep-seated, inherent, ingrained, innate, inborn, inbred, intrinsic.

home, inland, domestic, family, indoor.

Adv. **internally**; inwards, within, indoors, withindoors; at home.

222. CENTRALITY.—*N.* **centrality**; centralization, concentration; center; middle, midst; focus; center of gravity.

core, kernel, nucleus; heart, pole, axis, bull's-eye, nave, hub; marrow, pith; metropolis.

V. **centralize**, concentrate; bring to a focus; converge, etc., 290.

Adj. **central**; middle, axial, pivotal, nuclear, focal, concentric; middlemost; metropolitan.

223. COVERING.—*N.* **covering**, cover; canopy, awning, tent, marquee, wigwam, tepee; umbrella, parasol, sunshade; veil; shield, etc. (*defense*), 717.

roof, ceiling, thatch, tiles, slates, leads, shingles; dome, cupola.

coverlet, counterpane, sheet, quilt, blanket, rug; eiderdown quilt, comforter; pillowcase, pillowslip; linoleum, oilcloth; tarpaulin.

integument: skin, pellicle, fleece, fur, leather, lambskin, sable, beaver, ermine, hide, coat, buff, pelt, peltry [*collective noun*]; cuticle, cutis, epidermis; clothing, etc., 225.

peel, rind, crust, bark, husk, shell.

sheath, sheathing, capsule, pod, casing, case, wrapping, wrapper; envelope; cornhusk, corn shuck.

veneer, facing; scale, layer; incrustation, coating, paint, stain, varnish, enamel, whitewash, plaster, stucco.

V. **cover**, superimpose, overlay, overspread; wrap, incase, face, case, veneer, paper; clapboard, shingle; conceal, etc., 528.

coat, paint, stain, varnish, incrust, crust, cement, stucco, plaster; smear, daub, besmear, bedaub; gild, plate, japan, lacquer, enamel, whitewash.

Adj. **covered**, hooded, cowled, armored, armor-plated; ironclad; scaly.

224. LINING.—*N.* **lining**, coating, inner coating; filling, stuffing, wadding, padding; facing, bushing; sheathing.

V. **line**, stuff, incrust, wad, pad, fill, face, ceil, bush, wainscot, sheathe.

225. CLOTHING.—*N.* **clothing**, dress; covering, etc., 223; raiment, costume, attire, toilet, habiliment; vesture, vestment;

garment, garb, wardrobe, apparel, wearing apparel, clothes, finery, etc. (*ornament*), 847.

outfit, equipment, trousseau; uniform, khaki; livery, gear, harness, turnout, accouterment, caparison, suit, trappings.

dishabille, undress, tea gown, wrapper, negligee, dressing gown, kimono; rags, tatters, old clothes.

robe, habit, gown, dress, frock; blouse, middy blouse, waist, shirtwaist; suit; coat; toga, tunic, smock.

dress suit, dress clothes, evening dress, dinner coat, dinner jacket; Tuxedo [*colloq*.]; glad rags [*slang*]

cloak, mantle, shawl, veil; cape, plaid [Scot.], muffler, overcoat, greatcoat; oilskins, slicker, mackintosh, waterproof, ulster; poncho; pea-jacket; sweater, blazer, cardigan, jersey; Mackinaw coat.

jacket, vest, waistcoat; gaberdine.

skirt, petticoat, kilt; bloomers.

trousers, breeches, pants [*colloq*.]; overalls; shorts; tights; drawers; knickers [*colloq*.].

headdress, headgear, coiffure [F.], crush hat, opera hat; tam-o'-shanter, topee [India], sombrero; cap, hat, bonnet, panama, leghorn; derby; nightcap, skullcap; hood, coif; wimple: snood; crown, etc., 247; wig, front, peruke, periwig; turban, fez, tarboosh, shako, busby, bearskin; kepi, helmet; mask, domino.

body clothes, underclothing, linen; shirt, undervest, undershirt; smock, shift, chemise; nightgown, nightshirt, pajamas; bedgown.

tie, neckerchief, neckcloth; ruff, collar, cravat, stock, handkerchief, scarf; bib, tucker; boa; girdle, cummerbund [India].

shoe, Oxford shoe, Oxford tie, pump, sneakers, boot, slipper, moccasin, sandal, galosh, arctic, overshoe, rubber; patten, clog; snowshoes, ski.

stocking, hose, sock; hosiery.

glove, gauntlet; mitten, mitt.

V. clothe, array, dress, accouter, rig, fit out, deck, drape, robe, enrobe, gown, attire, apparel, equip; harness, caparison; cover, wrap, shroud, swathe, swaddle.

wear; don; put on, slip on; mantle.

Adj. clothed, clad, invested, habited.

226. DIVESTMENT.—*N.* divestment; nudity, bareness, nakedness: dishabille, etc., 225.

baldness, hairlessness.

V. divest, uncover, expose, lay open, lay bare, denude, bare, strip; undress, disrobe, dismantle; put off, take off, doff.

peel, bare, slough, excoriate, skin, scalp, flay, bark, husk.

Adj. naked, nude, bare, stark-naked, exposed; undressed, undraped, unclad, ungarmented, unclothed.

bald, hairless, beardless; shaven, clean-shaven.

227. ENVIRONMENT.—*N.* environment, encompassment; surroundings, outskirts, suburbs, purlieus, precincts, environs, entourage, neighborhood, vicinage, vicinity.

V. environ, surround, beset, compass, encompass, inclose, encircle, circle, girdle, hedge, embrace, gird, belt, engird; skirt, hem in; circumscribe, etc., 229; beleaguer, invest, besiege, beset, blockade.

Adj. surrounding, begirt; suburban.

Adv. **around,** about: without; on every side, on all sides.

228. INTERLOCATION.—*N.* **interlocation,** interjacence, interpenetration; interjection, interpolation, interlineation, interspersion, intercalation.

intervention, interference, interposition, intrusion; insinuation; insertion.

intermediary, go-between, interagent, middleman, medium.

partition, diaphragm, midriff; wall, party wall; panel, bulkhead.

V. **intervene,** come between, get between, interpenetrate.

introduce, import; throw in, edge in, run in, work in; interpose, insinuate, interject, interpolate, insert, intersperse, interlard, dovetail, splice, mortise.

interfere, intrude, obtrude; thrust in, etc. (*insert*), 300.

Adj. **intervening,** parenthetical, episodic; intrusive; embosomed.

Adv. **between,** among; amid, amidst; in the thick of; betwixt and between [*colloq.*]; parenthetically.

229. CIRCUMSCRIPTION.—*N.* **circumscription,** limitation, inclosure; confinement; etc. (*restraint*), 751; envelope, case.

V. **circumscribe,** limit, bound, confine, inclose; surround, etc., 227; hedge in, rail in, fence round, hedge round; picket; corral; imprison, restrain.

enfold, bury, incase, enshrine, enclasp; clothe, 225; embosom.

Adj. **circumscribed,** begirt, girt; lapped; buried in, immersed in; embosomed, imbedded, mewed up; imprisoned, etc., 751; landlocked.

230. OUTLINE.—*N.* **outline,** circumference; perimeter, periphery; circuit, lines, contour, profile, silhouette, lineaments, relief, bounds; coast line, horizon.

zone, belt, girdle; girth; band; baldric, zodiac; tire, pale, etc. (*inclosure*), 232; circlet, etc., 247.

V. **outline,** delineate, silhouette, block, sketch, circumscribe, etc., 229.

231. EDGE.—*N.* **edge,** verge, brink, brow, brim, margin, border, confine, skirt, rim, side; lip.

threshold, door, porch; portal, etc. (*opening*), 260.

shore, coast, strand, bank; quay, wharf, dock, mole, landing.

fringe, flounce, frill, furbelow; valance; trimming, edging, skirting, hem, selvage, welt; frame.

V. **edge,** coast, border, skirt; fringe, flounce, hem.

232. INCLOSURE.—*N.* **inclosure,** envelope; case, etc. (*receptacle*), 191; wrapper; girdle, etc., 230.

pen, fold; sty, paddock, pasture; pound; corral, yard; net, seine.

fence, pale, paling, balustrade, rail, railing, wall; hedge, hedgerow.

barrier, barricade, cordon, stockade; gate, gateway; weir; door, hatch, prison, etc., 752.

dike, ditch, trench, drain, moat.

V. **inclose,** circumscribe, etc., 229.

233. LIMIT.—*N.* limit, boundary, bounds, pale, confine, term, bourn, verge; termination, terminus, terminal; stint; frontier, border, marches.

boundary line, landmark; turning point.

V. **limit,** bound, compass, confine, define, circumscribe.

Adj. **definite;** terminal; frontier, bordering, border, boundary.

Adv. **thus far,** thus far and no further.

234. FRONT.—*N.* front, foreground, forefront; face, frontage, façade, proscenium, frontispiece; priority; obverse (*of a medal*).

van, vanguard, advanced guard; front rank; outpost; first line; scout.

brow, forehead; visage, physiognomy, features, countenance; bow, stem, prow; jib; bowsprit.

pioneer, etc. (*precursor*), 64.

V. **front,** face, confront, brave, dare, defy, oppose; breast; come to the front *or* fore.

Adj. **fore,** foremost, headmost; forward, anterior, front, frontal.

Adv. **before,** in front, in the van, in advance; ahead; in the foreground.

235. REAR.—*N.* rear, back; rear rank, rearguard; background, hinterland.

tail, scut (*as of a hare*), brush (*of a fox*).

afterpart; stern, poop; postern door; tailpiece, crupper.

wake; train, retinue, suite, cortege.

reverse; other side of the shield.

V. **be behind;** fall astern; bring up the rear; heel, tag, shadow, follow, pursue.

Adj. **back,** rear, hindmost; posterior; after.

Adv. **behind,** in the rear *or* background; at the heels of; after, aft, abaft, astern, rearward, backward.

236. SIDE.—*N.* side, flank, quarter, lee; wing; profile; gable, gable end; broadside.

points of the compass; East, sunrise, Orient, Levant; West, Occident, sunset.

V. **flank,** skirt, outflank; sidle; border; be on one side.

Adj. **lateral,** sidelong: collateral; flanking, skirting.

eastern, eastward, east, Orient, Oriental, auroral, Levantine.

western, west, westerly, westward, Occidental.

Adv **sidewise,** sidelong, sideling, broadside on; abreast, alongside, beside; aside; by, by the side of; side by side; to windward, to leeward; laterally; right and left.

237. OPPOSITE.—*N.* **opposite,** opposite side, reverse, inverse; counterpart, antithesis; opposition, polarity; inversion, etc., 218.

antipodes, opposite poles; North and South.

Adj. **opposite,** reverse, converse; antipodal, diametrical, antithetic, counter; fronting, facing.

northern, north, northerly, northward, hyperborean, boreal, polar, arctic.

southern, south, southerly, southward, austral, antarctic.

Adv. **over,** over the way, over against; against; face to face, vis-à-vis [F.].

238. RIGHT.—*N.* **right,** right hand; offside, starboard.

Adj. **dextral,** dexterous, right-handed, dexter.

ambidexter, ambidextrous.

239. LEFT.—*N.* **left,** left hand, south paw [*slang*]; near side; larboard, port.

Adj. **left-handed,** sinistral.

III. FORM

240. FORM.—*N.* **form,** figure, shape, make, formation, frame, construction, cut, build, contour, outline, stamp, type, cast, mold, fashion; structure, etc., 329; sculpture, architecture.

feature, lineament, turn; phase, etc. (*aspect*), 448; posture, attitude, pose.

V. **form,** shape, figure, fashion, carve, cut, chisel, hew, cast; roughhew, sketch, block out; trim, model, knead, mold, sculpture; cast, stamp; build, etc. (*construct*), 161.

Adj. **structural;** plastic, formative, impressible; creative.

shapely, well proportioned, symmetrical, well made, well formed, trim, neat.

241. ABSENCE OF FORM.—*N.* **formlessness,** shapelessness, misproportion, uncouthness; rough diamond; disorder, etc., 59; deformity, etc., 243; disfigurement, defacement; mutilation.

V. **deface,** disfigure, deform, mutilate, derange, etc., 61; blemish, mar.

Adj. **formless,** shapeless, amorphous, unshapely, misshapen, unsymmetrical, malformed, unformed; anomalous.

rough, rude, barbarous, rugged, scraggy; in the rough.

242. [Regularity of form] SYMMETRY.—*N.* **symmetry,** shapeliness, finish; beauty, etc., 845; proportion, eurythmics, uniformity, parallelism; centrality; radiation, branching, ramification; regularity, evenness.

Adj. **symmetrical**, shapely, well set, finished; beautiful, etc., 845; classic, chaste, severe.

regular, uniform, balanced, equal, even, parallel.

243. [Irregularity of form] DISTORTION.—*N.* distortion, contortion; knot, warp, buckle, screw, twist; crookedness, obliquity; grimace, deformity, malformation; monstrosity, misproportion, ugliness, disfigurement.

V. **distort,** contort, twist, warp, buckle, screw, wrench, wrest, writhe, deform, misshape.

Adj. **distorted,** out of shape, irregular, unsymmetric, awry, wry, askew, crooked, gnarled; not true, not straight; deformed; misshapen, misproportioned, ill-proportioned; ill-made; humpbacked, hunchbacked; bandy-legged, bow-legged; knock-kneed.

244. ANGULARITY.—*N.* angularity, bifurcation; fold, etc., 258; notch, etc., 257; fork, crotch, angle, bend, elbow, knee, knuckle; zigzag; right angle, acute angle, obtuse angle; obliquity, etc., 217.

corner, nook, recess, niche.

triangle; rectangle, square; lozenge, diamond; rhomb, rhombus, rhomboid; quadrangle, quadrilateral; parallelogram; polygon, pentagon, hexagon, heptagon, octagon, oxygon, decagon; cube, prism, pyramid.

V. **fork,** branch, ramify, bifurcate, bend hook.

Adj. **angular,** bent, crooked, aquiline, jagged, serrated; forked, bifurcate, crotched, zigzag, hooked; akimbo; oblique, etc., 217.

245. CURVATURE.—*N.* curvature, curvedness, incurvature, bend; flexure, crook, hook, bending; deflection, turn; deviation, detour; sweep; curl; sinuosity, etc., 248.

curve, arc, arch, arcade, vault, bow, cresent, half-moon, horseshoe, loop, festoon; parabola, hyperbola; tracery.

V. **be curved,** sweep, sag; deviate, etc., 279; turn; re-enter.

render curved, bend, curve, deflect, inflect; crook; turn, round, arch over, bow, coil, curl, recurve.

Adj. **curved,** curvate, devious; recurved, arched, vaulted; oblique, etc., 217; circular, etc., 247; bell-shaped; bow-shaped, embowed; crescent, crescent-shaped, horned; heart-shaped, cordate; hook-shaped, hooked, hooklike; moon-shaped, lunar, sickle-shaped.

246. STRAIGHTNESS.—*N.* straightness, directness; inflexibility; straight (*or* bee, right, direct) line; short cut.

V. **be straight,** have no turning, go straight, steer for.

render straight, straighten, rectify; set *or* put straight; unbend, unfold, uncurl, uncoil, unravel.

Adj. **straight,** rectilinear; direct, even, right, true, in a line; undeviating, unswerving, straight as an arrow; inflexible.

perpendicular, plumb, vertical, upright, erect.

247. [Simple circularity] CIRCULARITY.—*N.* circularity, roundness; rotundity, etc., 249.

circle, circlet, ring, hoop; bracelet, armlet; loop, wheel, cycle, orb, orbit, disk, circuit, zone, belt, cordon, band; hub, nave; sash, girdle, cestus, cincture, baldric, wreath, garland; crown, coronet, chaplet, snood, fillet; necklace, collar; noose, lasso.

ellipse, oval; ellipsoid, cycloid.

V. round; ring, encircle, etc., 227.

Adj. round, rounded, circular, oval, elliptic, elliptical, egg-shaped.

248. [Complex circularity] CONVOLUTION.—*N.* convolution, involution, winding, wave, undulation, sinuosity, sinuousness, meandering, twist, twirl; contortion.

coil, roll, curl, spiral, corkscrew, worm, tendril, scallop, kink; serpent, snake, eel; maze, labyrinth.

V. wind, twine, twirl, wreathe, entwine; wave, undulate, meander; twist, coil, roll; wrinkle; curl, friz, indent, scallop; wring, contort.

Adj. winding, twisted, convoluted; circling, snaky, serpentine, sinuous, undulating, undulated, wavy.

involved, intricate, mazy, tortuous, labyrinthine; circuitous, kinky, curly.

spiral, coiled, screw-shaped.

Adv. in and out, round and round.

249. ROTUNDITY.—*N.* rotundity, roundness, sphericity, globularity.

cylinder, barrel, drum; roll, roller, rolling pin, column.

sphere, globe, ball, spheroid, globule; bulb, bullet, pellet, pill, marble, pea, knob.

V. sphere, form into a sphere, roll into a ball, give rotundity, round.

Adj. rotund; round, etc. (*circular*), 247; cylindrical, conical, spherical, globular, bulbous; egg-shaped, ovoid, ovate; bell-shaped, etc., 245.

250. CONVEXITY.—*N.* convexity, prominence, projection, swelling, swell, bulge, protuberance, protrusion, excrescency.

excrescence, hump; bow; clump, bunch; bulb, bump, knob; knot; boss; tooth, peg; ridge, rib, snag; peak, etc. (*sharpness*), 253; growth, tumor; pimple, wart, wen; fungus, blister; nipple, teat, dug, breast.

proboscis, nose, beak, snout, nozzle.

belly, paunch; abdomen.

arch, cupola, dome, vault.

relief, cameo; low relief, bas-relief, high relief.

point of land, hill, mount, mountain; cape, promontory; foreland, headland; hummock, ledge, spur.

V. **project,** bulge, protrude; bag, belly, pout, bunch; jut out, stand out, stick out, stick up; hang over, beetle.

raise, etc., 307; emboss.

Adj. **prominent,** protuberant, projecting; bossed, bossy, convex, bunchy, hummocky, bulbous; bloated, swollen, distended; bowed, arched; bold; bellied; gibbous; club-shaped, knobby, gnarled; salient, in relief, raised.

251. FLATNESS.—*N.* **flatness;** smoothness.

plane; level, plain, tableland, plateau; stratum; plate, table, tablet, slab.

V. **flatten;** level, etc., 213; fell.

Adj. **flat,** plane, even, smooth; flush; level, horizontal; recumbent, supine, prostrate.

Adv. **flat,** flatwise. lengthwise, horizontally.

252. CONCAVITY.—*N.* **concavity,** depression, dip; hollow, hollowness; indentation, intaglio, cavity, dent, dint, dimple; honeycomb.

excavation, pit, sap, mine, shaft; caisson; trough, etc. (*furrow*), 259; bay, etc. (*of the sea*), 343.

cup, basin, crater; punch bowl; cell, etc.(*receptacle*), 191; socket.

valley, vale, dale, dell, dingle, glen.

cave, cavern, cove; grot, grotto; hole, burrow, kennel, tunnel; gully, etc., 198.

excavator, sapper, miner.

V. **render concave;** depress, hollow, gouge; stave in; scoop, scoop out; dig, delve, excavate, dent, dint, perforate; mine, sap, undermine, burrow, tunnel.

Adj. **concave,** hollow; funnel-shaped; retreating; cavernous; porous, perforated; honeycombed.

253. SHARPNESS.—*N.* **sharpness,** acuteness; saliency.

point, spike, spine, spit, needle, pin; prick, barb; spur; horn, antler; snag; tag; thorn, bristle; tooth, tusk; tine.

beard, porcupine, hedgehog, brier, bramble, thistle, bur; currycomb, comb.

peak, crag, crest, cone, sugar loaf; spire, pyramid, steeple.

cutting edge, knife edge, blade, edge tool, cutlery, knife, penknife, razor; scalpel, lancet; plowshare, colter; hatchet, ax, pick, cleaver, scythe, sickle, scissors, shears; sword, etc. (*arms*), 727; bodkin, etc. (*perforator*), 262.

sharpener; hone, strop; grindstone, whetstone, steel, emery, carborundum.

V. **be sharp;** taper to a point; bristle with; cut, etc., 44.

sharpen, whet, point, barb, set, strop, grind.

Adj. **sharp,** keen; acute, pointed; tapering; spiked, spiky, studded, peaked, salient; prickly, spiny, thorny, bristling, barbed, spurred, bearded, thistly, briery; craggy, jagged, snaggy; cone-shaped, conical.

keen-edged, cutting; sharp-edged, knife-edged; sharpened.

254. BLUNTNESS.—*N.* **bluntness,** dullness.

V. **be** *or* **render blunt,** dull; take off the point *or* edge; blunt, turn.

Adj. **blunt,** dull, dullish, obtuse, pointless, unpointed; unsharpened.

255. SMOOTHNESS.—*N.* **smoothness;** polish, gloss; lubrication.

smoother; roller, steam roller; sandpaper, emery paper; flatiron, sadiron; burnisher.

V. **smooth;** plane; file; mow, shave; level, roll; macadamize; polish, burnish, sleek, iron, press, mangle; lubricate, oil, grease, wax, anoint.

Adj. **smooth;** polished; even; sleek, glossy, silken, silky; velvety; slippery, glassy, oily.

256. ROUGHNESS.—*N.* **roughness,** asperity; corrugation.

hair, mat, thatch, mop; scalp lock; tress, lock, curl, ringlet; shag; mane; eyelashes, lashes; beard, whiskers; mustache; imperial, goatee; fringe; hair shirt.

plumage; plume, crest; feather, tuft.

nap, pile, grain, texture.

V. **roughen,** rough, rough up, crinkle, ruffle, crumple, rumple; corrugate; stroke the wrong way, rub the fur the wrong way.

Adj. **rough,** uneven; rugged, jagged; cross-grained, gnarled, gnarly, knotted, scraggly, scraggy; craggy, cragged; unkempt, unpolished, roughhewn; prickly, etc. (*sharp*), 253.

hairy, bristly, hirsute, tufted, bushy; nappy, bearded, shaggy.

Adv. **against the grain;** in the rough; on edge.

257. NOTCH.—*N.* **notch,** dent, nick, cut, indent, indentation; embrasure, battlement.

saw, tooth, scallop; jag.

V. **notch,** nick, mill, score, cut, dent, indent, jag, scarify, scallop.

Adj. **notched,** dentate, toothed, serrate *or* serrated.

258. FOLD.—*N.* **fold,** crease, flexure, pleat, plait, tuck, gather; joint, elbow, double; wrinkle, pucker, crow's-feet; crinkle, crumple; dog's-ear; ruffle, flounce; corrugation.

V. **fold,** double, pleat, plait, crease, wrinkle, cocker, crinkle, curl, shrivel, rumple, corrugate, ruffle, crumple, pucker; dog's-ear, tuck, ruck, hem, gather.

259. FURROW.—*N.* **furrow,** groove, rut, scratch, streak, crack, score, incision, slit.

trench, ditch, dike, moat, trough, channel, gutter, ravine, etc., 198; depression.

V. **furrow,** flute, groove, carve, corrugate, cut, chisel, plow; incise, engrave, etch, grave.

Adj. **furrowed,** ribbed, striated, fluted, corduroy.

260. OPENING.—*N.* **opening,** aperture, yawning; chasm, etc., 198.

outlet, inlet; pore; vent, venthole, blowhole, airhole; orifice, mouth, sucker, muzzle, throat, gullet, nozzle.

window, casement, lattice; embrasure; light; skylight, fanlight; bay window, bow window, oriel, dormer.

portal, porch, gate, postern, wicket, trapdoor, hatch, door; cellarway, driveway, gateway, doorway, hatchway, gangway.

way, path, etc., 627; thoroughfare; channel, gully; passage, passageway.

alley, lane, mall, aisle, glade, vista.

tube, pipe, main; water pipe, etc., 350; air pipe, etc., 351; vessel, canal, gut, fistula; smokestack, chimney, flue; bore, caliber.

tunnel, mine, pit, shaft; gallery.

hole, puncture, perforation; pinhole, loophole, peephole, eye, eyelet; slot.

sieve, strainer, colander, riddle, screen.

opener, key, master key; open-sesame.

V. **open,** gape, yawn, fly open.

perforate, pierce, tap, bore, drill; transpierce, transfix; enfilade, impale, spike, spear, gore, spit, stab, pink, puncture, lance; stick, prick, riddle.

uncover, unclose; punch, stave in; mine, etc. (*scoop out*), 252.

Adj. **open;** perforated, wide-open, agape, ajar, unclosed; gaping, yawning; patent.

tubular; pervious, permeable; porous, honeycombed.

261. CLOSURE.—*N.* **closure,** blockade, shutting up, sealing, obstruction; contraction, constipation; impermeability; blind alley; cul-de-sac [F.].

V. **close,** plug, block up, stop up, fill up, cork up, button up, stuff up, dam up; blockade; obstruct, bar, bolt, stop, seal; choke, throttle; ram down, dam, cram; clinch; shut, slam, snap.

Adj. **closed,** shut, unopened; unpierced, impervious, impermeable; impenetrable; impassable, pathless, wayless; untrodden.

tight, unventilated, airtight, watertight, hermetically sealed; snug.

262. PERFORATOR.—*N.* **perforator,** piercer, borer, auger, chisel, gimlet, drill, awl, scoop, corkscrew, dibble, trepan, lancet, probe, bodkin, needle, stiletto; punch, gouge; spear, etc. (*weapon*), 727; puncher; punching machine, punching press.

263. STOPPER.—*N.* **stopper**, stopple; plug, cork, bung, spike, spill, stopcock, tap, faucet; valve, spigot; rammer; ram, ramrod; piston; stopgap; wadding, stuffing, padding, sponge [*surg.*], tourniquet.

doorkeeper, gatekeeper, janitor, concierge [F.], porter, warder, beadle, usher, guard, sentinel; watchdog.

IV. MOTION

264. MOTION.—*N.* **motion**, movement; move; mobility, movableness, motive power; mobilization.

stream, flow, flux, run, course, stir.

rate, pace, tread, footfall, step, stride, gait; velocity, clip [*colloq.*]; progress, locomotion.

journey, etc., 266; voyage, sail, cruise, passage; transit, etc., 270.

unrest, restlessness, etc., 149.

V. **move**, go, hie, budge, stir, pass, flit; hover around *or* about; shift, slide, glide, roll, flow, stream, run, drift, sweep along; wander, etc. (*deviate*), 279; walk, etc., 266.

put in motion, set in motion; impel, etc., 276; propel, etc., 284; mobilize.

Adj. **moving**, in motion, traveling; transitional, shifting, movable, mobile, motive, motor; mercurial; restless, etc. (*changeable*), 149; nomadic, etc., 266; erratic, etc., 279; evolutionary.

Adv. **under way**; on the move (*or* wing, fly, tramp, march).

265. REST.—*N.* **rest**; stillness, quiescence; stagnation, stagnancy, fixity, immobility, catalepsy; quietism.

quiet, tranquility, calm; repose, relaxation; dead calm; silence, peace, hush; sleep, etc. (*inactivity*), 683.

pause, lull, etc. (*cessation*), 142; stand, standstill; deadlock, dead stand; full stop; embargo.

resting place; bivouac; home, abode; bed, etc. (*support*), 215; haven, etc (*refuge*), 666; goal, destination, bourn.

V. **be still**, stand still, stand fast, stand firm, lie still, keep quiet, repose, rest; vegetate, stagnate.

remain, stay; stand, tarry, mark time; pull up, draw up; hold, halt, stop, discontinue, stop short, pause; bring to, heave to, lay to; anchor, cast anchor, come to anchor, ride at anchor, lie to; rest on one's laurels, take breath.

dwell, etc., 186; settle, settle down; alight, dismount, arrive.

quell, becalm, hush, calm, still, tranquilize, stay, lull to sleep, lay an embargo on.

Adj. quiescent, still; silent, hushed, quiet; motionless, moveless; fixed; stationary; at rest, at a stand, at a standstill, at anchor; stock-still; sedentary, untraveled, stay-at-home; becalmed, stagnant, quiet; unmoved, calm, restful; immovable, stable; sleeping, etc. (*inactive*), 683.

266. [Locomotion by land] **JOURNEY.**—*N.* travel, traveling, wayfaring; campaigning.

excursion, journey, expedition, tour, trip, circuit, pilgrimage, march, walk, promenade, constitutional [*colloq.*], stroll, saunter, ramble, hike [*colloq.*], tramp, turn, stalk, perambulation; outing, ride, drive, airing, jaunt.

riding, equitation, horsemanship.

roving, vagrancy, nomadism; vagabondism, hoboism; migration; emigration, immigration. *Wanderlust*, [Ger.].

itinerary, route, guide; handbook; roadbook; Baedeker.

procession, parade, cavalcade, caravan, file, cortege, column.

vehicle, etc., 272.

traveler, etc., 268.

station, stop, stopping place, terminal, terminus, depot, railway station.

V. travel, journey, flit, take wing; migrate, emigrate, immigrate; trek; tour, peregrinate.

motor, bicycle, cycle [*colloq.*], spin, speed; trolley [*colloq.*].

motorize, electrify.

wander, roam, range, prowl, rove, jaunt, ramble, stroll, saunter, perambulate, meander, straggle; gad, gad about.

take horse, ride, drive, trot, amble, canter, gallop, prance, frisk, caracole.

walk, march, step, tread, pace; plod, trudge, wend; promenade; track; hike [*colloq.*], tramp; stalk, stride; strut, bowl along, toddle; paddle; peg on, jog on, shuffle on.

glide, slide, coast, skim, skate.

file off, march in procession, defile.

go to, repair to, resort to, hie to, betake oneself to.

Adj. traveling, journeying; itinerant, peripatetic, roving, rambling, vagrant, migratory, nomadic.

self-moving, automobile, automotive, locomotive.

wayfaring, wayworn; travel-stained.

267. [Locomotion by water or air] **NAVIGATION.**—*N.* voyage, cruise, sail, passage, aquatics; boating, yachting, cruising; ship, etc., 273.

headway, sternway, leeway; fairway.

oar, scull, sweep, pole; paddle, screw, propeller, turbine; sail, canvas.

aeronautics, aerial navigation, balloonery; balloon, etc., 273; ballooning; aviation, airmanship; flying, flight, volplaning, planing [colloq.], hydroplaning, volplane, glide, dive, nose-dive, spin, looping the loop; wing; pinion, aileron.

mariner, etc., 269, aviator, etc., 269a.

V. sail; embark, etc., 293; spread sail, gather way, make sail, carry sail; ride the waves, ride out the storm.

navigate, scud, boom, drift, course, cruise, steam; coast, hug the shore.

row, paddle, pull, scull, punt.

float, swim, skim, dive, wade.

Aeronautics: fly, soar, drift, hover, aviate; volplane, plane [colloq.], glide, dive, fly over, nose-dive, spin, loop the loop, land; take wing, take a flight.

Adj. nautical, maritime, naval; seafaring, seagoing; coasting; afloat; navigable.

aeronautic, aeronautical, aerial.

aquatic, natatory, natatorial.

Adv. under way (or sail, canvas, steam), in motion, in progress, on the wing; afloat.

268. TRAVELER.—N. traveler, wayfarer, voyager, passenger; commuter, straphanger [colloq.].

tourist, excursionist, globe-trotter [colloq.]; explorer, adventurer, mountaineer; wanderer, rover, straggler, rambler; landsman, landlubber, vagrant, loafer, tramp, hobo, vagabond, Bohemian, gypsy, nomad, Arab; pilgrim, palmer; immigrant; emigrant.

fugitive, refugee; runaway; renegade.

courier, messenger, runner; Mercury.

pedestrian, walker, foot passenger, hiker [colloq.], tramper.

rider, horseman, equestrian, cavalier; jockey, trainer, breaker, roughrider; huntsman, whip; postilion, postboy.

driver, coachman, charioteer, carter, wagoner, drayman, truckman; cabman, cab driver.

Railroad: engineer; fireman, stoker; conductor, motorman.

Automobile: driver, chauffeur, automobilist, motorist.

269. MARINER.—N. mariner, navigator; sailor, seaman, seafarer, seafaring man, sea dog [colloq.]; tar, bluejacket, gob [slang]; marine; midshipman, middy [colloq.]; able seaman, hand; crew; captain, commander, master mariner, skipper; mate, boatswain; boatman, ferryman, waterman, lighterman, longshoreman; gondolier; oar, oarsman, rower.

steersman, coxswain, cox [colloq.], helmsman, pilot.

269a. AERONAUT.—*N.* aeronaut, aviator, airman, flier, aviatress *or* aviatrix, pilot, observer, spotter [*mil. cant*], scout, bomber, ace; balloonist.

270. TRANSFERENCE.—*N.* transfer, transference; removal; deportation, extradition; conveyance, carriage; contagion, infection; transfusion; transfer, etc. (*of property*), 783.

transit, transition; passage, ferry; portage, carry; carting, cartage; shipment, freight; transmission, transport, transportation; translation; transposition, transposal.

deposit, moraine, drift, alluvium.

gift, bequest, legacy, deed, lease; quitclaim.

freight, cargo, mail, baggage, luggage, goods.

V. transfer, transmit, transport, transplant, transfuse; convey, carry, bear; hand, pass, forward; shift; bring, fetch, reach; conduct, convoy.

send, delegate, consign, relegate, deliver; ship, freight, embark; transpose; drag, etc., 285; mail, post.

Adj. transferable, assignable, negotiable, transmissible, movable, portable; contagious, infectious.

271. CARRIER.—*N.* carrier, porter, redcap, bearer, freighter; expressman; stevedore; coolie; conductor, chauffeur, truck driver; letter carrier, postman; pigeon post, carrier pigeon.

beast of burden, beast, cattle, horse, steed; charger, war horse; hunter; race horse, racer, courser, Arab, barb; blood horse, thoroughbred; palfrey, cob; nag, jade, hack; pack (*or* draft, cart, dray) horse; mare, filly, colt, foal.

pony, Shetland; broncho, cow pony, mustang.

ass, donkey, jackass, burro; mule.

reindeer; camel, dromedary, llama, elephant.

vehicle, etc., 272; ship, etc., 273.

Adj. equine, asinine; electric, motor, express.

272. VEHICLE.—*N.* vehicle, conveyance, carriage, caravan, car, van.

wagon, dray, cart, lorry, truck.

tumbrel, barrow, wheelbarrow, handbarrow; dump cart; baby carriage, gocart, perambulator; wheel chair; police van, patrol wagon, Black Maria [*colloq.*]; Conestoga wagon, prairie schooner; jinrikisha, ricksha [*colloq.*].

equipage, coach, chariot, phaeton, wagonette, break, drag, landau, barouche, victoria, brougham; sulky, runabout.

post chaise, mail stage, diligence, stage, stagecoach; horsecar, omnibus, bus [*colloq.*]; cab, hansom, four-wheeler, hack; dogcart, trap [*colloq.*], buggy, chaise.

team, pair, span, tandem, four-in-hand.

litter, palanquin, sedan; stretcher, hurdle; ambulance.

sled, bob, bobsled; toboggan; sledge, sleigh; ski, snowshoes, skates, roller skates.

cycle, bicycle, tricycle, tandem; machine [*colloq.*], wheel [*colloq.*], motorcycle; velocipede, hobbyhorse.

automobile, motorcar, limousine, sedan, touring car, roadster, coupé, motor [*colloq.*], machine [*colloq.*], car, auto [*colloq.*], autocar, runabout; truck, tractor; taxicab, taxi [*colloq.*], motorbus; flivver [*slang*], jitney [*colloq.*].

Allied automobile terms: tonneau, chassis, hood, top, ignition, spark plug, generator, distributor, magneto, self-starter, gear, gear box, differential, cylinder, manifold, intake, exhaust, carburetor, ammeter, speedometer, oil gauge, primer, clutch, universal joint, crank shaft, transmission, tire, rim; gasoline; trailer; garage; chauffeur, etc., 268.

train; express, mail; car, coach; baggage car; rolling stock; trolley, electric car, electric [*colloq.*].

Adj. vehicular; traveling, etc., 266.

273. SHIP.—*N.* ship, vessel, boat, sail; craft, bottom.

navy, marine, fleet, flotilla.

shipping, man-of-war, etc., 726; merchant ship, merchantman; packet, liner; whaler; slaver; collier; coaster, freight steamer, freighter, lighter; trawler, fishing boat; pilot boat; yacht.

ship, sailing vessel, clipper ship, windjammer [*colloq.*], bark; brig, brigantine, schooner; fore-and-after [*colloq.*]; sloop, cutter, revenue cutter, yawl, ketch, smack, lugger, barge, scow, cat, catboat.
steamer, steamboat, steamship; tug.
boat, rowboat; shallop, skiff, pinnace; launch; lifeboat, longboat, jolly boat, gig, cockboat, tender, cockleshell, dory, canoe, dugout, dinghy, punt, outrigger; float, raft, iceboat.
coracle, gondola, galley, argosy, galleon; junk, sampan [both Chinese]; dhow [Arab.]; trireme; derelict.

Aeronautics: aircraft; balloon, airship, dirigible, zeppelin, airplane, monoplane, biplane, triplane; air cruiser, flying boat, hydroplane; kite, parachute.

Allied aeronautical terms: fuselage, gondola, wings, controls, aileron, lifting power, rudder; tail, hangar.

Adj. marine, maritime, naval, nautical, seafaring, ocean-going; seaworthy.

aeronautic, aerial; airworthy.

Adv. afloat, aboard; on board, on shipboard.

274. VELOCITY.—*N.* velocity, speed, celerity, swiftness, rapidity; expedition, etc. (*activity*), 682; acceleration; haste, etc., 684.

spurt, sprint, rush, dash, race, steeplechase; round pace; flight.

pace, gallop, canter, trot, round trot, run, hand gallop.

V. speed, hie, hasten, spurt, sprint, scamper, scuttle, trip, post; scud, scurry, whiz; run, dart, swoop, fly, race, shoot, tear, whisk, sweep, skim, scorch [*colloq.*], rush, dash; bolt, run away; ride hard; hurry, hasten, haste; accelerate, quicken; carry sail, crowd sail.

Adj. fast, speedy, swift, rapid, quick, fleet; nimble, agile, expeditious; express; active, brisk, light-footed, nimble-footed; winged.

Adv. apace; at full speed, full gallop; posthaste; in double-quick time; whip and spur; by leaps and bounds; in high (gear *or* speed) [*automobiling*].

275. SLOWNESS.—*N.* **slowness,** tardiness; languor, etc. (*inactivity*), 683; drawl.

jog trot, dogtrot; amble, rack, pace, single-foot, walk; mincing steps; dead march, slow march.

retardation; slackening; delay, etc. (*lateness*), 133.

slow goer, slowpoke [*colloq.*]; loiterer, sluggard, dawdler; tortoise, snail.

V. **move slowly;** creep, crawl, lag, walk, linger, loiter, saunter; plod, trudge, lumber; trail, drag; dawdle, etc., 683; worm one's way, inch, inch along, jog on, toddle, waddle, slouch, shuffle, halt, hobble, limp, shamble; flag, falter, totter, stagger; mince, take one's time.

retard, relax, slacken, check, moderate, rein in, curb; reef, shorten *or* take in sail; brake, slacken speed, backwater, back pedal.

Adj. **slow,** slack; tardy; dilatory, etc. (*inactive*), 683; leisurely; deliberate, gradual; languid, sluggish, apathetic, phlegmatic, lymphatic; moderate.

dull, slow [*colloq.*], prosaic, boring, wearisome, uninteresting, humdrum.

Adv. at half speed, in slow time; with clipped wings; in low (gear *or* speed) [*automobiling*].

gradually, by degrees, step by step, bit by bit.

276. [Motion conjoined with force] IMPULSE.—*N.* **impulse,** impetus; momentum; push, thrust, shove, boom, boost, explosion, etc. (*violence*), 173; propulsion, etc., 284.

clash, collision, encounter, shock, brunt, crash, bump; impact; charge, onset; percussion, concussion.

blow, stroke, knock, tap, rap, slap, smack, pat, dab; fillip; bang; hit, whack, thwack, cuff, buffet, punch, thump, kick, cut, thrust, lunge; carom, cannon; jab.

Science of mechanical forces: mechanics, dynamics.

V. **impel,** push; start, set going; drive, urge; boom, boost; thrust, prod; elbow, shoulder, jostle, hurtle, shove, butt, jog, jolt; throw, etc. (*propel*), 284.

strike, knock, thump, beat, bang, slam, dash, punch, thwack, whack; batter, tamp, buffet, cudgel, belabor, lunge, jab, kick; hit, tap, rap, slap, pat.

collide, foul; telescope; bump, butt.

Adj. **impulsive,** propulsive, dynamic.

277. RECOIL.—*N.* **recoil,** rebound, ricochet, backlash, boomerang: kick; elasticity, etc., 325; reflex, reflux; reverberation, resonance, repulse; reaction, revulsion.

reactionary, recalcitrant.

V. recoil, react; balk, jib; rebound, reverberate, echo; ricochet.

Adj. refluent, recalcitrant, reactionary.

278. DIRECTION.—*N.* direction, bearing, course, set, trend, run, drift, tenor; tendency, etc., 176; dip, tack, aim.

points of the compass, cardinal points.

line, path, road, range, line of march, alignment; airline, beeline.

V. tend toward, conduct to, go to; point to, bend, verge, incline, dip; steer for, make for, aim at, level at; take aim; hold a course; be bound for; make a beeline for.

Adj. bound for; direct, straight; undeviating, unswerving.

directable, steerable, dirigible, guidable.

Adv. toward, on the road to; hither, thither, whither; directly; straight, point-blank; in a bee (*or* direct, straight) line to, as the crow flies; windward, in the wind's eye.

through, via, by way of.

279. DEVIATION.—*N.* deviation; warp, refraction; sweep; deflection, zigzag.

diversion, digression, aberration, drift, sheer, divergence, ramification, forking; detour.

Oblique motion: tack, yaw [*both naut.*]; echelon [*mil.*]; knight's move [*chess*].

V. deviate, alter one's course, turn, bend, curve, swerve, heel, bear off; jibe, yaw, wear, sheer, tack [*all naut.*]; sidle, edge, veer, diverge; wind, twist; turn aside, wheel, steer clear of; dodge, step aside, shy, jib; glance off.

deflect; divert, shift, switch, shunt; sidetrack.

stray, straggle; digress, wander, meander; go astray, ramble, rove, drift.

Adj. deviating, errant; excursive, discursive; devious, desultory, rambling; stray, vagrant, circuitous, roundabout, sidelong, indirect, crooked, zigzag; oblique.

280. PRECEDING.—*N.* preceding, leading, heading, precedence, priority, the lead, van, front; precursor, etc., 64.

V. precede, go before, forerun; introduce, herald; head, take the lead; lead, steal a march, get ahead, outstrip; take precedence.

Adv. in advance, before, ahead, in the van, in front.

281. FOLLOWING.—*N.* following, attendance; pursuant; sequence, sequel.

follower, attendant, satellite, pursuer, shadow, dangler, train.

V follow; pursue, etc., 622; go after; attend, dance attendance on, dog, shadow; hang on the skirts of; camp on the trail.

lag, loiter, linger, fall behind.

Adv. behind; in the rear; after, etc. (*order*), 63 (*time*), 117.

282. [Motion forward] PROGRESSION.—*N.* progression, progress, progressiveness; advance, advancement, headway; march, etc., 266; rise, improvement, etc., 658.

V. advance; proceed, go, go on, progress, get on, gain ground, forge ahead, press onward, step forward, make progress (*or* head, headway); go ahead, shoot ahead; distance.

Adj. progressive, advanced, up-to-date; enterprising, go-ahead [*colloq.*].

Adv. forward, onward; forth, on, ahead, under way.

283. [Motion backward] REGRESSION.—*N.* regression, retrogression, retreat, retirement, recession, withdrawal.

reflux, refluence, backwater, ebb, return; reflexion, recoil.

countermotion, countermovement, countermarch; tergiversation, backsliding, fall; deterioration, relapse, reversion.

V. recede, return, revert, retreat, retire; retrograde, back, back out [*colloq.*], back down [*colloq.*], balk; withdraw; recoil, rebound; turn back, fall back, put back; lose ground; drop astern; backwater, put about [*naut.*], veer, shy, double, wheel, countermarch, ebb, regurgitate.

Adj. retrograde, retrogressive; regressive, refluent, reflex, contraclockwise, counterclockwise; balky, perverse, reactionary.

284. PROPULSION.—*N.* propulsion, projection; push, etc. (*impulse*), 276; ejection; throw, fling, toss, shot, discharge, shy.

Science of propulsion: gunnery, ballistics.

missile, projectile; gun, etc. (*arms*), 727.

marksman, rifleman, good shot, dead shot, crack shot; sharpshooter, etc. (*combatant*), 726; gunner; archer, bowman.

V. propel, project, throw, fling, cast, pitch, toss, jerk, heave, shy, hurl.

dart, lance, tilt; drive, sling, pelt, pitchfork.

send; let off, fire off, discharge, shoot; launch, send forth, let fly; dash.

start, put *or* set in motion, set going, trundle, bundle off; impel, etc., 276; expel, eject.

Adj. propulsive, projectile, ballistic.

285. TRACTION.—*N.* traction, draft, pull, haul.

V. draw, pull, haul, lug, rake, trawl, draggle, drag, tug, tow, trail, train; take in tow.

Adj. tractile, tractional, ductile.

286. [Motion toward] APPROACH.—*N.* approach, approximation; access; advent.

pursuit, chase, hunt.

V. **approach,** converge, near, get (*or* draw) near; move toward, drift; gain upon; pursue, etc., 622; make land.

Adj. approximate, convergent; impending, imminent.

287. [Motion from] RECESSION.—*N.* **recession,** retirement, withdrawal; retreat; regression, etc., 283; departure, etc., 293; flight.

V. **recede,** go, go back, move back, retire, withdraw, ebb; shrink; drift away; depart, etc., 293; retreat, retire, fall back; run away, fly, flee.

288. ATTRACTION.—*N.* **attraction,** attractiveness; pull, magnetism, gravity.

loadstone, lodestar, polestar, magnet.

lure, bait, charm, decoy.

V. **attract,** pull, drag, draw, magnetize, bait, trap, decoy, charm, lure, allure.

Adj. **attractive,** attracting, seductive.

289. REPULSION.—*N.* **repulsion;** antipathy; repulse, abduction.

V. **repel,** push *or* drive from, etc., 276; chase, dispel; abduct; send away; repulse; keep at arm's length, turn one's back upon.

Adj. **repellent,** repulsive.

290. [Motion nearer to] CONVERGENCE.—*N.* **convergence,** confluence, concourse, concurrence, concentration; meeting.

assemblage, etc., 72; resort, etc., 74.

V. **converge,** concur; come together, unite, meet, close in upon; center, concentrate.

Adj. **convergent,** confluent, concurrent; centripetal.

291. [Motion farther off] DIVERGENCE.—*N.* **divergence,** ramification, forking; separation, detachment, dispersion, deviation, etc., 279.

V. **diverge,** ramify, branch off, fly off; spread, scatter, disperse, etc., 73; part, sever, separate, sunder.

Adj. **divergent,** radial, centrifugal.

Adv. **broadcast.**

292. ARRIVAL.—*N.* **arrival,** advent; landing; debarkation, disembarkation.

destination, bourn, goal; harbor, haven, port; terminus, terminal; home, journey's end; anchorage, refuge.

meeting, joining, encounter, rejoining; return, re-entry.

V. **arrive,** get to, come to; come; reach, attain; overtake; make, fetch; join, rejoin; return; enter, appear, drop in, visit.

alight, light, dismount, detrain.

land, cast anchor, put in, debark, disembark.

meet, encounter, come across; come (*or* light) upon.

Adv. **here, hither.**

293. DEPARTURE.—*N.* **departure,** embarkation; outset, start; removal; exit, etc. (*egress*), 295; exodus, hegira, flight.

leave-taking, adieu, farewell, good-by, Godspeed; valediction, valedictory, valedictorian.

V. **depart;** go, go away, go off, set out, start, issue, march out, debouch, sally forth; sally, go forth; retire, withdraw, remove; cut [*colloq. or slang*], take flight, take wing; fly, flit; strike tents, decamp, break camp, take leave; disappear, etc., 449; entrain; saddle, bridle, harness up, hitch up [*colloq.*].

quit, vacate, evacuate, abandon.

embark, go abroad; set sail, put to sea, sail, take ship; get under way, weigh anchor.

Adv. **hence,** whence, thence.

294. [Motion into] **INGRESS.**—*N.* **ingress;** entrance, entry; influx, inroad, incursion, invasion, irruption; penetration, infiltration; insinuation, insertion, etc., 300.

immigration, incoming, foreign influx.

import [*used esp. in pl.*], importation.

immigrant, incomer, newcomer, colonist.

inlet; mouth, door, etc. (*opening*), 260; path, etc., 627; conduit, etc., 350.

V. **enter;** come in, pour in, flow in; set foot on; burst *or* break in upon, invade; penetrate, infiltrate.

Adj. **incoming,** inbound, inward.

295. [Motion out of] **EGRESS.**—*N.* **egress,** exit, issue; emergence; outbreak; outburst, eruption; emanation; evacuation; leakage, percolation, oozing, drain, drainage; gush, outpour, effluence, outflow, discharge.

export [*used esp. in pl.*], exportation; shipment.

emigration, exodus, departure.

emigrant, migrant, colonist.

outlet, vent, spout, faucet, tap, sluice, floodgate; mouth, opening, door; pathway; conduit.

V. **emerge,** emanate, issue; go (*or* come, pass, pour, flow) out of.

exude, discharge, leak; run through, percolate; strain, distill; perspire, sweat; drain, seep, ooze, filter, infiltrate, gush, spout, flow out; pour, trickle; find vent; escape, etc., 671.

Adj. **eruptive,** porous, pervious, leaky; outgoing, outbound, outward bound.

296. [Motion into, actively] **RECEPTION.**—*N.* **reception;** admission, admittance, entree; importation; initiation, introduction, absorption; suction, sucking; eating, drinking, etc. (*food*), 298; insertion, etc., 300.

V. **give entrance to,** introduce, usher, admit, initiate; receive, import, bring in; absorb, imbibe, instill, implant, induct, inhale; let in, take in.

swallow, gulp; eat, drink, etc., 298.

Adj. **introductory,** initiatory, preliminary.

297. [Motion out of, actively] EJECTION.—*N.* **ejection,** rejection, expulsion, eviction, dislodgment, banishment, exile, deportation, expedition; discharge, evacuation, eruption, eruptiveness; tapping, drainage; emetic; vomiting.

V. **eject,** reject; expel, discard; ostracize, boycott; banish, exile, fire [*slang*], throw away *or* aside, push out *or* off, send off *or* away; discharge, dismiss, turn *or* cast adrift; turn out, throw overboard.

evict, oust, dislodge; turn out of doors, deport, expatriate.

emit, send out, pour out, dispatch, shed, void, evacuate; give vent to; tap, draw off; pour forth; squirt, spurt, spill; breathe, blow, exhale.

empty; drain, sweep off; clear off, draw off; clean out, purge; tap, broach.

root out, root up, unearth, eradicate; weed out, get out; eliminate, get rid of, do away with, shake off.

vomit, spew; cast up, bring up; disgorge.

unpack, unlade, unload, unship; dump.

298. [Eating] FOOD.—*N.* **eating,** mastication, rumination; gastronomy, carnivorousness, vegetarianism, gluttony, etc., 957.

mouth, jaws, mandible [*esp. of birds*], chops.

drinking, potation, draft, libation; carousal, etc. (*amusement*), 840; drunkenness, etc., 959.

food, meat, nourishment, nutriment, sustenance, nurture, subsistence, provender, corn, feed, fodder, provision, ration, board; commissariat, etc. (*provisions*), 637; prey, forage, pasture, pasturage; fare, cheer; diet, dietary; regimen; staff of life, bread.

eatables, victuals, edibles, grub [*slang*], meat; bread, viands, delicacy, dainty, creature comforts, ambrosia; good cheer, good living.

table, cuisine [F.], bill of fare, menu, table d'hôte [F.], à la carte [F.].

meal, repast, feed [*colloq.*], spread [*colloq.*]; mess; refreshment, entertainment; refection, collation, picnic, feast, banquet, potluck.

mouthful, tidbit, morsel.

drink, beverage, liquor, potion, dram, draft.

restaurant, café, eating house.

V. **eat,** feed, fare, devour, swallow, take; gulp, bolt; fall to; dispatch; tuck in [*slang*], dine, banquet, gormandize, etc., 957; crunch, chew, masticate, nibble, gnaw, mumble.

live on; feed upon; browse, graze, crop; bite, champ, munch, ruminate.

drink, quaff, sip, sup; lap; tipple, guzzle, carouse.

cater, purvey, etc., 637.

Adj. eatable, edible, esculent; dietetic; culinary; nutritive, nutritious; succulent.

underdone, rare; well done; overdone; high [*of game*]; ripe [*of cheese*].

drinkable, potable; bibulous.

omnivorous, carnivorous, flesh-eating, herbivorous, graminivorous, piscivorous.

299. EXCRETION.—*N.* excretion, discharge, emanation, exhalation, secretion, effusion, perspiration, sweat.

hemorrhage, bleeding; outpouring, etc. (*egress*), 295; diarrhea.

saliva, spittle, sputum (*pl.* sputa), spit; catarrh; lava.

V. excrete, etc. (*eject*), 297; secrete; exhale, emanate, etc. (*come out*), 295.

300. [Forcible ingress] INSERTION.—*N.* insertion, implantation, introduction; interpolation, interlineation, insinuation, etc. (*intervention*), 228; injection, inoculation, infusion; ingress, etc., 294; immersion; submersion; dip, plunge.

V. insert, introduce, put in (*or* into), run into; inject; imbed, inlay, inweave; interject, etc., 228; infuse, instill, inoculate, impregnate, imbue.

graft, ingraft, bud, plant, implant.

obtrude; thrust in, stick in, ram in, stuff in, tuck in, press in, drive in; pierce, etc. (*make a hole*), 260.

immerse, merge; bathe, soak, etc. (*water*), 337; dip, plunge, etc., 310.

301. [Forcible egress] EXTRACTION.—*N.* extraction; removal, elimination, extrication, eradication, extirpation, extermination; ejection, etc., 297; export, etc. (*egress*), 295; wrench.

V. extract, draw; take out, draw out, pull out, tear out, pluck out, pick out, get out; wring from, wrench; extort; root up, weed out; eradicate, uproot, pull up, extirpate.

elicit, evolve, bring forth, draw forth; extricate.

eliminate, etc. (*eject*), 297; remove.

express, squeeze out, press out, distill.

302. [Motion through] PASSAGE.—*N.* passage, transmission; permeation, penetration; infiltration; ingress; egress, exit, issue; path, road, way; conduit, opening; journey, voyage, sail, cruise.

V. pass, pass through; perforate, penetrate, permeate, thread, cut across; ford, cross; make (*or* work, thread, worm, force) one's way; find a way (*or* vent); transmit, make way, traverse.

303. [Motion beyond] OVERRUNNING.—*N.* overrunning, overrun, inroad, advance, infraction, transgression, encroachment, infringement; transcendence; redundance, etc., 641.

V. **overrun,** pass, go beyond, go by, shoot ahead of; steal a march upon, gain upon.

outstrip, override, overshoot the mark; outrun, outride, outrival, outdo; beat; distance; throw into the shade; exceed, transcend, surmount; tower above, surpass.

encroach, overstep, transgress, trespass, infringe, intrude, invade.

Adv. **ahead,** beyond the mark.

304. [Motion short of] SHORTCOMING.—*N.* shortcoming, failure, falling short; default, defalcation; delinquency; fizzle [*colloq.*], slump [*colloq.*]; flash in the pan.

incompleteness, deficiency; defect, imperfection, fault; insufficiency, etc., 640; noncompletion, nonfulfillment; failure, etc., 732.

V. **fall short,** come short of, not reach; want; keep within bounds (*or* the mark, compass).

collapse, fail, break down, flat out [*colloq.*], come to nothing; fall down, slump, fizzle out [*all colloq.*]; fall through, fall to the ground; cave in [*colloq.*], end in smoke, miss the mark.

Adj. **deficient;** at fault; short, short of; out of depth; perfunctory, remiss.

305. [Motion upward] ASCENT.—*N.* ascent, ascension; rising, rise, upgrowth, upward flight; upgrade; leap, etc., 309; grade, ramp, acclivity, hill, etc., 217.

stairway, staircase, stairs; flight of steps *or* stairs; ladder, scaling ladder; companionway [*naut.*]; escalator, elevator.

V. **ascend,** rise, mount, arise, uprise; go up, get up, work one's way up, start up, spring up, shoot up; aspire, aim high.

climb, shin [*colloq.*], swarm [*colloq.*], clamber, scramble, escalade, surmount, wind upward, scale.

tower, soar, spire, go aloft, fly aloft; surge; leap, etc., 309.

Adj. **rising;** ascendant; upcast; buoyant.

Adv. **up,** upward, skyward, heavenward; upturned; uphill.

306. [Motion downward] DESCENT.—*N.* descent, inclination, declension, declination; drop; cadence; subsidence, lapse; downcome, comedown, setback, fall; slump [*colloq.*], downfall, tumble, stumble, slip, tilt, trip, lurch.

avalanche, landslide, slide, snowslide, glissade.

declivity, dip, decline, pitch, drop, downgrade.

V. **descend,** go (*or* drop, come) down, fall, gravitate, drop, slip, skid, slide, settle; decline, sink, subside, droop, slump [*colloq.*].

get down, dismount, alight, light; swoop; stoop, etc., 308; fall prostrate, precipitate oneself; let fall.

tumble, trip, stumble, lurch, pitch, topple; tilt, sprawl.

Adj. **steep,** sloping, declivitous; beetling, overhanging; bottomless, fathomless, abysmal.

descending; down, downcast, descendent; deciduous.

Adv. downward, downhill.

307. ELEVATION.—*N.* **elevation;** raising; erection, lift; upheaval; sublimation, exaltation; prominence, relief.

lever, crowbar, crane, derrick, windlass, capstan, winch; dredge, dredger.

elevator, dumbwaiter; escalator.

V. **elevate,** raise, heighten, lift, erect; set up, tilt up; rear, hoist, heave; uplift, upraise, uprear; buoy, mount, exalt; sublimate.

take up, drag up, fish up; dredge.

Adj. **elevated,** upturned, stilted, rampant.

308. DEPRESSION.—*N.* **depression,** lowering; dip, etc. (*concavity*), 252.

overthrow, overturn; upset; prostration, reduction, abasement, subversion.

bow, curtsy, dip [*colloq.*], bob, duck, genuflexion, kowtow, obeisance, salaam.

V. **depress,** lower, cast down, let drop, let fall; sink, debase, bring low, abase, reduce, precipitate.

overthrow, overturn, overset, upset, prostrate, level, fell; down [*colloq.*], cast (*or* throw, fling, dash, pull, knock, hew) down, raze.

sit, sit down, squat; recline, sprawl.

crouch, stoop, bend, cower.

bow, curtsy, genuflect, kowtow, duck, bob, dip, kneel; incline, make obeisance, salaam, prostrate oneself, bow down.

Adj. **depressed;** at a low ebb; prostrate, horizontal.

309. LEAP.—*N.* **leap,** jump, hop, spring, bound, vault.

caper, dance, gambol, frisk, prance, curvet, caracole, buck; hop, skip, and jump.

V. **leap,** jump, hop, spring, bound, vault, clear, ramp, skip.

prance, dance, caper; buck; curvet, caracole, bob, bounce, flounce; frisk, jump about, romp, frolic, gambol; cavort, cut capers [*colloq.*].

Adj. **leaping,** saltatorial; frisky, lively, frolicsome.

Adv. on the light fantastic toe.

310. PLUNGE.—*N.* **plunge,** dip, dive, nose-dive [*aviation*], header [*colloq.*]; submergence, submersion, immersion.

diver; diving bird.

V. **plunge,** dip, souse, duck; dive, plump; take a header [*colloq.*]; make a plunge; bathe; pitch.

submerge, submerse; immerse; douse, sink, engulf, send to the bottom.

founder,welter,wallow; get out of one's depth; go to the bottom.

Adj. submergible, submersible.

311. CIRCULAR MOTION.—*N.* circulation, turn, excursion, circumnavigation, circumflexion; wheel, compass, lap, circuit; turning, evolution; coil, spiral.

V. **turn,** bend, wheel; go about, put about [*both naut.*]; go (*or* turn) round, round, turn a corner; double a point [*naut.*]; make a detour.

circle, encircle, circumscribe, circuit, describe a circle, circumnavigate; go the round.

wind, circulate, meander; whisk, twirl, twist, coil.

wallow, welter, roll.

Adj. circuitous, roundabout, devious.

312. ROTATION—*N.* rotation, revolution, gyration, circulation, roll; pirouette, convolution.

eddy, vortex, whirlpool, maelstrom; swirl, surge; whir, whirl; cyclone, tornado; vertiginousness, vertigo.

V. **rotate,** roll, revolve, spin, turn, turn round, encircle, circulate, swirl, gyrate,wheel,whirl, twirl, roll up, furl; box the compass.

Adj. rotating, rotary; vertiginous.

313. UNFOLDMENT.—*N.* unfoldment, unfolding, development; evolvement. evolution; inversion.

V. **evolve;** unfold, unroll, unwind, uncoil, untwist, unfurl, untwine, unravel; disentangle; develop.

Adj. evolutional, evolutionary.

314. [Motion to and fro] OSCILLATION.—*N.* oscillation, vibration, undulation, pulsation; pulse, beat, throb.

alternation; coming and going; ebb and flow, flux and reflux, systole and diastole; ups and downs.

fluctuation; vacillation, irresolution, indecision.

swing, wave, beat, shake, wag, seesaw, teeter.

V. **oscillate,** vibrate, undulate, wave; rock, teeter, sway, swing, dangle; pulsate, beat; wag, waggle; nod, bob, curtsy; wobble.

fluctuate, reel, quake; quiver, quaver, shake, flicker; wriggle; roll, toss, pitch; flounder, stagger, totter.

alternate, pass and repass, shuttle, ebb and flow, come and go; vacillate.

Adj. **oscillating;** undulatory, vibratory; pendulous.

Adv. **to and fro,** up and down, back and forth, in and out, seesaw, zigzag, from side to side, shuttlewise.

315. [Irregular motion] AGITATION.—*N.* agitation, stir, tremor, shuffling, shake, ripple, jog, jolt, jar, jerk, shock, trepidation, quiver, quaver, dance; tarantella; twitter, flicker, flutter.

disquiet, perturbation, commotion, turmoil, turbulence; tumult, hubbub, rout, bustle, fuss, racket.

twitching, chorea, St. Vitus' dance; staggers, blind staggers; epilepsy, fits.

spasm, throe, throb, palpitation, convulsion, paroxysm, seizure, grip, cramp.

disturbance, disorder; restlessness, changeableness, instability.

ferment, fermentation, ebullition, effervescence, hurly-burly; tempest, storm, whirlpool, vortex, etc., 312; whirlwind, tornado, cyclone, typhoon.

V. **be agitated;** shake, tremble, flutter, flicker; quiver, quaver, quake; shiver, writhe, toss; shuffle, tumble, stagger, bob, reel, sway; wag, waggle, wriggle; stumble, shamble, flounder, totter, flounce, flop, dance, curvet, prance, cavort; squirm; twitch; bustle.

throb, pulsate, beat, palpitate, go pitapat.

ferment, effervesce, foam, boil, boil over, bubble, bubble up; simmer.

agitate, shake, convulse, toss, tumble, wield, brandish, flap, flourish, whisk, jerk, jolt, jog, joggle, disturb, stir, shake up, churn.

Adj. **agitated,** shaking, tremulous; convulsive, jerky; effervescent, unquiet, restless.

Adv. by fits and starts; in convulsions, in fits, in a flutter.

CLASS III

Words Relating to MATTER

I. MATTER IN GENERAL

316. MATERIALITY.—*N.* **materiality,** corporality; substantiality, material existence; incarnation, flesh and blood.

matter, body, substance, brute matter, protoplasm, stuff, element, principle, material, substratum.

object, article, thing, something; still life; materials, etc., 635.

Science of matter: physics; natural philosophy; physical science.

materialist, physicist.

V. **materialize,** substantiate, incorporate, embody, incarnate.

Adj. **material,** bodily, corporeal, corporal, physical, incarnate, materialized, embodied; sensible, tangible, ponderable, palpable, substantial; unspiritual, materialistic.

objective, impersonal, nonsubjective.

317. IMMATERIALITY.—*N.* immateriality, insubstantiality, incorporality, unsubstantiality, spirituality; astral plane.

personality; I, myself, me.

ego, spirit, etc. (*soul*), 450; astral body, etheric double, subliminal self, subconscious self, higher self.

spiritualism, spiritism; animism.

spiritualist, spiritist; animist.

V. dematerialize, disembody, spiritualize.

Adj. immaterial, incorporeal, incorporate, unsubstantial; spiritistic, animistic; discarnate, bodiless, disembodied; extramundane, unearthly; spiritual, etc. (*psychical*), 450.

subjective, personal, nonobjective.

318. WORLD.—*N.* world, creation, nature, universe; earth, globe, sphere, wide world; cosmos, macrocosm.

heavens, sky, empyrean, starry cope (*or* host); firmament.

heavenly bodies, luminaries, stars, asteroids; galaxy, Milky Way; constellations, planets, satellites; comet, meteor, falling (*or* shooting) star; solar system.

sun, orb of day, daystar [*poetic*], Helios, Apollo, Phoebus, etc. (*sun god*), 423.

moon, Diana, Luna, Phoebe, Cynthia, Selene, silver-footed queen.

Adj. cosmic, mundane, terrestrial, earthly, sublunary.

celestial, empyreal, heavenly, solar; lunar; starry, stellar, sidereal, astral; nebular.

Adv. in all creation, on the face of the globe, here below, under the sun.

319. GRAVITY.—*N.* gravity, gravitation; weight, heft, heaviness, ponderousness, specific gravity, pressure, load, burden, ballast, counterpoise; mass.

Weighing instrument: balance, scales, steelyard, beam, weighbridge.

Science of gravity: statics.

V. weigh, load, press; counterweigh, poise; gravitate.

Adj. weighty, heavy, ponderous, ponderable; cumbersome, burdensome, cumbrous, unwieldy, massive; static.

320. LEVITY.—*N.* levity, lightness, imponderability, buoyancy, volatility.

ferment, leaven, yeast, pepsin.

V. be light, float, swim.

render light, lighten.

ferment, work, raise, leaven.

Adj. light, subtle, imponderous, imponderable, ethereal, airy, feathery, gossamery; volatile, vaporous, buoyant, floating, foamy, frothy; portable.

fermenting, fermentative, yeasty.

II. INORGANIC MATTER

(1) Solids

321. DENSITY.—*N.* **density**, solidity, solidness; impenetrability, impermeability; costiveness, constipation.

condensation; solidification, consolidation, concretion, coagulation; cohesion, etc., 46; petrifaction, etc. (*hardening*), 323; thickening, crystallization, precipitation.

solid body, mass, block, lump; concretion, concrete, conglomerate; stone, rock, cake; card.

sediment, lees, dregs, settlings.

V. **be dense**, compress, squeeze, ram down; solidify; cement, set, consolidate, condense, congeal, coagulate, curd, curdle; fix, clot, thicken, cake, candy, precipitate, deposit, cohere, crystallize; petrify, harden, stiffen.

compress, squeeze, ram down.

Adj. **dense**, solid, solidified; coherent, cohesive, compact; close, serried, thickset; substantial, massive, impenetrable, concrete, hard; crystalline, thick, stodgy.

undissolved, unmelted, unliquefied, unthawed.

indivisible; indissoluble, insoluble.

322. RARITY.—*N.* **rarity**, tenuity; subtlety.

rarefaction, attenuation, expansion, inflation; ether, etc. (*gas*), 334.

V. **rarefy**, expand, dilate, attenuate, thin.

Adj. **rare**, subtle, thin, fine, tenuous, compressible, flimsy, slight, light, porous; rarefied, unsubstantial.

323. HARDNESS.—*N.* **hardness**, firmness, rigidity, inflexibility, temper, callosity; induration, petrifaction, ossification; crystallization.

V. **harden**, render hard, temper, stiffen, cement, indurate, petrify, ossify.

Adj. **hard**, rigid, stubborn, stiff, firm; stark, unbending, unyielding, inflexible, tense.

adamantine, stony, granitic, rocky, horny, callous, bony, cartilaginous.

324. SOFTNESS.—*N.* **softness**, pliableness, flexibility, pliancy, pliability, malleability, ductility, tractility, plasticity, flaccidity, laxity, flabbiness, mollification, softening.

V. **soften,** render soft, mollify, mellow; mash; knead, massage.

bend, give, yield, relent, relax.

Adj. **soft,** tender; mollified; supple, pliant, pliable, flexible, lithe, lithesome, limber; plastic; ductile, malleable, tractable; yielding; flabby, flaccid, lax, limp, flimsy; mellow; spongy.

downy, woolly, fluffy, feathery.

325. ELASTICITY.—*N.* **elasticity,** springiness, spring, resilience *or* resiliency, buoyancy; recoil, rebound, reflex.

V. **be elastic;** spring back, recoil.

Adj. **elastic,** springy, resilient, buoyant.

326. INELASTICITY.—*N.* **inelasticity,** flaccidity, laxity; want of elasticity, etc., 325.

Adj. **inelastic,** flaccid, yielding; not elastic.

327. TENACITY.—*N.* **tenacity,** toughness, strength; cohesiveness, cohesion, adhesion; stubbornness, etc. (*obstinacy*), 606; gumminess, glutinousness, viscidity.

Adj. **tenacious,** cohesive, tough, strong, resisting; adhesive, stringy, viscid, gummy, glutinous, gristly, cartilaginous; stubborn, etc. (*obstinate*), 606.

328. BRITTLENESS.—*N.* **brittleness,** fragility; frailty; shortness.

V. **break,** crack, snap, split, shiver, splinter, crumble, crash, crush, burst, give way; fall to pieces; crumble to dust.

Adj. **brittle,** breakable, delicate, fragile, frail; splintery; crisp, short [*as of pastry*].

329. STRUCTURE.—*N.* **structure,** organization, constitution, organism, anatomy, frame, mold, fabric, construction; framework, architecture; stratification.

texture, contexture; tissue, grain, web, surface, nap; roughness; warp and woof (*or* weft); fineness (*or* coarseness) of grain.

Adj. **structural,** organic; anatomic *or* anatomical.

textile; fine-grained, coarse-grained, ingrained; ingrain; fine, delicate, subtile, subtle, gossamer, gossamery, filmy; coarse; homespun, linsey-woolsey.

330. POWDERINESS.—*N.* **powderiness,** grittiness, sandiness, friability.

powder, dust, sand, shingle; sawdust; grit; meal, bran, flour, rice, spore; crumb, seed, grain; particle.

Reduction to powder: pulverization, comminution, granulation, disintegration, abrasion, detrition; mill, grater, rasp, file, pestle and mortar, grindstone, quern, millstone.

V. **pulverize,** powder, comminute, granulate, reduce to powder; scrape, file, abrade, grind, grate, rasp, pound, bruise, beat, crush, craunch, crunch, crumble, disintegrate.

Adj. powdery, granular, mealy, floury, farinaceous, branny, dusty, sandy, gritty.

pulverable *or* pulverizable, friable, crumbly, shivery.

331. FRICTION.—*N.* friction, rubbing, abrasion, rub; massage; erasure; elbow grease [*colloq.*].

eraser, rubber, India rubber.

V. **rub,** abrade, scratch, scrape, scrub, fray, rasp, graze, curry, scour, polish, rub out, erase, file, grind, etc. (*pulverize*), 330; massage.

332. [Absence or prevention of friction] LUBRICATION.—*N.* lubrication, anointment, oiling.

smoothness, polish, gloss; unctuousness.

lubricant, lubricator; ointment, salve, balm, unguent.

V. **lubricate,** oil, grease; lather, soap; wax; anoint.

(2) Fluids

333. FLUIDITY.—*N.* fluidity, liquidity, liquidness; liquefaction; solubility; gaseity, etc., 334.

solution; fluid; liquid; juice, sap, lymph, serum.

Science of liquids at rest: hydrostatics, hydrodynamics, hydrokinetics.

V. **be fluid;** run; flow, etc. (*water in motion*), 348; liquefy, etc., 335.

Adj. **liquid,** fluid; juicy, succulent, sappy; rheumy; fluent, flowing; liquefied, uncongealed; soluble.

334. GASEITY.—*N.* gaseity, gaseousness, vaporousness; volatility; aeration; gasification; flatulence.

elastic fluid, gas, air, vapor, ether, steam, fume, effluvium; cloud, etc., 353.

Science of elastic fluids: pneumatics, aerostatics, aerodynamics, aerography, aeromechanics.

V. **gasify,** render gaseous; aerate; vaporize, etc., 336.

Adj. **gaseous,** ethereal, aery, aerial, airy, vaporous, volatile, flatulent.

335. LIQUEFACTION.—*N.* liquefaction, liquescence; deliquescence; melting, fusion; thaw; solubleness; solution.

mixture, decoction, infusion, solution.

V. **dissolve,** liquefy; run; melt, thaw, fuse; hold in solution; percolate

Adj. **liquefied;** soluble, dissolvable; solvent, dissolvent.

336. VAPORIZATION.—*N.* vaporization, atomization; fumigation, steaming; distillation; gasification; evaporation.

vaporizer, atomizer, spray, evaporator, still, retort.

V. **vaporize,** gasify, atomize; spray; distill, sublimate, evaporate; exhale, emit vapor; fumigate; fume, smoke, reek, steam.

Adj. **volatile,** vapory, vaporous, gaseous; volatilized.

337. WATER.—*N.* **water,** lymph; aqua [L.], *eau* [F.]; fluid, etc., 333.

washing, bathing, bath, immersion; dilution; infiltration, irrigation, seepage.

deluge, etc. (*water in motion*), 348; high water, flood tide, spring-tide.

sprinkler, shower *or* shower bath; nozzle; atomizer, etc., 336.

water, dilute, add water; moisten, etc., 339; steep, soak, drench, wet, dip, immerse, submerge; duck; drown; wash, lave, bathe, sprinkle, dabble; inundate, deluge; irrigate; infiltrate, percolate, seep.

inject; gargle, syringe.

Adj. **watery,** aquatic, lymphatic; infiltrative, seepy; drenching; diluted, weak; wet, etc. (*moist*), 339.

338. AIR.—*N.* **air,** etc. (*gas*), 334; atmosphere; ventilation.

the open air, open air; sky, blue sky.

weather, climate; rise and fall of the barometer (*or* mercury).

Science of air: aerology, aerometry, aerography; meteorology, climatology; pneumatics; aeronautics, etc., 267.

aeronaut, etc., 269*a*.

barometer, aneroid, weatherglass, weather gauge.

weather vane, weathercock, vane.

V. **air,** ventilate, fan, etc. (*wind*), 349.

fly, soar, drift, hover; aviate, etc. (*aeronautics*), 267.

Adj. **containing air,** flatulent, effervescent; windy, etc., 349.

atmospheric, airy; aerial, aeriform; aery, pneumatic.

meteorological, barometric, aerographic, weatherwise.

Adv. **in the open air,** in the open, under the stars, out of doors, outdoors; alfresco [It.].

339. MOISTURE.—*N.* **moisture;** moistness, humidity; dew; marsh, etc., 345.

V. **moisten,** wet, sponge, damp, bedew; infiltrate, saturate; soak, sodden, seethe, sop; drench, etc. (*water*), 337.

perspire, etc. (*exude*), 295.

Adj. **moist,** damp; watery, etc., 337; undried, humid, wet, dank, muggy; dewy; juicy.

sodden, soppy, soggy, dabbled; reeking, dripping, soaking, saturated, soft, sloppy, muddy: swampy, etc. (*marshy*), 345; irriguous.

340. DRYNESS.—*N.* **dryness,** aridness, aridity, drought. desiccation, evaporation; drainage.

V. **dry,** dry up, soak up; sponge, swab, wipe, drain, parch, sear; desiccate, evaporate.

Adj. **dry,** rainless, fair, pleasant, fine; arid, sear, droughty, waterless, dried, desiccated; juiceless, sapless; corky; husky, parched; waterproof, watertight.

341. OCEAN—*N.* **ocean,** sea, main, high seas, deep, salt water; waters, waves, billows; tide, etc. (*water in motion*), 348; offing, watery waste, pond [*humorous for Atlantic*], the seven seas; ocean lane, steamer track.

Neptune, Poseidon, Oceanus, Thetis, Triton, naiad, Nereid; sea nymph, siren, mermaid, merman; trident, dolphin.

oceanography; oceanographer.

Adj. **oceanic,** marine, maritime; seaworthy, seagoing.

342. LAND.—*N.* **land,** earth, ground, soil, dry land, terra firma [*L.*].

continent; mainland, main; peninsula, chersonese; delta; neck of land, isthmus; oasis: promontory, etc. (*projection*), 250; highland, etc. (*height*), 206; plain, etc., 344.

realty, real estate, property, acres.

coast, shore, strand, beach; bank; seaboard, seaside, seacoast, seashore; reclamation, made land.

fatherland, home, country, native land; region, etc., 181.

soil, glebe, clay, loam, marl, gravel, mold, subsoil, clod.

rock, crag, cliff, boulder.

landsman, landlubber, tiller of the soil; agriculturist, etc., 371.

V. **land,** disembark, debark, come to land, come (*or* go) ashore.

Adj. **earthy;** continental, midland; earthly, terrestrial; littoral, alluvial; landed, territorial; geographic *or* geographical.

Adv. **ashore,** on shore, on land, on dry land, on terra firma.

343. GULF, LAKE.—*N.* **gulf,** bay, inlet, bight, estuary, bayou, fiord, frith *or* firth; mouth; lagoon, cove, creek; natural harbor; roads; sound, strait, narrows.

lake, loch [*Scot.*], mere, tarn, pond, pool; well, artesian well; ditch, dike, dam, race, millrace; tank, reservoir.

344. PLAIN.—*N.* **plain,** open country; basin, downs, waste, desert, wild, steppe [*Russia*], grassland; tundra [*Arctic*], pampas [*esp. in Argentina*], savanna [*as in Brazil; also, a treeless plain, as in Florida*], campo [*S. Amer.*], llano [*S. Amer.*], prairie, heath, common, moor, moorland; bush; plateau, tableland, mesa; uplands; reach, stretch, expanse; alkali flat.

meadow, mead, pasture, lea, pasturage, field.

lawn, green, plot, grassplot.

greensward, sward, turf, sod, grass; heather.

grounds; estate, park, common, campus.

345. MARSH.—*N.* marsh, swamp, morass, peat bog, fen, bog, quagmire, slough; mud, slush.

Adj. marsh, marshy, fenny, swampy, boggy, soft; muddy, squashy, spongy.

346. ISLAND.—*N.* island, isle, islet; reef, atoll; archipelago; islander.

V. insulate, island.

Adj. insular, seagirt; archipelagic.

347. [Fluid in motion] STREAM.—*N.* stream, etc. (*of water*), 348 (*of air*), 349.

V. flow, etc., 348; blow, etc., 349.

348. [Water in motion] RIVER.—*N.* running water, jet, squirt, spout, splash, rush, gush, sluice.

waterspout, waterfall; fall, cascade, Niagara; cataract, inundation, deluge; chute, washout.

rain, rainfall; drizzle, shower; downpour, cloudburst; rains, rainy season, monsoon.

stream, course. flux, flow, current, tide, race, millrace, tiderace.

spring; fount, fountain; rill, rivulet, streamlet, brooklet; branch; brook, river; reach; tributary.

body of water, torrent, rapids, flood; spring (*or* high, flood, full) tide; bore, eagre; ebb, reflux; undercurrent, undertow; eddy, vortex, whirlpool, maelstrom.

wave, billow, surge, swell, ripple; tidal wave; comber, rollers, ground swell, surf, breakers, white horses.

Science of fluids in motion: hydrodynamics; hydraulics, hydrostatics, hydrokinetics, hydromechanics.

V. flow, run; meander; gush, pour, spout, roll, jet, well, issue; drop, drip, dribble, plash, trickle, distill, percolate; stream, surge, swirl, overflow, inundate, deluge, flow over, splash, swash; murmur, babble, purl, gurgle, spurt, ooze, flow out, etc. (*egress*), 295.

flow into, fall into, open into, drain into; discharge itself, disembogue.

Cause a flow: pour; pour out, etc. (*emit*), 297; shower down; irrigate, drench, etc. (*wet*), 337; spill, splash.

Stop a flow: stanch; dam, plug, stop up, cork, dam up, obstruct, choke, cut off.

rain; pour; shower, sprinkle, drizzle; set in.

Adj. flowing, fluent, meandering, flexuous; choppy, rolling; tidal.

rainy, showery, drizzly, drizzling, wet.

349. [Air in motion] WIND.—*N.* wind, draft, air; breath, puff, whiff, zephyr, blow, stream, current.

gust, blast, breeze, squall, half a gale, gale.

trade wind, trades, monsoon.

storm, tempest, hurricane, whirlwind, tornado, cyclone, typhoon, simoom [*as in Asia Minor*], harmattan [*W. coast of Africa*], sirocco [*as in W. Africa, Texas, and Kansas*], khamsin [*Egypt*], mistral [*Mediterranean*]; blizzard, norther, northeaster, northeast gale.

wind gauge, anemometer, anemograph; weathercock, weather vane, vane.

breathing, respiration, inspiration, inhalation, expiration, exhalation; blowing, fanning, inflation; ventilation.

V. blow, waft; storm.

respire, breathe, inhale, exhale; inspire, expire; puff, gasp, wheeze· snuff, snuffle; sniff, sniffle; sneeze, cough, hiccup.

inflate, pump, blow up.

whistle, scream, roar, howl, sing, sing in the shrouds, growl.

Adj. windy, breezy, gusty, squally.

stormy, tempestuous, blustering, cyclonic, typhonic; boisterous, violent.

350. [Channel for the passage of water] CONDUIT.—*N.* conduit, channel, duct, watercourse, canyon, coulee, water gap, gorge, ravine, chasm; race; aqueduct, canal; flume, dike, main· arroyo, gully, gulch; moat, ditch; gutter, drain, sewer, culvert; scupper; funnel, trough, siphon, pump, hose; pipe, tube; artery; spout, gargoyle; weir, floodgate, water gate, sluice, lock, valve.

Anatomy: artery, vein, blood vessel, pore; aorta; intestines, bowels; esophagus, gullet; throat.

351. [Channel for the passage of air] AIR PIPE—*N.* air pipe, airhole, blowhole, breathing hole, touchhole, venthole, spilehole, bung, bunghole; shaft, air shaft, smoke shaft, flue, chimney, funnel, vent, ventilator.

nostril, nozzle, throat; windpipe, trachea.

352. SEMILIQUIDITY.—*N.* semiliquidity; stickiness, pastiness, adhesiveness; thickening, jellification.

mud, slush, slime, ooze; moisture, humidity, marsh, etc., 345.

V. thicken, coagulate, gelatinize; jellify, jelly, jell [*colloq.*]; emulsify; mash, squash [*colloq.*], churn, beat up.

Adj. semifluid, semiliquid; half-melted, half-frozen; milky, muddy, curdled; thick, gelatinous, mucilaginous, glutinous, sticky; ropy; clotted.

353. [Mixture of air and water] BUBBLE, CLOUD.—*N.* bubble; foam, froth, spray, surf; spume, scum; lather, suds, yeast.

effervescence, babbling, fermentation; evaporation.

cloud, vapor, fog, mist, haze, steam; scud, rack, cumulus; nebula, cirrus, curl cloud; thunderhead; stratus.

V. **bubble,** boil, foam, spume, froth; effervesce, ferment, fizz; aerate.

cloud, overcast, overcloud, befog, becloud, mist, fog, overshadow, shadow.

Adj. **bubbling,** frothy, effervescent, sparkling, fizzy, heady. **cloudy,** nebulous; vaporous; overcast.

354. PULPINESS.—*N.* **pulpiness;** fleshiness; pulp, paste, dough, sponge, batter, curd, pap, jam, poultice.

V. **pulp,** mash, squash [*colloq.*], macerate; coagulate, etc., 352. *Adj.* **pulpy;** [*of fruit*] fleshy, succulent.

355. UNCTUOUSNESS.—*N.* **unctuousness,** oiliness; lubrication; unguent, salve, cerate; ointment, etc. (*oil*), 356; anointment; lubricant.

V. **oil,** anoint, lubricate, etc., 332; smear, salve, grease, lard. *Adj.* **unctuous,** oily, oleaginous, fat, fatty, greasy; waxy, soapy, slippery.

356. OIL.—*N.* **oil,** fat, butter, cream, grease, tallow, suet, lard, dripping, blubber; glycerin; coconut butter; soap, soft soap; wax; paraffin, benzine, kerosene, naphtha, gasoline, petroleum; ointment, pomade, unguent, liniment.

356a. RESIN.—*N.* **resin,** rosin, gum; shellac, varnish, mastic, lacquer, sealing wax; amber, ambergris; bitumen, pitch, tar, asphalt.

V. **varnish,** etc. (*overlay*), 223; rosin, resin.

Adj. **resinous,** lacquered, tarred, tarry, pitched, pitchy, gummed, gummy, waxed; bituminous, asphaltic.

III. ORGANIC MATTER

(1) Vitality

357. ORGANIZATION.—*N.* **organization,** structure, organized nature, animated nature; living beings; organic remains; organism; animal and plant life, fauna and flora.

fossils; fossilization, petrifaction; paleontology; paleontologist.

Science of living beings: biology, natural history;[1] zoology, etc., 368, botany; physiology, anatomy, organic chemistry; evolution, Darwinism.

protoplasm, bioplasm; cell, proteid, protein, albumen, germinal matter, germ plasm, germ cell; amoeba, protozoan.

naturalist, biologist, zoologist, botanist, bacteriologist, embryologist.

[1] The term *natural history* is also used as relating to all the objects in nature whether organic or inorganic, and including, therefore, *mineralogy, geology, meteorology,* etc.

V. **organize**, systematize, form, arrange, construct.

fossilize, petrify, mummify.

Adj. **organic**, organized, structural; cellular, protoplasmic.

fossilized, petrified.

358. INORGANIZATION.—*N.* **mineral kingdom,** mineral world; unorganized (*or* inorganic) matter.

Science of the mineral kingdom: mineralogy, geology, metallurgy.

V. **mineralize**; pulverize, turn to dust.

Adj. **inorganic**, inanimate, unorganized, mineral.

359. LIFE.—*N.* **life**; vitality; existence, etc.; animation.

vital spark, vital flame, lifeblood: respiration, breath, breath of life.

vivification; oxygen; life force; vitalization; revival; revivification, etc., 163; life to come, etc. (*destiny*), 152.

Science of life: physiology, biology, embryology.

nourishment, nutriment, etc. (*food*), 298.

V. **live**, be alive, breathe, subsist, exist, walk the earth.

be born, see the light, come into the world; quicken; revive; come to life.

give birth to, etc. (*produce*), 161; bring to life, put life into, vitalize; vivify, reanimate, restore, resuscitate.

Adj. **living**, alive; in life, in the flesh, breathing, quick, animated; lively, etc. (*active*), 682; vital, vivifying.

360. DEATH.—*N.* **death**, decease, demise; mortality; dying, dissolution, departure, release, rest, eternal rest; loss, bereavement.

cessation (*or* loss, extinction) of life.

river of death; Jordan, Stygian shore; the great adventure.

angel of death, death's bright angel; death, doom, fate, destiny.

death song, dirge, requiem, elegy, threnody.

V. **die**, expire, perish; breathe one's last; lose *or* lay down one's life; die a violent death; give (*or* yield) up the ghost.

die for one's country, make the supreme sacrifice, go West [*First World War euphemism*].

Adj. **dead**, lifeless, inanimate; deceased, late; departed, defunct; gone, no more; bereft of life.

deadly, mortal, fatal.

dying, moribund, at the point of death, at death's door, at the last gasp.

361. [Destruction of life; violent death] KILLING.—*N.* **killing**; homicide, manslaughter; murder, assassination; effusion of blood; bloodshed, slaughter, carnage, butchery, massacre.

war, warfare, organized murder; battle; war to the death, etc. (*warfare*), 722; Armageddon; deadly weapon, etc. (*arms*), 727.

deathblow, finishing stroke, *coup de grace* [F.], quietus; execution, etc. (*capital punishment*), 972; martyrdom.

suffocation, strangulation, garrote; hanging, etc., *v.*

slayer, butcher, murderer, Cain, assassin, cutthroat, garroter, thug, gallows, executioner, etc. (*punishment*), 975; apache, gunman [*colloq.*], bandit.

regicide, parricide, fratricide [*these words refer to both doer and deed*].

suicide, self-murder, self-destruction, hara-kiri [Jap.], suttee; immolation, holocaust.

fatal accident, violent death, casualty, disaster, calamity.

Destruction of animals: slaughtering, sport; the chase, venery; hunting, coursing, shooting, fishing; pigsticking.

sportsman, huntsman, hunter, Nimrod; fisherman, angler.

shambles, slaughterhouse.

V. **kill,** put to death, slay, shed blood; murder, assassinate, butcher, slaughter, immolate; massacre, decimate; put an end to; dispatch, do to death, do for [*colloq.*]; hunt, shoot, saber, stab, bayonet, put to the sword.

strangle, garrote, hang, throttle, choke, stifle, suffocate; smother, asphyxiate, drown.

execute; behead, guillotine; hang; electrocute.

die a violent death; commit suicide; kill (*or* make away with, put an end to) oneself.

Adj. **murderous,** slaughterous, sanguinary, bloody-minded, bloodthirsty; homicidal; red-handed, bloody, bloodstained, gory.

mortal, fatal, deadly, lethal; mutually destructive, internecine; suicidal.

362. CORPSE.—*N.* corpse, carcass, skeleton, relics, remains, dust, ashes, earth, clay; mummy; carrion.

ghost, shade, phantom, specter, apparition, spirit, revenant, spook [*colloq.*].

363. INTERMENT.—*N.* interment, burial, sepulture, entombment; obsequies, funeral, funeral rite, wake; knell, passing bell, death bell, tolling; dirge, etc. (*lamentation*), 839; dead march, muffled drum; pall, bier, litter, hearse, catafalque.

cremation, burning; pyre, funeral pile.

undertaker, funeral director.

mourner, mute; pallbearer, bearer.

graveclothes, shroud, winding sheet; cerecloth, cerements.

coffin, casket; urn; sarcophagus.

burial place, grave, pit, sepulcher, tomb, vault, crypt, catacomb, mausoleum; cemetery, burial ground, graveyard, churchyard; God's acre; potter's field; barrow, tumulus; charnel house, dead-house; morgue, mortuary; burning ghat [India]; crematorium, crematory.

gravedigger, sexton.

monument; gravestone, headstone, tombstone; hatchment, stone, marker, cross; epitaph, inscription.

autopsy, post-mortem examination *or* post mortem [L.].

disinterment, exhumation.

V. **inter**, bury, entomb; inurn; cremate.

disinter, exhume, unearth.

Adj. **funereal**, funeral, mortuary, sepulchral, cinerary; burial; elegiac.

364. ANIMAL LIFE.—*N*. **animal life**, animalism.

human system; breath; flesh, flesh and blood; physique, strength, power, vigor, force; spring, elasticity, tone.

V. **incarnate**, incorporate.

Adj. **fleshly**, carnal, human, corporeal.

365. VEGETATION.—*N*. **vegetation**, vegetable life, growth, herbage, flowerage.

V. **vegetate**, germinate, sprout, grow, shoot up, luxuriate, grow rank, flourish, flower, blossom; cultivate.

Adj. **vegetative**, vegetal, vegetable; leguminous, etc., 367.

luxuriant, rank, dense, lush, wild.

366. ANIMAL.—*N*. **animal kingdom**, fauna, brute creation.

animal, creature, created being, living thing; dumb animal, dumb friend, dumb creature; brute, beast.

mammal, quadruped, bird, reptile, fish, crustacean, shellfish, mollusk, worm, insect, zoophyte; animalcule, etc., 193.

beasts of the field, fowls of the air; flocks and herds, livestock, domestic animals, wild animals, game.

Domestic animals: horse, etc. (*beast of burden*), 271; cattle, ox; bull, bullock; cow, milch cow, Jersey, calf, heifer, shorthorn, yearling, steer; sheep; lamb, ewe, ram; pig, swine, boar, hog, sow; yak, zebu, buffalo.

dog, hound, canine; pup, puppy; whelp, cur [*contemptuous*], mongrel.

cat, feline, puss, pussy, tabby; tomcat *or* tom; mouser; Angora, Persian, Maltese, tortoise-shell; kitten, kitty.

Wild animals: deer, buck, doe, fawn, stag, hart, hind, roe, roebuck, caribou, elk, moose, reindeer, wapiti *or* American elk, fallow deer, red deer.

antelope, gazelle, American antelope *or* pronghorn, chamois.

ape, monkey, gorilla, marmoset, chimpanzee, lemur, baboon, orangutan.

fox, reynard, vixen [*fem*.]; dingo, coyote; wildcat, lynx, bobcat; skunk.

lion, tiger, etc. (*wild beast*), 913.

rat, mouse.

lizard, saurian, iguana, newt, chameleon, Gila monster, dragon; crocodile, alligator.

whale, shark, porpoise, walrus, seal, octopus, devilfish; swordfish; pike; salmon, trout, etc.

Birds: feathered tribes, singing bird, warbler, dickybird [*colloq*.].

canary, vireo, linnet, finch, goldfinch, siskin, crossbill, chewink, peewee, titmouse

or chickadee, nightingale, lark; magpie, cuckoo, mocking bird, catbird, starling; robin, sparrow, swallow, etc.

swan, cygnet, goose, gander, duck, drake, wild duck, mallard.

gull, sea gull, albatross, petrel, stormy petrel *or* Mother Carey's chicken; owl bird of night; hawk, vulture, buzzard; eagle, bird of freedom.

game, ruffed grouse, grouse, blackcock, duck, plover, rail, snipe, pheasant.

poultry, fowl, cock, rooster, chanticleer, barndoor fowl, barnyard fowl, hen, chicken, chick; guinea fowl, guinea hen; peafowl, peacock, peahen.

Insects: bee, honeybee, queen bee, drone; ant, white ant, termite; wasp, locust, grasshopper, cicada, cicala, cricket; dragonfly; beetle; butterfly, moth; fly, mo quito; earwig; bug, buffalo bug, gypsy moth, weevil.

vermin, lice, cooties [*slang*], flies, fleas, cockroaches *or* roaches, water bugs, bugs, bedbugs, mosquitoes; rats, mice, weasels.

snake, serpent, viper; asp, adder, coral snake *or* harlequin snake, krait [India], cobra, cobra de capello, king cobra, rattlesnake *or* rattler, copperhead, constrictor, boa constrictor, boa, python.

Mythological: basilisk, cockatrice, salamander; griffin; chimera; Python, Hydra, Cerberus.

Adj. animal; zoological; equine; bovine; canine; feline; piscatorial; ophidian, reptilian, snakelike.

367. VEGETABLE.—*N.* vegetable, vegetable kingdom; organism, plant, tree, shrub, bush, creeper, vine; herb, seedling exotic; annual, perennial; pulse, greens.

foliage, leafage, verdure; branch, bough, stem, trunk; leaf, spray, leaflet, frond, pad, flag, petal, needle, sepal; spray, runner, shoot, tendril.

flower, blossom, bud, floweret, flowering plant.

tree, sapling, seedling; oak, elm, beech, birch, timber tree, pine, palm, spruce, fir, hemlock, yew, larch, cedar, juniper, chestnut, maple, alder, ash, myrtle, magnolia, walnut, olive, poplar, willow, linden, lime; fruit tree; arboretum, etc., 371.

banyan, teak, acacia, deodar, fig tree, eucalyptus, gum tree.

woodlands, virgin forest, forest primeval, forest, wood, timberland, timber, wood lot; weald, park, greenwood, grove, copse, coppice, thicket, chaparral, jungle, bush.

undergrowth, underwood, brushwood, brake, scrub, heath, heather, fern, bracken, furze, gorse, broom, sedge, rush, bulrush, bamboo; weed, moss, lichen, turf, grass, herbage.

grassland, plain, etc., 344.

seaweed, alga (*pl.* algae), dulse, kelp, rockweed, sea lettuce, gulfweed, sargasso, sargassum; Sargasso Sea.

V. vegetate, grow, flourish, bloom, flower, blossom; bud, etc. (*expand*), 194; timber, retimber, plant, trim, graft, prune, cut.

Adj. vegetable, vegetative, vegetarian; leguminous, herbaceous, herbal, botanic *or* botanical; arboreous, arboreal, sylvan; grassy, verdant, verdurous; floral; ligneous, wooden, woody; bosky, copsy; mossy, turfy; deciduous, evergreen.

native, domestic, indigenous, native-grown, home-grown.

368. [Science of animals] ZOOLOGY.—*N.* zoology, zoography, morphology, anatomy, histology, embryology; comparative anatomy, animal physiology, comparative physiology, anthropology, ornithology, ichthyology, entomology, paleontology.

zoologist, zoographer, zoographist, anatomist, anthropologist, ornithologist, ichthyologist, entomologist, paleontologist.

Adj. **zoological,** zoologic; zoographical.

369. [Science of plants] BOTANY.—*N.* **botany,** phytology, phytobiology, vegetable chemistry; vegetable physiology, dendrology; flora; botanic garden, etc. (*garden*), 371.

botanist, phytologist, phytobiologist, dendrologist; horticulturist, etc., 371; herbalist, herbist, herbarian.

V. **botanize,** herborize.

Adj. **botanic** *or* botanical, dendroid, dendriform, herby, herbal; horticultural.

370. MANAGEMENT OF ANIMALS.—*N.* **domestication,** domesticity, manège, veterinary art; breeding, taming.

menagerie, zoological garden, zoo [*colloq.*]; bear pit; aviary, apiary, beehive, ⬚arium, fishery, fish hatchery, fish pond; hennery, incubator.

⬚: herder, cowherd, grazier, drover, cowkeeper; shepherd, shepherdess; ⬚eeper; trainer, breeder; cowboy, cowpuncher; horse trainer, bronchobuster ⬚, beekeeper, apiarist, apiculturist.

⬚eterinarian, veterinary surgeon, vet [*colloq.*], horse doctor, ⬚orseshoer.

inclosure, stable, barn; sheepfold, sty; cage, hencoop.

V. **tame,** domesticate; corral, round up; break in, gentle, break, bust [*slang*], break to harness, train; ride, drive; spur, prick, lash, goad, whip; yoke, harness, harness up [*colloq.*], hitch, hitch up [*colloq.*], cinch.

groom, tend, rub down, brush, currycomb; water, feed, fodder; bed down, litter.

tend stock, milk, shear; water, etc. (*groom*), *v.*; herd; raise, bring up.

hatch, incubate, sit, brood, cover.

Adj. **tame,** domestic, domesticated, housebroken, broken, gentle, docile.

371. MANAGEMENT OF PLANTS.—*N.* **agriculture,** cultivation, husbandry, farming; tillage, gardening, vintage; horticulture, arboriculture, forestry; floriculture; landscape gardening.

husbandman, horticulturist, gardener, florist; agriculturist, yeoman, farmer, granger, cultivator, tiller of the soil, plowman; logger, lumberman, lumberjack, forester, woodcutter, pioneer, backwoodsman.

garden; botanic (*or* flower, kitchen, market, truck) garden; nursery; greenhouse, hothouse, conservatory; grassplot, lawn; shrubbery, arboretum, orchard; vineyard, orangery.

field, meadow, mead, green, common.

V. **cultivate,** till, till the soil, farm, garden, sow, plant; reap, mow, cut; manure, dress the ground; dig, spade, delve, hoe, plow, harrow, rake, weed; force, seed, turf; transplant, thin out, bed, prune, graft.

Adj. **arable**, plowable, tillable.

rural, rustic, country, agrarian, pastoral, bucolic, Arcadian.

372. MANKIND.—*N.* **mankind**, man; human race (*or* species, kind, nature); humanity, mortality, generation.

Science of man: anthropology, ethnology, ethnography.

human being; person, personage; individual, creature, fellow creature, mortal, body, somebody, one, someone; soul, living soul; party [*slang or vulgar*].

people, persons, folk, public, society, world; community, general public; nation, state, realm, republic; commonweal, commonwealth; body politic; the masses, etc. (*commonalty*), 876; population; lords of creation; ourselves.

Adj. **human,** mortal, personal, individual; national, civic, public social.

373. MAN.—*N.* **man,** male; gentleman, sir, master; yeoman, chap [*colloq.*], swain, fellow, blade, beau; husband, etc. (*youth*), 129.

mister, Mr., *monsieur* (*abbr.* M., *pl.* Messrs.) [F.], *Herr* [Ger.], *signor* [It., *used before name*], *signore* [It.], *signorino* [It., *dim. of signore*], *señor* [Sp.], *senhor* [Pg.].

Male animal: cock, drake, gander, dog, boar, stag, hart, buck, horse, stallion, gelding; tom, tomcat; he-goat, billy goat [*colloq.*]; ram; bull, bullock; capon; ox, steer.

Adj. **male,** masculine, manly, virile; unwomanly, unfeminine.

374. WOMAN.—*N.* **woman,** female, petticoat.

womankind, womanhood; the sex, fair sex, softer sex.

dame [*archaic except as an elderly woman or as slang*], madam, lady, donna, belle, matron, dowager, good woman, squaw; wife.

spinster, old maid, bachelor girl, new woman, girl, etc. (*youth*), 129.

mistress, Mrs., *madame* (*pl. mesdames*) [F.], *Frau* [Ger.], *signora* [It.], *señora* [Sp.], *senhora* [Pg.]; miss, *mademoiselle* (*pl. mesdemoiselles*) [F.], *Fräulein* [Ger.], *signorina* [It.], *señorita* [Sp.], *senhorita* [Pg.].

Effeminacy: betty, molly, mollycoddle, old woman, tame cat [*all contemptuous*].

Female animal: hen; bitch, slut; sow, doe, roe, mare; she-goat, nanny goat [*colloq.*], nanny [*colloq.*]; ewe, cow; lioness, tigress; vixen.

harem, seraglio, purdah [India].

Adj. **female,** feminine, womanly, ladylike, matronly, girlish, maidenly; womanish, effeminate, unmanly.

(2) Sensation

375. PHYSICAL SENSIBILITY.—*N.* sensibility, sensitiveness, feeling, impressibility, susceptibility.

sensation, impression; consciousness.

V. feel, perceive, be sensitive to.

render sensitive, sharpen, refine, excite, stir, cultivate, tutor.

cause sensation, impress, excite (*or* produce) an impression.

Adj. sensitive, sensuous; perceptive, sentient, sensible; conscious, alive, alive to impressions, impressionable, responsive.

acute, sharp, keen, vivid, lively.

Adv. to the quick; on the raw [*slang*].

376. PHYSICAL INSENSIBILITY.—*N.* insensibility, obtuseness, paralysis, anesthesia, hypnosis, stupor, coma, sleep.

anesthetic; opium, ether, chloroform, chloral; nitrous oxide, laughing gas; cocaine, novocain; refrigeration.

V. render insensible, blunt, cloy, satiate; benumb, numb, deaden, freeze, paralyze; anesthetize; put to sleep, hypnotize, stupefy, stun.

Adj. insensible, unfeeling, senseless, callous, hard, hardened, casehardened, proof, obtuse, dull; paralytic, palsied, numb, dead.

377. PHYSICAL PLEASURE.—*N.* pleasure, bodily enjoyment, animal gratification, gusto, relish, delight, sensual delight, sensuality; luxuriousness, dissipation, round of pleasure; comfort, ease, luxury, lap of luxury; creature comforts; purple and fine linen; bed of roses.

treat; diversion, entertainment, banquet, refreshment, feast.

happiness, felicity, bliss, beatitude, etc. (*mental enjoyment*), 827.

V. enjoy, relish; luxuriate in, revel in, bask in, wallow in; feast on, gloat over, smack the lips.

please, charm, delight, enchant, etc., 829.

Adj. comfortable, cosy, snug, luxurious, in comfort, at ease, in clover [*colloq.*].

agreeable, etc., 829; grateful, refreshing, comforting, cordial, genial; gratifying, sensuous; palatable, delicious, sweet; fragrant; melodious, harmonious; lovely, etc. (*beautiful*), 845.

Adv. in comfort, on a bed of roses, on flowery beds of ease.

378. PHYSICAL PAIN.—*N.* pain, suffering, dolor, ache, smart; shoot, shooting, twinge, pang, gripe, hurt, cut; sore, soreness; discomfort.

spasm, cramp; crick, stitch; convulsion, throe; throb, colic, gripes.

torment, torture, agony, anguish, rack, crucifixion, martyrdom.

V. **suffer,** feel (*or* suffer, undergo) pain; ache, smart, bleed, tingle, shoot, twinge; writhe, wince.

pain, give pain, inflict pain; lacerate; hurt, chafe, sting, bite, gnaw, stab, grate, gall, fret, prick, pierce, wring, convulse; torment, torture; rack, agonize; crucify; flog, etc. (*punish*), 972.

Adj. painful, aching, poignant, excruciating, biting; on the rack; sore, raw.

(1) *Touch*

379. [Sensation of pressure] **TOUCH.**—*N.* **touch,** contact, tangency, impact, feeling; graze, glance, brush, lick; manipulation, rubbing, kneading, massage.

V. **touch,** feel, handle, finger, thumb, paw, fumble, grope; stroke, massage, rub, knead, manipulate, wield; throw out a feeler.

Adj. **tactual,** tangible, palpable, tangent, lambent.

380. SENSATIONS OF TOUCH.—*N.* itching, tickling, titillation.

itch, scabies; mange.

V. **itch,** tingle, creep, thrill, sting; prick, prickle.

tickle, titillate.

Adj. **ticklish,** titillative.

itchy, mangy; creepy, crawly.

381. [Insensibility to touch] **NUMBNESS.**—*N.* **numbness;** physical insensibility, etc., 376; anesthesia.

V. **benumb,** etc., 376; stupefy, drug, deaden, paralyze.

Adj. **numb,** benumbed, insensible, unfeeling, deadened; intangible, impalpable; dazed, comatose, narcotic.

(2) *Heat*

382. HEAT.—*N.* **heat,** caloric; temperature, warmth, incandescence.

summer, dog days, heat wave, broiling sun; sun, etc. (*luminary*), 423.

flush, glow, blush, redness; fever.

fire, spark, scintillation, flash, flame, blaze; bonfire; wildfire; sheet of fire, lambent flame.

hot springs, geysers; thermae, hot baths, Turkish bath; steam.

V. **be hot,** glow, flush, sweat, swelter, bask, smoke, reek, stew, simmer, seethe, boil, burn, singe, scorch, scald, broil, blaze, flame; smolder, parch, pant.

heat, etc. (*make hot*), 384; incandesce.

thaw, fuse, melt, liquefy.

Adj. **warm,** mild, genial; tepid, lukewarm.

hot, heated, fervid, fervent, baking, ardent, sunny, sunshiny, torrid, tropical, thermal.

close, sultry, stifling, stuffy, suffocating, oppressive, sweltering.

fiery; incandescent, ebullient, glowing, aglow, reeking, smoking; live; on fire, blazing, in flames, in a blaze; alight, afire, ablaze, smoldering.

feverish, febrile, inflamed, burning; in a fever.

383. COLD.—*N.* **cold,** coldness, frigidity, inclemency.

winter; depth of winter; hard winter; arctic, antarctic.

ice; sleet; hail, hailstone; frost, rime, hoarfrost; icicle, thick-ribbed ice; iceberg, floe, berg, ice field, ice pack, glacier.

snow, snowflake, snowball, snowdrift, snowstorm, snowslip, snow avalanche.

chill, chilliness, shivering, goose flesh, chilblains, frostbite, chattering of teeth.

V. **be cold,** shiver, quake, shake, tremble, shudder, chill, freeze.

Adj. **cold,** cool, chill, chilly, frigid; fresh, keen, bleak, raw, inclement, bitter, biting, cutting, nipping, piercing, pinching; shivering, anguish; frostbitten.

icy, glacial, frosty, freezing, wintry, boreal, arctic, snowbound, icebound, frost-bound, frozen.

Adv. with chattering teeth.

384. CALEFACTION.—*N.* **calefaction,** tepefaction, heating, melting, fusion, liquefaction, combustion; cremation; calcination; incineration; carbonization; cauterization.

ignition, kindling, inflammation, conflagration; incendiarism, arson; auto-da-fé [Pg.], the stake, burning at the stake; suttee.

incendiary, arsonist, pyromaniac, fire bug.

boiling, ebullition, ebullience, decoction; hot spring, geyser.

crematory, crematorium, incinerator; furnace, etc., 386.

wrap, blanket, flannel, wool, fur; wadding, lining, interlining; clothing, etc., 225.

Products of combustion: cinder, ash, embers, slag, clinker; coke, carbon, charcoal.

V. **heat,** warm, chafe, foment; make hot; sun oneself, bask in the sun.

fire, set fire to, set on fire; kindle, enkindle, light, ignite; rekindle.

melt, thaw, fuse; liquefy, dissolve.

burn, scorch, inflame; roast, toast, fry, grill, singe, parch, bake; brand, cauterize, sear, burn in; corrode, char, carbonize, calcine, incinerate, smelt; reduce to ashes.

take *or* catch fire· blaze, etc. (*flame*), 382.

boil, stew, cook, seethe, scald, parboil, simmer.
Adj. heated, warmed; burnt, scorched; molten; volcanic.
inflammable, inflammatory, combustible.

385. REFRIGERATION.—*N.* refrigeration, cooling, congelation, glaciation; solidification; ice; icebox, ice chest; refrigerator.
fire extinguisher, asbestos; fireman, fire brigade, fire department, fire engine.
V. cool, fan, refresh; ice, refrigerate, congeal, freeze, benumb, chill, petrify, pinch, nip, cut, pierce, bite.
extinguish, put out, stamp out; damp, slack, quench.
Adj. incombustible, asbestic, unflammable, uninflammable; fireproof.

386. FURNACE.—*N.* furnace, stove; cookstove, cooker, oven, brick oven, tin oven, Dutch oven, range, fireless cooker; forge, fiery furnace; volcano; kiln, brickkiln, limekiln.

brasier, tripod, salamander, heater, warming pan, footstove, foot warmer; radiator, register, coil; boiler, caldron, pot; urn, kettle; chafing dish; retort, crucible, alembic, still; flatiron, sadiron; toasting fork, toaster.
galley, caboose; hothouse, conservatory; bakehouse; washhouse, laundry.
fireplace, hearth, grate, firebox, andiron, firedog, fire irons; poker, tongs, shovel, hob, trivet; damper, crane, pothooks, chains, turnspit, spit, gridiron.
hot bath; thermae; Turkish (*or* Russian, vapor, electric, sitz, hip, shower) bath; bathroom, lavatory.

387. REFRIGERATOR.—*N.* refrigerator, icebox, ice chest; cold storage; refrigerating plant; icehouse; ice-cream freezer, freezer; ice bag, ice pack, cold pack; ice pail, cooler, wine cooler.
refrigerant, freezing, mixture, ice, ammonia.

388. FUEL.—*N.* fuel, firing, combustible, coal, anthracite, bituminous coal; carbon, slack, cannel coal *or* cannel, lignite, coke, charcoal; turf, peat; oil, gas, natural gas, electricity; ember, cinder, ash, slag, clinker; tinder, touchwood; punk.

log, backlog, yule log, firewood, fagot, kindling wood, kindlings, brushwood.
fumigator, incense, joss stick; smudge; disinfectant.
brand, firebrand, torch; fuse, wick; spill, match, light.

V. coal, stoke; feed, fire, etc., 384.
Adj. carbonaceous; combustible, inflammable; slow-burning, free-burning.

389. THERMOMETER.—*N.* thermometer, thermometrograph, thermostat, thermoscope; differential thermometer, telethermometer, pyrometer.

(3) *Taste*

390. TASTE.—*N.* taste, flavor, gusto, savor, relish; smack, tang; aftertaste.
palate; tongue; tooth; stomach.

V. taste, flavor, savor, smack; tickle the palate, etc. (*savory*), 394.

Adj. tasty, savory, flavored, spiced; palatable, etc., 394.

391. INSIPIDITY.—*N.* insipidity; tastelessness, unsavoriness.

Adj. insipid; tasteless, unsavory, unflavored, jejune, savorless; weak, stale, flat, vapid, wishy-washy [*colloq.*].

392. PUNGENCY.—*N.* pungency, piquancy, poignancy, tang, nip.

sharpness, acridity; sourness, unsavoriness.

dram, cordial, nip, bracer [*colloq.*], pick-me-up [*colloq.*], potion, liqueur.

tobacco, nicotine; smoke, cigar, cheroot, stogy; cigarette, fag [*slang*], Havana, Cuban tobacco; weed [*colloq.*]; snuff.

V. season, spice, bespice, salt, pepper, pickle, brine, devil, curry.

Adj. pungent, strong, high-flavored, full-flavored, high-seasoned; gamy, high; sharp, piquant, racy; biting, mordant; spicy; seasoned, spiced; hot, peppery; acrid, bitter; sour, acid, etc., 397; unsavory, etc., 395.

salt, saline, brackish, briny.

393. CONDIMENT.—*N.* condiment, flavoring, seasoning, sauce, spice, relish; pickle; chutney; appetizer.

V. season, etc. (*render pungent*), 392.

394. SAVORINESS.—*N.* savoriness, tastiness, palatability; delectability; relish, zest.

appetizer, hors d'oeuvre [F.].

delicacy, titbit, dainty, ambrosia, nectar.

V. be savory; tickle the palate (*or* appetite); tempt the appetite, taste good.

relish, like, smack the lips.

Adj. savory, tasty; good, palatable; pleasing, nice, dainty, exquisite, delicate; delectable, toothsome, appetizing, delicious; rich, luscious, ambrosial, nectareous; distinctive.

395. UNSAVORINESS.—*N.* unsavoriness; acridness, sourness, etc., 397; acerbity; gall and wormwood.

V. be unpalatable, sicken, disgust, nauseate, pall, turn the stomach.

Adj. unsavory, unpalatable, ill-flavored; bitter, acrid, acrimonious.

offensive, repulsive, nasty, sickening, nauseous; loathsome; unpleasant, etc., 830.

396. SWEETNESS.—*N.* sweetness, saccharinity.

sugar, saccharin; preserve, jam, sugar candy, sugarplum.

sweets, confectionery, caramel, lollipop, bonbon, jujube, comfit, sweetmeat, confection; honey, manna; glucose, sirup, treacle, molasses, maple sirup, maple sugar; taffy, butterscotch.

Sweet beverages: nectar; mead, liqueur, sweet wine.

pastry, cake, pie, tart, puff, pudding.

V. sweeten, sugar, sugar off [*local*]; candy.

Adj. sweet, sugary, saccharine, candied, honied, luscious, cloying, honey-sweet, nectareous; dulcet, mellifluous.

397. SOURNESS.—*N*. sourness, acerbity, acidity; acid.

V. render sour, acidify, acidulate, acetify; ferment.

Adj. sour; acid, acidulated; subacid; tart, crabbed; hard, unripe, green; astringent, styptic.

(4) *Odor*

398. ODOR.—*N*. odor, smell, scent; effluvium; emanation, exhalation; fume, trail, redolence.

V. have an odor (*or* scent); smell, exhale; give out a smell (*or* odor); scent.

smell, scent, snuff, sniff, inhale.

Adj. odorous, odoriferous; strong-scented, redolent, pungent.

Relating to the sense of smell: olfactory; quick-scented, keen-scented.

399. INODOROUSNESS.—*N*. inodorousness, absence (*or* want) of smell.

deodorization; deodorizer, deodorant.

V. be inodorous (*or* scentless); not smell.

Adj. inodorous, scentless; without smell (*or* odor).

400. FRAGRANCE.—*N*. fragrance, aroma, redolence, perfume, bouquet; sweet smell (*or* odor), scent.

perfumery; incense, frankincense; musk, myrrh, attar, bergamot, balm, civet, potpourri, tuberose, hyacinth, heliotrope, rose, jasmine, lily, lily of the valley, violet, pomander; toilet water; eau de cologne [F.], cologne, cologne water.

bouquet, nosegay, posy [*colloq*.], boutonniere [F.], buttonhole [*colloq*.].

spray; wreath, garland, chaplet.

Scent containers: smelling bottle, scent bottle, vinaigrette; scent bag, sachet; thurible, censer, incense burner, atomizer, spray.

V. be fragrant (*or* scented); have a perfume (*or* aroma); smell sweet, scent, perfume; embalm.

Adj. fragrant, aromatic, redolent, spicy, balmy, scented; sweet-smelling, sweet-scented; perfumed; incense-breathing, ambrosial.

401. FETOR—*N*. fetor, bad smell (*or* odor), stench, stink, fetidness, fustiness, mustiness; rancidity; foulness.

V. have a bad smell, smell, stink, smell strong, smell offensively.

Adj. fetid; strong-smelling; high, bad, strong, offensive, noisome, rank, rancid, moldy, tainted, musty; smelling, stinking; putrid, rotten, foul; suffocating.

(5) *Sound*

402. SOUND.—*N.* sound, noise; sonority, sonorousness; strain; accent, twang, intonation; tune, cadence; audibility; resonance, vibration; voice, etc., 580.

Science of sound: acoustics, phonetics, phonology, phonography; telephony, radiophony.

V. sound, make a noise; give out sound, emit sound; resound.

Adj. sounding, sonorous, resonant, audible, distinct; auditory, acoustic.

phonetic, phonic, sonant.

403. SILENCE.—*N.* silence, stillness, quiet, peace, hush, lull; rest [*music*]; muteness; silence of the tomb (*or* grave).

V. silence, still, hush, stifle, muffle, gag, stop; muzzle, put to silence.

Adj. silent; still, stilly; noiseless, quiet, calm, soundless, hushed; speechless; aphonic, surd, mute.

solemn, soft, awful, deathlike.

Adv. in dead silence.

404. LOUDNESS.—*N.* loudness, power, vociferation, uproariousness.

din, loud noise, clang, clangor, clatter, noise, roar, uproar, hubbub, racket, hullabaloo, pandemonium; fracas; outcry, etc., 411; explosion, detonation.

blare, trumpet blast, flourish of trumpets, fanfare, blast; peal, swell, alarum, boom; resonance, etc., 408.

V. be loud (*or* deafening); peal, swell, clang, boom, thunder, roar; deafen, stun, rend the air, awake the echoes; resound, etc., 408; speak up, shout, etc. (*vociferate*), 411; bellow, etc. (*cry as an animal*), 412.

Adj. loud, sonorous, deep, full, powerful; noisy, blatant; clangorous, thundering, deafening, earsplitting, piercing; shrill, etc., 410; obstreperous, uproarious; clamorous, vociferous, fullmouthed, stentorian.

Adv. loudly, noisily; aloud; at the top of one's lungs, lustily, in full cry.

405. FAINTNESS.—*N.* faintness, inaudibility; faint sound, whisper, breath; undertone; murmur, hum, buzz, purr, lap [*of waves*], plash; sough, moan, rustle; tinkle.

hoarseness, huskiness.

silencer, muffler; soft pedal, damper, mute, sordine [*all music*].

V. whisper, breathe; mutter, etc. (*speak imperfectly*), 583.

murmur, purl, hum, gurgle, ripple, babble, flow; rustle; tinkle.

muffle, deaden, mute, subdue.

Adj. **faint,** low, dull; stifled, muffled; inaudible; hoarse, husky; gentle, soft; floating; purling, flowing; muttered; whispered; liquid; soothing; dulcet, etc. (*melodious*), 413.

Adv. **in a whisper,** with bated breath, *sotto voce* [It.]; between the teeth; aside; piano, pianissimo [*both music*]; out of earshot; inaudibly, faintly.

406. [Sudden and violent sounds] SNAP.—*N.* snap, etc., *v.*; toot, shout, yell, yap [*dial.*], yelp, bark.

report, thump, knock, clap, thud; burst, thunderclap, thunderburst, eruption, blowout [*tire*], explosion, discharge, detonation, firing, salvo, volley.

V. **snap,** rap, tap, knock; click; clash; crack, crackle; crash; pop; slam, bang, clap; thump, toot, yelp, bark, fire, explode, rattle, burst on the ear.

407. [Repeated and protracted sounds] ROLL.—*N.* roll, etc., *v.*; drumming, rumbling, howl, dingdong; ratatat, rubadub, tattoo; pitapat; quaver, clutter, charivari; racket; peal of bells, devil's tattoo; drumfire, barrage; whir, rattle, drone; reverberation.

V. **roll,** drum, boom; whir, rustle, tootle, roar, drone, rumble, rattle, clatter, patter, clack.

hum, trill, shake; chime, peal, toll; tick, beat.

408. RESONANCE.—*N.* resonance; ring, chime, ringing, clangor, bell note, tintinnabulation, vibration, reverberation.

bass; basso [It.], basso profundo [It.]; baritone, contralto; pedal point, organ point; snoring, snore.

V. **resound,** reverberate, re-echo; ring, sound; chink, clink; jingle, tinkle; chime; gurgle, mutter, murmur; plash, echo, ring in the ear.

Adj. **resonant,** reverberant, resounding, reverberating; deeptoned, deep-mouthed; hollow, sepulchral; gruff, etc. (*harsh*), 410.

408a. NONRESONANCE.—*N.* nonresonance, dead sound; thud, thump, muffled drums, cracked bell; damper, sordine, mute; muffler, silencer.

V. **muffle,** deaden, mute; sound dead; stop (*or* deaden) the sound.

Adj. **nonresonant,** dead, mute; muffled, deadened.

409. [Hissing sounds] SIBILATION.—*N.* sibilation, hissing; zip; hiss, buzz; sneezing, sternutation.

V. **hiss,** buzz, whiz; rustle; fizz, fizzle; wheeze, whistle, sizzle, swish.

Adj. **sibilant;** hissing; rustling; wheezy.

410. [Harsh or high sounds] STRIDENCY.—*N* stridency; stridor, harshness, raucousness; sharpness; creak, jar; creaking, grating; discord, dissonance.

high note, shrill note; soprano, treble, tenor, alto, falsetto; head voice, head tone; shriek, yell, cry, wail, pipe.

V. **grate,** creak, saw, snore, jar, burr, pipe, twang, jangle, clank; scream, etc. (*cry*), 411; set the teeth on edge, pierce (*or* split) the ears; yelp, etc. (*animal sound*), 412; buzz, etc. (*hiss*), 409.

Adj. **grating,** creaking, jangling, jarring, strident, harsh, coarse, hoarse, raucous; metallic; rough, rude; gruff, grum, sepulchral, hollow.

high, sharp, acute, shrill; piercing, high-pitched; cracked; discordant.

411. CRY.—*N.* **cry,** shout; shriek; hubbub; bark, etc. (*animal*), 412.

outcry, vociferation, ejaculation, hullabaloo, chorus, clamor, hue and cry, plaint; lungs; stentor.

V. **cry,** roar, shout, bawl; halloo, halloa, yo-ho, whoop; yell, bellow, hoot, boo; howl, scream, screech, shriek; shrill, squeak, squeal, squall; whine, pipe.

cheer, huzza, hurrah, yell.

moan, grumble, groan.

snort, snore; grunt, etc., 412.

vociferate, raise (*or* lift) the voice; yell out, call out, sing out, cry out; exclaim, give cry, clamor; rend the air; make the welkin ring; shout at the top of one's voice.

Adj. **clamorous,** clamant, vociferous; stentorian, etc. (*loud*), 404; open-mouthed; full-mouthed.

412. [Animal sounds] ULULATION.—*N.* **ululation,** howling, cry, roar; call, note, howl, bark, yelp, bowwow, belling; woodnote; insect cry; twittering, drone.

V. **ululate,** howl; cry, roar, bellow; bark, yelp; bay, bay the moon; yap, growl, snarl, howl; grunt, snort, squeak; neigh, bray; mew, purr, caterwaul; bleat, low, moo; crow, screech, croak, caw, coo, gobble, quack, cackle, cluck; chirp, cheep, chirrup, peep, sing, twitter; chatter, hoot, wail; hum, buzz; hiss; blat [*colloq.*].

413. MELODY. CONCORD.—*N.* **melody,** rhythm, measure; rhyme, etc. (*poetry*), 597; euphony.

Musical terms: pitch, timbre, intonation, tone, overtone.
orchestration, harmonization, modulation, phrasing.
staff *or* stave, line, space, brace; bar, rest; passage, phrase; trill *or* shake, turn, arpeggio [It.].
note, musical note, notes of a scale; sharp, flat, natural; high note, etc., 410; low note, etc., 408; interval; semitone.
breve, semibreve *or* whole note, minim *or* half note, crotchet *or* quarter note, quaver *or* eighth note, semiquaver *or* sixteenth note, demisemiquaver *or* thirty-second note; sustained note, drone.
scale, gamut; diapason; key, clef, chord.
harmony, concord; tonality; consonance; part; unison; chime.
Science of harmony: harmony, harmonics; thorough bass, counterpoint; composer.

opus (*pl. opera*) [L.], piece of music, etc., 415.

V. **harmonize,** chime, symphonize, transpose, orchestrate; blend, put in tune, tune, accord, string.

Adj. **harmonious,** harmonic, in concord, in tune, in concert, in unison.

melodious, musical, tuneful, tunable; sweet, dulcet, mellow, mellifluous; soft; clear, silvery; euphonious; enchanting, etc. (*pleasure-giving*), 829; fine-toned, silver-toned, full-toned, deep-toned.

414. DISCORD.—*N.* **discord,** dissonance, want of harmony; harshness, etc., 410; charivari, racket; Babel, pandemonium.

V. **be discordant** (*or* harsh); jar, etc. (*sound harshly*), 410.

Adj. **discordant,** dissonant, out of tune, tuneless; unmusical, untunable; unmelodious, inharmonious; singsong; harsh, etc., 410; jarring.

415. MUSIC.—*N.* **music;** minstrelsy; strain, tune, air, melody; piece of music; rondo, rondeau, pastoral; cavatina, fantasia, toccata [It.]; fugue, canon; potpourri, medley; incidental music; variations, roulade, cadenza, cadence, trill; serenade, nocturne.

instrumental music; orchestral score, full score; composition, opus (*pl. opera*) [L.]; concert piece; concerto [It.]; symphony, sonata, symphonic poem, tone poem; chamber music; movement; overture, prelude, voluntary; string quartet (*or* quintet).

lively music, polka, reel, etc. (*dance*), 848; ragtime, jazz; syncopation. martial music, march; allegro, presto.

slow music, Lydian measures; adagio, largo, andante; lullaby, cradle song, berceuse [F.]; dirge, etc. (*lament*), 839; dead march; minuet.

vocal music, vocalism; chant; psalm, psalmody, hymnology; hymn; canticle; oratorio; opera, operetta; cantata; song, lay, ballad, ditty, carol; recitative, aria.

solo, duet, trio, quartet, quintet, sestet, septet, double quartet, chorus; part song, descant, glee, madrigal, catch, round, chorale; antiphon; accompaniment; inside part, second, alto, tenor, bass; score, piano score, vocal score.

concert, musicale, recital, chamber concert, popular concert *or* pop [*colloq.*], open-air concert; serenade; community singing, singsong [*colloq.*].

method, solfeggio [It.], tonic sol-fa, sight singing, sight reading.

V. **compose,** write, etc., 416; attune, tune.

perform, execute, play, etc., 416.

Adj. **musical;** instrumental, vocal, choral, lyric, melodic; operatic; classic, modern, orchestral, symphonic, contrapuntal; program, imitative; harmonious, etc., 413.

416. MUSICIAN. [Performance of music]—*N.* **musician,** virtuoso, performer, player, minstrel; bard, etc. (*poet*), 597; accompanist, instrumentalist, organist, pianist, violinist, fiddler; flutist, harpist, fifer, trumpeter, cornetist, piper, drummer

orchestra; strings, woodwind, brass; band, brass band, military band German band, jazz band; street musicians.

vocalist, singer, warbler; songbird; songster, songstress; chorister; chorus singer; choir, chorus.

Orpheus, Apollo, the Muses, Polyhymnia, Erato, Euterpe, Terpsichore

conductor, choirmaster, bandmaster, concertmaster, drum major, song leader, precentor.

performance, execution, touch, expression.

V. **play,** tune, tune up, pipe, pipe up, strike up, sweep the chords, fiddle, strike the lyre, beat the drum; blow (*or* wind) the horn; twang, pluck, pick; pound, thump; drum, thrum, strum, beat time; execute, perform; accompany.

compose, set to music, arrange, harmonize, orchestrate.

sing, troll, chant, intone, hum, warble, twitter, carol, chirp, chirrup, lilt, quaver, trill, shake.

Adj. **musical;** lyric, dramatic; bravura, florid, brilliant.

417. MUSICAL INSTRUMENTS.—*N.* **musical instruments;** orchestra (*including* strings, woodwind, brass, and percussive instruments); band; string band, military band, brass band.

418. [Sense of sound] HEARING.—*N.* **hearing,** audition; audibility; acoustics; ear for music.

ear; eardrum, tympanum.

Instruments: ear trumpet, audiphone, dentiphone, speaking trumpet; phonograph, gramophone, graphophone, microphone, victrola; stethoscope; telephone, radiophone, wireless telephone, radio.

hearer, auditor, audience, listener; eavesdropper.

V. **hear,** overhear; hark, hearken; list, listen; strain one's ears, attend to, give attention, prick up one's ears; give ear, give a hearing to.

Adj. **hearing,** auditory, acoustic, phonic; auricular; auditive.

419. DEAFNESS—*N.* **deafness,** hardness of hearing, inaudibility; deaf-mute; deaf-and-dumb alphabet.

V. **deafen,** render deaf, stun, split the ears (*or* eardrum).

Adj. **deaf,** hard (*or* dull) of hearing; stunned, deafened; stone-deaf; inattentive.

inaudible, out of earshot (*or* hearing).

(6) *Light*

420. LIGHT.—*N.* **light,** ray, beam, stream (*of light*), gleam, streak; sunbeam, moonbeam; aurora, dawn, daylight, day, sunshine; glint, glare, glow, afterglow; sun, etc., 423.

reflection, refraction, dispersion.

halo, glory, nimbus, aureole, aura.

spark, scintilla, scintillation, flash, blaze, coruscation; flame, glare, blaze; lightning; phosphorescence.

luster, sheen, shimmer, gloss, brightness, brilliancy, splendor, effulgence; illumination, radiance, radiation.

Science of light: optics, radiometry; photography; phototelegraphy, radiotelegraphy; actinic rays, radioactivity; Röntgen rays, X rays, ultraviolet rays.

illuminant, gas, etc., 423.

V. shine, glow, beam, glitter, glisten, gleam; flare, blaze, glare, shimmer, glimmer, flicker, sparkle, scintillate, coruscate, flash.

daze, dazzle, bedazzle.

lighten, enlighten, light, irradiate, illume, illumine, illuminate; kindle, etc., 384.

Adj. luminous, lucent; light, sunny, bright, vivid, splendid, resplendent, refulgent, lustrous, brilliant, radiant, lambent; aglow.

shiny, glossy, burnished, glassy.

clear, cloudless, unclouded.

421. DARKNESS.—*N.* darkness, duskiness; blackness, swarthiness; obscurity, gloom, murk, murkiness; dusk; dimness, etc., 422.

night; midnight; dead of night.

shadow, shade; obscuration, adumbration; eclipse; radiograph.

V. darken, obscure, shade, dim; lower, overcast, overshadow, cloud, becloud, bedim.

extinguish, put out, blow out, snuff out.

Adj. dark, darkling, obscure; black, etc. (*color*), 431; nocturnal.

somber, dusky; dingy, lurid, gloomy, murky; shady, umbrageous; overcast, etc. (*dim*), 422; cloudy, etc., 426.

422. DIMNESS.—*N.* dimness, paleness, dullness, duskiness, mistiness.

twilight, dusk, nightfall, gloaming; dawn, daybreak, break of day, Aurora; moonlight, moonshine [*poetic*], starlight.

V. cloud over, gloom, lower.

twinkle, glimmer, flicker.

pale, fade, grow dim.

dim, bedim, obscure, shade, shadow, darken, cloud, becloud.

Adj. dim, dull, dingy, dusky, lackluster; cloudy, misty, hazy.

leaden, lurid, dun; overcast, dirty.

423. [Source of light] LUMINARY.—*N.* luminary; light, ray, beam; flame, etc. (*fire*), 382; spark, scintilla; phosphorescence.

Heavenly bodies: sun, orb of day, daystar [*poetic*]; star; constellation; galaxy, Milky Way; polestar, Polaris, morning star, Lucifer; evening star, Venus; moon, etc., 318.

sun god, Helios, Phoebus, Apollo, Hyperion, Ra [*Egypt*].

phosphorus; *ignis fatuus* [L.]; jack-o'-lantern, will-o'-the-wisp.

polar lights, northern lights, aurora borealis [L.], aurora australis [L.]; aurora.

Artificial light: gas, gaslight, electric light, electric torch; headlight, searchlight; spotlight, flashlight, limelight, calcium light; lamplight, lamp, lantern, dark lantern, bull's-eye; candle, taper, rushlight; torch, flambeau, brand; gaselier, chandelier; candelabrum, sconce, luster, candlestick; fireworks, pyrotechnics.

signal light, rocket, balefire, beacon fire; lighthouse.

V. illuminate, etc. (*light*), 420.

Adj. self luminous; phosphorescent; radiant, etc. (*light*), 420.

424. SHADE.—*N.* shade; awning, etc. (*cover*), 223.

screen, curtain, portiere [F.]; shutter, blind.

veil, mantle, mask.

cloud, mist, shadow; smoke screen [*mil.*].

blinkers, blinders; smoked glasses, colored spectacles.

V. veil, draw a curtain; cast a shadow, etc. (*darken*), 421.

Adj. shady, umbrageous, shadowy.

425. TRANSPARENCY.—*N.* transparency, transparence, translucence, diaphanousness; lucidity, limpidity; fluorescence; translumination.

V. be transparent (*or* pellucid); transmit light.

Adj. transparent, pellucid, lucid, diaphanous; translucent, limpid, clear, serene, crystalline.

426. OPACITY.—*N.* opacity, opaqueness; cloudiness; film; cloud, etc., 353.

V. be opaque; obstruct the passage of light.

Adj. opaque, impervious to light; dim, etc., 422; turbid, thick, muddy, cloudy, foggy, vaporous; smoky, murky, smeared, dirty.

427. SEMITRANSPARENCY.—*N.* semitransparency, opalescence, milkiness, pearliness; mist, haze, steam.

V. cloud, frost, cloud over, frost over.

Adj. semitransparent, semidiaphanous, semiopaque; opalescent, opaline; pearly, milky; frosted, hazy, misty.

428. [Specific Light] COLOR.—*N.* color, hue, tint, tinge, dye, complexion, shade, tincture; coloration; glow, flush; tone, key.

primary color, complementary color; coloring, keeping, tone, value.

spectrum, spectrum analysis; prism, spectroscope, kaleidoscope.

pigment, coloring matter, paint, dye, wash, distemper, stain; medium.

V. color, dye, tinge, stain, tint, tone; paint, wash, distemper, ingrain, grain, illuminate, emblazon.

Adj. colored, dyed; chromatic, prismatic; double-dyed.

bright, vivid, intense, deep; fresh, rich, gorgeous; bright-colored, gay.

gaudy, florid; garish; showy, flaunting; flashy; many-colored, parti-colored, variegated; raw, crude; glaring, flaring.

mellow, harmonious, pearly, sweet, delicate, subtle, tender.

dull, sad, somber, sad-colored, grave, gray, dark.

429. ABSENCE OF COLOR.—*N.* **decoloration,** discoloration; pallor, paleness, sallowness.

neutral tint, monochrome, black and white.

V. **lose color,** fade, become colorless, turn pale; pale, fade out.

deprive of color, decolor, wash out, tone down; whiten, bleach, blanch.

Adj. **colorless,** uncolored, hueless, pale, pallid; pale-faced, anemic; faint, dull, cold, muddy, leaden, dun, wan, sallow, dingy, ashy, ashen, ghastly, cadaverous, glassy, lackluster; discolored.

light-colored, fair, blond, ash-blond; white, etc., 430; towheaded.

430. WHITENESS.—*N.* **whiteness,** showiness, hoariness.

whitewash, whiting, whitening, calcimine.

V. **whiten,** bleach, blanch, silver, frost.

whitewash, calcimine, white.

Adj. **white,** snow-white, snowy, frosted, hoar, hoary; silvery, silver, milk-white, milky.

whitish, creamy, pearly, ivory, fair, blond, ash-blond; blanched; light.

431. BLACKNESS.—*N.* **blackness,** darkness, obscurity; swarthiness, swartness; lividness.

Negro, Negress, blackamoor, man of color, colored man, colored woman, nigger [*colloq.*, *usually contemptuous*], darky [*colloq.*], black, Ethiop, Ethiopian, Hottentot, Pygmy, Bushman, African.

V. **black,** blacken, blot, blotch, smut, smudge, smirch; darken, etc., 421.

Adj. **black,** sable, somber, livid, dark, inky, ebon, pitchy, sooty; swart, swarthy, dusky, dingy, murky; blotchy, smudgy; low-toned.

432. GRAY.—*N.* **gray,** etc., *adj.*; grayness; neutral tint, silver, dove color, pepper and salt, chiaroscuro [It.].

V. **render gray,** gray.

Adj. **gray;** iron-gray, dun, drab, dingy, leaden, pearly, dove-colored, silver, silvery, silvered; dapple-gray; ashen, ashy; grizzly, grizzled.

433. BROWN.—*N.* **brown,** etc., *adj.*; brownness.

V. **render brown,** brown, tan, embrown, bronze.

Adj. **brown,** nut-brown, seal-brown, mahogany, chocolate; fawn, ecru, tawny; tan, fawn-colored, snuff-colored, liver-colored.

reddish-brown, terra cotta, russet, foxy, bronze, coppery, copper-colored, maroon; bay, roan, sorrel; chestnut, henna, auburn, hazel.

sunburned; tanned, etc., *v.*

434. RED.—*N.* **red,** etc., *adj.*; flesh color, flesh tint, color, warmth, redness, ruddiness, blush.

V. **redden,** rouge, crimson, incarnadine; ruddle, rust.

blush, flush, color, color up, mantle, redden.

Adj. **red,** scarlet, cardinal, vermilion, carmine, crimson, pink, rose, cerise, cherry, salmon, maroon, carnation, magenta, solferino, damask.

reddish; sanguine, bloody, gory; coral, coralline, rosy, roseate; blood-red, wine-red, wine-colored, ruby, rufous, bricky, reddish-brown, etc., 433; rose (*or* ruby, cherry, claret, flame, flesh, peach, salmon, brick, rust) -colored.

red-complexioned, red-faced, florid, burned, rubicund, ruddy, red, high-colored, glowing, sanguine, blooming, rosy, hectic, flushed, inflamed.

Of hair: sandy, carroty, brick-red, Titian, auburn, chestnut.

435. GREEN.—*N.* green, etc., *adj.*; greenness, verdancy, verdure.

Adj. **green,** verdant, olive; verdurous; emerald (*or* pea, grass, apple, sea, leaf, bottle, Irish, Kelly) green; greenish, aquamarine, blue-green.

436. YELLOW.—*N.* **yellow,** etc., *adj.*; yellowness; jaundice.

V. **render yellow,** yellow, gild.

Adj. **yellow,** aureate, golden, gold, gilt, gilded, lemon, fallow; sallow, jaundiced; tawny, cream, creamy; flaxen, yellowish, buff; gold (*or* saffron, citron, lemon, amber, straw, primrose, cream) -colored.

437. PURPLE.—*N.* **purple,** etc., *adj.*; royal purple; gridelin, amethyst; damson, heliotrope.

V. **render purple,** purple, empurple.

Adj. **purple,** violet, plum-colored, lavender, lilac, puce, mauve, purplish, amethystine, magenta, solferino, heliotrope; livid; purplish.

438. BLUE.—*N.* **blue,** etc., *adj.*; azure [*her.*]; indigo; sapphire, blueness, bluishness; bloom.

Adj. **blue,** azure, cerulean, sky-blue, navy-blue, midnight-blue, cadet-blue, robin's-egg-blue, baby-blue, ultramarine, aquamarine, electric-blue, steel-blue; bluish; cold.

439. ORANGE.—*N.* **orange,** old gold; gold color, etc., *adj.*

Adj. **orange,** orange (*or* gold, brass, apricot) -colored; warm, hot, glowing, flame-colored.

440. VARIEGATION.—*N.* **variegation;** iridescence, play of colors, spottiness; tricolor.

check, plaid, tartan, patchwork; marquetry, parquet, parquetry, mosaic, checkerwork; chessboard, checkers; harlequin.

V. **variegate,** stripe, streak, checker, fleck, speckle, besprinkle,

sprinkle; stipple, dot, tattoo, inlay, tessellate; damascene; embroider, quilt.

Adj. **variegated,** many-colored, many-hued, divers-colored, parti-colored, polychromatic; kaleidoscopic.

iridescent, opaline, opalescent, prismatic, pearly, shot, tortoise-shell.

mottled, pied, piebald, skewbald; motley, marbled, pepper-and-salt, dappled.

checkered, checked, plaid, mosaic, tessellated.

spotted, spotty; powdered; speckled, freckled, flea-bitten, studded; flecked.

barred, veined, brindled, tabby, watered.

441. [Perception of light] **VISION.**—*N.* vision, sight, optics, eyesight.

view, look, glance, ken, glimpse, glint, peep, peek; gaze, stare, leer; contemplation, regard, survey; inspection, reconnaissance, watch, espionage, autopsy; sight-seeing, globe-trotting [*colloq.*].

viewpoint, standpoint, point of view; loophole, watchtower.

field of view; theater, amphitheater, arena, vista, horizon; bird's-eye view, panoramic view.

eye, visual organ, organ of vision, naked eye; clear (*or* sharp, quick, eagle) sight.

V. **see,** behold, discern, perceive, descry, sight, make out; discover, distinguish, recognize, spy, espy, command a view of; witness, contemplate, look on, see at a glance.

look, view, eye, survey, scan, inspect; reconnoiter, glance, cast a glance; observe, etc. (*attend to*), 457; watch, keep watch · watch for, etc. (*expect*), 507; peep, peek, peer, pry, take a peep.

look intently; strain one's eyes; rivet the eyes upon, stare, gaze; pore over, gloat on, gloat over; leer, ogle, glare; goggle; squint, gloat, look askance.

Adj. **ocular,** visual, optic *or* optical; ophthalmic; visible, etc , 446.

clear-sighted, clear-eyed, farsighted; eagle-eyed, hawk-eyed, lynx-eyed, keen-eyed, Argus-eyed.

Adv. **at sight,** at first sight, at a glance, at the first blush

442. BLINDNESS.—*N.* blindness, sightlessness, benightedness, cataract; dim-sightedness, etc., 443; Braille.

V. **be blind,** not see; lose one's sight; grope in the dark.

blind, blindfold, hoodwink, dazzle; put one's eyes out; throw dust into one's eyes; screen, hide.

Adj. **blind,** eyeless, sightless, visionless; dark; stone-blind, stark-blind, undiscerning; dim-sighted, etc., 443.

Adv. **blindly,** blindfold; darkly.

443. DIM-SIGHTEDNESS.—*N.* **Imperfect vision:** dim (*or* short, near, long) -sightedness; purblindness, blearedness, myopia, astigmatism; color blindness, snow blindness; ophthalmia; cataract.

squint, cross-eye, cast in the eye, swivel eye, cockeye, goggle-eyes.

Limitation of vision: blinker, blinder; screen, curtain, veil.

Fallacies of vision: refraction, distortion, illusion, mirage, phantasm, phantom; vision; specter, apparition, ghost; will-o'-the-wisp, etc., 423.

V. **be dim-sighted,** see double; see through a glass darkly; wink, blink, squint, look askance, screw up the eyes, glare, glower.

dazzle, glare, swim, blur.

Adj. **dim-sighted,** myopic, nearsighted, shortsighted, astigmatic; blear-eyed, goggle-eyed, one-eyed; half-blind, purblind; cockeyed [*colloq.*], dim-eyed, mole-eyed.

444. SPECTATOR.—*N.* **spectator,** beholder, observer, looker-on, onlooker, witness, eyewitness, bystander, passer-by; sight-seer; rubberneck [*slang*].

spy, scout; sentinel, etc. (*warning*), 668.

grandstand [*fig.*], bleachers [*fig.*], gallery.

V. witness, behold, etc. (*see*), 441; look on, etc. (*be present*), 186.

445. OPTICAL INSTRUMENTS.—*N.* **optical instruments;** lens, magnifier, microscope; spectacles, glasses, goggles, eyeglass, pince-nez; periscope; telescope, glass, lorgnette, binocular; spyglass, opera glass, field glass; burning glass, convex lens; prism.

camera, hand camera, kodak [*trade name*]; moving-picture machine, magic lantern, stereopticon; stereoscope, kaleidoscope.

mirror, reflector, speculum; looking glass, pier glass, cheval glass.

optics, optician; photography, photographer; optometry, optometrist; microscopy, microscopist.

446. VISIBILITY.—*N.* **visibility,** perceptibility, conspicuousness, distinctness, appearance, etc., 448; exposure; manifestation, etc., 525; ocular demonstration; field of view, vista, horizon.

V. **appear,** open to the view; catch the eye; present (*or* show, manifest, reveal, expose, betray) itself; stand forth, stand out; materialize; show; arise; peep out, peer out; start up, spring up; gleam, glimmer, glitter, glow, loom; glare; burst forth; burst upon the view; heave in sight [*naut. or colloq.*]; come into view, come out, come forth, come forward; attract the attention, etc., 457.

expose to view, show, display.

Adj. visible, perceptible, discernible, apparent; in view, in full view, in sight; exposed to view.

distinct, plain, clear, definite; obvious, etc. (*manifest*), 525; recognizable; glaring, palpable, staring, conspicuous.

Adv. before one, under one's very eyes, in sight of.

447. INVISIBILITY.—*N.* invisibility, imperceptibility; indistinctness; mystery; latency, obscurity; concealment, mystification.

V. **be invisible** (*or* imperceptible); be hidden, etc. (*hide*), 528; escape notice.

render invisible; conceal, etc., 528; put out of sight.

Adj. **invisible,** imperceptible; out of sight, not in sight, unseen; viewless; inconspicuous; covert, latent.

indistinct; dim; mysterious, dark, obscure; confused, indistinguishable, shadowy, indefinite, undefined, ill-defined, blurred, out of focus; misty, veiled, concealed.

448. APPEARANCE.—*N.* **appearance,** phenomenon, sight, show, scene, view; lookout, outlook, prospect, vista, perspective, bird's-eye view, scenery, landscape, seascape, picture, tableau; display, exposure, rising of the curtain.

spectacle, pageant; peep show, magic lantern, biograph, cinematograph, cinema [*colloq.*], moving pictures, movies [*colloq.*], photoplay, photodrama; panorama.

aspect, angle, phase, shape, form, guise, look, complexion, color, image, mien, air, cast, carriage, port, demeanor; presence, expression, point of view, light.

lineament, feature, trait, lines; outline, outside; contour, silhouette, face, countenance, visage, profile; physiognomy.

V. **appear,** be visible, seem, look, show; cut a figure, figure; present to the view; show, etc. (*make manifest*), 525; look like, resemble.

Adj. **apparent,** seeming, ostensible; on view.

Adv. **to all appearance,** ostensibly, seemingly, on the face of it, at the first blush, at first sight, to the eye.

449. DISAPPEARANCE.—*N.* **disappearance,** evanescence, eclipse; departure, exit; vanishing point.

V. **disappear,** vanish, dissolve, fade, melt away, pass, go, depart, be gone, leave no trace; be lost to view (*or* sight), pass out of sight.

efface, etc., 552.

Adj. **disappearing,** evanescent; missing, lost; lost to sight.

CLASS IV

I. FORMATION OF IDEAS

450. INTELLECT.—*N*. **intellect,** mind, understanding, reason; rationality; intellectual faculties (*or* powers); senses, consciousness, observation, intellectuality, mentality, intelligence; conception, judgment, wits, brains, parts, capacity, genius; wit; ability; wisdom; ideality, idealism.

ego, soul, spirit; heart, breast, bosom; subconscious self, subliminal consciousness.

seat of thought, brain; head, headpiece; skull, cranium.

Science of mind: psychology, psychoanalysis; psychophysics; metaphysics; philosophy.

psychical research; telepathy, thought transference, thought reading; clairaudience; clairvoyance, mediumship; spiritualism, etc., 992*a*.

V. **reason,** understand, think, reflect, cogitate, conceive, judge, contemplate, meditate; ruminate, etc. (*think*), 451.

note, notice, mark; take notice of; be aware of, realize; appreciate.

Adj. **intellectual,** mental, rational; psychological; conscious, percipient, brainy [*colloq*.].

hyperphysical, subconscious, subliminal; telepathic, clairvoyant; psychic *or* psychical, spiritual, metaphysical, transcendental.

450a. ABSENCE OF INTELLECT.—*N*. **want of intellect** (*or* mind, understanding); unintellectuality; imbecility, etc., 490.

Adj. **unendowed with** (*or* void of) reason; unintelligent, etc. (*imbecile*), 499.

451. THOUGHT.—*N*. **thought;** reflection, cogitation, consideration, meditation, study, speculation, deliberation, brainwork, cerebration; close study, application.

mature thought; afterthought, reconsideration, second thoughts; retrospection, examination.

abstraction, abstract thought, contemplation, musing; reverie, etc., 458; depth of thought.

V. **think,** reflect, cogitate, consider, reason, deliberate: contemplate, meditate, ponder, muse, dream, ruminate, speculate; brood over, con over, study; bend (*or* apply) the mind; digest, discuss, hammer at, hammer out; weigh, realize, appreciate; fancy.

harbor, cherish, entertain, nurture (*as an idea*), imagine; bear in mind; reconsider.

suggest itself, present itself, occur to; come into one's head; strike one, come uppermost; enter (or cross, flash across, occupy) the mind.

Adj. thoughtful, pensive, meditative, reflective, cogitative, contemplative, speculative, deliberative, studious, introspective, philosophical.

absorbed, rapt; lost in thought; engrossed in, intent.

Adv. all things considered, taking everything into consideration (or account).

452. ABSENCE OF THOUGHT.—*N.* vacancy of mind, poverty of intellect; thoughtlessness, etc. (*inattention*), 458; inanity, fatuity, vacuity.

V. put away thought; relax (or divert) the mind; make the mind a blank, let the mind lie fallow; indulge in reverie, etc. (*be inattentive*), 458.

Adj. vacant, inane, unintellectual, unoccupied, unthinking, irrational, unreasoning, thoughtless, inattentive; diverted; bigoted, narrow-minded.

453. [Object of thought] IDEA.—*N.* idea, notion, conception, thought; apprehension, impression, perception; sentiment. reflection, observation, consideration; abstract idea.

view, opinion, theory; conceit, fancy; fantasy, etc., 515.

viewpoint, point of view; aspect, angle; field of view.

454. [Subject of thought] TOPIC.—*N.* subject, subject matter; matter, motif. theme, topic, thesis, text, business, affair. matter in hand, argument; motion, resolution, case, point, proposition, theorem· field of inquiry; moot point, point at issue; problem, etc. (*question*), 461.

V. enter the mind, etc., 451.

Adv. under consideration, under advisement; in question. in the mind; at issue, before the house, on foot, on the carpet.

455. [Desire of knowledge] CURIOSITY.—*N.* curiosity; inquisitiveness; interest, thirst for knowledge, mental acquisitiveness, inquiring mind.

investigator, inquirer, etc., 461.

busybody, newsmonger; Peeping Tom, Paul Pry, eavesdropper; gossip.

V. be curious; take an interest in, investigate; stare, gape; see the sights.

pry, nose, search, ferret out.

Adj. curious, inquiring, etc., 461; inquisitive, burning with curiosity, overcurious, prying; inquisitorial; agape, expectant.

456. [Absence of curiosity] INCURIOSITY.—*N.* incuriosity; incuriousness; apathy, unconcern, indifference.

V. be incurious (*or* indifferent); have no curiosity, etc., 455; be bored by, take no interest in.

Adj. incurious, uninquisitive, indifferent; impassive, etc., 823; uninterested, bored.

457. ATTENTION.—*N.* **attention;** intentness, alertness; thought, etc., 451; observance, observation; consideration, reflection; heed; heedfulness; notice, regard; circumspection, etc. (*care*), 459; study, scrutiny; inspection, revision, revisal.

minuteness, circumstantiality, attention to detail.

V. **attend,** watch, observe, look, see, view, notice, regard, take notice, mark; pay attention to, give heed to; occupy oneself with; contemplate, etc. (*think of*), 451, look to, see to; heed, mind, take cognizance of, entertain, recognize; make (*or* take) note of; note.

examine, scan, scrutinize, consider; overhaul, revise, pore over; inspect, review.

revert to, hark back to; come to the point.

meet with attention; attract notice, fall under one's notice; be under consideration.

call attention to, bring under one's notice; point out (*or* to, at), indicate; direct attention to; show; bring forward.

Adj. **attentive,** mindful, heedful, observant, regardful; alive to, awake to, on the job [*colloq.*], alert; taken up with, occupied with; engrossed in, wrapped in, absorbed, rapt; watchful; intent on, open-eyed; on the watch.

458. INATTENTION.—*N.* **inattention,** inconsideration, want of consideration, inconsiderateness; oversight; inadvertence, disregard; want of thought; heedlessness, etc. (*neglect*), 460; unconcern.

abstraction; absence of mind, absorption, preoccupation, distraction, reverie, brown study [*colloq.*], woolgathering.

V. **be inattentive** (*or* unobservant); overlook, disregard; pass by, neglect; think little of; pay no attention to; dismiss from one's mind; drop the subject, think no more of; turn a deaf ear to.

confuse, disconcert, discompose, perplex, bewilder, fluster, flurry; call off *or* distract the attention (thoughts, mind); put out of one's head.

Adj. **inattentive,** unobservant, undiscerning, unmindful, unheeding, regardless; listless, apathetic; blind, deaf; volatile, scatter-brained, flighty, giddy; unreflecting; inconsiderate, thoughtless; wild, harum-scarum [*colloq.*], heedless, careless, neglectful.

abstracted, absent, distrait [F.], woolgathering, dreamy; dazed, absent-minded; lost in thought; rapt, in the clouds, daydreaming; preoccupied, engrossed; in a reverie; off one's guard; caught napping.

459. CARE. [Vigilance]—*N.* **care,** solicitude, anxiety; heed, concern, heedfulness; scruple.

vigilance; watchfulness, surveillance, watch, vigil, lookout, watch and ward; espionage, reconnoitering; watching.

alertness, attention, prudence, forethought, circumspection, precaution, caution; accuracy, exactness; minuteness, attention to detail.

watcher, watchman, watchdog.

V. **be careful,** take care, be cautious; take precautions; pay attention to, etc., 457; take care of; look *or* see to, look after, keep an eye upon; chaperon, matronize, keep watch, mount guard, watch.

Adj. **careful,** regardful, heedful; prudent, discreet, cautious; considerate, thoughtful; provident; alert; sure-footed.

guarded, on one's guard; on the alert (*or* watch, lookout); awake, vigilant; watchful, wakeful, Argus-eyed, lynx-eyed.

scrupulous, punctilious, conscientious; tidy, orderly; clean; accurate, exact.

Adv. **carefully,** with care, gingerly.

460. NEGLECT.—*N.* **neglect;** carelessness; negligence; omission, procrastination; supineness, apathy; inattention, etc., 458; imprudence, improvidence, recklessness; slovenliness, untidiness; dirt; inexactness, inaccuracy.

trifler, waiter on providence; Micawber; slacker.

V. **neglect,** take no care of, let slip, let go; lose sight of.

delay, defer, procrastinate, postpone, adjourn, pigeonhole, shelve, table, lay on the table.

overlook, disregard; pass over, pass by; let pass; wink at, connive at.

scamp; trifle, slight, slur; skim, skip, take a cursory view of, run over, dip into; slur *or* slip over; push aside, throw into the background, sink; ignore; forget.

Adj. **neglectful,** negligent, remiss; heedless, careless; thoughtless, inconsiderate; perfunctory, offhand.

unwary, unwatchful, unguarded, off one's guard.

supine, apathetic; inattentive, etc., 458; nonchalant, indifferent; imprudent, reckless; slovenly, disorderly; dirty; inexact, inaccurate; improvident, unthrifty.

neglected, unheeded, uncared for, unattended to; abandoned, shunted, shelved.

461. INQUIRY. [Subject of inquiry. QUESTION.]—*N.* **inquiry;** request, etc., 765; search, research, quest; pursuit, prosecution.

examination, review, scrutiny, investigation; inquest, inquisition; trial; exploration; exploitation, ventilation; sifting; calculation, analysis, dissection; study, consideration.

reconnoitering, reconnaissance, espionage.

questioning, interrogation, interrogatory; challenge, examination, third degree [*colloq*.], cross-examination; discussion; catechism.

question, query, problem, poser, desideratum, point (*or* matter) in dispute; moot point; issue, question at issue; bone of contention, enigma, etc. (*secret*), 533; knotty point.

inquirer, investigator, inquisitor, inspector, querist, examiner, catechist; scrutator, scrutinizer; analyst.

V. inquire, seek, search, make inquiry, look for, scan, reconnoiter, explore, sound, rummage, ransack, pry, peer, look round; overhaul; look behind the scenes; nose, nose out, trace up; hunt out, fish out, ferret out; unearth.

track, seek a clue; hunt, trail, shadow, mouse, dodge, trace, pursue, experiment, etc., 463.

examine, study, consider, calculate; dip *or* dive into, probe, sound, fathom, scrutinize, analyze, anatomize, dissect, parse, resolve, sift, winnow, thresh out; investigate, look into, discuss, canvass, subject to examination, quiz, pose; audit, tax, pass in review.

question, ask, demand; interrogate, catechize, pump; cross-question, cross-examine; grill [*colloq*], put through the third degree [*colloq*.].

Adj. inquiring, inquisitive, catechetical, inquisitorial, analytic; interrogative.

undetermined, undecided, tentative; in question, in dispute, in issue, under consideration; moot, proposed; doubtful, etc. (*uncertain*), 475.

462. ANSWER.—*N.* answer, response, reply, rejoinder; retort, repartee; antiphon, acknowledgment; password; echo; counter-statement, countercharge, contradiction.

[Law] defense, plea, reply, rejoinder, rebutter, surrebutter, surrejoinder.

solution, explanation; discovery, disclosure; cause; clue.

oracle, etc., 513.

V. answer, respond, reply, rebut, retort, rejoin; give answer; acknowledge, echo.

[Law] defend, reply, surrejoin, surrebut, plead, rebut.

explain, interpret; solve, etc. (*unriddle*), 522; discover, fathom, hunt out, inquire; satisfy, set at rest, determine.

Adj. responsive, respondent, antiphonal; oracular; conclusive.

463. EXPERIMENT.—*N.* experiment, essay, trial, attempt;

analysis, investigation; verification, probation, proof, criterion, diagnosis, test, crucial test; assay, ordeal.

speculation, random shot, leap in the dark; feeler, pilot balloon.

experimenter, experimentalist, assayer, analyst; prospector, adventurer; speculator, gambler, stock gambler, plunger [*slang*].

V. experiment, essay, try, venture, make an experiment, make trial of; rehearse; put to the test, prove, verify, test.

grope, grope for, feel one's way, fumble, throw out a feeler; send up a pilot balloon; see how the land lies (*or* wind blows); feel the pulse; fish for, angle, trawl, cast one's net.

Adj. experimental, probationary; analytic, speculative, tentative, empirical.

on trial, on examination, on *or* under probation, under suspicion; on one's trial.

464. COMPARISON.—*N.* comparison, contrast, parallelism, balance; identification; simile, similitude, allegory, etc. (*metaphor*), 521.

V. compare, collate, confront, contrast, balance; parallel.

Adj. comparative, relative, contrastive; metaphorical, etc., 521.

Adv. relatively; as compared with.

465. DISCRIMINATION.—*N.* discrimination, distinction, differentiation, diagnosis, nice perception; estimation; nicety, refinement, taste, judgment; tact, discernment, acuteness, penetration.

V. discriminate, distinguish, separate; draw the line, sift; estimate, etc. (*measure*), 466; sum up, criticize; take into account, weigh carefully.

Adj. discriminating, critical, diagnostic, perceptive, discriminative, distinctive; nice, acute.

465a. INDISCRIMINATION.—*N.* indiscrimination, indistinction; want of discernment; uncertainty, etc. (*doubt*), 475.

V. confound, confuse, jumble, heap indiscriminately; swallow whole.

Adj. indiscriminate, indistinguishable, lacking distinction, undistinguished, undistinguishable; promiscuous, undiscriminating.

466. MEASUREMENT.—*N.* measurement, mensuration, survey, valuation, appraisement, assessment, estimate, estimation; dead reckoning [*naut.*]; reckoning, gauging; horsepower, candle power.

measure, gauge; yard measure, standard, rule, foot rule, spirit level, plumb line; square, T-square, steel square, compass, dividers, calipers; log, log line, patent log [*naut.*]; meter, line, rod, check.

flood mark, high-water mark, load-line mark.

scale; graduation, graduated scale; vernier, quadrant, theodolite; beam, steelyard, weighing machine, balance

latitude and longitude, altitude and azimuth.

geometry: topography, cartography; surveying, land surveying

surveyor, land surveyor, topographer, cartographer.

V. measure, meter; value, assess, rate, appraise, estimate, form an estimate; standardize; span, pace, step, inch, divide, gauge, balance, poise, weigh; plumb, probe, sound, fathom; survey, plot, block in, block out, rule, draw to scale.

Adj. metrical, metric; measurable; topographic *or* topographical, cartographic *or* cartographical.

467. [Materials for reasoning] **EVIDENCE.**—*N.* evidence; facts, premises, data, grounds, proof; confirmation, corroboration, ratification, authentication.

testimony, attestation; affirmation, declaration; deposition.

authority, warrant, credential, diploma, voucher, certificate, document, deed, warranty; autograph, handwriting, signature, seal, countersign; exhibit; citation, reference, quotation; admission, etc. (*assent*), 488.

witness, eyewitness, deponent [*law*]; sponsor.

writ, summons, etc. (*lawsuit*), 696.

V. evince, show, betoken, indicate, denote, imply, involve, argue, bespeak.

have weight, carry weight; tell, speak volumes, speak for itself.

testify, bear witness, give evidence, depose, witness, vouch for; certify, attest, acknowledge.

confirm, ratify, corroborate, indorse, support, bear out, vindicate, uphold, warrant.

adduce, evidence, cite, quote; refer to, call, call to witness; bring forward, bring into court; allege, plead.

establish, make out a case; authenticate, substantiate, verify, make good.

Adj. evidential, indicative, deducible, inferential, firsthand, authentic, documentary; cumulative, corroborative, confirmatory; significant, weighty, overwhelming, conclusive.

oral, hearsay, circumstantial, presumptive.

Adv. by inference; according to, in corroboration of.

468. COUNTEREVIDENCE.—*N.* counterevidence, rejoinder, disproof, refutation, negation, denial; plea, etc., 617; vindication.

V. refute, rebut, oppose; confute, etc. (*refute*), 479; subvert; destroy, check, weaken; contravene; contradict, deny, alter the case; turn the tables; prove a negative.

Adj. contradictory, conflicting; unattested, unauthenticated, unsupported, supposititious, trumped up.

Adv. on the other hand (*or* side), in opposition; in rebuttal.

469. QUALIFICATION.—*N.* qualification, limitation, modification, coloring; allowance, consideration, extenuating circumstances; mitigation.

condition, proviso, exception; exemption; saving clause.

V. **qualify,** limit, modify, affect, give a color to, narrow, temper; allow for, take into account.

Adj. **qualifying,** extenuating, palliative; conditional; exceptional; hypothetical, contingent.

Adv. **provided,** if, unless, but, yet; according as; conditionally, admitting, supposing; even, although, though.

470. POSSIBILITY.—*N.* **possibility,** potentiality, practicability, feasibility, workableness; potency; compatibility, etc. (*agreement*), 23.

contingency, chance, etc., 156.

V. **be possible,** stand a chance; admit of, bear.

render possible, put in the way of, bring to bear, bring together.

Adj. **possible,** conceivable, imaginable, credible; compatible, etc., 23; likely.

practicable, feasible, workable, achievable; within reach, accessible, surmountable; attainable, obtainable.

Adv. **possibly,** perhaps, perchance, peradventure, haply.

471. IMPOSSIBILITY.—*N.* **impossibility,** impracticability, incredibility, hopelessness, infeasibility; discrepancy.

V. **attempt impossibilities;** square the circle, find the elixir of life, discover the philosopher's stone, discover the grand panacea, find the fountain of youth, discover the secret of perpetual motion; make bricks without straw; weave a rope of sand; be in two places at once; gather grapes from thorns.

Adj. **impossible,** not possible, absurd, contrary to reason, unlikely, unreasonable, incredible, visionary, impractical, inconceivable, improbable, unimaginable, unthinkable.

impracticable, unachievable, infeasible; insuperable, insurmountable, inaccessible, unattainable, unobtainable; out of the question; incompatible, etc., 24; impassable, impervious, self-contradictory.

472. PROBABILITY.—*N.* **probability,** likelihood, likeness, verisimilitude, plausibility; color, semblance, show of; presumption; credibility; prospect; chance, etc., 156.

V. **be probable,** lend color to; point to; imply, bid fair, promise, stand (*or* run) a good chance.

presume, infer, venture, suppose, take for granted, flatter oneself; expect, etc., 507; count upon, etc. (*believe*), 484.

Adj. **probable,** likely, hopeful, presumable, presumptive, apparent.

plausible, specious, ostensible, colorable, reasonable, credible.

Adv. **in all probability,** most likely, apparently, seemingly, to all appearance.

473. IMPROBABILITY.—*N.* **improbability,** unlikelihood; bare possibility; long odds; incredibility.

V. **be improbable,** go beyond reason, strain one's credulity; have a small chance.

Adj. **improbable,** unlikely, rare, unheard of, inconceivable; unimaginable, incredible.

474. CERTAINTY.—*N.* **certainty;** necessity, etc., 601; certitude, sureness, surety, assurance; infallibility, reliability, inevitableness; fact; positive fact, matter of fact.

bigotry, positiveness, dogmatism, dogmatization; fanaticism.

dogmatist, doctrinaire, bigot; zealot, fanatic.

V. **render certain,** insure, assure; clinch, make sure; determine, decide; know, etc. (*believe*), 484.

Adj. **certain,** sure, inevitable, assured, solid, well founded.

unqualified, absolute, positive, definite, clear, unequivocal, categorical, unmistakable, decisive.

conclusive, undeniable, unquestionable; indisputable, incontestable, indubitable; irrefutable; final; undoubted, unquestioned, undisputed; questionless.

authoritative, authentic, official.

evident, manifest; self-evident, axiomatic.

infallible, unerring; unchangeable, etc., 150; trustworthy, reliable.

dogmatic, opinionated, dictatorial, doctrinaire; fanatical, bigoted.

Adv. **certainly,** undoubtedly, indubitably; for certain, surely, no doubt, doubtless, to be sure, of course, as a matter of course, in truth, truly, without fail.

475. UNCERTAINTY.—*N.* **uncertainty,** incertitude, doubt, doubtfulness, dubiousness.

hesitation, suspense, perplexity, embarrassment, dilemma, bewilderment; puzzle, quandary; timidity, etc. (*fear*), 860; vacillation, wavering, indetermination.

vagueness, haze, fog, obscurity, ambiguity, open question, blind bargain, pig in a poke, leap in the dark.

fallibility, unreliability, untrustworthiness; precariousness.

V. **hesitate,** flounder, miss one's way, wander aimlessly, beat about; lose oneself, lose one's head.

perplex, pose, puzzle, confuse, confound, bewilder, nonplus.

doubt, etc. (*disbelieve*), 485.

Adj. **uncertain,** unsure; casual, random, aimless, doubtful, dubious; insecure, unstable, indecisive, irresolute; unsettled, undecided, undetermined, in question; experimental, tentative.

vague, indefinite, ambiguous, equivocal, undefined, confused; mysterious, cryptic, veiled, obscure, undefinable; oracular.

perplexing, enigmatic, paradoxical, apocryphal, problematical.

fallible, questionable, debatable, untrustworthy, unreliable.

puzzled, perplexed; lost, astray, adrift, at sea, at fault, at a loss, at one's wit's end, distracted, distraught.

476. REASONING.—*N.* **reasoning,** ratiocination; inference, induction, generalization.

logic, art of reasoning, dialectics; deduction, induction; synthesis, analysis; syllogism.

discussion, comment; ventilation; inquiry, etc., 461.

argumentation, controversy, debate; polemics, wrangling, contention.

argument, case, plea, proposition, terms, premises, data, principle.

arguments, reasons, pros and cons.

reasoner, logician, dialectician, casuist; disputant, controversialist; wrangler, arguer, debater.

V. **reason,** argue, discuss, debate, dispute, contend, wrangle; chop logic; controvert, deny; canvass; consider, examine.

Adj. **reasoning,** rational; argumentative, controversial, dialectic, polemical; disputatious.

logical, syllogistic, inductive, deductive, synthetic *or* synthetical, analytic *or* analytical; relevant, germane.

Adv. **for,** because, hence, whence, seeing that, since, then, thence, so; whereas, considering, therefore, wherefore; consequently, *ergo* [L.], thus, accordingly.

finally, in conclusion, in fine, after all, on the whole.

477. [Absence of reasoning] INTUITION. [Specious reasoning] SOPHISTRY.—*N.* **intuition;** instinct, association of ideas; rule of thumb; presentiment.

sophistry, casuistry, equivocation, evasion, mental reservation, chicanery; perversion, mystification; speciousness; nonsense, etc., 497; hairsplitting, quibbling; begging of the question.

sophism, quibble, quirk, fallacy, subterfuge, shift, subtlety; inconsistency; claptrap.

V. **pervert,** quibble, equivocate, mystify, evade, elude; gloss over, varnish; misteach, etc., 538; mislead, etc. (*error*), 495; misrepresent, etc. (*lie*), 544; cavil, refine, split hairs; misjudge, etc., 481; beg the question, reason in a circle.

Adj. **intuitive,** instinctive, impulsive.

illogical, unreasonable, false, unsound, invalid; unwarranted, gratuitous; incongruous, inconsequent, inconsequential; unconnected; inconsistent; unscientific; untenable, inconclusive, incorrect, fallacious, groundless, unproved.

specious, sophistic *or* sophistical, casuistic; deceptive, illusive, illusory, hollow, plausible; evasive; irrelevant, inapplicable.

weak, feeble, poor, flimsy, loose, vague, irrational; nonsensical, absurd, foolish, etc. (*imbecile*), 499; frivolous; pettifogging, quibbling.

478. DEMONSTRATION.—N. demonstration, proof; conclusiveness; evidence, etc., 467; verification, etc., 462.

V. **demonstrate,** prove, establish, make good; show, evince, verify, etc., 467; settle the question.

follow; stand to reason; hold good, hold water [*colloq.*].

Adj. **demonstrative;** demonstrable; unanswerable, conclusive, decisive, convincing; irresistible, irrefutable, undeniable.

demonstrated, proved; unconfuted, unanswered, unrefuted; evident, self-evident, axiomatic.

deducible, inferential, following.

Adv. **of course,** in consequence, consequently, as a matter of course.

479. CONFUTATION.—N. confutation, refutation; answer, disproof, conviction, invalidation; exposure, exposé [F.], retort.

V. **confute,** refute, parry, negative, disprove, expose, show up; rebut, defeat, demolish, upset, subvert, overthrow, overturn, confound; invalidate; convince, silence; clinch an argument.

Adj. **confutable,** refutable; capable of refutation.

480. [Results of reasoning] JUDGMENT.—N. judgment, decision, determination, finding, verdict, sentence, decree; opinion, etc. (*belief*), 484; good judgment.

result, conclusion, upshot; deduction, inference, corollary.

estimation, valuation, appreciation; arbitrament, arbitration; assessment.

estimate, award; review, criticism, critique, notice, report.

plebiscite, voice, casting vote; vote, suffrage, election.

arbiter, arbitrator; judge, umpire; assessor, referee; inspector; censor.

reviewer, critic; connoisseur; commentator, annotator.

V. **judge,** conclude, opine; come to (*or* arrive at) a conclusion; ascertain, determine.

deduce, derive, gather, collect, infer.

estimate, form an estimate, appreciate, value, count, assess, rate, rank, account; regard, consider, think of; size up [*colloq.*].

decide, settle; try, pronounce, rule; find, pass judgment, sentence, doom, decree; give (*or* deliver) judgment; adjudge, adjudicate; arbitrate, award; confirm.

review, comment, criticize; examine, etc., 457; investigate, etc., 461.

Adj. **judicious,** judicial; determinate, conclusive, confirmatory.

critical, hypercritical, hairsplitting, censorious.

Adv. on the whole, all things considered, therefore, wherefore.

480a. [Result of search or inquiry] DISCOVERY.—*N.* discovery, detection, disclosure, find, revelation.

V. **discover,** find, determine, evolve; fix upon; find (*or* trace, make, root) out; spot [*colloq.*], fathom, bring out, draw out, educe, elicit, bring to light, dig up, unearth, disinter.

solve, resolve; unriddle, unravel, find a clue to; interpret; disclose; see through, detect; catch; scent, smell out.

recognize, realize, verify, make certain of, identify.

481. MISJUDGMENT.—*N.* **misjudgment,** obliquity of judgment, warped judgment; miscalculation, misconception, misinterpretation, etc., 523; hasty conclusion.

preconception, prejudgment, foregone conclusion; presumption, preconceived idea; prejudice, predilection, prepossession; presentiment, foreboding; fixed idea, obsession.

partisanship, clannishness; *esprit de corps* [F.], prestige, party spirit, class prejudice, class consciousness, race prejudice, provincialism.

quirk, shift, quibble, equivocation, evasion, subterfuge.

bias, warp, twist; hobby, whim, craze, cult, fad, crotchet, partiality.

V. **misjudge,** misconjecture, misconceive, misunderstand; miscalculate, misreckon; overestimate, etc., 482; underestimate, etc., 483.

prejudge, dogmatize; have a bias, run away with the notion; jump to a conclusion; blunder, etc., 699.

bias, warp, twist; prejudice, prepossess.

Adj. **misjudging,** ill-judging, wrong-headed; superficial; prejudiced, prepossessed; shortsighted, purblind; partial, one-sided; warped.

narrow, narrow-minded, provincial, parochial, insular; mean-spirited, confined, illiberal, intolerant, infatuated, fanatical, positive, dogmatic, dictatorial, pragmatic; egotistical, conceited, opinionated; bigoted, etc. (*obstinate*), 606; unreasonable, stupid, etc., 499; credulous, gullible.

482. OVERESTIMATION.—*N.* **overestimation,** exaggeration, hyperbole; optimism, much ado about nothing; tempest in a teacup; fine writing, rodomontade, gush [*colloq.*], hot air [*slang*].

egoism, egotism, bombast, conceit; vanity; megalomania.

egoist, egoist, megalomaniac; optimist; braggart, boaster, braggadocio, swaggerer.

V. **overestimate,** overrate, overpraise; strain, magnify; exaggerate, etc., 549.

eulogize, gush over [*colloq.*], boost; puff [*colloq.*]; extol.

Adj. **inflated,** puffed up; grandiose, stilted, pompous, pretentious, bombastic.

483. UNDERESTIMATION.—*N.* **underestimation,** undervaluation; depreciation, etc. (*detraction*), 934; pessimism; self-detraction, self-depreciation; modesty, etc., 881.

pessimist, depreciator, knocker [*slang*], crapehanger [*slang*].

V. **underrate,** underestimate, undervalue; depreciate; disparage, detract, decry, ridicule, deride; slight, etc. (*despise*), 930; neglect; slur over.

make light (*or* little) **of,** belittle, run down [*colloq.*], minimize, set no store by, set at naught, disregard.

Adj. **depreciating,** depreciative, depreciatory; pessimistic.

depreciated, unappreciated, unvalued, unprized.

484. BELIEF.—*N.* **belief,** credence; credit; assurance; faith, trust, confidence, presumption; hope.

conviction, principle; persuasion, certainty, opinion, view, conception, impression, surmise; conclusion.

doctrine, tenet, dogma, articles, canons; view, gospel; article (*or* declaration, profession) of faith, creed; assent, avowal, confession; propaganda.

credibility, probability; plausibility.

V. **believe,** credit, give faith (*or* credit, credence) to; realize; assume, take it; consider, presume; count (*or* depend, rely, build) upon; take for granted.

confide in, believe in, put one's trust in, place reliance on, trust.

think, hold, opine, conceive; have (*or* hold, entertain, adopt, embrace, foster, cherish) a belief *or* an opinion.

persuade, assure, convince, satisfy, bring to reason, convert, indoctrinate; wean, bring round, bring (*or* win) over; carry conviction.

Adj. **certain,** sure, assured, positive, cocksure [*colloq.*], satisfied, confident, unhesitating, convinced, secure.

confiding, trustful, unsuspecting, unsuspicious; credulous, gullible.

believed, trusted, unsuspected, undoubted.

credible, reliable, trustworthy, accredited, satisfactory; probable.

485. UNBELIEF. DOUBT.—*N.* **unbelief,** disbelief, incredulity; infidelity, etc. (*irreligion*), 989; wrangling, nonconformity; dissent, change of opinion; retractation, etc., 607.

doubt, uncertainty, skepticism, misgiving, demur; discredit; distrust, mistrust; misdoubt, suspicion, jealousy, scruple, qualm.

incredibility, incredibleness, unbelievability.

agnostic, skeptic; unbeliever, etc., 487.

V. **disbelieve,** discredit, misbelieve, dissent; refuse to believe.

doubt, distrust, mistrust; question, challenge, dispute; deny, etc., 536; cavil, wrangle; suspect, scent, smell, smell a rat [*colloq.*], harbor suspicions; have one's doubts.

demur, stick at, pause, hesitate, shy at, scruple; waver.

stagger, startle; shake one's faith, stagger one's belief.

Adj. **unbelieving,** skeptical, incredulous; distrustful of, suspicious of.

doubtful, etc. (*uncertain*), 475; disputable, questionable, suspicious; incredible, unbelievable, inconceivable.

Adv. with caution, with grains of allowance.

486. CREDULITY.—*N.* credulity, credulousness, gullibility; infatuation; self-delusion, self-deception; superstition; bigotry.

credulous person, dupe, gull.

V. **be credulous;** follow implicitly; swallow, swallow whole, gulp down; take on faith.

impose upon, etc. (*deceive*), 545.

Adj. **credulous,** gullible, easily deceived *or* convinced; simple, silly, childish; infatuated, superstitious; confiding, trustful, unsuspicious.

487. INCREDULITY.—*N.* incredulity, incredulousness; skepticism, doubt, disbelief, etc., 989; unbelief, etc., 485.

unbeliever, skeptic, doubting Thomas, disbeliever, agnostic, infidel, misbeliever; heretic, etc. (*heterodox*), 984.

V. **be incredulous,** distrust, doubt, suspect, refuse to believe; turn a deaf ear to.

Adj. **incredulous,** skeptical, suspicious; dissenting, unbelieving; heterodox.

488. ASSENT.—*N.* assent, acquiescence, admission; nod, consent, compliance; agreement, understanding; affirmation; recognition, acknowledgment, avowal, confession.

unanimity, common consent, consensus, acclamation, chorus, public opinion; concurrence, accord.

ratification, confirmation, corroboration, approval, acceptance; indorsement.

consenter, indorser, subscriber; upholder, etc. (*auxiliary*), 711.

V. **assent,** give assent, acquiesce, agree, accept, accede, accord, concur, consent, coincide, echo, reciprocate, go with; recognize; subscribe to, conform to, defer to; go with the stream; be in the fashion, join in the chorus.

acknowledge, own, admit, confess; concede, yield; abide by; permit, etc., 760.

confirm, ratify, approve, indorse, countersign; corroborate, etc., 467.

Adj. assenting, of one accord (*or* mind); of the same mind, at one with, agreed, acquiescent.

uncontradicted, unchallenged, unquestioned, unanimous.

Adv. yes, yea, aye, true; granted; even so, just so; to be sure, as you say; surely, assuredly; exactly, precisely, certainly, of course, unquestionably, no doubt, doubtless.

unanimously, by common consent, to a man, as one man; with one consent (*or* voice, accord).

489. DISSENT.—*N.* dissent, nonconsent, discordance, disagreement.

nonconformity, heterodoxy, protestantism, schism; disaffection, secession, recantation.

dissension, discord, caviling, wrangling; discontent, etc., 832.

protest, contradiction, denial; noncompliance, rejection.

dissentient, dissenter, nonconformist; sectary; separatist, protestant; heretic, etc., 984.

V. dissent, demur, call in question, disagree, refuse to admit; cavil, wrangle, protest, repudiate; contradict, deny.

secede; recant, etc., 607.

Adj. dissenting, negative; contradictory; dissentient; unconvinced, unconverted.

sectarian, denominational, schismatic; heterodox; intolerant.

Adv. at variance with, at issue with; under protest.

490. KNOWLEDGE.—*N.* knowledge; cognizance; cognition, acquaintance, experience, ken, insight, familiarity; comprehension, apprehension; recognition; appreciation, judgment, etc., 480; intuition, consciousness, perception.

enlightenment, light; impression, perception, discovery, revelation.

learning, erudition, lore, scholarship; letters, literature; book learning, bookishness, general information; education, culture, cultivation, attainments, acquirements, accomplishments, proficiency.

V. know, be aware of; conceive, apprehend, comprehend; realize, understand, appreciate; fathom, make out; recognize, discern, perceive, see, experience.

learn, imbibe knowledge; discover, evolve.

Adj. aware of, cognizant of, conscious of; acquainted with, privy to, in the secret; alive to; apprized of, informed of; undeceived.

educated, erudite, instructed, learned, lettered, well informed, well versed, well read, well grounded, well educated; high-brow [*slang*], bookish, scholastic, profound, deep-read, book-learned, accomplished; self-taught, self-educated, knowing, shrewd.

known, ascertained, well known, recognized, noted, received, notorious, proverbial; familiar, hackneyed, trite, commonplace.

Adv. to the best of one's knowledge; as every schoolboy knows.

491. IGNORANCE.—*N.* ignorance, illiteracy, unlearnedness, unacquaintance, unconsciousness, darkness, blindness; incomprehension, simplicity.

sealed book; virgin soil, unexplored ground; dark ages.

Imperfect knowledge: smattering, superficiality, half learning, shallowness, glimmering; incapacity.

Affectation of knowledge: pedantry, charlatanry, charlatanism.

V. be ignorant (*or* uninformed); be uneducated; know nothing of; ignore, be blind to.

Adj. **ignorant;** unknowing, unaware, unacquainted, uninformed, uninitiated, unwitting, unconscious; witless, unconversant.

illiterate, unread, low [*slang*], uncultivated, uninstructed, untaught, untutored, unschooled, uneducated, unlearned, unlettered, empty-headed.

shallow, superficial, green, rude, empty, half-learned, half-baked [*colloq.*], unscholarly.

in the dark; benighted, blinded, blindfold, hoodwinked; misinformed.

unknown, unapprehended, unexplained, uninvestigated, unexplored, unheard of; concealed, etc., 528.

Adv. unawares; for aught one knows; not that one knows.

492. SCHOLAR.—*N.* scholar, savant [F.], pundit [India], schoolman, professor, academician, doctor, fellow, don [Eng.], graduate, postgraduate, classicist, philosopher, scientist, linguist, etymologist, philologist, lexicographer; man of learning.

bookworm, bibliophile, bibliomaniac, bluestocking [*colloq.*], high-brow [*slang*].

pedant, doctrinaire; pedagogue, Dr. Pangloss; instructor, etc., 540.

student, learner, pupil, schoolboy, etc. (*learner*), 541.

Adj. learned, etc., 490.

493. IGNORAMUS.—*N.* **ignoramus,** illiterate, dunce, duffer, numskull [*colloq.*]; no scholar.

smatterer, dabbler, half scholar; charlatan; wiseacre.

novice, greenhorn, plebe [*West Point cant*]; tyro, etc. (*learner*), 541.

Adj. **bookless,** shallow, simple, dull, dumb [*colloq.*], dense, crass; illiterate, etc., 491.

494. [Object of knowledge] TRUTH.—*N.* truth, verity; fact, reality, authenticity, gospel; veracity, etc., 543.

accuracy, exactitude, exactness, preciseness, precision, regularity, fidelity, nicety.

V. **hold true,** stand the test, have the true ring, hold good.

trace, solve, etc. (*discover*), 480a.

Adj. **true,** real, actual, veritable; certain, etc., 474; unimpeachable; veracious, etc., 543.

pure, sound, sterling, true-blue; natural, unsophisticated, unadulterated, simon-pure [*colloq.*], unvarnished, undisguised.

exact, accurate, definite, concrete, precise, well defined, just, right, correct, strict, severe, rigid, rigorous, scrupulous, literal, punctilious, mathematical, scientific, unromantic; faithful, constant, unerring; particular, nice, meticulous, delicate, fine; clean-cut, clear-cut.

authentic, genuine, legitimate; orthodox, etc., 983a; official.

valid, well grounded, well founded, solid, substantial, tangible.

Adv. **truly,** verily, indeed, in reality; in very truth, in fact, as a matter of fact, beyond doubt.

495. ERROR.—*N.* **error,** fallacy, misconception, misapprehension, misunderstanding; aberration, inexactness, laxity; misconstruction, misinterpretation; misjudgment, heresy, misstatement, anachronism; fable, etc. (*untruth*), 546.

mistake, fault, blunder, oversight, misprint, erratum (*pl.* errata). slip, blot, flaw, trip, stumble, bungle; slip of the tongue, slip of the pen, clerical error; bull, etc. (*absurdity*), 497; spoonerism, malapropism.

delusion, illusion, false impression; bubble; self-deceit, self-deception; hallucination, mirage, etc., 443; dream, etc. (*fancy*), 515.

V. **mislead,** misguide, lead astray, beguile, misinform, delude; falsify, misstate; deceive, etc., 545; lie, etc., 544.

err, be in error, be mistaken, be deceived; mistake, deceive oneself, blunder, misapprehend, misconceive, misunderstand, miscalculate, misjudge.

trip, stumble, lose oneself, go astray; fail, etc., 732; take the shadow for the substance.

Adj. **erroneous,** untrue, false, faulty, erring, fallacious, unreal, ungrounded, groundless, unsubstantial, unsound, inexact, inaccurate, incorrect.

illusive, illusory, delusive; mock, imaginary, spurious, etc., 545; deceitful, etc., 544; untrustworthy.

exploded, refuted, discarded.

mistaken, in error, deceived, out in one's reckoning; wide of the mark, at fault, at cross-purposes, at sea, bewildered.

496. MAXIM.—*N.* maxim, aphorism, dictum, saying, adage, saw, proverb, motto, epigram, sentence, mot [*Gallicism*], commonplace, moral.

axiom, theorem, formula, truism.

principle, profession of faith, conclusion, etc. (*judgment*), 480.

Adj. **aphoristic,** proverbial, axiomatic; hackneyed, trite.

Adv. as the saying is, as they say.

497. ABSURDITY.—*N.* absurdity, absurdness, imbecility, etc., 499; nonsense, paradox, inconsistency.

blunder, muddle, Irish bull; anticlimax, bathos.

farce, burlesque, parody, limerick; farrago, extravagance.

pun, sell [*colloq.*], catch [*colloq.*], verbal quibble, joke.

jargon, gibberish, balderdash, bombast, claptrap, twaddle, moonshine, stuff.

tomfoolery, mummery, monkeyshine [*slang*], monkey trick, frisk, practical joke, escapade.

V. **play the fool,** blunder, muddle; be guilty of absurdity; romance, talk nonsense, exaggerate; be absurd, frisk, caper, joke, play practical jokes.

Adj. **absurd,** nonsensical, farcical, burlesque, preposterous, egregious, senseless, inconsistent, ridiculous, extravagant, self-contradictory, paradoxical; foolish, etc., 499; meaningless, fantastic, bombastic, high-flown.

498. [Faculties] **INTELLIGENCE. WISDOM.**—*N.* **intelligence,** capacity, comprehension, understanding; intellect, etc., 450; brains, parts, sagacity, mother wit, wit, gumption [*colloq.*], acuteness, acumen, longheadedness, subtlety, penetration, perspicacity, discernment, good judgment; discrimination, cunning, refinement.

wisdom, sapience, sense, common sense, clear thinking, rationality, reason; reasonableness, judgment, solidity, depth, profundity, caliber.

genius, inspiration, talent, etc., 698.

Wisdom in action: prudence, etc., 864; vigilance, etc., 459; tact, etc., 698; foresight, etc., 510; sobriety, self-possession, ballast, mental poise, balance.

V. **have all one's wits about one;** be brilliant, scintillate, coruscate; understand, etc. (*intelligible*), 518.

penetrate, see through, see at a glance, discern; foresee, etc., 510; discriminate.

Adj. **Applied to persons: intelligent,** quick of apprehension, keen, acute, alive, awake, bright, quick, sharp, quick-witted, wide-awake; shrewd, astute; clearheaded, long-sighted, calculating, thoughtful, farsighted, discerning, perspicacious, penetrating, piercing; sharp as a needle; alive to, etc. (*cognizant*), 490; clever, etc. (*apt*), 698.

wise, sage, sapient [*often in irony*], sagacious, rational, sensible, judicious, strong-minded; worldly-wise, sophisticated.

impartial, unprejudiced, unbiased, unbigoted, equitable, fair.

prudent, etc. (*cautious*), 864; sober, staid, solid; watchful; provident, prepared, etc., 673.

Applied to actions: wise, sensible, judicious, well judged, well advised; prudent, politic; expedient, etc., 646.

499. IMBECILITY, FOLLY.—*N.* imbecility, want of intelligence (*or* intellect), shallowness, silliness, foolishness, stupidity, stolidity; incompetence.

simplicity, puerility; senility, dotage, second childhood; fatuity; idiocy.

folly, frivolity, irrationality, trifling, ineptitude, inconsistency, giddiness; eccentricity, etc., 503; extravagance, etc. (*absurdity*), 497; rashness, etc., 863.

V. trifle, drivel, dote; ramble, play the fool, fool, stultify oneself, talk nonsense.

Adj. Applied to persons: unintelligent, unintellectual, unreasoning; mindless, brainless; half-baked [*colloq.*], bovine, thick [*colloq.*], blockish, unteachable; ungifted, unenlightened, unwise; thick-skulled, muddleheaded, addleheaded, weak-minded, feeble-minded.

stupid, dull, heavy, obtuse, blunt, stolid, asinine, inapt.

childish, childlike; infantine, infantile, babyish, puerile, senile, anile; simple, credulous.

imbecile, fatuous, idiotic, driveling; vacant, bewildered.

foolish, silly, senseless, irrational, insensate, nonsensical, maudlin.

narrow-minded, bigoted, etc., 606; rash, etc., 863; eccentric, odd.

Applied to actions: foolish, unwise, injudicious, improper, unreasonable, ill-advised, ridiculous, silly, stupid, asinine; inconsistent, irrational; extravagant, nonsensical, frivolous, trivial; useless, etc., 645; inexpedient, etc., 647.

500. SAGE.—*N.* sage, wise man; master mind, thinker, philosopher, savant [F.], pundit, etc. (*scholar*), 492; wiseacre [*ironical*]; expert, etc., 700.

authority, oracle, mentor, Solon, Solomon, Buddha, Confucius.

Adj. venerable, venerated, reverenced, revered, honored; authoritative, oracular; wise, erudite, etc., 490.

501. FOOL.—*N.* fool, idiot, tomfool, wiseacre, simpleton,

Simple Simon; donkey, ass, owl, goose, dolt, booby, noodle, imbecile, nincompoop [*colloq.*], oaf, lout, blockhead, bonehead [*slang*], calf [*colloq.*], colt, numskull [*colloq.*], clod, clodhopper; soft *or* softy [*colloq. or slang*], mooncalf, saphead [*slang*], gawk, rube [*slang*].

greenhorn, etc. (*dupe*), 547; dunce, etc. (*ignoramus*), 493; lubber, etc. (*bungler*), 701; madman, etc., 504; dotard, driveler, old fogy [*colloq.*].

502. SANITY.—*N.* **sanity,** soundness, rationality, sobriety, lucidity, senses, common sense, horse sense [*colloq.*], sound mind.

V. **become sane,** come to one's senses, sober down, cool down, see things in proper perspective.

render sane, bring to one's senses, sober, bring to reason.

Adj. **sane,** rational, normal, wholesome, right-minded, reasonable, sound, sound-minded, in possession of one's faculties.

Adv. **sanely,** in reason, within reason, within bounds.

503. INSANITY.—*N.* **insanity,** lunacy; madness, mania, dementia, idiocy; delirium tremens, d.t.'s, the horrors [*colloq.*]; frenzy, raving, wandering, delirium, delusion, obsession, hallucination, derangement, unsoundness of mind.

vertigo, dizziness, swimming, sunstroke.

oddity, eccentricity, twist, monomania; fanaticism, infatuation, craze.

V. **be** *or* **become insane,** lose one's senses (*or* reason), go mad, rave, dote, ramble, wander; lose one's head, drivel.

derange, render *or* drive mad, madden, infatuate, obsess, befool; turn the brain, turn one's head.

Adj. **insane,** mad, lunatic; crazy, crazed, crackbrained, cracked [*colloq.*], touched; bereft of reason; unhinged, insensate, beside oneself, demented, maniacal, daft, frenzied, deranged, maddened, moonstruck, off one's head.

giddy, vertiginous, wild, flighty, distracted, distraught, bewildered.

odd, fanatical, infatuated, eccentric.

delirious, lightheaded, rambling, wandering, frantic, raving, stark mad.

504. MADMAN.—*N.* **madman,** lunatic, maniac; crank [*colloq.*], nut [*slang*].

dreamer, visionary, rhapsodist, seer, enthusiast, fanatic; Don Quixote, Ophelia.

idiot, etc., 501.

505. [The Past] MEMORY.—*N.* **memory,** remembrance; retention, retentiveness; retentive (*or* tenacious, trustworthy, ready) memory.

recollection, retrospect, reminiscence; recognition; afterthought.

reminder, hint, suggestion, memorandum (*pl.* memoranda), token, memento, souvenir, keepsake, relic; memorial, monument; commemoration, jubilee.

mnemonics; art of memory, artificial memory; Mnemosyne.

fame, celebrity, renown, reputation; repute, notoriety.

V. **remember,** retain the memory of, keep in mind; bear in mind, haunt one's mind (*or* thoughts); rankle; keep the wound open, brood over.

recollect, recall, call up, conjure up, retrace; look back upon, review; call (*or* bring) to mind.

remind, suggest, hint, prompt; put (*or* keep) in mind; bring to mind, call up, summon up, renew; redeem from oblivion; commemorate.

memorize, commit to memory; con, con over; fix in the mind, engrave upon the memory; learn by heart, know by rote, have at one's fingers' ends.

make a note of, put down, record.

Adj. **remembering,** mindful, reminiscent; fresh, still vivid; enduring, unforgotten; never to be forgotten, indelible; within one's memory; memorable, suggestive.

Adv. **by heart,** by rote, without book, word for word.

506. OBLIVION.—*N.* **oblivion;** forgetfulness; Lethe; obliteration of the past; short (*or* treacherous, untrustworthy, slippery, failing) memory; decay (*or* failure, lapse) of memory; amnesia.

amnesty, general pardon.

V. **forget,** be forgetful; fall (*or* sink) into oblivion; have a short memory; lose, lose the memory of, lose sight of.

efface, from the memory; unlearn; consign to oblivion, think no more of; let bygones be bygones.

Adj. **forgotten,** unremembered, out of mind; buried (*or* sunk) in oblivion.

forgetful, oblivious; heedless, deaf to the past; Lethean.

507. [The Future] EXPECTATION.—*N.* **expectation,** expectancy, anticipation, prospect, contingency, reckoning, calculation; foresight; suspense; abeyance.

assurance, confidence, reliance, hope, trust, presumption; prognostication; prediction, etc., 511.

V. **expect;** look for, look out for, look forward to; hope for, anticipate; have in prospect, keep in view, contemplate; wait for, watch for, await; foresee, prepare for, forestall

predict, prognosticate, forecast.

Adj. **expectant;** expecting, in expectation, vigilant; open-eyed, open-mouthed; agape, gaping, on tenterhooks, on tiptoe; ready, prepared, provided for, provident.

expected, foreseen; in prospect, prospective, provisional; future, coming; in view, on the horizon; impending.

Adv. **expectantly,** on the watch, with muscles tense, on edge [*colloq.*], with eyes (*or* ears) strained, with bated breath.

soon, shortly, forthwith, presently.

508. NONEXPECTATION.—*N.* **nonexpectation,** unforeseen contingency, the unforeseen; miscalculation, false expectation; disappointment; disillusion.

surprise, blow, shock; bolt out of the blue; astonishment, amazement; wonder, bewilderment.

V. **be unexpected,** come unawares, turn up, burst *or* flash upon one; take by surprise, catch unawares.

surprise, startle, stun, stagger, astound; throw off one's guard; spring upon, astonish, etc. (*strike with wonder*), 870.

Adj. **nonexpectant,** surprised; unwarned, unaware; off one's guard.

unexpected, unanticipated, unlooked for, unforeseen; unheard of; startling; sudden.

Adv. **unexpectedly,** abruptly, suddenly, unawares; without notice *or* warning.

509. DISAPPOINTMENT.—*N.* **disappointment,** blighted hope, disillusion, balk; blow, false (*or* vain) expectation; miscalculation; fool's paradise.

V. **be disappointed;** look blank, look *or* stand aghast; find to one's cost.

disappoint, crush (*or* dash, blight) one's hope, balk *or* disappoint one's expectation, balk, tantalize; dumfounder, dumfound, disconcert, disillusionize; dissatisfy; disgruntle.

Adj. aghast; disgruntled; out of one's reckoning.

510. FORESIGHT.—*N.* **foresight,** prevision, long-sightedness, farsightedness; anticipation; prudence; forethought.

foreknowledge, prescience; presentiment, foreboding; second sight.

prospect; foregone conclusion; forecast.

V. **foresee;** look forward to, look ahead *or* beyond; look into the future; see one's way; see how the land lies.

anticipate, expect, surmise, contemplate; predict; forewarn.

Adj. **foreseeing,** prescient, anticipatory; farseeing, farsighted, long-sighted; provident; weatherwise; prospective; expectant.

Adv. against the time when; for a rainy day.

511. PREDICTION.—*N.* **prediction,** announcement; program;

platform; premonition, presage, foreboding; phophecy, prognostication, augury, forecast; omen, etc., 512; horoscope; soothsaying, fortunetelling, divination; oracle, etc., 513.

astrology; spell, charm, etc., 993; sorcery, magic, etc., 992.

V. **predict**, forecast, prognosticate, prophesy, divine, foretell; tell fortunes, cast a horoscope (*or* nativity); forewarn.

presage, augur, bode, forebode; foretoken, betoken; portend, signify, point to.

herald, usher in, announce; lower; threaten.

Adj. **prophetic**, oracular, sibylline; weatherwise.

ominous, portentous; auspicious; premonitory, significant of.

512. OMEN.—*N.* **omen**, portent, presage, augury; sign, token; harbinger; bird of ill omen; halcyon birds; signs of the times; warning, etc., 668.

Adj. **auspicious**, favorable, halcyon, of good omen.

inauspicious, ill-boding, ill-omened, ill-starred.

513. ORACLE.—*N.* **oracle**; prophet, seer, soothsayer, prophetess, witch, sibyl; augur, haruspex; medium, clairvoyant, palmist; fortuneteller; sorcerer, etc., 994; interpreter, etc., 524.

Delphic oracle; Cumaean Sibyl, Sibyl, Cassandra, Witch of Endor, Sphinx.

weather prophet, weather bureau.

514. [Creative Thought] SUPPOSITION.—*N.* **supposition**, assumption, presumption, condition, hypothesis, postulate, theory, data; thesis, theorem; conjecture, guess, guesswork, speculation; surmise, suspicion, inkling, suggestion, hint.

theorist, theorizer, doctrinaire, doctrinarian.

V. **suppose**, conjecture; surmise, suspect, guess, divine; theorize, speculate; presume, presuppose, assume, predicate; believe, take for granted.

propound, propose, put forth; put a case, submit; move, make a motion; hazard *or* put forward a suggestion (*or* supposition); suggest, allude to, hint.

Adj. **assumed**, given; conjectural, presumptive, hypothetical; theoretical, academic.

suggestive, allusive, stimulating.

Adv. **if**, if so be; on the supposition, in case, in the event of; as if, provided; perhaps, for aught one knows.

515. IMAGINATION.—*N.* **imagination**, originality, invention; fancy; inspiration.

ideality, idealism; romanticism, utopianism, castle-building, dreaming; frenzy, rhapsody, ecstasy, reverie, daydream.

conception; flight of fancy; creation of the brain; imagery; word painting.

fantasy, conceit; figment, myth; romance, extravaganza; dream, vision; shadow, chimera, phantasm, illusion, phantom, fancy, whim, vagary; bugbear, nightmare; flying Dutchman, great sea serpent, man in the moon, castle in the air, castle in Spain, Utopia, fairyland; land of Prester John.

Creative works: work of fiction, etc. (*novel*), 594; poetry, etc., 597; drama, etc., 599; music, etc., 415; painting, sculpture, architecture; art.

idealist, romanticist, visionary, romancer, daydreamer, dreamer, castle-builder; creative artist.

V. **imagine,** fancy, conceive; idealize, realize; dream, dream of; indulge in reverie; fancy (*or* represent, picture, figure) to oneself.

create, originate, devise, invent, make up, coin, fabricate; improvise.

Adj. **imaginative,** original, inventive, creative, productive.

extravagant, romantic, high-flown, flighty, preposterous; unreal; unsubstantial.

ideal; intellectual, impracticable, imaginary, visionary, utopian, quixotic.

fanciful; fantastical; fictitious; fabulous, legendary, mythic *or* mythical, mythological, chimerical; whimsical; fairy, fairylike.

II. COMMUNICATION OF IDEAS

516. MEANING.—*N.* **meaning** [*idea to be conveyed*], signification, significance; sense, import, purport; pith, essence; force; drift, bearing, tenor, spirit; allusion; suggestion, interpretation; acceptation.

Thing signified: matter, subject, subject matter, substance, gist, argument.

V. **mean,** signify, denote, express; import, purport; convey, imply, indicate; tell of, speak of; touch on; point to, allude to; drive at; involve; declare; affirm, state.

paraphrase, state differently; express by a synonym.

Adj. **meaning,** expressive, significant, pithy; intelligible, explicit, clear; suggestive; allusive.

literal, word-for-word, verbatim; exact, real.

synonymous; tantamount, equivalent.

implied; understood, tacit.

Adv. to that effect; that is to say.

517. UNMEANINGNESS.—*N.* **unmeaningness,** absence of meaning, drivel, senselessness; empty sound.

nonsense, jargon, gibberish, mere words, rant, bombast, balderdash, babble, inanity, twaddle, trash, rubbish; absurdity; imbecility, folly; ambiguity, vagueness, etc., 519.

V. **mean nothing;** be unmeaning; gibber; jabber, twaddle, rant, babble.

scribble, scrawl, scratch.

Adj. **unmeaning,** meaningless, senseless; nonsensical; inexpressive; vague; not significant.

trashy, inane, trumpery, trivial, insignificant.

518. INTELLIGIBILITY.—*N.* **intelligibility;** comprehensibility; clearness, clarity, explicitness, lucidity, perspicuity; precision; plain speaking.

V. **render intelligible,** popularize, simplify, elucidate, explain, interpret.

understand, comprehend; take in, catch, grasp, follow; master.

Adj. **intelligible;** clear, lucid; perspicuous, transparent.

plain, distinct, clear-cut, hard-hitting, to the point, explicit; positive; definite, precise; unequivocal, legible, obvious, etc., 525.

graphic, telling, vivid; expressive.

519. UNINTELLIGIBILITY.—*N.* **unintelligibility,** incomprehensibility, vagueness, obscurity, ambiguity, confusion; mystification; jargon.

enigma, riddle; sealed book.

V. **render unintelligible,** conceal, darken, confuse, mystify, perplex.

Adj. **unintelligible,** incomprehensible, unaccountable, undecipherable, unfathomable, inexplicable, inscrutable, insoluble, impenetrable; puzzling, enigmatic; indecipherable, illegible.

obscure, crabbed, dark, muddy, dim, nebulous, mysterious, hidden, latent, occult; abstruse; indefinite, vague, loose, ambiguous.

inexpressible, unutterable, ineffable.

520. [Having a double sense] EQUIVOCALNESS.—*N.* **equivocalness,** equivocation, double meaning; ambiguity; quibble; conundrum, riddle; pun, word play; sphinx, Delphic oracle.

equivocation, etc. (*duplicity*), 544; white lie, mental reservation, etc., 528.

V. **equivocate,** etc. (*palter*), 544; prevaricate; have a double meaning.

Adj. **equivocal,** ambiguous; double-tongued; enigmatical; indeterminate, doubtful.

521. FIGURE OF SPEECH.—*N.* **figure,** trope, phrase, expression; euphemism; image, imagery; personification, metaphor; simile, satire, irony.

allegory, apologue, parable, fable.

V. **employ figures of speech;** personify, allegorize, fable, shadow forth, allude to.

Adj. **figurative,** metaphorical, euphuistic, allusive; allegoric *or* allegorical, ironic, ironical, satiric *or* satirical; euphemistic.

522. INTERPRETATION.—*N.* **interpretation,** definition, explanation; elucidation, diagnosis; solution, answer; meaning, etc., 516; clue.

translation; rendering, rendition; metaphrase, literal (*or* word-for-word) translation; free translation; key; crib, horse, pony, trot [*school cant*].

comment, commentary; exegesis, exposition; inference, deduction; illustration, exemplification; gloss, annotation, note, construction, version, reading.

equivalent, equivalent meaning, synonym; paraphrase, convertible terms.

dictionary, etc., 562.

prediction, etc., 511; chiromancy, palmistry; astrology.

V. **interpret,** explain, define, construe, translate, render; decipher, make out, unravel, disentangle, solve; read between the lines.

elucidate, account for, throw *or* shed light upon; clear up, popularize, simplify; illustrate, exemplify; unfold, expound, comment upon, annotate.

Adj. **explanatory,** expository; interpretative, elucidative, inferential, illustrative.

equivalent, convertible, synonymous.

metaphrastic, literal, word-for-word.

Adv. **in explanation;** that is to say, to wit, namely.

literally, strictly speaking; in plain terms (*or* words).

523. MISINTERPRETATION.—*N.* misinterpretation, misapprehension, misconception, misunderstanding, misconstruction; misapplication; cross-purposes; mistake, etc., 495.

misrepresentation, perversion, misstatement, exaggeration; abuse of terms; play upon words, pun, parody, travesty; falsification, etc. (*lying*), 544.

V. **misinterpret,** misapprehend, misunderstand, misconceive; misjudge, misspell; mistranslate, misconstrue, misapply; mistake, etc., 495.

misrepresent, pervert, misstate, garble, falsify, distort; travesty, play upon words; stretch (*or* strain, twist, wrest) the sense *or* meaning.

Adj. **misinterpreted,** mistranslated; confused, tangled, snarled, mixed.

dazed, perplexed, bewildered, rattled [*slang*], benighted.

Adv. **at cross-purposes,** at sixes and sevens [*colloq.*]; in a maze.

524. INTERPRETER.—*N.* **interpreter,** translator, expositor, expounder, exponent; demonstrator; commentator, annotator; oracle, etc., 513.

spokesman, speaker, mouthpiece, foreman of the jury, mediator, advocate, delegate, representative, diplomatic agent, ambassador, plenipotentiary.

guide, courier, cicerone, showman, barker [*colloq.*].

525. MANIFESTATION.—*N.* **manifestation,** indication, expression; plain speaking, candor, openness; showing, exposition, demonstration; séance, materialization; exhibition, production, display, show.

Thing shown: exhibit, exhibition, exposition, show [*colloq.*], performance.

publicity, etc., 531; disclosure, etc., 529; openness, candor; saliency, prominence.

V. **make manifest,** materialize, express, represent, set forth, evidence, exhibit, produce, show, show up, expose; hold up, show forth, unveil, display, demonstrate, lay open; draw out, bring out; manifest oneself; speak out, proclaim, publish.

indicate, point out; disclose, discover; translate, transcribe, decipher, decode; elicit, bring to light, disinter.

be manifest *or* plain, appear, etc., 446; transpire, come to light, be disclosed; go without saying, be self-evident.

Adj. **manifest,** apparent; salient, striking, prominent, in the foreground, ostensible, notable, pronounced.

plain, intelligible, clear, defined, definite, distinct, conspicuous, obvious, evident, unmistakable; conclusive, indubitable, palpable, self-evident; open, patent, express, explicit; naked, bare, literal, downright, unreserved, frank, plain-spoken.

barefaced, brazen, bold, shameless, daring, flaunting, loud [*colloq.*]; flagrant, arrant, notorious; glaring.

Adv. **manifestly,** openly, plainly, above board, in plain sight, in the open, in broad daylight; without reserve.

526. LATENCY.—*N.* **latency,** hidden meaning; obscurity, ambiguity; secret, mystery, occultism, mysticism, symbolism; reserve, reticence; concealment, mystification, suppression, evasion; Delphic oracle; undercurrent; snake in the grass.

allusion, insinuation, implication; innuendo.

latent influence, power behind the throne, friend at court, wire-puller [*colloq.*], kingmaker.

V. **lurk,** smolder, underlie, make no sign; escape observation (*or* detection, recognition); lie hid, lie in ambush.

keep back, etc. (*conceal*), 528.

involve, imply, connote, import, allude to, leave an inference; symbolize.

Adj. **latent,** lurking; dormant, secret, occult; esoteric, recondite, veiled, symbolic, cryptic, mystic, mystical.

unapparent, unknown, unseen, unsuspected; invisible; unexpressed, undisclosed, tacit.

indirect, crooked, underhand, underground; by inference, by implication; implied, implicit, understood, tacit; allusive, covert, undercover, concealed.

Adv. secretly, stealthily, incognito; in the background; behind the scenes, between the lines; below the surface.

527. INFORMATION.—*N.* **information,** enlightenment, acquaintance, knowledge; publicity, notoriety.

mention; instruction, communicativeness, intercommunication.

notification, intimation, communication, notice, annunciation, announcement, communiqué; representation; message, etc., 532.

report, advice, monition; news, tidings, return, record, account, description; statement, estimate, specification.

informant, authority, teller, harbinger, herald, reporter, exponent, mouthpiece; spokesman, etc. (*interpreter*), 524; spy, informer, eavesdropper, detective, sleuth [*colloq.*]; newsmonger; messenger, etc., 534.

guide, cicerone; pilot; guidebook, handbook; map, plan, chart, gazetteer; itinerary.

hint, suggestion, insinuation, innuendo, inkling, whisper, cue, byplay; gesture; word to the wise.

V. **tell,** inform, acquaint, impart, apprise, advise, instruct, enlighten.

mention, express, intimate, represent, communicate, make known; publish, disseminate; notify, signify, specify; retail, describe; state, declare, assert, affirm.

announce, report, bring (*or* send, leave) word; telegraph, wire [*colloq.*], telephone, phone [*colloq.*].

disclose, etc., 529; explain.

hint, insinuate, allude to, glance at, let fall, indicate; suggest, prompt, give the cue.

undeceive, set right, correct, disabuse.

Adj. **informational,** advisory.

expressive, explicit, plain-spoken; declaratory; expository; communicative.

528. CONCEALMENT.—*N.* **concealment,** mystification; reticence, reserve, reservation; mental reservation, aside; suppression, evasion, white lie; silence, closeness, secretiveness, mystery.

screen, cloak; ambush, ambuscade; stowaway; blind baggage [*slang*].

cipher, code, sympathetic ink.

stealth, stealthiness, slyness, caution, cunning.

secrecy, privacy, secretness; disguise, mask, masquerade; incognito (*fem.* incognita).

masquerader, masker, mask, domino.

V. **conceal,** hide, secrete; lock up; cover, screen, cloak, veil, shroud; curtain, muffle; mask, camouflage, disguise; ensconce.

keep from, keep to oneself, keep secret; bury, sink, suppress; keep in the background; stifle, hush up; withhold, reserve.

code, use a code *or* cipher, reduce to a code.

hoodwink, blind, blindfold; mystify, puzzle, deceive, lead astray.

be concealed, hide oneself, couch; lie in ambush, lurk, sneak, skulk, slink, prowl, gumshoe [*slang*].

Adj. **concealed,** hidden, secret, private, privy; recondite, mystic, mystical, occult, dark, cryptic; in secret, tortuous; close, inviolate, confidential, behind a screen, undercover, in ambush, in hiding, in disguise; undisclosed, untold, covert, mysterious.

furtive, stealthy, skulking, surreptitious, underhand, sly, cunning, evasive; secretive, clandestine; reserved, reticent, uncommunicative, close, taciturn.

Adv. **secretly,** in secret, in private, incognito.

behind closed doors, under the rose, *sub rosa* [L.]; on the sly [*colloq.*]; in a whisper.

confidentially, in strict confidence, between ourselves, between you and me.

underhand, by stealth, like a thief in the night; stealthily.

529. DISCLOSURE.—*N.* **disclosure,** revelation, divulgence, exposition, exposure, publication, exposé.

acknowledgment, avowal, confession, confessional.

narrator, etc., 594; talebearer, etc., 532; informant, etc., 527.

V. **disclose,** discover, unmask, unveil, unfold, uncover, unseal, lay bare, expose, bare, bring to light, disabuse, open the eyes of, turn informer.

divulge, reveal, let into the secret, tell, etc. (*inform*), 527; breathe, utter, peach |*slang*]; let slip *or* drop, betray; blurt out, vent, whisper about, speak out, break the news, publish, etc., 531.

acknowledge, allow, concede, grant, admit, own, confess, avow, make a clean breast, unbosom oneself; turn informer.

be disclosed, transpire, come to light, become known, escape the lips; ooze out, leak out, come to one's ears.

530. AMBUSH. [Means of concealment]—*N.* **ambush,** ambuscade, lurking place, trap, snare, pitfall, etc., 667.

hiding place, secret place, recess, hole, cubbyhole, crypt; safe, safe-deposit box, safety-deposit box.

screen, cover, shade, blinker; veil, curtain, blind, cloak, cloud.

mask, visor, disguise, masquerade, domino.

V. **ambush,** ambuscade, lie in ambush, lie in wait for; set a trap for, ensnare.

531. PUBLICATION.—*N.* **publication,** public announcement, promulgation, propagation, proclamation, pronouncement, edict.

publicity, notoriety, currency, flagrancy, cry, hue and cry, bruit; report, etc. (*news*), 532; telegram, etc., 532.

the press, the fourth estate, public press; newspaper, journal, gazette.

advertisement, placard, bill, flier [*cant*], leaflet, handbill, poster; circular, notice, program, manifesto.

V. **publish,** make public, broach, utter, circulate, propagate, promulgate, spread, spread abroad, rumor, diffuse, disseminate; issue; bring before the public; give to the world; report, voice, bruit; proclaim, herald, blazon, noise abroad, advertise.

telegraph, cable, wireless [*colloq.*], broadcast, wire [*colloq.*].

Adj. **published,** current; public, notorious, flagrant.

Adv. **publicly,** in public, in open court, with open doors.

532. NEWS—*N.* **news,** information, etc., 527; intelligence, tidings; beat *or* scoop [*newspaper cant*], story, copy [*cant*].

message, word, advice, communication, bulletin, broadcast, dispatch; telegram, cable [*colloq.*], wire [*colloq.*], radio, radiogram, wireless telegram, wireless [*colloq.*]; telephone, radiophone, wireless telephone.

report, rumor, hearsay, cry, bruit, fame; talk, scandal, gossip; tittle-tattle.

narrator, historian; newsmonger, scandalmonger; talebearer, telltale, gossip, tattler, tattletale; chatterer, busybody; informer.

V. **transpire,** etc. (*be disclosed*), 529; rumor, etc. (*publish*), 531.

Adj. **rumored,** rife, current, in circulation.

533. SECRET.—*N.* **secret,** mystery; problem, etc. (*question*), 461; unintelligibility, etc., 519.

enigma, riddle, puzzle, conundrum, charade, rebus.

maze, labyrinth, intricacy.

Adj. **secret,** concealed, etc., 528; involved, tortuous, circuitous, labyrinthine; enigmatic *or* enigmatical.

534. MESSENGER.—*N.* **messenger,** intermediary, go-between; envoy, emissary, legate, nuncio, delegate; angel; Gabriel, Hermes, Mercury.

courier, runner; commissionaire, errand boy; herald, crier, trumpeter, bellman.

mail, post, post office; air mail; postman, mailman, letter carrier; carrier pigeon.

telegraph, cable, wire [*colloq.*], radiotelegraph, wireless telegraph, wireless [*colloq.*], radio.

telephone, phone [*colloq.*], radiotelephone, radiophone, wireless telephone.

reporter, newspaperman, journalist; gentleman (*or* representative) of the press; special correspondent; scout, spy, informer.

535. AFFIRMATION.—*N.* **affirmation,** statement, allegation, profession, assertion, declaration; confirmation; asseveration, swearing, oath, affidavit, deposition; assurance, protest, protestation.

positiveness, emphasis, peremptoriness, dogmatism, weight.

vote, voice; ballot, suffrage.

remark, observation, saying, dictum, sentence.

V. **assert,** say, affirm, declare, state; protest, profess; acknowledge; put forward; advance, allege, propose, propound; announce, enunciate, broach, set forth, maintain, contend, pronounce.

depose, aver, avow, avouch, asseverate, swear, affirm; take one's oath; make an affidavit; vow, vouch, warrant, certify, assure; attest, adjure.

emphasize, insist upon, lay stress on; lay down the law; dogmatize, repeat, reassert, reaffirm.

Adj. **affirmative,** declaratory, positive; unmistakable, clear; certain, etc., 474; express, explicit, absolute, emphatic, decided, insistent, dogmatic, formal, solemn, categorical, peremptory.

Adv. with emphasis, ex cathedra, without fear of contradiction.

536. NEGATION.—*N.* **negation,** denial; disavowal, disclaimer; contradiction, protest; dissent, etc., 489.

qualification, etc., 469; repudiation, rejection, recantation, revocation; retractation, rebuttal, confutation; refusal, etc., 764.

V. **deny;** contradict, contravene; controvert, gainsay, negative, give the lie to, belie.

disclaim, disown, repudiate, disaffirm, disavow, abjure, forswear, renounce; recant, revoke.

dispute, impugn, confute, rebut, join issue upon; bring (*or* call) in question, set aside, ignore; refuse, etc., 764.

Adj. **contradictory;** negative; recusant, dissentient, at issue upon.

Adv. **no,** nay, not, nowise, not at all, not in the least, quite the contrary, by no means.

537. TEACHING.—*N.* **teaching,** pedagogics, pedagogy, instruction, edification, education, tuition, tutorship, tutelage; direction, guidance.

preparation, qualification, training, schooling, discipline; drill, practice.

lesson, lecture, recitation, sermon, homily, harangue, disquisition; apologue, parable; discourse; explanation; exercise, task; curriculum; course.

V. **teach,** instruct, educate, edify, school, tutor, cram [*colloq.*], grind [*colloq.*], prime, coach; enlighten, inform, etc., 527; direct, guide.

inculcate, infuse, instill, imbue, impregnate, implant; disseminate, propagate.

expound, etc. (*interpret*), 522; lecture; hold forth, preach; sermonize, moralize.

train, discipline, form, ground, prepare, qualify, drill, exercise, practice, familiarize with, inure, initiate, graduate.

Adj. **educational,** scholastic, academic, disciplinary, instructive, pedagogic, didactic; cultural, humanistic, humane; pragmatic, practical, utilitarian.

538. MISTEACHING.—*N.* **misteaching,** misinformation, misguidance, misdirection, perversion, sophistry; the blind leading the blind.

V. **misinform,** misteach, misinstruct, misdirect, misguide, pervert; deceive, mislead, misrepresent, lie.

render unintelligible, bewilder, mystify, conceal.

539. LEARNING.—*N.* **learning,** acquisition of knowledge, acquirement, attainment; mental cultivation, scholarship, erudition; lore; wide reading; study, grind [*colloq.*]; inquiry, etc., 461. apprenticeship, tutelage, novitiate.

V. **learn,** acquire (*or* gain, imbibe, pick up, obtain) knowledge *or* learning; master, grind [*college slang*], cram [*colloq.*], get up, learn by heart.

study, read, peruse; con, pore over, wade through, plunge into. burn the midnight oil; be taught.

Adj. **studious;** industrious, etc., 682; scholastic, scholarly, well read, widely read, erudite, learned.

540. TEACHER.—*N.* **teacher,** preceptor, instructor, master, tutor, schoolmaster, dominie, pedagogue; kindergartner, governess, mistress; coach [*colloq.*], crammer [*colloq.*]; professor, don [*Univ. cant*], lecturer, reader, preacher; pastor, etc. (*clergy*), 996; schoolmistress.

guide, counselor, adviser, mentor, pioneer, apostle, missionary, propagandist; example.

professorship, chair, fellowship, tutorship, mastership, instructorship.

Adj. **pedagogic,** tutorial, professorial; scholastic, etc., 537.

541. LEARNER.—*N.* **learner,** scholar, student, alumnus (*pl.* alumni; *fem.* alumna, *pl.* alumnae), pupil, schoolboy, schoolgirl;

monitor, prefect; undergraduate, freshman; graduate student, postgraduate student.

class, form, grade, room; promotion, graduation.

disciple, follower, apostle, proselyte.

classmate, fellow student, schoolmate, schoolfellow, fellow pupil.

novice, beginner, tyro, recruit, tenderfoot [*slang or colloq.*], neophyte, probationer; apprentice.

Adj. in leading strings, pupillary, probationary.

542. SCHOOL.—*N.* school, academy, lyceum, seminary, college, educational institution, institute; university, varsity [*colloq.*], alma mater [L.].

General: day (*or* boarding, preparatory, elementary, denominational, secondary, military, naval, technical, library, secretarial, business, correspondence) school; kindergarten, nursery school; Sunday (*or* Sabbath, Bible) school.

United States: district (*or* grade, parochial, public, primary, grammar, junior high, high, Latin) school; private school, normal school, kindergarten training school; summer school; military academy (West Point); naval academy (Annapolis); college, fresh-water college [*colloq. or slang*], state university; graduate school, postgraduate school.

class, division, form, etc., 541; seminar.

classroom, room, schoolroom, recitation room; lecture room, lecture hall, theater, amphitheater.

desk, reading desk, pulpit, forum, stage, rostrum, platform.

schoolbook, textbook; grammar, primer, reader.

Adj. scholastic, academic, collegiate; educational, cultural; gymnastic, athletic, physical, eurythmic.

543. VERACITY.—*N.* veracity, truthfulness, frankness, truth, sincerity, candor, honesty, fidelity, love of truth; probity, etc., 939.

V. speak the truth, tell the truth; speak on oath; speak without equivocation (*or* mental reservation), make a clean breast, disclose, etc., 529; speak one's mind.

Adj. truthful, true; veracious, scrupulous, punctilious; sincere, candid, frank, open, outspoken, straightforward, unreserved, truth-telling, honest, trustworthy; guileless, pure, truth-loving; true-blue, as good as one's word; unfeigned, ingenuous.

544. FALSEHOOD.—*N.* falsehood, falseness, falsity, falsification, misrepresentation, deception, etc., 545; untruthfulness, lying; untruth, etc., 546; mendacity, guile, perjury, false swearing; forgery, invention, fabrication; perversion, distortion, exaggeration, prevarication, equivocation, evasion, fraud; simulation, dissimulation, dissembling; deceit; sham, pretense; malingering.

duplicity, double dealing, insincerity, hypocrisy, cant, pharisaism; casuistry, Machiavellism; lip service, hollowness, mere show; quackery, charlatanism, charlatanry; humbug; cajolery, flattery; Judas kiss; perfidy, etc., 940; cunning, etc., 702; misstatement, false report.

V. **lie,** tell a lie (*or* an untruth), fib, swear falsely, forswear, perjure oneself, bear false witness.

falsify, misstate, misquote; misrepresent, etc., 523; belie; garble, gloss over, disguise, color, varnish, doctor [*colloq.*], dress up, embroider; exaggerate, etc., 549.

prevaricate, equivocate, quibble; trim, shuffle, fence, beat about the bush.

fabricate, invent; trump up; forge; coin; hatch, concoct; romance.

dissemble, dissimulate; feign, assume; pretend, make believe; play false, play a double game; coquet; act *or* play a part; affect, pose; simulate, pass off for; counterfeit, sham; malinger; deceive, etc., 545.

Adj. **false,** untrue, deceitful, mendacious, lying, untruthful, fraudulent, dishonest; faithless, forsworn; evasive, disingenuous, hollow, insincere; artful, cunning, tricky, wily, sly; perfidious, treacherous, perjured; spurious, etc., 545; falsified.

hypocritical, canting, pharisaical; Machiavellian, double-tongued, double-dealing; two-faced, double-faced; smooth-spoken, smooth-tongued; plausible, mealy-mouthed; affected, canting, insincere.

545. DECEPTION.—*N.* **deception;** falseness, etc., 544; untruth, etc., 546; imposition, imposture; fraud, deceit, guile, fraudulence, misrepresentation, bluff; trickery, knavery, sharp practice, collusion, chicanery; treachery, double-dealing.

delusion, jugglery, sleight of hand, legerdemain, conjuring.

trick, cheat, wile, blind, feint, chicane, juggle, swindle; stratagem, artifice; hoax; bunk [*slang*], gold brick [*colloq.*].

snare, trap, pitfall, gin; bait, decoy duck, stool pigeon; cobweb, net, meshes, toils; ambush, ambuscade.

disguise, false colors, camouflage, masquerade, mask, mummery, borrowed plumes; dissembler, hypocrite, etc., 548.

sham, mockery, copy, counterfeit, make-believe, forgery, fraud, untruth, etc., 546; hollow mockery; whited sepulcher, tinsel, paste.

illusion, delusion, self-deception, *ignis fatuus* [L.], mirage, etc., 443.

V. **deceive,** mislead, lead astray, take in, defraud, cheat, cozen, swindle; victimize; betray, play false; lie, etc., 544: mystify; blind, hoodwink; throw dust into the eyes; impose upon, practice upon, palm off on; bluff.

outwit, circumvent, overreach, steal a march on.

insnare, ensnare, entrap, decoy, waylay, lure, beguile, delude, inveigle, trick.

fool, befool, dupe, gull, hoax, humbug, stuff [*slang*], sell [*slang*]; trifle with, cajole, flatter; dissemble, dissimulate, sham, counterfeit.

practice chicanery, live by one's wits, juggle, conjure, play off, palm off, foist off.

Adj. **deceptive,** deceitful, tricky, cunning, etc., 702; elusive, insidious; delusive, illusory.

make-believe; untrue, etc., 546; mock, sham, counterfeit, pseudo, spurious, so-called, pretended, feigned, bogus [*colloq.*], fraudulent, surreptitious, illegitimate, contraband; adulterated, disguised; unsound, meretricious, jerry-built; tinsel.

Adv. under false colors, under cover of.

546. UNTRUTH.—*N.* untruth, falsehood, lie, story, fib, whopper [*colloq.*].

fabrication, forgery, invention; misstatement, misrepresentation, perversion, falsification, false coloring, exaggeration.

fiction; fable, nursery tale, fairy tale, romance, extravaganza; canard; yarn [*colloq.*], fish story [*colloq.*], traveler's tale, cock-and-bull story, myth, moonshine, bosh [*colloq.*].

half truth, white lie, pious fraud; suppression; irony.

pretense, pretext, subterfuge, evasion, shift, shuffle, make-believe, sham, etc., 545; profession, Judas kiss, cajolery, flattery; disguise, etc., 530.

V. **feign,** make-believe, pretend, sham, counterfeit; lie, etc., 544.

Adj. **untrue,** false, trumped up; unfounded, invented, fictitious, fabulous, fabricated, fraudulent, forged; evasive.

547. DUPE.—*N.* dupe, gull, victim, April fool; sucker [*slang*]; laughingstock, etc., 857; greenhorn; fool, etc., 501; puppet, cat's-paw.

V. **be deceived,** be the dupe of; fall into a trap; swallow *or* nibble at the bait; swallow whole; bite.

Adj. **credulous,** gullible, etc., 486.

mistaken, etc. (*error*), 495.

548. DECEIVER.—*N.* deceiver, dissembler, hypocrite, Pharisee; sophist; serpent, snake in the grass, Judas, wolf in sheep's clothing.

liar, storyteller, perjurer, false witness, faker [*slang*], fraud, four-flusher [*slang*], confidence man, decoy, stool pigeon; rogue, knave, cheat, swindler.

impostor, pretender, malingerer, humbug; adventurer, adventuress.

trickster, conjurer, juggler, necromancer, sorcerer, magician, wizard, medicine man, witch doctor; quack, charlatan, mountebank.

549. EXAGGERATION.—*N.* **exaggeration,** expansion, amplification; fringe, embroidery; extravagance, hyperbole, stretch, high coloring, caricature; yarn [*colloq.*], traveler's tale, fish story [*colloq.*]; tempest in a teacup; much ado about nothing; puffery, etc. (*boasting*), 884; rant, etc., 577.

V. **exaggerate,** magnify, pile up, aggravate; amplify, expand, overestimate, overstate, overdraw, overshoot the mark, overpraise; stretch a point; draw a long bow [*colloq.*], out-Herod Herod. overcolor, heighten; embroider, color; puff, etc. (*boast*), 884

Adj. **exaggerated,** overwrought; bombastic, etc. (*magniloquent*), 577; hyperbolical, extravagant; preposterous, egregious.

550. [Means of communication] INDICATION.—*N.* **indication,** sign, symbol; index, indicator, pointer, cue, note, token, symptom; type, figure, emblem, cipher, device; motto, epitaph

means of recognition; lineament, feature, trait, trick, earmark, characteristic.

gesture, gesticulation; pantomime; wink, glance, leer; nod, shrug, beck; touch, nudge; byplay, dumb show; deaf-and-dumb alphabet, dactylology.

track, spoor, trail, footprint, scent; clue, key.

signal, rocket, watch fire, beacon fire, watchtower; telegraph, semaphore; fiery cross; calumet, peace pipe; heliograph; searchlight, flashlight.

mark, line, stroke, score, streak, scratch, tick, dot, notch, nick, blaze; red letter, underlining, impression.

Map drawing: hachure, contour line; isobar, isopiestic line, isobaric line; isotherm, isothermal line; latitude, longitude, meridian, equator.

For identification: badge, countercheck, countersign, counterfoil, stub, duplicate, tally; label, ticket, counter, check, chip, voucher, stamp; trade-mark, hall mark; card, visiting card; credentials; handwriting, sign manual, autograph, signature; monogram, seal, signet; fingerprint; brand; caste mark; mortarboard [*colloq.*], cap and gown, hood; shibboleth; watchword, catchword, password, cue, sign, countersign, pass, grip; open-sesame.

Insignia: banner, flag, colors, streamer, pennant, pennon, ensign, standard eagle, oriflamme, blue peter, jack, Union Jack; Old Glory [*colloq.*], Stars and Stripes

Heraldry: crest, arms, coat of arms, armorial bearings; hatchment, escutcheon or scutcheon; shield, supporters; livery, uniform; cockade, brassard, epaulet, chevron; garland, chaplet, love knot, favor.

Of locality: beacon, flagstaff, hand, pointer, vane, cock, weathercock, weather vane; guidepost, signpost; sign, signboard; North Star, polestar; landmark, seamark; lighthouse; address, direction, name.

Of the future: warning, premonition; omen, portent, sign.

Of the past: trace, record.

Of danger: warning, alarm, fire alarm, burglar alarm.

Of authority: scepter, etc., 747.

Of triumph: trophy, etc., 733.

Of mourning: mourning, etc., 839.

Of quantity: gauge, etc., 466.

Of distance: milestone, milepost.

Of disgrace: brand, foolscap, mark of Cain, stigma, stripes, broad arrow.

call, word of command; bugle call, trumpet call; bell, alarum, battle cry, reveille, taps, last post; sacring bell, Sanctus bell, angelus; dirge

V. **indicate,** denote, betoken, connote, signify; represent, stand for; typify, symbolize; mark, note, stamp, nick, blaze; label, ticket.

make a sign, signalize; beckon, nod, wink, glance, leer, nudge, shrug, gesticulate.

sign, seal, attest, underscore, underline; call attention to.

Adj. **indicative,** indicatory; connotative, denotative, representative, typical, individual, symbolic *or* symbolical, symptomatic, characteristic, significant, diagnostic, emblematic, armorial.

551. RECORD.—*N.* **trace,** vestige, relic, remains; scar, cicatrix; footstep, footmark, footprint; track, mark, wake, trail, scent, spoor.

monument, hatchment; escutcheon *or* scutcheon; slab, tablet, trophy, obelisk, pillar, column, monolith; memorial; memento; testimonial, medal, Congressional medal; cross, Victoria cross [Eng.], iron cross [Ger.]; ribbon, garter; commemoration, etc. (*celebration*), 883.

record, note, minute; register, registry; roll, list; entry, memorandum, endorsement, inscription, copy, duplicate, docket; mark, etc., 550; deed; document; deposition, affidavit; certificate.

notebook, memorandum book; bulletin, bulletin board, scoreboard, score sheet; card index, file, letter file, pigeonholes.

newspaper, daily, gazette, magazine, paper [*colloq.*].

calendar, diary, log, journal, daybook, ledger, cashbook.

archive, scroll, state paper, return, bluebook; almanac, gazetteer, census report; statistics; Congressional Records; minutes, chronicle, annals; legend; history, biography, etc., 594.

registration, registry, enrollment, tabulation; entry, booking; signature, sign manual; recorder, etc., 553; journalism.

mechanical record, recording instrument; phonograph, etc., 418; speedometer, pedometer, patent log [*naut.*]; ticker, tape; time clock; turnstile; cash register.

V. **record,** put *or* place upon record, chronicle, calendar, hand down to posterity; commemorate, etc. (*celebrate*), 883; report, commit to writing, note, put *or* set down; mark, etc. (*indicate*), 550; sign, etc. (*attest*), 467; enter, book, post, insert; mark off, tick off; register, list, enroll, inscroll; file.

552. [Suppression of sign] OBLITERATION.—*N.* **obliteration,** erasure, cancellation, deletion; blot; effacement, extinction.

V. **efface,** obliterate, erase, expunge, cancel; blot (*or* rub, scratch, strike, wash, wipe) out; deface, render illegible; rule out.

be effaced, leave no trace.

Adj. **obliterated,** erased; unrecorded, unregistered.

553. RECORDER.—*N.* **recorder,** notary, clerk; registrar, register; amanuensis, secretary, recording secretary, stenographer, bookkeeper, scribe.

annalist, historian, historiographer, chronicler; biographer, etc.

(*narrator*), 594; antiquary, antiquarian, archeologist; memorialist.

journalist, newspaperman, reporter, interviewer; publicist, author, editor.

554. REPRESENTATION.—*N.* **representation,** depiction, imitation, illustration, delineation, imagery, portraiture; design, designing; art, fine arts; painting, etc., 556; sculpture, etc., 557; engraving, etc., 558.

photography; radiography, X-ray photography, skiagraphy.

personation, impersonation; personification; drama, etc., 599.

drawing, picture, sketch, draft; tracing; copy, etc., 21.
photograph, photo [*colloq.*], daguerreotype, print, cabinet, snapshot.
image, effigy, icon, portrait, likeness, facsimile.
figure, figurehead, puppet, doll, manikin, lay figure, model, marionette, statue, statuette, bust.
map, plan, chart; diagram; ground plan, projection, elevation; atlas; outline, view.
radiograph, radiogram, skiagraph, skiagram, X-ray photograph, Xray [*colloq.*].
delineator, draftsman; artist, etc., 559; photographer, radiographer, X-ray photographer, skiagrapher, daguerreotypist.

V. **represent,** delineate, depict, portray, picture, limn, photograph, snapshot; figure, shadow forth, adumbrate; describe, etc., 594; trace, copy; mold; illustrate, symbolize; paint, etc., 556; sculpture, etc., 557; engrave, etc., 558.

personate, impersonate, dress up [*colloq.*], pose as, act; personify; play, etc. (*drama*), 559; mimic, etc. (*imitate*),19.

Adj. **representative;** illustrative; imitative, figurative; similar, like, etc., 17; descriptive, etc., 594.

555. MISREPRESENTATION.—*N.* **misrepresentation,** misstatement, falsification, exaggeration, distortion; bad likeness, daub, scratch.

burlesque, travesty, parody, take-off, caricature, extravaganza.

V. **misrepresent,** distort, overdraw, exaggerate, daub, falsify, understate, overstate, stretch.

burlesque, travesty, parody, caricature.

556. PAINTING, BLACK AND WHITE.—*N.* **painting,** depicting, drawing; design; perspective; composition; treatment; arrangement, values, atmosphere, tone, technique.

palette; easel; brush, pencil, stump, black lead, charcoal, crayons, chalk, pastel; paint, etc. (*coloring matter*), 428; water (*or* oil) colors; oils, oil paint; varnish; distemper, fresco, enamel, mosaic, encaustic painting; batik.
style, school; the grand style, high art; futurist, cubist, vorticist.
picture, painting, piece, tableau, canvas; fresco, cartoon; drawing, draft; still life, genre (*or* landscape) painting; sketch, outline, study.
portrait; head; miniature; silhouette; profile.

view, landscape, seascape, sea view, seapiece; scene, prospect; interior; panorama, bird's-eye view.

picture gallery, art gallery, art museum; studio, atelier [F.].

photograph, radiography, etc., 554; photograph, radiograph, etc., 554.

V. **paint,** design, limn, draw, sketch, pencil, color; stencil; depict, etc. (*represent*), 554.

Adj. **pictorial,** graphic; picturesque, historical; futurist, cubist, vorticist; in the grand style.

557. SCULPTURE.—*N.* **sculpture,** carving, modeling, statuary; ceramics.

marble, bronze, terra cotta; ceramic ware, pottery, porcelain, china, earthenware; cloisonné, enamel, faïence.

relief, low relief, bas-relief, high relief; intaglio; cameo; medal, medallion.

statue, statuette, bust; cast.

V. **sculpture,** carve, cut, chisel, model, mold; cast.

558. ENGRAVING.—*N.* **engraving,** etching, chiseling; plate (*or* copperplate, steel, half-tone, wood) engraving; lithography, chromolithography, photolithography.

printing; color printing, lithographic printing; type printing; three-color process. impression, print, engraving, plate; steel-plate, copperplate; etching; aquatint, mezzotint; cut, woodcut; lithograph, chromolithograph, photolithograph. illustration, illumination; half-tone; photogravure; rotogravure; vignette, initial letter, tailpiece.

V. **engrave,** grave, etch; bite; bite in; lithograph; print.

559. ARTIST.—*N.* **artist;** painter, drawer, sketcher, designer, engraver, graver, line engraver, draftsman; chaser; copyist; enameler, enamelist; cartoonist, caricaturist.

historical (*or* landscape, marine, flower, portrait, genre, miniature, scene) painter; carver, modeler, statuary, sculptor.

(1) Language generally

560. LANGUAGE.—*N.* **language;** phraseology, etc., 569; speech, etc., 582; tongue, lingo [*chiefly humorous or contemptuous*], vernacular, mother (*or* vulgar, native) tongue; king's English; dialect, brogue, patois, idiom.

confusion of tongues, Babel; universal language, Esperanto, Ido; pantomime, dumb show.

literature, letters, polite literature, belles-lettres [F.], muses, humanities, republic of letters, dead languages, classics.

linguist, etc. (*scholar*), 492.

V. **express,** say, express by words.

Adj. **lingual,** linguistic; dialectal, dialectic; vernacular, current; bilingual; polyglot; literary; colloquial, slangy.

561. LETTER.—*N.* **letter;** character; hieroglyphic; alphabet,

ABC; consonant, vowel, diphthong, mute, surd, sonant, liquid, labial, palatal, cerebral, dental, guttural.

syllable; monosyllable, dissyllable, polysyllable; prefix, suffix.

spelling, orthography; phonetic spelling, phonetics.

cipher, code; monogram, anagram; acrostic, double acrostic. *V.* spell; transliterate.

cipher, decipher; code, decode.

Adj. literal; alphabetical, syllabic.

phonetic, voiced, tonic, sonant; voiceless, surd; mute, labial, palatal, cerebral, dental, guttural, liquid.

562. WORD.—*N.* word, term, vocable; name, etc., 564; phrase, etc., 566; root, derivative; part of speech.

dictionary, lexicon, vocabulary, wordbook, index, glossary, thesaurus.

Science of language: etymology, philology; terminology; pronunciation, orthoëpy; lexicography.

verbosity, verbiage, wordiness; loquacity, etc., 584.

V. vocalize; etymologize, derive; index; translate.

Adj. verbal, literal; derivative.

verbose, wordy, etc., 573; loquacious, etc., 584.

563. NEOLOGY.—*N.* neology, neologism; barbarism; corruption.

dialect, brogue, patois, provincialism, broken English, Anglicism, Briticism, Gallicism, Americanism; gypsy lingo, Romany.

lingua franca, pidgin English, Hindustani; Esperanto, Ido.

jargon, dog Latin, gibberish; confusion of tongues, Babel; lingo, slang, cant, argot, billingsgate.

pseudonym, pen name; nickname; alias.

neologist, word coiner, coiner of words.

V. coin words; Americanize, Anglicize, Gallicize.

Adj. neologic, neological; slang, cant, barbarous.

564. NOMENCLATURE.—*N.* nomenclature; naming, nicknaming; baptism.

name, appellation, appellative, designation, denomination; nickname, etc., 565; epithet; title, head, heading; style, proper name, cognomen, patronymic, surname; title, handle to one's name; namesake.

term, expression, noun; technical term; cant.

V. name, call, term, denominate, designate, style, entitle, dub [*colloq. or humorous*], christen, baptize, nickname, characterize, specify, label.

Adj. named, yclept [*humorous*]; known as; titular, nominal.

565. MISNOMER.—*N.* misnomer; malapropism, Mrs. Malaprop.

nickname, sobriquet, pet name, assumed name, alias; stage name; *nom de guerre* [F.], nom de plume [English formation], pen name, pseudonym.

V. **misname,** miscall, nickname; take an assumed name.

Adj. **misnamed;** self-styled; so-called, quasi.

nameless, anonymous; unacknowledged; pseudo.

566. PHRASE.—*N.* **phrase,** expression, locution; sentence, paragraph; paraphrase, metaphor, euphemism, euphuism; motto, proverb; figure of speech; idiom, turn of expression; phraseology, etc., 569.

V. **express,** phrase; word, voice; put into (*or* express by) words; call, denominate, designate, dub.

Adv. in round (*or* set) terms; in set phrases; by the card.

567. GRAMMAR.—*N.* **grammar,** accidence, syntax, analysis, parts of speech; inflection, case, declension, conjugation; philology.

V. parse, analyze, conjugate, decline.

Adj. **grammatical,** syntactic *or* syntactical, inflectional, declensional, synthetic *or* synthetical.

568. SOLECISM.—*N.* **solecism;** grammatical blunder; error, slip; slip of the pen, slip of the tongue, bull; barbarism, impropriety.

V. **solecize,** commit a solecism; murder the king's English.

Adj. **ungrammatical,** incorrect, inaccurate, faulty; improper.

569. STYLE.—*N.* **style,** diction, phraseology, wording; manner, strain; composition; mode of expression, idiom, choice of words; mode of speech, literary power, command of language; authorship, artistry.

V. **word,** phrase, express by words, write; apply the file.

Various Qualities of Style

570. PERSPICUITY.—*N.* **perspicuity,** perspicacity, explicitness, lucidness, lucidity, limpidity, clearness; plain speaking, expression, definiteness, definition; exactness, etc., 494.

Adj. **lucid,** intelligible, etc., 518; limpid, pellucid, clear, explicit; exact, etc., 494.

571. OBSCURITY.—*N.* **obscurity,** unintelligibility, involution, confusion; hard words; ambiguity, indefiniteness, vagueness, inexactness, inaccuracy; darkness of meaning.

Adj. **obscure,** involved, confused.

572. CONCISENESS.—*N.* **conciseness,** terseness, brevity, laconicism, abridgment, compression, condensation, epitome, etc., 596.

Portmanteau word [Lewis Carroll]; brunch [breakfast + lunch], slithy, *adj.* [slimy + lithe], torrible, *adj.* [torrid + horrible].

V. be concise, telescope, compress, condense, abridge, abbreviate, abstract, etc., 596; come to the point.

Adj. concise, brief, short, laconic, succinct, curt, compact, summary, compendious, etc., 596; terse, to the point; compressed, condensed, pointed; pithy, crisp, trenchant, epigrammatic, sententious.

Adv. briefly, summarily; in brief, in short, in a word.

573. DIFFUSENESS.—*N.* diffuseness, profuseness, amplification, verbosity, wordiness; verbiage, flow of words, etc. (*loquacity*), 584; looseness; tautology, exuberance, redundance, prolixity, periphrase, expletive; padding [*editors' cant*]; drivel, twaddle.

V. expand, expatiate, enlarge, dilate, amplify, inflate, pad [*editors' cant*], rant; maunder, prose; harp upon, dwell on.

digress, ramble, beat about the bush, protract.

Adj. diffuse, profuse, wordy, verbose, copious, exuberant; lengthy, long, long-winded, protracted, prolix, diffusive, roundabout, digressive, discursive, loose; rambling, frothy.

574. VIGOR.—*N.* vigor, power, force; boldness, intellectual force; spirit, punch [*slang*], point, piquancy, raciness; verve, ardor, enthusiasm, glow, fire, warmth; gravity, weight.

loftiness, elevation, sublimity, grandeur.

eloquence; command of words, command of language.

Adj. vigorous, nervous, powerful, forcible, forceful; mordant, biting, trenchant, incisive; graphic, impressive.

spirited, lively, glowing, sparkling; racy, bold, pungent, piquant, pithy.

lofty, elevated, sublime, poetic, grand, weighty, ponderous; eloquent.

vehement, passionate, burning, impassioned, petulant.

575. FEEBLENESS.—*N.* feebleness, baldness, enervation, flaccidity, vapidity, poverty.

Adj. feeble, tame, meager, insipid, watery, nerveless, vapid, trashy, poor, dull, dry, languid; bald, colorless, enervated; prosy, prosaic, weak, slight; careless, slovenly, loose, lax; slipshod, inexact; puerile, childish; rambling, etc. (*diffuse*), 573.

576. PLAINNESS.—*N.* plainness, homeliness, simplicity, severity; household words.

V. speak plainly, waste no words, come to the point.

Adj. plain, simple, unornamented, unadorned, unvarnished; homely, homespun; neat; severe, chaste, pure, Saxon; commonplace, matter-of-fact, natural, prosaic, sober.

Adv. **point-blank;** in plain English; in common parlance.

577. ORNAMENT.—*N.* **ornament,** floridness, grandiloquence, magniloquence, declamation, well-rounded periods; elegance, etc., 578; flourish, trope; euphuism, euphemism.

bombast, inflation, pretension; rant, fustian, highfalutin [*slang*], buncombe, balderdash; fine writing; purple patches.

V. **ornament,** overcharge, overload; euphuize, euphemize.

Adj. **ornate;** ornamented, beautified, florid, rich, flowery; euphuistic, euphemistic; sonorous, inflated, swelling, tumid; turgid, pedantic, pompous, stilted, high-flown, sententious, rhetorical, declamatory; grandiose; grandiloquent, magniloquent, bombastic; frothy, flashy, flamboyant.

578. ELEGANCE.—*N.* **elegance,** distinction, clarity, purity, grace, felicity, ease; gracefulness, euphony; taste, good taste, restraint, propriety, correctness.

purist, classicist, stylist.

Adj. **elegant,** polished, classic *or* classical, correct, artistic; chaste, pure; graceful, easy, fluent, unaffected, natural, mellifluous, euphonious; restrained.

felicitous, happy, neat; well expressed.

579. INELEGANCE.—*N.* **inelegance,** impurity, vulgarity; poor diction, poor choice of words; loose construction; ill-balanced sentences; barbarism, slang; solecism, mannerism, affectation.

Adj. **inelegant,** graceless, ungraceful; harsh, abrupt; dry, stiff, cramped, formal, forced, labored; artificial, mannered, affected, ponderous, awkward; unpolished; turgid, barbarous, uncouth, rude, crude, halting, vulgar.

(2) Spoken Language

580. VOICE.—*N.* **voice;** intonation; utterance; vocalization; cry, exclamation, expletive, ejaculation; vociferation, enunciation, articulation; distinctness; clearness; delivery, attack.

accent, accentuation; emphasis, stress; pronunciation; euphony, etc. (*melody*), 413.

V. **speak,** utter, breathe; cry, etc. (*shout*), 411; ejaculate, rap out; articulate, enunciate, vocalize, pronounce, accentuate, deliver, emit; whisper, murmur.

Adj. **vocal,** phonetic, oral; ejaculatory, articulate, distinct, euphonious, melodious.

581. DUMBNESS.—*N.* **dumbness;** silence, etc. (*taciturnity*), 585; deaf-mutism, deaf-muteness, deaf-dumbness, mute, dummy, deaf-mute.

V. **silence,** muzzle, muffle, suppress, smother, gag, strike dumb, dumfound.

Adj. **dumb,** mute, mum; tongue-tied; voiceless, speechless, wordless; silent, etc. (*taciturn*), 585; inarticulate.

582. SPEECH.—*N.* **speech,** locution, talk, parlance, word of mouth, prattle.

oration, recitation, delivery, speech, address, discourse, lecture, harangue, sermon, tirade, soliloquy, etc., 589; conversation, etc., 588; salutatory; valedictory.

oratory, elocution, eloquence, rhetoric, declamation; grandiloquence.

speaker, spokesman, mouthpiece, orator, rhetorician, lecturer, preacher, elocutionist, reciter, reader; spellbinder.

V. **speak,** talk, say, utter, pronounce, deliver, breathe, let fall, rap out, blurt out.

soliloquize, etc., 589; tell, etc. (*inform*), 527; address, etc., 586; converse, etc., 588.

declaim, hold forth, harangue, stump [*colloq.*], spout, rant; recite, lecture, sermonize, discourse, expatiate.

Adj. **oral,** lingual, phonetic, unwritten, spoken.

eloquent, oratorical, rhetorical, elocutionary, declamatory, grandiloquent.

583. [Imperfect Speech] STAMMERING.—*N.* inarticulateness; stammering, hesitation, impediment in one's speech; lisp, drawl, nasal accent; twang; falsetto, brogue.

V. **stammer,** stutter, hesitate, falter.

mumble, mutter, maunder; mince, lisp; jabber, gabble, gibber; splutter, sputter; drawl, mouth; croak.

murder the language, murder the king's English; mispronounce.

Adj. **inarticulate;** stammering, guttural, throaty, nasal; tremulous.

584. LOQUACITY.—*N.* **loquacity,** loquaciousness, effusion; talkativeness, garrulity.

gabble, gab [*colloq.*], jaw [*low*], hot air [*slang*]; jabber, chatter; prate, prattle, twaddle, small talk.

fluency, volubility, flow of words; verbosity, etc. (*diffuseness*), 573; eloquence.

talker; chatterer, chatterbox; babbler, ranter, proser, driveler, gossip, magpie.

V. **be loquacious,** talk glibly, pour forth, prate, palaver, prose, maunder, chatter, blab, gush, prattle, jabber, jaw [*low*], babble, gabble; expatiate, gossip, talk at random, talk nonsense.

Adj. **loquacious,** talkative, garrulous, chattering, chatty, declamatory, fluent, voluble, effusive, glib, flippant.

585. TACITURNITY.—*N.* **taciturnity,** silence, muteness, curtness; reserve, reticence.

man of few words; Spartan.

V. **be silent,** keep silence; hold one's tongue, say nothing; render mute.

Adj. **silent,** mute, mum, still, dumb.

taciturn, laconic, concise, sententious, close, close-mouthed, curt; reserved; reticent.

586. ADDRESS.—*N.* **address,** allocution; speech, etc., 582; appeal, invocation, salutation, salutatory.

V. **address,** speak to, accost, apostrophize, appeal to, invoke; hail, salute; call to, halloo.

lecture, preach, harangue, spellbind.

587. RESPONSE, etc., *see* **Answer** 462.

588. CONVERSATION.—*N.* **conversation,** colloquy, converse, interlocution, talk, discourse, dialogue, duologue.

chat, tattle, gossip, tittle-tattle; babble.

conference, parley, interview, audience, reception; congress, etc. (*council*), 696; powwow.

debate, palaver, war of words, controversy.

talker, gossip, tattler; chatterer, etc. (*loquacity*), 584; speaker, etc., 582; conversationalist.

V. **converse,** talk together, hold (*or* carry on, join in, engage in) a conversation; parley; palaver; chat, gossip, tattle; prate, etc., 584.

confer with, discourse with, commune with, talk it over.

Adj. **conversational,** conversable; chatty, colloquial.

589. SOLILOQUY.—*N.* **soliloquy,** monologue, apostrophe.

V. **soliloquize,** monologize, talk to oneself; think aloud, apostrophize.

Written Language

590. WRITING.—*N.* **writing,** chirography, penmanship; type-writing; manuscript; script; character, letter, etc., 561.

shorthand, stenography, phonography; secret writing, cipher, cryptography.

handwriting; signature, mark, autograph, hand, fist [*colloq.*]; calligraphy.

composition, authorship; lucubration, production, work, screed, article, paper; book, etc., 593; essay, theme, thesis; novel, text-book; poem, book of poems (*or* verse), anthology.

writer, scribe; author, etc., 593; amanuensis, secretary, clerk, penman, copyist; stenographer, typewriter, typist.

V. **write,** pen, typewrite, type [*colloq.*]; copy, engross; transcribe; scribble, scrawl, scratch; note down, write down, record.

compose, indite, draw up, draft, formulate; dictate; inscribe.

Adj. **written,** in writing, in black and white; stenographic.

591. PRINTING.—*N.* **printing,** typography; type, linotype, monotype; composition, print, letterpress, text, context, matter; copy, impression, proof, galley, galley proof, page proof.

printer, compositor; reader, proofreader, corrector of the press; printer's devil; copyholder, copyeditor.

V. **print;** compose; go to press; publish, issue, bring out.

Adj. **typographical,** printed, in type.

592. CORRESPONDENCE.—*N.* **correspondence,** letter, epistle, missive, note, post card, postal card; dispatch; bulletin, circular.

correspondent, writer, letter writer.

V. **correspond,** write to, send a letter to; communicate, communicate by writing (*or* letter); circularize, follow up, bombard; reply.

593. BOOK.—*N.* **book,** booklet; writing, work, volume, tome, tract, treatise, brochure, monograph, pamphlet, libretto; handbook, manual, novel, etc. (*composition*), 590; publication; magazine, periodical.

work of reference, encyclopedia, cyclopedia, dictionary, thesaurus, concordance, anthology, compilation.

writer, author, essayist, contributor; hack writer, hack; journalist, publicist, reporter, correspondent; editor, scribe, etc., 590; playwright, etc., 599; poet, etc., 597.

publisher, bookseller; librarian; bookworm.

bookstore, bookshop, bookseller's shop, publishing house.

library, public library, lending library.

594. DESCRIPTION.—*N.* **description,** account, statement, report, record; brief, etc. (*abstract*), 596; delineation, sketch, pastel, vignette; monograph; narration, recital, rehearsal, relation.

narrative, history, memoir; annals, etc., (*chronicle*), 551; journal, letters, biography, autobiography, life, adventures.

Fiction· novel, romance, story, tale, short story, anecdote; detective story, fairy tale, fable, parable, allegory.

narrator, historian, biographer, novelist, storyteller, romancer, anecdotist, word painter; writer, etc., 593.

V. **describe,** set forth, picture, portray, characterize, delineate, narrate, relate, recite, recount, romance, tell, report; detail, particularize.

Adj. **descriptive,** graphic, narrative, epic, romantic, historic *or* historical, biographical, autobiographical; traditional, legendary, mythical, fabulous; anecdotic, idealistic; realistic, true to life.

595. DISSERTATION.—*N.* **dissertation,** treatise, essay, thesis, theme; tract, discourse, memoir, disquisition, lecture, sermon, homily, investigation, study, discussion, exposition.

commentary, review, critique, criticism, article, leader, editorial.

commentator, critic, essayist, publicist, reviewer, leader writer, editor.

V. comment, explain, interpret, criticize, illuminate; treat of (or ventilate, discuss, deal with, go into) a subject.

596. COMPENDIUM.—N. compendium, abstract, précis, epitome, analysis, digest, brief, condensation, abridgment, abbreviation, etc., 201; summary, draft, minute, note; excerpt, extract; synopsis, textbook, outlines, syllabus, contents, heads, prospectus.

fragments, extracts, cuttings; fugitive pieces, anthology, miscellany, compilation.

recapitulation, résumé, review; symposium.

V. abridge, abstract, epitomize, summarize; abbreviate, etc. (shorten), 201; condense, etc. (compress), 195.

compile, etc. (collect), 72; note down, collect, edit.

recapitulate, review, skim, run over, sum up.

Adj. compendious, synoptic, abridged, analytic or analytical.

Adv. in short, in substance, in few words, in a nutshell.

597. POETRY.—N. poetry, poetics, poesy, muse, Apollo, Parnassus, inspiration, fire of genius.

poem; epic, ballad, lyric, ode, idyl, eclogue, pastoral, sonnet, elegy; dramatic (or didactic, satirical, narrative, lyric) poetry; satire; anthology.

versification, rhyming, prosody; scansion, scanning.
canto, stanza, verse, line, couplet, triplet, quatrain; refrain, chorus, burden; octave, sextet.
verse, rhyme, assonance, alliteration, meter, measure; foot, numbers, rhythm; ictus, beat, accent, accentuation, iambus, iambic, dactyl, spondee, trochee, anapest, etc.; hexameter, pentameter; Alexandrine; blank verse, heroic verse; doggerel.

poet, genius, creator; poet laureate; laureate; bard, lyrist, sonneteer, rhapsodist, satirist, troubadour; minstrel; minnesinger, Meistersinger; jongleur, versifier, rhymer, rhymester, minor poet, poetaster.

V. poetize, sing, write poetry; string verses together, versify, make verses, rhyme.

Adj. poetic or poetical; lyric or lyrical; tuneful; metrical; elegiac, iambic, dactylic, spondaic, trochaic, anapestic.

598. PROSE.—N. prose, prosaicness; poetic prose; narrative, etc., 594.

prose writer, essayist, novelist, etc., 594.

V. prose; write prose (or in prose).

Adj. prosaic, prosy, unpoetical, unrhymed, in prose.

599. THE DRAMA.—*N.* **the drama,** the stage, the theater, the play; theatricals, histrionic art.

play, drama, piece, tragedy, comedy, opera, vaudeville, curtain raiser, interlude, afterpiece, farce, extravaganza, harlequinade, pantomime, burlesque, ballet, spectacle, masque, melodrama; comedy of manners; charade, mystery, miracle play, morality play.

act, scene, tableau, curtain; introduction, prologue, exposition, epilogue; libretto, book, text, prompter's copy.

performance, representation, show [*colloq.*], stage setting, stagecraft; acting; impersonation, stage business; slapstick [*slang*], buffoonery.

theater, playhouse, amphitheater, moving-picture theater, moving pictures, movies [*colloq.*]; puppet show, marionettes, Punch and Judy.

cast, dramatis personae [L.], role, part, character; star, headliner; comedian, tragedian.

actor, player, performer; masker, mime, mimic; star, headliner; comedian, tragedian.

buffoon, mummer, pantomimist, clown; pantaloon, harlequin, columbine; punch.

company, first tragedian, prima donna, leading lady; lead; leading man; comedian, comedienne; juvenile lead, juvenile; villain, heavy lead, heavy, heavy father; ingenue, soubrette; character man, character woman, extra, mute, supernumerary, super [*theat. cant*].

dramatist, playwright, playwriter; dramatic author (*or* writer).
audience, house; orchestra, gallery.

V. **act,** play, perform; put on the stage, dramatize, stage, produce, set; personate, mimic, enact; rehearse, spout, rant; tread the stage (*or* boards); make one's debut, take a part, star.

Adj. **dramatic;** theatrical; scenic, histrionic, comic, tragic, farcical, tragicomic, melodramatic, operatic; stagy, spectacular.

Adv. **on the stage,** on the boards; in the limelight, in the spotlight; before the footlights, before an audience; behind the scenes.

CLASS V

Words Relating to the VOLUNTARY POWERS

I. Individual Volition

600. WILL.—*N.* **will,** volition, free will; freedom, etc., 748; discretion; choice, inclination, intent, purpose, option, etc. (*choice*), 609; spontaneity, spontaneousness; originality.

determination, etc. (*resolution*), 604; force of will, will power, autocracy, bossiness [*colloq.*].

wish, desire, pleasure, mind, disposition, etc., 602; intention, etc., 620.

V. **will,** see fit, think fit; determine, etc. (*resolve*), 604; enjoin; settle, etc. (*choose*), 609; volunteer; do what one chooses, etc. (*freedom*), 748; have one's own way; use one's discretion; boss, [*colloq.*]; originate.

Adj. voluntary, volitional, willful; free, etc., 748; optional, discretionary; autocratic, dictatorial, bossy [*colloq.*].

willing, etc., 602; unbidden, spontaneous; original.

Adv. voluntarily, at will, at pleasure.

of one's own accord, on one's own responsibility; by choice, purposely, intentionally.

601. NECESSITY.—*N.* **necessity,** obligation; compulsion, etc., 744; subjection, etc., 749; stern (*or* dire) necessity, last resort.

instinct, blind impulse, natural tendency (*or* impulse), predetermination.

destiny, fatality, fate, kismet, doom, election, predestination; lot, fortune; fatalism.

Fates, God's will, heaven, will of heaven; stars; planets; wheel of fortune.

V. **be obliged,** be forced, be driven; be fated, be doomed, be destined, have no alternative.

destine, doom, foredoom, devote; predestine, preordain; necessitate; compel, etc., 744.

Adj. **necessary,** needful, etc. (*requisite*), 630; compulsory, etc. (*compel*), 744; inevitable, unavoidable, irresistible, irrevocable, inexorable, binding.

fated; destined, fateful, set apart, devoted, elect.

involuntary, instinctive, automatic, blind, mechanical; unconscious, unwitting, unthinking; unintentional.

Adv. **necessarily,** of necessity, of course; willy-nilly.

602. WILLINGNESS.—*N.* **willingness,** disposition, inclination, liking, turn, propensity, leaning, frame of mind, humor, mood, vein, bent, aptitude.

geniality, cordiality, good will; alacrity, readiness, zeal, enthusiasm, earnestness, eagerness.

assent, etc., 488; compliance, etc., 762.

volunteer, unpaid worker, amateur, nonprofessional.

V. **be willing,** incline, lean to, mind, hold to, cling to; desire, etc., 865; acquiesce, assent, comply with; jump at, catch at; take up, plunge into, have a go at [*colloq.*].

volunteer, offer, proffer.

Adj. **willing,** fain, disposed, inclined, favorable, content, well disposed; ready, forward, earnest, eager, zealous, enthusiastic; bent upon, desirous.

docile, amenable, easily persuaded, facile, easygoing, tractable, genial, gracious, cordial.

voluntary, gratuitous, free, unconstrained, spontaneous, unasked, unforced.

Adv. **willingly,** fain, freely, with pleasure, of one's own accord; graciously, with a good grace, without demur.

603. UNWILLINGNESS.—*N.* **unwillingness,** indisposition, disinclination, aversion, averseness, reluctance; indifference, etc., 866; backwardness, slowness; obstinacy, etc., 606.

scruple, scrupulousness, delicacy, qualm, shrinking, recoil; hesitation, fastidiousness.

dissent, etc., 489; refusal, etc., 764.

V. **be unwilling,** dislike, etc., 867; demur, stick at, scruple, stickle; hang fire, shirk, slack, recoil, shrink, hesitate; avoid, etc., 623; oppose, etc., 708; dissent, etc., 489; refuse, etc., 764.

Adj. **unwilling,** loath, disinclined, indisposed, averse, reluctant, opposed, adverse, laggard, backward, remiss, slack, indifferent, scrupulous; repugnant, restive; grudging, forced, under compulsion, irreconcilable.

Adv. **unwillingly,** grudgingly, with an ill grace; against one's will, against the grain; under protest.

604. RESOLUTION.—*N.* **determination,** will, decision, resolution; backbone; clear grit, grit; sand [*slang*]; strength of mind, resolve, firmness, energy, manliness, vigor, resoluteness; zeal, devotion.

self-control, self-mastery, self-command, self-reliance, self-restraint, self-denial.

tenacity, perseverance, etc., 604*a*; obstinacy, etc., 606; pluck.

V. **resolve,** will, determine, decide, form a resolution, conclude, fix, bring to a crisis, take a decisive step, take upon oneself.

take one's stand, stand firm, insist upon, make a point of, set one's heart upon; stick at nothing, make short work of, not stick at trifles; persevere, etc., 604*a*.

Adj. **resolved,** determined; strong-willed, strong-minded; resolute, self-possessed, earnest, serious; decided, peremptory, unflinching, firm, iron, game, plucky, tenacious, gritty, indomitable, inexorable, relentless; obstinate, etc., 606; unyielding; grim, stern, inflexible, irrevocable.

Adv. **resolutely,** in earnest, earnestly; on one's mettle, manfully, like a man.

604a. PERSEVERANCE.—*N.* **perseverance,** continuance, constancy, steadiness, persistence, patience; pertinacity, industry.

grit, bottom, pluck, stamina, backbone, sand [*slang*]; tenacity, staying power, endurance; bulldog courage.

V. **persevere,** persist, hold on, hold out; stick to, cling to, adhere to; keep on, carry on, hold on; bear up, keep up, hold up; plod; continue, die in harness, die at one's post.

Adj. persevering, constant; steady, steadfast, unwavering, unfaltering, unflinching, unflagging, plodding; industrious, etc., 682; strenuous, pertinacious, persistent; indomitable, indefatigable.

Adv. **without fail**, through thick and thin, through fire and water; sink or swim, rain or shine, fair or foul.

605. IRRESOLUTION.—*N.* **irresolution**, indecision, indetermination, instability, uncertainty; demur, suspense, hesitation, hesitancy, vacillation, changeableness, fluctuation; caprice, etc., 608; lukewarmness.

fickleness, levity, pliancy, weakness, timidity; cowardice, etc., 862.

waverer, shilly-shally, turncoat, opportunist, timeserver.

V. **be irresolute**, remain neuter; dilly-dally, hesitate, hover, shilly-shally, hem and haw, demur, debate, balance; dally with, coquet with; go halfway, compromise, be afraid.

vacillate, falter, waver, fluctuate, change, alternate, shuffle, palter, shirk, trim.

Adj. **irresolute**, drifting, halfhearted; undecided, undetermined, uncertain, at a loss; fickle, unreliable, irresponsible, unstable; capricious, etc., 608.

weak, feeble-minded, frail, timid, cowardly, pliant.

Adv. **irresolutely**, in faltering accents; off and on.

606. OBSTINACY.—*N.* **obstinacy**, tenacity, cussedness; perseverance, etc., 604*a*; immovability, inflexibility, obduracy, doggedness, stubbornness, self-will, contumacy, perversity; resolution, etc., 604.

bigotry, intolerance, dogmatism; fixed idea, fanaticism, zealotry, infatuation, monomania.

bigot, dogmatist, zealot, fanatic, bitter-ender [*colloq.*]; mule.

V. **be obstinate**, stickle, take no denial, be wedded to an opinion, persist, die hard, not yield an inch, stand out.

Adj. **obstinate**, tenacious, stubborn, obdurate, inflexible, balky; immovable, unchangeable, inexorable, determined, mulish, dogged; sullen, sulky; unmoved.

arbitrary, dogmatic, positive, bigoted, opinionated, stiff-necked, hidebound, unyielding; incorrigible.

willful, self-willed, perverse; ungovernable, wayward, refractory, unruly, headstrong; contumacious; cross-grained.

Adv. with set jaw; no surrender.

607. APOSTASY.—*N.* **apostasy**, recantation; renunciation; abjuration, defection, retraction, withdrawal, disavowal, revocation, tergiversation, reversal; backsliding.

turncoat, apostate, renegade, pervert, deserter, backslider, crawfish [*slang*].

timeserver, trimmer, double-dealer; weathercock.

V. **apostatize,** veer round, turn round; change one's mind, abjure, renounce, relinquish, back down, shift one's ground, change sides, go over, recant, retract, revoke, rescind, forswear.

trim, shuffle, blow hot and cold, be on the fence, straddle.

Adj. **changeful,** irresolute, ductile, slippery, trimming, timeserving.

608. CAPRICE.—*N.* **caprice,** fancy, humor, whim, fit, crotchet, quirk, freak, fad, vagary, prank, escapade.

V. **be capricious,** take it into one's head, blow hot and cold, play fast and loose.

Adj. **capricious,** erratic, eccentric, fitful, inconsistent, fanciful, whimsical, crotchety, freakish, wayward, wanton; contrary, captious, unreasonable, arbitrary; fickle, etc. (*irresolute*), 605.

Adv. **by fits,** by fits and starts, without rhyme or reason.

609. CHOICE.—*N.* **choice,** option, selection, pick; discretion, alternative, preference, adoption, decision.

Scylla and Charybdis.

election, poll, ballot, vote, voice, suffrage, plebiscite, referendum; electioneering; voting, elective franchise; ticket; ballot box.

voter, elector, constituent, electorate, constituency.

V. **choose;** elect, make one's choice; make choice of, fix upon, settle, decide, make up one's mind; adopt, take up, embrace, espouse.

vote, poll, hold up one's hand, give a (*or* the) voting sign; divide.

select, pick, cull, glean, winnow; pitch upon, indulge one's fancy; set apart, mark out for.

prefer, fancy, have rather, had (*or* would) as lief; reserve.

Adj. **optional,** discretional, at choice, on approval.

chosen, choice, elect, select, popular; preferential.

Adv. **optionally,** at pleasure, at the option of.

by choice, by preference; in preference; rather, before.

609a. ABSENCE OF CHOICE.—*N.* **no choice;** Hobson's choice; first come first served; necessity, etc., 601.

neutrality, indifference; indecision, etc. (*irresolution*), 605.

V. **be neutral,** have no preference, waive, not vote.

Adj. **neutral,** neuter; indifferent; undecided, etc. (*irresolute*), 605.

610. REJECTION.—*N.* **rejection,** repudiation, exclusion; refusal, etc., 764.

V. **reject,** set (*or* lay) aside, give up; decline, etc. (*refuse*), 764; exclude, except; pluck up, spurn, cast out; repudiate, scout, disclaim, discard.

Adv. **neither,** neither the one nor the other.

611. PREDETERMINATION.—*N.* **predetermination,** predestination, premeditation, foregone conclusion; resolve, project; intention, etc., 620; fate, necessity.

list, schedule, calendar, docket, slate [*pol. cant*], register, roster, poll, muster, draft.

V. **predetermine,** predestine, premeditate, resolve beforehand.

list, schedule, docket, slate, register, poll, empanel, draft.

Adj. **premeditated,** predesigned, prepense [*as,* malice *prepense*], studied, designed, calculated, aforethought; foregone.

well laid, well devised, well weighed; maturely considered; cut-and-dried.

Adv. **deliberately,** with eyes open, in cold blood; intentionally.

612. IMPULSE.—*N.* **impulse,** sudden thought; impromptu, improvisation; inspiration, flash, spurt.

V. **improvise,** extemporize; say what comes uppermost, act on the spur of the moment, rise to the occasion; spurt.

Adj. **extemporaneous,** impulsive, snap, improvised, unpremeditated, unprompted, natural, unguarded; spontaneous.

Adv. **extempore,** extemporaneously; offhand, impromptu.

613. HABIT.—*N.* **habit,** addiction, wont, run, way, matter of course, beaten path, second nature; trick, knack, skill.

custom, use, usage, prescription, practice; prevalence, observance; conventionalism, conventionality, mode, fashion, vogue, etiquette.

rule, standing order, precedent, routine, red tape, rut, groove.

V. **habituate,** inure, harden, season, caseharden; accustom, familiarize; acclimatize.

cling to, adhere to; acquire a habit; follow the beaten track (*or* path), move in a rut.

prevail; come into use, become a habit, take root; grow upon one.

Adj. **habitual,** customary, accustomed, wonted, usual, general, ordinary, common, frequent, everyday, household, familiar, trite, hackneyed, commonplace, conventional, regular, set, stock, established, stereotyped; fixed, rooted, permanent, inveterate, besetting, ingrained, current.

wont; used to, given to, addicted to, in the habit of; seasoned, imbued with, devoted to, wedded to.

Adv. **as usual,** as things go, as the world goes; as you were [*mil.*].

as a rule, for the most part, generally, most frequently.

614. DESUETUDE.—*N.* **desuetude,** disusage; disuse, etc., 678; want of practice.

V. **be unaccustomed,** leave off (*or* break off, shake off, violate) a habit *or* custom; be weaned from; disuse, etc., 678; wear off.

Adj. **unaccustomed,** unused, unwonted, unseasoned, untrained; new, fresh, original; unskilled.

unconventional, unfashionable, unusual; disused, etc., 678.

615. MOTIVE.—*N.* motive, reason, ground, call, principle, mainspring, pro and con, reason why; ulterior motive; intention, etc., 620.

inducement, consideration; attraction, loadstone, magnet, magnetism, temptation, enticement, allurement, glamour, witchery; charm, spell; fascination, blandishment, cajolery; seduction.

influence, prompting, dictate, instance; impulse, incitement, press, insistence, instigation; inspiration, persuasion, encouragement, exhortation, advice, solicitation, pull [*slang*].

incentive, stimulus, spur, fillip, whip, goad, provocative, whet.

bribe, lure, sop, decoy, bait, bribery and corruption.

tempter, prompter, instigator, coaxer, wheedler, siren; firebrand.

V. **induce,** move, draw, inspire; put up to [*slang*], prompt, stimulate, rouse, arouse, animate, whet, incite, provoke, instigate, actuate, encourage, advocate.

influence, bias, sway, incline, dispose, predispose; lead, lobby.

persuade, prevail upon, overcome, carry, bring round, conciliate, win (*or* talk) over; enlist, engage; invite, court.

tempt, overpersuade, entice, allure, captivate, fascinate, bewitch, hypnotize, charm, magnetize, wheedle, coax, lure, inveigle.

bribe, tamper with, suborn, grease the palm, corrupt.

enforce, force, impel, propel, whip, lash, goad, spur, prick, urge, egg on, hound on, hurry on.

Adj. **persuasive,** inviting, tempting, suasive, seductive, attractive, fascinating; provocative.

Adv. **because,** therefore, for, by reason of, for the sake of, on account of; out of, from, as, forasmuch as.

615a. ABSENCE OF MOTIVE.—*N.* absence of motive; caprice, etc., 608; chance, etc. (*absence of design*), 621.

V. **scruple,** etc. (*be unwilling*), 603; have no motive.

Adj. **aimless,** capricious, without rhyme or reason.

Adv. **capriciously,** out of mere caprice.

616. DISSUASION.—*N.* dissuasion, expostulation, remonstrance; deprecation, etc., 766; discouragement, damper, wet blanket.

curb, restraint, constraint, check.

V. **dissuade,** cry out against, remonstrate, expostulate, warn.

disincline, indispose, shake, stagger; discourage, dishearten, disenchant; deter, hold back, restrain, repel, turn aside, damp, cool, chill, blunt, calm, quiet, quench.

Adj. averse, etc. (*unwilling*), 603; repugnant, etc. (*dislike*), 867.

617. [Ostensible motive, ground, or reason] PLEA.—*N.* plea, pretext; allegation, excuse, vindication, justification; color; gloss, guise.

pretense, subterfuge, dust thrown in the eye; blind, lame excuse, makeshift, shift.

V. **plead,** allege, excuse, vindicate; color, gloss over, make a pretext of, use as a plea, take one's stand upon; pretend.

Adj. ostensible, alleged, pretended.

Adv. ostensibly; under the plea of, under the pretense of.

618. GOOD.—*N.* good, benefit, advantage; improvement, etc., 658; interest, service, behoof, behalf; commonweal; gain, profit, harvest; boon, etc. (*gift*), 784; good turn, blessing, prize, windfall, godsend, good fortune; happiness, etc., 827; goodness, etc., 648.

V. **benefit,** profit, advantage, serve, help, avail, do good to.

gain, prosper, flourish, thrive.

Adj. commendable, etc., 931; useful, etc., 644; good, beneficial, etc., 648.

Adv. **well,** aright, satisfactorily, favorably, in one's interest.

619. EVIL.—*N.* evil, ill, harm, hurt, mischief, nuisance, drawback, disadvantage; ills that flesh is heir to, mental suffering, pain; bane, etc., 663.

badness, etc., 649; painfulness, etc., 830; evildoer, etc., 913.

blow, buffet, stroke, scratch, bruise, wound, gash, mutilation; mortal blow (*or* wound); damage, loss.

disaster, accident, casualty, mishap, misfortune, calamity, woe, fatal mischief, catastrophe, tragedy, ruin; adversity, etc., 735.

outrage, wrong, injury, foul play; bad turn, disservice, grievance.

V. **harm,** injure, hurt, do disservice to.

Adj. disastrous; hurtful, etc., 649; disadvantageous, injurious, harmful.

Adv. amiss, wrong, ill; to one's cost.

620. INTENTION.—*N.* intention, intent, purpose; project, etc., 626; undertaking, design, ambition; view, proposal; contemplation.

object, aim, end; drift, tendency; destination, mark, point, goal, target, prey, quarry, game.

decision, determination, resolve; fixed purpose, resolution; ultimatum.

V. **intend,** purpose, design, mean, have in view, bid for, labor for, aspire to, aim at; contemplate, meditate, think of, dream of, talk of; premeditate, destine, propose; project, etc. (*plan*), 626; desire, etc., 865; pursue, etc., 622.

Adj. intentional, advised, express, determinate; bound for; disposed, inclined, bent upon, at stake; in prospect.

Adv. intentionally, advisedly, wittingly, knowingly, designedly, purposely, on purpose, by design, studiously, pointedly; deliberately.

621. [Absence of purpose] CHANCE.[1]—*N.* chance, etc., 156; lot, destiny, etc., 601; luck; hoodoo [*colloq.*], jinx [*slang*], Jonah, voodoo; wheel of chance, fortune's wheel; mascot.

speculation, venture, random shot, blind bargain, leap in the dark; fluke [*sporting cant*], flier [*slang*]; flutter [*slang*]; futures.

gambling, betting, drawing lots; wager; gamble, risk, stake, bet.

gambler, gamester, speculator; bookmaker, man of the turf.

V. chance, etc., 156; toss up, cast (*or* draw) lots; tempt fortune; speculate.

risk, venture, hazard, stake; wager, bet, gamble, game, play for.

Adj. chance; fortuitous, etc., 156; unintentional, unintended, accidental; random, undesigned, purposeless.

Adv. at random, at a venture, by chance, as it may happen.

622. [Purpose in action] PURSUIT.—*N.* pursuit, prosecution; pursuance, enterprise, undertaking, business, etc., 625; adventure, quest, hobby.

chase, hunt, race, steeplechase; hunting, coursing, sport, shooting, angling, fishing.

pursuer; hunter, huntsman, the field; sportsman, Nimrod; hound.

V. pursue, prosecute, follow, shadow; carry on, undertake, engage in, set about, endeavor, seek, trace, aim at, fish, fish for; press on, follow up, take up; go in for.

chase, give chase, stalk, course, hunt, hound.

Adj. in quest of, in pursuit, in full cry, on the scent.

623. [Absence of pursuit] AVOIDANCE.—*N.* avoidance, evasion, flight; escape, retreat, recoil, departure.

abstention, abstinence; forbearance; inaction, etc., 681; neutrality.

shirker, slacker [*colloq.*], shirk, quitter, truant; fugitive, refugee, runaway, deserter, renegade, backslider.

V. abstain, refrain, spare; eschew, keep from, let alone.

avoid, shun, steer (*or* keep) clear of; fight shy of, evade, elude, shirk.

shrink, hang (*or* hold, draw) back; recoil, retire, flinch, shy, dodge, parry.

[1] See note on 156.

beat a retreat; turn tail, take to one's heels; run, run away, cut and run [*colloq.*]; fly, flee, take flight; desert, make off, sneak off, sheer off; slip, play truant, decamp, flit, bolt, abscond; escape, etc., 671; abandon, etc., 624.

Adj. elusive, evasive; fugitive, runaway; shy, wild.

624. RELINQUISHMENT.—*N.* relinquishment, abandonment; desertion, defection, secession, withdrawal; discontinuance, renunciation, abrogation, resignation, retirement; cession, etc. (*of property*), 782.

V. relinquish, give up, abandon, desert, forsake, leave in the lurch; go back on [*colloq.*]; leave, quit, vacate, resign.

renounce, forego, have done with, drop, discard, give up the point (*or* argument), table, table the motion.

625. BUSINESS.—*N.* business, occupation, employment, undertaking, pursuit; affair, concern, matter, case.

task, work, job, chore, errand, commission, mission, charge, duty; avocation, hobby.

function, part, role, capacity, province, department, sphere, field, line; walk, round, routine; race, career.

office, place, position, post, incumbency, living; situation, berth, billet, appointment, engagement; undertaking, etc., 676.

vocation, calling, profession; cloth, faculty; craft, handicraft; trade.

V. occupy oneself with; employ oneself in *or* upon; undertake, etc., 676; turn one's hand to; be engaged in, be occupied with, be at work on; have in hand; ply one's trade.

officiate, serve, act, do duty; discharge (*or* perform) the duties of; hold (*or* fill) an office; hold a portfolio.

Adj. businesslike; workaday; professional, official, functional; busy.

in hand, on hand, afoot, on foot, going on; acting.

626. PLAN.—*N.* plan, scheme, design, project, proposal, proposition, suggestion; resolution, motion; organization, arrangement, system.

outline, sketch, skeleton, draft, rough draft, copy; forecast, program, prospectus; order of the day, memoranda, platform, plank, slate, ticket; role; policy.

contrivance, invention, expedient, receipt, nostrum, artifice, device; stratagem, trick; shift.

measure, step; stroke, master stroke; trump, trump card.

intrigue, cabal, plot, conspiracy, machination; mine.

promoter, designer, organizer, founder, projector; author, artist.

V. plan, scheme, design, frame, contrive, project, forecast, sketch, devise, invent, hatch, concoct; hit upon; map out, shape out a course; prepare, etc., 673.

systematize, organize; cast, recast, arrange; digest, mature.

plot, intrigue; counterplot, mine, countermine, lay a train.

Adj. under consideration, on the carpet, on the table.

627. METHOD. [Path]—*N.* **method,** way, manner, form, mode, fashion, guise; procedure.

path, road, route, course, tack; trajectory, orbit, track, beat.

means of access, entrance, approach, passage, cloister, covered way, lobby, corridor, aisle; alley, lane, avenue, artery, channel; gateway, door; secret passage; covert way.

roadway, thoroughfare; highway, turnpike, state road, causeway, king's highway; parkway, boulevard, speedway; walk, footpath, pathway, pavement, sidewalk, byroad, crossroad; railroad, railway, trolley track, tramway; towpath; street, etc. (*abode*), 189; bridge, viaduct.

Adv. **how;** in what way, in what manner; by what mode; so, thus; anyhow.

628. MID-COURSE.—*N.* **mid-course,** middle way, middle course; moderation; mean, etc., 29; golden mean.

compromise, half measures, neutrality.

V. **keep the golden mean,** steer a middle course; go straight. compromise, make a compromise, concede half, go halfway.

Adj. **neutral,** average, even; impartial, moderate; straight.

Adv. in the mean; in moderation.

629. CIRCUIT.—*N.* **circuit,** roundabout way, digression, detour, loop, winding.

V. **go round about,** make a circuit, make a detour; meander, deviate.

Adj. **circuitous,** indirect, roundabout; zigzag.

Adv. in a roundabout way; by an indirect course.

630. REQUIREMENT.—*N.* **requirement,** need, wants, necessities; stress, exigency, pinch, case of need; desideratum; necessity, indispensability, urgency.

requisition, demand, request, claim; run, call for.

charge, command, injunction, precept, mandate, order, ultimatum.

V. **require,** need, want, stand in need of, lack; desire, etc., 865.

Adj. **necessary,** requisite, needful, imperative, essential, indispensable, called for; in demand, in request.

urgent, exigent, pressing, instant, crying.

Adv. of necessity; at a pinch.

631. INSTRUMENTALITY.—*N.* **instrumentality;** aid, etc., 707; subservience, mediation, intervention; pull [*slang*], influence; medium, intermediary, vehicle, tool, agency; instrument, expedient; means, etc., 632.

minister, handmaid, servant; friend at court, go-between.

V. **mediate,** minister, intervene, come (*or* go) between; interpose; use one's influence, be instrumental; subserve.

Adj. **instrumental;** useful, etc., 644; subservient, serviceable; intermediary, intermediate, intervening; conducive.

Adv. **through,** by, whereby, thereby, hereby; by the agency of, by dint of; by (*or* in) virtue of; by means of.

somehow, by fair means or foul; somehow or other; by hook or by crook.

632. MEANS.—*N.* **means,** resources, wherewithal, ways and means; capital, etc. (*money*), 800; revenue, income; stock in trade, provision, reserve, remnant, last resource, appliances, conveniences; expedients, wheels within wheels; sheet anchor; aid, etc., 707; medium, etc., 631.

V. **provide the wherewithal,** find (*or* possess) means, have powerful friends, have friends at court; have something to draw on.

Adj. **instrumental,** etc., 631; **mechanical,** etc., 633.

trustworthy, reliable, efficient; honorable, etc. (*upright*), 939.

Adv. **by means of,** with; wherewith, herewith, therewith; wherewithal.

633. INSTRUMENT.—*N.* **instrument,** organ, tool, implement, utensil, machine, engine, lathe, gin, mill; motor; machinery, mechanism.

equipment, gear, tackle, tackling; rigging, apparatus, appliances; plant, harness, trappings, fittings, accouterments, appointments, furniture, upholstery; chattels; paraphernalia.

mechanical powers; leverage; fulcrum, lever, crow, crowbar, jimmy, marline spike, handspike; arm, limb, wing; wheel and axle; wheelwork, clockwork; wheels within wheels; pinion, crank, winch, capstan, wheel, flywheel, turbine, water wheel, pump; pulley, crane, derrick; inclined plane; wedge; screw; jack; spring, mainspring; loom, shuttle, jenny.

handle, hilt, haft, shaft, shank; tiller, rudder, helm; treadle, pedal.

Adj. **mechanical;** propulsive, driving, hoisting, elevating, lifting.

useful, labor-saving, ingenious; well made, well fitted, well equipped.

634. SUBSTITUTE.—*N.* **substitute,** etc., 147; proxy, alternate, understudy; deputy, etc., 759.

635. MATERIALS.—*N.* **material,** raw material, stuff, stock, staple; ore.

636. STORE.—*N.* **store,** accumulation, hoard; stock, fund, mine, vein, lode, quarry; spring, fount, fountain; well; orchard, garden, farm; stock in trade, supply; treasure; reserve, reserve fund, savings.

crop, harvest, vintage, yield, product, gleaning.

storehouse, storeroom, store closet; depository, depot, cache, warehouse, magazine; garner, granary, grain elevator, silo; safe-deposit vault; armory; arsenal; stable, barn.

reservoir, cistern, tank, pond, millpond; gasometer.

V. **store,** put by, lay by, set by, stow away, store up, hoard up, treasure up, lay up, save, preserve, save up, bank; cache, deposit; stow, stack, load; harvest; accumulate, amass, hoard.

reserve; keep back, hold back; husband, husband one's resources.

Adj. in store, in reserve, spare, supernumerary.

Adv. for a rainy day, for a nest egg, to fall back upon; on deposit.

637. PROVISION.—*N.* provision, supply; grist, resources, etc. (*means*), 632; groceries, purveyance, commissariat.

caterer, purveyor, commissary, quartermaster, steward, purser, housekeeper; innkeeper, landlord, mine host; grocer, fishmonger, provision merchant.

V. **provide,** make provision, lay in, lay in a stock (*or* store).

supply, furnish; cater, victual, provision, purvey, forage; stock, make good, replenish, fill; recruit, feed.

store, etc., 636; conserve, keep, preserve, lay by, gather into barns.

638. WASTE.—*N.* consumption, expenditure, exhaustion; dispersion, leakage, loss, wear and tear, waste; prodigality.

V. **consume,** spend, expend, use, swallow up; exhaust, spill, drain, empty, deplete; disperse, etc., 73; waste; squander.

labor in vain, etc. (*useless*), 645; cast pearls before swine; waste powder and shot.

run to waste; ebb, leak, melt away, run dry, dry up.

Adj. wasted, gone to waste, useless, run to seed; dried up.

wasteful, etc. (*prodigal*), 818; penny wise and pound foolish.

639. SUFFICIENCY.—*N.* sufficiency, adequacy, enough, wherewithal, competence.

abundance, plenitude, plenty, copiousness, amplitude, profusion, full measure; fill; luxuriance, affluence, fat of the land.

rich man, etc. (*wealth*), 803; financier, banker, plutocrat.

V. **suffice,** do, just do [*both colloq.*], satisfy, pass muster; have enough, have one's fill.

abound, teem, flow, stream, rain, shower down; pour, pour in; swarm; bristle with.

Adj. **sufficient,** enough, adequate, up to the mark, commensurate, competent, satisfactory; ample; plenty, plentiful, plenteous; copious, abundant; replete, unstinted, inexhaustible.

rich, affluent, etc. (*wealthy*), 803; luxuriant, etc. (*fertile*), 168.

Adv. without stint; to the good.

640. INSUFFICIENCY.—*N.* **insufficiency,** inadequacy, incompetence, deficiency, imperfection, shortcoming; paucity, stint, bare subsistence; poverty, etc., 804.

scarcity, dearth; want, need, lack, poverty, starvation, famine, drought.

dole, mite, pittance; short allowance; half rations.

depletion, emptiness, vacancy; ebb tide; low water; insolvency, etc. (*nonpayment*), 808.

poor man, pauper, etc., 804; bankrupt.

V. **want,** lack, need, require; be in want, etc. (*poor*), 804; live from hand to mouth.

impoverish, drain, drain of resources; stint, etc., 819.

Adj. **insufficient,** inadequate, too little, not enough; incompetent, perfunctory, deficient, wanting; imperfect; ill-furnished, ill-provided, ill-stored.

short of, out of, destitute of, devoid of, bereft of, slack, at a low ebb; empty, vacant, bare; dry, drained.

unprovided, unsupplied, unfurnished; unfed; empty-handed.

meager, poor, thin, spare, stinted, starved, emaciated, undernourished, underfed, half-starved, famine-stricken, famished.

scarce, scant, not to be had, scurvy, stingy, etc., 819; at the end of one's tether; without resources, in want.

Adv. in default of, for want of; failing.

641. REDUNDANCE.—*N.* **redundance,** too much, too many, superabundance, superfluity, exuberance, profuseness; profusion, plenty, repletion, plethora, glut, congestion, surfeit, overdose, oversupply, overflow; excess, surplus, remainder.

V. **superabound,** overabound, swarm; bristle with, overflow, run over; run riot; overrun, overstock, overdose, overfeed, overload, overburden, overwhelm, overshoot the mark; gorge, glut, load, drench, inundate, deluge, flood; send (*or* carry) coals to Newcastle.

cloy, choke, suffocate; pile up, lay on thick, lavish.

Adj. **redundant,** turgid; exuberant, inordinate, superabundant, excess, overmuch, replete, profuse, lavish, prodigal; exorbitant, extravagant, overflowing; gorged, stuffed.

superfluous, unnecessary, needless, over and above, supernumerary, spare, duplicate, supererogatory.

Adv. **over and above;** over much, too much; too far; over, too; over head and ears, over one's head; up to one's eyes; extra.

642. IMPORTANCE.—*N.* **importance,** consequence, moment, prominence, consideration, mark; weight, influence; value, usefulness; greatness, etc., 31; superiority, etc., 33; notability.

salient point, outstanding feature; cardinal point: substance, gist, sum and substance, cream, salt, core, kernel, heart, nucleus; key, keynote; keystone.

import, significance, concern; emphasis, interest.

gravity, seriousness, solemnity; pressure, urgency, stress.

V. be important, be somebody, be something; import, signify, matter, carry weight; come to the front, lead the way, take the lead.

value, care for, set store upon *or* by.

accentuate, emphasize, lay stress on; mark, underline, underscore.

Adj. important, of importance, momentous, material, considerable, weighty, influential, notable, prominent, salient, signal; memorable, remarkable; stirring, eventful.

grave, serious, earnest, grand, solemn, impressive, commanding, imposing.

urgent, pressing, critical, crucial, instant.

foremost, principal, leading, chief, main, prime, primary; capital; superior, etc., 33; marked, rare; paramount, essential, vital, radical, cardinal.

significant, telling, trenchant, emphatic, pregnant.

Adv. in the main; above all, in the first place, before everything else.

643. UNIMPORTANCE.—N. unimportance, insignificance, nothingness, immateriality.

triviality, levity, frivolity, paltriness, smallness, matter of indifference; no object.

nothing, small (*or* trifling) matter; joke, jest, snap of the fingers, fudge, fiddlestick, incident, mere nothing, nonentity.

toy, plaything, gewgaw, bauble, trinket, bagatelle, kickshaw, knickknack.

trumpery, trash, rubbish, stuff, frippery; chaff, dross, froth, scum, bubble, smoke; weed; refuse.

trifle, straw, pin, fig, button, feather, continental, jot, mote, rap, old song; cent, red cent; picayune [*colloq*].

nine days' wonder, flash in the pan, much ado about nothing, tempest in a teapot.

minutiae, details, minor details.

V. be unimportant, not matter, matter (*or* signify) little, not matter a straw.

make light of, catch at straws, make mountains out of molehills.

Adj. unimportant, immaterial; nonessential, unessential, irrelevant; indifferent, mediocre, passable, fair, tolerable, commonplace; mere, common, ordinary, insignificant.

trifling, trivial; slight, slender, light, airy, flimsy, idle, shallow, weak, powerless, frivolous, petty, finical.

paltry, poor, pitiful, contemptible, puerile; sorry, mean, meager, shabby, miserable, wretched, vile, niggardly, scurvy, beggarly, worthless, two-by-four [*colloq.*], cheap, trashy, catchpenny, gimcrack, trumpery; one-horse [*colloq.*]

Adv. rather, somewhat, fairly, fairly well, tolerably.

644. UTILITY.—*N.* utility, usefulness, efficacy, efficiency, adequacy; helpfulness, service, use, help, aid, applicability, subservience; value, worth, productiveness, utilization.

commonweal, public good; utilitarianism.

V. avail, serve, conduce, tend, answer (*or* serve) one's turn; benefit, bear fruit, profit, remunerate.

act a part, etc. (*action*), 680; discharge a function, render a service; bestead, stand one in good stead; help, etc., 707.

Adj. **useful,** of use, serviceable, subservient, conducive, helpful.

advantageous, beneficial, profitable, gainful, remunerative, valuable; invaluable, beyond price; effective, prolific.

adequate; efficient, efficacious; effective, effectual.

applicable, available, ready, handy, at hand, commodious, adaptable.

645. INUTILITY.—*N.* inutility, uselessness, inefficacy, futility; ineptitude, inadequacy, unfitness; inefficiency, incompetence, unskillfulness, labor in vain; worthlessness; triviality, etc., 643.

rubbish, junk, lumber, litter, odds and ends, shoddy; rags, leavings, dross, trash, refuse, sweepings, offscourings, waste, rubble, debris; chaff, stubble, dregs, weeds, tares.

V. **labor in vain;** seek (*or* strive) after impossibilities; use vain efforts, beat the air, pour water into a sieve, bay at the moon; cast pearls before swine, carry coals to Newcastle.

render useless, dismantle, dismast, disqualify; disable, hamstring, cripple, lame; spike guns, clip the wings; put out of gear.

Adj. **useless,** inutile, futile, unavailing, bootless; inoperative, inadequate, inept, inefficient, ineffectual, incompetent.

worthless, valueless, unsalable; not worth a straw, good for nothing, dear at any price; vain, empty, inane; gainless, profitless, fruitless; unserviceable, unprofitable; ill-spent; effete, barren, sterile, impotent, worn out, unproductive; uncalled for; unnecessary, unneeded, superfluous.

646. EXPEDIENCE.—*N.* expedience, desirability, fitness, propriety, utility, advantage, opportunity; opportunism; pragmatism.

V. **be expedient,** suit, befit; suit (*or* befit) the occasion.

Adj. **expedient,** desirable, advisable, acceptable; convenient; worth while, meet; fit, fitting, due, proper, eligible, seemly, becoming, befitting; opportune, advantageous, etc., 644; suitable.

practical, practicable, effective, pragmatic, pragmatical.

Adv. in the nick of time; in the right place.

647. INEXPEDIENCE.—*N.* **inexpedience,** undesirability, impropriety, unfitness, inutility, disadvantage, inconvenience, inadvisability.

V. **be inexpedient,** come amiss, embarrass, put to inconvenience.

Adj. **inexpedient,** undesirable; inadvisable, ill-advised, unsuitable, troublesome, objectionable, ineligible, inadmissible, inconvenient, discommodious, disadvantageous; inappropriate, unfit; unsatisfactory, unprofitable, inept, inopportune, improper, unseemly.

clumsy, awkward; cumbrous, cumbersome, lumbering, unwieldy, hulky.

648. [Good qualities] GOODNESS.—*N.* **goodness,** excellence, merit; beneficence, benevolence, etc., 906; virtue, etc., 944; value, worth, price.

perfection, quintessence; superiority, etc., 33; prime, flower, cream, elite, pick, A 1 *or* A number 1 [*colloq.*], pick of the crop, salt of the earth; prodigy, wonder; gem of the first water, treasure, one in a thousand.

good man, etc., 948.

V. **be beneficial,** produce (*or* do) good, profit, benefit, improve, be the making of, make a man of; do a good turn, confer an obligation.

be good, be pure gold, look good to [*colloq.*]; excel, transcend, stand the test; pass muster, pass an examination.

vie, challenge, comparison, emulate, rival.

Adj. **beneficial,** valuable, of value; useful, etc., 644; advantageous, profitable; edifying, salutary.

harmless, innocuous, innocent, inoffensive.

favorable; propitious, etc. (*hope-giving*), 858; fair.

good, excellent; better; superior, etc., 33; above par; nice, fine; genuine, etc. (*true*), 494.

choice, best, select, picked, elect, rare, priceless, matchless, peerless, unequaled, unparalleled, inimitable, crack [*colloq.*], crackajack [*slang*], gilt-edge [*colloq.*]; superfine, of the first water; first-rate, first-class; high-wrought, exquisite, admirable, capital, estimable, precious, priceless, invaluable, inestimable.

satisfactory, up to the mark, unexceptionable, unobjectionable.

Adv. for one's benefit.

649. [Bad qualities] BADNESS.—*N.* **badness,** hurtfulness, virulence; abomination, pestilence, guilt, depravity, vice, etc., 945; malignity, malevolence.

bane, etc., 663; plague spot, evil star, ill-wind; hoodoo [*colloq.*], jinx [*slang*], Jonah; snake in the grass, skeleton in the closet; thorn in the flesh.

ill-treatment, annoyance, molestation, abuse, oppression, persecution, outrage, misusage, scathe, injury.

bad man, etc., 949, evildoer, etc., 913.

V. **hurt,** harm, scathe, injure; pain, etc., 830.

wrong, aggrieve, oppress, persecute, trample upon; overburden, weigh down; victimize.

maltreat, abuse; ill-use, ill-treat; buffet, bruise, scratch, maul; smite, molest, do violence; stab, pierce.

Adj. **hurtful,** harmful, baneful, baleful, injurious, deleterious, detrimental, noxious, pernicious, mischievous, mischief-making, malignant, prejudicial; oppressive, burdensome, onerous; malign.

corrupting, virulent, venomous, corrosive; poisonous, deadly, destructive.

bad, ill, arrant, dreadful; horrid, horrible; dire; rank, foul, rotten.

unsatisfactory, indifferent, deteriorated, below par, imperfect, ill-conditioned.

deplorable, wretched, sad, grievous, lamentable, pitiful, pitiable, woeful.

evil,wrong; depraved,wicked, etc., 945; shocking; reprehensible.

hateful, abominable, vile, base, villainous, detestable, execrable, cursed, accursed, damnable, diabolic.

Adv. to one's cost; where the shoe pinches.

650. PERFECTION.—*N.* **perfection;** paragon, pink, pink (*or* acme) of perfection.

model, standard, pattern, mirror.

masterpiece, master stroke, prize winner, prize; superexcellence.

V. **perfect,** bring to perfection, ripen, mature; consummate, crown, put the finishing touch to (*or* upon); complete.

Adj. **perfect,** faultless, immaculate, spotless, impeccable, unblemished, sound, scathless, intact; consummate, finished.

best, model, standard; inimitable, unparalleled, beyond all praise.

Adv. clean as a whistle; with a finish; to the limit.

651. IMPERFECTION.—*N.* **imperfection;** deficiency, inadequacy, defection, badness, immaturity.

fault, defect, weak point; screw loose, flaw, taint, blemish, weakness, shortcoming, drawback.

V. **be imperfect,** have a defect, lie under a disadvantage; not pass muster, fall short.

Adj. **imperfect,** deficient, defective, faulty, unsound, tainted, out of order; warped, injured; inadequate, crude, incomplete, below par.

indifferent, middling, ordinary, mediocre, average, tolerable, fair, passable; decent; not bad, not amiss; admissible, bearable.

inferior, secondary, second-rate, one-horse [*colloq.*]; two-by-four [*colloq.*].

Adv. to a limited extent, pretty, moderately, considering.

652. CLEANNESS.—*N.* **cleanness,** purity, purification, purgation; ablution, lavation; disinfection, drainage, sewerage.

bath, bathroom, swimming pool, swimming bath, public bath, baths, bathhouse, lavatory; laundry, washhouse.

cleaner, washerwoman, laundress, laundryman, washerman; scavenger, sweeper; street sweeper, white wing [*local*]; dustman.

brush; broom, vacuum cleaner, carpet sweeper; mop, swab, hose.

cathartic, purgative, aperient, laxative.

V. **clean,** cleanse; rinse, flush, mop, sponge, scour, swab, scrub; wash, lave, launder; purify; purge, expurgate, clarify, refine.

strain, separate, filter, filtrate, drain; percolate.

sift, winnow, sieve, bolt, screen, riddle; pick, weed.

comb, rake, scrape, rasp; card.

sweep, brush, brush up, rout out; clean house, spruce up [*colloq.*].

disinfect, fumigate, ventilate, deodorize; whitewash.

Adj. **clean,** cleanly, pure, immaculate, spotless, stainless, unspotted, unsoiled, unsullied, untainted, sweet.

neat, spruce, tidy, trim, cleaned.

653. UNCLEANNESS.—*N.* **uncleanness,** impurity; defilement, contamination, abomination; taint.

decay, putrefaction; corruption; mold, mildew, dry rot, caries [*med.*].

squalor, squalidness, slovenliness.

dirt, filth, soil, slop; dust, smoke, soot, smudge, smut, grime.
dregs, grounds, lees, sediment, heeltap; dross, ashes, cinders; scum, froth.

sty, pigsty, lair, den, Augean stable, sink of corruption; slum, rookery.

mud, mire, quagmire, silt, slime, slush.

V. **rot,** putrefy, fester, rankle, reek; mold, molder, go bad.

soil, smoke, tarnish, spot, smear; daub, blot, blur, smudge, smutch, smirch; drabble, besmear, befoul, splash, stain, sully.

pollute, defile, debase, contaminate, taint, corrupt.

Adj. **unclean,** dirty, filthy, grimy, soiled, dusty, smutty, sooty; mussy [*colloq.*].

uncleanly, slovenly, slatternly, untidy, frowzy, sluttish, unkempt, unwashed, squalid.

offensive, nasty, coarse, foul, impure, abominable, beastly, reeky, fetid; moldy, musty, rancid, bad, touched, rotten, corrupt, tainted, putrid; gory, bloody.

654. HEALTH.—*N*. health, sanity; soundness, vigor; good (*or* perfect, excellent, robust) health; bloom, convalescence, strength, poise.

V. be in health, bloom, flourish, enjoy good health.

return to health; recover, etc., 660; get better, convalesce, be convalescent, recruit; restore to health, cure.

Adj. healthy, healthful, in health, well, sound, whole, strong, blooming, hearty, hale, fresh, green, florid, hardy, robust, vigorous, in fine fettle; chipper [*colloq.*].

uninjured, unscathed, unmarred, without a scratch, safe and sound.

655. DISEASE.—*N*. disease; illness, sickness; infirmity, ailment, indisposition; complaint, disorder, malady, loss of health, delicacy, delicate health, invalidism, malnutrition, want of nourishment; prostration, decline, collapse, decay.

visitation, attack, seizure, stroke, fit, epilepsy, apoplexy, palsy, paralysis; shock; shell shock.

taint, virus, pollution, infection, contagion; epidemic, plague, pestilence.

Science of disease: pathology, therapeutics; diagnostics, diagnosis.

V. ail, suffer, be affected with, droop, flag, languish, sicken, pine, dwindle; waste away, fail, lose strength, be laid by the heels; lie helpless.

Adj. sick, ill, not well, indisposed, ailing, squeamish, poorly, seedy [*colloq.*], laid up, confined, bedridden, in hospital, on the sick list; out of health, out of sorts [*colloq.*], under the weather [*colloq.*]; valetudinary.

sickly, infirm, unsound, unhealthy, weakly, drooping, flagging, lame, halt, crippled, halting.

diseased, morbid, tainted, poisoned, septic; mangy, leprous, cankered; rotten, withered; palsied, paralytic; consumptive, tubercular, tuberculous.

656. HEALTHINESS.—*N*. healthiness, wholesomeness; healthfulness, salubrity.

Preservation of health: hygiene, pure air, exercise, nourishment, tonic; immunity; sanitarium, sanatorium.

V. be salubrious, make for health, conduce to health; be good for, agree with.

Adj. healthy, healthful; salubrious, salutary, wholesome, sanitary, prophylactic; benign, bracing, tonic, invigorating, nutritious; hygienic.

innocuous, innocent; harmless, uninjurious, immune.

657. UNHEALTHINESS.—*N*. unhealthiness, plague spot; malaria, insalubrity; contagion; poisonousness.

V. **be unhealthy,** disagree with; shorten one's days.

Adj. **unhealthy,** insalubrious, unwholesome, noxious, noisome; pestiferous, pestilential; virulent, venomous, poisonous, septic, toxic, deadly.

infectious, contagious, catching, communicable, epidemic, sporadic, endemic; epizootic [*of animals*].

658. IMPROVEMENT.—*N.* **improvement,** amelioration, betterment; recovery, mend, amendment, emendation; advancement, advance, promotion, preferment, elevation, increase.

cultivation, culture, march of intellect, civilization.

reform, reformation; revision, radical reform; correction, refinement, elaboration; purification, repair.

reformer, progressive, radical.

V. **improve,** mend, amend, better, ameliorate, relieve; correct, repair, restore.

improve upon; rectify; enrich, mellow, elaborate, fatten.

refresh, revive; invigorate, strengthen, recruit, renew, revivify, freshen.

promote, cultivate, advance, forward, enhance, bring forward, foster.

revise, edit, review, make corrections, make improvements.

reform, remodel, reorganize, reclaim, civilize, lift, uplift, inspire.

Adj. **better,** better off, all the better for; improving, progressive, improved.

corrigible, improvable, curable.

Adv. **on consideration,** on reconsideration, on second thought.

659. DETERIORATION.—*N.* **deterioration,** debasement; wane, ebb, recession, retrogradation, decrease.

degeneracy, degeneration, degradation, depravation, depravity, demoralization.

injury, damage, loss, detriment, harm, impairment, outrage, havoc, inroad, ravage, vitiation, discoloration, pollution, poisoning, contamination, canker, corruption, adulteration, alloy.

decline, declension, declination; decadence, falling off; senility, decrepitude.

decay, dilapidation, wear and tear, erosion, corrosion, rottenness; moth and rust, dry rot, blight, atrophy.

V. **deteriorate,** degenerate, fall off, wane, ebb; retrograde, decline, droop, run to seed *or* waste, lapse, break down, crack, shrivel, fade, wither, molder, rot, rankle, decay, go bad; rust, crumble, shake, totter, perish.

corrupt, taint, infect, contaminate, poison, envenom, canker, blight, rot, pollute, defile, vitiate, debase, deprave, degrade; alloy, adulterate, tamper with, prejudice; pervert, demoralize, brutalize.

embitter, exasperate, irritate.

injure, impair, damage, harm, hurt, spoil, mar, despoil, waste; overrun, ravage, pillage.

wound, stab, pierce, maim, lame, cripple, hamstring, mangle, mutilate, disfigure, blemish, deface, warp.

Adj. deteriorated, unimproved, injured, degenerate, imperfect; battered, weathered, weather-beaten, stale, dilapidated, faded, worn, wasted, wilted, shabby, threadbare, frayed.

decayed, moth-eaten, worm-eaten, mildewed, rusty, moldy, seedy [*colloq.*], timeworn, effete, crumbling, moldering, rotten, cankered, blighted, tainted; decrepit, broken-down, worn-out, used up [*colloq.*].

stagnant, backward, unprogressive.

Adv. on the downgrade, on the downward track; beyond hope.

660. RESTORATION.—*N.* restoration, replacement, rehabilitation, reconstruction, reproduction, renovation, renewal, revival, resuscitation, reanimation, reorganization; redemption, restitution, relief, redress, retrieval, reclamation, recovery, convalescence, resumption.

renaissance, renascence, rebirth, new birth, regeneration, regeneracy, resurrection.

repair, repairing, reparation, mending; recruiting.

mender, repairer, tinker, cobbler.

V. recover, rally, revive; come to, come round, come to oneself; pull through, weather the storm, be oneself again; get well, survive, reappear.

restore, put back, reinstate, replace, rehabilitate, re-establish, reconstruct, rebuild, reorganize, convert, recondition, renew, renovate; regenerate; rejuvenate.

redeem, reclaim, recover, retrieve; rescue, etc. (*deliver*), 672.

cure, heal, remedy, doctor, bring round, set on one's legs.

resuscitate, revive, reanimate, revivify, reinvigorate, refresh.

repair, mend, put in repair, retouch, tinker, cobble, patch up, darn; stanch, calk, splice.

Adj. restored, convalescent, rejuvenated, renascent.

restorative, recuperative, curative, remedial.

restorable, remediable, retrievable, curable.

661. RELAPSE.—*N.* relapse, lapse; falling back, retrogradation; deterioration, etc., 659; backsliding.

V. relapse, lapse, fall (*or* slip) back, have a relapse, be overcome, be overtaken, yield again to, fall again into, return, retrograde.

Adj. backsliding, retrograde.

662. REMEDY.—*N.* remedy, help, redress, febrifuge; antipoison, antidote, emetic; stimulant, tonic; prophylactic, antiseptic, germicide, disinfectant; restorative; specific; cure, sovereign remedy, panacea.

materia medica, pharmacy, pharmaceutics; pharmacopoeia.

narcotic, opium, morphine, cocaine, hashish, dope [*slang*]; sedative.

physic, medicine, simples, drug, potion, draft, dose, pill, medicament; recipe, receipt, prescription; patent medicine, nostrum; elixir, balm, balsam, cordial.

salve, ointment, oil, lenitive, lotion, embrocation, liniment.

treatment, regimen, diet; dietary, dietetics; operation, the knife [*colloq.*], surgical operation; major operation.

healing art, practice of medicine, therapeutics; allopathy, homeopathy, osteopathy, eclecticism, surgery; faith cure, faith healing, mind cure, psychotherapy, psychotherapeutics; vocational therapy; dentistry.

hospital, surgery, infirmary, clinic, sanitarium, sanatorium; springs, baths, spa; asylum, home; Red Cross; ambulance.

dispensary, drugstore.

doctor, physician, medical man, general practitioner; specialist, consultant; surgeon.

intern, anesthetist, aurist, oculist, dentist, dental surgeon; osteopath, osteopathist; nurse, sister, nursing sister; apothecary, druggist, pharmacist, pharmaceutical chemist, Hippocrates, Galen; masseur (*fem.* masseuse), rubber.

V. **apply a remedy,** doctor [*colloq.*], dose, physic, nurse, minister to, attend, dress the wounds; relieve, palliate, heal, cure, remedy, restore.

Adj. **remedial,** restorative, corrective, palliative, healing; sanatory, sanative; prophylactic; medical, medicinal; therapeutic, surgical; tonic, sedative, lenitive; allopathic, homeopathic, eclectic; aperient, laxative, cathartic, purgative; septic; aseptic, antiseptic.

dietetic, dietary, alimentary; nutritious, nutritive; digestive, digestible.

663. BANE.—*N.* **bane,** curse, thorn in the flesh; bête noir [F.], bugbear; evil, scourge; fungus, mildew; dry rot; canker, cancer; poison, virus, venom; stench, fetor, poison gas.

sting, fang, thorn, bramble, brier, nettle.

Science of poisons: toxicology.

Adj. baneful, poisonous, etc. (*unwholesome*), 657.

664. SAFETY.—*N.* **safety,** security, surety, impregnability, invulnerability, escape, means of escape; safeguard, palladium; sheet anchor; rock, tower.

guardianship, wardship, wardenship; tutelage, custody, safekeeping, protection; auspices.

protector, guardian; warden, warder; preserver, lifesaver, custodian, duenna, chaperon.

safe-conduct, escort, convoy; guard, shield, guardian angel; tutelary deity (*or* saint).

watchman, patrolman, policeman, police officer, officer [*colloq.*]; cop, copper [*both slang*], bluecoat [*colloq.*], constable; detective, spotter [*slang*]; sheriff, deputy; sentinel, sentry, scout.

armed force, garrison, lifeguard, state guard, militia, regular army, navy; volunteer; marine, etc., 726; battleship, man-of-war, etc., 726.

judge, justice, judiciary, magistrate, justice of the peace.

V. protect, watch over, take care of, preserve, cover, screen, shelter, shroud, flank, ward, guard; defend, take precautions.

escort, support, accompany, convoy.

watch, mount guard, patrol, scout, spy.

Adj. safe, secure, sure, on terra firma [L.]; on the safe side; undercover, under lock and key; out of danger, protected; at anchor, high and dry, above-water; safe and sound.

snug, seaworthy, watertight, weatherproof, waterproof, fireproof; bombproof, shellproof.

defensible, tenable, proof against, invulnerable, unassailable, impregnable.

guardian, tutelary, protective.

Adv. with impunity.

665. DANGER.—*N.* danger, peril, insecurity, jeopardy, risk, hazard, venture, precariousness, instability; exposure, vulnerability, vulnerable point, heel of Achilles; forlorn hope.

Sense of danger: apprehension, etc., 860.

V. endanger, expose to danger, imperil, jeopardize, beard the lion in his den; sail too near the wind.

risk, hazard, venture, adventure, stake, set at hazard; run the gantlet.

Adj. dangerous, hazardous, perilous, unsafe, unprotected, insecure.

defenseless, guardless, unsheltered, unshielded; vulnerable, exposed; at bay.

precarious, critical, ticklish; slippery, between Scylla and Charybdis, between two fires; under fire; at stake, in question.

unsteady, unstable, shaky, tottering, top-heavy, tumble-down, ramshackle, crumbling, helpless, trembling in the balance; nodding to its fall.

threatening, ominous, ill-omened, alarming.

666. [Means of safety] REFUGE.—*N.* refuge, sanctuary, retreat, fastness, stronghold, fortress, castle, keep; asylum, shelter, covert, ark, home, hiding place.

anchorage, roadstead; breakwater, port, haven, harbor, pier, jetty, embankment, quay, wharf.

anchor, sheet anchor, grapnel, grappling iron, mainstay, support, safeguard.

667. [Source of danger] **PITFALL.**—*N.* pitfall, ambush, trap, snare, mine, spring gun.

rocks, reefs, sunken rocks, snags; sands, quicksands; breakers, shoals, shallows, lee shore, rockbound coast.

abyss, abysm, pit, void, chasm.

whirlpool, eddy, vortex, rapids, undertow; current, tiderace, maelstrom; eagre, bore, tidal wave.

pest, ugly customer, incendiary, firebug [*slang*]; firebrand; hornet's nest.

sword of Damocles; wolf at the door, snake in the grass, snake in one's bosom.

668. WARNING.—*N.* warning, caution, notice, premonition, prediction; symptom; lesson, admonition; handwriting on the wall, monitor, warning voice; stormy petrel, bird of ill omen, gathering clouds.

watchtower, beacon, signal post; lighthouse, etc., 550.

sentinel, sentry; watch, watchman; watch and ward; watchdog; patrol, picket, scout, spy, lookout, flagman.

V. warn, caution; forewarn, admonish, forbode, give warning; put on one's guard; sound the alarm.

beware, take warning, look out, keep watch and ward.

Adj. premonitory, cautionary; ominous, threatening, lowering, minatory; symptomatic.

Adv. with alarm, on guard, after due warning, with one's eyes open.

669. [Indication of danger] **ALARM.**—*N.* alarm; alarum, alarm bell, tocsin, beat of drum, sound of trumpet, hue and cry; signal of distress, SOS; fog signal, siren; yellow flag; danger signal; red light, red flag; fire alarm, still alarm; burglar alarm; police whistle.

V. alarm, give (*or* raise, sound) an alarm, warn, ring the tocsin.

670. PRESERVATION.—*N.* preservation, safekeeping, conservation, economy, maintenance, support, salvation, deliverance, etc., 672.

Means of preservation: prophylaxis; preserver, preservative; hygiene, hygienics; ensilage; dehydration, evaporation, drying, canning, pickling.

V. preserve, maintain, keep, sustain, support; save, rescue, make safe, take care of, guard; husband, economize.

embalm, dry, cure, salt, pickle, season, bottle, pot, tin, can; dehydrate, evaporate.

Adj. preserved, unimpaired, unbroken, uninjured, unhurt, unmarred; safe, safe and sound, intact, with a whole skin.

671. ESCAPE.—*N.* escape, flight, evasion, loophole, retreat; narrow (*or* hairbreadth) escape; close call [*colloq.*]; impunity.

refugee, etc. (*fugitive*), 623.

V. escape, make one's escape; break jail; get off, get clear off, elude, make off, give one the slip; wriggle out of; break loose, break away.

Adj. stolen away; fled; scot-free.

672. DELIVERANCE.—*N.* deliverance, extrication, rescue, ransom, reprieve, respite; armistice, truce; liberation, emancipation; redemption, salvation.

V. deliver, extricate, rescue, save, free, liberate, set free, release, emancipate, redeem, ransom; come to the rescue.

673. PREPARATION.—*N.* preparation, provision, arrangement, anticipation, precaution, forecast, rehearsal; dissemination, propaganda.

groundwork, steppingstone; foundation; scaffold, scaffolding.

elaboration, ripening, evolution; concoction, digestion; hatching, incubation.

Preparation of men: training, education, equipment, inurement; novitiate.

Preparation of food: cooking, cookery, culinary art; brewing.

Preparation of the soil: tilling, plowing, sowing, cultivation.

preparedness, readiness, ripeness, mellowness; maturity.

preparer, trainer, coach, teacher, pioneer; prophet; forerunner, etc. (*precursor*), 64; sappers and miners.

V. prepare, prime, get (*or* make) ready, arrange, make preparations, settle preliminaries, get up; prepare the ground, lay the foundations, erect the scaffolding.

elaborate, mature, ripen, mellow, season, bring to maturity; nurture; cook, brew.

equip, arm, man; fit out, fit up; furnish, rig, dress, accouter, array.

prepare for, guard against, forearm; make provision for; provide, provide against; set one's house in order, make all snug; clear decks, clear for action.

be prepared, be ready, watch and pray, keep one's powder dry, lie in wait for, anticipate, foresee.

Adj. preparatory, precautionary, provident; provisional, preliminary; in embryo, in hand, in train; afoot, afloat, on foot, brewing, hatching, forthcoming.

prepared, ready, cut and dried; available, at one's elbow, ready for use, all ready; handy.

ripe, mature, mellow; seasoned, practiced, experienced.

elaborate, labored, high-wrought, worked up.

Adv. **in preparation,** in anticipation of; afoot, astir, abroad.

674. NONPREPARATION.—*N.* nonpreparation, unpreparedness; improvidence.

immaturity, crudity, rawness; disqualification.

Absence of art: nature, state of nature; virgin soil, unweeded garden; rough diamond; raw material.

improvisation, etc. (*impulse*), 612.

V. **be unprepared;** lie fallow; live from hand to mouth.

extemporize, improvise; cook up, fix up.

surprise, drop in [*colloq.*], take (*or* catch) unawares; take by surprise.

Adj. **unprepared,** incomplete, premature, rudimental, embryonic, immature, unripe, callow, unfledged, unhatched; uncooked, raw, green, crude; coarse; rough, roughhewn; in the rough.

untaught, uneducated, untrained, untutored, unlicked.

fallow, unsown, untilled, uncultivated

unfitted, disqualified, unqualified, ill-digested; unready, unorganized, unfurnished, unprovided, unequipped.

shiftless, improvident, unthrifty, thriftless, happy-go-lucky; slack, remiss.

Adv. **inadvertently,** by surprise, without premeditation; extempore.

675. ESSAY—*N.* essay, trial, endeavor, attempt; aim, struggle, venture, adventure, speculation, probation, experiment.

V. **try,** essay; experiment, etc., 463; endeavor, strive; tempt, attempt, venture, adventure, speculate, tempt fortune.

Adj. **tentative,** experimental, empirical, problematic, probationary.

Adv. **on examination,** on trial, at a venture; by rule of thumb.

676. UNDERTAKING.—*N.* undertaking, adventure, venture, engagement, compact, enterprise; pilgrimage.

V. **undertake,** engage in, embark in, launch (*or* plunge) into, volunteer; apprentice oneself to; engage, contract, devote oneself to, take up, take on, take in hand; tackle [*colloq.*]; set about; launch forth; betake oneself to, turn one's hand to, have in hand, begin, broach, institute.

Adj. **energetic;** full of pep [*slang*]; enterprising, adventurous, venturesome.

677. USE.—*N.* use, employ, exercise, application, appliance; disposal; consumption; agency, usefulness, etc., 644; benefit, recourse, resort, avail.

Conversion to use: utilization, utility, service, wear.

Way of using: usage, employment, *modus operandi* [L.].

user, consumer, market, demand.

V. **use,** make use of, employ, put to use, apply, put in action, set in motion, set to work; ply, work, wield, handle, manipulate; exert, exercise, practice, avail oneself of, profit by; resort to, have recourse to, recur to, take up, try.

utilize, turn to account (*or* use); exploit; administer, apply, bring into play; task, tax, put to task; devote, dedicate, consecrate.

consume, use up, devour, swallow up; absorb, expend; wear.

Adj. **useful,** etc., 644; instrumental, subservient, utilitarian, pragmatic.

678. DISUSE.—*N.* disuse; forbearance, abstinence; relinquishment, abandonment; desuetude, disusage.

V. **not use;** do without, dispense with, let alone, forbear, abstain, spare, waive, neglect; keep back, reserve.

disuse; lay up, lay by, shelve; set aside, lay aside, leave off, have done with; supersede, discard, throw aside, relinquish; destroy, make away with, cast (*or* throw) overboard; dismantle.

Adj. **disused,** done with, run down, worn out; unemployed, unapplied, unexercised, uncalled for, not required.

679. MISUSE.—*N.* misuse, misusage, misapplication, misappropriation; abuse, profanation, desecration; waste.

V. **misuse,** misemploy, misapply; exploit; misappropriate; desecrate, abuse, profane.

overtask, overtax, overwork; squander, waste.

680. ACTION.—*N.* action, performance, perpetration, exercise, movement, operation, evolution, work, employment; labor, exertion, execution; procedure, conduct; handicraft; business, agency.

deed, act, stitch, touch, transaction, job, doings, dealings, proceeding, measure, step, maneuver, bout, passage, move, stroke, blow; feat, exploit, achievement; handiwork, craftsmanship, workmanship; manufacture; stroke of policy.

doer, worker, agent, etc., 690.

V. **do,** perform, execute, achieve, transact, enact; commit, perpetrate, inflict; exercise, prosecute, carry on, work, labor, practice, play; employ oneself, ply one's task; officiate, have in hand; shape one's course.

act, operate, take action, take steps, take in hand, put in practice, carry into execution, act upon.

Adj. **in action,** acting, in harness, on duty; at work; operative.

Adv. **in the act,** in the midst of; red-handed.

681. INACTION.—*N.* inaction, passiveness, watchful waiting; noninterference; neglect, etc., 460; inactivity, etc., 683; stagnation, vegetation, rest, loafing, want of occupation, unemployment; sinecure; soft snap, cinch [*both slang*].

V. **not do,** not act, not attempt; be inactive, abstain from doing, do nothing, hold, spare; leave (*or* let) alone; let be, let pass, let things take their course, live and let live; rest upon one's oars; stand aloof; refrain, relax one's efforts; desist, stop, pause, wait; waste time.

undo, do away with; take down, take to pieces; destroy, etc., 162.

Adj. **passive;** unoccupied, unemployed, out of employ (*or* work, a job); uncultivated, fallow.

Adv. at a stand.

682. ACTIVITY.—*N.* **activity,** animation, life, vivacity, spirit, verve, pep [*slang*], dash, go [*colloq.*], energy, snap, vim.

smartness, nimbleness, agility; quickness, velocity, alacrity, promptitude; dispatch, expedition, haste, etc., 684; punctuality.

eagerness, zeal, ardor, enthusiasm, earnestness, intentness, vigor, devotion, exertion.

industry, assiduity, assiduousness, sedulousness, laboriousness, drudgery, diligence, perseverance, etc., 604*a.*

vigilance, etc., 459; wakefulness; sleeplessness, restlessness; insomnia.

bustle, hustle [*colloq.*], movement, stir, fuss, ado, bother, fidget, flurry.

officiousness, dabbling, meddling; interference, intermeddling; butting in [*slang*], intrusiveness, intrigue.

man of action, busy bee; new broom; devotee, enthusiast, fanatic, zealot, hustler [*colloq.*], live wire, human dynamo [*both colloq.*].

meddler, intriguer, busybody.

V. **be active,** busy oneself in; stir, stir about, bestir oneself; speed, hasten, bustle, fuss; push, go ahead, push forward; make progress; toil, moil, drudge, plod, persist, persevere, hustle [*colloq.*], push [*colloq.*], keep moving, seize the opportunity, lose no time, dash off, make haste.

have a hand in, take an active part, put in one's oar, have a finger in the pie, dabble, intrigue; agitate.

meddle, tamper with, interfere, interpose; obtrude; butt in, horn in [*both slang*].

Adj. **active,** brisk, lively, animated, vivacious, alive, frisky, spirited; nimble, agile, light-footed, nimble-footed.

quick, prompt, instant, ready, alert, spry [*colloq. and dial.*], sharp, smart; fast, etc. (*swift*), 274; capable, expeditious, awake, go-ahead [*colloq.*], live [*colloq.*], hustling [*colloq.*], wide-awake.

enterprising, eager, ardent, strenuous, zealous, resolute.

industrious, assiduous, diligent, sedulous, painstaking, intent, indefatigable, persevering, unwearied, sleepless; busy, occupied; hard at work, hard at it; plodding, hard-working, businesslike.

bustling, restless, fussy, fidgety, pottering.

meddlesome, pushing, officious.

astir, stirring, afoot, on foot, in full swing; on the alert.

Adv. with life and spirit, with might and main, full tilt.

683. INACTIVITY.—*N.* **inactivity;** inaction, etc., 681; inertness, lull, quiescence; rust.

idleness, remissness, sloth, indolence, dawdling, puttering, relaxation.

languor, dullness, sluggishness, procrastination, torpor, stupor, somnolence, drowsiness, heaviness, hypnotism, lethargy.

sleep, slumber; Morpheus; coma, trance, catalepsy, hypnosis, dream; nap, doze, siesta; hibernation.

idler, drone, dawdler, truant; dead one [*slang*], dummy, bum [*slang*], tramp, hobo, beggar, lounge lizard [*slang*], lounger, loafer, slow-poke, laggard, sluggard.

V. **be inactive,** do nothing; dawdle, drawl, lag, hang back, slouch, loll, lounge, loaf, loiter; sleep at one's post; take it easy.

dally, dilly-dally, idle (*or* fritter, fool) away time; putter, dabble.

sleep, slumber, be asleep, oversleep, hibernate; doze, drowse, nap, take a nap; fall asleep, drop asleep; get sleepy, nod, go to bed, turn in.

languish, expend itself, flag, hang fire; relax.

Adj. **inactive,** motionless; unoccupied, unemployed.

indolent, lazy, slothful, idle, remiss, slack, inert, torpid, sluggish, logy, languid, listless; lackadaisical, maudlin; heavy, dull, leaden; dilatory, laggard, slow, flagging; puttering.

sleeping, asleep, comatose; in the arms (*or* lap) of Morpheus.

sleepy, dozy, drowsy, somnolent, lethargic, heavy, heavy with sleep; soporific, hypnotic; dreamy.

Adv. with half-shut eyes, half asleep; in dreams, in dreamland.

684. HASTE.—*N.* **haste,** urgency, dispatch, acceleration, spurt, forced march, rush, scurry, scuttle, dash; velocity, etc., 274; precipitancy, precipitation, impetuosity; hurry, drive, scramble, bustle, fidget, flurry.

V. **haste,** hasten, make haste, dash on, push on, press on *or* forward, hurry, scurry, bustle, flutter, scramble, plunge, dash off, rush, express; bestir oneself, etc. (*be active*), 682; lose no time, make short work of; work against time, work under pressure.

quicken, accelerate, expedite, precipitate, urge, whip, spur, flog, goad.

Adj. **hasty,** hurried, cursory, precipitate, headlong, furious, boisterous, impetuous, hotheaded; feverish, pushing.

in haste, in a hurry, in hot haste, breathless, hard-pressed, urgent.

Adv. **with haste,** with speed, in haste, apace, amain; at short notice, immediately, posthaste; by cable, by telegraph, by wireless [colloq.], by airplane, by return mail, by forced marches.

hastily, precipitately, helter-skelter, hurry-scurry, slapdash, slap-bang; full-tilt, full-drive; heels over head, headlong.

685. LEISURE.—*N.* leisure, convenience; spare time, vacant hour; time, time to spare; holiday, ease.

V. have leisure, take one's time (*or* leisure, ease); repose, etc., 687; move slowly, while away the time, be master of one's time, be an idle man.

686. EXERTION.—*N.* exertion, effort, strain, stress, tug, pull, throw, stretch, struggle, spell, spurt; dead lift, heft [*dial.*]; trouble, pains, duty; energy, etc. [*physical*], 171.

exercise, practice, play, gymnastics, field sports; breather [*colloq.*].

labor, work, toil, manual labor, sweat of one's brow, drudgery, slavery.

worker, plodder, laborer, drudge, slave; man of action; Hercules.

V. labor, work, toil, sweat, fag, drudge, slave, strive, strain; pull, tug, ply; ply the oar; exert oneself, bestir oneself (*be active*), 682.

work hard; rough it; put forth one's strength, buckle to, set one's shoulder to the wheel, do double duty; burn the candle at both ends, work (*or* fight) one's way; do one's best, do one's utmost; take pains; strain every nerve; spare no efforts *or* pains.

Adj. laborious, elaborate; strained; toilsome, wearisome, burdensome; uphill; herculean.

hard-working, painstaking, strenuous, energetic, never idle.

Adv. with might and main, with all one's might, to the best of one's abilities, tooth and nail, hammer and tongs, heart and soul.

687. REPOSE.—*N.* repose, rest, sleep, etc., 683; relaxation, breathing time; halt, stay, pause, respite.

day of rest, Sabbath, Lord's day, Sunday; holiday, red-letter day, gala day; vacation, recess.

V. repose, rest, take rest, take one's ease; lie down, recline, go to rest (*or* bed, sleep).

relax, unbend, slacken, take breath, rest upon one's oars; pause, etc. (*cease*), 142; stay one's hand.

take a holiday, shut up shop; lie fallow.

Adj. holiday, festal; sabbatic *or* sabbatical.

688. FATIGUE.—*N.* fatigue; weariness, etc., 841; yawning, drowsiness, lassitude, tiredness, sweat.

faintness, fainting, swoon, exhaustion, collapse, prostration.

V. be fatigued, yawn, droop, sink; flag; gasp, pant, puff, blow, drop, swoon, faint, succumb.

fatigue, tire, bore, weary, flag, jade, harass, exhaust, wear out, prostrate.

tax, task, strain; overtask, overwork, overburden, overtax, overstrain, fag, fag out.

Adj. **fatigued;** weary, etc., 841; drowsy, haggard, toilworn, way-worn, footsore, faint; done up [*colloq.*], exhausted, prostrate, spent, ready to drop, all in [*slang*], dog-tired, tired to death, played out.

worn, worn out; battered, shattered, seedy [*colloq.*], enfeebled.

breathless, short of (*or* out of)breath, blown, puffing and blowing, short-breathed, broken-winded.

689. REFRESHMENT.—*N.* recuperation; recovery of strength, restoration, revival, etc., 660; repair, refreshment; relief, etc., 834.

V. **refresh,** brace, strengthen, reinvigorate; air, freshen up, recruit, regale, repair, restore, revive; get better, recover (*or* regain) one's strength, recuperate.

Adj. refreshing, recuperative.

690. AGENT.—*N.* agent, doer, actor, performer, perpetrator, operator; executor, executrix; practitioner, worker; minister, etc. (*instrument*), 631; representative, etc. (*commissioner*), 758, (*deputy*), 759; factor, steward; servant, etc., 746; factotum.

workman, artisan, craftsman, handicraftsman, mechanic, operative; working-man, laboring man; hewers of wood and drawers of water; laborer; hand, man, day laborer, journeyman, hack, drudge, roustabout.

maker, artificer, artist, wright, manufacturer, architect, contractor, builder, machinist, engineer, electrician.

workwoman, charwoman, dressmaker, modiste, seamstress, needlewoman, milliner, laundress, washerwoman.

coworker, associate, fellow worker, co-operator, colleague, confrere; force, staff, personnel.

691. WORKSHOP.—*N.* **workshop,** laboratory, manufactory, armory, arsenal, mill, factory, studio, atelier; hive, hive of industry, beehive; bindery; dock, dockyard, slip, yard, wharf; foundry, forge, furnace.

melting pot, crucible, caldron, mortar, alembic; matrix.

692. CONDUCT.—*N.* **conduct,** behavior; deportment, carriage, demeanor, guise, bearing, manner; course of conduct, line of action; role; process, ways, practice, procedure, method; dealing, transaction, business.

policy, tactics, game, generalship, statesmanship, strategy, plan.

management; government, etc., 693; stewardship, husbandry; housekeeping, ménage, regime, regimen, economy; economics, political economy.

career, life, course, walk, province, race, record; execution, treatment; campaign.

V. **transact,** execute; dispatch, proceed with, discharge; carry on (*or* through, out, into effect); work out; go through, get through; enact.

adopt a course, shape one's course, play one's part; shift for oneself, paddle one's own canoe; conduct; manage, etc. (*direct*), 693.

behave, conduct (*or* acquit, carry, comport, bear, demean) oneself.

Adj. **directive,** methodical, businesslike, practical, executive, strategic, economic.

693. DIRECTION.—*N.* **direction;** management, government, conduct, legislation, regulation, guidance, reins; steerage, pilotage, helm, rudder, needle, compass; guiding star, lodestar, polestar, cynosure.

ministry, administration; stewardship, proctorship; chair; agency.

supervision, superintendence; surveillance, oversight; eye of the master; control, charge; auspices; command, etc. (*authority*), 737.

statesmanship, statecraft, kingcraft, reins of government; director, etc., 694; seat, portfolio.

V. **direct,** manage, govern, conduct; order, prescribe, head, lead, regulate, guide, steer, pilot, take the helm, be at the helm; hold the reins, drive.

superintend, supervise; overlook, oversee, control, handle, look after, see to, administer, patronize; rule, etc. (*command*), 737; hold office.

Adj. **directing,** executive, gubernatorial, supervisory; statesmanlike.

Adv. **in charge of,** under the guidance of, under the auspices of; in control of, at the helm, at the head of.

694. DIRECTOR.—*N.* **director,** manager, governor, controller, superintendent, supervisor, overseer, supercargo, inspector, foreman, surveyor, taskmaster; master, etc., 745; leader, ringleader, agitator, demagogue, conductor, precentor, bellwether, file leader.

guide, pilot; helmsman, steersman; adviser, etc., 695.

driver, whip, charioteer; coachman, carman, cabman; postilion, muleteer, teamster; chauffeur, motorman, engine driver.

head, headman, chief, principal, president, speaker; chair, chairman; captain, etc. (*master*), 745; superior; prime minister, premier.

officer, functionary, minister, official, bureaucrat, officeholder.

statesman, strategist, legislator, lawgiver, politician, boss [*slang*], political dictator, wirepuller [*colloq.*], power behind the throne, kingmaker.

steward, factor, agent, bailiff, factotum, major-domo, seneschal, housekeeper, shepherd; proctor, curator, librarian.

695. ADVICE.—*N.* advice, counsel, word to the wise, suggestion, recommendation, advocacy; consultation; exhortation, expostulation, dissuasion, admonition; guidance.

instruction, charge, injunction, message, speech from the throne.

adviser, prompter; counsel, counselor; monitor, mentor, sage, wise man; teacher, etc., 540; physician; arbiter, referee, judge.

consultation, conference, parley, powwow; reference.

V. **advise,** counsel, suggest, prompt, recommend, prescribe, advocate, exhort, persuade.

enjoin, enforce, charge, instruct, call, call upon, request, dictate.

expostulate, dissuade, admonish, warn.

confer, consult, refer to, call in; follow, take (*or* follow) advice.

696. COUNCIL.—*N.* council, committee, privy council, court, chamber, cabinet, board, directorate, syndicate, bench, staff.

Ecclesiastical: convocation, synod, congregation, church, chapter, vestry, consistory, conventicle, conclave, convention.

legislature, parliament, congress, national council, states-general, diet.

Duma [Russia], Storthing *or* Storting [Norway], Rigsdag [Denmark], Riksdag [Sweden], Cortes [Spain], Reichsrath *or* Reichsrat [Austria], Volksraad [Dutch], Dail Eireann [Sinn Fein].

upper house, upper chamber, first chamber, senate, legislative council, House of Lords, House of Peers; Bundesrath *or* Bundesrat [Ger.], federal council, Lagting [Nor.], Landsthing [Den.].

lower house, lower chamber, second chamber, house of representatives, House of Commons, the house, legislative assembly, chamber of deputies; Odelsting [Nor.], Folkething [Den.], Reichstag [Ger.].

assembly, caucus, clique; meeting, sitting, séance, conference, hearing, session, palaver; council fire, powwow.

Representatives: congressman, M.C., senator, representative; member, member of parliament, M.P., assemblyman, councilor.

Adj. **curule,** congressional, senatorial, parliamentary; synodic *or* synodical.

697. PRECEPT.—*N.* precept, direction, instruction, charge; prescript, prescription; recipe, receipt; golden rule; maxim, etc., 496.

rule, canon, law, code, convention; unwritten law; canon law; act, statute, rubric, stage direction, regulation; model, form, formula, technicality.

order, etc. (*command*), 741.

698. SKILL.—*N.* skill, skillfulness, address, dexterity, adroitness, expertness, proficiency, competence, craft; facility, knack, trick, sleight; mastery, excellence, sleight of hand, etc. (*deception*), 545.

accomplishment, acquirement, attainment; art, science; finish, technique.

worldly wisdom, knowledge of the world, *savoir-faire* [F.]; tact; mother wit, discretion, finesse; management.

cleverness, talent, ability, ingenuity, capacity, talents, faculty, endowment, forte, turn, gift, genius, intelligence, sharpness, readiness, aptness, aptitude, resourcefulness; felicity, capability, qualification.

expert, adept, etc., 700.

masterpiece, masterwork, chef-d'oeuvre [F.].

V. **be skillful,** excel in, be master of; have a turn for.

take advantage of, make the most of, profit by, make a hit, make a virtue of necessity, make hay while the sun shines.

Adj. **skillful,** dexterous, adroit, expert, apt, handy, quick, deft, ready, smart, proficient, good at, at home in, master of, conversant with; masterly, crack [*colloq.*], crackajack [*slang*], accomplished.

experienced, practiced, skilled, up in, in practice, competent, efficient, qualified, capable, fitted, fit for, trained, initiated, sophisticated, prepared, primed, finished.

clever, able, ingenious, felicitous, gifted, talented, resourceful, inventive; shrewd, sharp, cunning; neat-handed, fine-fingered; nimble-fingered, ambidextrous, sure-footed.

technical, artistic, scientific, workmanlike, businesslike, statesmanlike.

Adv. **skillfully,** artistically, with skill, with fine technique, with consummate skill; like a machine.

699. UNSKILLFULNESS.—*N.* unskillfulness, want of skill, incompetence, inability, infelicity, clumsiness, inaptitude, inexperience; disqualification.

mismanagement, misconduct, bad policy, impolicy; maladministration; misrule, misgovernment.

blunder, act of folly, bungle, botch, bad job, sad work.

bungler, etc., 701; fool, etc., 501.

V. **bungle,** blunder, muff [*esp. baseball*], boggle, fumble, botch, mar, spoil, flounder, stumble, trip; mismanage, misdirect, misapply.

mistake, take the shadow for the substance, bark up the wrong tree; be in the wrong box [*colloq.*]; lose one's way, miss one's way; fall into a trap.

Adj. **unskillful,** unskilled, inexpert, incompetent, bungling, awkward, clumsy, gawky, unhandy, maladroit; stupid, ill-qualified, unfit; raw, green, inexperienced; rusty, out of practice.

unaccustomed, unused, untrained, uninitiated; unbusinesslike, unpractical, shiftless; unstatesmanlike.

ill-advised, misadvised; ill-devised, ill-judged, ill-contrived, ill-conducted; misguided, foolish, wild; infelicitous.

700. EXPERT.—*N.* **expert,** adept, proficient, connoisseur, master, master hand; top sawyer; prima donna, first fiddle; past master.

picked man; medalist, prizeman.

veteran, old stager, old campaigner, man of business, man of the world.

genius; mastermind, master spirit; prodigy of learning, walking encyclopedia, mine of information.

man of cunning, diplomatist, diplomat, Machiavellian; politician, tactician strategist.

701. BUNGLER.—*N.* **bungler,** blunderer, blunderhead; fumbler, lubber, clown, lout, duffer [*colloq.*]; butter-fingers, muff, muffer [*all colloq.*]; awkward squad; novice, greenhorn.

landlubber, fresh-water sailor, fair-weather sailor, horse marine.

sloven, slattern, slut.

702. CUNNING.—*N.* **cunning,** craft, subtlety, maneuvering, temporization; circumvention; chicane, chicanery; sharp practice, knavery, jugglery, concealment, a nigger in the woodpile [*colloq.*], guile, duplicity, foul play.

diplomacy, politics, Machiavellianism; gerrymander, jobbery, back-stairs influence.

artifice, art, device, machination; plot, maneuver, stratagem, dodge, wile, trick, trickery, ruse, finesse, subterfuge, evasion, white lie, gold brick [*colloq.*], imposture, deception, net, trap.

schemer, trickster, sly boots [*humorous*], fox, reynard; intriguer, man of cunning.

V. **intrigue,** live by one's wits; maneuver, gerrymander, finesse, double, temporize, circumvent, outdo, get the better of, throw off one's guard; surprise, waylay, undermine, flatter; have an ax to grind.

Adj. **cunning,** crafty, artful, skillful; subtle, feline, deep, profound, designing, timeserving, tricky, wily, sly, insidious, stealthy, underhand, double-faced, shifty, deceptive; deceitful, crooked; shrewd, acute; sharp, canny, astute, knowing.

703. ARTLESSNESS.—*N.* **artlessness,** unsophistication, simplicity, innocence, candor, sincerity, singleness of purpose, honesty.

rough diamond, matter-of-fact man; *enfant terrible* [F.].

V. **be artless,** think aloud; speak one's mind; be free with one, call a spade a spade; tell the truth, the whole truth, and nothing but the truth.

Adj. **artless,** natural, pure, confiding, simple, plain, unsophisticated, unaffected, naïve; sincere, frank, open, candid, ingenuous, guileless; unsuspicious, honest, childlike; innocent straightforward, aboveboard; single-minded.

matter-of-fact, plain-spoken, outspoken; blunt, downright, direct, unflattering, unvarnished.

Adv. in plain words (*or* English); without mincing the matter.

704. DIFFICULTY.—*N.* difficulty, hardness, impracticability, uphill work, herculean task; dead weight, dead lift.

dilemma, predicament, fix [*colloq.*], quandary, embarrassment, deadlock, perplexity, intricacy, entanglement, knot, Gordian knot, maze, coil, strait, pass, pinch, rub, critical situation, exigency, crisis, trial, emergency, scrape, slough, quagmire, hot water [*colloq.*], pickle, stew, imbroglio, mess, muddle, botch, hitch, stumbling block.

vexed question, poser, puzzle, knotty point, paradox; hard nut to crack, crux.

V. be difficult, go against the grain, try one's patience, go hard with one, pose, perplex, bother, nonplus.

flounder, boggle [*local*], struggle, stick fast; come to a deadlock.

render difficult, enmesh, encumber, embarrass, entangle; spike one's guns.

Adj. difficult, hard, tough [*colloq.*]; troublesome, toilsome, irksome; laborious, onerous, arduous, herculean, formidable.

awkward, unwieldy, unmanageable, intractable, stubborn, perverse, refractory, knotted, knotty, thorny; pathless, trackless, intricate.

embarrassing, perplexing, delicate, ticklish, critical, thorny.

in difficulty, in hot water [*colloq.*], in a fix [*colloq.*], in a scrape, between Scylla and Charybdis; on the horns of a dilemma; on the rocks; reduced to straits; hard-pressed; run hard; pinched, straitened; hard up [*slang*]; puzzled, at a loss, at one's wits' end, at a standstill; nonplused, stranded, aground.

Adv. with much ado; uphill, upstream; in the teeth of; against the grain.

705. FACILITY.—*N.* facility, ease, easiness, capability, feasibility, practicability; flexibility, pliancy, smoothness, plain sailing; mere child's play; cinch, snap [*both slang*].

V. be easy, run smoothly; have full play, obey the helm, work well, work smoothly.

facilitate, smooth, ease, lighten, free, clear, disencumber, disembarrass, disentangle, extricate, unravel, unknot; humor, leave a loophole, leave the matter open; give full play, make way for, pave the way, bridge over.

Adj. easy, facile; feasible, practicable, within reach, gettable, accessible.

manageable, tractable; submissive; yielding, ductile, tractable, pliant.

unburdened, unencumbered, unloaded, unobstructed, untrammeled; unrestrained, free, at ease, light.

Adv. **easily,** readily, expertly, adroitly, smoothly, swimmingly, with no effort.

706. HINDRANCE.—*N.* **prevention,** obstruction, stoppage, interruption, interception, hindrance, embarrassment, constriction, restriction, restraint, etc., 751.

interference, interposition, obtrusion; discouragement, disapproval, disapprobation, opposition.

impediment, obstacle, obstruction, knot, snag, hitch, contretemps, stumbling block, lion in the path.

check; encumbrance; clog, brake, anchor; bit, snaffle, curb; drag, load, burden, onus, impedimenta; dead weight; lumber, pack; nightmare, incubus; stay, stop; preventive, prophylactic.

drawback, objection; difficulty, etc., 704; obstacle; ill-wind, head wind; trammel, tether.

damper, wet blanket, kill-joy, dog in the manger, usurper, interloper, opponent; filibusterer.

V. **hinder,** impede, filibuster, embarrass.

avert, keep off, stave off, ward off; obviate; turn aside, draw off, prevent, nip in the bud; retard, slacken, check, counteract, countercheck, preclude, debar, inhibit, restrict.

obstruct, stop, stay, bar, bolt, lock; block, barricade; dam up, put on the brake, put a stop to, interrupt, intercept, oppose, interfere, interpose.

encumber, cramp, hamper; clog, cumber, handicap; choke, saddle with, load with, overload, overwhelm, lumber, entrammel, trammel, incommode, discommode, discompose, corner.

thwart, frustrate, disconcert, balk, foil; circumvent, baffle, override, defeat, spoil, mar, clip the wings of, cripple, damp, dishearten, discountenance, undermine.

Adj. **obstructive,** intrusive, meddlesome; onerous, burdensome; cumbrous, cumbersome.

Adv. **in the way,** with everything against one, through all obstacles, under many difficulties.

707. AID.—*N.* **aid,** assistance, help, succor; support, lift, advance, furtherance, promotion.

patronage, auspices, countenance, favor, interest, advocacy.

sustenance, maintenance, nutrition, nourishment; manna in the wilderness, food, means, subsidy, bounty.

relief, rescue; ministry, ministration; supernatural aid; *deus ex machina* [L.].

supplies, re-enforcements, contingents, recruits, support, ally.

V. **aid,** assist, help, succor, lend a hand; contribute, subscribe to;

take by the hand, take in tow; relieve, rescue; set on one's legs, give new life to, be the making of; re-enforce, recruit; promote, further, forward, advance; speed, expedite, quicken, hasten.

support, sustain, uphold, prop, hold up, bolster.

nourish, nurture, nurse, cradle, dry-nurse, suckle, foster, cherish, cultivate.

serve; do service to, tender to, pander to, minister to; tend, attend, wait on; take care of; entertain, regale.

oblige, accommodate, consult the wishes of; humor, cheer, encourage.

second, stand by, back, back up; abet, work for, stick up for [*colloq.*], stick by, take up (*or* espouse) the cause of; advocate, countenance, patronize, smile upon, favor, befriend, side with.

Adj. aiding, auxiliary, adjuvant, helpful, subservient, accessary, accessory, subsidiary.

friendly, amicable, favorable, propitious, well disposed, neighborly, obliging, at one's beck.

Adv. in aid of, on (*or* in) behalf of, in favor of, in the name of, in furtherance of, on account of, for the sake of.

708. OPPOSITION.—*N.* opposition, antagonism, contrariness, contrariety; contravention, counteraction; resistance, etc., 719; hindrance, restraint, etc., 751.

collision, conflict, discord, want of harmony; filibuster, clashing.

competition, rivalry, emulation, race, contest; tug of war.

V. oppose, counteract, withstand, etc. (*resist*), 719; hinder, restrain; obstruct, etc., 706; antagonize, cross, thwart, pit against, face, confront, cope with; protest (*or* vote) against; disfavor; contradict, contravene, belie.

encounter, meet, stem, breast, resist, grapple with, kick against the pricks; contend with (*or* against), do battle with (*or* against).

compete, emulate, rival; force out, drive one out of business.

Adj. adverse, antagonistic, oppugnant, contrary, at variance, at issue, at war with, in opposition, at daggers drawn.

unfavorable, unpropitious, unfriendly, hostile, inimical, cross.

competitive, emulous, cutthroat; in rivalry with, in friendly rivalry.

Adv. against, counter to, in conflict with, at cross-purposes.

in spite, in despite, in defiance; in the teeth (*or* face) of; across; athwart.

709. CO-OPERATION.—*N.* co-operation, concert, concurrence, complicity, collusion; participation; union, combination.

association, alliance, joint stock, partnership, pool, gentleman's agreement; confederation, coalition, federation, fusion; logrolling; freemasonry.

unanimity, *esprit de corps* [F.], party spirit, school spirit; clanship, partisanship; concord.

V. co-operate, concur; conduce, combine, pool, unite one's efforts, pull together, stand shoulder to shoulder; act in concert, join forces, fraternize; conspire, concert.

side with, take sides with, go along with, join hands with, make common cause with, unite with, join with, take part with, cast in one's lot with; rally round.

participate, be a party to, lend oneself to; chip in [*colloq.*], bear part in, second, espouse a cause.

Adj. co-operating, in league, hand in glove with; favorable to, unopposed.

Adv. unanimously, as one man, shoulder to shoulder.

710. OPPONENT.—*N.* opponent, antagonist, adversary; opposition; assailant, enemy, etc., 891.

oppositionist, wrangler, disputant; filibuster, filibusterer, extremist, bitter-ender, irreconcilable, obstructionist.

malcontent; demagogue, reactionist; anarchist, Red.

rival, competitor, contestant; the field.

711. AUXILIARY.—*N.* auxiliary, recruit, assistant, help, helper, helpmate, helping hand; colleague, partner, confrere, co-operator, coadjutor, collaborator, associate, right hand, right-hand man.

ally; friend, etc., 890; confidant (*fem.* confidante), alter ego [L.], pal [*slang*], chum [*colloq.*], mate.

puppet, cat's-paw, creature, tool; satellite, adherent, parasite, dependent.

confederate; accomplice; accessory.

upholder, seconder, backer, supporter, abettor, advocate, partisan, champion, patron, friend at court, mediator.

friend in need, special providence, guardian angel, fairy godmother, tutelary genius.

712. PARTY.—*N.* party, faction, denomination, class, communion, side, crew, team; band, horde, posse, phalanx; caste, family, clan.

community, body, fellowship, party spirit, solidarity, freemasonry; fraternity, sodality, brotherhood, sisterhood, sorority; fraternal order.

gang, tong [Chin.], bolsheviki, bolshevists, ring, machine, junto, cabal.

clique, knot, circle, set, coterie; club, casino.

corporation, corporate body, guild, company, partnership, firm, house; combine [*colloq.*], trust; holding company, merger.

society, association; institute, institution; union; trade-union;

league, syndicate, alliance, combination, coalition, federation, confederation, confederacy.

staff; cast, dramatis personae [L.].

V. **unite**, join, band together, club together, co-operate, etc., 709; associate, federate, federalize.

Adj. **joint**, federal, corporate, confederated, organized, leagued, syndicated; fraternal, Masonic, institutional, denominational; cliquish, cliquy.

Adv. **side by side**, hand in hand, shoulder to shoulder, in the same boat.

713. DISCORD.—*N.* **discord**, dissidence, dissonance, disagreement, jar, clash, break, shock.

variance, difference, dissension, misunderstanding, cross-purposes, odds, division, split, rupture, disruption, disunion, breach, schism, feud, faction.

polemics; litigation, strife, warfare, outbreak, open rupture, declaration of war.

quarrel, dispute, tiff, bicker, squabble, altercation, words, high words, family jars.

broil, brawl, row [*colloq.*], racket, hubbub, imbroglio, fracas, scrimmage, rumpus [*colloq.*], squall, riot, disturbance, commotion.

subject of dispute, ground of quarrel, battleground, disputed point, bone of contention, apple of discord, question at issue.

V. **disagree**, clash, jar, conflict, misunderstand, live like cat and dog; differ; dissent, etc., 489.

quarrel, fall out, dispute, litigate; controvert, squabble, altercate, row [*colloq.*], wrangle, bicker, nag, spar, brawl.

split, break with; declare war, try conclusions, join issue, pick a quarrel; sow dissension, embroil, entangle, disunite, widen the breach; set (*or* pit) against.

Adj. **discordant**, dissident, out of tune, dissonant, harsh, grating, jangling, unmelodious; on bad terms, dissentient, unreconciled, unpacified; inconsistent, contradictory, incongruous.

quarrelsome, heated, unpacific, controversial, polemic, disputatious, factious.

at strife, at odds, at loggerheads, at daggers drawn, at variance, at issue, at cross-purposes, at sixes and sevens, embroiled, torn, disunited.

714. CONCORD.—*N.* **concord**, accord, harmony, homologue, correspondence, agreement, sympathy, response; union, unison, unity, peace, unanimity; happy family.

amity, etc. (*friendship*), 888; alliance, *entente cordiale* [F.], good understanding, conciliation, arbitration, reunion.

peacemaker, intercessor, interceder, mediator.

V. **agree,** accord, harmonize with, fraternize, go hand in hand, run parallel, concur, co-operate, pull together, sing in chorus.

side with, sympathize with; go with, chime in with, fall in with; assent, etc., 488; reciprocate.

smooth, pour oil on the troubled waters, keep in good humor, meet halfway; mediate, intercede.

Adj. **concordant,** congenial; in accord, harmonious, united, cemented, allied, friendly, fraternal, conciliatory, of one mind.

Adv. **unanimously,** with one voice, in concert with, hand in hand.

715. DEFIANCE.—*N.* **defiance,** dare, defial; challenge; threat, etc., 909; war cry, war whoop.

V. **defy,** dare, beard, brave, set at defiance, set at naught, hurl defiance at; laugh to scorn; disobey, etc., 742; threaten; challenge.

Adj. **defiant;** rebellious, bold, insolent, reckless, contemptuous, greatly daring, regardless of consequences.

Adv. in the teeth of; under one's very nose; in open rebellion.

716. ATTACK.—*N.* **attack,** assault, onset, onslaught, charge.

aggression, offense; incursion, inroad, invasion; irruption, outbreak; sally, sortie, raid, foray.

storm, storming, boarding, escalade; siege, investment, bombardment, cannonade, barrage; zero hour.

fire, volley, fusilade; sharpshooting, broadside, cross-fire.

thrust, lunge, pass, home thrust; cut.

assailant, aggressor, invader; sharpshooter, dead shot.

V. **attack,** assault, assail; set upon, pounce upon, fall upon, charge; enter the lists.

show fight, take the offensive; strike at, thrust at; aim (*or* deal) a blow at; be the aggressor, strike the first blow, fire the first shot; advance (*or* march) against, march upon, invade, harry.

close with, come to close quarters, bring to bay, come to blows.

fire upon, fire at, draw a bead on, shoot at, pop at, level at, open fire, pepper, bombard, shell, fire a volley.

besiege, beset, beleaguer, invest; sap, mine; storm, board, scale the walls, go over the top.

cut and thrust, bayonet, butt; kick, strike, etc., 276; horsewhip, whip.

Adj. **aggressive,** offensive; up in arms; amuck.

Adv. on the warpath; over the top; at bay.

717. DEFENSE.—*N.* **defense,** protection, guard, ward; guardianship.

self-defense, self-preservation; resistance, etc., 719.

safeguard, screen, fortification, bulwark, trench, mine, dugout;

moat, ditch, intrenchment; rampart, dike; parapet, battlement, bastion, redoubt, embankment, mound, bank, breastwork, earthwork, fieldwork; buttress, abutment, fence, wall, paling, palisade, stockade; barrier, barricade, boom; portcullis, barbed-wire entanglements.

stronghold, hold, fastness, asylum, keep, donjon, citadel, capitol, castle; tower, fortress, fort, barrack; blockhouse.

[**protective devices**] buffer, fender, cowcatcher, armor; mail, shield, buckler.

defender, protector, guardian, bodyguard, champion; knight-errant, paladin; garrison.

V. **defend,** guard, ward (*or* beat) off, shield, screen, shroud; garrison, man; fence, intrench, arm, accouter.

repel, parry, put to flight; hold (*or* keep) at bay; resist invasion, stand siege, stand (*or* act) on the defensive, show fight; stand one's ground, hold, stand in the gap.

Adj. **defensive;** armed, armed at all points (*or* to the teeth); panoplied, accoutered; iron-plated, ironclad; bulletproof, bombproof; protective.

Adv. on the defensive, in defense, in self-defense; at bay.

718. RETALIATION.—*N.* **retaliation,** reprisal, retort; counterstroke, counterblast; retribution.

requital, desert; tit for tat, give-and-take, blow for blow, an eye for an eye; boomerang.

recrimination, accusation; revenge, etc., 919; compensation.

V. **retaliate,** retort, turn upon; pay, pay off, pay back; cap, match; reciprocate, turn the tables upon, return the compliment; exchange blows; give and take, be quits, be even with; pay off old scores.

Adj. **retaliatory,** retaliative, retributive, recriminatory, reciprocal.

719. RESISTANCE.—*N.* **resistance,** stand, front, opposition, recalcitrance, repugnance, repulsion.

repulse, rebuff, snub.

insurrection, revolt, etc., 742; strike, lockout; boycott; riot.

V. **resist;** withstand; stand, stand firm (*or* fast, one's ground), stick it out [*colloq.*].

face, confront, breast the wave, stem the tide; grapple with; show a bold front, make a stand.

oppose, etc., 708; fly in the face of; withstand an attack, rise up in arms, strike, turn out, boycott; revolt, rebel; repel, repulse.

Adj. **resistant,** resistive, refractory, repugnant, recalcitrant, repulsive, repellent; up in arms.

unconquerable, stubborn, unconquered; indomitable, unyielding.

720. CONTENTION.—*N.* **contention,** strife, contest, struggle; belligerency, pugnacity, opposition.

controversy, polemics; debate, war of words, paper war, high words, quarrel, litigation.

competition, rivalry, match, race; athletics, athletic sports; games of skill.

conflict, skirmish; encounter, rencounter, rencontre, collision, affair, brush, fracas, etc. (*discord*), 713; clash of arms; tussle, scuffle, bout, broil, fray, affray, fight, battle, combat, action, engagement, joust, tournament, tourney; pitched battle; guerrilla (*or* irregular) warfare; death struggle, Armageddon.

duel, single combat, satisfaction, passage of arms, affair of honor; hostile meeting, appeal to arms.

V. **contend,** contest, strive, struggle, scramble, wrestle; spar, exchange blows, tussle, tilt, box, fence; skirmish, fight; wrangle; oppose, etc., 708; join issue.

compete (*or* cope, vie, race) with, emulate, rival; run a race.

Adj. **contentious,** combative, bellicose, belligerent, warlike, quarrelsome, pugnacious, pugilistic.

athletic, gymnastic, competitive, rival.

721. PEACE.—*N.* **peace,** amity, etc. (*friendship*), 888; harmony, concord, tranquillity, truce, pipe of peace, calumet.

piping time of peace, quiet life; neutrality; pacifism.

V. **be at peace,** keep the peace, make peace, pacify; be a pacifist.

Adj. **pacific;** peaceable, peaceful; calm, tranquil, untroubled, halcyon; bloodless; neutral, pacifistic.

722. WARFARE.—*N.* **warfare,** fighting, hostilities; war, arms, the sword, bloodshed; Mars.

appeal to arms (*or* the sword); ordeal (*or* wager) of battle; declaration of war.

battle array, campaign, crusade, expedition; warpath.

art of war, rules of war, the war game, tactics, strategy, generalship.

battle, conflict, etc. (*contention*), 720; service, campaigning, active service, tented field; war to the death (*or* knife).

war medal, military medal, Congressional Medal, Victoria Cross, V. C. [Eng.], *Croix de guerre* [F.], *Médaille militaire* [F.], Iron Cross [Ger.].

V. **war,** make war, go to war, declare war, wage war, arm, take up (*or* appeal to) arms; take the field, give battle, engage, fight, combat, contend, battle with.

serve; enroll, enlist; be on service (*or* active service), campaign;

smell powder, be under fire; be on the warpath, keep the field; take by storm; go over the top [*colloq.*]; sell one's life dearly.

Adj. **armed,** in (*or* under) arms, in battle array, in the field; embattled; battled.

warlike, belligerent, combative, bellicose, martial, military, militant; soldierly, chivalrous; civil, internecine; irregular, guerrilla.

Adv. in the thick of the fray, in the cannon's mouth; at the sword's point, at the point of the bayonet.

723. PACIFICATION.—*N.* **pacification,** conciliation, reconciliation, reconcilement; accommodation, arrangement, adjustment; terms, compromise; amnesty.

peace offering; olive branch; calumet, peace pipe.

truce, armistice; suspension of arms (*or* hostilities); truce of God; flag of truce, white flag.

V. **pacify,** tranquillize, compose, allay, reconcile, propitiate, placate, conciliate, meet halfway, hold out the olive branch, heal the breach, make peace, restore harmony, bring to terms.

raise a siege, sheathe the sword, bury the hatchet, lay down one's arms, turn swords into plowshares.

Adj. **conciliatory,** pacificatory.

724. MEDIATION.—*N.* **mediation,** mediatorship, intervention, interposition, interference, intercession; parley, negotiation, arbitration, good offices.

mediator, intercessor, peacemaker, negotiator, go-between, diplomatist, propitiator; umpire, arbitrator.

V. **mediate,** intercede, interpose, interfere, intervene; step in; negotiate; meet halfway; arbitrate, propitiate.

Adj. **mediatory,** propitiatory, diplomatic.

725. SUBMISSION.—*N.* **submission,** yielding, acquiescence, compliance, submissiveness, deference, nonresistance, obedience.

surrender, cession, capitulation, resignation, backdown [*colloq.*].

obeisance, homage, kneeling, genuflection, curtsy, kowtow [Chinese], salaam [Oriental], prostration.

V. **submit,** succumb, yield, defer to; bend, stoop; accede, resign oneself.

surrender, cede, capitulate, come to terms, lay down one's arms, strike one's flag, give way (*or* ground, in, up); obey.

yield obeisance, kneel to, bow to, pay homage to, cringe to, truckle to; kneel, bow submission, curtsy, kowtow [Chinese].

Adj. **submissive,** resigned, crouching, prostrate; unresisting, humble.

untenable, indefensible, insupportable, unsupportable.

726. COMBATANT.—*N.* **combatant;** belligerent, assailant, swashbuckler, duelist, swordsman; competitor, rival.

fighter, fighting man, prize fighter, pugilist, bruiser; gladiator.

soldier, warrior, brave, man at arms, guardsman, gendarme [F.]; campaigner, veteran; military man; knight; myrmidon, mercenary, irregular, free lance, franctireur; private, Tommy Atkins [Brit.], doughboy [*slang*], rank and file; sepoy [India], spearman, pikeman; archer, bowman; musketeer, rifleman, sharpshooter, skirmisher; grenadier, fusileer, infantryman, foot soldier, chasseur, zouave, artilleryman, gunner, cannoneer, engineer; cavalryman, trooper, dragoon; cuirassier, hussar, lancer; recruit, rookie [*slang*], conscript, drafted man, enlisted man.

officer, etc. (*commander*), 745; subaltern, ensign, standard-bearer.

horse and foot; cavalry, horse, light horse; infantry, foot, rifles; artillery, horse artillery, field artillery, gunners; military train.

armed force, troops, soldiery, military, forces, the army, standing army, regulars, the line; militia, national guard, state guard, yeomanry, volunteers, minutemen [*Am. hist.*]; posse; guards, yeomen of the guard, beefeaters [Eng.], lifeguards, household troops, bodyguard.

levy, draft; raw levies, awkward squad.

army, army corps; division, column, wing, detachment, garrison, flying column, brigade, regiment, battalion, squadron, company, battery, section, platoon, squad; picket, guard, legion, phalanx, cohort.

navy, first line of defense, wooden walls, naval forces, fleet, flotilla, armada, squadron; man-of-war's man, etc. (*sailor*), 269; marines.

man-of-war, line-of-battle ship, ship of the line, battleship, warship, ironclad, war vessel, superdreadnought, dreadnought, cruiser; torpedo boat, destroyer, gunboat, submarine, submersible, U-boat [Ger.]; submarine chaser, monitor; frigate, sloop of war, corvet, flagship; privateer; troopship, transport, tender.

airplane, hydroplane, seaplane, flying boat; glider; divebomber, bomber, Flying Fortress; dirigible, blimp [*cant*]; zeppelin, etc. (*aeronautics*), 273.

727. ARMS.—*N.* arms; arm, weapon, deadly weapon; armament; armor.

side arms, sword, cold steel, naked steel, steel, blade; broadsword, saber, cutlass, scimitar, rapier, foil, dagger, poniard, dirk, stiletto, bowie knife, bayonet.

ax, battle-ax, poleax, halberd, tomahawk, bill, partisan.

spear, lance, pike, assagai, javelin, dart, arrow; harpoon, boomerang; oxgoad, ankus.

club, war club, mace, truncheon, staff, bludgeon, cudgel, shillelagh, quarterstaff; billy, life preserver, blackjack.

bow, crossbow, long bow; catapult, sling.

firearms; gun, piece; artillery, ordnance; park, battery; cannon, fieldpiece, field gun, siege gun, mortar, howitzer, pompom, seventy-five [*French rapid-fire 75-mm. field gun*]; Lewis gun.

small arms; musketry; musket, firelock, fowling piece, rifle, carbine, blunderbuss, matchlock, harquebus, shotgun, breechloader, muzzle-loader, magazine rifle, automatic pistol, automatic, revolver, repeater; shooting iron [*slang*], six-shooter [*colloq.*], gun [*colloq. for revolver or pistol*], pistol.

missile, bolt, projectile, shot, ball, slug; grape, shrapnel, grenade, shell, bomb, depth bomb, smoke bomb, gas bomb; bullet; dumdum (*or* explosive, expanding) bullet; torpedo.

ammunition; powder, powder and shot; explosive; gunpowder; dynamite, cordite; cartridge; poison gas, mustard gas, chlorine gas, tear gas, etc.

728. ARENA.—*N.* arena, field, platform; scene of action, theater, walk, course; hustings; stage, boards, amphitheater,

coliseum, colosseum; hippodrome, circus, race course, turf, cockpit, bear garden, gymnasium, ring, lists; campus, playing field, playground.

battlefield, battleground, field of battle; no man's land [*First World War*]; theater (*or* seat) of war.

729. COMPLETION.—*N.* completion; accomplishment, achievement, fulfillment, performance, execution; dispatch, consummation, culmination; finish, conclusion; limit, close, finale, denouement, issue, upshot, result.

V. **complete,** perfect, effect, accomplish, achieve, compass, consummate, bring to maturity (*or* perfection); elaborate.

do, execute, make, work out, enact, dispatch, knock off [*colloq.*], finish off, dispose of, perform, discharge, fulfill, realize; carry out (*or* into effect).

do thoroughly, not do by halves, drive home; carry through, deliver the goods [*colloq.*].

finish, bring to a close, wind up, clinch, seal, put the last (*or* finishing) touch to; crown, crown all; cap.

Adj. **conclusive,** final, crowning, exhaustive, complete, mature, perfect, consummate, thorough.

Adv. to crown all, as a last stroke, as a fitting climax.

730. NONCOMPLETION.—*N.* noncompletion, nonfulfillment, nonperformance, neglect, etc., 460; shortcoming, incompleteness; drawn battle, drawn game.

V. leave unfinished, leave undone, neglect, etc., 460; let alone, let slip; lose sight of.

fall short of, do things by halves, hang fire; collapse.

Adj. **incomplete,** uncompleted, unfinished, unaccomplished, unperformed, unexecuted; sketchy; sterile.

Adv. without (*or* lacking) the final touches.

731. SUCCESS—*N.* success, successfulness; progress; advance; good fortune, prosperity, etc., 734; profit.

trump card; hit, stroke, master stroke; ten-strike [*colloq.*]; checkmate; prize.

mastery, advantage over; upper hand, whip hand; ascendancy, conquest, victory, walkover [*colloq.*], triumph.

victor, conqueror, master, champion, winner; master of the situation (*or* position).

V. **succeed,** be successful, gain one's end (*or* ends); crown with success; gain (*or* attain, carry, secure) a point *or* an object; get there [*slang*]; manage to, contrive to; accomplish; effect; come off successfully, take (*or* carry) by storm; gain the day (*or* prize, palm); carry all before one, score a success.

make progress, etc. (*advance*), 282; win (*or* make, work) one's way; speed; turn to account, prosper, etc., 734; strike oil [*slang*], make one's fortune.

triumph, be triumphant, gain a victory (*or* an advantage); surmount (*or* overcome) a difficulty, stem the torrent, weather the storm, master; distance, surpass, win.

defeat, conquer, discomfit, vanquish, overcome, overthrow, overpower, overmaster, outwit, outdo, outmaneuver, outgeneral, checkmate, beat, rout, floor, worst, lick to a frazzle [*colloq.*]; settle [*colloq.*], do for [*colloq.*], subdue, subjugate, reduce.

quell, silence, put down, confound, nonplus, baffle, circumvent, elude; drive to the wall.

avail, answer, answer the purpose; prevail, take effect, do, turn out well, take [*colloq.*], tell, bear fruit.

Adj. **successful**; prosperous, etc., 734; triumphant, crowned with success, victorious; unbeaten.

Adv. **successfully**, with flying colors, in triumph, swimmingly.

732. FAILURE.—*N.* **failure,** unsuccess, nonsuccess, nonfulfillment; labor in vain, no go [*colloq.*], inefficacy; vain attempt; frustration, disappointment.

blunder, error, etc., 495; fault, omission, miss, oversight, slip, trip, stumble; step, *faux pas* [F.]; scrape, mess, muddle, botch, fiasco.

mishap, etc. (*misfortune*), 735; split, collapse, smash, blow, explosion.

repulse, rebuff, defeat, rout, overthrow, discomfiture; beating, drubbing; subjugation, checkmate.

fall, downfall, ruin, perdition, wreck; deathblow; bankruptcy.

V. **fail,** be unsuccessful, make vain efforts, labor in vain; flunk [*colloq.*]; bring to naught, make nothing of, fall short of, go to the wall [*colloq.*], lick the dust; be defeated, have the worst of it, lose the day, lose; succumb.

miss, miss one's aim (*or* the mark), slip, trip, stumble, blunder, miscarry.

flounder, falter, limp, halt, hobble, fall, tumble, run aground, split upon a rock, break down, sink, drown, founder, come to grief.

come to nothing, end in smoke; flat out [*colloq.*]; fall through, hang fire, flash in the pan, collapse, go to wrack and ruin.

Adj. **unsuccessful,** successless, at fault; unfortunate, etc., 735; abortive, sterile, fruitless, bootless; ineffectual, ineffective, inefficient, lame, insufficient, unavailing.

stranded, aground, grounded, swamped, wrecked, shipwrecked, foundered, capsized.

undone, lost, ruined, broken, bankrupt, played out; done up, done for [*colloq.*]; broken down, overborne, overwhelmed; all up with [*colloq.*].

frustrated, thwarted, crossed, disconcerted; unhorsed, hard hit, stultified, befooled, dished [*colloq.*], foiled, defeated, victimized, sacrificed.

Adv. to little or no purpose, in vain.

733. TROPHY.—*N.* trophy; medal, prize, palm. laurel, laurels, bays, crown, chaplet, wreath; eulogy, citation; scholarship; garland; triumphal arch; war medal, etc., 722; Carnegie medal, Nobel prize; blue ribbon; decoration, etc., 877.

734. PROSPERITY.—*N.* prosperity, welfare, well-being; affluence, etc. (*wealth*), 803; success, etc., 731; luck, good fortune, good luck, blessings, godsend; bed of roses; fat of the land.

upstart, parvenu, *nouveau riche* [F.], mushroom.

V. **prosper,** thrive, flourish, swim with the tide: rise (*or* get on) in the world; light on one's feet; bask in the sunshine; have a run of luck; make one's fortune, feather one's nest, make one's pile [*slang*].

flower, blossom, bloom, fructify, bear fruit; fatten, batten.

Adj. **prosperous,** thriving, well off, well to do, at one's ease; rich, etc., 803; fortunate, lucky; palmy, halcyon.

auspicious, propitious, providential.

Adv. **prosperously,** swimmingly; as good luck would have it.

735. ADVERSITY.—*N.* adversity, evil, etc., 619; failure, etc., 732; bad (*or* ill, evil, adverse, hard) fortune *or* luck, frowns of fortune; broken fortunes; slough of despond; evil day, hard times, rainy day, cloud, gathering clouds, ill-wind; affliction, trouble, hardship, curse, blight, load, pressure, humiliation.

misfortune, mishap, mischance, misadventure, disaster, calamity, catastrophe; accident, casualty, blow, trial, sorrow, visitation, infliction, reverse, check, setback, contretemps [F.].

downfall, fall; losing game; ruin, undoing, extremity.

V. **come to grief,** go downhill, go to wrack and ruin, go to the dogs [*colloq.*]; fall, decay, sink, decline, go down in the world; have seen better days; be all up with [*colloq.*].

Adj. **unfortunate,** unblest, unhappy, unlucky, unprosperous, hoodooed [*colloq.*], luckless, hapless, out of luck; under a cloud; badly off; in adverse circumstances; poor, etc., 804; decayed, undone, on the road to ruin.

ill-fated, ill-starred, ill-omened; devoted, doomed; inauspicious, ominous, sinister, unpropitious, unfavorable.

adverse, untoward; disastrous, calamitous, ruinous, dire, deplorable.

Adv. from bad to worse, out of the frying pan into the fire.

736. MEDIOCRITY.—*N.* mediocrity, golden mean, moderation; moderate (*or* average) circumstances; respectability.

middle classes, *bourgeoisie* [F.].

V. strike the golden mean; preserve a middle course.

jog on, get along [*colloq.*], get on tolerably (*or* respectably).

Adj. middling, so-so, fair, medium, moderate, mediocre, ordinary.

Adv. with nothing to brag about.

II. INTERSOCIAL VOLITION[1]

737. AUTHORITY.—*N.* authority; influence, patronage, power, prestige, prerogative, jurisdiction.

right, divine right, authoritativeness, royalty, absolutism, despotism, tyranny.

command, empire, sway, rule; dominion, domination; sovereignty, supremacy, suzerainty, kingship; lordship, headship, leadership, mastership, government, dictation, control, hold, grasp; grip, iron sway, rod of empire.

reign, dynasty, administration; dictatorship, protectorate, presidency, presidentship, consulship, magistracy.

Governments: empire; monarchy; limited (*or* constitutional) monarchy; aristocracy; oligarchy, democracy, republic; triumvirate; autocracy; dictatorship, totalitarian state.

representative government, constitutional government, home rule, dominion rule [Brit.], colonial government; self-government, autonomy, self-determination; republicanism, federalism; socialism; communism; authoritarianism; totalitarianism; bureaucracy; martial law; feudal system, feudalism.

state, realm, commonwealth, country, power, body politic.

ruler, person in authority, lord, etc., 745; judicature, etc., 965; cabinet, etc. (*council*), 696; seat of government, headquarters.

V. authorize, empower, etc., 760; warrant, dictate.

rule, sway, command, control, administer, govern, direct, lead, preside over, be at the head of, reign.

dominate, have the upper (*or* whip) hand; preponderate, boss [*colloq.*]; override, overrule, overawe; lord it over, keep under, bend to one's will, have it all one's own way, be master of the situation, take the lead, lay down the law.

Adj. ruling, regnant, dominant, paramount, supreme, predominant, preponderant, in the ascendant, influential; imperious, dictatorial, peremptory; authoritative, executive, administrative, official, gubernatorial, bureaucratic, departmental.

sovereign; regal, royal, royalist, monarchical, kingly; dynastic, imperial, autocratic; oligarchic, democratic, republican.

[1]Implying the action of the will of one mind over the will of another.

Adv. in the name of, by the authority of, at one's command, in virtue of, under the auspices of.

738. [Absence of authority] LAXITY.—*N.* laxity; laxness, looseness, slackness; toleration, lenity, etc., 740; relaxation; freedom, etc., 748.

anarchy, interregnum; misrule, license, insubordination, mob rule, mob law, lynch law, nihilism, reign of violence.

Deprivation of power: dethronement, impeachment, deposition, abdication; usurpation.

V. **be lax,** hold a loose rein; give the reins to, give rope enough, give free rein to; tolerate; relax; misrule.

have one's fling, act without authority, act on one's own responsibility, usurp authority.

dethrone, depose; abdicate.

Adj. **lax,** loose; slack, remiss, negligent, etc., 460; weak.

relaxed, licensed, unbridled; anarchic *or* anarchical, nihilistic; unauthorized.

739. SEVERITY.—*N.* **severity;** strictness, harshness, rigor, stringency, austerity, inclemency; arrogance, etc., 885.

arbitrary power; absolutism, despotism; dictatorship, autocracy, tyranny, domination, oppression, assumption, usurpation; inquisition, reign of terror, iron rule, coercion, etc., 744; martial law.

bureaucracy, red-tapism, officialism.

tyrant, disciplinarian, martinet, stickler, despot, autocrat, oppressor, inquisitor, extortioner.

V. **arrogate,** assume, usurp, take liberties; domineer, bully, tyrannize, put on the screw, be hard upon, ill-treat, rule with a rod of iron, oppress, override, trample under foot, ride roughshod over; coerce, etc., 744.

Adj. **severe,** strict, hard, harsh, dour [Scot.], rigid, stern, rigorous, uncompromising, exacting, searching, inexorable, inflexible, obdurate, austere, relentless, stringent, strict, strait-laced, peremptory, absolute, arbitrary, imperative, coercive, tyrannical, extortionate, oppressive, cruel, arrogant; formal, punctilious.

Adv. with a high (*or* strong, tight, heavy) hand.

740. MILDNESS.—*N.* **mildness,** lenity, moderation, temperateness; tolerance, toleration, mildness, gentleness; favor; indulgence, clemency, mercy, forbearance, quarter, compassion, etc., 914.

V. **be lenient,** tolerate, bear with; spare the vanquished, give quarter; indulge, spoil.

Adj. **lenient,** mild, gentle, tolerant, indulgent, easy, moderate, complaisant, easygoing; clement, compassionate, forbearing; longsuffering.

741. COMMAND.—*N.* command, order, ordinance, act, fiat, bidding, word, call, beck, nod; direction, injunction, charge, instructions; dispatch, message.

demand, exaction, imposition, requisition, claim, requirement, ultimatum; request, etc., 765.

decree, dictate, dictation, mandate, precept; prescript, writ, ordination, bull, edict, dispensation, prescription, enactment, law, act; warrant, passport, summons, subpoena, citation; word of command, order of the day.

V. command, order, decree, enact, ordain, dictate, direct, give orders, issue a command; call to order; assume the command.

prescribe, set, appoint, mark out; set (*or* prescribe, impose) a task; set to work.

bid, enjoin, charge, instruct; require, demand, exact, impose, tax.

claim, lay claim to, reclaim.

cite, summon, call for, send for; subpoena; beckon.

Adj. commanding, authoritative, imperative, decisive, final.

Adv. in a commanding tone; by a stroke (*or* dash) of the pen; by order.

742. DISOBEDIENCE.—*N.* disobedience, insubordination, contumacy; infraction, infringement, violation.

revolt, rebellion, mutiny, outbreak, rising, uprising, insurrection, riot, tumult, strike.

sedition, treason; lese majesty; defection, secession, revolution; bolshevism.

insurgent, mutineer, rebel, traitor, communist, Fenian, Sinn Feiner, Red, Bolshevist, seceder, Secessionist [esp., U. S. hist.] *or* Secesh [*colloq. or slang*, U. S.]; apostate, renegade, anarchist.

V. disobey, violate, infringe; shirk, slack; defy, set at defiance, run riot, take the law into one's own hands; kick over the traces; refuse to support, bolt [*politics*].

resist, strike, rise, rise in arms; secede, mutiny, rebel.

Adj. disobedient, unruly, ungovernable; insubordinate, restive, refractory, defiant, contumacious; recusant, recalcitrant.

lawless, riotous, mutinous, seditious, insurgent, revolutionary.

743. OBEDIENCE.—*N.* obedience, observance, compliance; submission, subjection; nonresistance, passivity, resignation, submissiveness, ductility, obsequiousness, servility.

allegiance, loyalty, fealty, homage, deference, devotion; constancy, fidelity.

V. obey, submit, etc., 725; comply, do one's bidding, attend to orders, serve faithfully (*or* loyally, devotedly, without question); be resigned to, be submissive to; serve, etc., 746; play second fiddle.

Adj. **obedient**, law-abiding, complying, compliant; loyal, faithful, devoted; under beck and call, under control.

resigned, passive; submissive, etc., 725; unresisting, pliant.

Adv. as you please, if you please; in compliance with, in obedience to.

744. COMPULSION.—*N.* **compulsion**, coercion, constraint; restraint, etc., 751; enforcement, draft, conscription; eminent domain.

force; brute (*or* main, physical) force; the sword; mob law, martial law.

necessity, etc., 601; spur of necessity, Hobson's choice.

V. **compel**, force, make, drive, dragoon, coerce, constrain, enforce, necessitate, oblige.

extort, wring from, force upon, drag into; bind, pin down; require; tax, put in force; commandeer; restrain, etc., 751.

Adj. **compelling**, coercive, inexorable, compulsory, obligatory, stringent, peremptory, binding.

Adv. **forcibly**, by force, by force of arms; on compulsion, perforce, under protest, in spite of, in one's teeth; against one's will.

745. MASTER.—*N.* **master**, lord, commander, commandant, captain, chief, chieftain; paterfamilias [*Rom. law*], patriarch; sahib [India], head, senior, governor, ruler, dictator, leader, director, boss; sachem, sagamore.

potentate; liege, liege lord, suzerain, overlord, sovereign, monarch, crowned head, emperor, king, majesty, protector, president; autocrat, despot, tyrant, oligarch, dictator.

caesar, kaiser, czar, sultan, caliph, mogul, great mogul, mikado, inca; prince, duke, etc. (*nobility*), 875; archduke, doge; maharaja, raja, emir, nizam, nawab [*Indian ruling chiefs*].

empress, queen, sultana, czarina, princess, infanta, duchess, maharani, rani [both Hindu], begum [Moham.].

regent, viceroy, khedive, pasha, bey, mandarin.

the authorities, the powers that be, the government; staff, official, man in office, person in authority.

Military authorities: marshal, field marshal, generalissimo; commander in chief, general, brigadier general, brigadier, lieutenant general, major general, colonel, lieutenant colonel, major, captain, lieutenant, sublieutenant; officer, staff officer, aide-de-camp, adjutant, ensign, cornet, cadet, subaltern; noncommissioned officer; sergeant, top sergeant, corporal.

Civil authorities: mayor, prefect, chancellor, magistrate, syndic; burgomaster, seneschal, alderman, warden, constable.

Naval authorities: admiral, admiralty; commodore, captain commander, lieutenant; skipper, master, mate.

746. SERVANT.—*N.* **servant**, retainer, follower, henchman, servitor, domestic, menial, help [*local*], employee, attaché [F.], official.

subject, liege, liegeman.

retinue, suite, cortege, staff, court; office force, clerical staff, clerical force, workers, associate workers, employees, the help.

attendant, squire, usher, apprentice; page, buttons [*colloq.*]; trainbearer, cupbearer; waiter, butler, lackey, footman, flunky [*colloq.*]; boy [*any colored male servant, as in the Orient, South Africa, etc.*]; valet, equerry, groom, jockey, hostler *or* ostler, orderly, messenger, caddie; secretary, stenographer, clerk, agent, underling, understrapper; man.

maid, maidservant; girl, help [*local*], handmaid, lady's maid, nurse, ayah [India], nursemaid; cook, scullion, Cinderella; general servant [Brit.], general-housework maid [U. S.], general [*colloq.*]; washerwoman, laundress, charwoman.

dependent, hanger-on, satellite, parasite, protégé [F.], ward, hireling, mercenary, puppet, creature; serf, vassal, thrall, slave, Negro, helot; bondsman, bondswoman; bondslave; villein [*hist.*], churl [*hist.*].

V. serve, minister to, help, co-operate; wait (*or* attend, dance attendance) upon; squire, valet, tend, do for [*colloq.*].

Adj. serviceable, useful, helpful, co-operative; at one's call.

servile, slavish, subject, thrall, bond; subservient, obsequious, base, fawning, truckling, sycophantic, parasitic, cringing.

747. [Insignia of authority] SCEPTER.—*N.* Regal: scepter, orb; pall; robes of state, ermine, purple; crown, coronet, diadem; triple plume; flail [Egyptian]; signet seal.

Ecclesiastical: tiara, triple crown; ring, keys; miter, crozier, crook, staff; cardinal's hat; bishop's apron (*or* sleeves, lawn, gaiters), fillet.

Military: epaulet, star, bar, eagle, crown [Brit.], oak leaf, Sam Browne belt; chevron, stripe.

caduceus; Mercury's staff (*or* rod, wand); mace, fasces, ax, truncheon, staff, baton, wand, rod; flag, etc. (*insignia*), 550; regalia; toga, mantle; decoration, title, etc., 877; portfolio.

throne, divan; woolsack [*seat of English Lord Chancellor in the House of Lords*], chair, seat, dais.

talisman, amulet, charm, sign.

748. FREEDOM.—*N.* freedom, liberty, independence; license, indulgence.

scope, range, latitude, play, free play (*or* scope), swing, full swing, elbowroom, margin, rope, wide berth.

franchise; prerogative, etc., 924.

freeman, freedman, citizen, denizen.

immunity, exemption; emancipation, etc., 750; right, privilege.

autonomy, self-government; free trade; self-determination, noninterference; Monroe Doctrine [U. S.].

independent, free lance, freethinker, free trader.

V. be free, have scope (*or* one's own way), do what one likes, go at large, feel at home, stand on one's rights.

free, liberate, set free, etc., 750; give the reins to; make free of, enfranchise.

Adj. free, independent, at large, loose, scot-free; unconstrained, unconfined, unchecked, unhindered, unobstructed, uncontrolled, ungoverned, unchained, unshackled, unfettered, unbridled, uncurbed, unmuzzled, unvanquished.

unrestricted, unlimited, unconditional; absolute; with unlimited power (*or* opportunity); discretionary.

unbiased, unprejudiced, uninfluenced; spontaneous.

free and easy, at ease, at one's ease; quite at home.

exempt, immune, freed, freeborn; autonomous, freehold.

gratuitous, gratis, etc., 815; for nothing, for love.

Adv. **freely,** at will, with no restraint.

749. SUBJECTION.—*N.* subjection; dependence, subordination; thrall, thralldom, subjugation, bondage, serfdom; feudalism, vassalage, slavery, enslavement; conquest.

service; servitude, employ, tutelage, constraint, yoke, submission, obedience.

V. **be subject,** be at the mercy of, depend upon; fall a prey to, fall under, play second fiddle; serve, etc., 746; obey, etc., 743; submit, etc., 725.

subjugate, subject, tame, break in; master, tread down, weigh down, keep under, enthrall, enslave, lead captive, rule, etc., 737; hold in bondage (*or* leading strings).

Adj. **subject,** dependent, subordinate; feudal, feudatory; under control; in leading strings, in harness; servile, slavish, enslaved, downtrodden; henpecked; under one's thumb, tied to one's apron strings, at one's beck and call; liable.

Adv. **under;** under orders (*or* command), at one's orders.

750. LIBERATION.—*N.* liberation, disengagement, release, emancipation, Emancipation Proclamation; enfranchisement, manumission; discharge, dismissal.

deliverance, etc., 672; redemption, extrication, acquittance, absolution, acquittal, escape.

V. **liberate,** free, set free, emancipate, release; enfranchise, manumit; demobilize, disband, discharge, dismiss; let go, let loose, let out, deliver, etc., 672; absolve, acquit.

unfetter, untie, loose, loosen, relax; unbolt, unbar, unhand, unbind, unchain, disengage, disentangle; clear, extricate; reprieve.

Adj. **liberated,** freed; foot-loose, one's own master.

Adv. **at large,** at liberty; adrift.

751. RESTRAINT.—*N.* restraint; hindrance, etc., 706; coercion, compulsion, constraint, repression; discipline, control; limitation, restriction, protection, monopoly; prohibition, economic pressure.

confinement, durance, duress; imprisonment, incarceration, thrall, thralldom, limbo, captivity; blockade.

keep, care, charge, custody, ward.

repressionist, monopolist, protectionist.

V. **restrain,** check, restrict, debar, hinder, constrain, coerce, compel, curb, harness, control; hold in leash, withhold, repress, suppress, keep under; smother, pull in, rein in, hold, prohibit.

fasten, enchain, fetter, shackle, trammel; bridle, muzzle, gag, pinion, manacle, handcuff, hobble, bind, swathe, swaddle; tether, picket, tie, secure.

confine, shut up (*or* in), lock up, box up, bottle up, cork up, seal up, blockade, hem in, bolt in, wall in, rail in; impound, pen, coop; inclose, cage, imprison, immure, incarcerate, entomb; put in irons, cast into prison.

arrest, take into custody; take (*or* make) prisoner, lead captive, send to prison, commit; give in charge (*or* custody).

Adj. **restrained,** constrained, repressive, suppressive; imprisoned, pent up, wedged in; on parole; doing time [*colloq. or slang*], in custody.

stiff, narrow, prudish, strait-laced, hidebound.

Adv. **under restraint** (*or* lock and key, hatches), under discipline; in prison, in jail, in durance vile, in confinement; behind bars, in captivity, under arrest.

752. [Means of restraint] PRISON.—*N.* prison, prisonhouse; jail, cage, coop, den, cell; stronghold, fortress, keep, donjon, dungeon, Bastille, penitentiary, state prison, lockup, station house, station [*colloq.*], pen [*also slang for penitentiary*], pound; penal settlement; workhouse [U. S.; *in England, a workhouse is a poorhouse*], reformatory, reform school.

Restraining devices: shackle, bond, gyve, fetter, irons, pinion, manacle, handcuff, straight jacket, stocks, pillory; vise, bandage, splint, strap; yoke, collar, halter, harness; muzzle, gag, bit, curb, snaffle, bridle; rein, reins, lines [U. S. and dial. Eng.], ribbons [*colloq.*]; tether, picket, band, chain, cord.

bar, bolt, lock, padlock; rail, paling, palisade; wall, fence, barrier, barricade.

drag, brake, check, etc. (*hindrance*), 706.

753. KEEPER.—*N.* **keeper,** custodian, ranger, gamekeeper, warder, jailer, turnkey, castellan, guard; watch, watchdog, watchman, concierge [F.], sentry, sentinel; coastguard.

escort, bodyguard; convoy.

guardian, protector, governor; duenna, governess, nurse.

754. PRISONER.—*N.* **prisoner,** convict, captive, close prisoner.

V. stand committed; be imprisoned.

Adj. **imprisoned,** in prison, in custody, in charge, behind bars, under lock and key, under hatches.

755. [Vicarious authority] COMMISSION.—*N.* **commission,**

delegation; consignment, assignment; proxy, power of attorney, deputation, legation, mission, embassy; agency.

errand, charge, brevet, diploma, permit.

appointment, nomination, charter; ordination; installation, inauguration, investiture; accession, coronation, enthronement.

V. **commission,** delegate, depute; consign, assign, commit, charge, intrust, authorize.

accredit, engage, hire, bespeak, appoint, name, nominate, return; ordain, install, induct, inaugurate, invest, crown; enroll, enlist; employ, empower.

Adv. instead of, in one's stead, in one's place; as proxy for.

756. ANNULMENT.—*N.* **annulment,** nullification, cancellation, abrogation, revocation, repeal.

dismissal, *congé* [F.], sack [*slang*], deposition, dethronement; disestablishment, disendowment.

countermand, repudiation, retractation, recantation; abolition, abolishment; dissolution.

V. **annul,** cancel, destroy, abolish, abrogate, revoke, repeal, rescind, reverse, retract, recall; overrule, override; set aside; disannul, dissolve, quash, nullify, nol-pros [*law, short for nolle prosequi*], disestablish; countermand, counterorder, throw overboard.

disclaim, deny, ignore, repudiate; recant, break off.

dismiss, discard; turn out, cast off (*or* adrift, aside, away); send off, send away, discharge, get rid of, bounce [*slang*]; fire, sack [*both slang*].

cashier, oust, unseat, dethrone, depose, unfrock, strike off the roll, disbar.

757. RESIGNATION.—*N.* **resignation,** retirement, abdication; renunciation, retractation, retraction, disclaimer, abandonment, relinquishment.

V. **resign,** give up, throw up, lay down, abjure, renounce, forego, disclaim, retract, deny, desert.

vacate, abdicate, retire; tender (*or* hand in) one's resignation.

758. CONSIGNEE.—*N.* **consignee,** trustee, nominee; committee.

functionary, curator; treasurer, etc., 801; agent, factor, steward, bailiff, clerk, secretary, attorney, solicitor, proctor, broker, underwriter, commission agent, factotum, caretaker, employee; servant, etc., 746.

negotiator, go-between; middleman.

delegate, commissioner; emissary, envoy, messenger.

diplomatist, diplomat, ambassador, plenipotentiary, diplomatic agent, representative, resident, consul, legate, etc., 534; attaché [F.].

salesman, traveler, traveling salesman, commercial traveler, drummer, traveling man.

759. DEPUTY.—*N.* **deputy,** substitute, proxy, delegate, representative, alternate; vice-president.

regent, vicegerent, viceroy, minister, premier, chancellor, provost, warden, lieutenant, consul, ambassador; delegate, etc., 758.

team, eight, nine, eleven; captain, champion.

V. **represent,** stand for, appear for, hold a brief for, answer for; stand in the shoes of; stand in the stead of.

delegate, depute, empower, commission, substitute, accredit.

Adj. **acting,** vice, viceregal; accredited to; delegated, representative.

Adv. **in behalf of,** in the place of, as representing, by proxy.

760. PERMISSION.—*N.* **permission,** leave, allowance, sufferance, tolerance, toleration, connivance; liberty, law, license, concession, grace; indulgence, favor, dispensation, exemption, release; authorization, accordance, admission.

permit, warrant, sanction, authority, pass, passport; license, carte blanche [F.], grant, charter, patent.

V. **permit,** let, allow, admit; suffer, tolerate, recognize; concede, etc., 762; accord, vouchsafe, favor, humor, gratify, indulge, wink at, connive at.

grant, empower, charter, enfranchise, privilege, license, authorize, warrant, sanction; intrust, commission.

absolve, release, exonerate, dispense with.

Adj. **permitted,** permissible, allowable, lawful, legitimate, legal, legalized, chartered, unforbidden.

Adv. **by** (*or* with) **leave,** under favor of, by all means.

761. PROHIBITION.—*N.* **prohibition,** inhibition; veto, interdict, interdiction, injunction, embargo, ban, taboo, proscription, restriction; contraband; forbidden fruit; Volstead Act, 18th amendment [all U. S.].

V. **prohibit,** inhibit, forbid, disallow; bar, debar, hinder, restrain, etc., 751; withhold, limit, circumscribe, clip the wings of, restrict; interdict, taboo, proscribe; exclude, shut out.

Adj **prohibitive,** prohibitory; proscriptive; restrictive, exclusive.

prohibited, unlicensed, contraband, taboo, illegal, unauthorized.

762. CONSENT.—*N.* **consent;** assent, etc., 488; acquiescence, approval, compliance, agreement, concession, accession, acknowledgment, acceptance; permit, etc. (*permission*), 760; promise, etc., 768.

settlement, adjustment, ratification, confirmation.

V. **consent;** assent, etc., 488; yield assent, admit, allow, concede, grant, yield; acknowledge, give consent, comply with, acquiesce, agree to, accede, accept, close with, satisfy, settle, come to terms; deign, vouchsafe, promise.

Adj. **willing,** compliant, agreeable [*colloq.*], eager.

763. OFFER.—*N.* **offer,** proffer, tender, bid, overture, proposal, proposition; motion, invitation, offering.

V. **offer,** proffer, present, tender; bid; propose, move, make a motion, start, invite, place at one's disposal; make possible, put forward, press, urge upon, hold out.

volunteer, come forward, be a candidate, offer (*or* present) oneself, stand for, bid for; seek; be at one's service.

Adj. in the market, for sale, to let, disengaged, on hire; at one's disposal.

764. REFUSAL.—*N.* **refusal,** rejection, denial, declension, flat (*or* point-blank) refusal; repulse, rebuff; discountenance, disapprobation.

negation, abnegation, protest, renunciation, disclaimer; dissent, etc., 489; revocation, annulment.

V. **refuse,** reject, deny, decline, turn down [*slang*], dissent, etc., 489; negative, withhold one's assent, grudge, begrudge; stand aloof, be deaf to, turn one's back upon, discountenance, forswear, set aside.

resist, repel, repulse, rebuff, deny oneself, discard, repudiate, rescind, disclaim, protest.

Adj. **uncomplying,** deaf to, noncompliant, unconsenting; recusant, dissentient.

Adv. on no account, not for the world, not on your life! [*colloq.*].

765. REQUEST.—*N.* **request,** requisition; claim, demand, etc., 741; petition, suit, prayer, solicitation, invitation, entreaty, importunity, supplication, invocation.

motion, overture, application, canvass, address, appeal, imprecation; proposal, proposition.

V. **request,** ask, beg, crave, sue, pray, petition, solicit, canvass, invite, beg leave, beg a boon, apply to, call to, call for; make a request, make application, claim, demand; offer up prayers.

entreat, beseech, plead, supplicate, implore; conjure, adjure; apostrophize, cry to, kneel to, appeal to; invoke, evoke; press, urge, importune, dun, clamor for, cry aloud, cry for help.

Adj. **importunate,** clamorous, urgent, solicitous; cap in hand.

Adv. **please,** prithee, do, pray; be so good as, be good enough; have the goodness, vouchsafe, will you, I pray thee, if you please.

766. [Negative request] DEPRECATION.—*N.* **deprecation,** expostulation; intercession, mediation, protest, remonstrance.

V. **deprecate,** protest, expostulate, enter a protest, remonstrate.

Adj. deprecatory, expostulatory, intercessory.

unsought, unbesought; unasked.

767. PETITIONER.—*N.* **petitioner,** solicitor, applicant, suppliant, supplicant, suitor, candidate, claimant, aspirant, competitor, bidder; place hunter.

salesman, drummer, etc., 758; canvasser.

beggar, mendicant, panhandler [*slang*], cadger.

hotel runner, runner [*both cant*], steerer [*colloq.*], barker [*colloq.*].

sycophant, parasite, etc. (*servility*), 886.

768. PROMISE.—*N.* **promise,** undertaking, word, troth, plight, pledge, parole, word of honor, vow, oath, profession, assurance, warranty, guarantee, insurance, obligation, contract, stipulation.

engagement, affiance, betrothal, marriage contract (*or* vow); plighted faith.

V. **promise,** undertake, engage; make (*or* form, enter into) an engagement; bind (*or* pledge) oneself; vow, swear, give (*or* pledge) one's word; betroth, plight faith.

assure, warrant, guarantee, covenant, agree, vouch for, attest; answer for, be answerable for; secure, give security, underwrite.

Adj. **promissory,** votive, under hand and seal, upon oath, upon affirmation.

promised, affianced, pledged, bound, committed, compromised.

Adv. as true as I live; in all soberness; upon my honor; my word for it.

769. COMPACT.—*N.* **compact,** contract, specialty, deal [*colloq.*], agreement, bargain; pact, bond, covenant, indenture [*law*]; stipulation, settlement, convention; compromise, negotiation.

treaty, protocol, concordat, charter, Magna Charta, pragmatic sanction.

ratification, completion, signature, seal, bond.

V. **contract,** covenant, agree for; engage, etc. (*promise*), 768.

negotiate, treat, stipulate, make terms; bargain.

conclude, close, close with, complete, strike a bargain; come to terms (*or* an understanding); compromise, settle; confirm, ratify, clinch, subscribe, underwrite; indorse, sign, seal.

Adj. **contractual,** complete, agreed; signed, sealed, and delivered.

Adv. **as agreed upon,** as promised, according to the contract.

770. CONDITIONS.—*N.* **conditions,** terms, articles, articles of agreement; memorandum, clauses, provisions, proviso, covenant, stipulation, obligation, ultimatum.

V. **condition,** stipulate, insist upon, make a point of; bind, tie up; fence in, hedge in, make (*or* come to) terms.

Adj. **conditional**, provisional, guarded, fenced, hedged in.

Adv. **conditionally**, provisionally, on condition; with a string to it [*colloq.*], with a reservation.

771. SECURITY.—*N.* **security**, guaranty, guarantee; gage, bond, tie, pledge, mortgage, debenture; bill of sale, lien, collateral, bail, stake, deposit, earnest.

promissory note; bill, bill of exchange; I O U; personal security, covenant.

acceptance, indorsement, signature, execution, stamp, seal.

sponsor, surety, bail, hostage; godchild, godfather, godmother.

authentication, verification, warrant, certificate, voucher, receipt.

deed, instrument, title deed, indenture; charter, paper, parchment, settlement, will, testament, codicil.

V. **give security**, give bail, go bail; pawn, put in pawn, pledge, mortgage.

guarantee, warrant, assure; accept, indorse, underwrite, insure.

execute, stamp; sign, seal.

Adj. **pledged**, pawned, in pawn, at stake, on deposit, as earnest.

772. OBSERVANCE.—*N.* **observance**, performance, compliance, acquiescence, concurrence; obedience, etc., 743; fulfillment, satisfaction, discharge; acquittance, acquittal; adhesion, ackowledgment; fidelity.

V. **observe**, comply with, respect, acknowledge, abide by; cling to, adhere to, be faithful to, act up to; meet, fulfill, carry out, execute, perform, discharge, keep one's word (*or* pledge).

Adj. **observant**, faithful, true, loyal, honorable, etc., 939; punctual, punctilious, scrupulous, as good as one's word.

Adv. **to the letter.**

773. NONOBSERVANCE.—*N.* **nonobservance**, noncompliance, evasion, failure, omission, neglect, slackness, laxness, laxity, informality; lawlessness, disobedience, etc., 742; bad faith, etc., 940.

infringement, infraction; violation, transgression; piracy, literary theft.

V. **evade**, fail, neglect, omit, elude, cut [*colloq.*], set aside, ignore; shut (*or* close) one's eyes to.

infringe, transgress, violate, steal, pirate [*a book, etc.*].

discard, repudiate, protest, nullify, declare null and void, cancel, forfeit.

Adj. **elusive**, evasive, slack, lax, casual, slippery; nonobservant.

774. COMPROMISE.—*N.* **compromise**, composition, middle term, compensation, adjustment, mutual concession.

V. **compromise**, commute, compound, split the difference, meet one halfway, give and take, come to terms, submit to arbitration, patch up, arrange, straighten out, adjust, agree, make the best of, make a virtue of necessity.

Possessive Relations[1]

(1) Property

775. ACQUISITION.—*N.* **acquisition,** procurement; purchase, inheritance; gift, etc., 784.

recovery, redemption, salvage, find.

gain, thrift, money-making, pelf, lucre, filthy lucre, the main chance.

profit, earnings, wages, salary, emolument, income, remuneration; winnings, pickings, perquisite; proceeds, produce, product; outcome, output; return, fruit, crop, harvest; benefit; prize; wealth, etc., 803.

V. **acquire,** get, gain, win, earn, obtain, procure, gather; collect, pick, pick up, glean, find, light upon, come across, come at; scrape up (*or* together); get in, net, bag, secure; derive, draw, get in the harvest.

profit, turn to profit (*or* account), make capital out of, make money by, obtain a return, reap the fruits of; gain an advantage; make (*or* coin, raise) money, raise funds; realize, clear, produce, take, receive, come by, inherit.

recover, get back, regain, retrieve, redeem.

Adj. **profitable,** productive, advantageous, gainful, remunerative, paying, lucrative.

Adv. in the way of gain; for money; at interest.

776. LOSS.—*N.* **loss,** forfeiture, lapse; privation, bereavement, deprivation, riddance; damage, squandering, waste.

V. **lose,** incur a loss, miss, mislay, let slip, be deprived of, be without, forfeit.

squander, lavish, get rid of, waste.

Adj. **bereft,** bereaved, deprived of, shorn of, denuded, minus [*colloq., exc. in math.*], cut off; rid of, quit of, out of pocket, lost.

777. POSSESSION.—*N.* **possession,** ownership, proprietorship, occupancy, hold, holding, tenure, tenancy, dependency.

exclusive possession, monopoly, retention, corner.

future possession, heritage, inheritance, heirship, reversion; primogeniture.

V. **possess,** have, hold, occupy, enjoy, be possessed of, own, command, inherit.

[1] That is, relations which concern property.

monopolize, corner, engross, forestall, appropriate.

belong to, appertain to, pertain to; be in one's possession, vest in.

Adj. possessing, worth, possessed of, master of, in possession of; endowed (*or* blest, fraught, laden, charged) with.

possessed, on hand, in hand, in store, in stock; at one's command, at one's disposal.

777a. EXEMPTION.—*N.* exemption, exception, immunity, privilege, release.

V. not have, not possess, not own, be without.

Adj. devoid of, exempt from, without, unpossessed of, unblest with; immune from.

unpossessed; untenanted, vacant, without an owner.

778. [Joint possession] PARTICIPATION.—*N.* participation, joint tenancy; joint (*or* common) stock; partnership; communion; community of possessions, communism, collectivism, socialism; co-operation.

participator, sharer, partner; shareholder; joint tenant; tenants in common; coheir.

communist, communalist, collectivist, socialist.

V. participate, partake, share, share in, join in, go shares, go cahoots [*slang*], go halves; share and share alike.

communize, communalize; have (*or* possess) in common.

Adj. communistic, socialistic; co-operative, profit-sharing.

Adv. in common, share and share alike; on shares.

779. POSSESSOR.—*N.* possessor, holder, occupant, occupier, tenant, tenant at will, lessee, lodger.

owner; proprietor, proprietress, master, mistress, lord.

landholder, landowner, landlord, landlady; lord of the manor, laird [*Scot.*], landed gentry.

Future possessor: heir, heir apparent, heir presumptive; inheritor, heiress, inheritrix.

780. PROPERTY.—*N.* property, possession, tenure; ownership, etc., 777.

estate, interest, right, title, claim, demand, holding, vested interest; use, trust, benefit; term, lease, settlement; remainder, reversion.

dower, dowry, jointure, inheritance, heritage, patrimony, legacy.

assets, belongings, means, resources, circumstances; wealth, etc., 803; money, etc., 800; estate and effects.

realty, real estate, land, lands, landed (*or* real) property; tenements; plant, fixtures; ground; freehold, copyhold, leasehold.

manor, domain, demesne; farm, plantation, ranch.

territory, state, kingdom, principality, realm, empire, protectorate, dependency, sphere of influence, mandate.

personalty, personal property (*or* estate, effects), chattels, goods, effects, movables· stock, stock in trade, things, paraphernalia, equipage, appurtenances; income, etc., 810.

baggage, luggage [esp. in Eng.], impedimenta, bag and baggage; cargo.

V. **possess,** etc., 777; be the possessor, own; inherit.

Adj. landed, hereditary, entailed, real, personal.

Adv. to one's credit, to one's account; to the good.

781. RETENTION.—*N.* **retention,** detention, custody; tenacity, firm hold, grasp, gripe, grip, clutches, talon, claw, fang, tentacle.

captive, prisoner, bird in hand.

V. **retain,** keep, hold, hold fast, clinch, clench, clutch, grasp, gripe, hug; secure, withhold, detain; hold (*or* keep) back; husband, reserve; have (*or* keep) in stock; entail, tie up, settle.

Adj. retentive, tenacious.

782. RIDDANCE.—*N.* **riddance,** relinquishment, abandonment, renunciation, dereliction; cession, surrender, dispensation; resignation.

derelict, jetsam; abandoned farm [U. S.]; waif, foundling.

V. **relinquish,** give up, surrender, yield, cede; let go, let slip; spare, drop, resign, forego, renounce, abandon, give away, dispose of, part with; lay aside, set aside, discard, cast off, dismiss; maroon.

cast (*or* throw, fling) away, jettison.

supersede, give notice to quit, give warning; be (*or* get) rid of; eject.

divorce, cut off, desert, disinherit; separate.

Adj. **relinquished,** cast off, derelict; disowned, disinherited, divorced.

783. TRANSFER [of property].—*N.* **transfer,** conveyance, assignment, alienation, conveyancing, transmission, sale, lease, release, exchange, barter; succession, reversion.

V. **transfer,** convey, alienate, assign, grant, consign; make over, hand over, transmit, negotiate; hand down; exchange.

change hands, devolve, succeed; require, come into possession.

disinherit; dispossess, etc., 789; substitute.

Adj. **transferable,** alienable, negotiable, reversional, transmissive; inherited.

784. GIVING.—*N.* **giving,** bestowal, presentation, concession, cession; delivery, consignment, dispensation, endowment; investment, investiture; award, recompense, etc., 973.

charity, almsgiving, liberality, generosity.

gift, donation, present, boon, favor, benefaction, grant, offering, bonus, oblation, sacrifice.

allowance, contribution, subscription, subsidy, tribute.

bequest, legacy, devise, will, dot, dowry, dower.

gratuity, alms, largess, bounty, dole, help, offertory, honorarium, Christmas box, tip, baksheesh, consideration.

bribe, bait, peace offering; graft [*colloq*.].

giver, grantor, donor, testator; investor, subscriber, contributor; fairy godmother.

V. deliver, hand, pass, assign, hand (*or* make, deliver, turn) over.

pay, etc., 807; render, impart, communicate.

concede, cede, yield, part with, shed; spend, sacrifice.

give, bestow, donate, confer, grant; accord, award, assign, offer; present, give away, dispense, dispose of; give (*or* deal) out, fork out [*slang*]; allow, contribute, subscribe.

invest, endow, settle upon; bequeath, leave, devise.

furnish, supply, help, administer to, afford, spare, accommodate with, indulge with, favor with; lavish, pour on, thrust upon.

bribe, tip; grease the palm [*slang*].

Adj. charitable, eleemosynary, tributary; gratis, etc., 815; donative.

785. RECEIVING.—*N.* receiving, acquisition, etc., 775; reception, acceptance, admission.

recipient, receiver; assignee, legatee, grantee, lessee; beneficiary, pensioner.

income, etc. (*receipt*), 810.

V. receive; take, etc., 789; pocket; acquire, etc., 775; admit, take in, catch, accept.

be received; come in, come to hand, go into one's pocket; fall to one's lot (*or* share), accrue.

Adj. receiving, recipient; stipendiary, pensionary.

received, given, allowed; secondhand.

786. APPORTIONMENT.—*N.* apportionment, allotment, consignment, assignment, allocation, appropriation; distribution, division, deal; partition, administration.

portion, dividend, share, allotment, lot, measure, dose; dole, meed, pittance; ration; ratio, proportion, quota, modicum, allowance.

V. apportion, divide; distribute, administer, dispense; allot, allocate, detail, cast, share, mete; portion (*or* parcel, dole) out; deal, carve.

partition, assign, appropriate, appoint.

Adv. respectively, each to each; by lot; in equal shares.

787. LENDING.—*N.* lending, loan, advance, accommodation, mortgage, etc., 771; investment.

lender, pawnbroker, my uncle [*slang*], moneylender, usurer, Shylock.

V. **lend**, advance, accommodate with; lend on security; loan; pawn.

invest, intrust, place (*or* put) out to interest; place, put; embark, risk, venture, sink.

let, lease, sublet, sublease.

Adv. in advance; on loan, on security.

788. BORROWING.—*N.* **borrowing**, pledging, pawning.

V. **borrow**, pledge, pawn, put up the spout [*slang*], raise money, raise the wind [*slang*]; run into debt.

hire, rent, farm; take a lease.

appropriate, adopt, apply, imitate, make use of, take; plagiarize, pirate.

789. TAKING.—*N.* **taking**, reception, appropriation, capture, apprehension, seizure; abduction, abstraction.

dispossession; deprivation, bereavement, disinheritance; attachment, execution, sequestration, confiscation, eviction.

rapacity, rapaciousness, extortion, bloodsucking; theft, etc.,791.

taker, captor, capturer; extortioner *or* extortionist; vampire.

V. **take**, catch, hook, bag, sack, pocket, receive, accept.

reap, crop, cull, pluck, gather, draw.

appropriate, assume, possess oneself of; commandeer [*colloq.*]; help oneself to, make free with, lay under contribution; intercept, scramble for; deprive of.

seize, snatch, abstract, take away (*or* off), run away with; abduct, kidnap, capture, steal, pounce (*or* spring) upon; swoop down upon; take by storm; take prisoner; grapple, embrace, grip, gripe, clasp, grab [*colloq.*], clutch, collar, throttle, claw.

dispossess, take from, take away from; tear from, tear away from, wrench (*or* wrest, wring) from, extort; deprive of, bereave; disinherit, oust, evict, eject, divest; levy, distrain [*law*], confiscate; sequester, sequestrate, usurp; despoil, strip, fleece, bleed [*colloq.*].

Adj. **predatory**, wolfish, rapacious, ravening, ravenous; parasitic; all-devouring, all-engulfing.

790. RESTITUTION.—*N.* **restitution**, return, restoration, reinstatement, reinvestment, rehabilitation, reparation, atonement; compensation, indemnification; recovery.

V. **restore**, return, give back, render, give up, let go, release, remit; disgorge, recoup, reimburse, compensate, indemnify, reinvest, reinstate, rehabilitate, repair, make good.

recover, get back, retrieve, redeem; take back again.

Adj. **compensatory**, indemnificatory; reversionary, redemptive.

Adv. in full restitution; as partial compensation; to atone for.

791. STEALING.—*N.* **stealing**, theft, thievery, robbery, rapacity, thievishness, abstraction, appropriation, plagiarism, depredation; kidnaping.

pillage, spoliation, plunder, sack, rapine, brigandage, highway robbery, holdup [*slang*]; raid, foray, piracy, privateering, buccaneering, filibustering; burglary, housebreaking; shoplifting, blackmail.

peculation, embezzlement, fraud, forgery, larceny, pilfering; kleptomania.

V. **steal**, thieve, rob, purloin, pilfer, filch, bag, crib [*colloq.*], palm; abstract; appropriate, plagiarize.

abduct, convey away, carry off, kidnap, impress, make (*or* run) off with, run away with, spirit away, seize.

plunder, pillage, filibuster, rifle, sack, loot, ransack, spoil, despoil, strip, sweep, gut, forage, levy blackmail, maraud, poach, smuggle, bunko; hold up.

swindle, peculate, embezzle; sponge, pluck, fleece, defraud, obtain under false pretenses.

counterfeit, forge, coin, circulate bad money.

Adj. **thievish**, light-fingered, piratical; predatory, raptorial.

792. THIEF.—*N.* **thief**, robber, spoiler, depredator, pillager, marauder; pilferer, plagiarist; harpy, shark [*slang*], **smuggler**, poacher, kidnaper; crook [*slang*], shoplifter.

pirate, corsair, viking, buccaneer, privateer.

brigand, bandit, filibuster, freebooter, thug, cattle thief, bushranger, moss-trooper [*hist.*], highwayman, footpad, strong-arm man.
pickpocket, cutpurse, light-fingered gentry; sharper; cardsharper, trickster.
swindler, peculator, forger, coiner, counterfeiter; fence, receiver of stolen goods.
burglar, housebreaker, yegg [*slang*], cracksman [*slang*], sneak thief; second-story thief (*or* man).

793. BOOTY.—*N.* **booty**, spoil, plunder, prize, prey, loot, swag [*cant*]; perquisite, boodle [*polit. cant*], graft [*colloq.*], pork barrel [*polit. cant*], pickings; blackmail; stolen goods.

Adj. **looting**, plundering, spoliative.

794. BARTER.—*N.* **barter**, exchange, interchange, Indian gift [*colloq.*].

trade, commerce, buying and selling, traffic, business, custom, transaction, negotiation, bargain; speculation, jobbing, stock-jobbing.

free trade [*opp. to* protection].

V. **barter**, exchange, truck, swap *or* swop [*colloq. and dial.*]; interchange.

trade, traffic, buy and sell, give and take, carry on (*or* ply) a trade; deal in, speculate.

bargain; drive (or make, strike) a bargain; negotiate, bid for; haggle, stickle, dicker, cheapen, beat down, underbid; outbid.

Adj. **commercial,** mercantile, trading; marketable, staple, in the market, for sale; at a bargain, marked down; retail; wholesale.

Adv. across the counter; in the marts of trade.

795. PURCHASE.—*N.* **purchase,** buying, purchasing, shopping.

buyer, purchaser, client, customer, patron, clientele.

V. **buy,** purchase, invest in, procure; shop, market, go a-shopping; rent, hire, repurchase, buy in.

796. SALE.—*N.* **sale,** disposal; auction, custom.

salableness, salability, marketability, vendibility.

seller, vender, vendor [*law*]; merchant, auctioneer.

salesmanship, selling ability.

V. **sell,** vend, dispose of, make a sale, effect a sale; auction, sell at auction, put up to (or at) auction; hawk, dump, unload, place, undersell; dispense, offer, retail; deal in, sell off (or out), turn into money, realize.

Adj. **salable,** marketable, staple, in demand, popular.

unsalable, unpurchased, unbought, on the shelves, on one's hands.

797. MERCHANT.—*N.* **merchant,** trader, dealer, salesman; money-changer, shopkeeper, shopman; tradesman, tradespeople, tradesfolk.

peddler, hawker, huckster, sutler, vivandière; costermonger; canvasser, solicitor; faker [*slang*].

moneylender, usurer, banker; money-changer, money broker.

jobber, broker; buyer, seller; bear, bull [*Stock Exchange*].

firm, company, house, corporation, concern, trust.

798. MERCHANDISE.—*N.* **merchandise,** ware, commodity, effects, goods, article, stock, produce, staple commodity; stock in trade, cargo.

799. MART.—*N.* **mart,** market, market place; fair, bazaar, exchange, stock exchange, Wheat Pit [*Chicago*]; bourse, curb.

shop, store, department store, chain store, warehouse, depot, emporium, establishment; stall, booth; office, chambers, counting-house, bureau; counter.

(2) Monetary Relations

800. MONEY.—*N.* **money,** finance, funds, treasure, capital, stock; assets, wealth, etc., 803; supplies, ways and means, wherewithal *or* wherewith, sinews of war, almighty dollar, cash.

solvency, responsibility, reliability, solidity, soundness.

sum, amount; balance, balance sheet; sum total; proceeds, receipts.

currency, circulating medium, specie, coin, piece, hard cash; dollar, sterling; pounds, shillings, and pence, £ s. d.; guinea; wallet, roll, wad [*slang*], purse, ready money.

precious metals, gold, silver, copper, bullion, ingot, bar, nugget.

petty cash, pocket money, pin money, spending money, change, small coin.

wampum.

great wealth, money to burn [*colloq.*]; power or mint of money [*colloq.*], good sum, millions, thousands.

Science of coins: numismatics.

paper money; bill, money order; note, note of hand; bank note, promissory note; I O U, bond; bill of exchange; draft, check, order, warrant, coupon, debenture, greenback.

V. **total,** amount to, come to, mount up to.

issue, utter, circulate; fiscalize, monetize.

demonetize, deprive of standard value; cease to issue.

Adj. **monetary,** pecuniary, fiscal, financial; sterling.

solvent, sound, substantial, good, reliable, responsible, solid, having a good rating; able to pay 100 cents to the dollar.

801. TREASURER.—*N.* **treasurer,** bursar, purser, banker, financier; receiver, liquidator, steward, trustee, accountant, expert accountant, almoner, paymaster, cashier, teller; money-changer.

802. TREASURY.—*N.* **treasury,** bank, exchequer, bursary; strongbox, stronghold, strong room; coffer, chest, safe, depository, cash register, cashbox, money box, till.

purse, moneybag, pocketbook, wallet; pocket.

securities, stocks; public stocks (*or* funds, securities); bonds, government bonds, Liberty bonds [U. S.], gilt-edged securities.

803. WEALTH.—*N.* **wealth,** riches, fortune, opulence, affluence; easy circumstances; independence, competence.

capital, money; great wealth, bonanza, El Dorado; philosopher's stone; the golden touch.

pelf, mammon, lucre, filthy lucre.

means, resources, substance, command of money; property, income, livelihood.

rich man, moneyed man, man of substance; capitalist, millionaire, multimillionaire, plutocrat; nabob, Croesus, Midas.

V. **be rich,** roll (*or* wallow) in wealth, have money to burn [*colloq.*]; afford, well afford, command money.

become rich, fill one's pocket, feather one's nest, make a fortune; make money; worship mammon, worship the golden calf.

Adj. **wealthy,** rich, affluent, opulent, moneyed, well-to-do, well off, rolling in riches.

804. POVERTY.—*N.* **poverty,** indigence, penury, pauperism, destitution, want; need, neediness; lack, necessity, privation, distress, difficulties, wolf at the door, straits; low water [*slang*], impecuniosity.

mendicancy, beggary, mendicity; broken (*or* loss of) fortune; insolvency.

poor man, pauper, mendicant, beggar.

V. **be poor,** want, lack, starve, live from hand to mouth, have seen better days, go to rack and ruin; beg one's bread, run into debt.

impoverish, reduce, reduce to poverty, pauperize, fleece, ruin.

Adj. **poor,** indigent; poverty-stricken, badly off, moneyless, penniless; impecunious, short of money, hard up, seedy [*colloq.*]; barefooted, beggarly, beggared, destitute, reduced, needy, necessitous, distressed, pinched, straitened, embarrassed, involved, insolvent.

805. CREDIT.—*N.* **credit,** trust, score, tally, account.

paper credit, letter of credit, circular note; duplicate; mortgage. lien, draft, securities.

creditor, lender, lessor [*law*], mortgagee; dun, usurer.

V. **credit,** accredit, intrust, keep (*or* run up) an account with; place to one's credit (*or* account); give (*or* take) credit.

Adj. **accredited;** of good credit, of unlimited credit; well rated; credited.

Adv. on credit, to the account of, to the credit of.

806. DEBT.—*N.* **debt,** obligation, liability, debit, score.

arrears, deferred payment, deficit, default, insolvency; bad debt.

interest; premium, usury.

debtor; mortgagor, defaulter, borrower.

V. **be in debt,** owe; incur (*or* contract) a debt, run up a bill, (*or* an account); borrow, run into debt, be in difficulties.

answer for, go bail for; back one's note.

Adj. **liable,** chargeable, answerable for.

indebted, in debt, in embarrassed circumstances, in difficulties; encumbered, involved; insolvent.

unpaid; unrequited, unrewarded; owing, due, in arrear, outstanding.

807. PAYMENT.—*N.* **payment,** discharge, settlement, clearance, liquidation, satisfaction, reckoning, arrangement.

acknowledgment, release; receipt, voucher.

repayment, reimbursement, retribution; pay, money paid.

V. **pay,** defray, make payment; pay one's way, expend, put down, lay down; discharge, settle, foot the bill [*colloq.*]; settle with, satisfy, pay in full, clear, liquidate, pay up; cash, honor a bill, acknowledge; redeem.

repay, refund, reimburse, disgorge, make repayment.

Adj. out of debt, owing nothing, all clear, clear of debt, above-water; solvent.

Adv. money down, cash down, cash on delivery, C.O.D.

808. NONPAYMENT.—*N.* nonpayment; default, defalcation; protest, repudiation.

insolvency, bankruptcy, failure; run upon a bank; overdrawn account.

defaulter, bankrupt, insolvent, insolvent debtor; absconder, welsher [*slang*].

V. **not pay**, fail, break, stop payment; become insolvent (*or* bankrupt), swindle, run up bills.

protest, dishonor, repudiate, nullify.

Adj. in debt, behindhand, in arrear; beggared, insolvent, bankrupt, ruined.

809. EXPENDITURE.—*N.* **expenditure**, outgoings, outlay, expenses, disbursement; circulation.

Money paid: payment, etc., 807; pay, etc. (*remuneration*), 973; fee, footing, subsidy, tribute, ransom, bribe, donation, gift; investment; purchase.

deposit, earnest, installment.

V. **expend**, spend; run (*or* get) through, pay, disburse; lay out, fork out [*slang*]; invest, sink money.

reward, fee, remunerate; give, subscribe, subsidize; bribe.

Adj. **lavish**, free, liberal; beyond one's income.

expensive, costly, dear, high-priced, precious, high.

810. RECEIPT.—*N.* **receipt**, value received, income, revenue, return, proceeds; earnings.

rent, rent roll; rental.

premium, bonus, prize, drawings, handout [*slang*].

pension, annuity, pittance, jointure, alimony.

V. **receive**, get, be in receipt of, have coming in; take money; draw from, derive from; acquire, take.

yield, bring in, afford, pay, return; accrue.

Adj. **remunerative**, profitable, gainful, well paying, interest-bearing, well invested.

Adv. within one's income.

811. ACCOUNTS.—*N.* **accounts**, money matters, finance, budget, bill, score, reckoning, account.

bookkeeping, audit, single entry, double entry; ledger, cash-book, journal; balance sheet; receipts, assets; expenditure, liabilities; profit and loss account (*or* statement).

accountant, auditor, actuary, bookkeeper; expert accountant, certified accountant; bank examiner.

V. **keep accounts,** enter, post, post up, book, credit, debit, balance.

812. PRICE.—*N.* **price,** amount, cost, expense, charge, figure, demand, fare, hire; wages.

dues, duty, toll, tax, impost, tariff, levy; capitation, poll tax; custom, excise, assessment, taxation, tithe, ransom, salvage, towage; brokerage, wharfage, freightage.

worth, rate, value, par value, valuation, appraisement, money's worth; price current, market price, quotation.

V. **price,** set (*or* fix) a price, appraise, assess, charge, demand, ask, require, exact.

fetch, sell for, cost, bring in, yield, afford.

Adj. **taxable,** dutiable, assessable.

813. DISCOUNT.—*N.* **discount,** abatement, concession, reduction, depreciation, allowance, qualification, setoff, drawback, percentage, rebate.

V. **discount,** bate, rebate, abate, deduct, strike off, mark down, reduce, take off, allow, give, make allowance; depreciate.

Adv. **at a discount,** at a bargain, below par.

814. DEARNESS.—*N.* **dearness,** expensiveness, costliness, high price; overcharge, extravagance, exorbitance, extortion.

V. **overcharge,** bleed [*colloq.*], skin [*slang*], fleece, extort, profiteer.

pay too much, pay dearly, pay through the nose [*colloq.*].

Adj. **dear,** high, high-priced, expensive, costly, precious; extravagant, exorbitant, extortionate.

at a premium, beyond price, above price; priceless, of priceless value.

Adv. **dear,** dearly; at great cost, at heavy cost, at a high price.

815. CHEAPNESS.—*N.* **cheapness,** low price, depreciation, bargain, drug in the market.

V. **be cheap,** cost little; come down (*or* fall) in price, be marked down.

buy at a bargain, buy dirt-cheap, have one's money's worth; beat down, cheapen.

Adj. **cheap,** low-priced, low, moderate, reasonable, inexpensive, cheap at the price; dirt-cheap, catchpenny.

reduced, half-price, depreciated, shopworn, marked down, unsalable.

gratuitous, gratis, free, for nothing; costless, without charge, scot-free, complimentary, honorary.

Adv. **at a bargain,** for a mere song; at cost price, at prime cost.

816. LIBERALITY.—*N.* **liberality,** generosity, munificence;

bounty, bounteousness, hospitality, charity, open (*or* free) hand, open (*or* large) heart.

cheerful giver, free giver, patron; benefactor.

V. **be liberal,** spend freely; shower down upon, spare no expense, give with both hands; keep open house.

Adj. **liberal,** free, generous, charitable, hospitable; bountiful, bounteous, ample, handsome; unsparing, ungrudging; unselfish; open-handed, large-hearted; munificent, princely.

Adv. ungrudgingly; with open hands, with both hands.

817. ECONOMY.—*N.* **economy,** frugality; thrift, thriftiness; care, husbandry, retrenchment.

savings; prevention of waste, save-all; parsimony, etc., 819.

V. **economize,** save; retrench, cut down expenses; make both ends meet, meet one's expenses, pay one's way; husband, save (*or* invest) money; provide against a rainy day.

Adj. **economical,** frugal, careful, thrifty, saving, chary, spare, sparing; parsimonious, etc., 819; sufficient; plain.

818. PRODIGALITY.—*N.* **prodigality,** wastefulness, unthriftiness, waste; profusion, profuseness; extravagance, lavishness.

prodigal, spendthrift, waster, high roller [*slang*], squanderer, spender, prodigal son.

V. **squander,** lavish, sow broadcast, pay through the nose, spill, waste, dissipate, exhaust, drain, overdraw, spend money like water.

Adj. **prodigal,** profuse, thriftless, unthrifty, improvident, wasteful, extravagant, lavish, dissipated; penny-wise and pound-foolish.

Adv. with an unsparing hand.

819. PARSIMONY.—*N.* **parsimony,** parsimoniousness, stinginess, stint, illiberality, avarice, avidity, rapacity, extortion, venality, cupidity, selfishness.

miser, niggard, churl, screw, skinflint, curmudgeon, harpy, extortioner, extortionist, usurer.

V. **grudge,** begrudge, stint, pinch, gripe, screw, dole out, hold back, withhold, starve, famish.

drive a bargain, cheapen, beat down; have an itching palm, grasp, grab.

Adj. **parsimonious,** penurious, stingy, miserly, mean, shabby, near, niggardly, close, sparing, grudging, illiberal, ungenerous, churlish, sordid, mercenary, venal, covetous, avaricious; greedy, grasping, extortionate, rapacious.

Adv. with a sparing hand.

CLASS VI

WORDS RELATING TO THE SENTIENT AND MORAL POWERS

I. AFFECTIONS IN GENERAL

820. AFFECTIONS.—*N.* **character,** qualities, disposition, affections, nature, spirit, temper, temperament, idiosyncrasy, predilection, turn of mind, bent, bias, predisposition, proneness, proclivity, propensity, vein, humor, mood, sympathy.

soul, heart, bosom, inner man; inmost recesses of the heart.

passion, pervading spirit; ruling passion, fullness of the heart.

energy, fervor, fire, verve, force.

Adj. **characterized,** affected, formed, molded, cast, tempered; framed.

prone, predisposed, disposed, inclined; having a bias.

inborn, inbred, ingrained; deep-rooted, congenital, inherent.

Adv. at heart; in the vein, in the mood.

821. FEELING.—*N.* **feeling,** suffering, endurance, sufferance, response; sympathy, impression, inspiration, affection, sensation, emotion, pathos.

fervor, unction, gusto, vehemence, heartiness, cordiality, earnestness, eagerness, gush [*colloq.*], ardor, warmth, zeal, passion, enthusiasm, ecstasy.

excitement; thrill, shock, agitation, quiver, flutter, flurry, fluster, twitter, tremor, throb, throbbing, pulsation, palpitation, panting; blush, flush.

V. **feel,** receive an impression, be impressed with, respond, enter into the spirit of.

bear, suffer, support, sustain, endure, brook, brave, stand, abide, experience, taste, prove.

be agitated, be excited, glow, flush, blush, crimson, change color, mantle; darken, whiten, pale, tingle, thrill, heave, pant, throb, palpitate, tremble, quiver, flutter, shake, stagger, reel; wince.

Adj. **sentient,** sensuous, emotional; of (*or* with) feeling.

keen, sharp, lively, quick, acute, cutting, piercing, incisive, trenchant, pungent, racy, piquant, poignant, caustic.

impressive, deep, profound, indelible, deep-felt, heartfelt, soul-stirring, electric, thrilling, rapturous, ecstatic, rapt; pervading, penetrating, absorbing.

earnest, wistful, eager, fervent, fervid, gushing [*colloq.*], warm, passionate, hearty, cordial, sincere, zealous, enthusiastic, glowing, ardent.

rabid, raving, feverish, fanatical, hysterical, impetuous.

Adv. **heartily,** heart and soul, from the bottom of one's heart, devoutly.

822. SENSITIVENESS.—*N.* **sensitiveness,** sensibleness, sensibility, impressibility, susceptibility, vivacity, tenderness, sentimentality, sentimentalism.

excitability, etc., 825; physical sensibility, etc., 375.

V. **be sensitive,** have a tender heart; take to heart, shrink, wince, blench, quiver.

Adj. **sensitive,** sensible, impressible, impressionable; susceptive, susceptible; warmhearted, tenderhearted, softhearted, tender; sentimental, romantic; enthusiastic, impassioned, spirited, mettlesome, vivacious, lively, expressive, mobile, excitable, oversensitive, thin-skinned, fastidious.

Adv. to the quick, on the raw.

823. INSENSITIVENESS.—*N.* **insensitiveness,** insensibility, insensibleness, inertness, inertia, impassibility, impassivity, apathy, dullness, insusceptibility, lukewarmness.

coldness, coolness, frigidity, stoicism, nonchalance, unconcern, indifference, callousness, heart of stone.

torpor, torpidity, lethargy, coma, trance; sleep, stupor, stupefaction; paralysis, numbness.

stoic, Indian, man of iron.

V. **be insensitive,** not mind, not care, not be affected by; take no interest in; disregard.

blunt, numb, benumb, paralyze, deaden, stun, stupefy; brutalize. **inure;** harden, steel, caseharden, sear.

Adj. **insensitive,** insensible, unconscious, impassive, insusceptible, unimpressible; passionless, spiritless, heartless, soulless, unfeeling.

apathetic, unemotional, phlegmatic; dull, frigid, cold, cold-blooded, coldhearted; inert, supine, sluggish, torpid, sleepy, languid, halfhearted; numb, numbed; comatose.

indifferent, lukewarm, careless, mindless, inattentive, unconcerned, nonchalant.

unaffected, unruffled, unimpressed, unexcited, unmoved, unstirred, untouched, unshocked, unblushing.

callous, thick-skinned, impervious, hard, hardened, inured, casehardened; imperturbable, unfelt.

Adv. in cold blood; with dry eyes.

824. EXCITEMENT.—*N.* **excitement,** excitation, stimulation, piquancy, provocation, inspiration, animation, agitation, perturbation; fascination, intoxication, impressiveness; irritation, passion, thrill.

emotional appeal, melodrama, sensationalism, yellow journalism.

V. **excite,** affect, touch, move, impress, strike, interest, animate, inspire, smite, infect, awake, wake; awaken, waken; call forth; evoke, provoke; raise up, summon up, call up, wake up, raise; rouse, arouse, stir, fire, kindle, enkindle, illumine, illuminate, inflame.

stimulate, inspirit; stir up, infuse life into, give new life to; introduce new blood, quicken; sharpen, whet, fillip; fan, foster, heat, warm, foment, revive, rekindle.

penetrate, pierce; go to one's heart, touch to the quick, possess the soul, rivet the attention; prey on the mind.

agitate, perturb, ruffle, fluster, flutter, flurry, shake, disturb, startle, shock, stagger, strike dumb, stun, astound, electrify, galvanize, petrify.

irritate, sting, cut, pique, infuriate, madden, lash into fury.

flare up, flash up, seethe, boil, simmer, foam, fume, flame, rage, rave.

Adj. **excited,** wrought up, overwrought, hot, red-hot, flushed, feverish; raging, flaming, ebullient, seething, foaming, fuming, stung to the quick; wild, raving, frantic, mad, distracted, beside oneself.

exciting, impressive, telling, warm, glowing, fervid, spirit-stirring, thrilling; soul-stirring, heart-stirring, agonizing, sensational, yellow [*colloq.*], melodramatic, hysterical; overpowering, overwhelming.

piquant, spicy, appetizing, stinging, provocative, tantalizing.

Adv. at a critical moment, under a sudden strain.

825. [**Excess of sensitiveness**] **EXCITABILITY.**—*N.* **excitability,** impetuosity, vehemence, boisterousness, turbulence; impatience, intolerance, irritability; disquiet, disquietude, restlessness, fidgets, agitation.

trepidation, perturbation, ruffle, hurry, fuss, flurry, fluster, flutter; ferment; whirl; stage fright, thrill.

passion, excitement, flush, heat, fever, fire, flame, fume, tumult, effervescence, ebullition; gust, storm, tempest; burst, fit, paroxysm, explosion, outbreak, scene, outburst; agony.

fury; violence, fierceness, rage, furor, desperation, madness, distraction, raving, delirium; frenzy, hysterics; intoxication; towering rage, anger, etc., 900.

fixed idea, monomania; fascination, infatuation; fanaticism; quixotism, quixotry.

V. fidget, fuss.

fume, rage, foam; bear ill, wince, chafe, champ the bit, lose one's temper, break out, burst out, fly out, explode, flare up, flame up, fire up, boil, rave, rant, tear, go into hysterics; run riot, run amuck; raise Cain [*slang*].

Adj. **excitable,** easily excited, mettlesome, high-mettled, skittish, high-strung, nervous, irritable, hasty, impatient, intolerant, moody; feverish, hysterical, delirious, mad.

restless, unquiet, mercurial, galvanic, fidgety, fussy.

vehement, demonstrative, violent, wild, furious, fierce, fiery, hotheaded; overzealous, enthusiastic, impassioned, fanatical; rabid, rampant, clamorous, uproarious, turbulent, tempestuous, boisterous.

impulsive, impetuous, passionate, uncontrolled, uncontrollable, ungovernable, irrepressible, volcanic.

Adv. in confusion, pellmell.

826. INEXCITABILITY.—*N.* **inexcitability,** imperturbability, even temper, tranquil mind, dispassion; toleration, tolerance, patience; passiveness, inertia, etc., 172; impassibility, etc. (*insensibility*), 823; stupefaction.

calmness, composure, placidity, *sang-froid* [F.], coolness, tranquillity, serenity, content; quiet, quietude; peace of mind.

equanimity, poise, staidness, gravity, sobriety, philosophy, stoicism, self-possession, self-control, self-command, self-restraint; presence of mind.

resignation, submission, sufferance, endurance, long-sufferance, forbearance, longanimity, fortitude, patience of Job, moderation, restraint.

V. **endure,** bear, go through, support, brave, disregard; tolerate, suffer, stand, bide; abide, bear with, put up with, acquiesce, submit, resign oneself to, brook, digest, eat, swallow, pocket, stomach; carry on, carry through; make light of, make the best of, put a good face on.

compose, appease, assuage, propitiate, repress, restrain, master one's feelings, set one's mind at ease (*or* rest), calm down, cool down.

Adj. **inexcitable,** imperturbable; unsusceptible, dispassionate, cold-blooded, enduring, stoical, philosophical, staid, sober, grave; sedate, demure, coolheaded, levelheaded.

easygoing, peaceful, placid, calm; quiet, tranquil, serene, cool, undemonstrative.

composed, collected, temperate, unstirred, unruffled, unperturbed.

meek, mild, tame, subdued, unoffended, unresisting, submissive, gentle, patient, tolerant, clement, long-suffering.

Adv. in cold blood; more in sorrow than in anger.

II. PERSONAL AFFECTIONS[1]

827. PLEASURE.—*N.* **pleasure,** gratification, enjoyment, delectation, relish, zest, gusto, satisfaction, complacency; well-being; good, etc., 618; comfort, ease, luxury; physical pleasure, etc., 377.

joy, gladness, delight, glee, cheer, sunshine; cheerfulness, etc., 836; treat, luxury; amusement, etc., 840.

happiness, felicity, bliss, beatitude, enchantment, transport, rapture, ecstasy; paradise, heaven.

V. **enjoy oneself,** joy, be in clover [*colloq.*], tread on enchanted ground; go into raptures; feel at home, breathe freely, bask in the sunshine.

enjoy, like, relish, be pleased with, derive pleasure from, take pleasure in, delight in, rejoice in, indulge in, gloat over, love; take to, take a fancy to [*both colloq.*].

Adj. **pleased,** gratified, glad, gladsome; comfortable, etc. (*physical pleasure*), 377; at ease; content, etc., 831.

happy, blessed, blissful, beatified, joyful, in raptures, in ecstasies.

overjoyed, entranced, enchanted; raptured, enraptured, ravished, transported; fascinated, captivated.

pleasing, delightful, ecstatic, beatific, painless, unalloyed, cloudless.

828. PAIN.—*N.* **pain,** mental suffering, dolor, suffering, ache; physical pain, etc., 378.

displeasure, dissatisfaction, discomfort, discomposure, disquiet; inquietude, uneasiness, discontent.

annoyance, irritation, worry; infliction, visitation; plague, bore; bother, vexation, mortification, chagrin.

care, anxiety, solicitude, concern, trouble, trial, ordeal, shock, blow, fret, burden, load.

grief, sorrow, distress, affliction, woe, bitterness, heartache, heavy (*or* aching, bleeding, broken) heart.

misery, unhappiness, infelicity, tribulation, wretchedness, desolation; despair, etc., 859; extremity, prostration, depth of misery, slough of despond; nightmare, incubus.

anguish, pang, agony, torture, torment; crucifixion, martyrdom, rack, hell upon earth; reign of terror.

sufferer, victim, prey, martyr, wretch, shorn lamb.

V. **suffer,** ail, feel (*or* suffer, undergo, bear, endure) pain, smart, ache, bleed, bear the cross; fall on evil days, come to grief.

fret, chafe, sit on thorns, wince, worry oneself, fret and fume; take to heart.

[1]Or those which concern one's own state of feeling.

grieve, mourn, lament, etc., 839; yearn, repine, pine, droop, languish, sink, despair, break one's heart.

Adj. pained, afflicted, suffering, worried, displeased, aching, griped, sore, raw, on the rack.

uneasy, uncomfortable, ill at ease; disturbed; discontented; weary, etc., 841.

unfortunate, etc., 735; doomed, devoted, accursed, undone, crushed, lost, stranded; victimized, ill-used.

unhappy, infelicitous, poor, wretched, miserable, woebegone, comfortless, cheerless, etc. (*dejected*), 837; careworn; heavy-laden, stricken.

sorry, concerned, sorrowful, cut up [*colloq.*], chagrined, horrified, horror-stricken; heartbroken, brokenhearted.

829. [Capability of giving pleasure] PLEASURABLENESS.— *N.* pleasurableness, pleasantness, agreeableness, pleasure giving, amusement, etc., 840; treat, etc. (*physical pleasure*), 377; dainty titbit, sweets, sweetmeats, nuts, salt, savor.

attraction, attractiveness, charm, fascination, captivation, enchantment, witchery, seduction, winning ways, winsomeness; loveliness, beauty, etc., 845.

V. delight, charm, gladden, bless, captivate, fascinate; enchant, entrance, enrapture, transport, bewitch, ravish.

please, satisfy, gratify, satiate, quench, indulge, humor, flatter, tickle; tickle the palate, refresh, enliven, treat, amuse, take one's fancy; attract, allure; stimulate, excite, interest.

Adj. pleasurable, pleasure-giving, pleasing, pleasant, amiable, agreeable, grateful, gratifying; acceptable; dear, beloved, welcome, favorite.

refreshing, comfortable, cordial, genial, glad, gladsome; sweet, delectable, nice, dainty, delicate, delicious.

attractive, inviting, prepossessing, engaging; winning, winsome, magnetic, fascinating, seductive; alluring, enticing, appetizing, cheering, bewitching, enchanting, entrancing.

delightful, charming, felicitous, exquisite, lovely, ravishing, rapturous; heartfelt, thrilling, ecstatic, heavenly.

Adv. to one's delight, in utter satisfaction; at one's ease; in clover [*colloq.*].

830. [Capability of giving pain] PAINFULNESS.—*N.* painfulness, trouble, care, trial, affliction, infliction, misfortune, mishap; cross, blow, stroke, burden, load, curse.

annoyance, pique, grievance, nuisance, vexation, mortification, worry, bore, bother, hornet's nest, plague, pest, wound; sore subject, skeleton in the closet; thorn in the flesh.

V. pain, hurt, wound, cause (*or* occasion, give, inflict) pain;

pierce, prick, cut, etc. (*physical pain*), 378; pierce (*or* break, rend) the heart; make the heart bleed.

sadden, make unhappy, grieve, afflict, distress; cut up [*colloq.*], cut to the heart.

annoy, incommode, displease, discompose, trouble, disturb, cross, thwart, perplex, molest; tease, tire, irk, fret, vex, mortify, worry, plague, bother, pester, bore, harass, harry, badger, heckle [*Brit.*], bait, beset, infest, persecute.

torment, wring, harrow, torture, rack, crucify, convulse, agonize.

irritate, provoke, sting, nettle, pique, fret, roil, rile [*colloq. & dial.*], chafe, gall; aggrieve, affront, enrage, ruffle, give offense.

maltreat, bite, snap at, assail, smite, etc., 972.

repel, revolt, sicken, disgust, nauseate, disenchant, offend, shock, rankle, gnaw, corrode, horrify, appall.

Adj. **painful,** hurtful, dolorous; distressing, cheerless, dismal, disheartening, depressing, dreary, melancholy, grievous, piteous, woeful, mournful, deplorable, pitiable, lamentable, sad; affecting, touching, pathetic.

unpleasant, unpleasing, displeasing, disagreeable, unpalatable, bitter, distasteful, uninviting, unwelcome, undesirable, obnoxious; unacceptable.

inauspicious, unlucky, ill-starred, unsatisfactory; untoward.

irritating, provoking, annoying, aggravating [*colloq.*], exasperating, galling, vexatious; troublesome, tiresome, irksome, wearisome.

importunate, pestering, bothering, harassing, worrying, tormenting.

insufferable, intolerable, insupportable, unbearable, unendurable.

shocking, terrific, grim, appalling, crushing; dreadful, fearful, frightful, tremendous, dire, heartbreaking, heart-rending, harrowing, rending.

odious, hateful, execrable, repulsive, repellent, horrid, horrible; offensive; nauseous, disgusting, revolting, nasty, loathsome, vile, hideous.

acute, sharp, sore, severe, grave, hard, harsh, cruel, biting, caustic; cutting, corroding, consuming, excruciating, agonizing.

cumbrous, cumbersome, burdensome, onerous, oppressive.

desolating, withering, tragical, disastrous, calamitous, ruinous.

Adv. in agony, out of the depths.

831. CONTENT.—*N.* **content,** contentment, contentedness; complacency, satisfaction, ease, peace of mind, serenity, cheerfulness; comfort.

patience, moderation, endurance; conciliation, reconciliation; resignation.

V. be content, rest satisfied, let well enough alone; take in good part; be reconciled to, take heart, take comfort.

content, set at ease, comfort; conciliate, reconcile, win over, propitiate, disarm, beguile; content, satisfy; gratify, etc., 836.

Adj. content, contented, satisfied, at ease, at one's ease, easy-going, not particular; conciliatory, unrepining, resigned, cheerful, serene, at rest; snug, comfortable.

satisfactory, adequate, sufficient, ample, equal to; satisfying.

Adv. to one's heart's content.

832. DISCONTENT.—*N.* discontent, dissatisfaction; disappointment, mortification; cold comfort; regret, repining, inquietude, vexation of spirit, soreness; heartburning.

malcontent, grumbler, growler, grouch [*slang*], croaker, fault-finder.

the opposition; bitter-enders [*politics*, U. S.], die-hards.

V. be discontented, repine, regret, take to heart, make a wry face, look blue, look black, look glum.

grumble, take ill, take in bad part; fret, chafe, croak; lament.

dissatisfy, disappoint, mortify, put out [*colloq.*], disconcert, dishearten.

Adj. discontented, dissatisfied, unsatisfied, regretful, dejected, etc., 837; dissentient, malcontent, exacting.

glum, sulky, in high dudgeon, in a fume, in the sulks (*or* dumps), in bad humor; sour, soured, sore; out of humor, out of temper.

833. REGRET.—*N.* regret, repining; homesickness, nostalgia; bitterness, heartburning; lamentation, penitence, etc., 950.

V. regret, deplore, bewail, lament, etc., 839; repine, rue, rue the day; repent, etc., 950; leave an aching void.

Adj. regretful, rueful; homesick.

834. RELIEF.—*N.* relief, deliverance, alleviation, mitigation, palliation, solace, consolation, comfort, unction; encouragement.

V. relieve, ease, alleviate, mitigate, palliate, soothe; salve; soften, assuage, allay; remedy, cure, restore, refresh.

cheer, comfort, console; enliven; encourage, give comfort, inspirit, invigorate.

Adj. soothing, assuaging, balmy, lenitive, palliative, curative.

835. AGGRAVATION.—*N.* aggravation, heightening, intensification, overestimation, exaggeration.

V. aggravate, render worse, heighten, embitter, sour, intensify, enhance [*Note*: aggravate *in the sense of* provoke *is colloquial*].

Adj. aggravated, worse, unrelieved, aggravative.

Adv. from bad to worse, worse and worse.

836. CHEERFULNESS.—*N.* cheerfulness, geniality, gayety, cheer, good humor, spirits; high spirits, animal spirits, glee, high glee, light heart.

liveliness, life, alacrity, vivacity, animation, joviality, jollity, levity, jocularity.

mirth, merriment, hilarity, exhilaration, laughter, merrymaking, rejoicing, etc., 838.

optimism, hopefulness, etc., 858.

V. be cheerful, have the mind at ease, smile, keep up one's spirits, cheer up, take heart, cast away care, perk up; rejoice, etc., 838; carol, chirp, chirrup, lilt.

cheer, enliven, elate, exhilarate, gladden, delight, inspirit, animate, inspire.

Adj. cheerful; happy, etc., 827; cheery, sunny, smiling; blithe, in good spirits, chipper [*colloq.*], gay, debonair, light, lightsome, lighthearted; buoyant, bright, airy, jaunty, sprightly, spirited, lively, animated, vivacious, sparkling, sportive.

merry, joyful, joyous, jocund, jovial; jolly, blithesome, gleeful, hilarious.

winsome, bonny, hearty, buxom.

playful, tricksy, frisky, frolicsome, jocose, jocular, waggish, mirthful, rollicking.

elate, elated; exulting, jubilant, flushed, rejoicing.

cheering, inspiriting, exhilarating, pleasing, palmy, flourishing.

Adv. cheerfully, cheerily, with relish, with zest.

837. DEJECTION.—*N.* dejection, depression, mopishness, low (*or* depressed) spirits; heaviness, gloom; weariness, disgust of life; prostration, broken heart; despair, hopelessness.

melancholy, sadness, melancholia, blue devils [*colloq.*], blues [*colloq.*], dumps [*chiefly humorous*], doldrums, horrors, hypochondria, pessimism; despondency, slough of despond; disconsolateness, hope deferred.

gravity; demureness, solemnity; long face, grave face.

hypochondriac, self-tormentor, croaker, pessimist, damper, wet blanket.

V. be dejected, grieve, mourn, lament, give way, lose heart, despond, droop, sink, despair.

lower, frown, pout; look blue, lay to heart, take to heart.

mope, brood over, fret, sulk, pine, pine away; yearn, repine.

depress, discourage, dishearten, dispirit, damp, dull, deject, sink, dash, unman, prostrate, break one's heart; sadden, dash one's hopes, prey on the mind, damp the spirits.

Adj. cheerless, joyless, spiritless; unhappy, etc., 828; melancholy, dismal, dreary, depressing, somber, dark, gloomy, lowering, frowning, funereal, mournful, lamentable, dreadful.

downcast, downhearted, down in the mouth [*colloq.*], down on one's luck [*colloq.*], heavyhearted; sullen, mopish, moody, glum; sulky, etc. (*discontented*), 832; out of heart (*or* spirits); lowspirited; weary, etc., 841; discouraged, disheartened, despondent, crestfallen.

sad, pensive, doleful, woebegone, melancholic, bilious, jaundiced, saturnine, lackadaisical.

serious, sedate, staid, earnest, grave, sober, solemn, demure, grim, grim-faced, rueful, wan, long-faced.

disconsolate, forlorn, comfortless, desolate, sick at heart, heartsick.

overcome, broken-down, prostrate, cut up [*colloq.*], unnerved, unmanned; downfallen, downtrodden; brokenhearted; careworn.

Adv. with a long face, with tears in one's eyes.

838. [Expression of pleasure] REJOICING.—*N.* rejoicing, exultation, triumph, jubilation, heyday, flush, reveling, merrymaking, pæan, *Te Deum* [L.]; congratulation.

smile, simper, smirk, grin; broad grin, sardonic grin.

laughter, giggle, titter, snicker, snigger, crow, cheer, chuckle, shout; guffaw, burst (*or* fit, shout, roar, peal) of laughter.

cheer, huzza, hurrah, cheering; shout, yell [U. S. and Can.], college yell; tiger [*colloq.*].

V. rejoice, congratulate oneself, hug oneself, clap one's hands; skip; sing, carol, chirrup, chirp, hurrah, cry for joy, leap with joy; exult, triumph; make merry.

smile, simper, smirk, grin, laugh in one's sleeve.

laugh, giggle, titter, snigger, snicker, chuckle, cackle; burst out, shout, roar, shake (*or* split) one's sides.

Adj. rejoicing, jubilant, exultant, triumphant, flushed, elated; laughing, convulsed with laughter.

laughable, ludicrous, etc. 853.

Adv. in fits of laughter; in triumph.

839. [Expression of pain] LAMENTATION.—*N.* lamentation, lament, wail, complaint, plaint, murmur, mutter, grumble, groan, moan, whine, whimper, sob, sigh; frown, scowl.

cry, scream, howl; outcry, wail of woe.

weeping, flood of tears, fit of crying, crying; melting mood.

plaintiveness; languishment; condolence, etc., 915.

mourning, weeds [*colloq.*], widow's weeds, crape, deep mourning; sackcloth and ashes; death song, dirge, requiem, elegy, threnody, jeremiad, keen [Ir.].

mourner, keener [Ir.]; Niobe.

V. lament, mourn, deplore, grieve, keen [Ir.], weep over; bewail, bemoan, condole with, etc., 915; fret.

sigh, give (*or* heave) a sigh; wail.

cry, weep, sob, blubber, snivel, whimper, shed tears, burst into tears.

scream, groan, moan, whine, yelp, howl, yell, roar; rend the air.

complain, murmur, mutter, grumble, growl, clamor, croak, grunt.

Adj. lamenting, in mourning, in sackcloth and ashes, clamorous, sorrowing, sorrowful, mournful, lamentable, tearful, lachrymose, plaintive, querulous; in tears.

840. AMUSEMENT.—*N.* amusement, entertainment, diversion, recreation, relaxation, solace; pastime, sport; labor of love; pleasure, etc., 827.

fun, frolic, merriment, jollity, joviality, laughter, etc., 838; pleasantry, quip, jocoseness; drollery, buffoonery, tomfoolery; mummery, pageant.

play, game, gambol, romp, prank, antic, lark [*colloq.*], spree, skylarking, vagary, monkey trick, escapade, practical joke.

dance, hop [*colloq.*]; ball, masquerade, ballet; step dance, skirt dance, folk dance, morris dance; gavot, minuet, Highland fling, reel, jig, hornpipe, sword dance, cakewalk; country dance, Scotch reel, Virginia reel, quadrille, lancers, cotillion; waltz, polka, mazurka, schottische, one-step, fox-trot.

festivity, fete, festival, merrymaking; party, etc. (*social gathering*), 892; revels, revelry, reveling, carnival, saturnalia, jollification [*colloq.*], junket, picnic.

holiday, red-letter day, play day; high days and holidays; high holiday.

place of amusement, theater; concert hall, ballroom, dance hall, assembly room; moving-picture theater; movies [*colloq.*]; music hall; vaudeville theater; circus, hippodrome.

Sports and games: athletic sports, track events, gymnastics; tournament.
skating, tobogganing; cricket, tennis, lawn tennis, rackets, squash, fives; croquet, golf, curling, hockey, polo, football, Rugby, rugger [*colloq.*]; association, soccer [*colloq.*]; quoits, discus, putting the weight (*or* shot), tug of war; baseball, basketball, pushball, lacrosse.
billiards, pool, pyramids, bagatelle; bowls, skittles, ninepins, tenpins; chess, draughts, checkers, dominoes, dice; card games, etc.

toy, plaything, doll, bauble.

sportsman (*fem.* sportswoman), hunter, Nimrod.

gamester, sport, gambler; dicer, punter, plunger.

devotee, enthusiast, follower, fan [*slang*], rooter [*slang or cant*].

V. amuse, entertain, divert, enliven, raise a smile, excite (*or* convulse with) laughter; cheer, rejoice, solace, please, interest.

amuse oneself, sport, disport, revel, junket, feast, carouse.

banquet, make merry; frolic, gambol, frisk, romp, caper, dance.

Adj. amusing, entertaining, diverting, recreative, pleasant, laughable, etc. (*ludicrous*), 853; witty, etc., 842; festive, festal, jovial, jolly, roguish, arch, playful, sportive.

Adv. at play, in sport.

841. WEARINESS.—*N.* **weariness,** ennui, boredom, lassitude, fatigue, etc., 688; drowsiness, languor.

disgust, nausea, loathing, sickness; satiety, repletion.

tedium, wearisomeness, tediousness, monotony.

bore, buttonholer, proser, dry-as-dust, fossil [*colloq.*], wet blanket.

V. **weary,** tire, fatigue, bore, send to sleep; buttonhole.

pall, sicken, nauseate, disgust; harp on the same string.

Adj. **wearying,** wearing, wearisome, tiresome, irksome, uninteresting, stupid, monotonous, dull, dry, arid, tedious, humdrum, flat; prosy, prosing; slow, soporific, somniferous.

weary, tired, drowsy, sleepy, etc., 683; uninterested, flagging, used up, worn out, blasé [F.].

842. WIT.—*N.* **wit,** wittiness, Attic salt, Atticism; point, fancy, whim, humor, drollery, pleasantry.

buffoonery, fooling, farce, tomfoolery, broad farce, fun.

jocularity, jocoseness, facetiousness, waggishness, comicality.

smartness, ready wit, banter, persiflage, retort, repartee.

witticism, smart saying, sally, flash, scintillation, flash of wit; jest, joke, epigram, conceit.

wordplay, play upon words, pun, riddle, conundrum, quibble.

V. **joke,** jest, cut jokes; crack a joke, pun; make merry with.

retort, flash back, flash, scintillate; banter, etc. (*ridicule*), 856.

Adj. **witty,** clever, keen, keen-witted, brilliant, pungent, quick-witted, smart, jocular, jocose, funny, waggish, facetious, comic, whimsical, humorous, sprightly, sparkling, epigrammatic.

843. DULLNESS.—*N.* **dullness,** heaviness, flatness, stupidity, want of originality, dearth of ideas; matter of fact, commonplace, platitude.

V. **be dull,** hang fire, fall flat, platitudinize, prose.

depress, damp, throw cold water on, lay a wet blanket on.

Adj. **dull,** jejune, dry, uninteresting, heavy-footed, elephantine; insipid, tasteless, unimaginative; prosy, prosaic, matter-of-fact, commonplace, platitudinous, pointless.

stupid, slow, flat, humdrum, monotonous, stolid.

844. HUMORIST.—*N.* **humorist,** wag, wit, epigrammatist, punster; life of the party; joker, jester, buffoon, comedian, merry-andrew, mime, tumbler, acrobat, mountebank, harlequin, pantaloon, punch, punchinello, clown; motley fool; caricaturist.

845. BEAUTY.—*N.* beauty, form, elegance, grace, symmetry, bloom, delicacy, refinement, charm, style; comeliness, fairness, polish, gloss; good effect, good looks.

brilliancy, radiance, splendor, gorgeousness, magnificence; sublimity.

beau ideal, Venus, Aphrodite, Hebe, the Graces, peri, houri, Cupid, Apollo, Hyperion, Adonis; Helen of Troy, Cleopatra; Venus de Milo. Apollo Belvedere.

loveliness, pleasurableness, etc., 829.

beautifying, decoration, ornamentation, etc., 847.

V. **beautify,** set off, grace; decorate, etc., 847.

Adj. **beautiful,** beauteous, handsome; pretty; lovely, graceful, elegant, exquisite, delicate, dainty.

comely, fair, goodly, bonny, good-looking, well favored, well formed, well proportioned, shapely, symmetrical, harmonious.

bright, bright-eyed; rosy-cheeked, rosy, ruddy, blooming, in full bloom.

trim, trig, tidy, neat, spruce, smart, jaunty, dapper.

brilliant, shining, sparkling, radiant, splendid, resplendent, dazzling, glowing, glossy, sleek; rich, gorgeous, superb, magnificent, grand, fine.

artistic, aesthetic, picturesque, pictorial, enchanting, attractive, becoming, ornamental.

perfect, unspotted, spotless, immaculate; undeformed, undefaced.

passable, presentable, tolerable, not amiss.

846. UGLINESS.—*N.* ugliness, deformity, inelegance, disfigurement, blemish, want of symmetry, distortion; squalor.

eyesore, object, figure, sight [*colloq.*], fright, scarecrow, hag, harridan, satyr, witch, monster.

V. **deface,** disfigure, deform, distort, blemish, injure, spoil; soil.

Adj. **ugly,** inartistic, unsightly, unseemly, uncomely, unshapely, unlovely; unbeautiful; coarse, plain, homely.

misshapen, misproportioned, shapeless, monstrous, gross; ill-made, ill-shaped, ill-proportioned, crooked, distorted.

unprepossessing, hard-featured, ill-favored, ill-looking; squalid, haggard; grim, grisly, ghastly, cadaverous, gruesome.

uncouth, ungainly, graceless, inelegant, ungraceful, stiff, rough, gross, rude, awkward, clumsy, gawky, lumbering, unwieldy.

repellent, forbidding, frightful, hideous, odious, repulsive; horrid, horrible, shocking.

disfigured, tarnished, smeared, besmeared, discolored, spotted, spotty.

showy, specious, pretentious, garish.

847. ORNAMENT.—*N.* **ornament,** ornamentation, ornateness, adornment, decoration, embellishment.

embroidery, needlework; lace, trimming, drapery; tapestry, arras; millinery.
wreath, festoon, garland, chaplet, flower, nosegay, bouquet, posy [*colloq.*].
tassel, knot; shoulder knot, epaulet, star, rosette, bow; feather, plume, fillet, snood.
jewelry: tiara, crown, coronet, diadem; jewel, gem, precious stone, trinket.

finery, frippery, tinsel, spangle, excess of ornament; pride, show, ostentation.

illustration, illumination; purple patches.

virtu, article of virtu, work of art, bric-a-brac, curio; rarity, a find.

V. **ornament,** embellish, enrich, decorate, adorn, beautify; garnish, furbish, polish, gild, varnish, enamel, paint.

spangle, bespangle, bead, embroider, chase, tool; emblazon, blazon, illuminate.

smarten, trim, bedizen, prink, trick up, trick out, deck, bedeck, array; spruce up [*colloq.*]; smarten up, dress, dress up.

Adj. **ornamental,** ornate, ornamented, rich, gilt, begilt, festooned.

smart, gay, flowery, glittering, new-spangled, fine, well groomed.

showy, gorgeous, flashy, gaudy, garish, tawdry, etc., 851.

848. BLEMISH.—*N.* **blemish,** disfigurement, deformity, defect, flaw, injury, eyesore.

stain, blot, spot, speck, speckle, blur, freckle, patch, blotch, smudge, birthmark, scar, mole, pimple, blister.

V. **disfigure,** etc. (*injure*), 659.

Adj. **disfigured,** imperfect, injured; discolored, specked, speckled, freckled, pitted, bruised.

849. SIMPLICITY.—*N.* **simplicity,** plainness, homeliness; chasteness, chastity, restraint, severity, naturalness, unaffectedness.

V. **simplify,** reduce to simplicity, strip of ornament, chasten, restrain.

Adj. **simple,** plain, homelike, homely, homespun [*fig.*], ordinary.

unaffected, natural, native; inartificial, free from affectation; chaste, severe; unadorned, unornamented.

simple-minded, childish, credulous, etc., 486.

850. [Good taste] TASTE.—*N.* **taste,** good (*or* refined, cultivated) taste; delicacy, refinement, fine feeling, discrimination, tact, polish, elegance, grace, culture, cultivation.

Science of taste: aesthetics.

man of taste, connoisseur, judge, critic, virtuoso, amateur, dilettante; purist, precisian.

V. **display taste,** appreciate, judge, criticize, discriminate.

Adj. **in good taste,** tasteful, unaffected, pure, chaste, classical, cultivated; graceful, attractive, charming, aesthetic, artistic.

refined, elegant, prim, precise, formal.

Adv. **with quiet elegance;** with elegant simplicity; without ostentation.

851. [Bad taste] VULGARITY.—*N.* **vulgarity,** vulgarism, barbarism, vandalism, bad taste; want of tact; ill-breeding, coarseness, indecorum, misbehavior, boorishness.

lowness, low life, brutality, blackguardism, rowdyism, ruffianism; ribaldry.

Excess of ornament: gaudiness, tawdriness, cheap jewelry; flashy clothes (*or* dress), finery, frippery, trickery, tinsel.

vulgarian, rough diamond, clown, Goth, vandal; snob, cad [*colloq.*], cub; parvenu, upstart; frump [*colloq.*], dowdy, slattern.

V. **be vulgar,** misbehave; show a want of tact (*or* consideration); be a vulgarian.

Adj. **in bad taste,** vulgar, unrefined, coarse, indecorous, ribald, gross; unseemly, unpresentable, ungraceful; dowdy, slovenly; lew, extravagant, monstrous, horrid, shocking.

ill-mannered, ill-bred, underbred, snobbish, uncourtly, uncivil, discourteous, ungentlemanly, unladylike.

uncouth, unkempt, unpolished, plebeian; rude, awkward; homely, homespun, provincial, countrified, rustic; boorish, clownish; savage, brutish, blackguardly, rowdy, wild; barbarous, barbaric, outlandish; uncultivated.

antiquated, obsolete, out of fashion, old-fashioned, out of date, unfashionable.

newfangled, fantastic, fantastical, odd, affected.

tawdry, gaudy, meretricious, obtrusive, flaunting, loud, crass, showy, flashy, garish.

852. FASHION.—*N.* **fashion,** style, society, good (*or* polite) society, civilized life, civilization; court, high life, world, fashionable world; upper ten [*colloq.*], elite, smart set [*colloq.*], the four hundred; Vanity Fair; Mayfair.

manners, breeding, politeness; air, demeanor, *savoir-faire* [F.], gentility, decorum, propriety, Mrs. Grundy; convention, conventionality, the proprieties, punctiliousness, form, formality, etiquette.

mode, vogue, style, the latest thing, the rage, prevailing taste; custom.

V. **be fashionable,** be the rage, have a run, pass current, follow the fashion, go with the stream

Adj. **fashionable,** in fashion, *à la mode* [F.], presentable; punctilious, genteel, decorous, conventional; well bred, gentlemanly, ladylike.

polished, refined, thoroughbred, gently bred, courtly, distinguished, aristocratic, self-possessed, poised, easy, frank, unconstrained.

modish, stylish, swell [*slang*], all the rage, all the go [*colloq.*]. *Adv.* for fashion's sake; in the latest style (*or* mode).

853. RIDICULOUSNESS.—*N.* ridiculousness, comicality, oddity, drollery; farce, comedy, burlesque, buffoonery, bull, Irish bull, spoonerism; bombast, anticlimax, bathos; absurdity, laughingstock.

V. **be ridiculous,** play the fool, make a fool of oneself, commit an absurdity.

Adj. **ridiculous,** ludicrous, comic *or* comical, waggish, quizzical, droll, funny, laughable, farcical, seriocomic, tragicomic.

odd, grotesque, whimsical, fanciful, fantastic, queer, quaint, bizarre, eccentric, strange, outlandish, out-of-the-way.

extravagant, monstrous, preposterous, absurd, bombastic, inflated, stilted, burlesque, mock heroic.

854. FOP.—*N.* fine gentleman, fop, swell [*colloq.*], dandy, exquisite, coxcomb, beau, man about town, spark, popinjay, puppy [*contemptuous*], prig, jackanapes, carpet knight; dude [*colloq.*].

fine lady, belle, flirt, coquette, toast.

855. AFFECTATION.—*N.* affectation, affectedness, pretense, pretension, airs, pedantry, stiffness, formality, mannerism, euphuism; boasting, charlatanism, quackery.

prudery, demureness, mock modesty, false shame; sentimentalism.

foppery, dandyism, coxcombry, puppyism, conceit; coquetry.

poser, actor; pedant, pedagogue, doctrinaire, purist, euphuist, mannerist; bluestocking, prig, charlatan; prude, puritan, precisian, formalist.

V. **affect,** act a part, give oneself airs, boast, simper, mince, attitudinize, pose, languish; overact, overdo.

Adj. **affected,** pretentious, pedantic. stilted, stagy, theatrical, canting, insincere, unnatural; self-conscious, artificial; overdone, overacted.

stiff, formal, prim, smug, complacent; demure, puritanical, prudish.

priggish, conceited, foppish, finical, finicking, mincing, simpering, namby-pamby, sentimental, languishing.

856. RIDICULE.—*N.* ridicule, derision, snicker *or* snigger, grin, scoffing, mockery, banter, irony, persiflage, raillery, chaff.

squib, satire, skit, quip.

burlesque, parody, travesty, farce, caricature.

buffoonery, practical joke, horseplay, roughhouse [*slang*].

V. ridicule, deride; laugh at, grin at, smile at; snicker *or* snigger; banter, chaff, joke, guy [*colloq.*], rag [*slang*], haze [*colloq.*].

burlesque, satirize, parody, caricature, travesty.

Adj. derisive, sarcastic, ironical, satirical, quizzical, burlesque, mock.

Adv. as a joke, to raise a laugh.

857. [Object and cause of ridicule] LAUGHINGSTOCK.—*N.* laughingstock, butt, game, fair game, April fool, original, oddity; queer fish [*colloq.*], figure of fun [*colloq.*]; monkey; buffoon.

858. HOPE.—*N.* hope; desire, etc., 865; trust, confidence, reliance, faith, assurance, security; reassurance.

hopefulness, buoyancy, optimism, enthusiasm, aspiration; assumption, presumption; anticipation.

optimist, utopian.

daydream, castles in the air, utopia, millennium; golden dream, airy hopes, fool's paradise, fond hope.

mainstay, anchor, sheet anchor; staff.

V hope, trust, confide, rely, lean upon; live in hope, rest assured.

hope for, etc. (*desire*), 865; anticipate; presume, aspire; promise oneself; expect.

be hopeful, look on the bright side of, make the best of it, hope for the best; hope against hope, take heart, flatter oneself.

encourage, hearten, inspirit, hold out hope, cheer, assure, reassure, buoy up, embolden; promise, bid fair, augur well.

Adj. hopeful, confident, in hopes, secure, sanguine, buoyant, elated, flushed, exultant, enthusiastic.

fearless, unsuspecting, unsuspicious, undespairing, self-reliant; dauntless, etc. (*courageous*), 861.

propitious, promising; probable, auspicious, reassuring; encouraging, cheering, inspiriting, bright, roseate.

859. HOPELESSNESS.—*N.* hopelessness, despair, desperation; despondency, dejection, etc., 837; pessimism, hope deferred, dashed hopes.

pessimist, hypochondriac; bird of ill omen.

V. despair; lose (*or* give up, abandon) all hope, give up, give over, yield to despair; falter; despond.

Adj hopeless, desperate, despairing, gone, in despair, forlorn, inconsolable, brokenhearted.

undone, ruined; incurable, cureless, incorrigible; irreparable, irrecoverable, irretrievable, irreclaimable, irredeemable, irrevocable.

unpropitious, unpromising, inauspicious, ill-omened, threatening, lowering, ominous.

860. FEAR.—*N.* **fear,** timidity, diffidence, apprehensiveness, fearfulness, solicitude, anxiety, care, apprehension, misgiving, mistrust, suspicion, qualm; hesitation.

trepidation, flutter, fear and trembling, perturbation, tremor, quivering, shaking, trembling, palpitation, nervousness, restlessness, disquietude, funk [*colloq.*].

fright, alarm, dread, awe, terror, horror, dismay, consternation, panic, scare; stampede [*of horses*].

intimidation, bullying; terrorism, reign of terror; terrorist, bully.

V. **fear,** be afraid, apprehend, dread, distrust; hesitate, falter, funk [*colloq.*], cower, crouch, skulk, take fright, take alarm; start, wince, flinch, shy, shrink, fly.

tremble, shake, shiver, shudder, flutter, quake, quaver, quiver, quail.

frighten, fright, terrify, inspire (*or* excite) fear, bulldoze [*colloq.*], alarm, startle, scare, dismay, astound; awe, strike terror, appall, unman, petrify, horrify.

daunt, intimidate, cow, overawe, abash, deter, discourage; browbeat, bully, threaten, terrorize.

haunt, obsess, beset, besiege; prey (*or* weigh) on the mind.

Adj. **afraid,** frightened, alarmed, fearful, timid, timorous, nervous, diffident, fainthearted, tremulous, shaky, afraid of one's shadow, apprehensive; aghast, awe-struck, awe-stricken, horror-stricken, panic-stricken.

dreadful, alarming, redoubtable, perilous, dread, fell, dire, direful, shocking, frightful, terrible, terrific, tremendous; horrid, horrible, ghastly, awful, awe-inspiring, revolting.

861. [Absence of fear] COURAGE.—*N.* **courage,** bravery, valor, resoluteness, boldness, spirit, daring, gallantry, intrepidity, prowess, heroism, chivalry, audacity, rashness, dash, defiance, confidence, self-reliance; manhood, manliness, nerve, pluck, mettle, grit, virtue, hardihood, fortitude, firmness, backbone, resolution, tenacity.

exploit, feat, deed, act, achievement.

brave man, man of courage, a man, hero, demigod; Hercules, Achilles, Sir Galahad.

brave woman, heroine; Amazon, Joan of Arc.

V. **dare,** venture, make bold; face (*or* front, confront, brave, defy, despise) danger; face; meet, brave, beard, defy.

nerve oneself, summon up (*or* pluck up) courage, take heart, stand to one's guns, bear up, hold out; present a bold front, show fight, face the music.

hearten, inspire courage, reassure, encourage, embolden, inspirit, cheer, nerve, rally.

Adj. **courageous**, brave, valiant, valorous, gallant, intrepid, spirited, high-spirited, mettlesome, plucky; manly, manful, stouthearted, lionhearted, bold, daring, audacious, fearless, dauntless, undaunted, undismayed, unflinching, unshrinking, confident, self-reliant.

enterprising, adventurous, venturous, venturesome; dashing, chivalrous, warlike, soldierly, heroic.

fierce, savage, pugnacious, bellicose.

strong-minded, strong-willed, hardy, doughty [*archaic or humorous*]; firm, resolute, determined, dogged, indomitable.

862. [Excess of fear] COWARDICE.—N. cowardice, pusillanimity, cowardliness, timidity, effeminacy; baseness, abject fear, funk [*colloq.*]; fear, etc., 860; white feather, cold feet [*slang*], yellow streak [*slang*].

coward, poltroon, dastard, sneak, recreant, cur [*contemptuous*], craven.

alarmist, terrorist, pessimist.

shirker, slacker; fugitive, etc., 623.

V. **quail**, funk [*colloq.*], cower, skulk, sneak; flinch, shy, fight shy, slink, run away; show the white feather.

Adj. **cowardly**, coward, fearful, shy, timid, timorous, spiritless, soft, effeminate, fainthearted; white-livered; dastard, dastardly, base, craven, sneaking, recreant; unwarlike.

Adv. with fear and trembling, in fear of one's life, in a blue funk [*colloq.*].

863. RASHNESS.—N. rashness, temerity, imprudence, indiscretion; overconfidence, presumption, audacity, precipitancy, impetuosity, foolhardiness, heedlessness, thoughtlessness, carelessness, desperation.

gaming, gambling; blind bargain, leap in the dark.

desperado, madcap, daredevil; scapegrace, Don Quixote, knight-errant, adventurer; fire-eater, bully, bravo.

gambler, gamester, etc. (*chance*), 621.

V. **be rash**, stick at nothing, play a desperate game, run into danger, play with fire (*or* edged tools); rush on destruction, tempt providence, go on a forlorn hope.

Adj. **rash**, incautious, indiscreet, injudicious, imprudent, improvident, uncalculating, impulsive, heedless, careless, without ballast.

reckless, wild, madcap, desperate, devil-may-care, death-defying, hotheaded, headlong, headstrong; breakneck, foolhardy, harebrained, precipitate.

overconfident, overweening; venturesome, venturous, adventurous, quixotic.

Adv. posthaste, headforemost.

864. CAUTION.—*N.* **caution,** cautiousness, discretion, prudence, heed, circumspection, calculation, deliberation, foresight, etc., 510; vigilance, etc., 459; warning, etc., 668.

worldly wisdom; safety first, Fabian policy, watchful waiting.

coolness, self-possession, self-command; presence of mind, *sangfroid* [F.].

V. **be cautious,** take care, take heed, mind, be on one's guard; think twice, look before one leaps, count the cost, feel one's way, see how the land lies; pussyfoot [*colloq.*], keep out of harm's way, stand aloof; keep (*or* be) on the safe side.

warn, caution, etc., 668.

Adj. **cautious,** wary, guarded, on one's guard, suspicious, vigilant, careful, heedful, chary, sure-footed, circumspect, prudent, noncommittal, canny [Scot.], discreet, politic, strategic.

unenterprising, unadventurous, cool, steady, self-possessed; overcautious.

865. DESIRE.—*N.* **desire,** wish, fancy, inclination, leaning, bent, mind, whim, partiality, predilection, propensity, liking, love, fondness, relish.

longing, hankering, yearning, aspiration, ambition, eagerness, zeal, ardor, solicitude, anxiety.

need, want, exigency, urgency, necessity.

appetite, keenness, hunger, stomach, thirst, drought.

avidity, greed, greediness, covetousness, ravenousness, grasping, craving, rapacity, voracity.

mania, passion, rage, furor, frenzy, itching palm, cupidity, kleptomania, dipsomania; monomania.

Person desiring: lover, votary, devotee, aspirant; parasite, sycophant.

attraction, magnet, loadstone, lure, allurement, fancy, temptation, fascination; hobby.

V. **desire,** wish, wish for, care for, affect, like, take to, cling to, fancy; prefer, have an eye to, have a mind to; have a fancy for, have at heart, be bent upon; set one's heart (*or* mind) upon, covet, crave, hanker after, pine for, long for; hope, etc., 858.

woo, court, ogle, solicit; fish for.

want, miss, need, lack, feel the want of.

attract, allure, whet the appetite; appetize, take one's fancy, tempt, tantalize, make one's mouth water.

Adj. **desirous,** desiring, appetitive, inclined, fain, wishful, longing, wistful; anxious, solicitous, sedulous.

eager, keen, burning, fervent, ardent; agog; breathless; impatient.

ambitious, aspiring, vaulting.

craving, hungry, sharp-set, peckish [*colloq.*], ravening, famished; thirsty, athirst, dry [*colloq. when meaning thirsty*], droughty.

greedy, voracious, ravenous, omnivorous, covetous, rapacious, grasping, extortionate, exacting, sordid, insatiable, insatiate.

desirable, desired, in demand, popular, pleasing, appetizing.

Adv. fain; with eager appetite.

866. INDIFFERENCE.—*N.* **indifference,** neutrality; unconcern, nonchalance, apathy, supineness, disdain, inattention, coldness.

V. **be indifferent,** stand neuter, take no interest in, have no desire for, have no taste for, not care for, care nothing for (*or* about); not mind; spurn, disdain.

Adj. **indifferent,** cold, frigid, lukewarm; cool, neutral, unconcerned, phlegmatic, easygoing, careless, listless, halfhearted, unambitious, undesirous, unsolicitous.

unattractive, unalluring, undesired, undesirable, unwished.

867. DISLIKE.—*N.* **dislike,** distaste, disrelish, disinclination, unwillingness, reluctance, backwardness.

repugnance, disgust, nausea, loathing, aversion, abomination, antipathy, abhorrence, horror, hatred, detestation; hate, etc., 898.

V. **dislike,** disrelish; mind, object to, have no taste for, shudder at, turn up the nose at, look askance at; shun, avoid, eschew, shrink from.

loathe, abominate, detest, abhor; hate, etc., 898.

repel, disincline, sicken, pall, nauseate, disgust, shock, make one's blood run cold.

Adj. **loath,** averse; shy of, sick of, disinclined, heartsick.

repugnant, repulsive, repellent, abhorrent, insufferable, fulsome, nauseous, loathsome, offensive, disgusting.

unpopular, undesirable, uncared for, disliked, out of favor.

uneatable, inedible, unappetizing, unsavory.

Adv. to satiety, to one's disgust.

868. FASTIDIOUSNESS.—*N.* **fastidiousness,** nicety, hypercriticism, epicurism.

discrimination, discernment, perspicacity, keenness, sharpness, insight.

epicure, gourmet.

Excess of delicacy: prudery, prudishness, primness.

V. **be fastidious,** split hairs; mince the matter; turn up one's nose at, disdain.

discriminate, have nice discrimination; have exquisite taste; be discriminative.

Adj. fastidious, nice, delicate, meticulous, finicking *or* finicky, exacting, hard to please, difficult, dainty, squeamish, thin-skinned; querulous; particular, scrupulous; critical, hypercritical, overcritical.

prudish, strait-laced, prim.

discriminative, discriminating, discerning, judicious, keen, sharp, perspicacious.

869. SATIETY.—*N.* satiety, satisfaction, saturation, repletion, glut, surfeit, satiation.

V. sate, satiate, satisfy, saturate, cloy, quench, slake, pall, glut, gorge, surfeit; bore, tire, spoil.

Adj. satiated, overgorged, overfed, blasé [F.], sick of.

870. WONDER.—*N.* wonder, astonishment, amazement, wonderment, bewilderment, admiration, awe; stupor, stupefaction, fascination, surprise.

V. wonder, marvel, admire, be surprised, start, stare; gape, hold one's breath, stand aghast.

astonish, surprise, amaze, astound; dumfound, dumfounder, startle, dazzle, daze, strike, electrify, stun, stupefy, petrify, confound, bewilder, stagger, fascinate, take away one's breath, strike dumb.

Adj. astonished, surprised, aghast, breathless, agape, openmouthed, thunderstruck, spellbound; lost in amazement (*or* wonder, astonishment).

wonderful, wondrous, surprising, striking, marvelous, miraculous; unexpected, mysterious, monstrous, prodigious, stupendous, inconceivable, incredible, strange.

indescribable, inexpressible, ineffable; unutterable, unspeakable.

Adv. for a wonder, strange to say, to one's great surprise.

871. [Absence of wonder] EXPECTANCE.—*N.* expectance, expectancy, expectation, etc., 507.

calmness, imperturbability, *sang-froid* [F.], coolness, steadiness, lack of nerves, want of imagination.

V. expect, etc., 507; not wonder, make nothing of, take it coolly.

Adj. expecting, unamazed, astonished at nothing, blasé [F.], expected, foreseen.

calm, imperturbable, nerveless, cool, coolheaded, unruffled, steady, unimaginative.

common, ordinary, etc. (*habitual*), 613.

872. PRODIGY.—*N.* prodigy, phenomenon, wonder, wonderment, marvel, miracle; freak, freak of nature, monstrosity, monster; curiosity, infant prodigy, lion, sight, spectacle; sign, portent.

873. REPUTE.—*N.* **repute,** reputation, distinction, mark, name, figure, note, notability, éclat, vogue, celebrity, fame, renown, popularity, credit, prestige, account, regard, respect, fair name.

dignity, stateliness, solemnity, grandeur, luster, splendor, nobility, majesty, sublimity, glory, honor.

rank, standing, precedence, station, place, status, position, order, degree, caste, condition.

eminence, greatness, height, importance, pre-eminence, supereminence, elevation, exaltation.

celebrity, worthy, hero, man of mark (*or* rank), lion, notability, somebody.

scholar, savant; paragon, star; elite.

ornament, honor, feather in one's cap, halo, aureole, nimbus; laurels.

posthumous fame, memory, celebration, canonization, enshrinement, glorification, immortality, immortal name.

V. **be distinguished,** shine, etc. (*light*), 420; shine forth, figure, cut a figure, flourish, flaunt, play first fiddle, bear the palm, take precedence; win laurels (*or* golden opinions).

surpass, outshine, outrival, outvie, eclipse; throw into the shade, overshadow.

rival, emulate, vie with.

honor, give (*or* do, pay) honor to, accredit, dignify, glorify, pledge, toast, look up to, exalt, aggrandize, elevate, enthrone, signalize, immortalize, deify.

consecrate; dedicate to, devote to; enshrine, inscribe, blazon, lionize.

Adj. **distinguished,** noted, of note, honored, popular, remarkable, notable, celebrated, renowned, famous, famed, far-famed, conspicuous, foremost.

reputable, in good odor, in favor, in high favor, respectable, creditable, worthy.

imperishable, deathless, immortal, never fading, fadeless.

illustrious, glorious, splendid, brilliant, radiant; bright, etc., 420.

eminent, prominent, high, etc., 206; peerless, pre-eminent, great, dignified, proud, noble, honorable, lordly, grand, stately, august, princely, imposing, solemn, transcendent, majestic, sacred, sublime.

874. DISREPUTE.—*N.* **disrepute,** discredit, ill-repute, ill-favor, ingloriousness, derogation, abasement, debasement, degradation; odium, obloquy, opprobrium, ignominy, dishonor, disgrace, shame, humiliation, scandal, infamy.

stigma, brand, reproach, imputation, slur, stain, blot, spot, blur, tarnish, taint, badge of infamy.

V. **be inglorious,** have a bad name; disgrace oneself, lose caste; fall from one's high estate, cut a sorry figure.

shame, disgrace, put to shame, dishonor; tarnish, stain, blot, sully, taint; discredit, degrade, debase, expel.

stigmatize, vilify, defame, slur, brand, post, send to Coventry, snub, show up [*colloq.*], reprehend.

disconcert, put out [*colloq.*], upset, discompose; put to the blush.

Adj. **disgraced,** overcome, downtrodden, in bad repute, under a cloud, in the shade (*or* background); down in the world, down and out [*colloq.*].

inglorious, nameless, obscure, unknown to fame, unnoticed, unnoted, unhonored, unglorified.

discreditable, questionable, shameful, disgraceful, disreputable, despicable; unbecoming, unworthy, derogatory, degrading, humiliating, scandalous, infamous, opprobrious, arrant, shocking, outrageous, notorious, ignominious, base, abject, vile.

beggarly, pitiful, mean, petty, shabby.

875. NOBILITY.—*N.* **nobility,** rank, condition, distinction, blood, birth, high descent, order, quality.

high life, upper classes, upper ten [*colloq.*], the four hundred; elite, aristocracy, fashionable world.

celebrity, bigwig [*humorous*], magnate, great man, star, great gun [*colloq.*].

The nobility: peerage, baronage; House of Lords (*or* peers); lords, noblesse.

peer, noble, nobleman; lord, grandee, don, hidalgo; aristocrat, swell [*colloq.*], gentleman, squire, patrician.

gentry, gentlefolk, magnates.

king, etc., 745; prince, duke, marquis, earl, viscount, baron, baronet, knight, chevalier, count, esquire, laird [Scot.]; signior, seignior; signor [It.], señor [Sp.], senhor [Pg.]; sheik, pasha, sahib.

empress, queen, princess, duchess, marchioness, viscountess, countess; lady, doña [Sp.], dona [Pg.]; signora [It.], señora [Sp.], senhora [Pg.].

Hindu titles: raja, rana (*fem.* rani), maharaja, maharana (*fem.* maharani), Gaekwar [*lit.* cowherd; *Baroda*].

Mohammedan titles: nawab, sultan (*fem.* sultana), amir.

Rank or office: kingship, dukedom, marquisate, earldom; viscountship, county, lordship, baronetcy, knighthood.

Adj. **noble,** exalted, princely, titled, patrician, aristocratic; highborn, well born, courtly.

Adv. in high quarters.

876. THE PEOPLE.—*N.* **the people,** commonalty, democracy; obscurity; *bourgeoisie* [F.], the four million; lower classes (*or* orders), common herd, rank and file, the many, the general, the crowd, the ruck, the populace, the multitude, the million, the masses, the mobility [*humorous*], the peasantry, proletariat; *hoi polloi* [Gr.].

rabble, horde, canaille, dregs of society, mob, trash, riffraff, ragtag and bobtail.

commoner, one of the people, democrat, plebeian, republican, bourgeois [F.].

peasant, countryman, boor, churl, serf; swain, clown, clodhopper, yokel, lout, bumpkin; plowman, hayseed [*slang*], rustic, lunkhead [*colloq.*], rube [*slang*]; tiller of the soil; hewers of wood and drawers of water; gamin, street Arab.

rough, rowdy, roughneck [*slang*], ruffian, tough [*colloq.*], scullion, low fellow, cad.

upstart, parvenu, nobody, snob, mushroom, adventurer, *nouveau riche* (*pl. nouveaux riches*) [F.].

vagabond, beggar, caitiff, ragamuffin, pariah, outcast, tramp, panhandler [*slang*], bum [*slang*], hobo.

Adj. ignoble, common, mean, low, base, vile, sorry, scrubby, beggarly; vulgar, low-minded; snobbish, parvenu, low-bred; menial, servile.

plebeian, proletarian, lowborn, baseborn, risen from the ranks, obscure, untitled.

rustic, country, uncivilized; loutish, boorish, clownish, churlish, rude.

barbarous, barbarian, barbaric.

Adv. below the salt.

877. TITLE.—*N.* title, honor; earldom, etc. (*nobility*), 875.

highness, excellency, grace, lordship, reverence; reverend; esquire, sir, master, Mr., *signor* [It.], *señor* [Sp.], etc., 373; your (*or* his) honor.

madam, etc. (*mistress*), 374; empress, queen, etc., 875.

decoration, laurel, palm, wreath, garland, bays; medal, ribbon, cordon, cross, crown, coronet, star, garter; epaulet, chevron, colors, cockade; livery; order, arms, coat of arms, shield, escutcheon *or* scutcheon, crest; handle to one's name.

878. PRIDE.—*N.* pride, haughtiness, high notions, hauteur, vainglory, arrogance, self-importance, pomposity, side [*slang*], swagger, toploftiness [*colloq.*].

dignity, self-respect, self-esteem, decorum, stateliness, seemliness.

V be proud, presume, swagger, strut, hold one's head high, look big, carry with a high hand; ride the high horse, give oneself airs.

Adj. dignified, stately, lordly, lofty-minded, high-souled, high-minded, high-mettled, high-flown.

proud, haughty, lofty, high, mighty, swollen, puffed up, flushed, vainglorious; purse-proud, fine.

supercilious, disdainful, bumptious, magisterial, imperious, high and mighty, overweening, consequential; pompous, toplofty [*colloq.*]; arrogant.

stiff, stiff-necked; starched, stuck up [*colloq.*]; strait-laced, prim, affected, etc., 855.

Adv. with head erect, with nose in air, with nose turned up; with a sneer, with curling lip.

879. HUMILITY.—*N.* humility, humbleness, meekness, lowliness, abasement, self-abasement, submission, resignation.

modesty, timidity; confusion, humiliation, mortification.

V. **be humble,** deign, vouchsafe, condescend, humble oneself, stoop, submit, yield the palm, sing small [*colloq.*], hide one's face.

be humiliated, be put out of countenance, be shamed, be put to the blush, receive a snub, eat humble pie.

humble, humiliate, snub, abash, abase, strike dumb, lower, cast into the shade, put to the blush, confuse, shame, mortify, disgrace, crush.

Adj. **humble,** lowly, meek, modest, etc., 881; humble-minded, sober-minded; submissive, servile.

humbled, bowed down, abashed, ashamed, dashed, crestfallen, shorn of one's glory.

Adv. with downcast eyes, with bated breath, on bended knee.

880. VANITY.—*N.* vanity, conceit, conceitedness, self-conceit, self-sufficiency, self-praise, self-glorification, self-applause, self-admiration; selfishness, etc., 943.

pretension, airs, affected manner, mannerism; egoism, egotism, priggishness; vainglory, arrogance, pride, ostentation.

egoist, egotist; peacock; coxcomb.

V. **be vain,** pique oneself, have too high opinion of oneself, strut, put oneself forward; give oneself airs, boast, etc., 884.

render vain, inflate, puff up, turn one's head.

Adj. **vain,** conceited, overweening, forward, vainglorious, high-flown, ostentatious, etc., 882; puffed up, inflated, flushed, elate.

self-satisfied, complacent, self-confident, self-sufficient, self-admiring, pretentious, priggish, egotistic *or* egotistical, arrogant, assured.

881. MODESTY.—*N.* modesty; humility, etc., 879; diffidence, demureness, timidity, bashfulness, retiring disposition, unobtrusiveness; blush, blushing; reserve, constraint.

V. **be modest,** retire, give way to, hide one's face; keep in the background; hide one's light under a bushel.

Adj. **modest,** diffident, retiring, humble, etc., 879; timid, timorous, bashful, shy, coy, demure, sheepish, shamefaced, blushing.

unpretending, unpretentious, unobtrusive, unassuming, unostentatious; reserved, constrained.

Adv. **modestly,** quietly, privately; without ceremony.

882. OSTENTATION.—*N.* ostentation, display, show, flourish, parade, pomp, magnificence, splendor, pageantry, array, state, solemnity; dash [*colloq.*], splash [*colloq.*], glitter, pomposity, pretense, pretensions.

demonstration, pageant, spectacle, exhibition, exposition, procession, turnout [*colloq.*]; fete, field day, review, march past, promenade.

ceremony, ceremonial, ritual, form, formality, etiquette, punctilio.

V. **flaunt**, show off, parade, display, exhibit, brandish, blazon forth; dangle, emblazon.

Adj. **ostentatious**, showy, dashing, pretentious, grand, pompous; garish, gaudy, flaunting, glittering, gay.

splendid, magnificent, sumptuous, palatial.

theatrical, theatric, dramatic, spectacular, scenic.

ceremonial, ceremonious, ritualistic; solemn, stately, majestic, formal, punctilious.

Adv. with flourish of trumpet, with beat of drum, with flying colors.

883. CELEBRATION.—*N.* **celebration**, solemnization, commemoration; jubilation, ovation, triumph; inauguration, installation, presentation; coronation; debut, coming out [*colloq.*].

birthday, anniversary, biennial, triennial, etc.; centenary, centennial; bicentenary, bicentennial; tercentenary, tercentennial, etc.; festivity, festival, fete, holiday.

triumphal arch; salute, salvo, salvo of artillery; flourish of trumpets, fanfare; colors flying; illuminations.

jubilee, 50th anniversary; diamond jubilee.

V. **celebrate**, keep, signalize, do honor to, commemorate, solemnize; rejoice, etc., 838; paint the town red [*colloq.*].

inaugurate, install, instate, induct, chair.

Adj. **commemorative**, celebrated, kept in remembrance; immortal.

Adv. in honor of, in commemoration of, in celebration of, in memory of, in memoriam [L.].

884. BOASTING.—*N.* **boasting**, boast, vaunt, pretensions, braggadocio, puff [*colloq.*], flourish, bluff, highfalutin, swagger, jingoism, chauvinism, brag, bounce, bluster, bravado, buncombe [*cant or slang*]; rodomontade, bombast, hot air [*slang*], tall talk [*colloq.*], exaggeration, magniloquence, heroics.

boaster, braggart, pretender, bluffer, hot-air artist [*slang*]; chauvinist, jingo, jingoist; blusterer, swaggerer.

V. **boast**, brag, vaunt, puff, show off, flourish, strut, swagger, bluff; talk big, draw the long bow, blow one's own trumpet.

exult, crow [*colloq.*], triumph, glory, rejoice, cheer; gloat, gloat over, chuckle.

Adj. **boastful**, braggart, pretentious, vainglorious, highfalutin.

elate, elated, jubilant, triumphant, exultant; in high feather.

885. [Undue assumption of superiority] INSOLENCE.—*N.* insolence, brazenness, haughtiness, arrogance, airs; bumptiousness, assumption, presumption; disdain, insult, bluster, swagger.

impertinence, cheek [*colloq. or, slang*], nerve [*slang*], sauce [*colloq.*], abuse; flippancy.

impudence, self-assertion, assurance, audacity, hardihood, gall [*slang*], shamelessness, effrontery.

V. be insolent, bluster, swagger, give oneself airs, arrogate, assume, presume; make bold, make free, take a liberty.

outface, outlook, outstare, outbrazen, brazen out; look big.

domineer, bully, dictate, hector; lord it over; snub, browbeat, intimidate; dragoon, bulldoze [*colloq.*], terrorize.

Adj. insolent, haughty, arrogant, imperious, dictatorial, arbitrary, highhanded, supercilious, overbearing, toplofty [*colloq.*], intolerant, domineering, overweening, bumptious.

pert, flippant, fresh [*slang*], saucy, forward, impertinent, assuming, impudent, audacious, presumptuous.

brazen, shameless, unblushing, unabashed; barefaced, brazenfaced; lost to shame.

blustering, swaggering, hectoring, rollicking, roistering, devil-may-care.

jingo, jingoistic, chauvinistic.

Adv. with nose in air; with arms akimbo; with a high hand.

886. SERVILITY.—*N.* servility, slavery, obsequiousness, toadying, subserviency; abasement, prostration, toadeating, fawning, flunkyism, sycophancy; humility, etc., 879.

sycophant, parasite, toady, toadeater, flunky, hanger-on, timeserver, flatterer, tool; beat [*slang*], dead beat [*slang*]; heeler, ward heeler [*both polit. cant*]; sponge, sponger, truckler.

V. cringe, bow, stoop, kneel; fawn, crouch, cower, sneak, crawl, sponge, toady, grovel; be servile.

go with the stream, follow the crowd, worship the rising sun; be a timeserver.

Adj. servile, obsequious, oily, pliant, cringing, fawning, slavish, groveling, sniveling, mealy-mouthed; sycophantic, parasitical; abject, prostrate, base, mean, sneaking, timeserving.

887. BLUSTERER.—*N.* blusterer, swaggerer, braggart; roisterer, brawler, bully, terrorist, rough, ruffian, roughneck [*slang*], tough [*colloq.*], rowdy, hoodlum [*colloq.*], hooligan [*slang*], swashbuckler; desperado, daredevil, fire-eater [*colloq.*], jingo.

dogmatist, doctrinaire, stump orator.

III. SYMPATHETIC AFFECTIONS

888. FRIENDSHIP.—*N.* friendship, amity, friendliness; harmony, concord, peace, etc., 721; cordiality, *entente cordiale* [F.], good understanding, sympathy, fellow feeling, response; affection, etc. (*love*), 897; benevolence, good will; partiality, favoritism.

brotherhood, fraternization, association; acquaintance, familiarity, intimacy, intercourse, fellowship.

fraternity, sodality; sisterhood, sorority, sorosis.

V. **be friendly**, be friends, be acquainted with, know; have dealings with, sympathize with, have a leaning to, bear good will, love, befriend.

become friendly, make friends with, break the ice, be introduced to, make (*or* scrape) acquaintance with, get into favor, gain the friendship of; shake hands with, fraternize.

Adj. **friendly**, amicable, neighborly; brotherly, fraternal, sisterly; ardent, devoted, sympathetic, harmonious, hearty, cordial, warmhearted.

friends with, at home with, on good (*or* friendly, amicable, cordial, familiar, intimate) terms, on speaking terms, on visiting terms.

acquainted, familiar, intimate, hail fellow well met, free and easy; welcome.

Adv. with open arms; arm in arm.

889. ENMITY.—*N.* **enmity**, hostility, antagonism, unfriendliness; discord, etc., 713; bitterness, rancor; heartburning, animosity; malevolence, etc., 907.

alienation, estrangement; dislike, aversion, hate, etc., 898.

V **be unfriendly**, keep (*or* hold) at arm's length; be at loggerheads, bear malice, fall out; take umbrage; alienate, estrange.

Adj. **unfriendly**, inimical, hostile; at enmity, at variance, at daggers drawn, up in arms against.

on bad terms, not on speaking terms; cool, cold, estranged, alienated, disaffected, irreconcilable.

890. FRIEND.—*N.* **friend**, alter ego [L.], other self; intimate, confidant (*masc.*), confidante (*fem.*); best (*or* bosom, fast) friend, well-wisher; neighbor, acquaintance.

patron, backer, tutelary saint, good genius, advocate, partisan, sympathizer; ally, friend in need.

associate, comrade, mate, companion, confrere, colleague, partner, consort, chum [*colloq.*], pal [*slang*], buddy [*slang, First World War*]; playfellow, playmate, schoolmate, schoolfellow, classmate; bedfellow, bunkie [*colloq.*], roommate, shopmate, shipmate, messmate; fellow (*or* boon) companion.

Famous friendships: Pylades and Orestes, Castor and Pollux, Achilles and Patroclus, Damon and Pythias, David and Jonathan; Soldiers Three, the Three Musketeers.

host, hostess (*fem.*).

guest, visitor, frequenter, habitué, protégé.

compatriot, countryman, fellow countryman; fellow townsman.

891. ENEMY.—*N.* enemy, antagonist, foe, foeman, open (*or* bitter) enemy, opponent; mortal aversion (*or* antipathy); snake in the grass.

public enemy, enemy to society; anarchist, seditionist, traitor, traitress (*fem.*).

892. SOCIALITY.—*N.* sociality, sociability, social intercourse, intercourse, companionship, comradeship, fellowship; urbanity, intimacy, familiarity, condescension, *esprit de corps* [F.]; morale.

conviviality, good fellowship, joviality, jollity, festivity, merry-making; hospitality, heartiness; cheer.

welcome, greeting; hearty (*or* warm) reception; hearty welcome (*or* greeting), the glad hand [*slang*].

social gathering, social reunion, assembly, barbecue; bee; cornhusking, corn shucking [U. S.]; husking, husking-bee [U. S.]; hen party [*colloq.*]; house raising, housewarming, hanging of the crane, smoker [*colloq.*]; Dutch treat [*colloq.*]; stag, stag party [*both colloq.*]; sociable [U. S.], party, entertainment, reception, levee, at home, soiree, matinee; garden party, coming-out party [*colloq.*], surprise party; ball, hunt ball, dance festival.

Social meals: breakfast, wedding breakfast, hunt breakfast; luncheon, lunch; picnic lunch, basket lunch, picnic; tea, afternoon tea, five-o'clock tea, cup of tea, dish of tea [*esp.* Brit.], coming-out tea [*colloq.*]; tea party, tea fight [*slang*]; dinner, potluck, bachelor dinner, stag dinner [*colloq.*], hunt dinner; church supper, high tea, banquet.

visit, visiting; round of visits; call, morning call, interview; tryst, appointment.

V. be sociable, know, be acquainted, associate with, consort with, club together, join; make advances, fraternize.

visit, pay a visit, call at, call upon, leave a card, drop in, look in.

entertain, give a party; see one's friends, keep open house, do the honors, receive, welcome; kill the fatted calf.

Adj. sociable, companionable, clubbable [*colloq.*], cozy, chatty, conversational; convivial, festive, festal, jovial, jolly, hospitable.

free and easy, hail fellow well met, familiar, intimate, social, neighborly.

Adv. en famille [F.], in the family circle; on terms of intimacy; in the social whirl.

893. SECLUSION. EXCLUSION.—*N.* seclusion, privacy, retirement, concealment, rustication, solitude, isolation, loneliness, voluntary exile, aloofness.

retreat, cell, hermitage, cloister, convent; sanctum sanctorum [L.], study, library, den [*colloq.*].

exclusion, excommunication, banishment, exile, ostracism, cut.

unsociability, unsociableness, inhospitality, domesticity, self-sufficiency.

recluse, hermit; caveman, cave dweller, troglodyte, cynic, Diogenes.

outcast, pariah, leper; outsider, rank outsider; castaway, foundling.

V. seclude oneself, keep aloof, shut oneself up; deny oneself, rusticate, retire, retire from the world; take the veil.

exclude, repel, cut; send to Coventry, turn one's back upon, shut the door upon; blackball, excommunicate, exile, expatriate; banish, outlaw, maroon, ostracize, keep at arm's length; boycott, embargo, blockade, isolate.

Adj. secluded, sequestered, retired, private, out of the world.

unsociable, unsocial, inhospitable; domestic, stay-at-home.

excluded, unfrequented, unvisited, uninvited, unwelcome, under a cloud.

friendless, homeless, desolate, lorn, forlorn; solitary, lonely, lonesome, isolated, single, estranged; derelict, outcast, deserted, banished.

uninhabited, unoccupied, untenanted, tenantless, abandoned.

894. COURTESY.—*N.* courtesy; respect, etc., 928; good manners (*or* behavior, breeding); manners, politeness, urbanity, gentility, breeding, gentle breeding, cultivation, culture, polish, civility, amenity, suavity; good temper, good humor, amiability, complacency, affability, complaisance, compliance, gallantry, chivalry.

pink of courtesy, pink of politeness; flower of knighthood; Chesterfield; Lancelot.

ceremonial; salutation, reception, presentation, introduction, welcome, greeting; respects, regards, remembrances; deference, love.

Forms of greeting: bow, curtsy, salaam, kowtow [China], obeisance, bowing and scraping; kneeling, genuflection; capping, pulling the forelock, nod, shaking hands; embrace, hug, squeeze, kiss; salute, accolade.

V. be courteous, show courtesy; behave oneself, conciliate, speak one fair, take in good part.

do the honors, usher, usher in, receive, greet, hail, bid welcome, welcome; bid Godspeed; speed the parting guest.

salute; nod to; smile upon; uncover, touch (*or* raise) the hat, doff the cap, bow, make one's bow, curtsy, bob a curtsy, kneel; bow (*or* bend) the knee; salaam, kowtow [China], prostrate oneself.

Adj. courteous, polite, civil, mannerly, urbane; well behaved, well mannered, well bred, gently bred, of gentle breeding; polished, cultivated, refined; gallant, chivalrous, chivalric, knightly.

tactful, ingratiating, winning; gentle, mild; good-humored,

cordial, gracious, amiable, familiar; neighborly; obliging, complacent, conciliatory.

bland, suave, affable, honey-tongued; oily, unctuous, obsequious.

Adv. with a good grace; with open arms, with outstretched arms, with perfect courtesy, in good humor.

895. DISCOURTESY.—*N.* **discourtesy,** ill-breeding, bad manners; tactlessness; discourteousness, rusticity, incivility, lack (*or* want) of courtesy, disrespect, impudence, misbehavior, barbarism, barbarity; vulgarity, brutality, blackguardism, conduct unbecoming a gentleman.

bad temper, ill-temper, peevishness, surliness, churlishness, perversity; moroseness, etc., 901*a*; sternness, austerity; moodishness, captiousness, tartness, acrimony, asperity.

scowl, black looks, frown; sulks, short answer, rebuff; hard words, unparliamentary language, personality.

bear, brute, blackguard, beast; unlicked cub; crosspatch [*colloq.*], grouch [*slang*].

V. **be rude,** insult, treat with discourtesy, make bold with, make free with; take a liberty; stare out of countenance, ogle, point at.

sulk, frown, scowl, glower, pout; snap, snarl, growl.

cut; turn one's back upon, turn on one's heel; give the cold shoulder, keep at a distance.

Adj. **discourteous,** uncourteous, uncourtly, ill-bred, ill-mannered, ill-behaved, unmannerly, uncivil, impolite, unaccommodating, unneighborly, ungallant, ungracious, unpolished; ungentlemanly; unladylike; vulgar.

pert, forward, obtrusive, impudent, rude, saucy, flippant.

rough, rugged, bluff, blunt, short, gruff; churlish, boorish, bearish; brutal, brusque, stern, harsh, austere; cavalier.

bad-tempered, ill-tempered, ill-humored, crusty, tart, sour, crabbed, sharp, trenchant, sarcastic, caustic, virulent, bitter, acrimonious, venomous, contumelious, snarling, surly, perverse, grim, sullen, peevish, bristling, thorny.

Adv. with a bad grace.

896. CONGRATULATION.—*N.* **congratulation,** felicitation, compliment; compliments of the season; good wishes, best wishes.

V. **congratulate,** felicitate, wish one joy, compliment, tender (*or* offer) one's congratulations; wish many happy returns of the day.

897. LOVE.—*N.* **love,** affection, sympathy, fellow feeling; tenderness, heart, brotherly love; charity, good will, benevolence; attachment, fondness, liking, inclination; regard, admiration, fancy.

yearning, tender passion, gallantry, passion, flame, devotion, fervor, enthusiasm, rapture, enchantment, infatuation, adoration, idolatry.

mother love, maternal love, natural affection.

attractiveness, charm; popularity; idol, favorite, etc., 899.

god of love, Cupid, Eros, Venus; myrtle.

lover, suitor, fiancé [F.], follower [*colloq.*], admirer, adorer, wooer, beau, sweetheart, swain, young man [*colloq.*], flame [*colloq.*], love, truelove.

ladylove, sweetheart, mistress, inamorata, darling, idol, angel, goddess; betrothed, fiancée [F.].

flirt, coquette.

V. **love**, like, fancy, care for, take an interest in, sympathize with; be in love with, regard, revere, take to, set one's affections on, adore, idolize, dote on (*or* upon), make much of, hold dear, prize; hug, cling to, cherish, caress, fondle, pet.

charm, attract, attach, fascinate, captivate, bewitch, enrapture, turn the head.

Adj. **loving**, affectionate, tender, sympathetic, amorous, love-sick, fond, ardent, passionate, rapturous, devoted, motherly.

loved, beloved, well beloved, dearly beloved; dear, precious, darling, pet; favorite, popular.

lovable, adorable, lovely, sweet, attractive, winning, winsome, charming, enchanting, captivating, fascinating, bewitching, amiable.

898. HATE.—*N.* **hate**, hatred, vials of hate; hymn of hate; disaffection, disfavor; alienation, estrangement, coolness; enmity, etc., 889; animosity, malice, implacability.

umbrage, pique, grudge, spleen, bitterness, bitterness of feeling; ill-blood, bad blood; acrimony.

repugnance, etc. (*dislike*), 867; odium, unpopularity; detestation, abhorrence, loathing, execration, abomination, aversion, antipathy.

object of hatred, an abomination, an aversion, bête noire [F.]; enemy, etc., 891; bitter pill.

V. **hate**, detest, abominate, abhor, loathe; recoil at, shudder at; shrink from, revolt against, execrate; dislike, etc., 867.

alienate, estrange, repel, horrify, set against, sow dissension, set by the ears, envenom, incense, irritate, ruffle, vex.

Adj. **abhorrent**, averse from, set against; bitter, etc. (*acrimonious*), 895; implacable.

unloved, unbeloved, unlamented, undeplored, unmourned, uncared for, unvalued; disliked.

lovelorn, jilted, crossed in love, forsaken, rejected.

hateful, obnoxious, odious, abominable, repulsive, offensive, shocking; disgusting, reprehensible.

invidious, spiteful; malicious, etc., 907.

899. FAVORITE.—*N.* **favorite,** pet, idol, jewel, spoiled child, apple of one's eye, man after one's own heart.

love, dear, darling, duck, honey, sweetheart, etc. (*ladylove*), 897.

general (*or* universal) favorite; idol of the people; matinee idol.

900. RESENTMENT.—*N.* **resentment,** displeasure, animosity, anger, wrath, ire, indignation; exasperation, vexation, wrathful, indignation.

pique, umbrage, huff, soreness, acerbity, virulence, bitterness, acrimony, asperity; irascibility, etc., 901; sulks, etc., 901*a*; hate, etc., 898; revenge.

irritation; warmth, ferment, excitement, ebullition; angry mood, pet, tiff, passion, fit, tantrum [*colloq.*].

rage, fury, towering rage, passion; outburst, explosion, paroxysm, storm, violence, vials of wrath; hot blood, high words.

Furies, Erinyes (*sing.* Erinys), Eumenides.

provocation, affront, offense, indignity, insult, grudge; last straw, sore subject; ill-turn, outrage; buffet, blow, box on the ear, rap on the knuckles.

V. **resent,** take amiss, take offense (*or* umbrage, exception); pout, frown, scowl, lower, snarl, growl, gnash, snap; redden, color; look black, look daggers.

be angry, fly into a rage, bridle up, fire up, flare up; chafe, mantle, fume, kindle, fly out, boil, boil with indignation (*or* rage); rage, storm, foam; hector, bully, bluster; lose one's temper; raise Cain [*slang*]; breathe revenge.

anger, affront, offend, give offense (*or* umbrage); hurt the feelings; insult, ruffle, heckle [Brit.], nettle, huff, pique; excite, irritate, fret, sting, provoke, chafe, wound, incense, inflame, enrage, envenom, embitter, exasperate, infuriate, madden; rankle.

Adj. **angry,** wroth, irate, ireful, wrathful; irascible, etc., 901; bitter, virulent, acrimonious, offended, indignant, hurt, sore.

fuming, raging, hot under the collar [*slang*]; convulsed with rage; fierce, wild, furious, fiery, rabid, savage, violent.

Adv. in the height (*or* heat) of passion; in an ecstasy of rage.

901. IRASCIBILITY.—*N.* **irascibility,** temper; crossness, petulance, irritability, tartness, acerbity, acrimony, asperity; pugnacity, excitability.

shrew, vixen, virago, dragon, scold, spitfire, fury.

V. **be irascible,** have a temper, be possessed of the devil, have the temper of a fiend; fire up, flare up.

Adj. **irascible,** bad-tempered, irritable, excitable; thin-skinned, sensitive; hasty, quick, warm, hot, testy, touchy, huffy, pettish, petulant, fretful, querulous, captious, moody, cross, fractious, peevish.

quarrelsome, contentious, disputatious, pugnacious, cantankerous [*colloq.*], cross-grained; waspish, peppery, fiery, passionate, choleric, shrewish.

901a. SULLENNESS.—*N.* **sullenness,** moroseness, spleen; churlishness, irascibility, moodiness, perversity, obstinacy, crabbedness.

sulks, dudgeon, dumps [*humorous*], doldrums; black looks, scowl; grouch [*slang*], huff.

V. **sulk,** frown, scowl, lower, glower, pout, grouch [*slang*].

Adj. **sullen,** sulky, ill-tempered, ill-humored, ill-disposed; crusty, crabbed, sour, sore, surly, moody, cross, cross-grained; perverse, wayward, refractory, restive, ungovernable, cussed [*vulgar or euphemistic*]; grumpy, glum, grum, grim, morose, grouchy [*slang*].

902. [Expression of affection] ENDEARMENT.—*N.* **endearment,** caress, blandishment, fondling, billing and cooing, dalliance, caressing, embrace, salute, kiss, smack, osculation.

courtship, wooing, suit, addresses, love-making; calf love [*colloq.*]; amorous glances, ogle, side glance, sheep's eyes, goo-goo eyes [*slang*].

flirting, flirtation, gallantry; coquetry, spooning [*slang*].

engagement, betrothal; marriage, etc., 903; honeymoon; love letter, billet-doux; valentine.

flirt, coquette; male flirt, philanderer; spoon [*slang*].

V. **caress,** fondle, pet; smile upon, coax, wheedle, coddle, make much of, cherish, foster.

clasp, hug, cuddle; fold to the heart, press to the bosom, fold in one's arms; snuggle, nestle, nuzzle; embrace, kiss, salute.

court, make love, bill and coo, spoon [*slang*], toy, dally, flirt, coquet, philander, pay court to; serenade; woo.

propose, make (*or* have) an offer, pop the question [*colloq.*]; become engaged, become betrothed; plight one's troth.

Adj. lovesick, spoony [*slang*].

903. MARRIAGE.—*N.* **marriage,** matrimony, wedlock, union, intermarriage; nuptial tie, nuptial knot; match; betrothment.

wedding, nuptials, Hymen, bridal, espousals; leading to the altar; honeymoon.

bridesmaid, maid of honor, matron of honor; attendant, usher, best man, bridesman, groomsman; bride, bridegroom.

married man, partner, spouse, mate, husband, man [*dial.*], consort.

married woman, wife, wedded wife, spouse, helpmeet, helpmate, better half, lady [*obs. or uncultivated*]; squaw; matron.

married couple, man and wife, wedded pair, wedded couple, Darby and Joan.

Kinds of marriage: monogamy, bigamy, polygamy, polyandry; Mormonism; morganatic (*or* left-handed) marriage, *mésalliance* [F.].

matchmaker, matrimonial agency (*or* agent, bureau).

V. **marry,** wive, take to oneself a wife; be married, be spliced [*colloq.*]; wed, espouse, lead to the altar, join, couple, be made one.

Adj. **engaged,** betrothed, plighted, affianced.

Matrimonial, marital, conjugal, connubial, wedded; nuptial, hymeneal, spousal, bridal.

904. CELIBACY.—*N.* **celibacy,** singleness, single blessedness; bachelorhood, bachelorship; misogyny.

virginity, maidenhood, maidenhead.

unmarried man, bachelor, old bachelor; misogamist, misogynist; monk, priest, celibate, religious.

unmarried woman, maid, maiden, virgin, spinster, old maid; nun, sister, vestal, vestal virgin; Diana.

Adj. **unmarried,** unwedded; wifeless, spouseless; single, celibate, virgin.

905. DIVORCE. WIDOWHOOD.—*N.* **divorce,** divorcement; separation, judicial separation, separate maintenance.

widowhood, weeds.

widow, relict, dowager; divorcée; grass widow.

widower; grass widower.

V. **live separate;** separate, divorce, put away.

906. BENEVOLENCE.—*N.* **benevolence,** Christian charity; God's grace; good will, philanthropy, unselfishness, kindness, kindliness, good nature, loving-kindness, benignity, brotherly love, charity, humanity, kindly feelings, fellow feeling, sympathy, goodness of heart, warmheartedness, kindheartedness, amiability, tenderness, love, friendship; tolerance, consideration; mercy.

charitableness, bounty, almsgiving; good works, beneficence, generosity, a good turn.

philanthropist, salt of the earth; good Samaritan, sympathizer, well-wisher, altruist.

V. **bear good will,** wish well, take (*or* feel) an interest in; be interested in, sympathize with, feel for; treat well, give comfort, do good, do a good turn, benefit, assist, render a service, render assistance, aid.

enter into the feelings of others, practice the golden rule, do as you would be done by.

Adj. **benevolent,** kind, kindly, well meaning, amiable, cordial, obliging, accommodating, indulgent, gracious, tender, considerate, warmhearted, kindhearted, tenderhearted, largehearted, softhearted, merciful; sympathizing, sympathetic.

full of natural affection, fatherly, motherly, brotherly, sisterly; paternal, maternal, fraternal; friendly.

charitable, beneficent, philanthropical, generous, humane, benignant, unselfish, altruistic, bountiful.

Adv. with the best intentions; out of deepest sympathy.

907. MALEVOLENCE.—*N.* **malevolence,** bad intent, bad intention, unkindness, uncharitableness, ill-nature, ill-will, enmity, hate, malice, malignance, malignity, maliciousness; spite, resentment; gall, venom, rancor, virulence, hardness of heart, heart of stone, obduracy; evil eye, cloven foot (*or* hoof).

ill-turn, bad turn; affront, indignity; tender mercies (*ironical*).

cruelty, brutality, savagery, ferocity; outrage, atrocity, illusage, persecution; barbarity, inhumanity, truculence, ruffianism; inquisition, torture.

V. **bear malice,** harbor a grudge; hurt, annoy, injure, harm, wrong, outrage, malign; molest, worry, harass, harry, bait, hound, persecute, oppress, grind, maltreat, ill-treat; give no quarter, have no mercy.

Adj. **malevolent,** ill-disposed, ill-intentioned, ill-natured, ill-conditioned, evil-minded, evil-disposed, venomous, malicious, malign, malignant, maleficent; rancorous, spiteful, treacherous, caustic, bitter, envenomed, acrimonious, virulent; grinding, galling, harsh; disobliging, unkind, unfriendly; ungracious, churlish, surly, sullen.

cold-blooded, coldhearted, hardhearted, stonyhearted, cold, unnatural; ruthless, pitiless, relentless.

cruel, brutal, brutish, savage, ferocious, inhuman; barbarous, fell, truculent, bloodthirsty, atrocious, fiendish, diabolic *or* diabolical, devilish, infernal, hellish.

Adv. with bad intent; with the ferocity of a tiger.

908. MALEDICTION.—*N.* **malediction,** malison, curse, imprecation, denunciation, execration; anathema, ban, proscription, excommunication, commination, fulmination; disparagement, vilification, vituperation.

abuse, evil speaking, foul (*or* bad, strong, unparliamentary) language, billingsgate, blackguardism, cursing, profane, swearing, expletive, oath, foul invective, ribaldry, scurrility, invective.

V. **curse,** imprecate, damn, swear at; execrate, vituperate, scold; anathematize, denounce, proscribe, excommunicate, fulminate, thunder against.

909. THREAT.—*N.* threat, menace, defiance, abuse, intimidation, denunciation, fulmination, etc., 908; gathering clouds.

V. threaten, threat, menace; snarl, growl, mutter, bully; defy, intimidate, shake the fist at; thunder, fulminate, bluster.

Adj. threatening, menacing, minatory, abusive; ominous, defiant.

910. PHILANTHROPY.—*N.* philanthropy, altruism, humanity, humanitarianism, benevolence; public welfare.

public spirit, patriotism, nationality, love of country.

philanthropist, altruist, etc., 906; humanitarian, patriot.

Adj. philanthropic, altruistic, humanitarian, public-spirited, patriotic; humane, largehearted, benevolent, etc., 906; generous, liberal, etc., 942.

911. MISANTHROPY.—*N.* misanthropy, hatred of mankind; selfishness, egoism, egotism; sullenness, moroseness, cynicism; want of patriotism.

misanthrope, misanthropist, egoist, egotist, cynic, man hater.

woman hater, misogynist.

Adj. misanthropic, antisocial, unpatriotic; egoistical, egotistical, selfish; morose, sullen, cynical, etc., 901a.

912. BENEFACTOR.—*N.* benefactor, savior, protector, good genius, tutelary saint, guardian angel, good Samaritan; friend in need; salt of the earth; philanthropist, etc., 910; fairy godmother.

913. [Maleficent being] EVILDOER.—*N.* evildoer, evil worker, wrongdoer, etc., 949; mischiefmaker, marplot; oppressor, tyrant; incendiary, etc., 384; anarchist, nihilist, destroyer, vandal, iconoclast, terrorist.

savage, brute, ruffian, barbarian, desperado; apache, gunman, hoodlum [*colloq.*], redskin, tough [*colloq.*], bully, rough, hooligan [*slang*], dangerous classes; thief, etc., 792; cutthroat.

wild beast, tiger, leopard, panther, hyena, catamount [U. S.], catamountain, lynx, cougar, jaguar, puma; bloodhound, hellhound, sleuthhound; gorilla; vulture.

cockatrice, adder, snake, serpent, cobra, asp, viper, rattlesnake, boa; alligator, crocodile, octopus.

hag, hellhag, beldam, Jezebel.

monster, fiend, demon, etc., 980; devil incarnate, Frankenstein's monster; cannibal; bloodsucker, vampire, ogre, ghoul.

914. PITY.—*N.* pity, compassion, commiseration, sympathy, fellow feeling, tenderness, softheartedness, yearning forbearance, humanity, mercy, clemency; leniency, lenity, charity, ruth, longsuffering; quarter, grace.

sympathizer; advocate, friend, partisan, patron, well-wisher, defender, champion.

V. **pity,** have (*or* take) pity, commiserate, condole, sympathize, feel for, be sorry for.

forbear, relent, relax, give quarter.

excite pity, touch, soften, melt, melt the heart; propitiate,

Adj. **pitying,** pitiful, compassionate, sympathetic, touched.

merciful, clement, humane, humanitarian; tender, tender-hearted, softhearted, lenient, forbearing.

914a. PITILESSNESS.—*N.* **pitilessness,** inclemency, inexorability, inflexibility, hardness of heart; want of pity, severity, malevolence, etc., 907.

V. **be pitiless,** turn a deaf ear to; claim one's pound of flesh; have no mercy, give no quarter.

Adj. **pitiless,** merciless, ruthless, unpitying, unmerciful, inclement, grim-faced, grim-visaged; inflexible, relentless, inexorable, harsh, cruel, etc., 907.

915. CONDOLENCE.—*N.* **condolence,** sympathy, consolation; lamentation, etc., 839.

V. **condole with,** console, sympathize, express pity; afford consolation; lament with, express sympathy for, feel for, send one's condolences; share one's sorrow.

916. GRATITUDE.—*N.* **gratitude,** gratefulness, thankfulness; sense of obligation; acknowledgment, recognition, thanksgiving, giving thanks.

thanks, praise, benediction; paean; *Te Deum* [L.], grace, requital, thank offering.

V. **be grateful,** thank; give (*or* render, return, offer, tender) thanks, acknowledge, requite; lie under an obligation; never forget, overflow with gratitude.

Adj. **grateful,** thankful, obliged, beholden, indebted to, under obligation.

917. INGRATITUDE.—*N.* **ingratitude,** thanklessness, unthankfulness; thankless task, thankless office.

V. **be ungrateful,** feel no obligation, owe one no thanks, forget benefits, have a short memory for.

Adj. **ungrateful,** unmindful, unthankful; thankless, ingrate.

forgotten; unacknowledged, unthanked, unrequited, unrewarded; ill-requited; ill-rewarded.

918. FORGIVENESS.—*N.* **forgiveness,** pardon, grace, remission, absolution, amnesty, oblivion; reprieve.

conciliation; reconciliation, forbearance, propitiation.

exoneration, excuse, quittance, release, indemnity; acquittal, exculpation.

V. **forgive,** pardon, think no more of, let bygones by bygones, bury the hatchet. start afresh.

remit, exculpate, exonerate, absolve, give absolution; blot out one's sins (*or* offenses, transgressions), wipe the slate clean; reprieve, acquit.

excuse, pass over, overlook; condone, wink at; bear with, allow for, make allowances for; pocket the affront.

conciliate, propitiate, placate; beg (*or* ask) pardon, make up a quarrel.

Adj. forgiving, placable, conciliatory.

919. REVENGE.—*N.* revenge, vengeance; vendetta, death feud, eye for an eye, tooth for a tooth, retaliation; day of reckoning.

rancor, vindictiveness, implacability, ruthlessness; malevolence, etc., 907.

avenger, nemesis, Eumenides.

V. revenge, avenge, take revenge, have one's revenge; breathe vengeance; give no quarter, take no prisoners.

keep the wound open, harbor revenge, bear malice; rankle, rankle in the breast.

Adj. **revengeful,** vengeful, vindictive, rancorous; pitiless, ruthless, rigorous, avenging, retaliative; unforgiving, unrelenting; inexorable, implacable, relentless, remorseless.

920. JEALOUSY.—*N.* jealousy, distrust, mistrust, heartburn; envy, etc., 921; doubt, suspicion; green-eyed monster.

V. **be jealous,** view with jealousy, grudge, begrudge.

doubt, distrust, mistrust, suspect, misdoubt.

Adj. **jealous,** jaundice, yellow-eyed, envious.

921. ENVY.—*N.* envy, enviousness; rivalry; ill-will, spite; jealousy, etc., 920.

V. **envy,** covet, grudge, begrudge, break the tenth commandment.

Adj. **envious,** invidious, covetous, grudging, begrudged; belittling.

IV. MORAL AFFECTIONS

922. RIGHT.—*N.* right; what ought to be, what should be; fitness.

justice, equity, equitableness, propriety, fairness, fair play, square deal [*colloq.*], impartiality; lawfulness, legality.

morals, etc. (*duty*), 926; law, etc., 963; honor, etc., 939; virtue, etc., 944.

V. **be right,** stand to reason.

do right, see justice done, see fair play; do justice to, recompense, hold the scales even, give everyone his due.

Adj. **right**, good; just, reasonable; fit, etc., 924; equal, equable, equitable; even-handed, fair, square.

legitimate, justifiable, rightful, as it ought to be; lawful, legal.

Adv. in justice, in equity, in reason; upon even terms.

923. WRONG.—*N.* **wrong**, iniquity; what ought not to be, what should not be; unreasonableness, grievance; shame.

injustice, unfairness, foul play, partiality, leaning, favor, favoritism, partisanship; undueness, unlawfulness, illegality.

dishonor, etc., 939; vice, etc., 945.

V. **do wrong**, be inequitable, show partiality, favor, lean toward; encroach; impose upon; reap where one has not sown.

Adj. **wrong**, wrongful, iniquitous, bad, unjust, unfair, inequitable, unequal, partial, one-sided; injurious.

unjustifiable, unreasonable, unwarrantable, objectionable, improper, unfit, unjustified; unlawful; illegal, immoral.

924. AUTHORIZATION.—*N.* **authorization**, sanction, authority, charter, warrant; constitution; bond.

right, dueness, due, privilege, prerogative, prescription, title, claim, pretension, legality, demand, birthright.

immunity, license, liberty, franchise; vested interest (*or* right).

deserts, merits, dues.

claimant, appellant; plaintiff, etc., 938.

V. **deserve**, merit, be worthy of, make good.

demand, claim, lay claim to, reclaim, exact; insist on (*or* upon), make a point of, require, assert, assume, arrogate.

entitle, give (*or* confer) a right, authorize, sanction, legalize, ordain, prescribe, allot.

Adj. **privileged**, allowed, sanctioned, warranted, authorized; ordained, prescribed, constitutional, chartered, enfranchised.

prescriptive, presumptive, absolute, inalienable, inviolable, sacrosanct.

merited, due to, deserved, condign [*archaic, except of punishment*].

right, creditable, fit, fitting, correct, square, due, proper, meet, befitting, becoming, seemly; decorous.

lawful, legitimate, legal, legalized, allowable.

Adv. by right, by divine right; on the square [*colloq.*].

925. [Want of authorization] IMPROPRIETY.—*N.* **impropriety**, undueness, unrightfulness, illegality, unlawfulness; falseness, invalidity of title; illegitimacy.

loss of right, disfranchisement, forfeiture.

assumption, usurpation, tort [*law*], violation, breach, encroachment, seizure, exaction, imposition.

usurper, pretender, impostor.

V. **infringe,** encroach, trench on, exact, arrogate, usurp, violate; get under false pretenses, sail under false colors.

disentitle, disfranchise, disqualify; invalidate.

Adj. **undue,** unlawful, illegal, illicit, unconstitutional, unauthorized, unwarranted, unsanctioned, unjustified; disqualified, unqualified; unprivileged, unchartered.

undeserved, unmerited, unearned.

illegitimate, bastard, spurious, false; usurped.

improper, unfit, unbefitting, unseemly, unbecoming, misbecoming; preposterous, pretentious, would-be.

926. DUTY.—*N.* **duty,** moral obligation, accountability, liability, onus, responsibility.

allegiance, fealty, tie; engagement; function, part, calling.

observance, fulfillment, discharge, performance, acquittal, satisfaction, redemption; good behavior.

morality, morals, decalogue; conscientiousness, conscience, inward monitor, still small voice within, sense of duty.

propriety, fitness, seemliness, decorum, the thing, the proper thing.

Science of morals: ethics, moral (*or* ethical) philosophy, casuistry, polity.

V. **behoove,** become, befit, beseem; belong to, pertain to; rest with, fall to one's lot, devolve on.

take upon oneself, be (*or* become) sponsor for, incur a responsibility; perform (*or* discharge) a duty *or* an obligation; act one's part, redeem one's pledge, be at one's post, do one's duty.

impose a duty, enjoin, require, exact; bind, bind over; saddle with, prescribe, assign, call upon, look to, oblige.

Adj. **obligatory,** binding, imperative, peremptory, stringent, incumbent on.

amenable, liable, accountable, responsible, answerable.

right, meet, etc. (*due*), 924; moral, ethical, conscientious.

Adv. with a safe conscience, as in duty bound, on one's own responsibility, at one's own risk.

927. DERELICTION OF DUTY.—*N.* **dereliction,** nonobservance, nonperformance, nonco-operation; indolence, neglect, infraction, violation, transgression, failure, evasion; fault, etc. (*guilt*), 947.

slacker, loafer, time killer; eyeserver, eyeservant; striker; nonco-operator.

V. **violate,** break, break through; infringe, set aside, set at naught; encroach upon, trench upon, trample on; slight, get by [*slang*], neglect, evade, escape, transgress, fail.

927a. EXEMPTION.—*N.* **exemption,** freedom, irresponsibility, immunity, liberty, license, release, discharge, excuse, dispensation, absolution, exculpation, exoneration.

V. **exempt**, release, acquit, discharge, remit; free, set at liberty, let off [*colloq.*], pass over, spare, excuse, dispense with, license; absolve, exonerate.

Adj. **exempt**, free, immune, at liberty, scot-free, released, unbound; irresponsible, not accountable, excusable.

928. RESPECT.—*N.* **respect**, regard, consideration, courtesy, attention, deference, reverence, honor, esteem, estimation, veneration, admiration; approbation, etc., 931.

homage, fealty, obeisance, genuflection, kneeling, prostration; salaam, etc., 894.

V. **respect**, regard; revere, reverence, honor, venerate, hallow; esteem, think much of, entertain respect for, look up to, defer to, pay attention to, pay respect to, do honor to; do the honors, hail, show courtesy, pay homage to.

command respect, inspire respect; awe, impose, overawe, dazzle.

Adj. **respectful**, deferential, decorous, reverential, ceremonious, bareheaded, cap in hand; prostrate.

respected, estimable; time-honored, venerable.

Adv. **in deference to**; with all respect, with due respect, with the highest respect; with submission.

929. DISRESPECT.—*N.* **disrespect**, disfavor, disrepute, want of esteem, low estimation, disparagement, detraction; irreverence, slight, indignity, contumely, affront, dishonor, insult, outrage, discourtesy, scoffing; hiss, hissing, hoot, derision; mockery.

gibe, flout, jeer, scoff, taunt, sneer, fling.

V. **slight**, disregard, undervalue, humiliate, depreciate, trifle with, pass by, push aside, overlook, be discourteous.

disparage, call names; throw mud at; point at, indulge in personalities.

dishonor, desecrate; insult, affront, browbeat, outrage.

deride, scoff, sneer, laugh at, ridicule, gibe, mock, jeer, taunt, twit, flout, roast [*colloq.*], guy [*colloq.*], rag [*dial. Eng.* and *college slang*], burlesque, scout, hiss, hoot.

Adj. **disrespectful**, disparaging, etc., 934; insulting, supercilious, rude, derisive, sarcastic, scurrilous, contemptuous, insolent, disdainful; irreverent.

unrespected, unregarded, disregarded, unenvied, unsaluted.

930. CONTEMPT.—*N.* **contempt**, disdain, scorn, contemptuousness, derision, etc. (*disrespect*), 929; contumely; slight, sneer, spurn, byword.

V. **despise**, contemn, scorn, disdain, disregard, scout, slight, pass by, look down upon, sneer at, laugh at, curl up one's lip, think nothing of, make light of, underestimate, esteem slightly, care nothing for, set no store by; pooh-pooh, damn with faint praise.

spurn, turn one's back upon, trample underfoot; kick; fling to the winds, repudiate.

Adj. **contemptuous,** disdainful, scornful, withering, supercilious, cynical, haughty, cavalier; derisive; with the nose in air.

contemptible, despicable, despised, pitiable, pitiful, downtrodden.

931. APPROBATION.—*N.* **approbation,** approval, sanction, advocacy; esteem, estimation, good opinion, admiration; love, etc., 897; appreciation, regard, account, popularity, credit, repute.

commendation, compliment, praise, laud, laudation; good word; encomium, eulogy, eulogium, panegyric, blurb [*slang*]; benediction, blessing, benison.

applause, plaudit, clap, clapping, acclaim, acclamation; cheer; paean, shout (*or* peal, chorus, thunders) of applause.

V. **approve,** esteem, value, prize, set great store by; honor, hold in esteem, look up to, admire, like, appreciate; stand up for, stick up for [*colloq.*], uphold, countenance, sanction, indorse, recommend.

commend, praise, laud, compliment, applaud, clap, cheer, acclaim, encore; eulogize, boost [*colloq.*], root for [*slang*], cry up, puff; extol, magnify, glorify, exalt, sing the praises of.

Adj. **commendatory,** complimentary, laudatory, panegyrical, eulogistic, lavish of praise, uncritical.

approved, praised, popular, in good odor; in high esteem, in favor, in high favor.

praiseworthy, commendable, worthy of praise, good, meritorious, estimable, creditable, unimpeachable.

Adv. with credit, to admiration.

932. DISAPPROBATION.—*N.* **disapprobation,** disapproval, disesteem, odium, dislike, black list, blackball, ostracism, boycott.

disparagement, depreciation, dispraise, detraction, etc., 934; denunciation, condemnation, stricture, objection, exception, criticism; blame, censure, obloquy, sarcasm, satire, insinuation, innuendo, sneer, taunt.

reproof, reprehension, remonstrance, expostulation, reprobation, admonition, reproach; rebuke, reprimand, lecture, curtain lecture; wigging, dressing down [*both colloq.*]; rating, scolding, correction, rebuff, home thrust, hit; frown, scowl, black look.

abuse, personalities, personal remarks, vituperation, invective, contumely, hard words; bad language.

diatribe, tirade, philippic.

clamor, outcry, hue and cry; hiss, hissing, catcall; execration.

V. **disapprove,** dislike, object to, take exception to, think ill of, view with disfavor, frown upon, look askance, look black upon, set one's face against.

blame, censure, reproach, reprobate, impugn, impeach, accuse, denounce, expose, brand, gibbet, stigmatize; show up [*colloq.*].

reprove, reprehend, chide, admonish, berate, take to task, overhaul, lecture, rebuke, blow up [*colloq.*], correct, reprimand, snub; chastise, castigate, lash, trounce.

remonstrate, expostulate, recriminate.

abuse, scold, rate, upbraid, fall foul of; jaw [*low*], rail, rail at, call names, execrate, revile, vilify.

decry, cry down, run down, backbite; insinuate, damn with faint praise; hiss, hoot, catcall, mob; ostracize, blacklist, boycott, blackball.

disparage, depreciate, knock [*colloq.*], dispraise, deprecate, speak ill of, condemn, scoff at, sneer at, satirize, lampoon, defame, criticize.

incur blame, scandalize, shock, revolt; get a bad name, forfeit one's good opinion, be under a cloud.

Adj. **disparaging,** condemnatory, denunciatory, reproachful, abusive, vituperative, defamatory.

critical, satirical, sarcastic, sardonic, cynical, dry, sharp, cutting, biting, severe, withering, trenchant, censorious, captious, hypercritical.

blameworthy, reprehensible, blamable, answerable, bad; vicious, etc., 945.

Adv. with a wry face.

933. FLATTERY.—*N.* **flattery,** adulation, cajolery, fawning, wheedling, obsequiousness, sycophancy, flunkeyism, toadyism.

honeyed words, flummery, buncombe [*cant or slang*]; blarney, soft soap [*both colloq.*].

V. **flatter,** overpraise, puff, wheedle, cajole, fawn upon, humor, pet, coquet, butter [*colloq.*], jolly [*slang or colloq.*]; truckle to, pander to, court, curry favor with.

Adj. **flattering,** adulatory; mealy-mouthed, honeyed, smooth, smooth-tongued; oily, unctuous, specious, plausible, servile, sycophantic, fulsome.

934. DETRACTION.—*N.* **detraction,** disparagement, depreciation, vilification, obloquy, scandal, defamation, slander, calumny, evil-speaking, backbiting; sarcasm, cynicism, criticism; invective.

personality, libel, lampoon, skit, squib.

V. **detract,** derogate, decry, depreciate, disparage, run down, cry down, belittle, criticize, pull to pieces, asperse, bespatter, blacken, vilify, brand, malign, backbite, libel, lampoon, traduce, slander, defame, calumniate.

Adj. detracting, defamatory, detractory, derogatory, disparaging, libelous; scurrilous, abusive, foul-mouthed; slanderous, calumnious.

935. FLATTERER.—*N.* **flatterer,** adulator, eulogist, euphemist; optimist; puffer, booster [*colloq.*], whitewasher.

toady, sycophant, parasite, hanger-on; courtier.

936. DETRACTOR.—*N.* **detractor,** censor, censurer; cynic, critic, caviler, carper.

defamer, knocker [*colloq.*], backbiter, slanderer, lampooner, satirist, traducer, libeler, calumniator, reviler, vituperator.

Adj. defamatory, etc., 934.

937. VINDICATION.—*N.* **vindication,** justification, warrant; exoneration, exculpation, acquittal; whitewashing, extenuation, palliation, softening, mitigation.

plea, apology, gloss, varnish; excuse, extenuating circumstances; allowance; reply, defense; recrimination.

apologist, vindicator, justifier; defendant, etc., 938.

V. justify, warrant, lend a color, vindicate, exculpate, acquit, clear, exonerate, whitewash.

extenuate, palliate, excuse, soften, apologize.

advocate, defend, plead one's cause; contend for, speak for; bear out, make good; support, plead, say in defense.

Adj. vindicative, vindicatory, vindicating, palliative, extenuating, exculpatory, apologetic.

excusable, defensible, pardonable; venial, plausible, justifiable.

938. ACCUSATION.—*N.* **accusation,** charge, imputation, slur, incrimination, recrimination, denunciation.

libel, challenge, citation, arraignment, impeachment, indictment, true bill, lawsuit, condemnation.

accuser, prosecutor, plaintiff, complainant, libelant, informant, informer.

accused, defendant, prisoner, respondent, litigant.

V. accuse, charge, tax, impute, twit, taunt with, reproach, stigmatize, slur; incriminate, inculpate, implicate.

inform against, indict, denounce, arraign; charge with, saddle with; impeach, show up [*colloq.*], challenge, cite, prosecute; blow upon [*colloq.*], squeal [*slang*].

Adj. accusatory, denunciatory, recriminatory.

inexcusable, indefensible, unpardonable, unjustifiable.

939. PROBITY.—*N.* **probity,** integrity, rectitude, uprightness, respectability, honesty, faith, honor, good faith; constancy, faithfulness, fidelity, loyalty, trustworthiness, truth, veracity, candor, singleness of heart.

fairness, fair play, justice, equity, impartiality, principle.

punctiliousness, punctilio, delicacy, scrupulosity, scrupulousness, scruple; point of honor.

man of honor, man of his word, gentleman, trump [*slang*], brick [*slang or colloq.*].

V. **be honorable,** speak the truth, draw a straight furrow, make a point of; do one's duty, play the game [*colloq.*]; redeem one's pledge, keep one's promise (*or* word), keep faith with.

Adj. **upright,** honest, veracious, truthful, virtuous, noble, honorable, reputable, respectable; fair, right, just, equitable, impartial, square, white [*slang*].

manly, straightforward, frank, candid, openhearted.

loyal, constant, faithful, stanch; true; trusty, trustworthy; incorruptible.

conscientious, right-minded, high-principled, high-minded, scrupulous, religious, strict; nice, punctilious.

stainless, unstained, unsullied, inviolate, untainted, incorrupt, innocent, pure, undefiled, undepraved.

chivalrous, jealous of honor, high-spirited.

Adv. on the square [*colloq.*], in good faith, in all honor, by fair means, with clean hands.

940. IMPROBITY.—*N.* **improbity,** dishonesty, dishonor, disgrace; fraud, lying; bad faith, infidelity, faithlessness; Judas kiss, betrayal, perfidy, treachery, double-dealing; villainy, baseness, degradation, turpitude, moral turpitude.

breach of trust (*or* faith), disloyalty, divided allegiance, hyphenated allegiance [*cant*], treason, high treason; apostasy.

knavery, roguery, rascality, foul play; jobbing, jobbery, graft [*colloq.*], venality, corruption, sharp practice.

V. **play false;** break one's word (*or* promise), jilt, betray, forswear; grovel, sneak, lose caste; sell oneself, squeal [*slang*], go back on [*colloq.*].

Adj. **dishonest,** dishonorable; unconscientious, unscrupulous; fraudulent, knavish, falsehearted; unfair, one-sided; double, double-tongued, double-faced; timeserving, crooked, slippery; fishy [*colloq.*], questionable.

infamous, arrant, foul, base, vile, low, ignominious, perfidious, treacherous, perjured; contemptible, abject, mean, shabby, paltry, dirty, sneaking, groveling, rascally, corrupt, venal.

derogatory, degrading, undignified, unbefitting, ungentlemanly, unchivalric, unmanly, recreant, inglorious.

faithless, false, unfaithful, disloyal; untrustworthy; trustless, lost to shame, dead to honor.

Adv. like a thief in the night, by crooked paths, by foul means.

941. KNAVE.—*N.* knave, rogue, villain, rascal, etc., 949; shyster.

traitor, betrayer, archtraitor, conspirator, Judas; reptile, serpent, snake in the grass, wolf in sheep's clothing, sneak, squealer [*slang*], telltale, mischiefmaker; renegade, recreant, slacker.

942. DISINTERESTEDNESS.—*N.* disinterestedness, unselfishness, generosity; liberality, altruism, benevolence, loftiness of purpose, exaltation, magnanimity; honor, chivalry, heroism, sublimity.

self-denial, self-control, stoicism, self-abnegation, self-sacrifice, devotion, self-devotion; labor of love.

Adj. disinterested, unselfish, self-denying, self-sacrificing, altruistic.

magnanimous, high-minded; princely, great, high, elevated, lofty, exalted, greathearted, largehearted; generous, liberal; chivalrous, heroic, sublime.

943. SELFISHNESS.—*N.* selfishness, self-love, self-indulgence, self-worship, self-seeking, self-interest; egotism, egoism; illiberality, meanness.

self-seeker, timeserver, fortune hunter, monopolist, dog in the manger, trimmer; hog, roadhog [*colloq.*].

V. be selfish, feather one's nest; have an eye to the main chance, live for oneself alone.

Adj. selfish, self-seeking, self-indulgent, self-interested; self-centered; egotistic, egoistic.

illiberal, mean, ungenerous, narrow-minded; mercenary, venal; covetous.

worldly, unspiritual, earthly, earthly-minded, mundane, worldly-minded, worldly-wise; timeserving, interested.

Adv. from selfish motives.

944. VIRTUE.—*N.* virtue, morality, moral rectitude; integrity, probity, nobleness, well-doing, good actions, good behavior, well-spent life, innocence.

merit, worth, desert, excellence, credit; self-control, self-denial. morals; ethics, duty, etc., 926; cardinal virtues.

V. be virtuous, practice virtue, do one's duty, fight the good fight; acquit oneself well, keep in the right path.

Adj. virtuous, good, innocent, meritorious, deserving, worthy, dutiful, duteous; moral, right, righteous, right-minded; creditable, laudable, commendable, praiseworthy; sterling, pure, noble; whole-souled.

exemplary; matchless, peerless; saintly, saintlike; angelic, god-like.

945. VICE.—*N.* vice, evildoing, wrongdoing, wickedness, viciousness, iniquity, sin, immorality, want of principle, knavery, obliquity, backsliding, infamy, brutality.

depravity, demoralization, corruption, profligacy, flagrancy.

weakness, infirmity, frailty, imperfection, error; foible; failing, failure; besetting sin; defect, defection.

fault, crime; guilt, etc., 947.

reprobate; sinner, etc., 949.

V. be vicious, sin, commit sin, err, transgress; misconduct oneself, misbehave; fall, lapse, slip, trip, offend, trespass, go astray; sow one's wild oats.

demoralize, brutalize; corrupt, degrade, etc., 659.

Adj.[1] vicious, sinful; wicked, iniquitous, immoral, unrighteous, wrong, criminal; unprincipled, lawless, disorderly, disgraceful, recreant, disreputable; demoralized, corrupt, depraved, degenerate; evil-minded, heartless, graceless, shameless, abandoned.

base, sinister, foul, gross, vile, black, felonious, nefarious, shameful, scandalous, infamous, villainous, heinous; flagrant, atrocious.

diabolic *or* diabolical, devilish, fiendish, fiendlike, demoniacal, Mephistophelian, satanic, hellish, infernal, hellborn.

incorrigible, irreclaimable, obdurate, reprobate, reprehensible.

unjustifiable, indefensible, inexcusable, inexpiable, unpardonable.

improper, unseemly, indecorous, indiscreet, unworthy, blameworthy, discreditable; incorrect, undutiful, naughty.

weak, frail, lax, infirm, imperfect; spineless, invertebrate [*both fig.*].

946. INNOCENCE.—*N.* innocence; guiltlessness, incorruption, impeccability; clean hands, clear conscience.

innocent, newborn babe; lamb, dove.

Adj. innocent, not guilty, unguilty; guiltless, faultless, sinless, stainless, spotless, clear, immaculate, unerring, undefiled, inculpable, blameless, above suspicion, irreproachable, unimpeachable; virtuous, etc., 944.

harmless, inoffensive, innocuous, pure.

Adv. with clean hands; with a clear conscience.

947. GUILT.—*N.* guilt, guiltiness, culpability, criminality; vice, sinfulness, misconduct, misbehavior, misdeed; fault, sin, error, transgression; dereliction, delinquency.

indiscretion, lapse, slip, trip, flaw, blot, omission, failing, failure, blunder, break [*colloq.*].

---

[1]Most of these adjectives are applicable both to the act and to the agent.

offense, trespass: misdemeanor, malefaction, malversation, corruption, malpractice; crime, felony, capital crime.

enormity, atrocity, outrage; deadly sin, mortal sin.

Adj. guilty, blamable, culpable, reprehensible, blameworthy.

Adv. in the very act, red-handed.

948. GOOD MAN. GOOD WOMAN.—*N.* good man, worthy, model, paragon, pattern, good example; hero, demigod, angel, saint; benefactor, etc., 912; philanthropist, etc., 910.

salt of the earth; one in ten thousand; a man among men, white man [*slang*].

good woman, virgin, innocent; goddess, queen, Madonna, ministering angel, heaven's noblest gift.

949. BAD MAN. BAD WOMAN.—*N.* bad man, wrongdoer, worker of iniquity; evildoer, etc., 913; sinner, transgressor; bad example.

rascal, scoundrel, villain, knave, etc., 941; miscreant, wretch, reptile, viper, serpent, monster, devil, demon, devil incarnate, fallen angel, lost sheep, black sheep, castaway, prodigal.

bad woman, jade, Jezebel, hellcat.

ruffian, rowdy, bully, etc., 887; thief, murderer.

culprit, delinquent, criminal, malefactor, felon, convict, outlaw.

riffraff, scum of the earth; blackguard, loafer, sneak, vagabond.

scamp, scapegrace, ne'er-do-well, good for nothing, reprobate, scalawag [*colloq.*], limb [*colloq.*], rapscallion [*all the words in this paragraph are commonly applied jocularly or lightly*].

950. PENITENCE.—*N.* penitence, contrition, compunction, repentance, remorse, regret, self-reproach, self-reproof, self-accusation, self-condemnation, qualms of conscience.

acknowledgment, confession, apology, recantation; penance.

penitent, Magdalen, prodigal son, returned prodigal.

V. repent, be sorry for, rue, regret, think better of, recant; plead guilty, acknowledge, confess, humble oneself, beg pardon, apologize; turn over a new leaf.

reclaim, reform, regenerate, redeem, convert, amend, make a new man of, restore self-respect.

Adj. penitent, repentant, contrite, softened, melted, touched, conscience-stricken; self-accusing, self-convicted.

951. IMPENITENCE.—*N.* impenitence, irrepentance, recusancy, hardness of heart, heart of stone, seared conscience, obduracy.

V. be impenitent, steel the heart, harden the heart; die and make no sign.

Adj. impenitent, obdurate, hard, hardened, seared, recusant, unrepentant; relentless, remorseless, graceless.

lost, incorrigible, irreclaimable; unreclaimed, unreformed.

952. ATONEMENT.—*N.* atonement, reparation, compromise, composition, compensation, quittance, expiation, redemption, reclamation, conciliation, propitiation; indemnification, redress, amends, apology, satisfaction; sacrifice.

penance, fasting, sackcloth and ashes, shrift, purgation, purgatory.

V. atone, atone for, expiate, propitiate, make amends; reclaim, redeem, repair, ransom, absolve, purge, shrive, do penance, pay the penalty.

apologize, express regret, beg pardon, give satisfaction.

Adj. propitiatory, expiatory, sacrifice, sacrificial.

953. [Moral Practice] TEMPERANCE.—*N.* temperance, moderation, frugality, sobriety, soberness, forbearance, abnegation; self-denial, self-restraint, self-control.

abstinence, abstemiousness, asceticism; vegetarianism, prohibition, teetotalism, total abstinence.

abstainer; teetotaler, etc., 958; vegetarian, fruitarian; ascetic.

V. be temperate, abstain, forbear, refrain, deny oneself, spare.

Adj. temperate, moderate, sober, frugal, sparing, abstemious.

954. INTEMPERANCE.—*N.* intemperance, sensuality, animalism, pleasure, luxury, luxuriousness, freeliving, indulgence, high living, dissipation, self-indulgence; voluptuousness, debauchery.

revel, revels, revelry, orgy; drunkenness, debauch, carousal, drinking bout, saturnalia.

V. be intemperate, indulge, exceed; live high (*or* on the fat of the land), dine not wisely but too well; plunge into dissipation, revel, carouse, run riot, sow one's wild oats.

Adj. intemperate, excessive; sensual, self-indulgent, voluptuous, wild, dissipated, dissolute, fast.

brutish, swinish, piggish, hoggish, beastlike, beastly.

luxurious, epicurean, sybaritical; nursed in the lap of luxury; indulged, pampered; full fed, high fed.

intoxicated, drunk, etc., 959.

954a. SENSUALIST.—*N.* sensualist, sybarite, voluptuary, man of pleasure, epicure, epicurean, gourmet; gourmand, glutton, pig, hog; free liver, hard liver.

955. ASCETICISM.—*N.* asceticism, puritanism, austerity; total abstinence; mortification, sackcloth and ashes, penance, fasting; martyrdom.

ascetic, anchorite, hermit, recluse; puritan, yogi [Hindu]; dervish, fakir [both Moham.]; martyr.

Adj. ascetic, austere, puritanical.

956. FASTING.—*N.* **fasting,** famishment, starvation.

fast, fast day, Lent, spare (*or* meager) diet, lenten diet, Barme-cide feast; short rations.

V. **fast,** starve, famish, perish with hunger.

Adj. **fasting,** lenten, unfed; starved, half-starved, hungry.

957. GLUTTONY.—*N.* **gluttony;** greed, greediness, voracity; epicurism, gastronomy; high living; guzzling.

feast, banquet, good cheer, blow out [*slang*].

glutton, gormandizer, cormorant, hog, etc. (*sensualist*), 954a.

epicure, *bon vivant* [F.], gourmand [*obs. as* glutton], gourmet.

V. **gormandize,** gorge; overeat, glut, satiate, indulge, eat one's fill, cram, stuff, guzzle, bolt, devour, gobble up, gulp, raven, eat out of house and home.

Adj. **gluttonous,** greedy, gormandizing, omnivorous, voracious, devouring, overfed, gorged.

958. SOBRIETY.—*N.* **sobriety;** total abstinence, teetotalism.

water drinker; prohibitionist, dry [*slang*], teetotaler, total ab-stainer.

V. take the pledge; abstain, etc., 953.

Adj. **sober,** temperate, moderate, abstemious.

959. DRUNKENNESS.—*N.* **drunkenness,** intemperance, drink-ing, inebriety, inebriation, intoxication, winebibbing; baccha-nalia; libations.

alcoholism, dipsomania; delirium tremens, d.t.'s [*colloq.*].

drink, alcoholic drinks, alcohol, blue ruin [*slang*], booze [*colloq.*]; grog, punch; punchbowl, cup, rosy wine, flowing bowl; liquor, dram, beverage, beer, etc.; cocktail, highball, peg [*slang, orig.* India]; stirrup cup, parting cup.

illicit distilling; bootlegging [*slang*], moonshining, moonshine *or* moonshine whisky [*colloq.*], hooch [*slang*], home-brew; moon-shiner [*colloq.*]; bootlegger [*slang*].

drunkard, sot, toper, tippler, winebibber, hard drinker, soaker [*slang*], sponge [*slang*], boozer [*colloq.*], bum [*slang*]; reveler, carouser; dipsomaniac.

V. **get** (*or* **be**) **drunk,** see double; take a drop (*or* glass) too much; drink, tipple, booze [*colloq.*], soak [*slang*], have a jag on [*slang*], carouse; drink hard (*or* deep, like a fish).

liquor, liquor up [*both slang*], wet one's whistle [*colloq. or humor-ous*]; raise the elbow, hit the booze [*slang*], crack a bottle.

inebriate, fuddle [*colloq.*], befuddle.

sell illicitly, bootleg [*slang*].

Adj. **drunk,** tipsy, intoxicated, inebriate, inebriated; in a state of intoxication, overcome, fuddled [*colloq.*], boozy [*colloq.*], full [*vulgar*], lit up [*slang*], elevated [*colloq.*]; groggy [*colloq.*]; screwed, tight, primed [*all slang*], muddled, maudlin; blind drunk, dead drunk.

960. PURITY.—*N.* purity; decency, decorum, delicacy; continence, chastity, virtue, modesty; virginity.

virgin, vestal, prude; Diana.

Adj. pure, undefiled, modest, delicate, clean, decent, decorous; chaste, continent, virtuous, honest.

961. IMPURITY.—*N.* impurity, uncleanness; immodesty; grossness; indelicacy, indecency, obscenity; dissipation.

Adj. impure, unclean; immodest, shameless, indelicate, indecent, coarse, gross.

962. LIBERTINE.—*N.* libertine, voluptuary, rake, roué [F.], fast man.

5. Institutions

963. LEGALITY.—*N.* legality, legitimacy, legitimateness; legitimization.

law, code, constitution, charter, act, enactment, statute, rule, canon, ordinance, institution, regulation, bylaw, decree, standing order.

equity, common law; unwritten law; law of nations, international law; constitutionality; justice, etc., 922; jurisprudence; legislation.

V. legalize, legitimize; enact, ordain, decree, authorize, pass a law, legislate; codify, formulate, regulate.

Adj. legal, legitimate; according to law; vested, constitutional, chartered, legalized, lawful, statutory; legislative; judicial, juridical.

Adv. in the eye of the law.

964. [Absence or violation of law] ILLEGALITY.—*N.* lawlessness, illicitness; breach (*or* violation) of law; disobedience, violence, brute force, despotism, tyranny, outlawry; mob (*or* lynch) law.

illegality, informality, unlawfulness, illegitimacy; smuggling.

V. violate the law, set the law at defiance, make the law a dead letter, take the law into one's own hands.

smuggle, run, poach, bootleg [*slang*].

Adj. illegal, prohibited, unlawful, illegitimate, illicit, contraband, actionable.

unchartered, unconstitutional, lawless, unwarranted, unauthorized; unofficial.

arbitrary, despotic, summary, irresponsible.

Adv. with a high hand, in violation of law.

965. JURISDICTION. [Executive]—*N.* jurisdiction, judicature, administration of justice; judge, etc., 967; tribunal, etc., 966.

city government, municipal government, commission government, Oregon plan [U. S.]; municipality, corporation; police, police force, constabulary.

executive, officer, commissioner, lord lieutenant [Brit.], city manager, mayor, alderman, councilor, selectman; bailiff, beadle; sheriff, constable, policeman, police constable, police sergeant, patrolman, gendarme [F.].

bureau, department, portfolio, secretariat.

V. **judge,** adjudge, adjudicate, sit in judgment; have jurisdiction over.

Adj. **executive,** administrative; municipal; judiciary, judicial, juridical.

966. TRIBUNAL.—*N.* **tribunal,** court, board, bench, judicature, court of justice (*or* law); judgment seat, mercy seat; bar, bar of justice; town hall, statehouse, townhouse, courthouse; forum; sessions.

United States courts: U. S. Supreme Court, U. S. District Court, U. S. Circuit Court of Appeal; Federal Court of Claims, Court of Private Land Claims; Supreme Court, Superior Court, court of sessions, criminal court, police court, juvenile court.

court-martial, (*pl.* courts-martial), drumhead court-martial. *Adj.* judicial, etc., 965; appellate; curial.

967. JUDGE.—*N.* **judge,** justice, justice (*or* judge) of assize; magistrate, police magistrate, beak [*slang*]; his worship [Eng.], his honor, his lordship [Brit.]; the court.

Lord Chancellor, Master of the Rolls, Vice-Chancellor, Lord Chief Justice [all Brit.], Chief Justice.

arbiter, arbitrator; moderator; receiver, master; umpire, referee; censor.

jury, grand jury, petty jury, inquest, panel.

juror, juryman, talesman; grand juror, grand juryman; petty juror, petty juryman.

V. **adjudge,** etc. (*determine*), 480; try a case, try a prisoner. *Adj.* judicial, etc., 965.

968. LAWYER.—*N.* **lawyer,** jurist, legal adviser, advocate; barrister, barrister-at-law [Eng.]; counsel, counselor; king's counsel [Eng.]; pleader, special pleader.

attorney, solicitor; conveyancer, notary, notary public; pettifogger, shyster.

bar, legal profession; Inns of Court [Eng.].

V. **practice law;** practice at (*or* within) the bar, plead; be called to (*or* within) the bar; admitted to the bar.

disbar, degrade.

Adj. learned in the law; at the bar; forensic.

969. LAWSUIT.—*N.* **lawsuit,** suit, action, cause; litigation; suit in law.

writ, summons, subpoena, citation; habeas corpus [L.].

arraignment, prosecution, impeachment, accusation; present-
ment, true bill, indictment.

arrest, apprehension, committal, commitment; imprisonment.

pleadings; declaration, bill, claim; affidavit, libel; answer, plea,
demurrer, rebutter, rejoinder; surrebutter, surrejoinder.

litigant, suitor, libelant; plaintiff, defendant, etc., 938.

hearing, trial; judgment, sentence, finding, verdict; appeal,
writ of error.

case, decision, decided case, precedent.

V. litigate, go to law, appeal to the law; bring to justice (*or*
trial, the bar), put on trial, accuse, prefer (*or* file) a claim.

cite, summon, summons, serve with a writ, arraign; sue, prosecute, indict, impeach; attach, distrain; commit, apprehend, arrest, give in charge.

try, hear a cause; sit in judgment; adjudicate, etc., 480.

970. ACQUITTAL.—*N.* acquittal, exculpation, acquittance,
clearance, exoneration, discharge, release, absolution, reprieve,
respite, pardon.

Exemption from punishment: impunity, immunity.

V. acquit, exculpate, exonerate, clear; absolve, whitewash, discharge, release, liberate, reprieve, respite, pardon.

Adj. acquitted, uncondemned, unpunished; recommend to
mercy.

971. CONDEMNATION.—*N.* condemnation, conviction, judgment, penalty, sentence; death warrant.

V. condemn, convict, find guilty, damn, doom, sentence, pass
sentence on, attaint, confiscate, sequestrate.

proscribe, interdict; disapprove, etc., 932; accuse, etc., 938.

Adj. condemnatory, damnatory, condemned, self-convicted.

972. PUNISHMENT.—*N.* punishment, punition, chastise-
ment, chastening, correction, castigation; discipline, infliction,
trial; judgment, penalty, retribution, nemesis, retributive justice.

Forms of punishment: lash, scaffold, etc. (*instrument of punishment*), 975; imprisonment; transportation, banishment, expulsion, exile, involuntary exile, ostracism, penal servitude, hard labor, galleys; beating, flagellation, bastinado, blow,
stripe, cuff, kick, buffet, pummel; torture, rack.

capital punishment, execution; hanging, shooting, electrocution, decapitation,
strangling, strangulation, crucifixion, impalement, martyrdom, auto-da-fé (*pl.*
autos-da-fé) [Pg.], hara-kiri [Jap.], happy dispatch [*jocular*], lethal chamber,
hemlock.

V. punish, chastise, chasten, castigate, correct, inflict punishment; tar and feather; masthead, keelhaul.

visit upon, pay, settle, settle with, do for [*colloq.*], get even with,
make an example of; give it one [*both colloq.*].

strike, etc., 276; smite; spank, thwack, thump, beat, buffet,
thrash, pommel, drub, trounce, belabor; trim [*colloq.*], cowhide,

lambaste [*slang*], lash, flog, scourge, whip, birch, cane, switch, horsewhip, lay about one, beat black and blue; sandbag, blackjack; pelt, stone.

execute; bring to the block (*or* gallows), behead, decapitate, guillotine; hang [*p. p.* hanged, *not* hung, *for the death penalty*], electrocute, shoot, burn, crucify, impale, lynch.

torture, agonize, rack, put on (*or* to) the rack, martyr, martyrize.

banish, exile, transport, deport, expel, ostracize; rusticate; drum out; dismiss, disbar; unfrock [*as a priest*].

Adj. **punitive,** penal, punitory, inflictive, castigatory.

973. REWARD.—*N.* **reward,** recompense, remuneration, prize, meed, guerdon, indemnity, indemnification; quittance, compensation, reparation, redress, acknowledgment, requital, amends, sop, consideration, return; atonement.

perquisite, perks [*slang*]; donation, etc., 784; tip, bribe, hush money, blackmail.

allowance, salary, stipend, wages; pay, payment, emolument; tribute; premium, fee, honorarium; hire; mileage.

V. **reward,** recompense, repay, requite, remunerate, compensate; fee, tip, bribe; pay, etc., 807; make amends, indemnify, redress, atone, satisfy, acknowledge.

Adj. **remunerative,** compensatory; retributive.

974. PENALTY.—*N.* **penalty;** retribution, etc. (*punishment*), 972; pain, penance.

fine, mulct, forfeit, forfeiture, damages, sequestration, confiscation.

V. **penalize,** fine, mulct, confiscate, sequestrate, sequester; forfeit.

975. [Instrument of punishment] SCOURGE.—*N.* **scourge,** whip, lash, strap, thong, cowhide, knout, cat, cat-o'-nine-tails; rope's end; black snake, bullwhack, quirt, rawhide.

rod, cane, stick, rattan, birch, birch rod; rod in pickle; switch, ferule, cudgel, truncheon.

Various instruments: pillory, stocks, whipping post, ducking stool, iron maiden; thumbscrew, boot, rack, wheel; treadmill, crank, galleys; bed of Procrustes.
scaffold; block, ax, guillotine; stake; cross, gallows, gibbet, tree; noose, rope, halter, bowstring; death chair, electric chair.

prison, jail, etc., 752; jailer.

executioner; electrocutioner, headsman, hangman; lyncher, torturer.

malefactor, criminal, culprit, felon, victim, gallows bird [*slang*].

V. RELIGIOUS AFFECTIONS

976. DEITY.—*N.* Deity, Divinity, Godhead, Omnipotence, Omniscience, Providence.

GOD, Lord, Jehovah, The King of Kings, The Lord of Lords, The Almighty, The Supreme Being, The Absolute, The First Cause, Author of all things, Creator of all things, The Infinite, The Eternal, The All-powerful, The Omnipotent, The All-wise, The All-merciful, The All-knowing, The Omniscient.

Deus [L.], *Theos* [Gr. Θεος], *Dieu* [F.], *Gott* [Ger.], *Dio* [It.], *Dios* [Sp.], *Deos* [Pg.], *Gud* [Nor., Sw., and Dan.], *God* [Du.], *Bog* [Russ.], Brahma [Skr.], *Deva* [Skr.], *Khuda* (Hind.), Allah (Ar.).

THE TRINITY, The Holy Trinity, The Trinity in Unity, Triunity, Threefold Unity.

I. GOD THE FATHER, The Maker, The Creator, The Preserver.

Functions: creation, preservation, divine government, thearchy.

II. GOD THE SON, Jesus Christ; The Messiah, The Anointed, The Saviour, The Redeemer, The Mediator, The Intercessor, The Advocate, The Judge; The Son of God, The Son of Man; The Only-Begotten, The Lamb of God, The Word, Logos; The Man of Sorrows; Jesus of Nazareth, King of the Jews, The Son of Mary, The Risen, Immanuel, The King of Kings and Lord of Lords, The King of Glory, The Prince of Peace, The Good Shepherd, The Way, The Door, The Truth, The Life, The Bread of Life, The Light of the World, The Vine, The True Vine.

The Incarnation, The Word made Flesh.

Functions: salvation, redemption, atonement, propitiation, mediation, intercession, judgment.

III. GOD THE HOLY GHOST, The Holy Spirit, Paraclete, The Comforter, The Consoler, The Intercessor, The Spirit of God, The Spirit of Truth, The Dove.

Functions: inspiration, regeneration, sanctification, consolation, grace.

The Deity in other religions: Brahmanism *or* **Hinduism:** Brahma (*neuter*), the Supreme Soul *or* Essence of the Universe; Trimurti *or* Hindu trinity *or* Hindu triad: (1) Brahma (*masc.*), the Creator; (2) Vishnu, the Preserver; (3) Siva, the Destroyer and Regenerator.

Buddhism: the Protestantism of the East; Buddha, the Blessed One, the Teacher.

Zoroastrianism: Zerâna-Akerana, the Infinite Being; Ahuramazda *or* Ormazd, the Creator, the Lord of Wisdom, the King of Light (*opposed by* Ahriman, the King of Darkness).

Mohammedanism *or* **Islam:** Allah.

V. create, fashion, make, form, mold, manifest.
preserve, uphold, keep, perpetuate, immortalize.
atone, redeem, save, propitiate, expiate; intercede, mediate.

predestinate, predestine, foreordain, preordain; elect, call, ordain.

bless, sanctify, hallow, justify, absolve, glorify.

Adj. **almighty,** all-powerful, omnipotent; omnipresent, all-wise, all-seeing, all-knowing, omniscient, supreme.

divine, heavenly, celestial; holy, hallowed, sacred, sacrosanct. **supernatural,** superhuman, spiritual, ghostly, unearthly.

Adv. by God's will, by God's help, *Deo volente* [L.], God willing; in Jesus' name, in His name, to His glory.

977. [Beneficent spirits] ANGEL.—*N.* angel, archangel, messenger of God, guardian angel; ministering spirits, invisible helpers, choir invisible, heavenly host, sons of God; saint; seraphim (*sing.*, seraph, *E. pl.*, seraphs), Cherubim (*sing.*, cherub, *E. pl.*, cherubs· cherubim *or* cherubin *are often treated as sing.*).

Madonna, Our Lady, *Notre Dame* [F.], Holy Mary, The Virgin, The Blessed Virgin, The Virgin Mary.

Adj. **angelic,** seraphic, cherubic, archangelic.

978. [Maleficent spirits] SATAN.—*N.* Satan, the Devil, Lucifer, Belial, Beelzebub, Mephistopheles, Mephisto, Asmodeus, *le Diable* [F.], Deil [Scot.].

fallen angels, unclean spirits, devils; rulers of darkness, the powers of darkness; demon, etc.,980.

Moloch, Mammon; Belial, Beelzebub; Loki [*Norse Myth*].

diabolism, devil worship, demonism, demonology; Black Mass, black magic, demonolatry, witchcraft.

diabolist, demonologist.

V. **demonize;** bewitch, bedevil, etc. (*sorcery*), 992; possess, obsess.

Adj. **satanic,** diabolic *or* diabolical, devilish, demoniac *or* demoniacal, infernal, hellborn.

979. MYTHIC AND PAGAN DEITIES.—*N.* god, goddess; heathen gods and goddesses; pantheon.

Greek and Latin: Zeus, Jupiter *or* Jove (*King*); Apollo *or* Phoebus Apollo (*the sun*); Ares, Mars (*war*); Hermes, Mercury (*messenger*); Poseidon, Neptune (*ocean*); Hephaestus, Vulcan (*smith*); Dionysus, Bacchus (*wine*); Hades [Gr.], Pluto *or* Dis [L.] (*King of the lower world*); Kronos, Saturn (*time*); Eros, Cupid (*love*); Pan, Faunus (*flocks, herds, forests, and wild life*).

Hera, Juno (*Queen*); Demeter, Ceres (*fruitfulness*); Persephone, Proserpina *or* Proserpine (*Queen of the lower world*); Artemis, Diana (*the moon and hunting*); Athena, Minerva (*wisdom*); Aphrodite, Venus (*love and beauty*); Hestia, Vesta (*the hearth*); Rhea *or* Cybele ("Mother of the gods," *identified with* Ops, *wife of Saturn*); Gaea *or* Ge, Tellus (*earth goddess, mother of the Titans*).

Norse: Ymir (*primeval giant*), Odin *or* Woden (*the All-father* = Zeus); the Æsir: Thor (*the Thunderer*), Balder (= Apollo), Freyr (*fruitfulness*), Tyr (*war*), Bragi (*poetry and eloquence*), Höder (*blind god of the winter*), Heimdall (*warder of Asgard*), Loki (*evil*).

the Vanir: Njorth (*the winds and the sea*), Frey (*prosperity and love*), Freya (*goddess of love and beauty* = Venus).

Frigg or Frigga (*wife of Odin*), Hel (*goddess of death = Persephone*), Idun (*goddess of spring, wife of Bragi*), Sigyn (*wife of Loki*).

Egyptian: Ra or Amon-Ra (*the sun god*), Osiris (*judge of the dead*), Isis (*wife of Osiris*), Horus (*the morning sun; son of Osiris and Isis*), Anubis (*jackal-god, brother of Horus, a conductor of the dead*), Nephthys (*sister of Isis*), Set (*evil deity, brother of Osiris*), Thoth (*clerk of the underworld*), Bast or Bubastis (*a goddess with head of a cat*), the Sphinx (*wisdom*).

Various: Baal [Semitic]; Astarte or Ashtoreth (*goddess of fertility and love*) [Phoenician]; Bel [Babylonian]; The Great Spirit [N. Amer. Indian].

nymph, dryad, hamadryad, wood nymph; naiad, fresh-water nymph; oread, mountain nymph; nereid, sea nymph; Oceanid, ocean nymph; Pleiades, Hyades.

fairy, fay, sprite; nix (*fem.* nixie), water sprite; the good folk, brownie, pixy, elf (*pl.* elves), banshee; the Fates; kobold, troll, hobgoblin, gnome, kelpie; faun; peri, undine, sea maid, mermaid (*masc.* merman); Mab, Oberon, Titania, Ariel; Puck, Robin Goodfellow.

familiar spirit, familiar, genius, guide, good genius, daimon, demon.

mythology, mythical lore, folklore, fairyism, fairy mythology.

Adj. **mythical,** mythic, mythological, fabulous, legendary.

fairylike, sylphlike, elfin, elflike, elfish, nymphlike.

980. EVIL SPIRITS.—*N.* demon, fiend, devil, etc. (*Satan*), 978; evil genius, familiar, familiar spirit; bad (*or* unclean) spirit; incubus; ogre, ogress, ghoul, vampire, harpy; Fury, the Furies, the Erinyes, the Eumenides.

imp, bad fairy, sprite, jinni (*pl.* jinn), genius (*pl.* genii), dwarf. changeling, elf child, werewolf; satyr.

elemental, sylph, gnome, salamander, nymph [*Rosicrucian*]. siren, nixie, undine, Lorelei.

bugbear, bugaboo, bogy, goblin, hobgoblin.

Adj. demoniac, demoniacal, fiendish, fiendlike, evil, ghoulish; pokerish [*colloq.*], bewitched.

980a. SPECTER.—*N.* specter, ghost, apparition, vision, spirit, sprite, shade, shadow, wraith, banshee, spook [*now humorous*], phantom, phantasm, materialization [*spiritualism*], double.

will-o'-the-wisp, etc., 423.

Adj. **spectral,** ghostly, ghostlike, spiritual, wraithlike, weird, uncanny, eerie, spooky [*colloq.*] haunted; unearthly, supernatural.

981. HEAVEN.—*N.* **heaven;** kingdom of heaven (*or* God), heavenly kingdom; heaven of heavens, God's throne, throne of God; Paradise, Eden, Zion, Holy City, New Jerusalem, Heavenly City, City Celestial, abode of the blessed.

Mythological heaven or paradise: Olympus; Elysium, Elysian fields, Islands (*or* Isles) of the Blessed, Happy Isles, Fortunate Isles, garden of the Hesperides; third heaven, seventh heaven; Valhalla [Scandinavian]; Nirvana [Buddhist]; happy hunting grounds [N. Amer. Indian].

future state, life after death, eternal home, resurrection, translation; apotheosis, deification.

Adj. **heavenly**, celestial, supernal, unearthly, paradisaic, beatific; Elysian, Olympian.

982. HELL.—*N.* **hell**, bottomless pit, place of torment; pandemonium; hell-fire, everlasting fire (*or* torment); worm that never dies.

purgatory, limbo, Gehenna, abyss.

Mythological hell: Tartarus, Hades, Avernus; infernal regions, inferno, shades below, realms of Pluto.
Pluto, Rhadamanthus, Erebus, Charon, Cerberus; Persephone, Proserpina; Minos, Osiris.
Rivers of hell: Styx, Acheron, Cocytus, Phlegethon, Lethe.

Adj. **hellish**, infernal, stygian.

983. [Religious Knowledge] THEOLOGY.—*N.* **theology**, theosophy, divine wisdom, divinity, hagiography; monotheism, theism, religion; religious persuasion (*or* sect, denomination, affiliation); creed, articles (*or* declaration, profession, confession) of faith.

theologian, scholastic, divine, schoolman, the Fathers; monotheist, theist.

Adj. **theological**, religious, divine, canonical; denominational; sectarian.

983a. ORTHODOXY.—*N.* **orthodoxy**; strictness, soundness, religious truth, true faith; truth, etc., 494; soundness of doctrine; Christianity, Catholicism.

the church, Holy Church, Church Militant, Church Triumphant; Catholic (*or* Universal, Apostolic) Church; Established (*or* State) Church; The Bride of the Lamb; temple of the Holy Ghost; Church of Christ; Christians, Christendom.

canons; thirty-nine articles; Apostles' (*or* Nicene, Athanasian) Creed.

Adj. **orthodox**, sound, strict, faithful, catholic, Christian, evangelical, scriptural, literal, divine, monotheistic, true, etc., 494.

984. HETERODOXY. [Sectarianism]—*N.* **heterodoxy**; error, false doctrine, heresy, schism, recusancy, backsliding, apostasy; materialism, atheism; idolatry, superstition.

bigotry, fanaticism, iconoclasm; precisianism; sabbatarianism, puritanism, bibliolatry.

sectarianism, nonconformity, dissent, secularism; religious sects, the clash of creeds, the isms.

[*Generally speaking, each sect is* orthodox *to itself and* heterodox *to others.*]

paganism, heathenism, heathendom; animism, polytheism, pantheism; dualism.

pagan, heathen, paynim; kafir, non-Mohammedan; gentile; pantheist, polytheist, animist.

misbeliever, heretic, apostate; backslider; antichrist; idolater; skeptic, etc., 989.

bigot, dogmatist, fanatic, dervish, iconoclast.

sectarian, sectary; seceder, separatist, recusant, dissenter, non-conformist.

materialist, positivist, deist, agnostic, atheist, etc., 989.

Adj. **heterodox,** heretical, unorthodox, unscriptural, uncanonical, unchristian, apocryphal; antichristian; schismatic, recusant, iconoclastic; sectarian, dissenting, secular; agnostic, atheistic; skeptical, etc., 989.

bigoted, dogmatical, fanatical; superstitious, credulous; idolatrous.

pagan, heathen, heathenish, gentile, paynim; polytheistic, pantheistic, animistic.

985. REVELATION. [Biblical]—*N.* revelation, inspiration.

The Bible, the Book, the Book of Books, The Good Book, the Word, the Word of God, Scripture, the Scriptures, Holy Writ, Holy Scriptures, inspired writings, Gospel.

Old Testament, Septuagint, Vulgate, Pentateuch; the Law, the Prophets; Apocrypha.

New Testament; Gospels, Evangelists, Acts, Epistles, Apocalypse, Revelation; Good Tidings, Glad Tidings.

inspired writers, prophet, evangelist, apostle, disciple, saint; the Fathers, the Apostolic Fathers; Holy Men of old.

Adj. **scriptural,** biblical, sacred, prophetic; evangelical, evangelistic, apostolic, apostolical; inspired, apocalyptic, revealed; ecclesiastical, canonical.

986. SACRED WRITINGS. [Non-Biblical]—*N.* The Vedas, Upanishads, Puranas, Sutras, Bhagavad Gita [all Brahmanic]; Zendavesta, Avesta [Zoroastrian]; The Koran *or* Alcoran [Mohammedan]; Tripitaka, Dhammapada [Buddhist]; Granth, Adigranth [*Sikh*]; the Kings [Chinese]; the Eddas [Scandinavian].

Non-Biblical prophets and religious founders: Gautama (Buddha); Zoroaster, Confucius, Mohammed.

987. PIETY.—*N.* piety, religion, theism, faith; religiousness, religiosity, holiness, saintship; reverence, humility, veneration, devotion, worship, grace, sanctity, consecration.

beatification, regeneration, conversion, sanctification, salvation, inspiration, bread of life; Body and Blood of Christ.

believer, convert, theist, Christian, devotee, pietist, saint.

V. **be pious,** have faith, believe, receive Christ; venerate, adore, worship, revere, be converted, be on God's side, stand up for Jesus, fight the good fight, keep the faith, let one's light shine.

regenerate, convert, edify, sanctify, hallow, keep holy, beatify, inspire, consecrate, enshrine.

Adj. pious, religious, devout, devoted, reverent, godly, humble, pure, pure in heart, holy, spiritual, saintly, saintlike; believing, faithful, Christian.

regenerated; inspired, consecrated, converted, unearthly. elected, adopted, justified, sanctified.

988. IMPIETY.—*N.* impiety, sin, irreverence; profaneness, profanity, blasphemy, profanation; desecration, sacrilege; scoffing.

Assumed piety: hypocrisy, pietism, cant, pious fraud; lip devotion, lip service; formalism, austerity; sanctimony, sanctimoniousness, pharisaism, sabbatarianism; sacerdotalism; bigotry; blue laws.

apostasy, recusancy, backsliding, perversion, reprobation.

bigot, pharisee, sabbatarian, formalist, pietist, precisian, devotee, ranter, fanatic.

sinner, scoffer, blasphemer, sabbath breaker; worldling; hypocrite.

the wicked, the evil, the unjust, the reprobate.

V. profane, desecrate, blaspheme, revile, scoff, swear; commit sacrilege.

dissemble, simulate, play the hypocrite, snuffle.

Adj. impious, irreligious, etc., 989; profane, irreverent, sacrilegious, blasphemous.

unhallowed, unsanctified, unregenerate; hardened, perverted, reprobate.

hypocritical, canting, pietistical, sanctimonious, unctuous, pharisaical, overrighteous.

bigoted, fanatical, hidebound, narrow, narrow-minded, illiberal, prejudiced, little; provincial, parochial, insular.

989. IRRELIGION.—*N.* irreligion, impiety, ungodliness, laxity, apathy, indifference.

skepticism, doubt; unbelief, disbelief, incredulity, agnosticism, freethinking; materialism, rationalism, positivism; atheism, infidelity.

unbeliever, infidel, atheist, heretic, heathen, alien, gentile, Nazarene; freethinker, skeptic, rationalist; materialist, positivist, nihilist, agnostic.

V. disbelieve, lack faith; doubt, question, deny the truth.

Adj. irreligious; undevout, godless, graceless, ungodly; unholy, unsanctified, unhallowed; atheistic.

skeptical, freethinking, unbelieving, unconverted; incredulous, faithless.

worldly, mundane, earthly, carnal, worldly, worldly-minded, unspiritual.

990. WORSHIP.—*N.* worship, cult, adoration, devotion, vow, aspiration, homage, service; kneeling, genuflection, prostration.

prayer, invocation, supplication, intercession, orison, petition; collect, litany, Lord's prayer, paternoster; *Ave Maria* [L.], Hail, Mary.

thanksgiving; grace, praise, glorification, paean, benediction, doxology, hosanna, hallelujah, alleluia, *Te Deum* [L.], *Gloria* [L.].

psalm, hymn, chant, response, anthem.

offering, oblation, sacrifice, incense, libation, offertory, collection.

divine service, office, duty; exercises; morning prayer; Mass, matins, evensong, vespers, vigils, lauds.

worshiper, congregation, communicant, celebrant.

V. worship, lift up the heart, aspire; revere, adore, do service, pay homage, offer one's vows, vow; bow down and worship.

pray, invoke, supplicate; beseech; offer up prayers, say one's prayers, tell one's beads, recite the rosary.

give thanks, say grace, bless, praise, laud, glorify, magnify, sing praises.

Adj. devout, devotional, reverent, solemn, fervid.

991. IDOLATRY.—*N.* idolatry, idolatrousness, demonism, demonology, devil worship, fetishism.

idolization, deification, apotheosis, canonization; hero worship.

sacrifice, hecatomb, holocaust; human sacrifices, immolation, self-immolation, suttee.

idol, golden calf, graven image, fetish, joss [Chinese], *lares et penates* [L.]; god (*or* goddess) of one's idolatry; Baal, Moloch, Juggernaut.

idolater, idolatress, idolizer, fetishist.

V. idolize, idolatrize, worship idols, worship, put on a pedestal, prostrate oneself before; make sacrifice to, deify, canonize.

Adj. idolatrous, idolistic, prone before, prostrate before, in the dust before, at the feet of.

992. SORCERY.—*N.* sorcery, magic, black magic, the black art, necromancy, demonology, witchcraft, witchery, wizardry, fetishism, hoodoo, voodoo, voodooism; fire worship, incantation, enchantment, bewitchment, glamour; obsession, possession.

divination, etc. (*prediction*), 511; sortilege, ordeal, hocus-pocus.

V. practice sorcery, cast a nativity (*or* horoscope), conjure, charm, enchant, bewitch, bedevil, witch, voodoo, hoodoo [*colloq.*]; entrance, fascinate, hypnotize, cast a spell; call up spirits.

Adj. **magic**, magical, witching, weird, cabalistic, talismanic.

992a. PSYCHICAL RESEARCH.—*N.* **psychical research**, psychical (*or* psychic) investigation; abnormal (*or* mediumistic) phenomena; mysticism.

the subconscious, the subconscious self, the subliminal self, the higher self, ego, astral body; aura; subconsciousness, subliminal consciousness; intuition; dual personality, multiple personality, obsession, possession.

psychotherapy, psychotherapeutics, psychoanalysis; hysteria, neurasthenia, dreams, visions, apparitions, hallucinations.

mesmerism, animal magnetism; mesmeric trance; hypnotism; hypnosis.

Phenomena: telepathy, thought transference, thought transmission, telepathic transmission; second sight, clairvoyance, clairaudience, psychometry.

premonitions, previsions, premonitory apparition, fetch, wraith, double; death lights, ominous dreams.

automatism, automatic writing, planchette, ouija board, trance writing, spirit writing; trance speaking, inspirational speaking.

spiritualism, spiritism, spirit manifestations; trance, spirit control, spirit possession; mediumistic communications; séance; materialization.

medium, seer, clairvoyant, clairaudient, telepathist; guide, control; mesmerist, hypnotist.

V. **psychologize**; investigate the abnormal (*or* supernormal, subconscious, subliminal), traverse the borderland, know oneself.

mesmerize, magnetize, hypnotize, place under control, subject to suggestion, place in a trance, induce hypnosis.

Adj. **psychical**, psychic, psychological; spiritistic, spiritualistic, spiritual; subconscious, subliminal, supernormal, abnormal; mystic *or* mystical.

993. SPELL.—*N.* **spell**, charm, incantation, exorcism, abracadabra, open-sesame; evil eye.

talisman, amulet, phylactery, philter, fetish, wishbone; mascot, rabbit's foot, hoodoo [*colloq.*], jinx [*slang*], scarabaeus *or* scarab; veronica, swastika.

wand, caduceus, rod, divining rod, witch hazel, Aaron's rod.

Magic wish-givers: Aladdin's lamp, Aladdin's casket, magic casket, magic ring, magic belt, magic spectacles, wishing cap, Fortunatus' cap; seven-league boots; magic carpet; cap of darkness.

994. SORCERER.—*N.* **sorcerer**, magician, wizard, necromancer, conjuror, prestidigitator; charmer, exorcist, voodoo medicine man, witch doctor; astrologer, soothsayer, etc., 513.

sorceress, witch, hag; siren, harpy.

Cagliostro, Merlin; Circe, weird sisters, witch of Endor.

995. CHURCHDOM.—*N.* **churchdom**; church, ministry, priesthood, prelacy, hierarchy, church government; clericalism, sacerdotalism, episcopalianism.

monasticism, monkhood, monachism; celibacy.

Ecclesiastical offices and dignities: cardinalate, cardinalship; primacy, archbishopric, archiepiscopacy; prelacy, bishopric, episcopate, episcopacy, see, diocese; benefice, incumbency, living, cure, charge, cure of souls; rectorship, vicariate, vicarship; pastorate, pastorship, pastoral charge; deaconry, deaconship; curacy; chaplaincy, chaplainship, presbytery.

holy orders, ordination, institution, consecration, induction, installation, preferment, translation, presentation.

papacy, pontificate, See of Rome, the Vatican, the apostolic see.

V. **call,** ordain, induct, install, translate, consecrate, present, elect, bestow.

Adj. **ecclesiastical,** clerical, sacerdotal, priestly, pastoral, ministerial, hierarchical, episcopal, canonical; pontifical, papal, apostolic.

996. CLERGY.—*N.* **clergy,** clericals, ministry, priesthood, presbytery, the cloth, the pulpit, the desk.

clergyman, divine, ecclesiastic, priest, pastor, shepherd, minister, preacher, clerk in holy orders, parson, sky pilot [*slang*]; father, padre, *abbé* [F.], *curé* [F.]; reverend.

Dignitaries of the church: Pope, pontiff, Holy Father; cardinal, primate, metropolitan, archbishop, bishop, prelate, dean, archdeacon, canon, rector, vicar, beneficiary, incumbent, chaplain, curate; elder, deacon.

religious, abbot, prior, monk, friar, lay brother, pilgrim, palmer.

nun, sister, priestess, abbess, prioress, canoness; mother superior, the reverend mother; novice.

Adj. **ordained,** in orders, in holy orders, called to the ministry.

997. LAITY.—*N.* **laity,** flock, fold, congregation, assembly, brethren, people; society [U. S.]; class [Methodist].

layman, parishioner, catechumen.

V. laicize, secularize.

Adj. **secular,** lay congregational, civil, temporal, profane.

998. RITE.—*N.* **rite,** ceremony, observance, function, duty, form, solemnity, sacrament; service, ministry, ministration.

sermon, preaching, preachment, exhortation, religious harangue, homily, lecture, discourse.

worship, etc., 990; invocation of saints, confession, the confessional; absolution, remission of sins; reciting the rosary, telling one's beads.

Seven Sacraments: (1) baptism, immersion, christening; baptismal regeneration; font.

(2) confirmation, laying on of hands.

(3) Eucharist, Mass, Lord's supper, communion; the sacrament, the holy sacrament; consecrated elements, bread and wine, celebration; transubstantiation, real presence.

(4) penance, fasting, sackcloth and ashes, flagellation.

(5) **extreme unction,** last rites, viaticum.

(6) **holy orders,** ordination, etc. (*churchdom*), 995.

(7) **matrimony,** marriage, wedlock, etc., 903.

Sacred articles: relics, rosary, beads, reliquary, host, cross, rood, crucifix; pyx, censer, thurible; prayer wheel [Buddhist]; Sangraal, Holy Grail.

ritual, liturgy, rubric, canon, ordinal, missal, breviary, Mass book, beadroll, litany, prayer book, Book of Common Prayer; psalter, psalmbook, hymnbook, hymnal.

ritualism, ceremonialism; sabbatism, sabbatarianism; ritualist, sabbatarian.

V. **perform service,** do duty, minister, officiate, celebrate.

excommunicate; ban with bell, book, and candle.

preach, sermonize, address the congregation.

Adj. **ritual,** ritualistic, ceremonial, liturgic *or* liturgical; paschal.

999. CANONICALS.—*N.* **canonicals,** vestments, robe, gown, surplice, etc.

1000. TEMPLE.—*N.* **temple,** fane, place of worship; house of God, house of prayer; cathedral, minster, church, kirk [Scot.], chapel, meetinghouse.

synagogue, tabernacle; mosque [Moham.]; pagoda, Chinese temple, joss house [*colloq.*]; pantheon, shrine.

monastery, priory, abbey, friary, convent, nunnery, cloister.

parsonage, rectory, vicarage, manse, deanery, clergy house; bishop's palace; Vatican.

Adj. **churchly,** cloistered, monastic, monasterial, conventual.

INDEX

The numbers refer to the headings under which the words or phrases occur. When the same word or phrase can be used in various senses, the several headings under which it or its synonyms will be found are indicated by *italics*.

When the word given in the Index is itself the title or heading of a category, the word is printed in capitals and the reference number in bold-faced type, thus: **ACTIVITY 682.** When the word is the keyword to a group of synonyms, the reference number is also in bold-faced type.

Derivatives likewise have been sparingly admitted, since the allied or basic term will serve as a key to the various derived forms; thus *alarm* is given, but not *alarmed* or *alarming*. Adverbs ending in -*ly* should be looked for under the adjective, if not found in the Index.

IMPORTANT NOTE

The numbers following all references in this Index Guide refer to the *section* numbers in the text, and *not* to pages.

INDEX

A

abandon 624, 782
abandoned
 forsaken 893
 vicious 945
abandonment 757, 782
abase 879
abasement 874
abash 879
abashed 879
abatement 36
abbess 996
abbey 1000
abbot 996
abbreviation 201
abdicate 757
abdomen 250
abduct *repel* 289
 steal 791
aberration 83
abet 707
abhor 867, 898
abhorrence 867, 898
abhorrent *painful* 830
 hateful 898
abide *endure* 1, 106
 remain 110
 dwell 186
ability 157, 698
abject *vile* 874
 servile 886
abjure *deny* 536
 renounce 607
ablaze 382
able *capable* 157
 skillful 698
able-bodied 159
ablution 652
abnormal 83
aboard *present* 186
 afloat 273
abode 189
abolish 756
abolition 2, 162, 756
abominable *bad* 649
 hateful 898
abominate *dislike* 867
 hate 898
abomination 867
aboriginal 66, 124
aborigine 188
abound 639
about *nearly* 32, **197**
 around 227

above 206
abracadabra 993
abrade 330,331
abrasion 330,331
abreast 216, 236
abridge 36, 201
 in writing 596
abridgment 35, **201**
abroad 57, 196
abrupt *sudden* 113
 steep 217
abscond 623
ABSENCE 187
 -of mind 458
 -of time 107
absent 187, 458
absentee 187
absent-minded 458
absolute *not relative* 1
 great **31**
 certain 474
absolution 918
absolve 918, 952
absorb *combine* 48
 take in 296
absorbed 451
absorption 296
abstain *refrain* 623
 be temperate 953
abstainer 953, 958
abstemious 953, 958
abstention 623
abstinence 623, **953**
abstract, *v. take* 789
abstract, *n. epitome* 195,
 596
abstracted *inattentive* 458
abstraction 38, 451, **458**
absurd 471, 497, 583
ABSURDITY
 impossibility 471
 nonsense 497
 ridiculousness 853
abundance 31, **639**
abundant *great* 31
 enough 639
abuse, *v. illtreat* 649
 misuse 679
abuse, *n. in-vective* **908,**
 932
abusive 909, 932
abut 197
abysmal *deep* 208

abyss 198, 667
academic 537
academy 542
accede *assent* 488
 submit 725
 consent 762
accelerate 132, 274, 684
accent 402, 580
accentuate 580, **642**
accept *assent* 488
 receive 785
acceptable
 expedient 646
 agreeable 829
acceptance *security* 771
access *approach* 286
accessible *possible* 470
 easy 705
accession *increase* 35
accessory *extrinsic* 6
 adjunct 37, 39
 accompanying 88
accident 151, 619, 735
accidental *extrinsic* 6
 occasional 134
 fortuitous 156
acclaim 931
acclamation 488, 931
acclivity 217
accommodate *suit* 23
 aid 707
accommodation
 adaptation 23
 space 180
ACCOMPANIMENT
 adjunct 37, 39
 coexistence 88
 musical 415
accompany
 coexist 88
 escort 664
accomplice 711
accomplish *execute* 151
 complete 729
accomplishment
 learning 490
 talent 698
accord
 agree 23
 assent 488
 grant 760, 784
accordance 16, 23
accordingly 8, 476

311

aeronautics 267, **273**
aerostatics 267
aesthetic 845
afar 196
affable 894
affair *event* **151**
   battle 720
affect *relate to* 9
   qualify 469
   touch 824
   simper 855
   desire 865
AFFECTATION 579, 855
affected 579, 855
affection 879
affectionate 897
AFFECTIONS 820
affianced 903
affiliated 9, 11
affinitive 9
affinity *relation* 9
   similarity 17
affirm 535
AFFIRMATION 535
affirmative 535
affix *addition* 37
   sequel 39
   precedence 62
afflict 830
affliction 828, 830
affluence 734, 803
afford 803
affront 900, 929
afield 186
afire 382
afloat 267, **273**
afoot *ready* 673
aforesaid 104
afraid 860
afresh *repeated* 104
   new 123
aft 235
after *in order* **63**
   in time 117
   rear 235
   in pursuit 281
aftermath 154
afternoon 126
afterpart 235
afterthought 451
afterward 117
again 104
   -and again 136
against 708
   -the grain 256, 704
agape 455, 507
AGE *period* 108
   course 109
   long time 110
   oldness 124
   advanced life **128**
aged 128
AGENCY 170
AGENT 690
aggrandize *increase* 35
aggravate *increase* 35

heighten **835**
AGGRAVATION 35, **835**
aggregate 50
aggression 716
aggrieve 830
aghast 860
agile 274
agitate *move* 315
   excite 821, **824**
AGITATION
   [*see* agitate]
   energy 171
   motion 315
aglow 382, 420
agnostic 485, 984, 989
agnosticism 989
ago 122
agonizing 830
agony *physical* 378
   mental 828
agree *accord* 23, **714**
   concur 178
   assent 488
   -to 762
agreeable 82, 377
AGREEMENT 23, 82, 178
agriculture 371
agriculturist 342
aground *fixed* 150
   failure 732
ahead 234, 282, **303**
AID 707, 906
ail 655
aileron 267
ailment 655
aim *direction* 278
   purpose 620
aimless 615a
air *gas* 334
ATMOSPHERIC 338, 349
   tune 415
   appearance 448
aircraft 273
air line 278
airman 269
AIR PIPE 351
airplane 273, 726
airs *affectation* 855
   vanity 880
airwoman 269a
airy [*see* air]
   visionary 4
   light 320
aisle 260
ajar 260
akimbo 244
akin *related* 11
alacrity 682, 836
ALARM
   notice of danger **669**
   fear 860
alarmist 862
alarum 550, 669
album 593, 596
alcohol 959
alcove 191

alert *watchful* 457, 459
   active 682
alertness 457, 459
alias 18
alibi 187
alien *irrelevant* 10
   foreigner 57
alienate *disjoin* 44
   estrange 889
   set against 898
alight, *v. arrive* 292
   descend 306
alight, *adv. on fire* 382
align 278
alike 17
alive *living* 359
   intelligent 498
   active 682
all *whole* 50
   complete 52
allay 174, 834
allege 467, 535
allegiance *obedience* **743**
   duty 926
alleviate 174, 834
alleviation 174
alley 260
alliance *relation* 9
   kindred 11
   co-operation 709
allied 11, 48
alliteration 104
allot 786
allow *admit* 529
   permit 760
allowable 760
allowance
   qualification 469
   gift 784
   salary 973
alloy *mixture* 41
   combine 48
allude 521, 526
allure 865
allusion 526
ally, *v.* 48
ally, *n.*
   auxiliary 711
   friend 890
almanac 86, 114
almighty 157, 976
Almighty, the 976
almost 32
alms 784
aloft 206
alone 87
along 200
alongside *near* 197
   parallel 216
   laterally 236
aloof *distant* 196
   secluded 893
aloud 404
alphabet 561
already 118
also 37

apathy 823
ape *monkey* 366
ape, v. *imitate* 19
aperient 652
aperture 260
apex 206, 210
aphorism 496
apiary 370
apiece 79
Apocalypse 985
Apocrypha 985
apocryphal 475
apologetic 937
apologist 937
apology *substitution* 147
  vindication 937
  penitence 950
apostasy *recantation* 607
  impiety 988
apostate *turncoat* 607
  heretic 984
apostatize 607
apostle 985
apostolic 985, 995
apostrophe 589
apostrophize 765
apothecary 662
apotheosis 981, 991
appall *pain* 830
  terrify 860
apparatus 633
apparel 225
apparent *visible* 446
  appearing 448
  probable 472
  manifest 525
apparition
  phantom 4, 362
  spirit 980a, 992a
appeal *address* 586
  request 765
appear *arrive* 292
  come in sight 446, **448**
APPEARANCE **448**
appease 174, 826
append 37, 63
appendage *addition* 37
  adjunct 39
  sequel 65
  accompaniment 88
appendix 65
appertain 777
appetite 865
appetizer 394
appetizing 394
applaud 931
applause 931
appliance *use* 677
appliances 632
applicable *relevant* 9, 23
  useful **644**
applicant 767
application *study* 457
  request 765
apply *appropriate* 788
appoint 755, 786

appointment *business* 625
  charge 755
  interview 892
appointments *gear* 633
apportion 786
APPORTIONMENT 786
apposition 23, 199
appraise 466
appreciate *realize* 450
  know 490
apprehend *know* 490
  fear 860
  seize 969
apprehension *idea* 453
  fear 860
apprehensive 860
apprentice 541
apprenticeship 539
APPROACH 286
  of time 121
  nearness 197
  path 627
approbation 931
appropriate *fit* 23
  peculiar 79
  timely 134
  borrow 788
  take **789**
appropriation
  allotment 786
  taking 789
approval *assent* 488
  commendation 931
approve 488, **931**
approved 931
approximate
  related to 9
  resemble **17**
  near 197
  nearing 286
appurtenance 780
apt *consonant* 23
  clever 698
aquatic 267
aqueduct 350
aquiline 244
arable 371
arbiter *critic* 480
  judge 967
arbitrament 480
arbitrary 10
  willful 606
  severe 739
  lawless **964**
arbitrate 480, 724
arbitration 480
arbitrator 724
arbor 191
arboreal 367
arc 245
arcade 189
arch *curve* 245
  convexity 250
  roguish 840
archeologist 122
archeology 122

archaic *old* 124
archaism 122, 124
archangel 977
archbishop 996
archer 284, 726, **840**
archetype 22
archipelago 346
architect 164, 690
architecture 161
archive 551
arctic 237, 383
arctics 225
ardent *eager* 682
  loving 897
ardor *vigor* 574
  feeling 821
arduous 704
area 181
ARENA *space* 180
  field of battle 728
argosy 273
argot 563
argue 467, 476
argument 476
argumentation **476**
arid 169, 340
aright 618
arise *begin* 66
  happen 151
  mount 305
aristocracy 875
aristocrat 875
aristocratic 852
arithmetic 85
ark 666
arm *part* 51
  power 157
  prepare 673
  weapon 727
armada 726
armament 727
armchair 215
armed 722
  -force 664, **726**
armful 25
armistice 142, 723
armor 727
armorial 550
armory 636
ARMS 727 [see arm]
  heraldry 550
army *collection* 72
  multitude 102
  troops **726**
aroma 400
around 227
arouse *move* 615
  excite 824
arraign *accuse* 938
  indict 969
arraignment 969
arrange *set in order* 60
  organize 357
  harmonize 416
  plan 626
  compromise 774

B

betroth 768, 903
betrothal 902
betrothed 897, 903
better *improve* **658**
between 228
betwixt **228**
beverage 298
bevy 102
bewail 839
beware 668
bewilder *put out* 458
    perplex 475
    astonish 870
bewitch *fascinate* 615
    diabolize 978
    hoodoo 992
beyond *superior* **33**
    further 196
bias *influence* 175
    tendency 176
    slope 217
    prepossession **481**
bib *pinafore* 225
Bible 985
bicentenary 98, 138
bicentennial 98, 138
bicker *quarrel* 713
bicycle 272
bid *order* 741
    offer 763
bide *wait* 133
    remain 141
biennial 138
bier 363
big *in degree* 31
    in size 192, 206
bigot *dogmatist* 474
    mule 606
    heterodox **984**
    impious **988**
bigoted **988**
bigotry 474, 606, **984**
bill *money account* 811
    -of fare 86, 298
billet, *n. office* 625
billet, *v. locate* **184**
billingsgate 908
billows 341
bind *connect* 43
    compel 744
biography 594
biologist 357
biology 357, 359
biplane 273
bird 366
birth *beginning* 66
    production 161
birthday 138
birthright 924
bisect **91**
bisection **91**
bishop 996
bishopric 995
bit *small quantity* 32
    part 51
    curb 752

bite *eat* 298
biting *cold* 383
    pungent 392
bitter *cold* 383
    acrid 395
    malevolent 907
bitterness [*see* bitter]
bivouac 265
bizzare 83, 853
black *color* **431**
    -sheep 949
blackball 893, **932**
blacken 431
    defame 934
blacklist **932**
blackmail 793
BLACKNESS 431
blade *edge tool* 253
blamable **932**, 947
blame 155, **932**
blameless 946
blameworthy **932**, 947
blanch 429, 430
bland 894
blandishment 902
blank *inexistent* 2
    unsubstantial 4
blanket 223
blare 404
blarney 933
blasé 869, 871
blasphemy 988
blast, *n. destroy* 162
    explosion 173
blast, *v. wind* 349
blatant *loud* 404
blaze *heat* 382
    mark 550
blazer *coat* 225
blazon *publish* 531
    inscribe 873
    -forth 882
bleach 429
bleachers 444
bleak 383
blear-eyed 443
bleat 412
bleed *extort money* 814
    suffer 828
bleeding *hemorrhage* 299
BLEMISH *deface* 241
    imperfection 651
    defect **848**
blench *shrink* 821
blend *mix* 41
    combine 48
    harmonize 413
bless *sanctify* **976**
blessed 827
blessing 618, 931
blight 659
blighted 659
blind, *n. shade* 530
    pretext 617
blind, *adj. sightless* **442**
blind, *v. conceal* 528

blinders 443
blindfold 442, 491, 528
BLINDNESS 442
blink *wink* 443
blinker **424**, 443, 530
bliss 827
blister 848
blithe 836
blithesome 836
blizzard 349
bloat *inflate* 194
bloated *expanded* 194
    convex 250
block, *n. houses* 189
    mass 192
block, *v. hinder* 706
    execution 975
blockade *surround* 227
    close 261
    seclude 893
blockhead 501
blonde 429
blood *consanguinity* **11**
    -relation 11
bloodlessness 160
bloodshed 361
bloodthirsty 361
bloody *killing* 361
bloom *blossom* 367
    health 654
    flower 734
blossom
    flower 161, 365, **367**
    flower 734
blot *blacken* 431
    blemish 848
    disgrace 874
blotch *black* 431
    blemish 848
blotchy 431
blouse 225
blow *knock* **276**
    waft 349
    disappointment 509
    evil 619
    -up *explode* 173
    inflate 194, 349
    objurgate 932
blowhole 260, 351
bludgeon 727
BLUE *color* 438
bluestocking 492
bluff *high* 206
    brag 884
blunder *error* 495
    absurdity **497**
    bungle 699
    failure **732**
    indiscretion 947
blunt *obtuse* 254
    benumb 376
    plain-spoken 703
BLUNTNESS 254
blur *dim* 443
    blemish 848
blurred *invisible* 447

blush *heat* 382
  redden **434**
  feel 821
bluster *violence* 173
  brag 884
  resent 900
  threaten 909
BLUSTERER 884, **887**
blustering *insolent* **885**
boa 225
board *food* 298
  council 696
boarder 188
boast 855, **884**
boaster 482, **884**
boastful **884**
BOASTING 884
boat 273
boating 267
boatman 269
boatswain 269
bob *bow* 308
  oscillate 314
bodily 3, 50
body *substance* 3
  whole 50
  assemblage 72
  -clothes **225**
bodyguard 753
bog *swamp* 345
bogus 545
Bohemian 83
boil *be violent* 173
  effervesce 315
  bubble 353
  heat 382, 384
  flare up 824, 825
boisterous *violent* 173
  excitable 825
bold *prominent* 250
  unreserved 525
  defiant 715
  brave 861
boldness [see bold]
bolshevism 742
bolshevist 712, 742
bolster 707
bolt *sift* 42
  fasten 43
  close 261
  run away 623
  shackle 752
  -food 957
bomb 727
bombard 716
bombast 577
bombastic 577
bonanza *wealth* 803
bonbon 396
bond *tie* 9, 45
  security 771, 802
bondage 749
bonfire 382
bonnet 225
bonny *cheerful* 836
  pretty 845

bonus *gift* 784
  money 810
bony 323
BOOK, *n. volume* **593**
book, *v. register* 86
bookish 490
bookkeeper 811
bookkeeping 811
bookless *unlearned* **493**
bookshop 593
bookstore 593
bookworm **492**
boom *impulse* 276
  sound 404
  roll 407
boomerang *recoil* 277
  weapon 727
boon 784
boor *clown* 876
boorish *uncouth* 851
  rustic 876
boost *praise* 931
booster 935
boot 225
  to - *added* 37
booth 799
bootlegging 959
BOOTY 35, **793**
border, *n. edge* 231
  limit 233
border, *v. adjoin* 199
bordering 233
borderland 199
bore, *n. diameter* 202
  trouble 828
  plague 830
  wearier 841
bore, *v. perforate* 260
  satiate 869
boredom 841
borer 262
boring 275
born, be **359**
borough 189
borrow *imitate* 19
  receive **788**
borrowed plumes
  deception 545
borrower 806
BORROWING 788
bosh 546
bosky 367
bosom *breast* 221
  affections 820
boss *knob* 250
  politician 694
  rule 737
  master 745
botanic 369
botanist 369
BOTANY 369
botch *disorder* 59
  bungle 699
both 89
bother *trouble* 828
  harass 830

bottle *receptacle* 191
  preserve 670
bottom *lowest part* **211**
  ship 273
bottomless **208**
boudoir 191
bough 51, 367
boulder 342
boulevards 627
bounce *jump* 309
  dismiss 756
bound
  circumscribe 195, 229
  leap 309
boundary 233, -line **233**
boundless 105
bounds 230, 233
bountiful 816
bounty 707, 906
bouquet *fragrance* **400**
  beauty 847
bourgeois *medium* 29
bout *turn* 138
  fight 720
boutonniere 400
bovine 366, 499
bow, *n. fore part* 234
  curve 245
  weapon 727
bow, *v. stoop* **308**
  greet 894
bower 189, **191**
bowie knife 727
bowl, *vessel* 191
  -along *walk* 266
bow-legged 243
bowman 726
bowsprit 234
box, *n. chest* 191
box, *v. fight* 720
boy 129
boycott *eject* 297
  resist 719
  disapprove 932
boyhood 127
boylike 129
brace, *n. two* 89
  support 215
  music 413
brace, *v. strengthen* 159
  refresh 689
bracing *salubrious* 656
bracken 367
bracket *tie* 43
  couple 89
brackish 392
brag *boast* 884
braggadocio **884**
braggart 482, **884**
Brahmanism **976**
braid 219
brain *intellect* 450
brainless **499**
brainwork 451
brainy 450
brake, *n. copse* 367

curt 752
brake, v retard 275
bramble 253
branch, n 51, 367
branch, v ramify 244
brand, n. fuel 388
  torch 423
  mark 550
  sword 727
brand, v sear 384
  defame 874
brandish 315
brass alloy 41
bravado 884
brave, adj. 861
  -man 861
  -woman 861
brave, v. defy 234
  bear 826
bravery 861
brawl discord 713
brawny strong 159
brazen unreserved 525
  insolent 885
breach crack 44
  gap 198
  quarrel 713
  violation 925
bread 298
BREADTH 202
break fracture 44
  discontinuity 70
  gap 198
  faux pas 947
break, v. crumble 328
  train animals 370
  -in domesticate 370
  -out begin 66
  -up disjoin 44
  destroy 162
breakdown 162
breakers surf 348
breakneck
  rash 863
breast, n 221
breast, v. confront 234
breath breeze 349
  life 359
breathe exist 1
  blow 349
breathing 349
breathless
  out of breath 688
  astonished 870
breeches 225
breed, n. race 11
breed, v. multiply 161
breeding politeness 894
breeze wind 349
brethren 997
brevity 201, 572
brew 48
bribe, n. gift 784
bribe, v. tempt 615
  buy 795
  reward 973

bribery [see bribe]
bric-a-brac 847
bridal 903
bride 903
bridegroom 903
bridesmaid 903
bridge link 45
  -over join 43, 45
bridle depart 293
  restrain 751
brief time 111
  space 201
  concise 572
briefly awhile 111
  anon 132
  shortly 572
brier 253
brigade 726
brigand 792
bright shining 420
  color 428
  intelligent 498
  cheery 836
  beautiful 845
  cheering 848
brilliant shining 420
  witty 842
  beautiful 845
  glorious 873
brim 231
brimful 52
brindled 440
brine salt 392
bring 270
  -about cause 153
  -forth produce 161
  -forward adduce 467
  -over persuade 484
  -round persuade 615
  -together assemble 72
  -to mind 505
  -to terms 723
  -up develop 161
brink 231
briny 392
brisk prompt 111
  active 274, 682
bristle 253
bristling thorny 253
  discourteous 895
bristly rough 256
brittle 328
BRITTLENESS 328
broach begin 66
  tap 297
broad general 78
  space 202
broadcast
  disperse 73, 291
  publish 531
broaden 78
broadside side 236
  cannonade 716
broadsword 727
broil, n. fray 713
broil, v. heat 382

fry 384
broken divided 51
  discontinuous 70
  weak 160
  of horses 370
  -heart 837
broker 758
brokerage 812
bromide
  conventionalist 82
broncho 271
  -buster 370
bronze brown 433
brood multitude 102
  family 167
brook, n. stream 348
brook, v. bear 826
broom undergrowth 367
  sweeper 652
brother 17, 27
brotherhood 11, 17, 888
brotherly 888
brow top 210
  front 234
browbeat 860
BROWN 433
  -study 458
brownie 979
brownness 433
browse 298
bruise powder 330
  injure 649
bruised blemished 848
brunt 66, 276
brush, n. tail 235
  fight 720
brush, v. groom 370
  touch 379
  clean 652
brushwood 367
brusque 895
brutal savage 907
brutalize 945
brute animal 366
  rude person 895
  evildoer 913
  -force 964
brutish intemperate 954
BUBBLE, n.
  transience 111
  air 353
bubble, v. boil 315
bubonic plague 655
buccaneer 792
buck, n. stag 366
buck, v. leap 309
bucket receptacle 191
buckle, n. tie 43
buckle, v. distort 243
  -to labor 686
buckler 717
bucolic 371
bud, n. blossom 367
bud, v. expand 194
Buddhism 976
buddy chum 890

clash, *v. disagree* 24
  cross 179
  -of arms 720
clashing *contrariety* 14
clasp *fasten* 43
  stick 46
  embrace 902
CLASS, *n. category* 75
  learners 541
  school 542
  party 712
  laity 997
class, *v. arrange* 60
classfellow 890
classic *old* 124
  symmetry 242
classics 560
classification 60
classify 60
classmate 541
classroom 542
clatter *noise* 404
  rattle 407
clause 51
claw 781
clay *earth* 342
clean *perfect* 650
  unstained 652
  -cut 494
cleaner 652
cleanly 652
cleanness 652
cleanse 652
clear *simple* 42
  light 420
  transparent 425
  certain 474
  intelligible 518
  manifest 525
  distinct 535
  perspicuous 570
clear, *v. leap* 309
  vindicate 937, 970
clear-cut *true* 494
clear-sighted 441
clearness [see clear]
cleavage *cutting* 44
cleave *sunder* 44
  adhere 46
  bisect 91
clef 413
cleft *chink* 198
clement *lenient* 740
  compassionate 914
CLERGY 996
clergyman 996
clerical 995
clerk *recorder* 553
  writer 590
clever 698
cleverness 698
click 406
client *dependent* 711
  customer 795
clientele 795
cliff *height* 206

verticality 212
  steep 217
  crag 342
climate 338
climax *supremacy* 33
  summit 210
climb 305
clime 181
clinch *fasten* 43
cling *adhere* 46
  -to
  persevere 604a
  desire 865
  love 897
clink *resound* 408
clip *shorten* 201
clique 75, 712
cliquish 712
cloak, *n. dress* 225
cloak, *v. conceal* 528
  disguise 530
clock 114
clod *lump* 192
  earth 342
  fool 501
clog *hinder* 706
cloister *arcade* 189
  seclusion 893
close, *n. end* 67
close, *adj. similar* 17, 21
  tight 43
  near 197
  dense 321
  warm 382
  taciturn 585
  stingy 819
close, *v. shut* 261
  conclude 769
closely [see close]
closet 191
CLOSURE 261
clot 321
clothe 225
CLOTHING 225
cloture 142
CLOUD, *n. mist* 353
cloud, *v. darken* 421
  dim 422, 427
  -over 422, 427
cloudy *dim* 422
  opaque 426
clown 599, 844
cloy 641, 869
club, *n. place of meeting* 74
  association 712
  weapon 727
club, *v. combine* 48, 892
clue *answer* 462
  indication 550
clump 72, 250
  -of trees 367
clumsiness [see clumsy]
clumsy *unfit* 647
  awkward 699
cluster 72
clutch *seize* 781

throttle 789
clutter 59
coach, *n. carriage* 272
  tutor 540
coach, *v. teach* 537
coachman 268
coagulate *cohere* 46
  densify 321
coal 388
coalesce 13, 48
coalition 709, 712
coarse *harsh* 410
  vulgar 851
coast, *n. border* 231
coast, *v. glide* 266
  navigate 267
  land 342
coat *layer* 204
  paint 223
  dress 225
  -of arms 550
coating, inner - 224
coax *persuade* 615
  wheedle 902
cobble *mend* 660
cobbler 660
cobra 366
cobweb 205
cock *vane* 338
  bird 366
cockeyed 443
cockle 258
cocksure 484
coddle 902
code *concealment* 528
  cipher 561
  law 963
codicil *addition* 37
  testament 771
codify *arrange* 60
  legalize 963
coequal 27
coequality 27
coerce *compel* 744
  restrain 751
coeval 120
coexist *exist* 1
  concur 120
coexistence 120
coffer *chest* 191
  money chest 802
coffin 363
cog *tooth* 253
cogency 157
cogent *powerful* 157
cogitate 450, 451
cogitative 451
cognate *related* 9
  similar 17
cognition 490
cognizance 490
cohere 46
COHERENCE 46
coherent 23
cohesion 46
cohesive 46

cottager 188
couch, *n. bed* 215
couch, *v. lurk* 528
cough 349
COUNCIL *senate* 696
councilor 696
counsel *advice* 695
   lawyer 968
count, *n. item* 79
   lord 875
count, *v.*
   compute 37, 85
   estimate 480
countenance, *n. face* 234
   appearance 448
   favor 707
countenance, *v. approve*
   931
counter, *n. token* 550
counter, *adj. contrary* 14
   reverse 237
counteract 179, 706
COUNTERACTION 179
counterbalance 30, 179
countercharge 462
counterclaim 30
COUNTEREVIDENCE
   468
counterfeit *imitate* 19
   copy 21
   sham 545
   swindle 791
counterfeiter 792
countermand 756
countermarch 283
countermotion 283
counterpane 223
counterpart *identity* 13
   complement 14
   match 17
   copy 21
counterpoise
   compensate 30
countersign *n.*
   evidence 467
   mark 550
countersign, *v.* 488
countess 875
countless 105
countrified 189
country *region* 181
   abode 189
   land 342
   state 737
countryman 876
county 181
coupé 272
couple, *n. two* 89
couple, *v. unite* 43
   combine 48
COURAGE 861
courageous 861
courier *traveler* 268
   messenger 534
COURSE *order* 58
   continuity 69

time 106, **109**
layer 204
locomotion 267
direction 278
lesson 537
pursue 622
courser *horse* 271
court, *n. house* 189
   hall 191
   retinue 746
court, *v. invite* 615
   tribunal 966
   woo 902
   flatter 933
courteous 894
COURTESY
   politeness 894
courtier 935
courtly 852
court-martial 966
courtship 902
courtyard 182
cousin 11
cove *hollow* 252
   bay 343
covenant *compact* 769
   condition 770
   security 771
cover, *n. dress* 225
   lid 223
cover, *v. include* 76
   superpose 223
   conceal 528
   keep safe 664
covered 223
COVERING 220, **223**
coverlet 223
covert *abode* 189
   invisible 447
   latent 526
   refuge 666
coverture 903
covet *desire* 865
   envy 921
covetous *miserly* 921
covey 102
cow, *n. animal* 366
cow, *v. intimidate* 860
coward 862
COWARDICE 862
cowardly 862
cowboy 370
cower *stoop* 308
   fear 860
   quail 862
   fawn 886
cowherd 370
cowhide, *n. whip* 975
cowhide, *v. lash* 972
coworker 690
cowpuncher 370
coxcomb 854, 880
coxcombry *affectation* 855
coxswain 269
coy 881
cozy 377, 892

crabbed *sour* 397
   unintelligible 519
   uncivil 895
crack, *n. fissure* 44, 198
   furrow 259
crack, *v. split* 44
   crush 328
   sound 406
crack, *adj. excellent* 648
crack-brained *insane* 503
cracked *unmusical* 410
   mad 503
crackle 406
cracksman 792
cradle *beginning* 66
   infancy 127
   origin 153
   bed 215
   aid 707
craft *shipping* 273
   calling 625
   cunning 702
craftsman 690
craftsmanship 680
crag *cliff* 212, 253, 342
craggy *rough* 256
crake 884
cram *stuff* 194
   choke 261
   teach 537
   learn 539
   gorge 957
cramp, *n. spasm* 315
cramp, *v. paralyze* 158
   weaken 160
   hinder 706
crane *lever* 307
cranium 450
crank *fanatic* 504
   instrument 633
cranny 198
crash, *n. collision* 276
   sound 406
crash, *v. destroy* 162
   crack 328
crass *unintelligent* 493
   bad taste 851
cravat 225
crave *ask* 765
   desire 865
craven *cowardly* 862
craving 865
craw 191
crawl *elapse* 109
   creep 275
   cower 886
crazy *weak* 160
   mad 503
creak 410
cream, *n.* 356
   important part 642
   best 648
cream, *adj. yellow* 436
creamy 430
crease 258
create *cause* 153

compress 195
  shatter 328
  humble 879
crushed *unhappy* 828
crust 223
crusty *discourteous* 895
crutch *support* 215
crux *difficulty* 704
CRY *stridor* 410
  human **411**
  animal 412
  weep **839**
crying [*see* cry]
  urgent 630
crypt *cell* 191
  grave 207, 363
cryptic *uncertain* 475
  concealed 528
crystalline *dense* 321
  transparent 425
crystallization 321, 323
crystallize 321
cub *cad* 851
cubicle 191
cubist 556
cuddle 902
cudgel, *n.* 727
cudgel, *v. beat* 276
cue *hint* 527
  watchword 550
cuff *blow* 276
cuirass 717
cuisine 298
cul-de-sac 261
culinary 298
cull *choose* 609
  take 789
culminate *cap* 33
  tower 206
  crown 210
culprit 949, 975
cult 481, 990
cultivate *till* 371
  improve 658, 707
cultivated *courteous* 894
cultivation *tillage* 371
  knowledge 490
  improvement **658**
  courtesy 894
cultivator 371
cultural 537, 542
culture *knowledge* 490
  improvement 658
  courtesy 894
cumber 706
cumbersome *heavy* 319
  disagreeable 830
cumbrous 319, **830**
cumulative 467
CUNNING *artfulness* **702**
cup *vessel* 191

hollow 252
cupboard **191**
cupidity *avarice* 819
  desire 865
cupola *dome* 223, 250
cupping 662
cur *dog* 366
curable 658, 660
curate 996
curb, *n. bit* 752
curb, *v. moderate* 174
  slacken 275
  check 706
  restrain 751
curd 321
curdle *condense* 321
cure *reinstate* 660
  remedy 662
curio 847
CURIOSITY **455**
  phenomenon 872
curious *exceptional* 83
  inquisitive **455**
curl *bend* 245
  convolution 248
  hair 256
curly 248
currency *publicity* 531
  money **800**
current, *n.*
  of air 349
current, *adj. existing* 1
  general 78
  present 118
  happening 151
  rife 531, 532
currycomb 253
curse, *n. bane* 663
  adversity 735
curse, *v. execrate* **908**
cursory *transient* 111
  hasty 684
curt *short* 201
  concise 572
curtail *retrench* 38
  shorten 201
curtailment
  decrease 36
  [*see* curtail]
curtain *shade* 424
  screen 530
curtsy 308
CURVATURE **245**
curve 245, 252, 279
curved **245**
curvet *leap* 309
cushion *pillow* 215
cussedness 606
custodian 753
custody 664, 751
custom, *rule* 80

habit 124, **613**
  barter 794
  sale 796
  fashion 852
customary [*see* custom]
  regular 80
customer 795
cut, *n. bit* 51
  notch 257
  blow 276
  path 627
cut, *v. divide* 44
  absent 187
  curtail 201
  form 240
  depart 293
  reap 371
  carve 557
  ignore 893
  snub 895
  -across 302
  -adrift 44
  -away 38
  -off *subduct* 38
    disjoin 44
    bereft 776
    divorce 782
  -out *surpass* 33
    substitute 147
  -short *stop* 142
cuticle 223
cutlass 727
cutlery 253
cutter 273
cutthroat 361, 913
cutting *sharp* 253
  affecting 821
  painful 830
  -edge 253
cuttings 596
cycle *period* 138
  circle 247
  vehicle **272**
cyclic 138
cyclist 268
cyclone *rotation* 312
  wind 349
cyclonic 349
cyclopedia 593
cylinder 249, 272
cylindrical 249
cynic *recluse* 893
  misanthrope 911
  detractor 936
cynical *morose* 911
  contemptuous 930
  censorious 932
cynicism
  misanthropy 911
  discourtesy 895
czar 745

D

DESCENT 69
lineage 166
fall 306
describe 594
DESCRIPTION kind 75
narration 594
descriptive 594
desecrate misuse 679
profane 988
desert, n. waste 169, 180,
344
merit 924
desert, v. run away 187
relinquish 624
deserted empty 187
outcast 893
deserter 623
DESERTION 624
deserve be entitled to 924
deserving 924
deshabille
[see dishabille]
desiccate 340
desideratum 630
design prototype 22
delineation 554
painting 556
intention 620
plan 626
designate specify 79
call 564
designation kind 75
designer 559, 626
designing cunning 702
desirability 646
desirable 646, 865
DESIRE 865
will 600
desirous desiring 865
desist discontinue 142
desk box 191
school - 542
desolate, adj. dejected 837
secluded 893
desolate, v. ravage 162
desolating painful 830
desolation
[see desolate]
despair grief 828
hopelessness 859
despatch [see dispatch]
desperado 863, 887
desperate great 31
violent 173
hopeless 859
rash 863
despicable shameful 874
contemptible 930
despise 930
despite 30
despoil injure 659
take 789
rob 791
despond despair 859
fear 860
despot 739, 745

despotism severity 739
tyranny 964
destination end 67
rest 265
arrival 292
destine 152, 601, 620
DESTINY chance 152
fate 601
destitute 640, 804
destroy 2, 162
DESTROYER 165
naval 726
DESTRUCTION 21, 162
destructive ruinous 162
bad 649
DESUETUDE 614
desultory fitful 70
irregular in time 139
changeable 149
deviating 279
detach 44
detached irrelated 10
loose 47
detachment separation 44
part 51
army 726
detail, n. item 79
detail, v. describe 594
allot 786
in - 51
details minutiae 32
particulars 79
detain 781
detect 480a
detective 527
detention 781
deter dissuade 616
deteriorate 659
DETERIORATION 659
determine define 79
cause 153
satisfy 462
make sure 474
judge 480
discover 480a
resolve 604
determinant 153
determined resolute 604
detest dislike 867
hate 898
detestable 649
dethrone 738
dethronement 738, 756
detour 279, 629
detract subduct 38
underrate 483
defame 934
DETRACTION 934
DETRACTOR 936
detriment 619, 659
detrimental 649
devastate destroy 162
make havoc 162
depopulate 893
devastation 162
develop produce 161

evolve 313
development 35, 154
deviate change 140
turn 279
DEVIATION 20a, 140, 279
device motto 550
expedient 626
artifice 702
devil Satan 978
-worship 978
devious changeful 140
deviating 279
circuitous 311
devise imagine 515
plan 626
bequeath 784
devoid 777a
devolve 783
devote destine 601
employ 677
consecrate 873
devoted ill-fated 735
obedient 743
loving 897
devotee zealot 682
enthusiast 840
fanatic 988
devotion obedience 743
love 897
piety 987
worship 990
devour destroy 162
eat 298
cram 957
devout 987, 990
dew 339
dewy 339
dexter 238
dexterous 238, 698
dextral 238
dextrality 238
diabolic malevolent 907
wicked 945
satanic 978
diabolism 978
diabolist 978
diadem 747, 847
diagnosis 465, 522, 655
diagnostic 15, 465, 550
diagonal 217
diagram 554
dial 114
dialect 560, 563
dialogue 588
diameter 202
diametrical 237
diamond lozenge 244
diaphragm 68, 228
diary journal 114
diatribe 932
dichotomy 91
dicker haggle 794
dictate write 590
advise 695
command 741
dictator 745

dictatorial *narrow* 481
  willful 600
  insolent 885
diction 569
dictionary 86, **562**
dictum *maxim* 496
  affirmation 535
  command 741
didactic 537
die, *n. mold* 22
die, *v. expire* 67, **360**
  -away *dissolve* 4
  cease 142
  -out *pass away* 2
  vanish 4
diet *food* 298
  remedy 662
  council 696
dietetics 662
differ 15
  discord 713
DIFFERENCE **15, 24, 713**
different 15
  -time **119**
differentiate 7
difficult 704, 868
DIFFICULTY **704**
diffident *fearful* 860
  modest 881
diffuse *mix* 41
  disperse 73
  publish 531
  style 573
DIFFUSENESS **573**
diffusion 73
diffusive *verbose* 573
dig *deepen* 208
  excavate 252
  -up 480a
digest, *n.*
  compendium 596
digest, *v. think* 451
digestible 662
digestion 673
digestive 662
dignified 31, 873, **878**
dignify 873
dignitary *clergy* 996
dignity *greatness* 31
  glory 873
  pride 878
digress *deviate* 279
  ramble 573
digression *circuit* 629
digressive 573, 595
dike *gap* 198
  fence 232
  furrow 259
dilapidation 659
dilate *increase* 31, 35
  swell 194
  rarefy 322
  expatiate 573
dilation [*see* dilate]
dilatory *slow* 133, 275
dilemma 7, 475, **704**

dilettante 850
diligence 682
diligent *active* 682
dilly-dally *waver* 605
dilute *weaken* 160
  water 337
dim *dark* 421
  faint **422**
dime 800
dimension 192
diminish *lessen* 36, 38
  reduce 103
  contract 195
diminution 36, 195
diminutive *degree* 32
  size 193
DIMNESS **422**
dimple 252
DIM-SIGHTEDNESS **443**
din 404
dine 298
dingy 421, 422
dint *concavity* 252
  by - of 157, 631
diocese 995
dip, *n. slope* 217
  direction 278
  descent 306
dip, *v. plunge* 310
  immerse 337
  -into 461
diploma 467
diplomacy *artfulness* **702**
diplomatic
  [*see* diplomacy]
  -agent 758
diplomatist 700, **758**
dire *hateful* 649
  disastrous 735
  grievous 830
  fearful 860
direct, *adj.*
  straight 246, 278
direct, *v. teach* 537
  manage 693
  command 741
directable 278
DIRECTION [*see* direct]
  place 183
  tendency **278**
  management **693**
  precept 741
directive 692
directly *soon* 132
DIRECTOR **694**
directory *list* 86
dirge *lament* 839
dirigible, *n. balloon* 273
dirigible, *adj.* 278
dirk 727
dirt 653
dirty *opaque* 426
  unclean 653
disability *impotence* 158
disable 158
disabled 158

disabuse *inform* 527
  disclose 529
disadvantage 647
disadvantageous
  disastrous 619
  inexpedient 647
disaffection 489
disagree 24, 489, 713
disagreeable 830
DISAGREEMENT
  irrelation 10
  difference 15
  incongruity 24
  dissent 489
  discord 713
disallow 761
disappear 2, **449**
DISAPPEARANCE **449**
disappoint 509
DISAPPOINTMENT
  blighted hope 509
  discontent 832
DISAPPROBATION
  disapproval 932
disapprove 932
DISAPPROVAL **932**
disarm *disable* 158
disarrange 61
disaster *killing* 361
  evil 619
  adversity 735
  calamity 830
disastrous 619, 830
disavow 536
disband *separate* 44
  disperse 73
  liberate 750
disbar 968
disbelief 485
  religious 989
disbelieve **485, 989**
disburse 809
discard *eject* 297
  disuse 678
  abrogate 756
  repudiate **773**
discern *see* 441
  know 490
discerning 498
discernment 465, 498, 868
discharge, *n.*
  sound 406
discharge, *v.*
  be violent 173
  exude 295
  emit 297
  acquit oneself 692
  liberate 750
  abrogate 756
  pay 807
  exempt 927a
  acquit 970
disciple 65, **541**
discipline *order* 5?
  teaching 537
  restraint 751
  punishment 972

dispatch, v. eject 297
  kill 361
dispel scatter 73
  destroy 162
  repel 289
dispensation
  [see dispense]
  command 741
  license 760
  exemption 927a
dispense disperse 73
  give 784
  apportion 786
  retail 796
  -with disuse 678
  exempt 927a
disperse separate 44, 49
  scatter 73
DISPERSION 44, 73
dispirit 837
displace annihilate 2
  derange 61
  remove 185
DISPLACEMENT
  derangement 61
  removal 185
display show 525
  parade 882
displease 830
displeasure 828
  anger 900
disport 840
disposal [see dispose]
dispose arrange 60
  tend 176
  induce 615
  -of relinquish 782
  give 784
  sell 796
disposition temperament 5
  arrangement 60
  inclination 602
  mind 820
dispossess 789
disproof 479
disproportion
  irrelation 10
  disagreement 24
disprove 479
disputable uncertain 475
  doubtful 485
disputant 476
dispute disagree 24
  discuss 476
  doubt 485
  deny 536
  discord 713
disqualification 158, 699,
  925
disqualify 158, 925
disquiet changeability 149
  agitation 315
  uneasiness 828
disquietude 860
disregard overlook 458
  neglect 460

  make light of 483
  disrespect 929
disrelish dislike 867
disreputable 874
  vicious 945
DISREPUTE 874, 929
DISRESPECT 929
disrespectful 929
disrobe 226
disruption disjunction 44
  destruction 162
dissatisfaction 828, 832
dissatisfied 832
dissatisfy 832
dissect anatomize 44, 49
  investigate 461
dissemble 544, 988
dissembler 548
disseminate scatter 73
  publish 531
  teach 537
dissemination
  [see disseminate]
dissension 489, 713
DISSENT 489
  heterodoxy 984
dissenter 489, 984
dissentient 24, 489
dissenting 487
DISSERTATION 595
dissever 44
DISSIMILARITY 15,
  16a, 18
dissimilitude 15, 16a, 18,
  24
dissimulate 544
dissipate destroy 162
dissipated 954, 961
dissociate 44
dissociation 10, 44
dissoluble 51
dissolution
  [see dissolve]
  decomposition 49
  end 67
  destruction 162
  death 360
dissolvable 51
dissolve vanish 2, 4, 49
  destroy 162
  liquefy 335
  abrogate 756
dissonance
  disagreement 24
  discord 414, 713
dissonant 414
dissuade 616
DISSUASION 616
DISTANCE 196
  overtake 282
  go beyond 303
distant 196
distaste 867
distemper color 428
distend 194
distended 192, 250

distill extract 301
  evaporate 336
distillation 336
distinct audible 402
  visible 446
  intelligible 518
  manifest 525
distinction difference 15
  greatness 31
  discrimination 465
  elegance 578
  fame 873
distinctive 15
distinguish perceive 441
  discriminate 465
distinguished superior 33
  noted 873
distinguishing 15
distort 243, 523
DISTORTION twist 243
  of vision 443
  misinterpretation 523
  falsehood 544
distract 458
distracted confused 475
  excited 824
distraction passion 825
distrain take 789
  attach 969
distraught 475, 503
distress, n. poverty 804
  affliction 828
distress, v.
  cause pain 830
distressing 830
distribute arrange 60
  disperse 73
  allot 786
distribution
  [see distribute]
district 181
distrust disbelief 485
  fear 860
  mistrust 920
distrustful 487
disturb derange 61
  displace 185
  agitate 315
  distress 830
disturbance
  disorder 59, 61, 315
disunion disagreement 24
  separation 44
disunite separate 44
DISUSE 614, 678
disused 678
ditch inclosure 232
  trench 259
  conduit 350
ditto 13, 104
ditty 415
divarication 16a
dive 267, 310
diver 310
diverge 291
  [see divergence]

DIVERGENCE 291
 difference 15
 nonuniformity 16a
 dissimilarity 18
 variation 20a
 disagreement 24
diverse 15, 81
diversified 16a
diversify [*see* diversity]
 vary 18, 20a
 change 140
diversion *change* 140
 deviation 279
 pleasure 377
 amusement 840
diversity *difference* 15
 irregularity 16a
 dissimilarity 18
 multiformity 81
divert *turn* 279
 deceive 545
 amuse 840
divest *denude* 226
 -oneself of
DIVESTMENT 226
divide *separate* 44
 part 51
 bisect 91
 apportion 786
dividend *part* 51
 portion 786
divination 511, 992
divine, *n. clergyman* 996
divine, *v. predict* 511
 guess 514
divine, *adj. perfect* 650
 of God 976, 983, 983a
 -service 990
Divinity *God* 976
 theology 983
divisible 51
 [*see* divide]
division [*see* divide]
 separation 44
 part 51
 class 75
 interval 198
 discord 713
DIVORCE, n. 44, 905
divorce, *v. relinquish* 782
divulge 529
dizziness [*see* dizzy]
dizzy *confused* 458
 vertigo 503
do *suit* 23
 produce 161
 act 680
 complete 729
 -for *destroy* 162
 kill 361
docile *willing* 602
dock, *n. wharf* 231
 tribunal 966
dock, *v. shorten* 201
docket *list* 86

schedule 611
doctor *learned man* 492
 physician 662
doctrinaire 855
doctrine *tenet* 484
document 551
documentary 467
dodder 160
dodge, *n. stratagem* 702
dodge, *v. change* 140
 deviate 279
 avoid 623
doer 680, 690
doff 226
dog, *n.* 366
dog, *v. follow* 281
dogged *obstinate* 606
 valorous 861
doggerel *verse* 597
 ridiculous 851, 853
dogma 484
dogmatic *certain* 474
 positive 481
dogmatism 474
dogmatist 474, 887
doings *events* 151
 actions 680
doldrums *sulks* 901a
dole, *n. mite* 640
dole, *v. give* 784
doleful 837
doll 554
dollar 800
dolor *physical* 378
 moral 828
dolorous 830
domain 75, 181
dome 206, 223, 250
domestic, *n. servant* 746
domestic, *adj.*
 native 188, 367
 tame 370
 home 189, 221
 secluded 893
 -animals 366
domesticate *locate* 184
 acclimatize 613
 -animals 370
domestication 184, 370
domesticize 370
domicile 189
domiciled
 inhabitating 186
domiciliary 188
 -visit 461
dominant 175
dominate *influence* 175
 rule 737
domination 175, 737
domineer 739, 885
dominion 181, 737
 -rule 737
domino *dress* 225
 mask 530
don, *n. scholar* 492
 tutor 540

noble 875
don, *v. put on* 225
donate 784
donation 784
done
 -for 732
 failed 732
 -up *tired* 688
donjon *defense* 717
 prison 752
donkey *ass* 271
 fool 501
donor 784
doom, *n. fate* 152
 destruction 162
 death 360
 necessity 601
doom, *v. sentence* 971
door *entrance* 66, 260
 brink 231
 barrier 232
doorkeeper 263
dormancy 172
dormant *inert* 172
dormitory 191
dory 273
dose *quantity* 25
 medicine 662
dot *speck* 32, 193
dot *dowry* 784
dotage *age* 128
dotard 130, 501
dote *drivel* 499, 503
 -upon 897
double *similar* 17
 increase 35
 duplex 90
 substitute 147
 fold 258
 wraith 992a
double-dealing 544, 940
double-faced 940
DOUBT, n. uncertainty
 475
 disbelief 485
 skepticism 989
doubtful 475, 485
doubtless 474, 488
douceur *gift* 784
doughboy 726
doughty 159, 861
dour 739
douse 310
dovetail *agree* 23
 join 43
 insert 228
dowdy 851
dower *property* 780
 bequest 784
down, *n. upland* 180
down, *adj. below* 207
down, *v. cast down* 308
downcast *dejected* 837
downfall *destruction* 162
 failure 732
 misfortune 735

E

educate *teach* 537
educated **490**
education *teaching* 537
knowledge 490
educational **537**
educe *extract* 301
efface *destroy* 162
obliterate 552
EFFECT *consequence* **154**
complete 729
effective *capable* 157
influential 175
useful 644
effects *property* 780
goods 798
effectual 157, 175
effectually 52
effeminacy
[see effeminate]
effeminate *weak* 160
womanish 374
timorous 862
effervesce 173, 353
effervescence 353
effervescent 338, 353
effete *old* 128
weak 160
useless 645
efficacious [see efficient]
efficient *powerful* 157
operative 170
reliable 632
useful 644
effigy *copy* 21
efflorescence 161
effluence 295
effluvium *vapor* 334
odor 398
efflux *egress* 295
effort 686
effrontery 885
effulgence 420
effusion
loquacity 584
-of blood 361
effusive 584
egg *embryo* 153
-on 615
egg-shaped 247
ego 317, 450, 980a
egoism **482**, **880**, **911**
egoist **482**, **880**, **911**
egotism *overestimation* 482
vanity 880
cynicism 911
selfishness 943
egotist **482**, **880**, **911**
egotistical [see egotism]
narrow 481
egregious *exceptional* 83
absurd 497
EGRESS 295
Egyptian -deities 979
eight *number* 98
ejaculate *utter* 580
eject 284, **297**

EJECTION
displacement 185
propulsion 284
emission **297**
eke
-out *complete* 52
spin out 110
elaborate, *adj.* 686
elaborate, *v. improve* 658
prepare 673
work out 729
elaboration 673
elapse *flow* 109
pass 122
elastic 325
[see elasticity]
ELASTICITY
strength 159
energy 171
spring 325
elate, *adj. exulting* 836
vain 880
boastful **884**
elate, *v. gladden* 836
elated 838
[see elate]
elbow, *n. angle* 244
elbow, *v. push* 276
elbowroom 180, 748
elder, *adj.* 124, 128
elder, *n.* 996
elderly 128
elect *choose* 609
predestinate 976
election **609**
elector 609
electorate 609
electric *swift* 274
electricity 388
electrify *strengthen* 157
motorize 226
excite 824
astonish 870
electron 32
ELEGANCE *in style* **578**
beauty 845
elegy *poetry* 597
element *component* 56
beginning 66
cause 153
elemental, *adj. simple* 42
elemental, *n.*
Rosicrucian 980
elementary *simple* 42
elephantine *huge* 192
elevate 307
elevated 206
ELEVATION
height 206
raising **307**
repute 873
elevator 307
elf *fairy* 979
elicit *cause* 153
draw out 301
discover 480a

eligible 646
eliminate *subduct* 38
simplify 42
exclude 55
weed out 103, 297
extract 301
elimination **42**
eliminative 299, 350
elision 201
elixir 5
ellipse 247
ellipsis 201
elliptic 247
elocution 582
elocutionist 582
elongate 200
elongation 200
eloquence *style* 569, **574**
speech 582
eloquent 574, **582**
elsewhere 187
elucidate 522
elude *avoid* 623
escape 671
palter 773
elusive 623, **773**
elysian 981
Elysium 981
emaciated 203, 640
emaciation 203
emanate 295
emanation *egress* 295
odor 398
emancipate *deliver* 672
free 750
embalm 400
embankment
esplanade 189
fence 717
embargo 761
embark *sail* 267
depart **293**
-in *engage in* 676
embarrass 704
embarrassed *poor* 804
in debt 806
embarrassing **704**
embarrassment 704
embassy 755, 758
embellish 847
embers 384
embezzle 791
embitter *deteriorate* **659**
aggravate 835
emblazon *color* 428
ornament 847
emblem 550
embody *join* 43
combine 48
form a whole 50
include 76
materialize 316
embolden 861
emboss 250
embrace, *n.* 892, 902
embrace, *v. compose* 54

include 76
inclose 227
greet 888
embrasure 257
embrocation 662
embroider 847
embroil 61, 713
embryo *beginning* 66
cause 153
in - *preparing* 673
embryonic *initial* 66
immature 674
emendation 658
emerald *green* 435
emerge 295
emergency *circumstance* 8
juncture 43
occasion 134
event 151
emetic 297
emigrant 57, 268, 295
emigrate 266, 295
emigration 266, 295
eminence *height* 206
fame 873
eminent 873
eminently 33
emissary 758
emission 297
emit *eject* 297
emolument 775, 973
emotion 821
emotional 821
empale [*see* impale]
emperor 745
emphasis 535
emphasize 535, 642
emphatic 535, 642
emphatically *much* 31
empire 181, 737
empirical 463
employ *use* 677
-oneself 680
employee 746
employer 795
employment 625
empower *authorize* 157
delegate 759
permit 760
empress 745, 877
emptiness 2, 187
[*see* empty]
empty, *adj. vacant* 4, 187
empty, *v. deflate* 195
drain 297
empty-headed 491
emulate *imitate* 19
vie 648
rival 708, 873
enable 157
enact *act* 680
conduct 692
complete 729
order 741
ordain 963
enamel *coating* 223

enamor 897
encamp 184
encase [*see* incase]
enchain 751
enchant 377, 829
enchantment 827, 829
encircle *surround* 220, 227
go round 311
enclose [*see* inclose]
enclosure [*see* inclosure]
enclothe 225
encomium 931
encompass 227
encore 104, 931
encounter, *n.* 276, 720
encounter, *v. undergo* 151
meet 292
withstand 708
encourage *animate* 615
hearten 858
embolden 861
encroach 303, 925
-upon 927
encrust 223
encumber *hinder* 706
encumbrance 706
encyclopedia 593
END *termination* 67
cessation 142
effect 154
object 620
endanger 665
endear 897
ENDEARMENT 902
endeavor *pursue* 622
attempt 675
endemic 657
endless *infinite* 105
lasting 110
perpetual 112
spacious 180
endorse [*see* indorse]
endorsement
[*see* indorsement]
endow *confer power* 157
endowed with
possessed of 777
endowment *power* 157
talent 698
gift 784
endue 157
endurance [*see* endure]
perseverance 604a
patience 831
endure *exist* 1
last 106, 110
continue 141, 143
undergo 151
feel 821
submit to 826
endwise 212
ENEMY *foe* 891
-to society 891
energetic *powerful* 157
strenuous 171
enterprising 676

energize 157, 171
ENERGY *power* 157
strength 159
physical 171
activity 682
fervor 820
enervate *paralyze* 158
weaken 160
enervation 160, 575
enfeeble 158, 160
enfold 229
enforce *urge* 615
compel 744
enfranchise *free* 748
liberate 750
empower 760
engage *bespeak* 132
undertake 676
do battle 722
commission 755
promise 768
engaged *betrothed* 903
engagement *business* 625
battle 720
betrothal 768
engaging *pleasing* 829
engender 161
engine 633
engine driver 268
engineer *engine driver* 268
military 726
English broken - 563
king's - 560
plain-*intelligible* 518
(of style) 576
engorge *swallow* 296
engrave 550, 558
engraver 559
ENGRAVING 558
engross *write* 590
possess 777
engulf *swallow up* 296
plunge 310
enhance 35, 835
enhancement 35
enigma 519, 533
enigmatic 519, 533
enjoin *advise* 695
command 741
prescribe 926
enjoy *physically* 377
possess 777
morally 827
enjoyment [*see* enjoy]
enkindle *heat* 384
excite 824
enlarge *increase* 31, 35
swell 194
enlighten *illumine* 420
inform 527
teach 537
enlist 615, 722
enlisted man 726
enliven *inspirit* 834
cheer 836
enmesh 704

erudite 490, 500, 539
erudition 490, 539
eruption *revolution* 146
  violence 173
  egress 295
  ejection 297
  explosion 406
eruptive [*see* eruption]
escalade 305
escalator 305, 307
escapade 608, 840
ESCAPE, *n. flight* 671
escape, *v.* 671, 927
eschew *avoid* 623
  dislike 867
escort *companion* 88
  safeguard 664
  keeper 753
esculent 298
escutcheon 550, 551
esophagus 350
esoteric 528
especial 79
especially 33
espionage 441, 461
esplanade 189
espouse *choose* 609
  marry 903
  -a cause *aid* 707
  co-operate 709
esprit de corps 709
espy 441
esquire 875
essay, *n.*
  experiment 463
  dissertation 595
ESSAY, *v.*
  endeavor 675
essence *being* 1
  nature 5
  meaning 516
essential *real* 1
  intrinsic 5
  inherent 56
  important 642
establish *settle* 150
  create 161
  place 184
  evidence 467
  demonstrate 478
established 141
  church 983a
establishment
  fixture 150
  location 184
  shop 799
estate *condition* 7
  property 780
esteem 928, 931
estimable 648
estimate *number* 85
  measure 466
  adjudge 480
estimation 480, 928, 931
estrange *disjoin* 44
  alienate 889

hate 898
estuary 343
etch 259, 558
etching 558
Eternal, The - 976
eternal 112
eternalize 112
eternity 112
  an - 110
ether *space* 180
  vapor 334
  anaesthetic 376
ethereal 4, 820
etheric body 980a
ethical 926
ethics 926
ethnology 372
etiquette *custom* 613
  fashion 852
etymology 562
Eucharist 998
eulogist 935
eulogize 482
eulogy 931
Eumenides 173, 900
euphemism *metaphor* 521
  phrase 566
  style 577
euphemist 935
euphony *melody* 413
  elegant style 578
euphuism 579, 855
eurythmic 542
eurythmics 242
evacuate *vacate* 185
  quit 293
  emit 297
evade *elude* 477
  not observe 773
  exempt 927
evanescent 111
evangelical 983a, 985
Evangelists 985
evaporate *vanish* 4
  vaporize 336
  dry up 340
evaporation
  vaporization 336
  dryness 340
evasion *sophistry* 477
  quirk 481
  concealment 528
  falsehood 544
  avoidance 623
evasive [*see* evasion]
eve 126
even, *adj.*
  uniform 16
  equal 27
  level 213
  parallel 216
  straight 246
  flat 251
  smooth 255
even, *v. level* 213
even, *adv.* 469

EVENING 126
evenness
  [*see* even]
  symmetry 242
evensong 126, 990
event 151
  in the - of
  circumstance 8
  eventuality 151
  destiny 152
  supposition 514
  justified by the - 937
eventful 151, 642
eventide 126
eventual 121
EVENTUALITY 151
eventually 121, 151, 154
eventuate 151
ever 16, 112
everlasting 112
evermore 16, 112
every 78, 138
  -other 138
everybody 78
every one 78
everywhere 180, 186
evict 297, 789
EVIDENCE 467
evident *visible* 446
  certain 474
  proved 478
  manifest 525
evidential 467
EVIL *harm* 619
  badness 649
  -spirits 980
  -star 649
EVILDOER 913, 949
evildoing 945
evil-minded 907, 945
evil speaking 908, 934
evince *show* 467
  prove 478
evoke *cause* 153
  call upon 765
  excite 824
evolution 161, 311, 313
evolutionary 313
evolve 161, 313
ewer 191
exact, *adj. similar* 17
  copy 21
  true 494
  literal 516
exact, *v. require* 741
  claim 924, 926
exacting *discontented* 832
  fastidious 865
exaction 741
exactly *literally* 19
exactness [*see* exact]
  repetition 13
exaggerate *increase* 35
  overestimate 482
  magnify 549
  misrepresent 555

F

fence, *n. enclosure* 232,
752
thief 792
on the - 607
fence, *v. evade* 544
fight 720
fender 717
ferment, *n. disorder* 59
agitation 171, 315
lightness 320
excitement 825
ferment, *v. effervesce* 353
sour 397
fermentation
[see ferment]
fern 367
ferocity *violence* 173
brutality 907
ferret
-out *be curious* 455
ferry 270
ferryman 269
fertile 168
fertilization 161, 168
fertilize 168
ferule 975
fervent *hot* 382
desirous 865
fervid *hot* 382
heartfelt 821
fervor *passion* 820
animation 821
festal 687, 840
fester *corrupt* 653
festival 138, 883
festivity 840, 883
festoon 245
fetch *bring* 270
sell for 812
fete 840, 882
fetid 401
fetish 991, 993
FETOR 401, 663
fetter *restrain* 43, 751
shackle 752
feud *discord* 713
feudal 749
feudatory 749
fever *heat* 382
disease 655
excitement 825
feverish *hot* 382
hurry 684
excited 824
few 103, 137
FEWNESS 32, 103
fez 225
fiancée 897
fiasco 732
fiat 741
fib *falsehood* 546
fiber *filament* 205
fibrous 205
fickle *changeable* 149
irresolute 605
fickleness 605

fiction *untruth* 546
work of - 594
fictitious 515, 546
fiddle 417
fiddler 416
fidelity *identity* 13
truth 494
veracity 543
obedience 743
honor 939
fidget 682, 825
field *scope* 180
region 181
plain 344
agriculture 371
business 625
field day 882
field glass 445
field marshal 745
fiend *ruffian* 913
demon 980
fiendish 907, 945, 980
fierce *violent* 173
daring 861
angry 900
fiery *violent* 173
hot 382
excitable 825
angry 900
fifer 416
fight *contention* 720
warfare 722
-shy *avoid* 623
turn tail 862
fighter 726
figment 515
figurative 554
FIGURE, *n. number* 84
form 240
metaphor 521
price 812
cut a - *repute* 873
- of speech 521
figure, *v. represent* 554
figurehead *sign* 550
representation 554
FILAMENT 205
filch 791
file, *v. pare* 38
arrange 60
smooth 255
pulverize 330
record 551
-off *march* 266
file, *n. row* 69
list 86
on - 60
filial 167
filibuster, *n.*
obstructionist 710
freebooter 792
filibuster, *v. delay* 133
impede 706
pillage 791
filibusterer 706, 710
filigree 219

fill *complete* 52
occupy 186
load 190
stuff 224
-up *complete* 52
close 261
fillet *band* 45
filament 205
ornament 847
filling *stuffing* 224
fillip *impulse* 276
stimulus 615
film *layer* 204
opacity 426
filmy *scaly* 204
filter *percolate* 295
clean 652
filth 653
filthy 653
final 67, 729
finale *end* 67, 729
finality 67, 729
finally *eventually* 151
on the whole 476
finance 800
financier 639
find *experience* 151
adjudge 480
discover 480a
-out 480a
finding *judgment* 480
fine, *adj. rare* 322
not raining 340
delicate 329
exact 494
good 648
beautiful 845
adorned 847
proud 878
-arts 554
-gentleman *fop* 854
-lady 854
-writing 482, 577
in end 67
after all 476
fine, *v. mulct* 974
fineness [see fine)]
finery 847
finesse *tact* 698
artifice 702
finger *touch* 379
finical 855, 868
finicking 855, 868
finis 67
finish, *n. end* 67
symmetry 242
finish, *v. complete* 729
finished *symmetrical* 242
perfect 650
skilled 698
finite 32
fire, *n. energy* 171
heat 382
fuel 388
fire, *v. make hot* 384
shoot 716

dismiss 756
  excite 824
  -at 716
  -up *rage* 825
firearms 727
firebrand *fuel* 388
  instigator 615
fire bug 384, 949
fire-eater 863, 887
fire extinguisher **385**
fireman *stoker* 268
  extinguisher 385
fireplace **386**
fireproof 385
firm, *n. partnership* 712
  797
firm, *adj. fast* **43**
  steadfast 150
  hard 323
  resolute 604
firmness [*see* firm]
first **66**
firstborn 124, 128
first-class *best* 648
first fruits 154
first-rate 648
firth 343
fiscal 800
fish, *n.* 366
fish, *v.* 622
  -for *pursue* 622
  desire 865
  -out *inquire* 461
  -up *raise* 307
fisherman 361
fissure **44**, 198
fit, *n. paroxysm* **173**
  caprice 608
  disease 655
fit, *adj. expedient* 646
  right 922, 924
fit, *v. agree* 23
  -out *dress* 225
  prepare 673
fitful *irregular* 139
  changeable 149
fitness **23**, 926
fitting 924
FIVE **98**
fix, *n. dilemma* 7, 704
fix, *v. join* 43
  arrange 60
  establish 150
  place 184
fixed *intrinsic* 5
  durable 110
  permanent 141
  stable **150**
  -idea 825
fixity 141, 265
fixture **150**
fizz 353
fizzle 304, 353
flabby 324
flaccid 324, 326
flaccidity 326

flag, *n.* 550, 747
flag, *v. be weak* 160
  falter 275
  languish 683
  fatigue 688
flagon 191
flagrant *manifest* 525
  notorious 531
  atrocious 945
flagstaff 206
flake 204
flamboyant 577
flame *fire* 382
  light 420
  passion 824, 825
flank *side* 236
flap, *v. hang* 214
  move to and fro 315
flapper *girl* 129
flare *flash* 173
  glare 420
  -up *be excited* **824**
  get angry 900
flash *flare* 173
  fire 382
  light 420
flashy *gaudy* 428
  tawdry 851
flask 191
flat, *n. house* 191
  note 413
flat, *adj. low* 207
  horizontal 213
  even **251**
  vapid 391
  dull 843
flatiron 255
flatness 213, **251**
flatten 213, **251**
flatter *deceive* 545
  please 829
  adulate **933**
  -oneself 472, 858
FLATTERER **935**
flattering **938**
FLATTERY **933**
flaunt *flourish* 873
  display **882**
flaunting 882
flavor 390
flavoring 393
flaw *break* 70, 198
  error 495
  imperfection 651
  blemish 848
flaxen 436
flay 226
flea *insect* 366
fleck 440
fled *escaped* 671
flee 287
fleece, *n.* 223
fleece, *v. strip* 789
  rob 791
  surcharge 814
fleet, *n.* 273, 726

fleet, *adj. transient* 111
  swift 274
fleeting 111
flesh 364
flesh color 434
fleshy *of fruit* 354
flexible *pliant* 324
flicker *waver* 314
  flutter 315
  glimmer 420, 422
flier *aviator* 269a
  advertisement 531
flight *flying* 267
  swiftness 274
  departure 287, 293
  escape 671
flighty *inattentive* 458
  fanciful 515
flimsy *weak* 160
  slight 322
  soft 324
  sophistical 477
  trifling 643
flinch *fear* 860, 862
fling *propel* 284
flippant *pert* 885
  discourteous 895
flirt 854, **902**
flirtation 902
flit *elapse* 109, 111
  move 264
  depart 293
  run away 623
flivver 272
float *navigate* **267**
  buoy up 305
  be light 320
flock *multitude* 72, 102
  laity 997
floe *ice* 383
flog 684, 972
flood 337, 348
floodgate 350
flood tide 206, 337
floor, *n.* 211
floor, *v. overthrow* 731
flop 315
flora 367, 369
floral 367
floriculture 371
florid 428, 434
  (*style*) 577
florist 371
flotation [*see* float]
flotilla 273, 726
flounce, *n. trimming* 231
flounce, *v. jump* 309
flounder *toss* 315
  be uncertain 475
  bungle 699
  fail 732
flourish *brandish* 315
  vegetate 365, 367
  prosper 734
  flaunt 872
  boast 884

flourishing [*see* flourish]

flout 929

flow *course* 109
 motion 264
 stream 348
 -from *result* 154
 -into *river* 348

flower, *n. plant* 367
 ornament 847

flower, *v. produce* 161
 prosper 734

flowery *ornamental* 847

flowing [*see* flow] 348

fluctuate *change* 149
 oscillate 314, 605

fluctuation 314

flue 351

fluency 584

fluent *flowing* 348
 loquacious 584

fluffy 324

fluid 333
 -in motion 347

fluidity 333

fluke *chance* 156

flume 350

flunk 732

flunky *servant* 746

flunkyism 933

fluorescence 425

flurry, *n.*
 agitation 821, 824
 excitability 825

flurry, *v.* 458

flush, *n. heat* 382
 glow 420, 428

flush, *adj. even* 213
 flat 251

flush, *v. glow* 382
 redden 434
 wash 652
 blush 821

fluster, *n.* 821

fluster, *v.* 824, 825

flutter, *n. agitation* 315

flutter, *v. vary* 149
 excite 821
 tremble 860

flux *conversion* 144
 motion 264
 flow 348

fly, *n. insect* 366

fly, *v. vanish* 4
 elapse 109
 be transient 111
 aviate 267
 hasten 274
 recede 287
 depart 293
 soar 338
 shun 623
 -at 716
 -off 291
 -open 260

flying [*see* fly] 267

foal 271

foam, *n.* 353

foam, *v. boil* 315
 rage 824, 825

foamy 320

focal 222

FOCUS 74
 center 222

fodder *food* 298

foe 891

fog *mist* 353
 uncertainty 475

foggy *opaque* 426

fogy *fool* 501
 laughingstock 857

foible 945

foil, *n. weapon* 727

foil, *v. contrast* 14
 baffle 706
 defeat 731

FOLD, *n. inclosure* 232
 plait 258
 congregation 997

fold, *v.* 91, 258

foliage 367

folio 593

folk 372

folklore 124, 979

follow *be similar* 17
 -in *order* 63
 -in *time* 117
 pursue 235
 -in *motion* 281
 hold good 478
 understand 518
 pursue 622
 obey 743
 -up *continue* 143

follower [*see* follow]
 successor 65
 pursuer 281
 disciple 541
 servant 746
 lover 897

FOLLOWING 282

FOLLY 499

foment *stimulate* 173
 warm 384
 promote 707
 excite 824

fond 897

fondle 897, 902

fondness *desire* 865

FOOD *eatables* 298

FOOL, *n.* 501

fool, *v deceive* 545
 trifle 499
 ridicule 856

foolhardy 863

foolish 499, 699

foot *length* 200
 base 211
 on - *existing* 1
 preparing 673
 active 682

footfall *motion* 264

footing *circumstances* 8

influence 175
 situation 183
 support 215

foot-loose *liberated* 750

footman 746

footpad 792

footpath 627

footprint 550, 551

foot *soldier* 726

foot-sore 688

footstep 551

footstool 215

FOP 854

foppery 855, 882

foppish *affected* 855

for *because* 476

forage *food* 298

foray *attack* 716
 robbery 791

forbear *avoid* 623
 spare 678
 tolerate 826
 pity 914
 abstain 953

forbearance 826, 918

forbid 761

forbidding *ugly* 846

force, *n. assemblage* 72
 power 157
 strength 159
 energy 171
 violence 173
 significance 516
 troops 726

force, *v. urge* 615
 compulsion 744

forced *irrelative* 10
 unwilling 603

forceful 171, 574

forcible [*see* force]

forcibly *744*

ford 302

fore 234

fore-and-aft 200

fore-and-after 273

forebears 166

forebode 511

forecast *foresight* 510
 prediction 507, 511
 plan 626

forefathers 166

forefront 234

forego 624, 757

foregoing 116, **122**

foregone *past* 122

foreground 234

forehead 234

foreign *alien* 10
 extraneous 57

foreigner 57

foreknow 510

foreknowledge 510

foreland 206

foreman 694

foremost *superior* 33
 beginning 66

-nature 906
-offices *mediation* 724
-taste 578, 850
-turn *kindness* 906
-will *benevolence* 906
-woman **948**
-word 931
make - *restore* 790
substantiate 924
vindicate 937
good-for-nothing 158, **949**
good-looking 845
goodly *great* 31
handsome 845
good-natured 906
GOODNESS 648
goods *effects* 780
merchandise 798
goose *bird* 366
gore, n. *gusset* 43
blood 361
gore, v. 260
gorge, n. *ravine* **198**
gorge, v. *glut* 869
gormandize 957
gorgeous *gay* 428
beautiful 845
gorilla 366
gormandize **957**
gorse 367
gory *murderous* 361
red 434
gospel *doctrine* 484
truth 494
Gospels 985
gossamer 205
gossamery 320
gossip *news* 532
babbler 584
conversation 588
gouge 262
gourmand *glutton* 957
gourmet 868, 954*a*
govern 693, 737
governess 540
government 737, 745, 965
governor *director* 694
ruler 745
gown *dress* 225
grab *take* 789
grace *elegance* 845
polish 850
pity 914
forgiveness 918
worship 990
graceful *elegant* 578
beautiful 845
tasteful 850
graceless *inelegant* 579
ugly 846
impenitent 951
Graces 845
gracious *courteous* 894
kind 906
gradation *degree* 26
order 58

grade *degree* 26
classify 60
term 71
obliquity 217
ascent 305
class 541
crossing 219
gradual *degree* 26
continuous 69
slow 275
gradually **275**
graduate, n. 492
graduate, v. *adjust* 23
measure 26
arrange 60
initiate 537
graduation 541
graft, v. *insert* **300**
graft, n. *loot* 784
improbity 940
grain *humor* 5
tendency 176
roughness 256
texture 329
powder 330
against the-704
GRAMMAR 567
grammatical 567
gramophone 418
grand *august* 31
important 642
handsome 845
glorious 873
ostentatious 882
-juror 967
grandee 875
grandeur *greatness* 31
repute 873
grandfather 130, 166
grandmother 166
grandness [see grand]
granny 30
grant *admit* 529
permit 760
consent 762
confer 784
granular 330
graphic *intelligible* **518**
vigorous 574
descriptive 594
graphophone 418
grapnel 666
grapple 789
-with
-*a question* 461
-*difficulties* 704
oppose 708
resist 719
grasp, n. *power* 737
grasp, v. *comprehend* 518
retain 781
-at 865
grasping *miserly* 819
covetous 865
grass 367
-widow 905

grassland 367
grassplot 371
grassy 367
grate, n. *fireplace* 386
grate, v. *rub* 330
-on the ear
harsh sound 410
grateful *enjoyable* 377
agreeable 829
thankful 916
gratification 377, 827
gratify *permit* 760
please 829
grating *lattice* 219
stridor 410
gratis 815
GRATITUDE 916
gratuitous
inconsequent 477
free 748, 815
gratuity *gift* **784**
grave, n. 363
grave, adj. *somber* 428
important 642
distressing 830
sad 837
graveclothes **363**
gravedigger **363**
gravestone 363
gravitate *descend* 306
weigh 319
-towards 176
GRAVITY weight 319
importance 642
seriousness 837
[see grave]
GRAY *old* 128
color 428, **432**
graybeard 130
graze *touch* 199, 379
browse 298
rub 331
grease *lubricate* 332
oil 355, 356
greasy 355
great *much* 31
big 192
glorious 873
greater 33
greatness 33
GREATNESS 31
greed *desire* 865
gluttony 957
greedy 819, **865**, 957
Greek - *deities* 970
GREEN, n. lawn 344, 371
color **435**
green, adj. *new* 123
young 127
sour 397
credulous 486
novice 701
immature 674
greenhorn *novice* 493
bungler 701
greenness 435

greensward **344**
greet *hail* **894**
greeting **894**
gregarious **892**
grenade **727**
grenadier **726**
grey [*see* gray]
gridiron *crossing* 219
grief **828**
grievance **830, 923**
grieve *mourn* **828**
  pain 830
  complain 839
grievous *bad* 649
  painful 830
grievously *very* **31**
grill 384
  question 461
grim *resolute* **604**
  painful 830
  doleful 837
  sullen 901a
grimace 243
grimy 652
grin *laugh* **838**
grind *reduce* 195
  sharpen 253
  pulverize 330
  learn 539
  oppress 907
grip *bag* 191
  paroxysm 315
  indication 550
  power 737
  clutch 789
gripe [*see* grip] 378
grisly 846
grist 637
grit *strength* 159
  resolution 604, 861
  stamina 604a
gritty 323, 330
grizzled *gray* 432
groan *cry* 411
  lament 839
grocer 637
groceries 637
groin, 244
groom, *n.* 746
groom, *v.* 370
groomsman 903
groove *furrow* 259
  habit 613
grope *feel* 379
  experiment 463
gross *huge* 31
  whole 50
  ugly 846
  vulgar 851
grossness [*see* gross]
grotesque *odd* 83
  ridiculous 853
grotto 252
grouch 901a
ground *cause* 153
  situation 183

  base 211
  support 215
  land 342
  evidence 467
  teach 537
  motive 615
stand one's-
  defend 717
  resist 719
grounded *stranded* **732**
groundless
  unsubstantial 4
  illogical 477
  erroneous 495
grounds *estate* **344**
  dregs 653
groundwork *substance* 3
  cause 153
  basis 211
  support 215
  preparation 673
group, *n.* 72
group, *v.* 60
grove *group* 72
  wood 367
grovel *wallow* 207
  cringe 886
grow *increase* 31, **35**
  become 144
  expand 194
  vegetation 365, 367
grower 164
growl *cry* 412
  complain 839
  resent 900
  threat 909
grown up 131
growth [*see* grow]
  increase 35
  conversion 144
  development 161
  -*in size* 194
  vegetation 365
grub
  food 298
grudge *begrudge*
  refuse 764
  stint **819**
  envy 921
gruesome 846
gruff *harsh* 410
  discourteous 895
grum *morose* 901a
grumble *cry* 411
  complain 832, 839
grumpy 901a
Grundy, Mrs. 852
grunt *animal sound* 412
  complain 839
guarantee 768, **771**
guaranty 771
guard *stopper* 263
  defense 717
  soldier 726
guardian *safety* **664**
  keeper 753

  -*angel* 912
guardianship **664**
guardsman **726**
guerdon 973
guerrilla 722
guess 514
guesswork 514
guest 890
guffaw 838
guidable 278
guide, *n. model* 22
  itinerary 266, **527**
  courier 524
  teacher **540**
  director **694**
guide, *v. teach* 537
  indicate 550
  direct 693
  advise 695
guidebook 527
guidepost 550
guiding star 693
guild *society* 712
guile *deceit* 554, 545
  cunning 702
guileless *veracious* **543**
  artless 703
guillotine 975
guilt *state* 7
  dress 225
  appearance 448
GULF 343
gull, *n. bird* 366
  dupe 547
gull, *v. deceive* 545
gullet 260
gullible 486
gully *gorge* 198
gulp *swallow* 296
gum *fasten* 46
gumminess 327
gummy *tenacious* 327
  resinous 356a
gumption 498
gun *weapon* 727
gunboat 726
gunman 913
gunner 284, **726**
gunnery 284
gunpowder 727
gunshot 197
gurgle *flow* 348
  faint sound 405
gush, *n. ardor* 821
gush, *v. flow out* 295
gushing *emotional* 821
gusset 43
gust *wind* 349
gusto
  physical pleasure 377
  emotion 821
gusty 349

gut, *n.* 260
gut, *v. destroy* 162
gutter *groove* 259
guttural 561
guy *chaff* 856

guzzle *gourmandize* 957
gybe 279
gymnasium 189, 728
gymnast 159
gymnastic *strong* 159

athletic 720
gymnastics 159
gypsy 268
gyrate 312
gyve 752

H

habiliment 225
HABIT, *n. dress* 225
custom 613
habitat 189
HABITATION 189
habitual *normal* 80
ordinary 82
customary 136, **613**
habituate 613
habitude 613
hack, *n. horse* 271
vehicle 272
writer 593
hack, *v. cut* 44
hackneyed *trite* 496
habitual 613
Hades 982
haft 633
hag 846, 913
haggard *tired* 688
ugly 846
haggle *chaffer* 794
ha-ha *ditch* 198
hail, *n.* 383
hail, *v. welcome* 292
call 586
greet 894
hair 205, **256**
hairless 226
hair-splitting 480
hairy **256**
halcyon *calm* 174
prosperous 734
hale 654
half 91
-truth **546**
half-baked *ignorant* 491
half-blood *mixture* **41**
half-breed **41**
half-caste **41**
halfhearted
irresolute 605
insensible 823
indifferent 866
half-starved 640, 956
halfway 68
half-witted 499, 501
hall *chamber* 189
hallelujah 990
halloo 411, 586
hallow 976, 987
hallowed 976
hallucination 495, 992a
halo *light* 420
glory 873
halt *cessation* 142

rest 265
halt, *adj. lame* 655
halter 752
halve 91
hamadryad 979
hamlet 189
hammer *repeat* 104
hammock 215
hamper, *n. basket* 191
hamper, *v. obstruct* 706
hand, *n. side* 236
mariner 269
man 372
organ of touch 379
indicator 550
writing 590
at - *present* 118
destined 152
near 197
in - *incomplete* 53
hand, *v. transfer* 270
grasp 781
handbag 191
handbook *travel* 266
information 527
book 593
handcuff 751
handful 25
handicap, *n. race* 720
handicap, *v. equalize* 27
incumber 706
handicraft 625
handiwork 154, 680
handkerchief 225
handle, *n.* 633
handle, *v. touch* 379
use 677
manage 693
handmaid 631, 746
handsome *liberal* 816
beautiful 845
handwriting 590
handy *near* 197
useful 644
ready 673
dexterous 698
hang *loiter* 133
be *pendent* 214
kill 361
execute 972
-back 623
-fire *be late* 133
not finish 730
fail 732
-together 178
hangar 273

hanger-on
accompaniment 88
dependent 746
flunky 886
hangman 975
hanker 865
hansom 272
hap 156
haphazard 156
hapless 735
haply *possibly* 470
happen, 1, **151**
happening 151
happiness 377, **827**
[see happy]
happy *fit* 23
opportune 134
glad **827**
cheerful 836
harangue *speech* 582
harass *vex* 830
worry 907
harbinger *precursor* 64
omen 512
harbor, *n.* haven 189, 292
refuge 666
harbor, *v. cherish* **451**
hard *strong* 159
firm 323
difficult 704
severe 739
grievous 830
impenitent 951
-by 197
-pressed 684, 704
-up 704, 804
harden 323 [see hard]
strengthen 159
accustom 613
hardened *impenitent* 951
hardheaded 498
hardhearted 907
hardihood *courage* 861
insolence 885
hardiness [see hardy]
hardly *scarcely* 32, 137
-ever 137
HARDNESS **323**
hardpan 211
hardship 735
hard-working **686**
hardy *strong* 159
brave 861
harebrained 863
harem 374
hark *hear* 418

-back to 457
harlequin 599
harm, *n.* 649, 659
harm, *v injure* 659
harmful 619
harmless *impotent* 158
   good 648
   salubrious 656
   innocent 946
harmonious 413, 714
harmonize *agree* 23
   arrange 60, 416
   conform 82
   concur 178
   blend 413
harmony *agreement* 23
   music 413
   concord 714
   peace 721
harness, *n.* 225
harness, *v.*
   -a horse 370
   control 751
harp upon *repeat* 104
harpy *thief* 792
   demon 980
harrowing 830
harry *pain* 830
   attack 716
   persecute 907
harsh *acrid* 171
   discordant 410, 713
   severe 739
   disagreeable 830
   malevolent 907
harshness [*see* harsh]
harum-scarum 458
harvest 154, 636
hash *mixture* 41
hasp *fasten* 43
hassock 215
HASTE *velocity* 274
   hurry 684
hasten 274, 684
hasty *hurried* 684
   impatient 825
   irritable 901
hat 225
hatch *incubate* 370
   fabricate 544
hatchet 253
hatchway 260
hate *dislike* 867
   hatred 898
hateful *noxious* 649
   painful 830
   odious 898
hatred 867, 898
haughty *proud* 878
   insolent 885
   contemptuous 930
haul *drag* 285
haunt, *n. resort* 74
   abode 189
haunt, *v. alarm* 860
   persecute 907

have *possess* 777
haven 292, 666
hawser 45
hazard *chance* 156, 621
   danger 665
haze *mist* 353, 427
   uncertainty 475
hazel 433
hazy 427
head, *n. beginning* 66
   class 75
   summit 210
   person 373
   intellect 450
   director 694
   master 745
head, *v. precede* 62
   lead 280
   direct 693
headdress 225
header 310
headforemost 863
headgear 225
heading 66
headland 206, 250
headlong 684, 863
headquarters 74, 189
   authority 737
headstrong *violent* 173
   obstinate 606
   rash 863
headway *navigation* 267
   progression 282
heal *restore* 660
   cure 662
healing *art* 662
HEALTH 654
healthful 654
HEALTHINESS 656
healthy 654
heap *quantity* 31
   collection 72
hear *listen* 318
hearer 418
HEARING 418
   trial 969
hearken 457
hearsay 467, 532
heart *essence* 5
   center 68, 222
   cause 153
   interior 221
   affections 820
   courage 861
heartache 828
heartbreaking 830
heartbroken 828
heartburning
   discontent 832
   regret 833
   enmity 889
hearten 858, 861
heartfelt *profound* 821
hearth *home* 189
   fireplace 386

heartily [*see* hearty]
heartless 823, 945
heartrending 830
heartsick *dejected* 837
   loath 867
hearty *healthy* 654
   cordial 821
   cheerful 836
   friendly 888
HEAT, *n. warmth* 382
   excitement 824, 825
heat, *v.* 384
heated *hot* 384
   quarrelsome 713
heath *moor* 344
heathen *pagan* 984
heather 367
heave *raise* 307
   -to 265
HEAVEN *bliss* 827
   paradise 981
heavenly *celestial* 318
   rapturous 829
   divine 976
   of heaven 981
   -bodies 318
heavens 318
heavy *inert* 172
   weighty 319
   stupid 499
heavy-laden *unhappy* 828
heckle *harry* 830
hectic *red* 434
hector *domineer* 885
hedge, *n.* 232
hedge, *v.* 30
heed *attend* 457
   care 459
   caution 864
heedful 864
heedless *inattentive* 458
   neglectful 460
   forgetful 506
   rash 863
heel, *n.* 215
heel, *v. follow* 63
   lean 217
   tag 235
heft *weight* 319
   exertion 686
HEIGHT *degree* 26
   altitude 206
   summit 210
heighten *increase* 35
   uplift 206
   elevate 307
   exaggerate 549
   aggravate 835
heinous 945
heir 167, 779
heliotrope *purple* 437
HELL *gehenna* 982
hellish 982
helm 633
helmet 225
helmsman 269

help *benefit* 618
  utility 644
  aid 746
helper 711
helpful 746
helpless *incapable* 158
helpmate *wife* 903
helter-skelter 684
hem *edge* 231
  fold 258
  -in 751
hemisphere 181
hemorrhage 299
hen *bird* 366
hence *arising from* 155
  departing 293
  therefore 476
henchman 746
henpecked 749
herald, *n.* 64, 527
herald, *v. precede* 280
  predict 511
  proclaim 531
heraldry 550
herb 367
herbaceous 367
herculean *strong* 159
  difficult 704
herd 72, 102
here 183, 186
hereabouts 183
hereafter 121, 152
hereditary *intrinsic* 5
  derivative 154, 167
heredity 167
heresy 984
heretic 984, 989
heretical 984
hereupon 106
heritage 121
hermit *recluse* 893
  ascetic 955
hermitage *house* 189
hero 861, 873
heroic 861
  magnanimous 942
heroics 884
heroine 861
heroism 861, 942
hesitate *flounder* 475
  demur 485
  be reluctant 603
  be irresolute 605
heterodox 984
HETERODOXY 984
heterogeneity 10, 15, 16a
heterogeneous
  unrelated 10
  different 15
  mixed 41
  multiform 81
  exceptional 83
hew *cut* 44
  -down 213, 308
hiatus *interval* 198
hibernate 683

hidden 528
hide, *n. skin* 223
hide, *v conceal* 528
hidebound
  strait-laced 751
  bigoted 988
hideous 846
hiding place *ambush* 530
  refuge 666
hie *go* 264
  speed 274
hierarchy 995
high *lofty* 206
  gamy 298
  treble 410
  -life 875
  -note 410
  -principled 939
  -tide 106, 348
  -time 134
  -words *quarrel* 713
  anger 900
  on - 206
highborn 875
high-brow 490
higher 33
highest 210
high-flown *absurd* 497
  imaginative 515
  vain 880
highlands 206
high-minded 898, 942
high-priced 809
high-spirited *brave* 861
  honorable 939
high-strung 825
highway 627
highwayman 792
hike 260
hilarity 836
hill *height* 206
hillock 206
hilly 206
hilt 633
hind *deer* 366
hind, *adj. back* 235
hinder *impede* 706
Hinduism 976
HINDRANCE 706
hinge *fastening* 43
  cause 153
  -upon *depend upon* 154
hint, *n. reminder* 505
hint, *v. inform* 527
hire, *n. reward* 973
hire, *v.* 788
hireling 746
hirsute 256
hiss *sound* 409
  disrespect 929
  disapprobation 932
historian 553
historic 594
history 122, 594
  natural - 357
histrionic 599

hit *chance* 156
  strike 276
  reach 292
hitch, *n. stoppage* 142
  difficulty 704, 706
hitch, *v. fasten* 43
  hang 214
  -a horse 370
hither 278
hitherto 122
hive 184
  apiary 370
hoar *aged* 128
hoard 636
hoarse *husky* 405
hoary 124, 128, 430
hoax 545
hobble *limp* 275
  fail 732
  shackle 751
hobby 481, 625
hobgoblin 980
hobo 268, 876
Hobson's choice 609a
hodgepodge 41
hog *animal* 366
  selfishness 943
  glutton 957
hoist 307
hold, *n. influence* 175
  storage 191
  power 737
hold, *v. cohere* 46
  contain 54
  cease 142
  support 215
  believe 484
  defend 717
  restrain 751
  possess 777
  retain 781
  -forth *declaim* 537, 582
  -good 478, 494
  -on *continue* 141, 143
  persevere 604a
  -out *persevere* 604a
  offer 763
  -true 494
  -up *support* 215
  aid 707
holder 779
holding
  tenancy 777
  property 780
holdup 791
hole *hovel* 189
  cave 251
  opening 260
holiday *anniversary* 138
  leisure 685
  vacation 687
  amusement 840
  celebration 883
holiness *God* 976
  piety 987
holloa 411

hollow, n. 207, 252
hollow, adj.
  unsubstantial 4
  resonant 408
  gruff 410
  specious 477
hollowness [see hollow]
holocaust 991
Holy *of God* 976
  pious 987
  -Ghost 976
  -orders 995, 998
  -Scriptures 985
homage *submission* 725
  respect 928
home *habitation* 189
  interior 221
  country 342
  refuge 666
  -rule 737
  -thrust
   attack 716
   censure 932
homeless *unhoused* 185
  banished 893
homelike 849
homeliness 851
  [see homely]
homely *unadorned* 849
  common 851
homesick 833
homestead 189
homicide 361
homily *teaching* 537
  sermon 998
homogeneity *relation* 9
  identity 13
  uniformity 16
  simplicity 42
hone 253
honest 939
honeycomb 252
honeymoon, 902, 903
honor, n. *glory* 873
  respect 928
  approbation 931
  probity 939
honor, v. 873
honorable 873, 939
honorarium 784, 973
honorary 815
honored 873
hood *cap* 225
hoodoo 621, 992, 993
hoodwink *blind* 442
  hide 528
hoof 211
hook *fasten* 43
  hang 214
  fork 244
  curve 245
hooligan 887, 913
hoop *circle* 247
  cry 411
hoot *cry* 411, 412
  deride 929

  censure 932
hop *leap* 309
HOPE 858
hopeful 858
hopeless 859
HOPELESSNESS 859
horde 72
horizon 196, 230
horizontal 213, 251, 308
HORIZONTALITY 213
horny 323
horoscope 511
horrible *noxious* 649
  dire 830
  ugly 846
  fearful 860
horrid 649, 830, 846
horrify *terrify* 860
horror *fear* 860
  dislike 867
horror-stricken 828
horse *animal* 271
  translation 539
  cavalry 726
horseman 268
horsemanship 266
horseplay 856
horse power 466
horticulture 371
horticulturist 369
hosanna 990
hose *stockings* 225
  pipe 350
hospitable 816, 892
hospital 662
hospitality 816, 892
host *multitude* 102
  army 726
  friend 890
hostage 771
hostel 189
hostess 890
hostile 14, 24, 889
hostility 889
hot *warm* 382
  pungent 392
  excited 824
  irascible 901
  -air *bombast* 884
  -bath 386
  -springs 382
hotbed 153
hotel 189
  -runner 767
hotheaded 825, 863
hothouse *conservatory* 371
hound, n. *animal* 366
hound, v. *hunt* 622
  persecute 907
hourglass 114
house *lineage* 69
  family 166
  abode 189
  council 696
  firm 712
  -of Commons 966

  -of Lords 875
  -of Representatives 696
house, v 184
housebreaker 792
housebreaking 791
household *inhabitants* 188
  abode 189
householder 188
housemaid 746
housing *lodging* 189
hovel 189
hover *soar* 206, 267
  vacillate 605
how 627
however 30
howitzer 727
howl *cry* 411, 412
  lamentation 839
hoyden *tomboy* 129
hub 222, 247
hubbub 315, 404
huddle 72, 197
hue 428
huff 900
hug, v *clasp* 46
  border on 197
  love 897
huge 192
hulking 193
hulky *big* 192
  unwieldy 647
hullabaloo *noise* 404
hum *sound* 405, 407
  sing 416
human 364, 372
humane *benevolent* 906
  merciful 914
humanitarian 910
humanitarianism 910
humanity 906, 910
humble *inferior* 34
  meek 879
humbug, n. *falsehood* 544
  deceiver 548
humbug, v. 545
humdrum *dull* 843
humid 339
humiliate 879, 929
humiliation 735, 879
HUMILITY
  meekness 879
hummock 206, 250
humor, n *essence* 5
  tendency 176
  disposition 602
  caprice 608
  wit 842
humor, v. *indulge* 760
  please 829
  flatter 933
HUMORIST 844
humorous 842
hump 250
humpbacked 243
Hun *destroyer* 165
hunch 250

hunchbacked 243
hundred 98
hunger 865
hungry 865, 956
hunt *pursuit* 286, 622
  inquiry 461
hunter *horse* 271
  pursuer 622
hurl 284
hurrah 838
hurricane *tempest* 349
hurry 274, 684
hurt, *n. physical pain* 378
  evil 619
hurt, *v.*
  cause (physical) pain 378
  maltreat 649
  injure 659, 907
  pain 830
  more frightened than-
  860
hurtful 649
hurtle 276
hurtless 648

husband *store* 636
  director 694
  spouse 903
husbandman 371
husbandry *agriculture* 371
  conduct 692
  economy 817
hush *moderate* 174
  stop 265
  silence 403
  taciturn 585
  -up *conceal* 528
  pacify 723
husk *covering* 223
husky *strong* 159
  hoarse 405, 581
hussar 726
hustings 728
hustle 682
hustler 682
hut 189
hybrid 41
hydroplane 273
hydroplaning 267

hygiene 656
hygienic 656
hygienics 670
Hymen 903
hymeneal 903
hymn *song* 415
  worship 990
hyperbole 549
hypercriticism 868
hyperphysical **450**
hyphen 45
hypnosis 376, 992*a*
hypnotic 683
hypnotism 683, 992*a*
hypnotize 615, 992
hypochondriac **837**, 859
hypocrisy 544, 988
hypocrite 548
hypocritical 544, **988**
hypothesis 514
hypothetical 514
hysteria 992*a*
hysterical 821
hysterics 173

I

ice 383, 387
iceberg 383
ice chest 385
icon 554
iconoclasm 984
iconoclast 165
icy **383**
IDEA *notion* **453**
ideal 515
idealism 450, 515
idealist 515
ideality 450, **515**
idealize 515
identical 13
identification 13
IDENTITY 13, 27
idiocy 503
idiom 560, 566
idiosyncrasy 5, 79, 83
idiot 501
idiotic *foolish* 499
idle *trivial* 643
  slothful 683
idler 683
idol *favorite* 899
  fetich 991
idolater 991
IDOLATRY 991
idolize *love* 897
  idolatrize **991**
idyl 597
if 8, 469, **514**
igneous 382
ignis fatuus 4, 443
ignite 384
ignition *calefaction* **384**
ignoble 876

ignominious 940
ignominy *shame* 874
  dishonor 940
IGNORAMUS **493**
IGNORANCE **491**
ignorant 491
ignore *neglect* 460
  not known 491
ill, *n. evil* 619
  badness 649
  sick 655
ill, *adj. bad* 649
  -usage 807
  -will 907, 921
ill-adapted 24
ill-advised *inexpedient* **647**
  unskillful **699**
ill-assorted 24
ill-behaved 895
ill-bred *vulgar* 851
  rude 895
ill-disposed 907
illegal 964
ILLEGALITY **964**
illegible 519
illegitimate 925, 964
ill-fated 135, 735
ill-favored 846
illiberal *stingy* 819
  selfish **943**
  bigoted 988
illicit 925, 964
illiteracy 491
illiterate 491, 493
ill-made 243
ill-mannered 851
ill-natured 907

illness 655
illogical 477
ill-omened 135, 735
ill-proportioned 846
ill-spent 645
ill-starred 135
ill-timed 24, 135
ill-treat 649, 907
ill-treatment 649
illuminant 420
illuminate *enlighten* 420
  comment 595
illumine *lighten* 420
  excite 824
ill-use 649
illusion
  fallacy of vision 443
  error 495
  deception **545**
illusive 4, **495**
illusory 4, 495
illustrate *exemplify* 82
  interpret 522
  represent 554
illustration 558
illustrious 873
image *likeness* 17
  appearance 448
  metaphor 521
imagery *fancy* 515
  metaphor 521
imaginable 470
imaginary 2, 4, 515
IMAGINATION **515**
imaginative 515
imagine 515
imbecile, *adj. ignorant* 493

INEXPEDIENCE **647,** 699
inexpedient **647**
inexpensive **815**
inexperience
  ignorance 491
  unskillfulness 699
inexpert **699**
inexplicable **519**
inexpressible *great* 31
  unintelligible **519**
inexpressive **517**
infallibility **474**
infallible **474**
infamous **940**
infamy *shame* 874
  dishonor 940
infancy *beginning* 66
  youth 127
INFANT **129**
infantile **129**
infantine **129**
infantry **726**
infatuation *credulity* 486
  love 897
infect **659**
infection **270, 655**
infectious **270, 657**
infelicitous **24, 828**
infelicity *misery* 828
infer *presume* 472
  deduce 480
inference **476, 480**
inferior **34, 207, 651**
INFERIORITY
  in degree 28, **34**
  in size 195
  imperfection 651
infernal *malevolent* 907
  wicked 945
infertility **169**
infest **830**
infidel **487, 989**
infidelity *dishonor* 940
  irreligion 989
infiltrate *mix* 41
  interpenetrate 294
  ooze 295
infiltration **41, 302**
infinite **105, 180**
infinite, the - 976
infinitely *great* 31
infinitesimal **32**
INFINITY **105**
infirm *weak* 160
infirmary **662**
infirmity **160, 655**
inflame *give energy* 171
  render violent 173
  burn 384
  excite 824
inflamed *red* 434
inflammatory *heated* 384
  [*see* inflame]
inflate *increase* 35

expand 194
  blow **349**
inflated *vain* **482, 880**
inflation [*see* inflate]
inflect 245
inflexible *straight* 246
  hard 323
  resolved 604
  obstinate 606
  stern 739
inflict **680, 739**
infliction *adversity* 735
  mental pain 828, 830
  punishment 972
influence *cause* 153
  physical - 175
  tendency 176
  inducement 615
  instrumentality 631
  importance 642
  authority 737
  absence of - 175a
influential **175**
influx 294
inform 527
  - *against accuse* 938
informal *irregular* 83
informality **83**
informant **527, 938**
INFORMATION
  knowledge 490
  communication **527**
infraction
  infringement 303
  disobedience 742
INFREQUENCY **103, 137**
infrequent **137**
infringe *transgress* 303
  disobey 742
  not observe **773**
  violate **925**
infuriate *inflame* 173
  excite 824
  anger 900
infuse *mix* 41
  insert 300
  teach 537
infused 6
infusion [*see* infuse]
ingathering 72
ingenious *original* 515
  skillful 698
ingenuity **698**
ingenuous *artless* 703
inglorious **374**
ingot **800**
ingraft *join* 43
  insert 300
ingrafted 6
ingrain **329**
ingrained *intrinsic* 5
  inborn 820
ingratiate **897**
INGRATITUDE **917**
ingredient **56**
INGRESS **294**

inhabit **186, 188**
INHABITANT **188**
inhale *receive* 296
  breathe 349
inharmonious **15, 24**
inhere in **56**
inherence **5**
inherent **56, 221, 820**
inherit *acquire* 775
  possess 777
inheritance **777, 780**
inherited **5**
inheritor **779**
inhibit *hinder* 706
  restrain 751
  prohibit 761
inhospitable **893**
inhuman **907**
inimical **14, 708**
inimitable **20, 28, 650**
iniquity **923, 945**
initial **66**
initiate *begin* 66
  receive 296
  teach 537
initiatory **296**
inject **300, 337**
injudicious **499, 863**
injunction *command* 741
  prohibition 761
injure *harm* 619
  damage **659**
  spite 907
injurious **619, 923**
injury *evil* 619
  badness 649
  damage **659**
injustice **923**
inkling **514, 527**
inland **221**
inlay **300**
inlet **66, 294**
  -of the sea 343
inmate **188, 221**
inmost **221**
inn **189**
innate **5, 221**
inner **221**
  - *reality* **1**
innkeeper **188, 637**
INNOCENCE **946**
innocent, *n. child* 167
  fool 501
innocent, *adj. good* 648
  artless 703
  guiltless **946**
innocuous *healthy* **656**
  innocent 946
innovation **20a, 123, 140**
innuendo *hint* 527
innumerable **105**
inobservance **773**
inoculate *insert* 300
  influence 615
inodorous **399**
INODOROUSNESS **399**

J

concurrent 178
united 712
jointly **43**
joke *absurdity* 497
  trifle 643
  wit 842
  ridicule 856
joker 844
jollity 840
jolly, *adj. hay* 836
  merry 840
jolly, *v.* 933
jolt 276, 315
jongleur 597
jostle 276
jot 32
journal *annals* 114
  newspaper 531
journalism 551
journalist 534, **553**
JOURNEY 266
journeyman 690
joust 720
jovial 836, 840
joy **827**
joyful 836

joyless 837
jubilant 836, 838
jubilee 138
JUDGE, *n. justice* 664, **967**
judge, *v. decide* 480
  criticise 850
  adjudicate 965
JUDGMENT
  intellect 450
  discrimination 465
  decision **480**
  condemnation 971
  sentence 972
judicature 965, 966
judicial 965
judiciary 664
judicious 480, 868
jug 191
juggle 545, 702
juggler 548
juice 333
juicy 333
jumble, *n.* 41, 59
jumble, *v. derange* 61
  confuse 465a
jump *leap* 146, 309

JUNCTION **43**
juncture 8, 43, 134
jungle 59, 367
junior *secondary* 34
  younger 127
junk *vessel* 273
  lumber 645
JURISDICTION **965**
jurisprudence 963
jurist 968
juror 967
jury 967
juryman 967
just *accurate* 494
  right 922
  equitable 939
  pious 987
just *tilt* 720
justice *judge* 664, 967
  right 922
  honor 939
justifiable 922, 937
justification 937
justify 937
jut 214
juvenile *youth* 127
juxtaposition 199

K

keel 211
keen *energetic* **171**
  sharp 253
  sensible 375
  intelligent 498
  poignant **821**
  eager 865
  discriminative 868
keen-edged 253
keenness [*see* keen]
keep, *n. citadel* 717
  custody **751**
keep, *v. persist* 141
  continue 143
  provision 637
  preserve 670
  retain 781
  celebrate 883
  -away 187
  -from *conceal* 528
  -off *avoid* 623
    avert 706
  -on *do often* **136**
    continue 143
    persevere 604a
  -under *domineer* **737**
    subject 749
  -up *continue* 143
KEEPER 370, **753**
keepsake 505
keg 191
ken *sight* 441
  knowledge 490
kerchief 225

kernel *heart* 5, 68
  center 222
  importance 642
ketch *ship* 273
kettle 386
key *opener* 260
  music 413
  interpretation 522
keynote **22**
keystone *support* 215
  importance 642
kick *impulse* 276
  recoil 277
  assault 716
kid *child* 129, 167
kidnap 789, 791
kidnaper 792
kill 361
KILLING **361**
kiln 386
kilt 225
kimono 225
kin 11, 75
kind *class* **75**
  benevolent 906
kindergarten 542
kindergartner 540
kindle *quicken* 171
  inflame 173
  set fire to 384
  excite 824
kindly 906
kindness 906
kindred 11

king 745
kingdom *region* 181
kingly 737
kink 248
kinsfolk 11
kinsman 11
kirk 1000
kismet 601
kiss 379, 902
kit *knapsack* 191
kitchen *room* 191
kite *fly* 273
kith 11
kleptomania 791
knack 698
knapsack 191
KNAVE *deceiver* 548
  rogue **941**
knavery 545, **940**
knead *mix* 41
  soften 324
  touch 379
knee 244
kneel *stoop* 308
  submit 725
  beg 765
knell 363
knickers 225
knicknack 643
knife 253
knight 875
  -errant 863
knighthood 877
knit **43**

knob 249
knobby 250
knock
  blow 276
  sound 406
  -down *lay flat* 213

knockout 67
knoll 206
knot *ligature* 45
  group 72
  intersection 219
  difficulty 704

knotted *rough* 256
know 484, 490
knowing 702
knowingly 620
KNOWLEDGE 490, 539
known 490
kowtow 308, 725

L

label 550
labor 680, 686
  -in vain 645
laboratory 691
laborer 686, 690
laborious 686
labyrinth 248, 533
labyrinthine 248, 533
lace *stitch* 43
lacerate 378
lack 53, 630, 865
lackey 746
laconic 585
lacquer 223
lad 129
ladder 305
lade *load* 184, 190
ladle 191
lady 374, 875
ladylove 897
lag *linger* 275
  follow 281
laggard 603
lagoon 343
laicize 997
lair *den* 189
laird 875
LAITY 997
LAKE 343
lamb 366
lambent 379
lame 158
lament 839
lamentable 837
LAMENTATION 839
lamp 423
lampoon 934
lampooner 936
lance, *n. spear* 727
lance, *v pierce* 260
  throw 284
lancer 726
lancet 253, 262
LAND, *n.* 342
land, *v* 292
landholder 779
landing place 292
landlocked 292
landlord *innkeeper* 637
  possessor 779
landlubber 701
landmark 233, 550

landowner 779
landscape *prospect* 448
  -painting 556
landslide 306
landsman 342
lane 189, 260
LANGUAGE 560
languid *weak* 160
  inert 172
  slow 275
  inactive 683
languish *decrease* 36
  be inactive 683
  repine 828
  affect 855
languishing 855
languor 683
  [*see* languid]
lanky *tall* 200
lantern *lamp* 423
  -jawed 203
lap, *n. support* 215
  -of *weaves* 405
lap, *v. drink* 298
  circuit 311
lapse, *n. conversion* 144
  fall 306
  relapse 661
  guilt 947
lapse, *v. proceed* 109
  pass 122
  cease 142
  relapse 661
larceny 791
large *quantity* 31
  size 192
  at - *liberated* 750
largehearted 906, 942
lariat 45
lark *bird* 366
  spree 840
larva 193
lash *tie together* 43
  whip 370
  incite 615
  punish 972
lass *girl* 129
lassitude 688
lasso 45
last, *n. model* 22
last, *v. abide* 1
  -in *order* 67

endure 106, 110
  -in *time* 122
  continue 141
latch 43, 45
late *past* 122
  new 123
  tardy 133
  dead 360
lately 122, 123
LATENCY 526
LATENESS 133
latent *inert* 172
  concealed 526
  -influence 526
later 117
lateral 236
latest 118
lath 205
lathe 633
lather 353
Latin deities 979
latitude *breadth* 202
  freedom 748
latter 63, 122
latterly 122, 123
lattice 219
laud *praise* 931
laudable 944
laudatory 931
laugh 838
  -at *ridicule* 856
  sneer 929
laughable 853
LAUGHINGSTOCK 857
laughter 838
launch, *n. boat* 273
launch, *v. begin* 66
  propel 284
  -forth 676
  -into 676
  -out 573
laundress 652
laundry 652
laundryman 652
laurel *glory* 873
lavatory 652
lave *water* 337
  clean 652
lavender *color* 437
lavish, *adj. profuse* 809
lavish, *v. squander* 818
law *regularity* 80

budge 264
budget *finance* 811
buff *color* 436
buffer 717
buffet *strike* 276
 smite 972
buffet *café* 189
 cupboard 191
buffoon *actor* 599
 humorist 844
 butt 857
buffoonery
 humor 840, 842, 853
 horseplay 856
bug 193, 366
bugaboo 980
bugbear 980
build *construct* 161
 form 240
building 189
bulb 249, 250
bulge 250
bulk, *n. quantity* 25
 whole 50
 size 192
bulk, *v.* 31
bulkhead 228
bulky 31, 192
bull *animal* 366
 absurdity 495, 497
 stock exchange 797
bulldoze 860
bullet 717
bulletin *list* 86
 news 532
bullion 800
bully, *n.* 863, 887
bully, *v. frighten* 860
 bluster 885
 threaten 909
bulwark 717
bump, *n.* 250
bump, *v.* 276

bumptious *proud* 878
bunch *collection* 72
 protuberance 250
buncombe *bombast* 577
 boast 884
 flattery 933
bundle *packet* 72
bung 263
bungle 495, 699
bungler 701
bunkum
 [*see* buncombe]
buoy *raise* 307
buoyant
 floating 305
 light 320
 elastic 325
 hopeful 858
bur 53
burden *clog* 706
bureau *chest* 191
 department 965
bureaucracy 737
burgess 188
burgher 188
burglar 792
burglary 791
burial 363
 -place 363
burlesque, *n.*
 travesty 555, 853
 absurdity 497
 ridicule 856
burlesque, *v. imitate* 19
 ridicule 856
burn *heat* 382
 consume 384
burnish *polish* 255
burrow *excavate* 208, 252
burst, *n. sound* 406
 paroxysm 825
burst, *v.*
 -forth *begin* 66

expand 194
 be seen 446
bury 229, 363
bush *shrub* 367
bushy 256
BUSINESS 151, **625**
businesslike
 orderly 58
 business 625
 practical 692
bustle *energy* 171
 agitation 315
 activity 682
bustling 682
busy 625, 682
busybody 455
but 30
butcher *kill* 361
butchered 53
butler 746
butt, *n. cask* 191
 laughingstock 857
butt, *v.* 276
butter 356
button *fasten* 43
buttonhole, *n.*
 bouquet 400
buttonhole, *v.*
 to bore 841
buttress 717
buxom 836
buy 795
buyer 795
buzz 409
by 236, 631
 -and by 132
 -means of **632**
 -the by 134
 -the way 134
bygone *past* 122
byplay 550
bystander 197, 444
byword, *contempt* 930

C

cab 272
cabin *room* 189
cabinet *receptacle* 191
 council 696
cable, *n. link* 45
 dispatch 532
cable, *v.* 534
cabman 268
cackle (*of geese*) 412
 laugh 838
cad 851
cadaverous *pale* 429
 hideous 846
cadence *sound* 402
 music 415
cadet *junior* 129
 officer 745
caesura 44, 198

café 189, 298
cage, *n. prison* 752
cage, *v. restrain* 751
caisson 191, 252
cajole *flatter* 933
 [*see* cajolery]
cajolery *imposition* 544
 persuasion 615
 flattery 933
cake, *n.* 396
cake, *v. stick* 46
 consolidate 321
calamitous
 adverse 735, 935
 disastrous 830
calamity *killing* 361
 evil 619
 adversity 735

calcine 384
calculate 85
calculation 85
caldron 191
CALEFACTION **384**
calendar *list* 86, 611
 chronicle 114
calf *animal* 366
 fool 501
caliber *measure* 26, 192
 intellectual capacity 498
calipers 466
calisthenics 159
calk 660
call *signal* 550
 name 564
 visit 892
 ordain 995

loathsome 867
local 181, 183
locality 182
localize 184
locate 184
LOCATION 182, 184
lock *fasten* 43
  fastening 45
  tuft 256
  canal 350
  -up *hide* 528
  imprison 751
locker 191
lockout 55
lockup *prison* 752
locomotion 264
  -by air 267
  -by land 266
  -by water 267
locomotive 466
locution 566, 582
lodestar *attraction* 288
  direction 693
lodestone
  [see loadstone]
lodge *place* 184
  inhabit 186
lodgment 184
lodger 188
lodging 189
loft *garret* 191
lofty *high* 206
  style 574
  proud 878
log *fuel* 388
  measurement 466
  record 551
logic 476
logical 476
logician 476
logy 172, 683
loiter *be slow* 133, 275
  lag 281
loll *sprawl* 213
lone 87
lonely 893
lonesome 893
long -*in time* **110**
  -*in space* **200**
  diffuse 573
  -*for* 865
longevity 128
longing 865
long-lived 110
longshoreman
  waterman 269
long-suffering 826, 914
long-winded 110
look, *n. appearance* 448
look, *v. see* **441**
  attend to 457
  -after *care* 459
  -ahead 510
  -for *seek* 461
  expect 507
  -to 459

lookout *view* 448
  sentinel 668
loom *magnify* 31
  impend 152
  come in sight 446
loony 501
loop 245, 247
loophole *opening* 260
  escape 671
loose, *adj. incoherent* 47
  illogical 477
  vague 519
  lax 738
  free 748
loose, *v. detach* 44
  liberate 750
loosen *make loose* 47
  let loose 750
loot, *n. booty* 793
loot, *v. steal* 791
lop 201
lopsided 28
loquacious **584**
LOQUACITY 562, **584**
Lord *God* 976
lord *nobleman* 875
lordly 873, 878
lore 490, 539
lorgnette 445
lose *forget* 506
  fail 732
  incur loss 776
  -an opportunity **135**
LOSS *decrement* 40a
  death 360
  privation 776
  -of strength 160
lost *nonexisting* 2
  absent 187
  uncertain 475
  bereft 776
  impenitent 951
lot *state* 7
  quantity 25
  multitude 102
  necessity 601
  chance 621
lotion *liquid* 337
lottery *chance* 156
loud *noisy* 404
  bad taste 851
LOUDNESS 404
lounge, *n.* 191
lounge, *v.* 683
lout 501, 876
lovable 897
LOVE *desire* 865
  affection 897
loveliness 845
lovelorn 898
lovely *beautiful* 845
  lovable 897
lover 865, 897
lovesick 902
low, *adj. small* 32
  not high 207

  faint 405
  vulgar 851
  common 876
low, *v. moo* 412
  -spirits 837
  -tide 207
  -water *low* **207**
  poverty 804
lowborn 876
low-brow *ignorant* 491
lower, *adj.*
  inferior 34, **207**
  overcast 421, 422
lower, *v. decrease* 36
  depress 308
  frown 837
lowermost 207
lowlands 207
lowliness 879
lowly 879
LOWNESS 207, **851**
  [see low]
loyal 743, 939
lubber 701
lubricant 332
lubricate *oil* **332**
LUBRICATION 332
lucent 420
lucid *luminous* 420
  intelligible 518, **570**
  rational 502
lucidity 518, 570
luck *chance* 156
  prosperity 734
lucky *timely* 134
  successful 731
lucrative 775
lucre *gain* 775
  wealth 803
ludicrous 853
lug 285
luggage 270, 780
lukewarm *torrid* 823
  indifferent 866
lull 142, 174, 403
lullaby 415
lumber, *v.* 275
lumberman 371
LUMINARY *star* 318
  light 423
luminosity 420
luminous *light* **420**
lump *whole* 50
  chief part 51
  mass 192
  density 321
  -together 72
lunacy 503
lunar 318
lunatic 503, 504
luncheon 892
lunge 276, 716
lurch *tilt* 217
  fall 306
  sway 314
  leave in the-

relinquish 624
lure *charm* **288**
   deceive 545
   entice 615
lurid *dark* 421
   dim 422
lurk 526, 528
luscious *savory* 394
luster **420**, 873

lustily *loud* 404
lustrous *shining* 420
lusty *strong* 159
   big 192
luxuriant *fertile* 168
   rank **365**
luxurious *pleasant* 377
   intemperate **954**
luxury

enjoyment 377, **827**
   sensuality 954
lying 544
lymphatic *slow* **275**
lynch 972
   -*law* 964
lyncher **975**
lyric 597
lyrist 597

M

mace *weapon* 727
   scepter 747
machination 626, 702
machine *automobile* 272
   instrument 633
   party 712
machinery 633
machinist 690
mackintosh 225
mad *violent* 173
   insane 503
   excited 824
madam 374, 877
madden 824
MADMAN **504**
madness 503
Madonna 977
maelstrom *whirl* 312
magazine *book* 593
   store 636
magenta 434, 437
magic 992
magician 548, 994
magisterial 878, 885
magistrate 967
magnanimity 942
magnanimous 942
magnate 875
magnet *attraction* 288
   desire 865
magnetic 157, 829
magnetism *power* 157
   influence 175
   attraction 288
magnetize 157, 288
magnificent *fine* 845
   grand 882
magnify *increase* 31, **35**
   enlarge 194
   overrate 549
magnitude 25, 31, 192
maharajah 875
mahogany *color* 433
maid *girl* 129
   servant 746
   spinster 904
maiden *first* 66
   girl 129
maidenly 374
mail *post* 270, **534**
   armor 717
maim *injure* 659

main, *n. ocean* 341
   land 342
   conduit 350
   in the - *principally* **642**
main, *adj. principal* 642
   -*force strength* 159
   violence 173
   compulsion 744
mainland 342
mainspring *cause* 153
mainstay *support* 215
   refuge 666
   hope **858**
maintain *keep* 141
   continue 143
   sustain 170
   assert 535
   preserve 670
maintenance
   [*see* maintain]
majestic *grand* 31
   glorious 873
   stately 882
majesty 745, 873
major, *adj. greater* 33
major, *n. officer* 745
majority *superiority* 33
   plurality 100
   age 131
make *constitute* 54, 56
   render 144
   produce 161
   form 240
   complete 729
   compel 744
   create 976
   -*believe* **545**
   -*good*
   demonstrate 478
   -*out discover* 480a
   know 490
   interpret 522
   -*up complete* 52
maker *artificer* 690
Maker, the - 976
makeshift *substitute* 147
   excuse 617
make-up *composition* 54
makeweight 30
malady 655
malcontent 710, **832**
male *man* 373

MALEDICTION **908**
malefaction 947
malefactor **975**
maleficent 907
MALEVOLENCE **907**
malevolent **907**
malformation 243
malformed 241
malice *hate* 898
   spite 907
   bear - 907
malign, *adj. malevolent* 907
malign, *v. detract* 934
malignant 907
malignity 907
malinger 544
malison 908
malleable *soft* 324
maltreat *injure* 649
   aggrieve **830**
   molest 907
mamma 166
mammal 366
Mammon 803
mammoth 192
MAN, *n. mankind* 372
   male 373
   workman 690
   servant 746
   -*of action* **682**
man, *v. prepare* 673
   defend 717
manacle *fetter* 752
manage 175, 693
manageable *easy* **705**
management 692, 693
manage *director* 694
mandate *requirement* 630
   command 741
mane 256
manege 370
maneuver *operation* 680
   stratagem 702
manful *strong* 159
   resolute 604
   brave 861
manger 191
mangle *smooth* 255
   injure 659
manhood 131, 861
mania *insanity* 503
   desire **865**

fastidious 868
metrical *measured* 466
metropolis 189, 222
mettle *energy* 171
  spirit 820
  courage 861
mew *cry* 412
microbe 193
microscopic 32
mid 68
MID-COURSE 628
midday 125
MIDDLE *-in degree* 29
  -in order 68
  -in space 222
  -age 131
middle-aged 131
middle-class 29
middleman 228
middling 736
midmost 68
midnight 126
midriff 228
midshipman 269
midst 68
midsummer 125
midway 68
mien 448
might 31, 157
mighty *much* 31
  strong 157, 159
migrate 266
mild *moderate* 174
  warm 382
  lenient 740
  calm 826
MILDNESS 740
mile 200
militant 722
military 722
  soldiers 726
  -authorities 745
militia 726
milksop *coward* 862
milky 430
mill, *n.* 691
mill, *v. indent* 257
  pulverize 330
millennium *period* 108
  hope 858
millinery *ornament* 847
million 98, 876
millionaire 803
mimic *imitate* 19
mince *step short* 275
  lisp 583
  affect 855
mind, *n. intellect* 450
  will 600
  purpose 620
  desire 865
bear in - 505
mind, *v. attend to* 457
  dislike 867
mindful 457, 505
mine, *n.* 545, 636

mine, *v. sap* 162, 252, 717
miner 252
  sapper and - 726
mineral 358
mineralize 358
mingle 41
miniature *small* 32
minimize 36
minimum 32, 34
minister *deputy* 759
  clergy 996
  -to help 707, 746
ministerial 995
ministration *aid* 707
ministry *direction* 693
  aid 707
  church 995
  clergy 996
minor *inferior* 34
  infant 129
minority *few* 103
  youth 127
minster 1000
minstrel 416, 597
mint 22
minuend 38
minus *subtracted* 38
  absent 187
minute, *n. period* 108
  record 551
minute, *adj. -in degree* 32
  -in size 193
minutemen 726
minuteness 457, 459
minutiae 32, 643
miracle *exceptional* 83
  prodigy 872
miraculous *wonderful* 870
mirage 443
mire 653
mirror, *n. reflector* 445
mirror, *v. imitate* 19
mirth 836
misadventure 735
misanthrope 911
MISANTHROPY 911
misapply *misinterpret* 523
  misuse 679
  mismanage 699
misapprehend *mistake* 495
  misinterpret 523
misappropriate 679
misbehave 851, 945
misbehavior
  discourtesy 851, 895
  guilt 947
misbelief 485
misbeliever 984
miscalculate 481, 495
miscall 565
miscarry 732
miscellany 41, 72, 78
mischance *misfortune* 735
mischief 619
mischief-maker 913
mischievous 649

misconceive *mistake* 481, 495
  misinterpret 523
misconception 481, 495
misconduct *guilt* 947
misconstrue 523
miscreant 949
misdate 115
misdeed 947
misdemeanor 947
misdoubt 485
misemploy 679
miser 819
miserable *unhappy* 828
miserably 32
miserly 819
misery 828
misfire 732
misfortune *adversity* 735
misgiving 485, 860
misguide 495, 538
misguided 699
mishap *failure* 732
  misfortune 735
misinform 495, 538
misinstruct 538
MISINTERPRETATION 523
MISJUDGMENT 481, 495
mislay *derange* 61
  lose 776
mislead 495
mismanage 699
mismatch 15
misname 565
MISNOMER 565
misplace *derange* 61
  displace 185
misprint 495
mispronounce 583
misproportioned *ugly* 846
misreckon 481
misrepresent
  misinterpret 523
  misteach 538
  lie 544
  distort 555
MISREPRESENTATION 523, 555
misrule 699, 738
miss, *n. girl* 129
  error 495
miss, *v. neglect* 460
  fail 732
  lose 776
  want 865
misshapen *shapeless* 241
  distorted 243
  ugly 846
missile 284, 727
missing 2, 187
mission 625, 755
missionary 540
missive 592
misspell 523
misspend 818

misstate 495
misstatement *error* 495
  untruth 546
  misrepresentation 555
mist *cloud* 353
  semitransparency 427
mistake 495, 699
mistaken 495
MISTEACHING 538
mister 373
mistime 135
mistress *lady* 374
mistrust 485
misty [*see* mist]
misunderstand 495, 523
misunderstanding
  disagreement 24
  error 495
MISUSE 679
mite *bit* 32
  infant 129
  small 193
mitigate *decrease* 36
  abate 174
  relieve 834
mitigation
  [*see* mitigate]
mitten 225
mix 41
mixed 41
mixture 41, 335
mizzen 235
mnemonics 505
moan *cry* 411
  lament 839
moat *inclosure* 232
  canal 350
mob 72, 102, 876
  -law 738
mobile *inconstant* 149
  movable 264
  sensitive 822
mobilization 264, 722
mobilize 264
moccasin 225
mock, *v. imitate* 17, 19
mock, *adj. derisive* 856
  -modesty 855
mockery 19, 856
mode *state* 7
  habit 613
  method 627
  fashion 852
model *copy* 21
  prototype 22
  form 240
  sculpture 557
  perfection 650
  good man 948
moderate, *adj. small* 32
  slow 275
  lenient 740
  cheap 815
  temperate 953
moderate, *v. allay* **174**
MODERATION 174

  patience 831
  [*see* moderate]
moderator *lenitive* **174**
  judge 967
modern 123
modernism 123
modernization 123
modest *small* 32
  humble 879
  diffident 881
MODESTY 879, 881
modicum *little* 32
modification *difference* 15
  variation 20a
  change 140
  qualification 469
modify 469
modish 852
modulation 140
Mohammedanism 976
moiety 51
moil 682
moist 339
moisten 339
MOISTURE 339
mold, *n. matrix* 22
  form 240, 554
  structure 329
  earth 342
mold, *v. convert* 144
  carve 557
  decay 653
  create 976
moldy *fetid* 401
molecular 32
molecule 32, 193
molest 907
mollify *allay* 174
  soften 324
mollycoddle 158
molten *liquefied* 384
moment 113
momentous 151, 642
momentum 276
monarch 745
monarchy 737
monastery 1000
monasticism 995
monetary 800
MONEY 800
money-changer 797
moneylender 797
monger 797
mongrel 41, 83
monitor *oracle* 513
  director 694
  adviser 695
  warship 726
monitory *prediction* 511
  dissuasion 616
  warning 668
monk 996
monkey *imitator* 19
  ape 366
  butt 857
monocycle 272

monograph 594
monologue 589
monoplane 273
monoplanist 269a
monopolist 751, 943
monopolize 777
monopoly *restraint* 751
  possession 777
monotone 104
monotonous *uniform* 16
  equal 27
  repetition **104**
  weary 841
monotony 13
  [*see* monotonous]
monsoon 348, 349
monster *exception* 83
  giant 192
  prodigy 872
  evildoer 913
  ruffian 949
monstrosity
  [*see* monster]
  distortion 243
monstrous *excessive* 31
  exceptional 83
  huge 192
  wonderful 870
month 108
monument *tomb* **363**
  record 551
moo 412
mood *nature* **5**
  state 7
  tendency 176
  humor 602
moody *sad* 837
  sullen 901a
moon 108, **318**
  -shaped 245
moonbeam *light* 420
moonlight 422
moonshine *absurdity* 497
moonstruck *insane* 503
moor, *n. open space* 180
  plain 344
moor, *v. fasten* 43
  locate 184
moorings 184
moot -point *topic* 454
  question 461
mop 256, 652
mope 837
moraine 270
moral, *n. maxim* 496
moral, *adj. right* 922, 926
  virtuous 944
  -courage 604
  -obligation 926
morality 926, 944
moralize 476
morals *duty* 926
  virtue 944
morass 345
moratorium 133
morbid 655

hide 528
deceive 545

mythical 515, **979**
mythology **979**

N

nadir 211
nag, *n. horse* 271
nag, *v. quarrel* 713
nail *fasten* 43
naked 226
namby-pamby
  affected 855
name *indication* 550
  appellation **564**
nameless 565
namely 79
namesake 564
nap *texture* **256, 329**
  sleep 683
narcotic 662
narration 594
narrative 594
narrator 529, **532, 594**
narrow *thin* 203
  bigoted 481, **988**
narrow-minded
  bigoted 481
  foolish 499
  selfish 943
NARROWNESS 203
nasty *foul* 653
  offensive 830
nation 372
national 372
 -guard 726
nationality 372, 910
nationwide 78
native, *n.* 188
native, *adj.* 5, 367
 -land 342
nativity *birth* 66
natural *intrinsic* 5
  true 494
  artless 703
  simple 849
 -history 357
 -philosophy 316
naturalist 357
naturalization 184
naturalized 188
nature *essence* 5
  tendency 176
  world 318
naught 4, 101
naughty 945
nausea 841, 867
nauseate *sicken* 395, 867
  give pain 830
nauseous *unsavory* 395
  unpleasant 830
  disgusting 867
nautical 267, 273
naval 267, 273
 -authorities **745**

NAVIGATION 267
navigator 269
navvy *laborer* 690
navy 273, **726**
nay 536
neap *low* 207
 -tide 36
near *like* 17
 -in *space* 197
 -in *time* 121
 soon 132
 impending 152
 approach 286
 stingy 819
nearly 32
NEARNESS 9, 197
nearsighted 443
neat *orderly* 58
  trim 240, 845
  clean 652
nebula 353
nebulous *misty* 353
  obscure 519
necessarily 154
necessary 601, **630**
necessitate 630
NECESSITY *fate* 601
  predetermination 611
  compulsion 744
  indigence 804
  need 865
necromancy 511
necropolis 363
nectar 394, 396
need *necessity* 601
  requirement 630
  want 640
  indigence 804
  desire 865
needful 601, 630
needle 262
needless 641
needlework 847
nefarious 945
NEGATION 536, 764
negative, *n.* 22
negative, *adj. inexisting* 2
  denying 536
negative, *v. confute* 479
  deny 536
NEGLECT 460
  leave undone 730
  omit 773
  evade 927
negligence 460
negligent 460
negotiable 270
negotiate *mediate* 724
  bargain 769

negotiator 724, 758
Negro *black* **431**
neigh 412
neighbor *near* 197
  friend 890
neighborhood 197, 227
neighborly *aiding* **707**
  friendly 888
  social 892
nemesis 972
neologist 563
NEOLOGY 563
Nereid 979
nerve *strength* 159
  courage 861
nerveless *impotent* 158
  imperturbable 871
nervous *excitable* 825
  timid 860
nest 102, **153**
nestle 186, 902
net, *adj.* 40
net, *n.* 219, 232
nether 207
netlike 219
netting 219
nettle 830
network 59, **219**
neutral *mean* 29
  no choice 609a
  mid-course **628**
  indifferent 866
neutrality
  indifference 609a, 866
  [*see* neutral]
neutralize 179
never 107
 -more 107
new *different* 18
  novel **123**
newcomer 294
newfangled 851
NEWNESS 123
NEWS 532
newsmonger *gossip* 532
newspaper 531, 551
next 63, 121
nib *end* 67
nibble *eat* 298
nice *discriminative* **465**
  exact 494
  pleasing 829
  fastidious 868
niceness [*see* nice]
nicety 494
niche 191, 244
nick *notch* 257
nickel 800
nickname 565

O

P

misjudging 481
unjust 923
partiality desire 865
love 897
favor 923
partially 32, 51
participate co-operate 709
share 778
PARTICIPATION 778
participator 690
particle 32, 50, 193
particular, n. item 51
event 151
particular, adj. special 79
careful 494
exact 494
fastidious 868
particularize 79, 594
particularly 31, 33
particulars 79
parting 44
partisan follower 65
auxiliary 711
friend 890
partisanship 481, 709
partition divide 44
wall 228
partly 51
partner companion 88
auxiliary 711
partnership 88, 709
PARTY assemblage 72
person 372
association 712
sociality 892
-spirit warped judgment
481
co-operation 709
party-colored 428, 440
parvenu 123, 734, 876
paschal 998
pass, n. predicament 7
conjuncture 8
interval 198
defile 203
way 627
difficulty 704
thrust 716
pass, v. be superior 33
elapse 109, 122
happen 151
transfer 270
move through 302
vanish 449
an examination 648
away
cease 2, 142
-time 106
passable unimportant 643
imperfect 651
pretty 845
PASSAGE 302
conversion 144
corridor 191
opening 260
motion 264

navigation 267
transit 270
[see pass]
passenger 268
passing 31, 111
passion emotion 820
excitability 825
desire 865
love 897
anger 900
passionate impetuous 825
irascible 901
passionless 823
passive inert 172
obedient 743
passport 760
password 550
PAST 122
paste 352
pastime 840
pastor 996
pastoral 371
pastorate 995
pastry 396
pasture 232, 344
pat, adj. pertinent 23
pat, v. strike 276
patch change 140
blemish 848
-up restore 660
compromise 774
patchwork mixture 41
variegation 440
patent, n. 760
patent, adj. open 260
manifest 525
pater father 166
paternal father 166
benevolent 906
PATERNITY 166
paternoster 990
path direction 278
way 627
pathetic 830
pathless 180
pathos 821
patience
perseverance 604a
endurance 826
moderation 831
patient, n. 655
patriarch veteran 130
patriarchal 124, 166
patrician 875
patriot 910
patriotism 910
patrol safeguard 664
patrolman 664
patron auxiliary 711
customer 795
friend 890
patronage influence 175
aid 707
patronize aid 707
patter, n.
unmeaningness 517

talk 584
patter, v. strike 276
sound 407
pattern model 22
perfection 650
paucity 32, 103
Paul Pry 455
paunch 191, 250
pauper 640, 804
pause cessation 142
quiescence 265
pavement 211
pavilion 189
paving 211
paw handle 379
pawn 788
pawnbroker 787
pay, n. compensation 30
income 810
pay, v. defray 807
remunerate 973
PAYMENT 30, 807
remuneration 973
PEACE rest 265
silence 403
amity 721
peaceable 721
peaceful 174, 265, 721
peacemaker 714
peace offering 723
peace pipe 550
pea-coat 225
peak height 206
summit 33, 210
sharpness 253
peal 404, 407
pearly semitransparent 427
white 430
gray 432
peasant 876
peck, n. 31, 102
peculate 791
peculator 792
peculiar special 79
exceptional 83
peculiarity 5
peculiarly greatly 31
more 33
pecuniary 800
pedagogic 540
pedagogue scholar 492
teacher 450
pedal 633
pedant 492
pedantic 855
pedantry 491, 855
peddler 797
pedestal 215
pedestrain 268
pedigree 69, 166
pedlar [see peddler]
peek 441
peel pare 204
skin 223
uncover 226
peep chirp 412

Q

quaint *odd* 83
  ridiculous 853
quake *oscillate* 314
  shake 315
  fear 860
QUALIFICATION
  change 140
  power 157
  modification 469
qualify *change* 140
  modify 469
quality *attributes* 157
  tendency 176
  nobility 875
qualm 603
quandary 7, 475
quantitative 25
QUANTITY 25
  much 31
quarrel 24, 713
quarrelsome 713, 901
quarry *object* 620
  mine 636
quarter, n. *fourth* 95
  period 108
  region 181
  forbearance 740
  mercy 914
quarter, v. *cut up* 44
  quadrisect 97
  locate 184
quarters *abode* 189
quartet 95
quash *destroy* 162
  annul 756

QUATERNITY 95
quaver *oscillate* 314
  shake 315
  fear 860
quay *wharf* 231
queen 745, 877
queer *singular* 83
quell 265, 731
quench *cool* 385
  satiate 869
querulous *complaining* 839
  fastidious 868
  irritable 901
query 461
quest 461
question *inquire* 461
  doubt 485
questionable
  uncertain 475
  doubtful 485
  disreputable 874
questioner 455
queue 65
quibble *quirk* 481
  equivocation 520
quick *transient* 111
  rapid 274
  alive 359
  intelligent 498
  active 682
  irascible 901
quicken *work* 170
  hasten 274, 684
  come to life 359
  excite 824

quickly *soon* 132
quiescence 265
quiet *calm* 174
  rest 265
  silence 403
quietude 826
quietus *death* 361
quilt *covering* 223
QUINQUESECTION 99
quintessence 5
quip *amusement* 840
  wit 842
  ridicule 856
quirk 481
quit *depart* 293
  relinquish 624
quite 52
quits 27
quitter 623
quiver, n. 191
  agitation 315
quiver, v. *oscillate* 314
  shiver 383
  fear 860
quixotic *fanciful* 515
  rash 863
quiz *question* 461
  ridicule 856
quizzical 856
quota 25
quotation
  imitation 19
  evidence 467
  price 812
quote 82, 467

R

rabble 72, 876
rabid 821
race *relation* 111
  sequence 69
  kind 75
  lineage 166
  run 274
  stream 343, 348
racial 166
raciness 574
rack, n. *receptacle* 191
  frame 215
  gait 275
  instrument of torture 975
rack, v. *torture* 830
racket *uproar* 404
racy *strong* 171
  pungent 392
radiance *light* 420
  beauty 845
radiant *diverging* 291
  beautiful 845
radiate 73, 291
radiation 73, 291
radical, adj. *essential* 5
  complete 52

  important 642
radical, n. *reformer* 658
radically *greatly* 31
radio 534
radiograph 554
radiography 556
radiophone 534
radiotelegraphy 420
radiotelephone 534
radius 200, 202
raft 273
rafter 215
rag 32
ragamuffin 876
rage *violence* 173
  excitement 824, 825
  fashion 852
  desire 865
  wrath 900
rags 225
ragtime *music* 415
raid *attack* 716
  pillage 791
rail *inclosure* 232
railing 232
raillery 856

railroad 266, 627
railway 627
  -station 266
raiment 225
rain 348
rainy 348
raise *increase* 35
  produce 161
  elevate 212, 307
  leaven 320
raja 875
rake, v. *drag* 285
  clean 652
  -up *collect* 72
rally *meet* 74
  encourage 861
ramble *stroll* 266
  wander 279
  rave 503
  digress 573
rambler 268
rambling 279
ramification 291
ramify 291
rampage 173
rampant *prevalent* 175

reward 973
repeal 756
repeat *imitate* 19
  iterate 104, 136
  reproduce 163
  affirm 535
repeated 104
repeater *watch* 114
  firearm 727
repel *repulse* 289
  defend 717
  resist 719
  refuse 764
  give pain 830
  disincline 867
  banish 893
repellent 289, 846
  [see repel]
repent 950
repentant 950
repertory 599
REPETITION
  similarity 17
  imitation 19, 21
  iteration 104, 136
repine *grieve* 828
  regret 833
  mope 837
replace *substitute* 147
  restore 660
replenish *complete* 52
  fill 637
repletion *redundance* 641
  satiety 869
replica 21
reply *answer* 462
report *noise* 406
  judgment 480
  information 527
  rumor 532
  statement 594
reporter 534, 553
REPOSE *quiescence* 265
  leisure 685
  rest 687
reprehend 932
reprehensible 898
represent *exhibit* 525
  intimate 527
  denote 550
  delineate 554
  stand for 759
REPRESENTATION
  [see represent]
  copy 21
  portrait 554
representative, *adj.*
  typical 79
  illustrative 554
representative, *n.*
  delegate 524, 758
  legislator 696
  -government 737
repress *restrain* 751
  counteract 179
repressionist 751

repressive 751
reprieve *delay* 133
  pardon 918
  respite 970
reprimand 932
reprint *copy* 21
reprisal 148
reproach, *n. disgrace* 874
  blame 932
reproach, *v.* 932, 938
reprobate 945, 949
reproduce *match* 17
  imitate 19
  renovate 163
REPRODUCTION 163
  copy 21
reproductive 163
reproof 932
reprove *berate* 527
  disapprove 932
reptile *animal* 366
  knave 941, 949
republic 372, 737
republican 737, 876
repudiate *deny* 489
  reject 610
  abrogate 756
  violate 773
repugnance
  contrariety 14
  dislike 867
  hate 898
repugnant 24, 867
repulse *repel* 289, 764
  resist 719
  failure 732
REPULSION 289, 719
repulsive [see repulse]
  unsavory 395
  ugly 846
  disliked 867
  hateful 898
reputable *honored* 873
reputation 873
REPUTE 873
REQUEST 765
requiem *lament* 839
require *need* 630
  exact 741
  compel 744
  demand 924
  behoove 926
REQUIREMENT 630
requisite 630
requisition 630, 765
requital 148, 718
requite 973
rescind *abrogate* 756
  refuse 764
rescue *deliver* 672
  aid 707
research 461
resemblance 17
resemble 17, 23
resent 900
RESENTMENT 900

reservation
  concealment 528
reserve
  concealment 526, 528
  means 632
  store 636
  shyness 881
reservoir 153, 636
reside 186
residence 189
resident 186, 188
residential 186
residue 40
residuum *remainder* 40
  dregs 653
resign *give up* 757
  relinquish 782
  -oneself *submit* 725
  not mind 826
RESIGNATION
  [see resign]
  submission 725
  abdication 757
  endurance 831
  humility 879
resigned 743
resilience *elasticity* 325
RESIN 356a
resinous 356a
resist *oppose* 179
  withstand 719
  refuse 764
RESISTANCE 708, 719
  [see resist]
resistless 159
resolute *determined* 604
  brave 861
RESOLUTION
  [see resolve]
  concession 144
  topic 454
  mental energy 604
  intention 620
  courage 861
resolve *discover* 480a
  determine 604
  intend 620
resonance *repetition* 104
  sound 402
  ringing 408
resort, *n.* 189
resort, *v.* 72
  -to be present 186
  employ 677
resound 408
resourceful 698
resources *means* 632
  wealth 803
RESPECT, *n. fame* 873
  deference 928
respect, *v. observe* 772
  regard 928
respectability
  mediocrity 736
  probity 939
respectable

revolt *revolution* 146
  rebellion **742**
  shock 830
REVOLUTION
  periodicity 138
  change **146**
  rotation 312
  rebellion 742
revolutionary **146, 742**
revolutionize 140, **146**
revolve 138, 312
revolver 727
revulsion *reversion* 145
  recoil 277
REWARD 30, **973**
rhapsody 515
rhetoric *speech* 582
rhetorical 577
rhyme 597
rhythm 104, 138
  verse 597
rhythmic 413, 578
rib 250
ribald 851
ribaldry 908
ribbon 205
rich *abundant* **639**
  wealthy 803
  -man **639, 803**
riches 803
richly *much* 31
rickety *weak* 160
ricochet 277
RIDDANCE 672, 776, 782
riddle, *n. sieve* 260
  secret 533
  enigma 519
ride 266
  -*a horse* 370
rider *appendix* 39
  equestrian 268
ridge 206, 250
ridicule 856
ridiculous *absurd* 497
  foolish 499
  grotesque **853**
RIDICULOUSNESS 853
riding
  journey **266**
rife 78, 175
riffraff 876, **949**
rifle, *n.* 727
rifle, *v. plunder* 791
rift *fissure* 44, 198
rig *dress* 225
  prepare 673
rigging *ropes* 45
right, *n. justness* **922**
  privilege **924**
right, *adj. dextral* 238
  straight 246
  true 494
  proper **924**
  fitting **926**
  virtuous 944
righteous *virtuous* **944**

rightful 922
right-handed 238
rigid *regular* 82
  hard 328
  exact 494
rigor 739
rigorous *exact* 494
  severe 739
rile 830
rill 348
rim 231
rind *covering* 223
ring, *n. circle* 247
  clique 712
  arena 728
ring, *v. resound* 408
ringleader 694
ringlet 256
rinse 652
riot *confusion* 59
  violence 173
  mutiny 742
rioter 742
riotous 173
rip *open* 260
ripe 673
ripen *perfect* 650
  prepare **673**
ripple 315
  murmur 405
rise *ascend* 35, 305
  begin 66
  revolt 146, 742
  slope 217
rising 305 [*see* rise]
risk, 621, 665
RITE 998
ritual *ceremony* 882
  worship 990
  rite 998
ritualism 998
rival, *n.* 710
rival, *v. emulate* 648
  oppose 708
  compete 720
  outshine **873**
rivalry 708
rive 44
RIVER 348
rivet *fasten* 43
rivulet 348
road 278, 627
roadstead 666
roadster 272
roadway 627
roam 266
roan *color* 433
roar *be violent* **173**
  sound 404
  bellow 411, 412
  laugh 838
roast 384
rob *plunder* 791
robber 792
robbery 791
robe *dress* 225

robust *strong* 159
  healthy 654
rock, *n.* **342**, 667
rock, *v. oscillate* 314
rocket *signal* 550
rocky 323
rod *support* 315
  scourge **975**
rogue 941
roguery 940
roguish *playful* **840**
roisterer 887
role *drama* 599
  conduct 692
ROLL, *n. list* **86**
  sound **407**
  convolution 248
  rotundity 249
  rotate 312
  flow 348
roll, *v. make smooth* 255
  move 264
  wallow 311
roll call 85
roller 255
rollers *billows* 348
rollick 836
romance, *n.*
  imagination 515
  fiction 546, 594
romance, *v.* 497
romantic *imaginative* 515
  descriptive 594
  sentimental 822
romanticism 515
romp 309, 840
Röntgen ray 420
roof *house* 189
  summit 210
  cover 223
rookie 726
rookery *nests* 189
room *space* 180
  chamber 191
roommate 890
roomy 180
roost 189, 215
rooster 366
root *algebraic* - **84**
  cause 153
  place 184
  base 211
  -out *eject* **297**
  -up *extract* 301
rooted *old* 124
  firm 150
  located 184
rope *cord* 205
ropy 352
rosary 998
rose *fragrance* 4)0
  red 434
roseate *red* 434
  hopeful 858
rosin *resin* 356*a*
roster

rostrum 542
rosy 434, 845
rosy-cheeked 845
rot *decay* 49, 659
   putrefy 653
rotate 312
ROTATION 138, 312
rotten *foul* 653
   decayed 659
rotound 249
ROTUNDITY 249
rough, *n bully* 876, 887
   913
rough, *adj. violent* 173
   shapeless 241
   uneven 256
   harsh 410
   churlish 895
roughen 256
roughew 240
roughly *nearly* 197
ROUGHNESS 256
   [see *rough*]
roughrider 268
round, *n series* 69
   revolution 138
round, *adj*
   circular 247, 249
round, *v* 245, 311
roundabout 279, 311
roundup 72
rouse *stimulate* 615
   excite 502
rout, *n. tumult* 315
rout, *v. overcome* 731
   discomfit 732
route 266, 627
routine *order* 58, 138
   custom 613
   business 625
rove *travel* 266
rover 268
roving 266
row, *n. series* 69
   violence 173
   street 189
row, *v* 267
rowdy, *n. blusterer* 887
rowdyism 851
rower 269

royal 737
royalist 737
royalty 737
rub, *n. difficulty* 704
rub, *v* 331, 379, 662
rubber *overshoe* 225
   eraser 331
   masseur 662
rubbish 645
rube 876
Rubicon *limit* 233
rubicund 434
rubric *liturgy* 998
ruby *red* 434
ruck 876
rudder 273, 633, 693
ruddy *red* 434
rude *violent* 173
   shapeless 241
   vulgar 851
   uncivil 895
rudiment *beginning* 66
   cause 153
rudimentary 66
rudiments 66
rue *regret* 833
rueful *regretful* 833
   sad 837
ruff 225
ruffian *rough* 876, 913
   scoundrel 949
ruffianism 907
ruffle *disorder* 59
   derange 61
   roughen 256
   fold 258
   excite 824, 825
   irritate 898
rug *covering* 223
rugged
   shapeless 241
   rough 256
ruin *destruction* 162
   failure 732
   adversity 735
ruined 732, 859
ruinous *painful* 830
ruins *remains* 40
RULE *average* 29

regularity 80
   influence 175
   measure 466
   decide 480
   custom 613
   precept 697
   reign 737
ruler 737, 745
rumble 407
ruminate *chew* 298
   think 451
rummage 461
rumor 532
rump *remainder* 40
rumple *disorder* 59
   derange 61
   roughen 256
rumpus *confusion* 59
run, *n. rule* 29
   repetition 104
   motion 264
   speed 274
   habit 613
run, *v. flow* 109, 264, 348
   race 274
   -down *depreciate* 932
runaway 623
rung 215
runner *branch* 51
   courier 268, 271, 534
rupture 44
   quarrel 713
rural 189, 371
ruse *cunning* 702
rush *crowd* 72
   dash 274
   haste 684
russet 433
rust *decay* 659
rustic, *n.* 876
rustic, *adj.* 189, **371**
rustle 405, 407
rusty *decayed* 659
   unskillful 699
rut *regularity* 80
   furrow 259
ruthless
   savage 907
   revengeful 919

S

Sabbath 687
saber 727
sable 431
sabotage 162
saccharin 396
sacerdotal 995
sack, *n. bag* 191
   dismissal 756
sack, *v. plunder* 791
sacrament 998
SACRED *holy* 976

   -writings **986**
sacrifice, *n. worship* 990
   holocaust 991
sacrifice, *v.* 162
sacrilege 988
sad *dull* 428
   painful 830
   dejected 837
sadden 830, 837
saddle 155, 293
   -with *quarter on* 184

sadness 837
safe, *n.* 530
safe, *adj. secure* **664**
safeguard 717
SAFETY **664**
sag *curve* 245
sagacious 498
SAGE, *n.* **500**
sage, *adj.* 498
said *repeated* 104
sail *navigate* 267

learner 541
schoolfellow 541
schoolgirl 129, 541
schoolmaster 540
schoolmate 541, 890
schoolmistress 540
schoolroom 191, 542
schooner 273
science *knowledge* 490
skill 698
scientific *exact* 494
scientist 492
scimitar 727
scintilla *particle* 193
spark 420, 423
scintillate
[*see* scintillation]
be brilliant 498
scintillation *heat* 382
light 420
wit 842
scion *part* 51
scissors 253
scoff *deride* 929, 988
-at 932
scold, *n. shrew* 901
scold, *v. denounce* 908
censure 932
scollop *notch* 257
scoop *hollow out* 252
scope *degree* 26
extent 180
freedom 748
scorch 382
scorching *violent* 173
score *list* 86
twenty 98
furrow 259
music 415
scorn 930
scoundrel 949
scour *rub* 331
clean 652
SCOURGE 975
scout, *n vanguard* 234
aviator 269a
spectator 444
patrol 664
scout, *v. reject* 610
disregard 930
scowl *complain* 839
frown 895
sulk 901a
scraggy 241
scramble *climb* 305
contend 720
scrap *small* 32
piece 51
scrape, *n. difficulty* 704
mischance 732
scrape, *v. pare* 38
reduce 195
pulverize 330
abrade 331
clean 652
scratch, *n.* 619

scratch, *v. abrade* 331
write 590
wound 649
scrawl 517
scream *blow* 349
cry 411
wail 839
screech 411
screen, *n. sieve* 260
shade 424
hider 530
defense 717
screen, *v. hide* 528
shelter 666
screw, *n. distortion* 243
propeller 267
screw, *v. fasten* 43
distort 243
scribble 517, 590
scribe 590
scrimmage 713
script 590
scriptural 983a, **985**
Scripture 985
scroll *list* 86
scrub, *adj. short* 201
scrub, *v. rub* 331
clean 652
scruple *doubt* 485
reluctance 603
scrupulous *careful* **459**
exact 494
reluctant 603
fastidious 868
punctilious 939
scrutiny *attention* 457
inquiry 461
scud *sail* 267
speed 274
scuffle 720
scull *row* 267
sculptor 559
SCULPTURE *form* 240
carving 557
scum *foam* 353
scurrilous 929
scurry *haste* 274
scuttle *destroy* 162
speed 274
scythe 253
sea *ocean* 341
at - *uncertain* 475
seacoast 342
seafarer 269
seafaring 267, 273
seagirt 346
seagoing 267
seal, *n. matrix* 22
mark 550
seal, *v. close* 261
complete 729
seam 43
seaman 269
séance 525, 992a
sear *dry* 340
burn 384

deaden 823
search 461
searching 739
searchlight 423, 550
seashore 342
season, *n.* 106
season, *v. mix* 41
spice 392
accustom 613
seasonable *early* 132
opportune 134
seasoning *condiment* 393
seat *place* 183
support 215
seaweed 367
secede *dissent* **489**
disobey 742
seceder 984
Secessionist 742
seclude 893
SECLUSION 893
second, *n. instant* 113
second, *adj.* 90
second, *v. abet* 707
secondary *inferior* 34
seconder 711
second-rate 34, 651
secrecy 528
SECRET, *n.* 533
secret, *adj. latent* 526
secretary *desk* 191
recorder 553
writer 590
servant 746
secrete *conceal* 528
secretion 299
secretive 528
sect 75
religious - 984
sectarian *489, 984*
sectarianism 984
sectary 489, 984
section *division* 44
class 75
troops 726
sector *part* 51
secular 997
secure, *adj.* 664
secure, *v. fasten* 43
bespeak 132
restrain 751
gain 775
securities 802
SECURITY *safety* 664
pledge 771
sedan 272
sedan chair 272
sedate *thoughtful* 451
calm 826
grave 837
sedative 174
sedentary 265
sediment 321, 653
sedition 742
seditionist 891
seduction 829

gang 712
set, *adj. habitual* 613
set, *v. make firm* 150
  place 184
  sharpen 253
  -about *begin* 66
  undertake 676
  -apart *separate* 44
  exclude 55
  select 609
  -free 44, 750
set-off *compensation* 30
settee 215
settle *establish* 150
  be located 184
  come to rest 265
  subside 306
  decide 480, 609
  pay 807
  -down *become stable* 150
  locate oneself 184
settlement [*see* settle]
  location 184
  compact 769
  deed 771
  payment 807
settler 188
seven 98
seventy-five *gun* 727
sever 44, 291
several 100, 102
severally 44, 79
severe *exact* 494
  harsh 739
  painful 830
  simple 849
  critical 932
SEVERITY 739
  [*see* severe]
sew 43
sewer *drain* 350
sewerage 652
sex 75
sexton 363
shabbiness [*see* shabby]
  inferiority 34
shabby *paltry* 643
  deteriorated 659
  stingy 819
  mean 874
  disgraceful 940
shack 189
shackle, *n* 45, 752
shackle, *v restrain* 751
SHADE, *n degree* 26
  ghost 362, 980a
  darkness 421
  shadow 424
  color 428
  screen 530
shade, *v. dim* 422
shadow, *n. phantom* 4
  copy 21
  darkness 421
  shade 424
  ghost 980a

shadow, *v. follow* 63
  pursue 235, 281
  cloud 353, 422
  inquire 461
shadowy *inexistent* 2
  unsubstantial 4
  shady 424
shady 424
shaft *depth* 208
  pit 260
  air pipe 351
  handle 633
shaggy 256
shake *totter* 149
  vibrate 314, 315
  shiver 383
  dissuade 616
  fear 860
  -off 297
shaky *weak* 160
  unsteady 665
shallow *not deep* 209
  ignorant 491
SHALLOWNESS 209
sham *falsehood* 544
  deception 545
shamble *dawdle* 275
shambles 361
shame, *n. dishonor* 874
shame, *v. humiliate* 879
shamefaced 881
shameful *disgraceful* 940
shameless *unreserved* 525
  impudent 885
shanty 189
shape *state* 7
  form 240
  aspect 448
shapeless 241
shapely 240, 242
share, *n.* 51, 786
share, *v.* 778
shareholder 778
sharp *energetic* 171
  acute 253
  sensible 375
  pungent 392
  shrill 410
  intelligent 498
  active 682
  painful 830
  keen 868
  censorious 932
sharpen 253 [*see* sharp]
sharpener 253
SHARPNESS 253
  pungency 392
  fastidiousness 868
sharpshooter 716, 726
shatter 158, 162
shattered *weak* 160
shave *reduce* 195
  shorten 201
  smooth 255
shaving *layer* 204
shawl 225

sheaf 72
shear *reduce* 195
  shorten 201
shears 253
sheath 223
sheathe 224
shed, *n.* 189
shed, *v. scatter* 73
  emit 297
  -tears 839
sheen 420
sheep 366
sheepish 881
sheer *mere* 32
  complete 52
  deviation 279
sheet *layer* 204
  covering 223
shelf 215
shell, *n. cover* 223
  bomb 727
shell, *v bombard* 716
shelter 664, 666
shelve *defer* 133
  slope 217
  neglect 460
shepherd 370
sheriff 664
shibboleth 550
shield, *n heraldry* 550
  buckler 666
shield, *v. defend* 717
shift, *n. chemise* 225
  subterfuge 477
shift, *v. change* 140
  convert 144
  change 149
  displace 185
  transfer 270
  deviate 279
shiftless 674
shifty 702
shilling 800
shimmer 420
shin *climb* 305
shine *light* 420
shingle *cover* 223
shiny 420
SHIP, *n.* 273
ship, *v* 270
shipload *much* 31
  cargo 190
shipmate 890
shipment 270, 295
shipping 273
shipshape 58
shipwreck 162
shipwrecked 732
shirk *avoid* 623
shirker 623, 862
shirt 225
shiver *destroy* 162
  shake 315
  be cold 383
shoal, *n. multitude* 102
shoal, *adj. shallow* 209

shoals *rocks* 667
shock, *n. cluster* 72
  concussion 276
  seizure 655
  excitement 82
  ordeal 828
shock, *v. startle* 508
  agitate 824
  repel 830, 867
  scandalize 932
shocking *bad* 649
  painful 830
  fearful 860
  disreputable 874
  hateful 898
shoe 225
shoot, *n. tendril* 367
shoot, *v. expand* 194
  dart 274
  propel 284
  kill 361
  pain 378
shop 799
shopkeeper 797
shoplifter 792
shoplifting 791
shore 231, 342
shore up 215
shorn 51
short *incomplete* 53
  not long 201
  brittle 328
  concise 572
  uncivil 895
  -commons
    fasting 956
  -cut *straight* 246
  -of *lacking* 38
shortage 53
SHORTCOMING
  inequality 28
  inferiority 34
  incompleteness 53
  motion short of 304
shorten 36, 38, 201
shorthand 590
short-lived 111
SHORTNESS 201
shortsighted *myopic* 443
  misjudging 481
shot, *n.* 727
shotgun 727
shoulder, *v.* 215
shout *cry* 406, 411
  cheer 838
shove 276
shovel 191
show, *n. opportunity* 134
  drama 599
  ornament 847
  parade 882
show, *v. appear* 446, 448
  draw attention 457
  evince 467
  demonstrate 478
  manifest 525

-off *display* 882
  boast 884
  -up *censure* 932
  accuse 938
shower *assemblage* 72
  rain 348
showy *ugly* 846
  ornamental 847
  tawdry 851
  ostentatious 882
shrapnel 727
shred 32, 205
shrew 901
shrewd *knowing* 490
  wise 498
  cunning 702
shriek 410, 411
shrift 952
shrill 404, 410
shrine 1000
shrink *decrease* 36
  shrivel 195
  avoid 623
  blench 822
  fear 860
shrive 952
shrivel 195, 258
shroud, *n.* 223, 363
shroud, *v. invest* 225
  hide 528
shrub *plant* 367
shrug *sign* 550
shrunk 195
shudder *shiver* 383
  fear 860
  -at *hate* 898
shuffle *change* 140, 149
  move slowly 275
  prevaricate 544
  palter 605
shun *avoid* 623
  dislike 867
shut 261
  -out *exclude* 55
  prohibit 761
  -up 751
shutter 424
shuttle *alternate* 314
shy, *adj.* 862, 881
shy, *v. deviate* 279
  draw back 283
  propel 284
  avoid 623, 860
Shylock 787
SIBILATION *hiss* 409
sibyl *oracle* 513
sick *ill* 655
  -of *averse* 867
  satiated 869
sicken *nauseate* 395
  pain 830
  weary 841
  disgust 867
sickle 253
sickly *weak* 160
sickness 655

SIDE *edge* 231
  laterality **236**
  party 712
  -by side **712**
  -issue 39
  -with *aid* 707
  co-operate **709**
side arms 727
sidelong 236
sidereal 318
sidetrack 279
sidewalk 627
sidewise 217, **236**
sidle 217, 236, 279
siege 716
siesta 683
sieve 219, 260
sift *simplify* 42
  inquire 461
  clean 652
sigh 839
sight *vision* 441
  appearance 448
  prodigy 872
sightless *blind* 442
sight-seeing 441
sight-seer 444
sign, *n. omen* 512
  indication 550
  prodigy 872
sign, *v. attest* 467, 550
signal, *n. light* 423
  sign 550
signal, *adj. great* 31
  eventful 151
signalize *indicate* 550
  celebrate 883
signature 467
signet 550, 747
significant 642
  [see signify]
signify *forebode* 511
  mean 516
  indicate 550
SILENCE, *n.* 403, 585
silence, *v. confute* 479
  gag 581
  quell 731
silencer 408a
silent 403, 585
silhouette *outline* 230
silken 255
sill 215
silly *credulous* 846
  imbecile 499
silo 636
silt *dirt* 653
silver, *n. money* 800
silver, *adj. white* 430
  gray 432
SIMILARITY 9, 17, 27
simile *similarity* 17
  comparison 464
  metaphor 521
similitude *copy* 21
simmer *boil* 382, 384

spurious *deceptive* 545
  illegitimate 925
spurn *reject* 610
  disdain 866, **930**
spurt *sprint* 274
  gush 348
spy, *n.* 444, 664
spy, *v.* 441
squabble 713
squad 72, 726
squadron 726
squalid *dirty* 653
  unsightly 846
squall, *n.* 349
squall, *v. cry* 411
squalor 653
squander 776, 818
square, *n. four* 95
  place 182
  rectangle 244
  measure 466
square, *adj. just* 922, **924**
square, *v. compensate* 30
squash *quell* 162
  pulp 354
squat, *v.* 184, 308
squat, *adj. short* 201
  thick 202
  low 207
squatter 188
squaw 374
squeak *cry* 411
squeal 411
squeamish *sick* 655
  fastidious 868
squeeze *contract* 195
  condense 321
  -out *extract* **301**
squib *lampoon* 856
squint, *n.* 443
squint, *v. look* 441
squire *attendant* 746
  gentry 875
squirm 315
squirt *eject* 297
stab *pierce* 260
  kill 361
  pain 649
STABILITY 16, 141, **150**
stabilize 150
stable, *n.* 189, 370
stable, *adj.*
  permanent 141, 150
  quiescent 265
stack 72
staff *support* 215
  music 413
  council 696
  cast **712**
  weapon 727
  retinue 746
stag *deer* 366
  male 373
  socialty 892
stage *degree* 26
  term 71

time 106
  position 183
  platform 215
  drama 599
stagecoach 272
stagger, *n. be slow* 275
  reel 314, 821
  shake belief 485
  startle 508
  astonish 870
stagnant *inert* 172
  quiescent 265
  unprogressive **659**
stagnate 265
stagnation *inertness* 172
  quiescence 265
staid *grave* 837
stain *color* 223, 428
  blemish 848
  disgrace 874
stainless *clean* 652
  honorable **939**
  innocent 946
staircase 305
stairs 305
stairway 305
stake *wager* 621
  security 771
  execution 975
stale *old* 124
  insipid 391
stalk, *n.* 215
stalk, *v. walk* 266
  chase 622
stall *cot* 189
  booth 799
stalwart *strong* 159
stamina *strength* 159
STAMMERING 583
stamp *character* 7
  prototype 22
  kind 75
  form 240
  mark 550
  security 771
  -out *extinguish* 385
stampede 860
stanch, *adj.* **939**
stanch, *v.* 348
stand, *n. time* 106
  support 215
  quiescence 265
stand, *v. resist* 719
  brook 821
  endure 826
  -by *near* 197
  aid 707
  -fast 141
  -for *indicate* 550
standard *model* 22
  degree 26
  average 29
  rule 80
  measure 466
  flag 550
  perfection 650

standardize 58
standing *footing* 8
  degree 26
  permanence 141
  situation 183
  rank 873
standpatter 150
standpoint 441
stanza 597
staple, *n. whole* 50
  material 635
staple, *adj.* 794
star *luminary* 318, **423**
  actor 599
  glory 873
  -s and stripes 550
starched *proud* 878
stare *look* 441
  gape 455
  wonder 870
stark *very* 31
  sheer 32
starry 318
start *begin* 66
  arise 151
  move 284
  depart 293
  leap 309
  offer 763
  fear 860
  wonder 870
startle *doubt* **485**
  stagger 508
  fear 860
  amaze 870
starvation [*see* **starve**]
  insufficiency 640
  fasting 956
starve *be poor* 804
  stint 819
  fast 956
STATE, *n. condition* **7**
  position 71
  realm 372, 780
  government **737**
state, *v.* 535
statehouse 966
stately *grand* 873
  pompous 882
statement 535
stateroom 191
statesman 694
statesmanship **693**
static 319
statics 159, 319
station, *n. degree* 26
  term 71
  situation 183
  journey **266**
  prison 752
  rank 873
station, *v. locate* **184**
stationary 265
statistical 85
statistics 85, 86
statue 554

straggle *stroll* 266
  deviate 279
straggler 268
straight, *adj.* **246**
straight, *adv.* 278
straighten 246
straightforward
  truthful 543
  honorable 939
STRAIGHTNESS 246
straightway 132
strain, *n. race* 11
  melody 415
strain, *v. weaken* 160
  percolate 295
  overrate 482
  clarify 652
  tax 688
  effort 686
strainer *sieve* 260
strait *interval* 198
  water 343
  difficulty 704
straitened *poor* 804
strait-laced *severe* 739
  fastidious 868
  haughty 878
strand *thread* 205
  land 342
stranded *stuck fast* 150
  ruined 732
  lost 828
strange *unrelated* 10
  exceptional 83
  ridiculous 853
  wonderful 870
  -bedfellows 713
  -to say 870
stranger *alien* 57
strangle *contract* 195
  kill 361
strangulation 361
strap, *n.* 45
strap, *v. fasten* 43
strapping *strong* 159
stratagem *plan* 626
  artifice 702
strategic 692, 864
strategist 694, 700
strategy *conduct* 692
  warfare 722
stratification 204
stratum 204, 251
stray, *adj.* 73
stray, *v.* 279
streak 440
STREAM, *n. -of fluid* **347**
  -of water **348**
  -of air 349
  -of light 420
stream, *v.* 72, 264
streamer *flag* 550
street, 189, 627
STRENGTH *quantity* 25
  degree 26
  greatness 31

vigor **159**
  energy 171
  tenacity 327
strengthen *reinforce* 37
  invigorate **159**
strenuous *energetic* 171
  persevering 604a
  active 682
stress *emphasis* 580
  importance 642
  strain 686
stretch, *n. expanse* 180
  exertion 686
stretch, *v. expand* 194
  extend 200
  misrepresent 555
stretcher 272
strew 73
strict *rigid* 82
  exact 494
  severe 739
  conscientious 939
  orthodox 983a
stricture 932
stride, *n.* 264
stride, *v.* 266
STRIDENCY 410
strident 410
strife *discord* 713
  contention 720
strike *hit* 276
  resist 719
  disobey 742
  impress 824
  beat 972
  -off exclude 55
  -root 150
striking 525, 890
string 205
stringent *energetic* 171
  strict 739
  compulsory 744
stringy *filamentous* 205
  tough 327
strip, *n.* 205
strip, *v. divest* 226
  take 789
  rob 791
stripe, *n, line* 200
  insignia 747
  blow 972
stripe, *v.* 440
stripling 129
strive *endeavor* 675
  exert 686
  content 720
stroke *impulse* 276
  mark 550
  blow 619
  expedient 626
  disease 655
  action 680
  success 731
stroke, *v.* 379
stroll 266
strong *powerful* **159**

energetic 171
  tough 327
  pungent 392
  fetid 401
  healthy 654
stronghold 717
strong-minded 604, **861**
strong-willed 604, **861**
strop 253
structural 240, **329**
STRUCTURE 329
  production **161**
  organization 357
struggle, *n. essay* 675
  exertion 686
struggle, *v. flounder* 704
  contend 720
strum 416
strut *walk* 266
  swagger 878, 880
  boast 884
stub 550
stubble *remains* 40
stubborn *hard* 323
  obstinate 606
stubby 201
stucco 223
stuck [see stick]
  -fast firm **150**
stuck-up 878
studded *spiked* 253
  variegated 440
student 492, 541
studio room 191
  workshop 691
studious *thoughtful* 451
  docile **539**
study, *n. copy* 21
  room 191
  learning **539**
study, *v. think* 451
  examine 461
stuff, *n. matter* 316
  absurdity 497
  material 635
stuff, *v. fill* 190
  pad 194
  line 224
  fool 545
  overeat 957
stuffing *lining* 224
  stopper 263
stuffy *sultry* 382
stultify 499
stumble *fal.* 306
  flounder 315
  trip 495
stumbling block
  difficulty 704
  hindrance 706
stump *remainder* 40
  trunk 51
stumpy *short* 201
stun *stupefy* 376
  deafen 419
  startle 508

discourteous 895
sulky **901a**
SULLENNESS **901a**
sully *dirty* 653
  dishonor 874
sultan 745
sultry 382
sum *total* 50
  number 84
  money 800
  -up reckon 37, 85
  discriminate 465
  review 596
summarize 201, 596
summary, *n.* 596
summary, *adj. transient*
  111
  short 201
  concise 572
summer 125, 382
SUMMIT 33, 210
summon *command* 741
  indict 969
summons 741, 969
sumptuous 882
sun 318, 423
  -god **423**
sunbeam 420
sunburnt 433
Sunday 687
sunder 44
sundial 114
sundry 102
sunny *warm* 382
  cheerful 836
sunrise 125
sunset 126
sunshade 223
sunshine 420
sup *feed* 298
superabound 641
superannuated 128, 158
superb 845
supercilious *proud* 878
  insolent 885
  scornful 930
superficial *shallow* 209
  extrinsic 220
  ignorant 491
superficies 220
superfluity 40, 641
superfluous 641
superhuman *godlike* 976
superintend 693
superintendent 694
superior, *n. head* 694
superior, *adj. greater* **33**
  high 206
SUPERIORITY **33**
superlative 33
superman 33
supernatural 976, 980a
supersede *substitute* 147
  relinquish **782**
superstition 486
superstitious 486, 984

supervene *succeed* 117
supervise 693
supervision **693**
supervisor 694
supervisory 693
supine *flat* 213, 251
  sluggish 462
supplant 147
supple *soft* 324
supplement 37, 39
suppliant 767
supplicate *beg* 765
supplies 707
supply *store* **636**
  provide 637
  give 784
  -deficiencies 52
SUPPORT, *n. footing* 175
  foundation 215
support, *v. perform* 170
  evidence 467
  escort 664
  aid 707
  feel 821
  endure 826
supporter 215
suppose 472, **514**
SUPPOSITION **514**
suppress *destroy* 162
  conceal 528
  restrain 751
suppression [*see suppress*]
supremacy 33
supreme *superior* **33**
  highest 210
  ruling 737
Supreme Being 976
sure *certain* 474
  safe 664
sure-footed *careful* 459
  skillful 698
  cautious 864
sureness [*see sure*]
surety *certainty* 474
  safety 664
  sponsor 771
surf 348, 353
surface 220
surfeit *redundance* 641
  satiety 869
surge *swarm* 72
  swell 305
  wave 348
surgeon 662
surgery 662
surly *gruff* 895
  sullen **901a**
surmise 514
surmount *tower* 206
  overtop 210
  ascend 305
surname 564
surpass *be superior* 33
  go beyond 303
  outshine **873**
surplus *remainder* 40

redundance 33, 641
surprise, *n.* **508**
surprise, *v.*
  take unawares **674**
  wonder 870
surrender *submit* **725**
  relinquish 782
surreptitious
  furtive 528
  deceptive 545
surround 227
surrounding **227**
surroundings 227
surveillance *care* 459
  direction 693
survey *view* 441
  measure 466
surveyor **466**
survive *remain* 40, 141
  outlast 110
susceptibility
  tendency 176
  sensibility 375
  impressibility 822
suspect *doubt* 485, 920
  suppose 514
suspend *defer* 133
  discontinue 142
  hang 214
suspense *cessation* 142
  uncertainty 475
  irresolution 605
suspension *lateness* 133
  cessation 142
  hanging 214
suspicion *doubt* 485
  supposition 514
  fear 860
  jealousy 920
suspicious 485
sustain *continue* **143**
  strengthen 159
  support 215
  aid 707
  endure 821
sustenance 298, **707**
sustentation [*see sustain*]
swab *dry* 340
  clean 652
swag *booty* 793
swagger, *n. pride* 878
swagger, *v. boast* 884
  bluster 885
swain *man* 373
  rustic 876
  lover 897
swallow, *n.* 366
swallow, *v. gulp* **296**
  be credulous 486
  brook 826
swamp, *n. marsh* 345
swamp, *v.* 162
swampy 345
swan 366
swap *exchange* 148
  barter 794

narrative 594
talebearer 532
talent 698
talented 698
talisman 747, 993
talk, *n. rumor* 532
 conversation 588
talk, *v. speak* 582
 -over *confer* 588
 persuade 615
 -together 588
talkative 584
talkativeness 584
talker 584, 588
tall *lanky* 200
 high 206
tally, *n. numeration* 85
 list 86
 sign 550
tally, *v. agree* 23
tame, *adj. inert* 172
 feeble 575
 mild 826
tame, *v. moderate* 174
 domesticate 370
 subjugate 749
tamper with *alter* 140
 injure 659
 meddle 682
tan *color* 433
tandem 200, 272
tang *taste* 390
 pungency 392
tangent 379
tangible *material* 316
 touching 379
 exact 494
tangle 61, 219
tangled *disordered* 59
tank *reservoir* 636
tankard 191
tantalize *balk* 509
 desire 865
tantamount *equal* 27
 synonymous 516
tap, *n. faucet* 263
tap, *v. open* 260
 hit 276
 let out 297
 sound 406
tape *string* 205
taper, *n. candle* 423
taper, *adj.* 203
taper, *v. narrow* 203
tapestry 847
tar *sailor* 269
 pitch 356a
tardy *dilatory* 133
 slow 275
target 620
tariff 812
tarnish *soil* 653
 deface 848
 disgrace 874
tarry *remain* 110
 delay 133

continue 141
 stay 265
tart, *n. pastry* 396
tart, *adj. acid* 397
 rude 895
tartan 440
task, *n. lesson* 537
 business 625
 fatigue 688
task, *v. put to use* 677
taskmaster 694
TASTE *sapidity* 390
 elegance 578
 good taste 850
tasteful 850
tasteless *insipid* 391
tasty 390, 394
tatters 225
tattle 588
tattler *newsmonger* 532
 gossip 588
tattoo, *n. drumming* 407
tattoo, *v.* 440
taunt, *n. disrespect* 929
taunt, *v. reproach* 938
taut 43
tautology *repetition* 104
 diffuse style 573
tavern 189
tawdry 851
tawny *brown* 433
 yellow 436
tax, *n. impost* 812
tax, *v. inquire* 461
 employ 677
 fatigue 688
 command 741
 accuse 938
taxable 812
taxation 812
taxi 272
taxicab 272
tea 892
teach 537
teachable 539
TEACHER 540, 673
TEACHING 537
team *conveyance* 272
 crew 712
 representative 759
tear, *n. weeping* 839
tear, *v. separate* 44
 move rapidly 274
 rave 825
tease *annoy* 830
technical 698
 -school 542
technicality 697
technique 698
Te Deum 990
tedious 841
tedium 841
teem *produce* 168
 abound 639
teeter 314
teetotalism 958

telegram 532
telegraph, *n.* 534, 550
telegraph, *v.* 527, 531
telepathic 450
telepathy 450, 992a
telephone, *n.* 418, 534
telephone, *v.* 527
telephony 402
telescope, *n.* 445
telescope, *v. collide* 276
telescopic 196
tell *count* 85
 influence 175
 inform 527
 speak 582
 describe 594
teller *treasurer* 801
telltale 532
temerity 863
temper, *n. nature* 5, 820
 state 7
 pliability 324
 irascibility 901
temper, *v. moderate* 174
 qualify 469
temperament
 nature 5, 820
 tendency 176
TEMPERANCE 174, 953
temperate *moderate* 174
 abstemious 953, 959
temperature 382
tempest 315, 349
TEMPLE 1000
temporal *transient* 111
temporary 111
temporize *protract* 110
 defer 133
 cunning 702
tempt *entice* 615
 desire 865
temptation 615, 865
tempter 615
 Satan 978
ten 98
tenable 664
tenacious 327, 861
TENACITY
 toughness 327
 coherence 46
 resolution 604
 obstinacy 606
 retention 781
tenancy 777
tenant, *n.* 188, 779
tenant, *v.* 186
tend *conduce* 176
 aid 707
 serve 746
 -stock 370
 -toward 278
TENDENCY 176
tender, *n. boat* 273
tender, *adj. soft* 324
 affectionate 897
 benevolent 906

torpid *inert* 172
  inactive 683
  insensible 823
torpor **823**
torrent 348
torrid 382
tortuous *twisted* 248
torture, n. *physical* 378
  moral 828
  cruelty 907
torture, v. **972**
torturer **975**
toss *throw* 284
  oscillate 314
  -up 156
tot *child* 129
total, n. *whole* 50
  number 84, **85**
total, adj. **50**
  -abstinence 953, 955
total, v. *add* 37, **800**
totality **52**
totally **52**
totter 160
  limp 275
TOUCH, n. *mixture* 41
  sensation **379, 380**
  act 680
touch, v. *relate to* 9
  adjoin 199
  feel 379
  excite 824
  excite pity 914
touched *crazy* 503
  tainted 653
  penitent 950
touching 830
touchy **901**
tough, *ruffian* 876, 887, 913
tough, adj. *adhesive* 46
  tenacious 327
  difficult 704
tour 266
touring *car* 272
tourist 268
tournament 720
tourniquet 263
tousle 61
tow 285
toward **278**
tower, n. 150, 191, **206**
tower, v. *loom* 31
  soar 305
towering *great* 31
  high 206
town 189
township 181
toy, n. **643, 840**
toy, v. *fondle* 902
trace n. 550, 551
trace, v. *follow* 63
  inquire 461
  discover 480a
  delineate 554
tracing 21

track *trace* **461**
  spoor **550**
tract *region* 181
  book 593
  dissertation 595
tractable *malleable* 324
  willing 602
  easy 705
tractile **285**
TRACTION **285**
trade *business* 625
  traffic **794**
trader 797
trademark 550
tradesman 797
trade-union 712
trade wind **349**
tradition 124
traduce 934
traducer 936
traffic **794**
tragedian 599
tragedy *drama* 599
  evil 619
tragic *dramatic* 599
tragical 830
trail, n. *sequel* 65
  odor 398
  track 550
  record 551
trail, v. *dawdle* 275
  tow 285
  inquire 461
train, n. *sequence* 63
  sequel 65
  suite 88, 235, 281
  vehicle 272
train, v. *teach* **537**
trainer 370
training *education* 537
trait 79, 550
traitor 891, **941**
trajectory 627
tram 272
trammel *hinder* 706
  restrain 751
tramp, n. *stroller* 268
  vagabond 876
tramp, v. 266
trample upon 649
trance 992a
tranquil *calm* 174
  quiet 265
  peaceful 721
tranquilize *moderate* 174
  quell 265
  pacify 723
  soothe 826
transact 680, **692**
transaction 151, 680
transcend 33, 303
transcendency 33
transcendent *superior* 33
  glorious 873
transcendental 450
transcribe 19, 525

transcript *copy* 21
TRANSFER *copy* 21
  -of *things* **270**
  -of *property* **783**
transferable 270, 783
TRANSFERENCE 140, 270
transfiguration *change* 140
  divine - 908
transfix 260
transform 140
transformation **140**
transfuse *mix* 41
  transfer 270
transgress *go beyond* 303
  infringe 773
  sin 945
transgression 303, 947
transgressor 949
TRANSIENCE **111**
transient 111
transit 144, 270
transition 144, 270
transitional 140, 264
transitory 111
translate *interpret* 522
translation
  transference 270
  interpretation **522**
transmigration 144
transmission 270, 302
transmit 270, 302
transmutation 140
TRANSPARENCY **425**
transparent
  transmitting light **425**
  obvious 518
transpire *appear* 525
  be disclosed 529
transplant 270
transport, n. *ship* 273
  war vessel 726
  delight 827
transport, v. *transfer* 270
  enrapture 829
transportation 270
transposal 270
transpose *invert* 14, 218
  exchange 148
  transfer 270
transubstantiation
  change 140
  sacrament 998
transverse *oblique* 217
  crossing 219
trap *snare* 545
  pitfall 667
trappings *clothes* 225
  equipment 633
trash *trifle* 643
  rubbish 645
  riffraff 876
trashy 517
travel 266
traveler 268
  bagman 758

traveling 266
traverse 302
travesty *imitate* 19
  copy 21
  misinterpret 523
  burlesque 555
trawl 285
trawler 273
tray 191
treacherous 907, 940
treachery *deception* 545
  dishonesty 940
tread 266
treason *revolt* 742
  treachery 940
treasure 636, 800
TREASURER 801
TREASURY 802
treat
  physical pleasure **377**
  bargain 769
  delight 827, 829
  -of 595
treatise 593, 595
treatment
  conduct 692
  medical - 662
treaty 769
treble *three* 93
  shrill 410
tree *pedigree* 166
  plant 367
trellis 219
tremble *totter* 160
  shake 315
  fear 860
tremendous *painful* 830
  fearful 860
tremor *agitation* 315
  emotion 821
  fear 860
tremulous *changeable* 149
  agitated 315
  fearful 860
trench *dike* 232
  furrow 259
  defense 717
trenchant *energetic* 171
  concise 572
  vigorous 574
  keen 821
trend *tendency* 176
  bend 278
trepidation *agitation* 315
  excitement **825**
  fear 860
trespass *go beyond* 303
  sin 945
tress 256
triad 92
trial *inquiry* 461
  experiment 463
  essay 675
  adversity 735
  suffering 828
  lawsuit 969

TRIALITY 92
triangle 92
tribe *race* 11
  assemblage 72
  clan 166
tribulation 828
TRIBUNAL 966
tributary, *n. river* 348
tributary, *adj. giving* 784
tribute *donation* 784
  money paid 809
  reward 973
trick *deception* **545**
  habit 613
  contrivance 626
  skill 698
  artifice 702
trickery *deceit* 545
trickiness [see tricky]
trickle 295, 348
trickster *deceiver* **548**
  schemer 702
tricky *deceiving* 545
  cunning 702
tricycle 272
trident 92
trifle, *n.* 32, **643**
trifle, *v. neglect* 460
  fool 499
  -with *deceive* 545
trifler 460
trifling **643**
trig 845
trill *sound* 407
  sing 416
trim, *n. state* 7
trim, *adj. neat* 652, **845**
trim, *v. adjust* 27
  form 240
  lie 544
  waver 605
  change sides **607**
  adorn 847
trimmer
  timeserver 607, 943
trimming *border* 231
  ornament 847
trinity 92
Trinity, Holy - 976
trinket **643**, 847
trio 92
trip, *n. jaunt* 266
  fall 306
trip, *v. run* 274
  leap 309
  mistake **495**
triple 93
triplet 92
TRIPLICATION 93
triplicity 92
TRISECTION 94
trite *known* 490
  conventional 613
triumph *succeed* **731**
  exult 838
trivial *unmeaning* 517

trifling 643
triviality **643**
troglodyte 893
troll, *n.* 980
troll, *v.* 416
trolley 272
  -car 272
troop *assemblage* 72
  soldiers 726
trooper 726
troopship 726
trope 521
TROPHY 733
tropical 382
trot *run* 266, 274
  translation 522
troth 768
troubadour 597
trouble, *n. turmoil* 59
  exertion 686
  adversity 735
  care 828
trouble, *v. derange* 61
troublesome
  inexpedient 647
  difficult 704
  painful 830
troublous 59
trough 259
trounce *censure* 932
  punish 972
trousers 225
trousseau 225
trow 484
truant 187, 623
truce 133, 142, **723**
truck *vehicle* 272
  barter 794
truckman 268
truculent 907
trudge *walk* 266
  move slowly 175
true *real* 1
  straight 246
  accurate **494**
  veracious 543
  faithful 772
trueness [see true]
truism *axiom* 496
truly *really* **494**
trumpery 517, **643**
truncheon 727
trundle 284
trunk *stem* 166
  box 191
truss *bundle* 72
  support 215
trust, *n. belief* 484
  firm 712
  property 780
  credit 805
  hope 858
trust, *v.* 484, 858
trustee 758, 801
trustful 484, 486
trustworthy *certain* **474**

U

neutralize 179
  not do 681
undoing *ruin* 735
undone *ruined* **732**
  hopeless 859
undoubted 474
undress, *n. clothes* 225
undress, *v. strip* 226
undue **925**
undulate *wave* 248
  oscillate 314
undutiful 945
undying *perpetual* 143
unearth *eject* 297
  disinter 363
  discover 480a
unearthly *immaterial* 317
  spectral 980a
  heavenly 981
uneasy 828
uneatable 867
uneducated *ignorant* 491
  unprepared 674
unemotional 823
unemployed *not used* 678
  inactive 681
unemployment 681
unenterprising 864
unequal **28**, 139
unequaled 28, 33
unequivocal *great* 31
  sure 474
unerring *certain* 474
  exact 494
unessential *extrinsic* 6
  irrelative 10
  unimportant 643
uneven *diverse* 16a
  unequal 28
  irregular 139
  rough 256
unexampled
  unimitated 20
unexpected *sudden* 132
  unforeseen **508**
unfading 112
unfailing 141
unfair *unjust* 923
unfaithful 940
unfamiliar 83
unfashionable
  unconventional 614
  vulgar 851
unfasten 44
unfathomable *infinite* 105
  deep 208
  mysterious 519
unfavorable
  out of season 135
  obstructive 708
  adverse 735
unfeeling *insensible* 376
  numb 381
  heartless 823
unfeigned 543
unfetter *release* 750

unfettered *free* 748
unfinished 53, 730
unfit *inappropriate* 24
  impotence 158
  inexpedient 647
  unskillful 699
  wrong 923
  undue 925
unfitness *inaptitude* 24
  [see unfit]
unfitted *not prepared* 674
unfledged *young* 127
  callow 674
unflinching
  persevering 604a
  brave 861
unfold *evolve* 313
  interpret 522
  disclose 529
UNFOLDMENT 313
unforeseen
  unexpected 508
unforgiving 919
unfortunate *ill-timed* 135
  unlucky 735
  unhappy 828
unfriendly *opposed* 708
  hostile **889**
  malevolent 907
unfruitful 169
unfurl *unfold* 313
ungainly 846
ungenerous *stingy* 819
  selfish 943
ungentlemanly *rude* 895
  dishonorable 940
ungodly 989
ungovernable *violent* 173
  passionate 825
ungraceful 846
ungracious *uncivil* 895
  unfriendly 907
ungrammatical **568**
ungrateful 917
ungrounded
  unsubstantial 4
unguarded *neglected* 460
  spontaneous 612
unguilty 946
unhallowed 988
unhappy *unlucky* 735
  wretched 828
  dejected 837
UNHEALTHINESS 657
unhealthy *ill* 655
  unwholesome **657**
unheard of
  exceptional 83
  improbable 473
  ignorant 491
unhinge *derange* 61
  make powerless 158
unholy 989
unhonored 874
unhurt 670
uniform, *n.* 225, 550

uniform, *adj.*
  homogeneous **16**
  regular 80
  dress 225
  symmetrical 242
UNIFORMITY 16, 80, 242
unimitated 20
UNIMPORTANCE 643
unimportant 643
unimpressed 838
uninhabitable 187
uninhabited 187, **893**
uninitiated *ignorant* 491
  unskillful 699
uninjured *healthy* **654**
  preserved 670
unintellectual 452
unintelligent 499
UNINTELLIGIBILITY
  519
unintelligible 519
unintentional 601
  undesigned 621
uninteresting 841
uninterrupted
  continuous 69
  perpetual 112
uninvited 893
uninviting 830
union *agreement* 23
  junction 43
  combination 48
  party 712
  concord 714
unique *dissimilar* 18
  original 20
  unequal 28
  exceptional 83
  alone 87
unison *agreement* 23
  melody 413
unit 87
unite *join* 43, **712**
  combine 48
  compose 56
  assemble 72
  concur 178
  converge 290
United States courts **966**
UNITY *identity* 13
  uniformity 16
  agreement 23
  completeness 52
  oneness 87
  concord 714
universal 78
  -*language* 560
universe 318
university 542
unjust *wrong* 923
unjustifiable *wrong* **923**
  inexcusable 938
  wicked 945
unkempt *rough* 256
  vulgar 851
unkind 907

verge, *v. tend* 176
  incline 278
  -upon 197
verification *test* 463
  warrant 771
verify *test* 463
  evidence 467
  find out 480a
verily *truly* 494
veritable 1, 494
verity 1, 494
vermin 366
vernacular, *n.* 560
vernacular, *adj. native* 188
  lingual 560
vernal 125
versatile *changeable* 149
verse *poetry* 597
versify 597
version 522
vertical 212, 246
VERTICALITY 212
vertigo 503
very 31
vesper 126
vespers 126
vessel *receptacle* 191
  ship 273
vest 225
vested *fixed* 150
  legal 963
vestibule *entrance* 66
vestige 551
vestment *dress* 225
  canonicals 999
vestry *council* 696
vesture 225
VETERAN *old* 130
  adept 700
  warrior 726
veterinarian 370
veto 761
vex 830, 898
vexation 830, 900
vexatious 830
vexed question 704
viaduct 627
vial 191
viands 298
vibrate 149, 314
vibration 138, 314, 408
vicar 996
vicarage 1000
vicarious *substitute* 147
VICE 945
vice-president 759
viceroy *governor* 745
vicinity 227
vicious 945
vicissitude 149
victim *dupe* 547
  sufferer 828
  culprit 975
victimize *deceive* 545
  injure 649
victor 731

victoria *carriage* 272
victory 731
victual *provide* 637
victuals 298
videlicet *namely* 79, 522
vie 648
view, *n. sight* 441
  appearance 448
  opinion 453, 484
  landscape 556
view, *v.* 441, 457
viewpoint 441, 453
vigil *care* 459
vigilance *care* 459
  activity 682
vigilant 459, 864
VIGOR *energy* 157, 171
  strength 159
  style 574
  resolution 604
  health 654
vigorous 574
vile *hateful* 649
  disgraceful 874
  plebeian 876
  dishonorable 940
  vicious 945
vilification 908
vilify *censure* 932
  detract 934
villa 189
village 189
villager 188
villain *actor* 599
  rascal 949
villainous *evil* 649
  wicked 945
villainy 940
vim 171, 682
VINCULUM 45
vindicate *justify* 937
VINDICATION 937
vindictive *revengeful* 919
vine 367
violate *disobey* 742
  infringe 925
  fail 927
VIOLENCE 173, 825
violent 173, 825
violet 437
violinist 416
viper *snake* 366, 913
virago 901
Virgin, The 977
virgin, *n. girl* 129
  spinster 904
  good woman 948, 960
virgin, *adj. new* 123
virile *adolescent* 131
  strong 159
  manly 373
virtu 847
virtual *inexistent* 2
  unsubstantial 5
virtually 5
VIRTUE *power* 157

  goodness 944
  purity 960
virtuous 944, 960
virulence *noxiousness* 649
  anger 900
  malevolence 907
virulent *energetic* 171
  corrupting 649, 657
  angry 900
  malevolent 907
virus *disease* 655
visage *front* 234
  appearance 448
viscount 875
VISIBILITY 446
visible 446
vision *phantom* 4, 980a
  sight 441
  dream 515
visionary *inexistent* 2
  unsubstantial 4
  imaginary 515
visit *arrival* 292
  sociality 892
visitation *disease* 655
  adversity 735
  suffering 828
visitor *friend* 890
vista *glade* 260
  sight 441
  appearance 448
visual 441
  -organ 441
visualize 220
vital *living* 359
  important 642
  -principle 1
vitality *stability* 150
  strength 159
  life 359
vitalize 359
vitiate *deteriorate* 659
vituperate 908, 932
vituperation 908, 932
vivacious *active* 682
  sensitive 822
  cheerful 836
vivid *bright* 420, 428
  graphic 518
vivification 359
vivify 359
vixen *fox* 366
  shrew 901
viz. [*see* videlicet]
vizor 530
vocabulary 86, 562
vocal *musical* 415
  oral 580
  -music 415
vocalist 416
vocalize 562, 580
vocation *business* 625
vociferate 411
vociferation *loudness* 404
  cry 411
  voice 580

W

X

Y

Z

FOREIGN WORDS AND PHRASES

à bas. [F.] Down, down with.

ab initio. [L.] From the beginning.

à bon marché. [F.] Cheap; a good bargain.

ab origine. [L.] From the origin.

ab ovo. [L.] From the egg; from the beginning.

à cheval. [F.] On horseback.

addenda. [L.] Things to be added; list of additions.

ad finem. [L.] To the end.

ad hoc. [L.] To or with respect to this (object); said of a body elected or appointed for a definite work (as a school board for education).

ad infinitum. [L.] To infinity.

ad libitum. [L.] At pleasure; as much as one pleases.

ad nauseam. [L.] To the point of disgust or satiety.

ad rem. [L.] To the purpose; to the point.

adsum. [L.] I am present; here!

ad valorem. [L.] According to the value.

advocatus diaboli. [L.] Devil's advocate; a person chosen to dispute before the papal court the claims of a candidate for canonization.

æquo animo. [L.] With an equable mind; with equanimity.

ære perennius. [L.] More lasting than brass (*or* bronze).

affaire d'amour. [F.] A love affair.

affaire de cœur. [F.] An affair of the heart.

affaire d'honneur. [F.] An affair of honor; a duel.

a fortiori. [L.] With stronger reason.

Agnus Dei. [L.] Lamb of God.

à haute voix. [F.] Aloud.

à la belle étoile. [F.] Under the stars; in the open air.

à la bonne heure. [F.] In good time; very well.

à la carte. [F.] According to the bill of fare.

à la mode. [F.] According to the custom (*or* fashion).

al fresco. [It.] In the open air.

alter ego. [L.] Another self.

amende honorable. [F.] Satisfactory apology; reparation.

à merveille. [F.] Admirably; marvelously.

amour propre. [F.] Self-love; vanity.

ancien régime. [F.] The former order of things.

anglice. [NL.] In the English language or fashion.

anguis in herba. [L.] A snake in the grass; an unsuspected danger.

anno urbis conditæ. [L.] In the year (*or* from the time) of the founded city (Rome).

à outrance. [F.] To the utmost.

aperçu. [F.] A general sketch or survey.

à perte de vue. [F.] Till beyond one's view.

à peu près. [F.] Nearly.

à pied. [F.] On foot.

a posteriori. [L.] From effect to cause; empirical.

a priori. [L.] From cause to effect; presumptive.

arbiter elegantiarum. [L.] A judge or supreme authority in matters of taste.

arcana imperii. [L.] State secrets.

argumentum ad hominem. [L.] An argument to the individual man; *i.e.*, to his interests and prejudices.

arrière-pensée. [F.] Mental reservation.

ars est celare artem. [L.] It is true art to conceal art.

ars longa, vita brevis. [L.] Art is long, life is short.

au contraire. [F.] On the contrary.

au courant. [F.] Fully acquainted with matters.

au désespoir. [F.] In despair.

au fait. [F.] Well acquainted with; expert.

au fond. [F.] At bottom.

au reste. [F.] As for the rest; besides.

au revoir. [F.] Until we meet again.

autant d'hommes, autant d'avis. [F.] So many men, so many minds.

avant-propos. [F.] Preliminary matter, preface.

à votre santé! [F.] To your health!

ballon d'essai. [F.] A trial balloon; a device to test opinion.

bas bleu. [F.] A bluestocking; a literary woman.

beau idéal. [F.] The ideal of perfection.

beau monde. [F.] The world of fashion.

beaux esprits. [F.] Men of wit.

beaux yeux. [F.] Fine eyes; good looks.

bel esprit. [F.] A person of wit or genius; a brilliant mind.

ben trovato. [It.] Well found.

bête noire. [F.] A bugbear; a special aversion; *lit.*, black beast.

bis dat qui cito dat. [L.] He gives twice who gives quickly.

bona fides (bona fide). [L.] Good faith (in good faith).

bon ami. [F.] Good friend.

bon gré, mal gré. [F.] With good or ill grace; willing or unwilling.

bon jour. [F.] Good day; good morning.

bon mot. [F.] A witty saying.

bonne foi. [F.] Good faith.

bon naturel. [F.] Good nature.

bon soir. [F.] Good evening.

bon ton. [F.] Fashionable society; good style.

bon vivant. [F.] A lover of good living; a gourmet.

bon voyage! [F.] A good voyage or journey to you!

campo santo. [It.] A burying-ground; *lit.*, a holy field.

canaille. [F.] Rabble.

carpe diem. [L.] Enjoy the present day; improve the time.

casus belli. [L.] That which causes or justifies war.

catalogue raisonné. [F.] A catalogue arranged according to subjects.

cause célèbre. [F.] A celebrated or notorious case (in law).

caveat emptor. [L.] Let the purchaser beware (*i.e.,* he buys at his own risk).

cave canem. [L.] Beware of the dog.

cela va sans dire. [F.] That goes without saying; that is a matter of course.

c'est-à-dire. [F.] That is to say.

c'est égal. [F.] It's all one.

c'est magnifique, mais ce n'est pas la guerre. [F.] It is magnificent, but it is not war.

c'est autre chose. [F.] That's quite another thing.

ceteris paribus. [L.] Other things being equal.

chacun à son goût. [F.] Every one to his taste.

chef-d'œuvre. [F.] Masterpiece.

cherchez la femme. [F.] Look for the woman (who is at the bottom of the affair).

chère amie. [F.] A dear (female) friend.

chevalier d'industrie. [F.] One who lives by his wits; a swindler.

ci-gît. [F.] Here lies.

circa. [L.] About.

cogito, ergo sum. [L.] I think, therefore I exist.

comme il faut. [F.] As it should be; in good form.

compte rendu. [F.] An account rendered; a report.

con amore. [It.] With love; very earnestly.

confrère. [F.] Colleague.

contretemps. [F.] An unexpected or untoward event; a hitch.

coram populo. [L.] Publicly; in public.

corpus delicti. [L.] The body of the crime.

corrigenda. [L.] Things to be corrected; a list of errors.

coup. [F.] A stroke.—**coup d'essai,** a first attempt.—**coup d'état,** a sudden decisive blow in politics; a stroke of policy.—**coup de grâce,** a finishing stroke.—**coup de main,** a sudden attack or enterprise.—**coup de maître,** a master stroke.—**coup d'œil,** a rapid glance of the eye.—**coup de pied,** a kick.—**coup de soleil,** sunstroke.—**coup de théâtre,** a theatrical effect.

coûte que coûte. [F.] Cost what it may.

credat Judæus Apella. [L.] Let Apella, the superstitious Jew, believe it; I won't.

credo quia absurdum. [L.] I believe because it is absurd, or contrary to reason.

cui bono? [L.] For whose advantage?

cul-de-sac [F.] A blind alley (often used figuratively).

cum grano salis. [L.] With a grain of salt; with some allowance.

d'accord. [F.] In agreement.

débâcle. [F.] The break-up of ice in a river; *hence,* a general, confused rout.

de bonne grâce. [F.] With good grace; willingly.

de facto. [L.] In point of fact; actual or actually.

dégagé. [F.] Free; easy; unconstrained.

de gustibus non est disputandum. [L.] There is no disputing about tastes.

Dei gratia. [L.] By the grace of God.

de jure. [L.] From the law; by right.

delenda est Carthago. [L.] Carthage must be destroyed.

de mortuis nil nisi bonum. [L.] (Say) nothing but good of the dead.

dénoûement. [F.] The issue; the end of a plot.

de novo. [L.] Anew.

Deo gratias. [L.] Thanks to God.

de profundis. [L.] Out of the depths.

de rigueur. [F.] Indispensable; obligatory.

dernier ressort. [F.] A last resort.

de trop. [F.] Too much; more than is wanted; out of place.

deus ex machina. [L.] A god from a machine; used in reference to forced or unlikely events introduced in a drama, novel, etc., to resolve a difficult or awkward situation; derived from the use of deities in the ancient drama.

dies iræ. [L.] Day of wrath.

Dieu et mon droit. [F.] God and my right (British royal motto).

distingué. [F.] Distinguished; of elegant appearance.

dolce far niente. [It.] Sweet doing-nothing;sweet idleness.

Dominus vobiscum. [L.] The Lord be with you.

double entente (or, esp. in English, entendre). [F.] A double meaning; a play upon words.

dramatis personæ. [L.] Characters of the drama or play.

dulce et decorum est pro patria mori. [L.] It is sweet and glorious to die for one's country.

dum spiro, spero. [L.] While I breathe, I hope.

dum vivimus, vivamus. [L.] While we live, let us live.

ecce homo. [L.] Behold the man!

édition de luxe. [F.] A splendid and expensive edition of a book.

editio princeps. [L.] The first printed edition of a book.

ego et rex meus. [L.] I and my king.

élite. [F.] The best part; the pick.

emeritus. [L.] Retired or superannuated after long service.

en avant. [F.] Forward.

en déshabillé. [F.] In undress.

en effet. [F.] In effect; substantially; really.

en famille. [F.] With one's family; in a domestic state.

enfant gâté. [F.] A spoiled child.

enfants perdus. [F.] Lost children; a forlorn hope.

enfant terrible. [F.] A terrible child, that is, one who makes disconcerting remarks.

enfant trouvé. [F.] A foundling.

enfin. [F.] In short; at last; finally.

en masse. [F.] In a mass (*or* body).

en rapport. [F.] In harmony; in agreement.

en route. [F.] On the way.

en suite. [F.] In company; in a set.

entente cordiale. [F.] Cordial understanding, especially between two states.

entourage. [F.] Surroundings; friends, confidants, etc., closely associated with a person.

entre nous. [F.] Between ourselves.

en vérité. [F.] In truth; verily.

e pluribus unum. [L.] One out of many; one composed of many (motto of the United States).

errata. [L.] Errors; list of errors.

esprit de corps. [F.] The animating spirit of a collective body, *as* a regiment.

est modus in rebus. [L.] There is a medium in all things.

et cætera (or et cetera.) [L.] And the rest.

et id genus omne. [L.] And everything of the sort.

et tu, Brute! [L.] And thou also, Brutus!

eureka! [Gr.] I have found (it)!

Ewigkeit. [G.] Eternity.

ex cathedra. [L.] From the chair; with high authority.

excelsior. [L.] Higher, *that is*, taller, loftier.

exeunt omnes. [L.] All go out (*or* retire).

exit. [L.] He goes out.

ex nihilo nihil fit. [L.] Out of nothing, nothing comes.

ex officio. [L.] In virtue of (his) office.

ex parte. [L.] From one party or side.

ex pede Herculem. [L.] From the foot we recognize a Hercules; we judge of the whole from the specimen.

experto crede. [L.] Trust one who has had experience.

exposé. [F.] A statement; a recital.

ex post facto. [L.] After the deed is done; retrospective.

extra muros. [L.] Beyond the walls.

ex uno disce omnes. [L.] From one judge of the rest.

facile princeps. [L.] Easily preeminent; indisputably the first.

facilis est descensus Averni. [L.] The descent to Avernus (*or* hell) is easy.

façon de parler. [F.] Way of speaking.

fait accompli. [F.] A thing already done.

faux pas. [F.] A false step; a slip in behavior.

femme de chambre. [F.] A chambermaid; lady's maid.

festina lente. [L.] Hasten slowly.

feu de joie. [F.] A discharge of firearms as a sign of rejoicing.

fiat justitia, ruat cœlum. [L.] Let justice be done though the heavens should fall.

fiat lux. [L.] Let there be light.

fides Punica. [L.] Punic (*or*

Carthaginian) faith; treachery.

fidus Achates. [L.] Faithful Achates; a true friend.

fin de siècle. [F.] End of the (nineteenth) century.

finis coronat opus. [L.] The end crowns the work.

flagrante delicto. [L.] In the commission of the crime; red-handed.

fons et origo. [L.] The source and origin.

force majeure. [F.] Greater force or strength; overwhelming force; compulsion.

fortiter in re. [L.] With firmness in acting.

fortuna favet fortibus. [L.] Fortune favors the bold.

furor loquendi. [L.] A rage for speaking.

furor scribendi. [L.] A rage for writing.

gaucherie. [F.] Awkwardness.

gaudeamus igitur. [L.] So let us be joyful.

genius loci. [L.] The genius (or guardian spirit) of a place.

gens d'armes. [F.] Men at arms.

gloria in excelsis (Deo). [L.] Glory (to God) in the highest.

gloria Patri. [L.] Glory be to the Father.

goût. [F.] Taste; relish.

grâce à Dieu. [F.] Thanks to God.

habitué. [F.] One in the habit of frequenting a place.

hic et ubique. [L.] Here and everywhere.

hic jacet. [L.] Here lies.

hinc illæ lacrimæ. [L.] Hence these tears.

hodie mihi, cras tibi. [L.] Mine today; yours tomorrow.

hoi polloi. [Gr.] The many; the vulgar; the rabble.

homme d'esprit. [F.] A man of wit or genius.

homo sum; humani nihil a me alienum puto. [L.] I am a man; I count nothing human indifferent to me.

honi soit qui mal y pense. [O. F.] Shamed be he who thinks evil of it (motto of the Order of the Garter).

horribile dictu. [L.] Horrible to relate.

hors de combat. [F.] Out of the combat; disabled.

hors d'œuvre. [F.] A relish.

hôtel de ville. [F.] A town hall.

hôtel-Dieu. [F.] A hospital.

humanum est errare. [L.] To err is human.

ibidem. [L.] At the same place (in a book).

ich dien. [G.] I serve (motto of the Prince of Wales).

ici on parle français. [F.] French is spoken here.

ignotum per ignotius. [L.] The unknown (explained) by the still more unknown.

il n'y a pas de quoi. [F.] Don't mention it; it's not worth speaking of.

il n'y a que le premier pas qui coûte. [F.] It is only the first step that costs.

il penseroso. [It.] The pensive man.

impasse. [F.] A deadlock; an insurmountable difficulty.

impedimenta. [L.] Encumbrances; luggage; baggage.

in æternum. [L.] Forever.

in articulo mortis. [L.] At the point of death; in the last struggle.

index expurgatorius. [L.] A list of prohibited works.

in esse. [L.] In being; in actuality.

in extenso. [L.] At full length.

in extremis. [L.] At the point of death.

infra dignitatem. [L.] Below one's dignity.

in loco. [L.] In the place; in the natural (*or* proper) place.

in loco parentis. [L.] In the place of a parent.

in medias res. [L.] Into the midst of things.

in memoriam. [L.] To the memory of; in memory.

in nomine. [L.] In the name of.

in omnia paratus. [L.] Prepared for all things.

in perpetuum. [L.] Forever.

in posse. [L.] In possible existence; in possibility.

in præsenti. [L.] At the present moment.

in propria persona. [L.] In one's own person.

in puris naturalibus. [L.] Quite naked.

in re. [L.] In the matter of.

in rerum natura. [L.] In the nature of things.

in sæcula sæculorum. [L.] For ages on ages.

in situ. [L.] In its original position.

in statu quo. [L.] In the former state.

inter alia. [L.] Among other things.

inter nos. [L.] Between ourselves.

in terrorem. [L.] As a warning.

in toto. [L.] In the whole; entirely.

intra muros. [L.] Within the walls.

in transitu. [L.] In course of transit.

in vacuo. [L.] In empty space; in a vacuum.

in vino veritas. [L.] There is truth in wine; truth is told under the influence of liquor.

invita Minerva. [L.] Against the will of Minerva; without genius or natural abilities.

ipse dixit. [L.] He himself said it; a dogmatic saying or assertion.

ipsissima verba. [L.] The very words.

ipso facto. [L.] By that very fact.

ipso jure. [L.] By the law itself.

jacquerie. [F.] French peasantry; a revolt of peasants.

je ne sais quoi. [F.] I know not what; a something or other.

jeu de mots. [F.] A play on words; a pun.

jeu d'esprit. [F.] A display of wit; a witticism.

jeunesse dorée. [F.] Gilded youth; rich and fashionable young men.

jubilate Deo. [L.] Rejoice in God; be joyful in the Lord.

jure divino. [L.] By divine law.

jure humano. [L.] By human law.

juste milieu. [F.] The golden mean.

laborare est orare. [L.] To labor is to pray; work is worship.

labor omnia vincit. [L.] Labor conquers everything.

laissez-faire. [F.] Let alone; noninterference.

l'allegro. [It.] The merry man.

lapsus calami. [L.] A slip of the pen.

lapsus linguæ. [L.] A slip of the tongue.

lapsus memoriæ. [L.] A slip of the memory.

lares et penates. [L.] Household gods.

lasciate ogni speranza voi ch'entrate. [It.] All hope abandon ye who enter here (inscription on the entrance to the hell of Dante's Inferno).

laudator temporis acti. [L.] A praiser of past times.

laus Deo. [L.] Praise to God.

l'avenir. [F.] The future.

le beau monde. [F.] The fashionable world.

lebe wohl. [G.] Farewell.

la grand monarque. [F.] The great monarch; Louis XIV of France.

le pas. [F.] Precedence in place or rank.

le roi est mort, vive le roi! [F.] The king is dead, long live the king (his successor)!

le roy le veult. [Norm. F.] The king wills it; the formula used by the sovereign in assenting to a bill.

le roy s'avisera. [Norm. F.] The king will consider; the formula formerly used by the sovereign in rejecting a bill.

lèse-majesté. [F.] High treason.

l'état c'est moi. [F.] It is I who am the state.

le tout ensemble. [F.] The whole (taken) together.

lettre de cachet. [F.] A sealed letter containing private orders; a royal warrant.

lex non scripta. [L.] Unwritten law; common law.

lex scripta. [L.] Statute law.

l'homme propose, et Dieu dispose. [F.] Man proposes, and God disposes.

l'inconnu. [F.] The unknown.

littera scripta manet. [L.] The written word remains.

locum tenens. [L.] One occupying the place of another; a substitute.

longo intervallo. [L.] By or at a long interval.

lucus a non lucendo. [L.] Used as typical of an absurd derivation—*lucus*, a grove, having been derived by an old grammarian from *luceo*, to shine—"from not shining."

lusus naturæ. [L.] A sport or freak of nature.

ma chère. [F.] My dear (fem.).

ma foi. [F.] Upon my faith.

magna est veritas, et prevalebit. [L.] Truth is mighty, and will prevail.

magnum opus. [L.] A great work.

maison de santé. [F.] A private asylum *or* hospital.

maître d'hôtel. [F.] A house steward.

mala fide. [L.] With bad faith; treacherously.

mal-à-propos. [F.] Ill-timed; out of place.

mal de mer. [F.] Seasickness.

malgré nous. [F.] In spite of us.

mañana. [Sp.] Tomorrow.

mardi gras. [F.] Shrove Tuesday.

mare clausum. [L.] A closed sea; a sea belonging to a single nation.

mariage de convenance. [F.] Marriage from motives of interest rather than of love.

materfamilias. [L.] Mother of a family.

matériel. [F.] Baggage and munitions of an army; material equipment as opposed to men.

mauvaise honte. [F.] Bashfulness; shamefacedness.

mauvais goût. [F.] Bad taste.

mauvais sujet. [F.] A bad subject; a worthless scamp.

mea culpa. [L.] My fault; by my fault.

me judice. [L.] I being judge; in my opinion.

mêlée. [F.] A confused conflict.

memento mori. [L.] Remember that you must die; a reminder of death.

mens sana in corpore sano. [L.] A sound mind in a sound body.

mens sibi conscia recti. [L.] A mind conscious of rectitude.

meo periculo. [L.] At my own risk.

mésalliance. [F.] A bad match; marriage with one of a lower rank.

meum et tuum. [L.] Mine and thine.

mirabile dictu. [L.] Wonderful to relate.

mirabile visu. [L.] Wonderful to see.

mise en scène. [F.] Stage setting.

modus operandi. [L.] Manner of working.

modus vivendi. [L.] Manner of living; used of a temporary working agreement or compromise.

mon ami. [F.] My friend (masc.).

mon cher. [F.] My dear (masc.).

mont-de-piété. [F.] A public or municipal pawnshop.

monumentum ære perennius. [L.] A monument more lasting than brass.

more majorum. [L.] After the manner of our ancestors.

morituri te salutamus. [L.] We, about to die, salute thee:— said by the Roman gladiators to the emperor.

mot d'ordre. [F.] Watchword.

motu proprio. [L.] Of his own accord.

moyen âge. [F.] Middle Ages.

multum in parvo. [L.] Much in little.

mutatis mutandis. [L.] With the necessary changes.

natura non facit saltum. [L.] Nature does not make a leap.

née. [F.] Born; used in giving

the maiden name of a married woman.

négligé. [F.] Morning dress; an easy loose dress.

nemine contradicente. [L.] No one speaking in opposition; without opposition.

nemine dissentiente. [L.] No one dissenting; with a dissenting voice.

nemo me impune lacessit. [L.] No one assails me with impunity (motto of Scotland).

ne plus ultra. [L.] Nothing further; the uttermost point; perfection.

ne quid nimis. [L.] Avoid excess.

n'est-ce pas? [F.] Isn't that so?

nicht wahr? [G.] Isn't that so?

nil admirari. [L.] To be astonished at nothing.

nil desperandum. [L.] There is no reason for despair.

n'importe. [F.] It matters not.

nisi Dominus, frustra. [L.] Except the Lord (build the house, they labor) in vain (that build it). Ps. cxxvii. (motto of Edinburgh).

noblesse oblige. [F.] Rank imposes obligations.

Noël. [F.] Christmas.

nolens volens. [L.] Unwilling or willing.

noli me tangere. [L.] Touch me not.

nom de guerre. [F.] A war name; a pseudonym; a pen name.

nom de plume. [F.] A pen name. (Incorrect for *Nom de guerre*.)

non Angli sed angeli. [L.] Not Angles but angels.

non compos mentis. [L.] Not of sound mind.

non est. [L.] He (*or* it) is not.

non est inventus. [L.] He has not been found.

non libet. [L.] It does not please (me).

non liquet. [L.] The case is not clear.

non multa, sed multum. [L.] Not many things, but much.

non nobis solum. [L.] Not for ourselves alone.

non omnis moriar. [L.] I shall not wholly die.

non sequitur. [L.] It does not follow.

nosce te ipsum. [L.] Know thyself.

nota bene. [L.] Note well; take notice.

Notre Dame. [F.] Our Lady.

nous avons changé tout cela. [F.] We have changed all that.

nous verrons. [F.] We shall see.

novus homo. [L.] A new man; one who has raised himself from obscurity.

nuance. [F.] Shade; tint.

nulla dies sine linea. [L.] Not a day without a line; no day without something done.

nunc aut nunquam. [L.] Now or never.

obiit. [L.] He (*or* she) died.

obiter dictum. [L.] A thing said by the way.

odi profanum vulgus. [L.] I loathe the profane rabble.

odium theologicum. [L.] The hatred of theologians.

œuvres. [F.] Works.

ohne Hast, ohne Rast. [G.] Without haste, without rest:—motto of Goethe.

omnia vincit amor. [L.] Love conquers all things.

on dit. [F.] They say.

onus probandi. [L.] The burden of proof.

operæ pretium est. [L.] It is worth while.

ora et labora. [L.] Pray and work.

ora pro nobis. [L.] Pray for us.

ore rotundo. [L.] With round full voice; well-turned speech.

O! si sic omnia. [L.] Oh, if all things (were) so; Oh, if he had always so spoken or acted.

O tempora! O mores! [L.] Alas for the times! Alas for the manners (or morals)!

otium cum dignitate. [L.] Ease with dignity.

ouï-dire. [F.] Hearsay.

ouvrage de longue haleine. [F.] A work of long breath; a long work or one which lasts.

pace. [L.] By leave of; not to give offence to.

palmam qui meruit ferat. [L.] Let him who has won the palm wear it.

pardonnez-moi. [F.] Pardon me; I beg your pardon.

par excellence. [F.] Pre-eminently.

par exemple. [F.] For example.

par hasard. [F.] By chance.

pari passu. [L.] With equal pace; side by side.

par nobile fratrum. [L.] A noble pair of brothers; two just alike.

parole d'honneur. [F.] Word of honor.

particeps criminis. [L.] An accomplice in a crime.

parti pris. [F.] Preconceived opinion.

parvenu. [L.] A person of low origin who has risen suddenly to wealth or position; an upstart.

pas. [F.] A step; precedence.

passim. [L.] Everywhere; throughout; in all parts of the book, chapter, etc.

pâté de foie gras. [F.] Goose-liver pie.

paterfamilias. [L.] Father of a family; head of a household.

pater patriæ. [L.] Father of his country.

pax vobiscum. [L.] Peace be with you.

peccavi. [L.] I have sinned (or been to blame).

peine forte et dure. [F.] Strong and severe punishment; a kind of judicial torture.

penchant. [F.] A strong liking.

pensée. [F.] A thought.

per. [L.] For; through; by.—**per contra.** On the contrary.—**per annum.** By the year; annually.—**per capita.** By heads; for each individual.—**per centum.** By the hundred.—**per diem.** By the day; daily.—**per fas et nefas.** Through right and wrong.—**per se.** By itself.

persona non grata. [L.] An unacceptable person.

peu à peu. [F.] Little by little.

peu de chose. [F.] A trifle.

pièce de résistance. [F.] A resistance piece; the main dish of a meal.

pied-à-terre. [F.] A resting-place; a temporary lodging.

pis aller. [F.] The worst or last shift.

place aux dames. [F.] Make room for the ladies.

plebs. [L.] The common people.

poco a poco. [It.] Little by little.

point d'appui. [F.] Point of support; basis.

pons asinorum. [L.] The asses' bridge; a name for the fifth proposition of the first book in Euclid.

poste restante. [F.] To remain in the post office till called for.

post hoc ergo propter hoc. [L.] After this, therefore, on account of this; subsequent to, therefore due to this—an illogical way of reasoning.

pour faire rire. [F.] To excite laughter.

pour le mérite. [F.] For merit.

pour passer le temps. [F.] To pass the time.

preux chevalier. [F.] A brave knight.

prima donna. [It.] First lady; the chief female singer in an opera, etc.

prima facie. [L.] At first view (or consideration).

primo. [L.] In the first place.

primum mobile. [L.] The source of motion; the mainspring.

principia, non homines. [L.] Principles, not men.

pro bono publico. [L.] For the good of the public.

procès-verbal. [F.] An authenticated minute or statement.

pro et contra. [L.] For and against.

profanum vulgus. [L.] The profane herd.

pro forma. [L.] For the sake of form.

pro patria. [L.] For our country.

pro rata. [L.] According to rate or proportion.

pro tanto. [L.] For so much; as far as it goes.

protégé. [F.] One under the protection of another.

Punica fides. [L.] Punic (or Carthaginian) faith; treachery.

qualis rex, talis grex. [L.] Like king, like people.

quand même. [F.] Even if; whatever may happen.

quantum libet. [L.] As much as you please.

quantum sufficit. [L.] As much as suffices.

quelque chose. [F.] Something; a trifle.

quid pro quo. [L.] Something in return; an equivalent.

quién sabe? [Sp.] Who knows?

quis custodiet ipsos custodes? [L.] Who shall guard the guards themselves?

qui s'excuse s'accuse. [F.] He who excuses himself accuses himself.

qui va là? [F.] Who goes there?

qui vive? [F.] Who lives? Who goes there? To be on the qui vive means to be alert or watchful.

quoad hoc. [L.] To this extent.

quoad sacra. [L.] As far as sacred things are concerned; for ecclesiastical purposes only.

quem Deus vult perdere, prius dementat. [L.] Those whom God wishes to destroy, he first makes mad.

quod erat demonstrandum. [L.] Which was to be proved or demonstrated.

quod vide. [L.] Which see.

quorum pars magna fui. [L.] Of which things, I was an important part.

quot homines, tot sententiæ. [L.] Many men, many minds.

raconteur. [F.] A teller of stories.

raison d'être. [F.] The reason for a thing's existence.

rapprochement. [F.] The act of bringing (or coming) together.

rara avis. [L.] A rare bird; a paragon.

réchauffé. [F.] *Lit.*, something warmed up; *hence*, old literary material worked up into a new form.

reductio ad absurdum. [L.] A reducing to the absurd; a method of proof in which a proposition is shown to be true by demonstrating the absurdity of its contradictions.

rencontre. [F.] An encounter; a hostile meeting.

répondez, s'il vous plaît. [F.] Please reply. *R. S. V. P.*

requiescat in pace. [L.] May he rest in peace.

res angusta domi. [L.] Narrow circumstances at home; poverty.

res gestæ. [L.] Things done; exploits; history.

respice finem. [L.] Look to the end.

résumé. [F.] A summary or abstract.

resurgam. [L.] I shall rise again.

revenons à nos moutons. [F.] Let us return to our sheep; let us return to our subject.

rôle. [F.] A character represented on the stage; also other similar meanings.

rouge et noir. [F.] Red and black; a game of chance.

rus in urbe. [L.] The country in town.

salle à manger. [F.] Dining room

sanctum sanctorum. [L.] Holy of holies.

sang froid. [F.] Coolness; indifference.

sans façon. [F.] Without ceremony.

sans peur et sans reproche. [F.] Without fear and without reproach.

sans souci. [F.] Without care.

sartor resartus. [L.] The patcher repatched; the tailor patched (or mended).

satis superque. [L.] Enough, and more than enough.

satis verborum. [L.] Enough of words; no more need be said.

sauve qui peut. [F.] Let him save himself who can.

savoir-faire. [F.] The knowing how to act; tact.

savoir-vivre. [F.] Good breeding; refined manners.

scripsit. [L.] Wrote (it).

sculpsit. [L.] Engraved (it).

secundum artem. [L.] According to art (*or* rule).

semper idem. [L.] Always the same.

semplice. [It.] Simple; plain.

seriatim. [L.] In a series; one by one.

sic itur ad astra. [L.] Such is the way to the stars, or to immortality.

sic passim. [L.] So here and there throughout; so everywhere.

sic transit gloria mundi. [L.] Thus passes away the glory of this world.

sicut ante. [L.] As before.

similia similibus curantur. [L.] Like things are cured by like.

simplex munditiis. [L.] Elegant in simplicity.

sine cura. [L.] Without charge or care.

sine die. [L.] Without a day being appointed.

sine qua non. [L.] Without which, not; something indispensable.

siste, viator. [L.] Stop, traveler.

sit tibi terra levis. [L.] Light lie the earth upon thee.

soi-disant. [F.] Self-styled.

sotto voce. [It.] In an undertone.

spero meliora. [L.] I hope for better things.

splendide mendax. [L.] Nobly untruthful; untrue for a good object.

sponte sua. [L.] Of one's (*or* its) own accord.

status quo. [L.] The state in which; the existing condition.

stet. [L.] Let it stand; do not delete.

suaviter in modo, fortiter in re. [L.] Gentle in manner, resolute in execution.

sub judice. [L.] Under consideration.

sub rosa. [L.] Under the rose; confidentially.

succès d'estime. [F.] A partial success, or one based on certain merits.

sui generis. [L.] Of its own peculiar kind; in a class by itself.

summum bonum. [L.] The chief good.

sunt lacrimæ rerum. [L.] There are tears for things; misfortunes call for tears.

suppressio veri. [L.] A suppression of the truth.

sursum corda. [L.] Lift up your hearts.

suum cuique. [L.] Let every one have his own.

tableau vivant. [F.] A living picture; the representation of some scene by a group of persons.

table d'hôte. [F.] A public dinner at an inn or hotel.

tabula rasa. [L.] A smooth or blank tablet.

tant mieux. [F.] So much the better.

tant pis. [F.] So much the worse.

te Deum laudamus. [L.] We praise Thee, O God (*or rather*, as God).

te judice. [L.] You being the judge.

tempus fugit. [L.] Time flies.

terminus ad quem. [L.] The term (*or* limit) to which.

terminus a quo. [L.] The term (*or* limit) from which.

terra firma. [L.] Solid earth; a secure foothold.

terra incognita. [L.] An unknown country.

tertium quid. [L.] A third something; a nondescript.

tiers état. [F.] The third estate; the commons.

timeo Danaos et dona ferentes. [L.] I fear the Greeks, even when they bring gifts.

tot homines, quot sententiæ. [L.] So many men, so many minds.

toto cælo. [L.] By the whole heavens; diametrically opposite.

tour de force. [F.] A notable feat of strength or skill.

tout à fait. [F.] Wholly; entirely.

tout à l'heure. [F.] Instantly.

tout au contraire. [F.] On the contrary.

tout de suite. [F.] Immediately.

tout ensemble. [F.] The whole taken together.

tu quoque. [L.] You also.

ubi supra. [L.] Where above mentioned.

ultima Thule. [L.] Most distant Thule; utmost limit.

una voce. [L.] With one voice; unanimously.

und so weiter. [G.] And so forth.

urbi et orbi. [L.] To the city and to the world.

utile dulci. [L.] The useful with the agreeable.

ut infra. [L.] As below.

ut supra. As above.

væ victis. [L.] Woe to the vanquished.

vale. [L.] Farewell.

valet de chambre. [F.] A personal attendant; a body servant.

varium et mutabile semper femina. [L.] Woman is ever a changeful and capricious thing.

veni, vidi, vici. [L.] I came, I saw, I conquered. (Cæsar's message to the senate when he conquered Pharnaces, king of Pontus.)

verbatim et literatim. [L.] Word for word and letter for letter.

verbum sat sapienti. [L.] A word is enough for a wise man.

via, veritas, vita. [L.] The way, the truth, the life.

vice versa. [L.] The terms of the case being interchanged or reversed; conversely.

videlicet. [L.] Namely (*lit.*, one may see).

vide ut supra. [L.] See what is stated above.

vi et armis. [L.] By force and arms; by main force.

vincit qui se vincit. [L.] He conquers who conquers himself.

virginibus puerisque. [L.] For maidens and boys.

vis a tergo. [L.] A force from behind.

vis-à-vis. [F.] Opposite; face to face.

vis inertiæ. [L.] The power of

inertia; resistance to force applied.

vis medicatrix naturæ. [L.] The healing power of nature.

vis vitæ. [L.] Living force; energy.

vivat regina (rex)! [L.] Long live the queen (king)!

viva voce. [L.] By the living voice; orally.

vive la bagatelle! [F.] Long live trifles (*or* frivolity)!

vive le roi! [F.] Long live the king!

vogue la galère! [F.] Row the galley; come what may!

voilà. [F.] Behold; there is; there are.

voilà tout. [F.] That's all.

vox et præterea nihil. [L.] A voice and nothing more; sound but no sense.

vox populi, vox Dei. [L.] The voice of the people is the voice of God.

vraisemblance. [F.] Probability; apparent truth.

vulgo. [L.] Commonly.

Wanderjahr. [G.] Year of wandering.

Wanderlust. [G.] Passion for traveling (*or* wandering).

Weltanschauung. [G.] World view; theory or conception of life or of the world in all its aspects.

Weltschmerz. [G.] World sorrow; sentimental pessimism.

Zeitgeist. [G.] Time-spirit; spirit of the age.

zum Beispiel. [G.] For example.

ABBREVIATIONS USED IN WRITING AND PRINTING

A

a. About; acre; adjective; afternoon; answer; are (metric system); at.

A. Academician; Academy; America; American; artillery.

A. A. A. Amateur Athletic Association.

A. A. A. S. American Association for the Advancement of Science.

A. A. of A. Automobile Association of America.

A. A. U. Amateur Athletic Union.

ab. About.

A. B. Artium Baccalaureus (L., Bachelor of Arts); (also l. c.) able-bodied (seaman).

abbr., *or* **abbrev.** Abbreviated; abbreviation.

abd. Abdicated.

A. B. F. M. American Board of Foreign Missions.

abl. Ablative.

Abp. Archbishop.

abr. Abridged; abridgment.

abs. Absolutely; abstract.

A. B. S. American Bible Society.

A. C. Alpine Club; ambulance corps; ante Christum (L., before Christ); Army Corps.

Acad. Academy.

acc. Acceptance; account; accusative.

acct. Account.

ad. (*pl.* ads.) Advertisement.

a. d. After date; ante diem (L., before the day).

A. D. Anno Domini (L., in the year of our Lord).

A. D. C. Aid-de-camp; aide-de-camp.

ad fin. Ad finem (L., at the end).

ad inf. Ad infinitum (L., to infinity).

ad int. Ad interim (L., in the meantime).

adj. Adjective.

Adj., *or* **Adjt.** Adjutant.

Adj. Gen. Adjutant General.

ad. lib. Ad libitum (L., at pleasure).

Adm. Admiral; Admiralty.

admix. Administratrix.

admr. Administrator.

admx. Administratrix.

adv. Ad valorem; adverb; advocate.

Adv. Advent.

Adv. Gd. Advance guard.

advt. Advertisement.

æ., æt., ætat. Ætatis (L., of age, aged).

A. E. F. American Expeditionary Forces.

AF *or* **A.-F.** Anglo-French.

aff. Affectionate; affirmative; affirming.

afft. Affidavit.

Afr. Africa; African.

A. G. Adjutant General; Advance guard; Attorney-general.

agr., *or* **agric.** Agriculture; agricultural.

agt. Agent.

A. H. Anno Hegiræ (L., in the year of the Hegira).

A. H. C. Army Hospital Corps.

A. I. American Institute.

Ala. Alabama.

A. L. A. American Library Association; Automobile Legal Association.

ald., *or* **aldm.** Alderman.

Alex. Alexander.

alg. Algebra.

alt. Alternate; altitude; alto.

Alta. Alberta (Canada).

Am. America; American; ammunition.

a. m. Ante meridiem (L., before noon).

A. M. Anno mundi (L., in the year of the world); Annus Mirabilis (L., the Wonderful Year, i.e., 1666); Artium Magister (L., Master of Arts).

A. M. D. Army Medical Department.

Amer. America; American.

A. M. S. Army Medical Staff.

amt. Amount.

anal. Analogous; analogy; analysis; analytic.

anat. Anatomy.

anc. Ancient; anciently.

anon. Anonymous.

ans. Answer.

ant. Antonym; antiquarian.

Ant. Anthony; Antigua.

anthrop. Anthropology; anthropological.

antiq. Antiquities; antiquarian.

A. N. Z. A. C., *or* **Anzac.** Australian and New Zealand Army Corps.

A. O. Army order.

A. O. C. Army Ordnance Corps.

A. O. D. Army Ordnance Department.

A. O. F. Ancient Order of Foresters.

A. O. H. Ancient Order of Hibernians.

aor. Aorist.

A. P. C. Army Pay Corps.

A. P. D. Army Pay Department.

Apoc. Apocalypse; Apocrypha; Apocryphal.

app. Appendix; appointed.

App. Apostles.

approx. Approximately.

Apr. April.

aq., *or* **Aq.** Aqua (L., water).

Ar. Arabian; Arabic.

A. R. Anno regni (L., in the year of the reign); Army Regulations.

A. R. A. Associate of the Royal Academy (of Arts, London).

Arab. Arabian; Arabic.

arch. Archaic; archaism; archery; archipelago; architect; architecture.

Arch. Archibald.

archaeol. Archæology.

Archd. Archdeacon; Archduke.

arith. Arithmetic.

Ariz. Arizona.

Ark. Arkansas.

Arm. Armenian.

arr. Arranged; arrived; arrivals.

art. Article; artificial; artillery; artist.

Art. *or* **A.** Artillery.

AS., *or* **A.-S.** Anglo-Saxon.

A. S. C. Army Service Corps; Army Staff Corps (British Army).

A. S. C. E. American Society of Civil Engineers.

A. S. M. E. American Society of Mechanical Engineers.

assd. Assigned.

assn. Association.

assoc. Associate; association.

asst. Assistant.

A. S. S. U. American Sunday School Union.

astr., astron. Astronomer; astronomy.

astrol. Astrologer; astrology.

Atl. Atlantic.

att., atty. Attorney.

at. wt. Atomic weight.

A. U. C. Ab urbe condita (L., from the founding of the city; i.e., Rome, about 753 B. C.).

Aug. August.

Aus., Aust. Austria; Austrian.

Austral. Australasia; Australia.

Auth. Ver. Authorized Version.

auxil. Auxiliary.

av. Avenue; average.

A. V. Artillery Volunteers; Authorized Version.

A. V. C. Army Veterinary Corps.

A. V. D. Army Veterinary Department.

ave. Avenue.

A. W. L. Absent with Leave.

A. W. O. L. Absent without Leave.

ax. Axiom.

az. Azure.

B

b. Base; bass; battery; bay; book; born; brother.

B. A. Bachelor of Arts; British Academy; British America.

B. Agr. Bachelor of Agriculture.

bal. Balance.

bap. Baptized.

Bapt. Baptist.

bar. Barometer; barometric; barrel.

Barb. Barbados.

barr. Barrister.

Bart. Baronet.

bat., batt., *or* **bn.** Battalion.

batt. *or* **b.** Battery.

bbl. (*pl.* **bbls.**) Barrel.

B. C. Before Christ; British Columbia.

B. C. L. Bachelor of Civil Law.

bd. Board; bond; bound.

B. D. Bachelor of Divinity.

bdl. (*pl* **bdls.**) Bundle.

b. e. Bill of exchange.

B. E. F. British Expeditionary Forces.

Belg. Belgian; Belgium.

Benj. Benjamin.

B. ès L. Bachelier ès Lettres (F. Bachelor of Letters).

bg. (*pl.* **bgs.**) Bag.

b. h. p. Brake horse power.

B. I. British India.

Bib. Bible; Biblical.

biog. Biographer; biography.

biol. Biologist; biology.

bk. Bank; book.

bkg. Banking.

bkt. (*pl.* **bkts.**) Basket.

b. l. Bill of lading; breech-loading.

B. L. Bachelor of Laws.

bldg. (*pl.* **bldgs.**) Building.

B. Litt. Bachelor of Literature, *or* of Letters.

B. L. R. Breech-loading rifle.

b. m. Board measure.

B. M. Bachelor of Medicine; Brigade Major.

B. Mus. Bachelor of Music.

b. o. Branch office; buyer's option.

Boh. Bohemia; Bohemian.

Bol. Bolivia.

bor. Borough.

bot. Botanical; botanist; botany.

Bp. Bishop.

b. p. Below proof; bill of parcels; bills payable.

B. P. O. E. Benevolent and Protective Order of Elks.

br. Brig; brother; brown.

Br. British.

Br. Am. British America.

b. rec. Bills receivable.

brig. Brigade; brigadier.

Brit. Britain; British.

bro. (*pl.* bros.) Brother.

b. s. Balance sheet; bill of sale.

B. S. Bachelor of Surgery.

B. Sc. Bachelor of Science.

bu., bus. Bushel; bushels.

bul. Bulletin.

Bulg. Bulgaria; Bulgarian.

B. V. M. Beata Virgo Maria (L., Blessed Virgin Mary).

Bvt. Brevet; breveted.

Brig. Gen. Brigadier General.

C

c. Carton; cathode; cent; centime; centimeter; century; chapter, child; circa (L., about); cost; cubic; current.

C. Cape; Catholic; centigrade (thermometer); Chancellor; Congress; Conservative; Consul; Corps; Court.

C. A. Chartered Accountant; Chief Accountant; Confederate Army; Controller of Accounts; Court of Appeal.

cal. Calendar; calends; calorie.

Calif. California.

Cam., Camb. Cambridge.

Can. Canada; Canadian.

Cant. Canterbury, Canticles.

Cantab. Cantabrigiensis (L., of Cambridge).

Cantuar. Cantuaria (LL., Canterbury); Cantuariensis (LL., of Canterbury).

cap. Capital; capitalize; capitulum (L., chapter); captain.

Capt. Captain.

car. Carat; carpentry.

Card. Cardinal.

cash. Cashier.

cat. Catalogue; catechism.

cath. Cathedral.

Cath. Catherine; Catholic.

cav. Cavalry.

C. B. Cape Breton; Cavalry Brigade; Chief Baron; Common Bench; Companion of the Bath; Confined to Barracks.

cc. Cubic centimeter, *or* centimeters.

c. c. Compte courant (F., account current); cubic centimeter, *or* centimeters.

C. C. Caius College (Cambridge, Eng.); Circuit Court; Civil Court; County Clerk.

C. C. D. Commander of Coast Defenses.

C. C. P. Court of Common Pleas.

c. d. v. Carte de visite.

C. E. Church of England; Civil Engineer; Corps of Engineers.

cel. Celebrated.

Celt. Celtic.

cen. Central; century.

cent. Centigrade; central; century; centum.

cert. Certificate; certify.

certif. Certificate; certificated.

cf. Confer (i.e., compare).

C. F. A. Chief of Field Artillery.

c. f. & i. *or* **c. f. i.** Cost, freight, and insurance.

cg. Centigram.

C. G. Captain General; Captain of the Guard; Coast Guard; Commanding General; Consul General.

C. G. H. Cape of Good Hope.

C. G. S. *or* **c. g. s.** Centimeter-gram-second (system of units); Chief of General Staff in the field.

ch. Chapter; chief; child, church.

Ch. Chancery; Charles; China; Church.

C. H. Captain of the Horse; Courthouse; Customhouse.

chanc. Chancellor; chancery.

chap. Chaplain; chapter.

Chas. Charles.

chem. Chemical; chemist; chemistry.

Chin. China; Chinese.

Ch. J. Chief Justice.

Chr. Christ; Christian; Christopher.

chron. Chronological; chronology.

Chron. Chronicles.

chs. Chapters.

c. i. f. Cost, insurance, and freight.

circ. Circa. circiter, circum (L., about).

cit. Citation, cited; citizen.

civ. Civil; civilian.

C. J. Chief Justice.

cl. Centiliter; class; clause; clergyman; cloth.

class. Classic; classical; classification.

cld. Cleared; colored.

clk. Clerk.

cm. Centimeter.

cml. Commercial.

C. M. Certificated Master; common meter; Corresponding Member; court-martial.

C. M. G. Companion of St. Michael and St. George.

cml. Commercial.

Co. Company; county.

c. o. Care of; carried over.

C. O. Colonial Office; Commanding Officer; Crown Office.

coad. Coadjutor.

C. O. D. Cash, or collect, on delivery.

C. of S. Chief of Staff.

cog. Cognate.

col. College; collegiate; colonial; colony; colored; column.

Col. Colonel; Colossians.

coll. Colleague; collection; collector; college.

collat. Collateral; collaterally.

colloq. Colloquial; colloquially.

Colo. Colorado.

Col. Sergt. Color Sergeant.

com. Comedy; commentary; commerce; common; commonly; communication.

Com. Commander; Commission; Commissioner; Committee; Commodore.

comdg. Commanding.

Comdr. Commander.

Comdt. Commandant.

comp. Compare; comparative; composer; compositor; compound; comprising.

Com. Ver. Common Version.

con. Contra (L., against).

Cong. Congregational; Congress; Congressional.

conj. Conjunction.

Conn. Connecticut.

const. Constable; constitution.

cont. Containing; contents; continent; continue; continued.

contemp. Contemporary.

contr. Contracted; contraction; contrary.

cor. Corner; cornet; corrected; correction; correlative; correspondent; corresponding.

Cor. Corinthians.

Corp. Corporal.

cos. Cosine.

cosec. Cosecant.

cot. Cotangent.

cp. Compare.

c. p. Candle power; chemically pure.

C. P. Common Pleas; Common Prayer; Court of Probate.

C. P. A. Certified public accountant.

cps. Coupons.

C. P. S. Clerk of Petty Sessions.

cr. Created; credit; creditor; crown.

cresc. Crescendo.

C. S. Christian Science; Civil Service.

C. S. A. Confederate States Army; Confederate States of America.

C. S. C. Conspicuous Service Cross.

C. S. I. Companion of the Star of India (Brit. order).

C. S. N. Confederate States Navy.

C. S. O. Chief Signal Officer.

ct. Cent; county

cts. Cents; centimes.

cu., cub. Cubic.

cur. Currency; current.

C. V. Common Version.

c. w. o. Cash with order.

cwt. Hundredweight *or* hundredweights.

cyc., *or* **cyclo.** Cyclopedia; cyclopedic.

C. in C. Commander in Chief.

D

d. Date; daughter; day; dead; degree; denarius, *or* denarii (L., penny *or* pence); deputy; died; dime; dollar; dose.

D. Democrat; department; Deus (L., God); Duke; Dutch.

Dan. Danish, Daniel.

D. A. R. Daughters of the American Revolution.

dat. Dative.

dau. Daughter.

D. C. Da capo (It., from the beginning); Dental Corps; District Court; District of Columbia.

D. C. L. Doctor of Civil Law.

d. d. Days after date.

D. D. Divinitatis Doctor (L., Doctor of Divinity).

D. D. S. Doctor of Dental Surgery.

Dea. Deacon.

deb. Debenture.

dec. Declension; declination; decorative.

Dec. December.

def. Defendant; definition.

deft. Defendant.

deg. Degree.

del. Delegate; delineavit (L., he, *or* she, drew it).

Del. Delaware.

Dem. Democrat; Democratic.

Den. Denmark.

dep. Department; departs; deponent; deputy.

dept. Department; deponent.

der., *or* **deriv.** Derivation; derivative; derived.

Deut. Deuteronomy.

D. F. Dean of the Faculty; Defensor Fidei (L., Defender of the Faith).

dft. Defendant; draft.

dg. Decigram.

D. G. Dei gratia (L., by the grace of God); Deo gratias (L., thanks to God); Director General; Dragoon Guards.

diam. Diameter.

dict. Dictator; dictionary.

dim., *or* **dimin.** Diminuendo; diminutive.

dis. Discipline; discount.

disc. Discount; discovered.

disct. Discount.

disp. Dispensatory.

dist. Distant; distinguished; district.

div. Divide; divided; dividend; divine; division; divisor.

dl. Deciliter.

D. Lit. Doctor of Literature.

D. L. O. Dead Letter Office.

dm. Decimeter.

do. Ditto.

dol. (*pl.* dols.) Dollar; dollars.

dom. Domestic; dominion.

D. O. M. Deo Optimo Maximo (L., to God, the Best, the Greatest).

D. O. R. C. Dental Officers' Reserve Corps.

dow. Dowager.

doz. Dozen; dozens.

dpt. Department; deponent.

dr. Dram; drawer.

Dr. Debtor; doctor.

dram. pers. Dramatis personæ.

d. s. Dal segno (It., from the sign; — *musical direction*); day's sight; days after sight.

D. S. Director of Supplies.

D. Sc. Doctor of Science.

D. S. C. Distinquished Service Cross.

D. S. O. Distinquished Service Order (British, Army and Navy).

D T Double Time; "rush." (Signal).

D. T.'s. Delirium tremens. *Colloq.*

Du. Dutch.

D. V. Deo volente (L., God willing).

D. V. M. Doctor of Veterinary Medicine.

D. V. S. Director of Veterinary Services.

dwt. Pennyweight *or* pennyweights.

E

E. Earl; Earth; East; Eastern; Engineer; English.

ea. Each.

Ebor. Eboracum (L., York); Eboracensis (L., of York).

E. C. Eastern Central (Postal District, London); Established Church.

eccl., *or* **eccles.** Ecclesiastical.

Eccl., *or* **Eccles.** Ecclesiastes.

Ecclus. Ecclesiasticus.

Ecua. Ecuador.

ed. Edition; editor.

E. D. Eastern Department; Extra Duty.

Edin. Edinburgh.

edit. Edition.

Edw. Edward.

E. E. Early English; Electrical Engineer; errors expected.

E. E. & M. P. Envoy Extraordinary and Minister Plenipotentiary.

Eg. Egypt; Egyptian.

e. g. Exempli gratia (L., for example).

E. I. East India; East Indies.

elec. Electrical; electrician; electricity.

Eliz. Elizabeth; Elizabethan.

Em. Emmanuel; Emily; Emma.

E. M. F. Electromotive force.

Emp. Emperor; Empress.

ency., *or* **encyc.** Encyclopedia.

ENE. East-northeast.

eng. Engineer; engraving.

Eng. England; English.

engin. Engineer; engineering.

entom. Entomology.

E. O. Engineer Officer.

E. O. R. C. Engineer Officers' Reserve Corps.

Eph. Ephesians, Ephraim.

Epiph. Epiphany.

Epis., *or* **Episc.** Episcopal.

eq. Equal; equivalent.

ESE. East-southeast.

esp., *or* **espec.** Especially.

Esq. Esquire.

est., *or* **estab.** Established.

Esth. Esther.

et al. Et alibi (L., and elsewhere); et alii (L., and others).

etc. Et cetera (L., and others, and so forth).

et seq. Et sequens (L., and the following).

et sqq. Et sequentes (L., and the following), *masc. & fem. pl.*, or sequentia, *neut. pl.*

etym., *or* **etymol.** Etymology.

ex. Examined; example; excursion; executed; executive; export; extract.

ex div. Without dividend.

Exod. Exodus.

exp. Export; express.

Expl. Explosives.

exr. Executor.

exrx. Executrix.

ext. External; extinct; extra; extract.

Ezek. Ezekiel.

F

f. Farthing; fathom; feminine; fine; flower; folio; foot; forte; franc.

F. Fahrenheit; French.

F. A. Field Artillery.

fac. Facsimile.

Fahr. Fahrenheit.

F. A. I. A. Fellow of the American Institute of Architects.

fam. Familiar; family.

F. A. M. Free and Accepted Masons.

far. Farriery; farthing.

F. A. R. C. Field Artillery Reserve Corps.

F. B. A. Fellow of the British Academy (scientific society).

F. C. Free Church (of Scotland).
fcap. Foolscap.
fcp. Foolscap.
F. D. Fidei Defensor (L., Defender of the Faith).
Feb. February.
fem. Feminine.
ff. Folios; following (pages); fortissimo.
F. F. V. First Families of Virginia.
f. i. For instance.
fict. Fiction.
fig. Figurative; figuratively; figure.
Fin. Finland; Finnish.
fir. Firkin; firkins.
fl. Florin; flourished; fluid.
Fl. Flanders; Flemish.
Fla. Florida.
Flem. Flemish.
fm. Fathom.
F. M. Field Marshal; Foreign Mission.
fo. Folio.
F. O. Field Officer; Field Order.
f. o. b. Free on board.
fol. Folio; following.
for. Foreign.
fort. Fortification.
fr. Fragment; franc; from.
Fr. Father; France; Frau; French; Friar.
Fred. Frederick.
freq. Frequent; frequentative.
F. R. G. S. Fellow of the Royal Geographical Society (London).
Fri. Friday.
F. R. S. Fellow of the Royal Society (London).
frs. Francs.
F. S. Field Service.
ft. Feet; foot; fort; fortified.

fur. Furlong; further.
fut. Future.

G

g. Gauge; genitive; gram; guide; guinea or guineas; gulf.
G. German.
Ga. Georgia.
G. A. General Assembly.
gal. (*pl.* gals.) Gallon.
Gal. Galatians.
G. A. R. Grand Army of the Republic.
gaz. Gazette; gazetteer.
G. B. Great Britain.
G. B. & I. Great Britain and Ireland.
G. C. Grand Chancellor (*or* Chaplain, Chapter, Council, Conclave, etc.).
g. c. d. Greatest common divisor.
g. c. m. Greatest common measure.
G. C. M. General Court Martial.
Gd. Guard.
gen. Gender; general; generic; genitive; genus.
Gen. General; Genesis.
gent. Gentleman.
Geo. George.
geog. Geographer; geographic; geographical; geography.
geol. Geologic; geological; geologist; geology.
geom. Geometry.
ger. Gerund.
Ger. German; Germany.
G. H. Q. General Headquarters.
gi. Gill; gills.
G. L. Grand Lodge.

gm. Gram.

G. M. Grand Master.

G. O. General order.

G. O. C. General Officer Commanding.

gov. Government; governor.

Gov. Gen. Governor General.

govt. Government.

G. P. Gloria Patri (L., Glory to the Father); Graduate in Pharmacy.

G. P. O. General Post Office.

gr. Grain; grand; great; gross.

Gr. Greece; Greek; Grecian.

gram. Grammar.

Gr. Br., Gr. Brit. Great Britain.

G. S. General Secretary; General Service; General Staff; Grand Scribe; Grand Secretary.

gt. Gilt; great; gutta (L., drop).

gtt. Guttæ (L., drops).

gun. Gunnery.

H

h. Harbor; hard; hardness; height; high; hour; husband.

H., HQ., or Hqrs. Headquarters.

ha. Hectare.

H. A. Horse Artillery.

Hab. Habakkuk.

Hag. Haggai.

H. B. C. Hudson's Bay Company.

H. B. M. His (or Her) Britannic Majesty.

H. C. Heralds' College, House of Commons.

h. c. f. Highest common factor.

H. E. High explosive; His Eminence; His Excellency.

Heb. Hebrew; Hebrews.

hectol. Hectoliter.

hectom. Hectometer.

H. E. I. C. Honorable East India Company.

her. Heraldry.

hg. Hectogram; heliogram.

H. G. His (or Her) Grace; Horse Guards, High German.

H. H. His (or Her) Highness; His Holiness (the Pope).

hhd. Hogshead; hogsheads.

H. I. H. His (or Her) Imperial Highness.

H. I. M. His (or Her) Imperial Majesty.

Hind. Hindustan; Hindustani.

hist. Historian; historical; history.

H. J. Hic jacet (L., here lies).

hl. Hectoliter.

H. L. House of Lords.

hm. Hectometer.

H. M. His (or Her) Majesty.

H. M. S. His (or Her) Majesty's Service; or Ship.

ho. House.

Hon. Honorable; honorary.

hort. Horticulture.

Hos. Hosea.

Hosp. Hospital.

H. P., or h. p. Half pay; high pressure; horse power.

hr. (pl. hrs.) Hour.

H. R. House of Representatives.

H. R. E. Holy Roman Emperor, or Empire.

H. R. H. His (or Her) Royal Highness.

H. S. H. His (or Her) Serene Highness.

ht. Height.

Hun., Hung. Hungarian; Hungary.

H. W. M. High-water mark.
Hy. Henry.
hyd. Hydrostatics.
hyp. Hypothesis; hypothetical.

I

I. Imperator (L., Emperor); island.
I. A. Indian Army.
ib., *or* **ibid.** Ibidem (L., in the same place).
Ice., Icel. Iceland; Icelandic.
id. Idem (L., the same).
I. D. R. Infantry Drill Regulations.
i. e. Id est. (L., that is).
i. h. p. Indicated horse power.
IHS. A symbol representing Greek IH (ΣΟΤ) Σ Jesus.
ill., illus., illust. Illustrated; illustration.
Ill. Illinois.
imp. Imparted; imperative; imperfect; imperial; impersonal; imported; importer.
in. (*pl.* ins.) Inch.
inc. Including; inclusive; incorporated; increase.
incl. Including; inclusive.
incog Incognito.
incor. Incorporated.
ind. Independent; indicative; indigo.
Ind. India; Indian; Indiana.
inf. Infantry; infinitive.
I. N. R. I. Iesus Nazarenus, Rex Iudæorum (L., Jesus of Nazareth, King of the Jews).
ins. Inches; inscribed; inspector; insurance.
insp. Inspector.
inst. Instant; institute; institution.

int. Interest; interior; interjection; internal; international; interpreter; intransitive.
interj. Interjection.
intrans. Intransitive.
in trans. In transitu (L., on the way).
introd. Introduction; introductory.
I. O. O. F. Independent Order of Odd Fellows.
I. O. U. I owe you.
I. R. Inland Revenue; Internal Revenue.
I. R. C. Infantry Reserve Corps.
Ire. Ireland.
is. Island; isle.
Isa. Isaiah.
isl. Island; isle.
It. Italian; Italy.
ital. Italic, italics.
Ital. Italian; Italy.
I. W. Isle of Wight.

J

J. Judge; Justice.
J. A. Judge Advocate.
Jam. Jamaica.
Jan. January.
Jap. Japan; Japanese.
Jas. James.
Jav. Javanese.
J. C. Jesus Christ; Julius Cæsar; jurisconsult.
J. C. D. Juris Civilis Doctor (L., Doctor of Civil Law).
Jer. Jeremiah.
JJ. Justices.
Jno. John.
Jon., Jona. Jonathan.
Jos. Joseph.
Josh. Joshua.
Jour. Journal; journeyman

J. P. Justice of the Peace.
Jr. Junior.
Judg. Judges.
Jun., *or* **jun.** Junior.
Junc. Junction.
jus., **just.** Justice.

K

K. King; Kings; Knight.
Kans. Kansas
K. B. King's Bench.
K. C. Knights of Columbus.
K. C. B. Knight Commander of the Bath (Brit. order).
kg. Kilogram.
K. G. Knight of the Garter.
Ki. Kings.
kilom. Kilometer.
K. K. K. Ku-Klux Klan.
kl. Kiloliter.
km. Kilometer, kingdom.
K. M. Knight of Malta (European religious order).
knt. Knight.
K. O. Commanding Officer.
K. P. Kitchen Police; Knight *or* Knights of Pythias.
K. T. Knight Templar.
Ky. Kentucky.

L

l. Lake; land; latitude; leaf; league; left; length; libra (L., a pound); line; link; liter.
L. Lady; Latin; Law; Liber (L., book); Liberal; Low.
La. Louisana.
Lab. Labrador.
Lam. Lamentations.
lat. Latitude.
Lat. Latin.
lb. (*pl.* lbs.) Libra *or* libræ (L., pound *or* pounds).

l.c. Loco citato (L., in the place cited); lower case.
L. C. Lord Chamberlain; Lord Chancellor.
L/C Letter of Credit.
L. C. J. Lord Chief Justice.
l. c. m. Least common multiple.
Ld., **ld.** Lord.
L. D. Lady Day; (*or* LD.) Low Dutch.
Ldp. Lordship.
lea. League.
leg. Legal; legate; legato; legislative; legislature.
Lev. Leviticus.
LG., *or* **L. G.** Low German.
LGr., *or* **L. Gr.** Low Greek.
l. h. Left hand.
L. H. A. Lord High Admiral.
L. I. Light Infantry; Long Island.
lib. Liber (L., book); librarian; library.
Lieut. *or* **Lt.** Lieutenant.
lin. Lineal; linear.
liq. Liquid; liquor.
lit. Liter; literal; literally; literary; literature.
Lit. D. Literarum Doctor (L., Doctor of Letters).
Lith. Lithuanian.
Litt. D. Litterarum Doctor (L., Doctor of Letters).
LL., *or* **L. L.** Late Latin; Low Latin.
L. L. Lord Lieutenant.
LL. B. Legum Baccalaureus (L., Bachelor of Laws).
LL. D. Legum Doctor (L., Doctor of Laws).
log. Logarithm.
lon., *or* **long.** Longitude.
L. S. Licentiate in Surgery.
L. S. D., *or* **£. s. d.**, *or* **l. s. d.**

Libræ, solidi, denarii (L., pounds, shillings, pence).

Lt. *or* Lieut. Lieutenant.

l. t. Long ton.

M

m. Male; manual; married; masculine; measure; medicine; medium; meridian; meter; middle; mile; mill; minute; month; moon; morning; mountain.

M. Majesty; Manitoba; Marshal; Marquis; Monsieur.

M. A. Magister Artium (L., Master of Arts); Military Academy.

Mac., Macc. Maccabees.

mach. Machinery.

Mad. Madam.

mag. Magazine; magnitude.

Maj. Major.

Mal. Malachi.

man. Manège; manual.

Manit. Manitoba.

manuf. Manufactory; manufacture.

mar. Maritime.

Mar. March.

March. Marchioness.

Marq. Marquis.

mas., *or* masc. Masculine.

Mass. Massachusetts.

math. Mathematician; mathematics.

Matt. Matthew.

max. Maximum.

M. C. Medical Corps; Member of Congress.

Md. Maryland.

M. D. Medicinæ Doctor (L., Doctor of Medicine).

mdse. Merchandise.

Me. Maine.

ME., *or* M. E. Middle English.

M. E. Mechanical, Military, *or* Mining Engineer; Methodist Episcopal; Most Excellent.

meas. Measure.

mech. Mechanics; mechanical.

med. Medical; medicine; medieval; medium.

Medit. Mediterranean.

mem. Memento; memoir; memorandum; memorial.

mer. Meridian; meridional.

Messrs. Messieurs.

metal. Metallurgy.

meteor. Meteorology.

Meth. Methodist.

Mex. Mexican; Mexico.

Mf., *or* mf. Mezzo forte (It., moderately loud).

mfg. Manufacturing.

mfr. (*pl.* mfrs.) Manufacturer.

mg. Milligram.

Mgr. Monseigneur; Monsignore.

M. H. G., *or* MHG. Middle High German.

M. H. R. Member of the House of Representatives.

M. I. Mounted Infantry.

Mic. Micah.

Mich. Michaelmas; Michigan.

mid. Middle; midshipman.

mil. Military; militia.

min. Minim; minimum; mining; minister; minor; minute.

Minn. Minnesota.

Min. Plen. Minister Plenipotentiary.

misc. Miscellaneous.

Miss. Mississippi.

ml. Mail; milliliter.

M. L. A. Modern Language Association.

M. L. G., or **MLG.** Middle Low German.

Mlle. Mademoiselle.

mm. Millimeter.

MM. Their Majesties; Messieurs.

Mme. (*pl.* **Mmes.**) Madame (*pl.* Mesdames).

mo. (*pl.* mos.) Month.

Mo. Missouri.

M. O. Medical officer; money order.

mod. Moderate; moderato (It., moderately); modern.

Moham. Mohammedan.

mol. wt. Molecular weight.

Mon. Monastery; Monday.

Monsig. Monseigneur; Monsignor.

Mont. Montana.

Mor. Morocco.

M. O. R. C. Medical Officers' Reserve Corps.

M. P. Member of Parliament.

M. P. C. Member of Parliament, Canada.

m. p. h. Miles per hour.

Mr. Mister.

M. R. C. Medical Reserve Corps.

Mrs. Mistress.

MS., or **ms.** Manuscript.

M. S. Master of Science; Master of Surgery.

m. s. l. Mean sea level.

MSS. or **mss.** Manuscripts.

mt. (*pl.* mts.) Mount; mountain.

mun. Municipal.

mus. Museum; music; musician.

Mus. B. Musicæ Baccalaureus (L., Bachelor of Music).

Mus. D. or **Musc. Doc.** Musicæ Doctor(L., Doctor of Music).

M. W. Most Worshipful; Most Worthy.

myg. Myriagram.

myl. Myrialiter.

mym. Myriameter.

myth. Mythology.

N

n. Natus (L., born); nephew; neuter; new; nominative; note; noun; number.

N. Navy; Noon; Norse; North; Northern.

N. A. National Academy; National Army; North America; North American.

N. A. A. National Automobile Association.

Nah. Nahum.

nat. National; native; natural.

Nath. Nathanael; Nathaniel.

naut. Nautical.

nav. Naval; navigable; navigation.

N. B. New Brunswick; North Britain; North British; nota bene (L., note well, or take notice).

N. C. New Church; Nurses' Corps; North Carolina.

N. C. O. Noncommissioned Officer.

n. d. No date.

N. Dak. North Dakota.

N. E. New England.

N. E. A. National Education Association.

Nebr. Nebraska.

N. E. D. New English Dictionary;—better, O. E. D. (which see).

neg. Negative.

Neh. Nehemiah.

Neth. Netherlands.

neut. Neuter.

Nev. Nevada.

N. F. Newfoundland; (*or* NF.) Norman French.

Ng. Norwegian.

N. G. National Guard; New Granada; (*Slang*) no good.

N. Gr., *or* **NGr.** New Greek.

N. H. New Hampshire.

Nicar. Nicaragua.

N. J. New Jersey.

N. L., *or* **NL.** New Latin.

N. Lat. North latitude.

N. Mex. New Mexico.

NNE. North-northeast.

NNW. North-northwest.

N. O. Natural order (*Bot.*); New Orleans.

No., *or* **no.** (*pl.* Nos., nos.) Numero (L., [by] number).

nol. pros. Nolle prosequi (L., to be unwilling to prosecute).

nom. Nominative.

non seq. Non sequitur (L., it does not follow).

Nor. Norman; North.

Norw., *or* **Nor.** Norway; Norwegian.

Nov. November.

N. P. New Providence; Notary Public.

nr. Near.

N. R. North Riding; North River.

N. S. National Society; New Series; New Style (since 1752); Novia Scotia.

N. S. W. New South Wales.

N. T. New Testament; Northern Territory.

Num. Numbers.

NW. Northwest; Northwestern.

N. W. T. Northwest Territories.

N. Y. New York.

N. Z. New Zealand.

O

O. Old; Ontario; Order.

o/a. On account (of).

ob. Obiit (L., he, *or* she, died).

Obad. Obadiah.

obdt. Obedient.

obj. Object; objection; objective.

obl. Oblique; oblong.

obs. Observation; observatory; obsolete.

obt. Obedient.

oc. Ocean.

Oct. October.

O. D., *or* **OD.** Old Dutch.

O. E., *or* **OE.** Old English.

O. E. Omissions excepted.

O. E. D. Oxford English Dictionary.

O. F., *or* **OF.** Old French.

off. Offered; officer; official; officinal.

O. H. G., *or* **OHG.** Old High German.

O. H. M. S. On His (*or* Her) Majesty's Service.

O. K., *or* **OK.** Correct; all right. *Cant.*

Okla. Oklahoma.

ol. Oleum (L., oil).

O. M. Old measurement; Order of Merit.

Ont. Ontario.

O. O. R. C. Ordnance Officer' Reserve Corps.

op. Opera; opposite; opus.

opp. Opposed; opposite.

opt. Optative; optics.

Or. Oriental.

O. R. C. Order of the Red Cross; Officers' Reserve Corps.

ord. Ordained; order; ordinance; ordinary; ordnance.

Oreg. Oregon.

orig. Original; originally.

O. S. Old School; Old Series; Old Style; ordinary seaman.

O. T. Old Testament.

O. T. C. Officers' Training Camp.

Oxon. Oxonia (L., Oxford); Oxoniensis (L., Oxonian).

oz. Ounce; ounces.

P

p. Page; part; participle; past; penny; piano (It., softly); pint; pipe; pole; population; professional.

P. Pastor; pater (L., father); père (F., father); post; president; priest; prince.

Pa. Pennsylvania.

p. a. Participial adjective; per annum (L., by the year).

P/A. Power of attorney; private account.

Pac. Pacific.

pam. Pamphlet.

Pan. Panama.

par. Paragraph; parallel; parenthesis; parish.

Para. Paraguay.

parl. Parliament; parliamentary.

part. Participle.

pass. Passive.

P. B. Prayer Book.

p. c. Per cent; postal card; post card.

pd. Paid.

P. E. Presiding Elder; Protestant Episcopal.

P. E. I. Prince Edward Island.

pen. Peninsula.

Pent. Pentecost.

per an. Per annum (L., by the year).

per ct. Per cent.

perf. Perfect.

perh. Perhaps.

pers. Person; personal.

Pers. Persia; Persian.

pert. Pertaining.

Pet. Peter.

pf. Preferred.

Pg. Portugal; Portuguese.

P. G. M. Past Grand Master.

Phar. Pharmacy; Pharmacopœia.

Ph. B. Philosophiæ Baccalaureus (L., Bachelor of Philosophy).

Ph. D. Philosophiæ Doctor (L., Doctor of Philosophy).

Ph. G. Graduate in Pharmacy.

Phil. Philemon; Philip; Philippians; Philippine.

Phila. Philadelphia.

philol. Philology; philologist.

philos. Philosopher; philosophical; philosophy.

physiol. Physiologist; physiology.

P. I. Philippine Islands.

pinx. Pinxit (L., he, *or* she, painted it).

pk. (*pl.* pks.) Peck.

pkg. (*pl.* pkgs.) Package.

pl. Place; plural.

plf., *or* **plff.** Plaintiff.

plup., *or* **plupf.** Pluperfect.

plur. Plural.

pm. Premium.

P. M., *or* **p. m.** Post meridiem.

(L., afternoon); post mortem.

P. M. G. Postmaster-General.

P. O. Post office; Province of Ontario.

P. O. B. Post-office box.

P. O. D. Pay on delivery; Post Office Department.

Pol. Poland; Polish.

pol., polit. Political.

pol. econ. Political economy.

pop. Popular; population.

Port. Portugal; Portuguese.

pos. Positive; possessive.

poss. Possession; possessive.

pp. Pages; past participle; pianissimo.

p. p. Past participle; postpaid.

P. P. C. *or* **p. p. c.** Pour prendre congé (F., to take leave).

pph. Pamphlet.

p. pr. Present participle.

P. Q. Previous question; Province of Quebec.

pr. Pair; present; price; priest; prince.

Pr. Preferred stock.

P. R. Puerto Rico.

prep. Preparatory; preposition.

pres. President; presidency.

Presb. Presbyterian.

pret. Preterit.

prin. Principal.

priv. Privative.

prob. Probably; problem.

Prof. Professor.

pron. Pronominal; pronoun; pronounced; pronunciation.

propr. Proprietor.

pros. Prosody.

Prot. Protestant.

pro tem. Pro tempore (L., temporarily).

prov. Provident; province; provisional.

Prov. Provençal; Proverbs; Provost.

prox. Proximo (L., next, of the next month).

prs. Pairs.

Prus. Prussia; Prussian.

Ps. Psalm; Psalms.

P. S. Postscriptum (L., postscript); Privy Seal.

pseud. Pseudonym.

psychol. Psychologist; psychology.

pt. (*pl.* **pts.**) Part; payment; pint; point; port.

P. T., *or* **p. t.** Post town.

p. v. Post village.

pwt. Pennyweight; pennyweights.

pxt. See *pinx.*

Q

q. Quart; queen; query; question; quintal; quire.

Q. Quebec (province)

Q. E. D. Quod erat demonstrandum (L., which was to be demonstrated).

Q. F. Quick-Fire, *or* quick-firing.

ql. Quintal.

Q. M. Quartermaster.

Q. M. G. Quartermaster-General.

Q. M. O. R. C. Quartermaster Officers' Reserve Corps.

Q. M. S. Quartermaster-Sergeant.

qr. (*pl.* **qrs.**) Quadrans (L., a farthing); quarter; quire.

qt. Quantity; (*pl.* **qts.**) quart.

qu. Quart; quarterly; queen; query; question.

ques. Question.

qy. Query.

R

r. Railroad; railway; rare; received; rector; resides; retired; right; river; rises; road; rod; rood; royal.

R. Rabbi; Radical; Réaumur; Republican; response.

R. A. Rear Admiral; Regular Army; Royal Academy; Royal Artillery.

rad. Radical; radix.

R. C. Red Cross; Roman Catholic.

R. C. A. Reformed Church in America.

Re. Rupee.

R. E. Reformed Episcopal; Right Excellent; Royal Engineers.

Réaum. Réaumur.

rec. Receipt; recipe; record; recorded; recorder.

recd. Received.

rec. sec. Recording secretary.

rect. Receipt; rector; rectory.

ref. Referee; reference; referred; reformation; reformed.

Ref. Ch. Reformed Church.

reg. Regent; region; register; registered; registry; regular.

Reg. Regina (L., queen).

regt. Regiment.

rel. Relating; relative (-ly); religion; religious.

rep. Repeat; report; reporter; representative; republic.

Rep. Republican.

Repub. Republic; Republican.

retd. Returned.

rev. Revenue; reverse; review; revise; revised; revision; revolution.

Rev. Revelation; Reverend.

Rev. Ver. Revised Version.

R. F., *or* **r. f.** Rapid-fire.

R. F. D. Rural Free Delivery.

R. G. S. Royal Geographical Society (London).

r. h. Right hand.

R. H. Royal Highness.

rhet. Rhetoric; rhetorical.

R. I. Rhode Island.

R. I. P. Requiescat in pace (L., may he, *or* she, rest in peace).

riv. River.

rm. Ream.

R. M. Resident Magistrate; Royal Marines.

R. M. S. Royal Mail Steamer.

R. N. Royal Navy.

R. N. R. Royal Naval Reserve.

ro. Rood.

Robt. Robert.

Rom. Roman; Romance; Romans.

Rom. Cath. Roman Catholic.

R. O. T. C. Reserve Officers' Training Corps (*or* Camp).

R. P. O. Railroad Post Office.

rpt. Report.

R. R. Railroad.

Rs. Rupees.

R. S. Recording Secretary; Revised Statutes.

R. S. V. P. Répondez, s'il vous plaît (F., reply, if you please).

Rt. Hon. Right Honorable.

Rt. Rev. Right Reverend.

Rum. Rumania; Rumanian.

Rus., *or* **Russ.** Russia; Russian.

R. V. Revised Version; Rifle Volunteers.

R. W. Right Worshipful; Right Worthy.

Ry. Railway.

R. Y. S. Royal Yacht Squadron.

S

s., *or* S. Section; see; series; shilling; signed; singular; son; stem; sun; surplus.

S. Sabbath; Saint; Saxon; school; senate; Socialist; Society; Socius (L., Fellow); soprano; South; Southern.

S. A. Salvation Army; Small-arms; South Africa; South America; South Australia.

sa. Sable.

Sab. Sabbath.

S. Afr. South Africa; South African.

Salv. Salvador.

Sam. Samaritan; Samuel.

S. Amer., *or* S. Am. South America; South American.

S. & T. Supply and Transport.

Sans. Sanskrit.

S. A. R. South African Republic.

Sar. Sardinia; Sardinian.

Sask. Saskatchewan.

Sat. Saturday.

Sax. Saxon; Saxony.

sb. Substantive.

S. B. Bachelor of Science; South Britain.

sc. Scene; and see sci., scil., scr., sculp.

Sc. Scotch; Scottish.

s. c. Small capitals.

S. C. Signal Corps; South Carolina; Staff Corps; Supreme Court.

Scand. Scandinavia; Scandinavian.

S. caps. Small capitals.

sch. Scholium; schooner.

sci. Science; scientific.

scil. Scilicet (L., namely).

Scot. Scotch; Scotland; Scottish.

scr. Scruple.

Script. Scripture.

sculp. Sculpsit (L., he, *or* she, carved it).

s. d. Sine die (L., without [appointing] a day).

S. Dak. South Dakota.

SE. Southeast.

sec. Secant; second; secretary; section; secundum (L., according to).

Sec. Leg. Secretary of Legation.

sect. Section.

Sem. Seminary; Semitic.

Sen. Senate; Senator; Senior.

Sep., *or* Sept. September; Septuagint.

ser. Series; sermon.

serg., sergt., *or* Sgt. Sergeant.

Serv. Servian.

s. g. Specific gravity.

S. G. Solicitor-general; Surgeon-General.

Sgt. Maj. Sergeant-Major.

Sh., *or* sh. Share; shilling; shillings.

Shak. Shakespeare.

S. I. Sandwich Islands; Staten Island.

Sib. Siberia; Siberian.

Sic. Sicilian; Sicily.

sing. Singular.

S. J. Society of Jesus.

S. J. C. Supreme Judicial Court.

Skr., *or* Skt. Sanskrit.

S. L. Solicitor at Law.

S. Lat. South latitude.

Slav. Slavic; Slavonic.

sld. Sailed.

S. M. Sa Majesté (F., His, *or* Her, Majesty); Sergeant-Major; Society of Mary

sm. c., *or* **sm. caps.** Small capitals.

S. O., *or* **s. o.** Seller's option.

S. O. Staff Officer; Signal Officer; Special Order.

soc. Society.

S. of Sol. Song of Solomon.

sol. Solution.

sop. Soprano.

S. O. R. C. Signal Officers' Reserve Corps.

sov. Sovereign.

sp. Species; specimen; spelling; spirit.

Sp. Spain; Spaniard; Spanish.

s. p. Sine prole (L., without issue).

S. P. C. A. Society for Prevention of Cruelty to Animals.

S. P. C. C. Society for Prevention of Cruelty to Children.

specif. Specifically.

sp. gr. Specific gravity.

S. P. Q. R. Senatus Populusque Romanus (L., the Senate and People of Rome); small profits, quick returns.

spt. Seaport.

sq. Squadron.

sq. Sequens (L., the following [one]); square.

sqq. Sequentes (L., the following [ones]).

Sr. Sir; Senior.

S. R. S. Fellow (L., Socius) of the Royal Society.

ss. Scilicet (L., namely); semis (L., half).

S. S. Steamship; Supply Sergeant.

SSE. South-southeast.

SSW. South-southwest.

st. Stanza; stone; stet (L., let it stand).

St. Saint; Strait; Street.

stat. Statuary; statue; statutes.

S. T. D. Sacræ Theologiæ Doctor (L., Doctor of Sacred Theology).

str. Steamer.

Sub. Subaltern.

subj. Subject; subjunctive.

subst. Substantive; substitute.

suff. Suffix.

Sun. Sunday.

sup. Superior; superlative; supine; supplement; supra (L., above).

Sup. C. Superior Court; Supreme Court.

superl. Superlative.

Sup. O. Supply Officer.

supp. Supplement.

Supt. Superintendant.

surg. Surgeon; surgery.

surv. Surveying; surveyor.

s. v. Sub verbo (L., under the word); sub voce (L., under the title).

S. V. Sancta Virgo (L., Holy Virgin); Sanctitas Vestra (L., Your Holiness).

SW. Southwest.

Sw., *or* **Swed.** Sweden; Swedish.

Switz. Switzerland.

syn. Synonym; synonymous.

Syr. Syria; Syriac.

T

t. Temperature; tenor; time; tome; ton; town; township; transitive.

T. Territory; Testament; trains; Turkish.

tan. Tangent.

tel. Telegram; telegraph; telephone.

Tenn. Tennessee.

ter. Terrace; territory.

Test. Testament.

Teut. Teuton; Teutonic.

Tex. Texas.

Th. Thomas.

Theo. Theodore; Theodosia.

Theoph. Theophilus.

Thess. Thessalonians.

Tho., *or* **Thos.** Thomas.

Thurs. Thursday.

Tim. Timothy.

T. M. True mean.

T. N. T. Trinitrotoluene *or* Trinitrotoluol.

t. o. Telegraph office; turn over.

topog. Topographical; topography.

tp. Township.

tr. Translated; translation; translator; transpose; treasurer; trustee.

trav. Travel; traveler.

treas. Treasurer; treasury.

trig. Trigonometric; trigonometrical; trigonometry.

Trin. Trinity.

trop. Tropic; tropical.

T. S. Transport and Supply.

T. T. Telegraphic transfer; Trinity term.

T. U. Trade Union.

Tues. Tuesday.

Turk. Turkey; Turkish.

typ. Typographer; typographic (-ical); typography.

U

U. Uncle; Unionist; upper.

U. K. United Kingdom.

ult. Ultimately; ultimo.

Unit. Unitarian.

univ. Universally; university.

Univ. Universalist.

U. of S. Afr. Union of South Africa.

U. P. C. United Presbyterian Church.

Uru. Uruguay.

U. S. Uncle Sam; United States.

U. S. A. United States Army; United States of America.

U. S. C. United States of Colombia.

U. S. M. United States Mail; United States Marine.

U. S. M. A. United States Military Academy.

U. S. N. United States Navy.

U. S. N. A. United States Naval Academy.

U. S. N. G. United States National Guard.

U. S. S. United States Senate; United States Ship *or* Steamer.

usu. Usual; usually.

u. s. w. Und so weiter (G., and so forth).

V

v. Verb; verse; version; versus; very; vicar; vice-; vide (L., see); village; vocative; volume; von (G., of).

V. Venerable; Victoria; Viscount; Volunteers.

Va. Virginia.

v. a. Verb active.

V. A. Vicar Apostolic; Vice Admiral.

var. Variant; variation; variety; various.

Vat. Vatican.

vb. n. Verbal noun.

V. C. Veterinary Corps; Vice Chancellor; Victoria Cross.

Ven. Venerable; Venice.
Venez. Venezuela.
ver. Verse; verses.
Vet. Veterinary.
V. G. Vicar-general.
v. i. Verb intransitive.
Vic. Victoria.
vid. Vide (L., see).
vil. Village.
Vis., *or* **Visc.** Viscount.
viz. Videlicet (L., namely).
V. M. D. Veterinariæ Medicinæ Doctor (L., Doctor of Veterinary Medicine).
v. n. Verb neuter.
voc. Vocative.
vocab. Vocabulary.
vol. (*pl.* vols.) Volume; volunteer.
vol. Volcano; volcanic.
V. P. Vice-President.
v. r. Verb reflexive.
V. R. Victoria Regina (L., Queen Victoria).
V. Rev. Very Reverend.
vs. Versus.
v. s. Vide supra (L., see above).
V. S. Veterinary Surgeon.
Vt. Vermont.
v. t. Verb transitive.
Vul. Vulgate.
vv. Verses; violins.

W

w. Wanting; week; wide; wife; with.
W. Wales; Washington; Welsh; West; Western.
W. A. West Africa; Western Australia.
Wash. Washington.
W. C. Wesleyan Chapel; Western Central (Postal District, London).

W. C. T. U. Woman's Christian Temperance Union.
W. D., *or* **War D.** War Department.
Wed. Wednesday.
w. f. Wrong font.
w. g. Wire gauge.
W. G. C. Worthy Grand Chaplain.
W. G. M. Worthy Grand Master.
whf. Wharf.
W. I., *or* **W. Ind.** West Indies; West Indian.
Wis. Wisconsin.
Wisd. of Sol. Wisdom of Solomon.
wk. Week.
W. long. West longitude.
Wm. William.
W. M. Worshipful Master.
WNW. West-northwest.
W. O. War Office.
wp. Worship.
W. R. Water reserve; West Riding.
WSW. West-southwest.
wt. Weight.
W. Va. West Virginia.
Wyo. Wyoming.

X

X. Χριστος (Gr., Christ).
X-c., *or* **X-cp.** Ex coupon.
Xmas [no period] Christmas.
Xn. Christian.
Xnty., *or* **Xty.** Christianity.
Xper., *or* **Xr.** Christopher.
Xt. Christ.

Y

y. Yard; year.

yd. (*pl.* yds.) Yard.

Y. M. C. A. Young Men's Christian Association.

Y. M. Cath. A. Young Men's Catholic Association.

Y. M. C. U. Young Men's Christian Union.

Y. P. S. C. E. Young People's Society of Christian Endeavor.

yr. (*pl.* yrs.) Year; younger; your.

Y. W. C. A. Young Women's Christian Association.

Z

Zach. Zacharias; Zachary.

Zeb. Zebadiah; Zebedee.

zoogeog. Zoogeography.

zool. Zoological; zoologist; zoology.

Z. S. Zoological Society.

Zech. Zechariah.

Zeph. Zephaniah.